Communication Law
Practical Applications in the Digital Age

DOM **CARISTI**

Ball State University

WILLIAM R. **DAVIE**

University of Louisiana-Lafayette

PEARSON

Boston   Columbus   Indianapolis   New York   San Francisco   Upper Saddle River
Amsterdam   Cape Town   Dubai   London   Madrid   Milan   Munich   Paris   Montreal   Toronto
Delhi   Mexico City   São Paulo   Sydney   Hong Kong   Seoul   Singapore   Taipei   Tokyo

Editor-in-Chief, Communication: Karon Bowers
Editor: Ziki Dekel
Associate Development Editor: Angela Mallowes
Editorial Assistant: Stephanie Chaisson
Marketing Manager: Wendy Gordon
Senior Digital Editor: Paul DeLuca
Digital Editor: Lisa Dotson
Project Manager: Anne Ricigliano
Project Coordination, Editorial Services, and Text Design: Electronic Publishing Services Inc., NYC
Art Rendering and Electronic Page Makeup: TexTech
Cover Design Manager: Nancy Danahy
Cover Photo: George Doyle/Thinkstock
Manufacturing Buyer: Mary Ann Gloriande
Printer and Binder: R.R. Donnelley and Sons/Harrisonburg
Cover Printer: R.R. Donnelley and Sons/Harrisonburg

Library of Congress Cataloging-in-Publication Data

Caristi, Dom
  Communication law : practical applications in the digital age/Caristi [and] Davie.
    p. cm.
  Includes index.
  ISBN 978-0-205-50416-9
  1. Mass media—Law and legislation—United States.   2. Freedom of expression—United States.   I. Davie, William R.,   II. Title.

  KF2750.C368 2011
  343.7309'9—dc22

                                                                2011013855

10 9 8 7 6 5 4 3 2 1—DOH—14 13 12 11

www.pearsonhighered.com

ISBN-10:   0-205-50416-7
ISBN-13: 978-0-205-50416-9

*To our wives, Kimberly Ann Caristi
and
Yuling Huang-Davie*

BRIEF CONTENTS

CONTENTS

PREFACE

THERE ARE LOTS OF COMMUNICATION LAW TEXTBOOKS

Much like the discipline of communication, the specialization of communication law has evolved over time. Now most university communication programs require a law class, or a course that combines law and ethics. It is worth examining the reason behind that. We believe it is not because there is any expectation that the students will become lawyers, but because law is one of the best content areas for practicing analysis and criticism. Members of the business world and the academic world both stress the importance for graduates to be able to think critically and solve problems.

A number of texts in communication law have had an orientation toward specific subdisciplines. Because journalism was the largest of the areas, many texts heavily emphasized law most relevant to print reporters. In the twenty-first century, when the vast majority of communication students are *not* pursuing futures in print journalism, law texts need a broader focus: one that matches the broad variety of professions available to communication graduates.

THIS BOOK IS DIFFERENT

The style of this text varies considerably from others because it is targeted at individuals who are likely to become *communication professionals,* not lawyers, a point that seems to be missed often in textbooks. Communication professionals need to understand the major points of the law, the framework, but not every minor point about a particular area. Therefore, each chapter of our text contains *seminal cases* and does not overburden the student with dozens of major and minor cases on the same point. Communication professionals hire lawyers to help them navigate the complicated nuances of the system. What we try to do in our courses, and what we have tried to do with this text, is not to train lawyers but rather, to encourage critical thinking about the law and provide the framework for students who are working to become professionals in the field of communication.

THIS BOOK IS ENGAGING

Between the two of us, we have 50 years of experience teaching communication at the collegiate level. That experience includes private and public schools, small colleges, and major research universities. We have been students and/or faculty at a dozen different institutions across a half-dozen different states. While we may not be experts on higher education in America, we feel we have a good grasp of what it takes to engage students. Unlike so many other law texts, we've tried to make the text engaging with a writing style designed to draw the reader into the material.

The twenty-first-century student probably reads just as much as the student of a previous generation, but less of that reading is found in the pages of a book. Older textbooks would contain all the content a student needed for the class. Today's students spend a considerable amount of their reading time looking at screens. Research is not confined to libraries but can be conducted on a Smartphone while walking between classes. This book is not the sum total of all knowledge about communication law but rather a purposeful selection of what matters most.

While most students who take a course in communication law are majoring in a related field, very few "elect" a course in communication law but rather take it because it is a requirement of the major. As faculty we believe one of our responsibilities is to demonstrate the relevance of the content and convince the reader that it *does* matter.

THIS BOOK IS PRACTICAL

Another unique aspect of this text is the chapter on *business law*. More than ever, communication professionals must be familiar with the basics of contract law. Of course, many new employees are presented with multipage contracts and ought to be able to understand their rights. Media professionals are increasingly confronted by contracts stipulating their behavior away from work (morals clauses) and limiting their rights to accept other job offers (noncompete clauses). In addition, freelance work by writers, video professionals, web designers, etc. requires each to enter into a contractual agreement as to what rights belong to the freelancer and what rights are transferred to the purchaser.

Because the law changes constantly, faculty need to stress to students that even those who successfully complete the course have only a temporary mastery. Knowledge of any subject requires constant diligence, and anyone who wants to be well informed in a field needs to stay current. For that reason one of the most important things this text can provide is a framework for understanding communication law.

THIS BOOK IS ACCESSIBLE

We have included a set of features designed to help your students get the most out of the information provided.

Chapter Learning Objectives and Corresponding Summary Points

Each chapter of this book begins with focused learning objectives and ends with corresponding summary points to help your students prepare for the chapter concepts and efficiently review.

Bedrock Law

This feature, threaded throughout the text, highlights the indisputable points of law that relate to key points in the chapter.

Glossary

Throughout the text, readers will find relevant definitions when they need them, as well as compiled into a glossary at the end of the book.

From the Trenches

This feature gives students access to the experiences of actual practitioners, giving insight into practical perspectives on legal questions.

Iconography

One of the reasons law can be so difficult to grasp is that both sides often have plausible arguments. To demonstrate this clearly for students, we've inserted tug-of-war icons throughout the text to highlight examples of legal questions that are often hotly disputed between two sides.

THIS BOOK MAKES YOU THINK CRITICALLY

Up Close Boxes

This feature provides students with relevant connections to real-world examples, additional cases, and the sorts of thought-stimulating sidebars that become the departure point for critical discussions.

Unsolved Cases

Located at the conclusion of each chapter, these cases highlight that law is not some static subject, but rather a constantly changing body. As this book was going to press, the Supreme Court was considering a case involving government employees' free speech rights, the Federal Trade Commission was considering new privacy regulations for the Internet, and the Federal Communications Commission was drafting network neutrality rules that parties on the political left and right were threatening to litigate even before they had the opportunity to read the regulations. It is a good idea for students and faculty to speculate about the future. This can be done either as class discussion or a written assignment. Either way it provides a great opportunity for the application of previous models and case law to future dilemmas.

THIS BOOK HAS STRONG SUPPORT

Instructor's Manual and Test Bank

We prepared this comprehensive instructor resource to help you plan your Mass Media Law course with a concentration on creating an informed *communication professional*. It includes both chapter-by-chapter teaching material as well as a fully reviewed test bank. The Instructor's Manual portion contains learning objectives and linked summary points from the book, an instructional outline, discussion questions, and sample assignments. The test bank contains multiple-choice, true/false, completion, and matching questions organized by chapter. Each question is referenced by topic and page. This is available for download at http://www.pearsonhighered .com/irc (access code required).

ACKNOWLEDGMENTS

As anyone who has ever written a textbook knows, authors are only a part of the process. We both want to thank the many people who have also contributed to the process. Obvious among those are the contributors who have provided our unique "From the Trenches" features. We would also like to thank our many reviewers for providing valuable feedback during the writing process:

Chris Burnett, California State University—Long Beach; Edward L. Carter, Brigham Young University; Ralph Engelman, Long Island University; Paul H. Gates, Appalachian State University; Deb Geisler, Suffolk University; George Albert Gladney, University of Wyoming; Howard Kleiman, Miami University Ohio; George Padgett, Elon University; Kathy Brittain Richardson, Berry College; and Lorna Veraldi, Florida International University.

Not so obvious are the many production people at Pearson Education, most notably our editor Angela Mallowes, who have all spent hours trying to turn our words into something presentable. We are also grateful to Karon Bowers, Editor in Chief, for her continued support. We also wish to acknowledge the proofing work by Jean Gillespie and Bobbye Jo Hudson of Tarrant County Community College and glossary editing by Judson Eldredge of the University of Louisiana at Lafayette. Both of us are fortunate to work at wonderful universities with very supportive departments and colleagues. We thank the Department of Communication at the University of Louisiana Lafayette and the Department of Telecommunications at Ball State University. Our colleagues and students have been a great source of both formal and informal feedback, and our work has been guided by their wisdom.

DOM CARISTI
MUNCIE, INDIANA

WILLIAM R. DAVIE
LAFAYETTE, LOUISIANA

ABOUT THE AUTHORS

Photo by Tim Underhill

Dom Caristi, Associate Professor of Telecommunications

Caristi joined the Ball State faculty in 1998. He previously taught at Saint Mary's of Minnesota, Iowa State University, and Missouri Southern, where he also managed the university's low-power television station. He was a Fulbright professor in Slovenia in 1995 and in Greece in 2009, and has been a visiting professor in Italy with the Kentucky Institute for International Studies and AHA-International. His B.A. is from the University of Miami, his M.A. from the University of Central Missouri, and his Ph.D. is from the University of Iowa. He has served fellowships with the Radio Television News Directors Association and the National Association of Television Program Executives. In 1998 he received the Distinguished Service Award from the Iowa Broadcasters Association. A member of the Broadcast Education Association for more than 20 years, he served on the Board of Directors 1997–2002, including a term as its Vice President.

William R. Davie, Associate Professor of Communication

Davie has been a member of the University of Louisiana at Lafayette faculty since 1993. He is the head of the Mass Communication/Broadcast sequence, and has served as interim department head and graduate program coordinator. He taught previously at Texas Christian University and Texas A&M University, where he served as news director for the university's NPR radio and PBS television stations. In 2003, he co-authored *Principles of Electronic Media* with James R. Upshaw and has contributed chapters, articles, and essays to books and journals in journalism and mass communication. Davie has served as division head for the Broadcast Education Association's News Division and the Radio-Television Journalism Division for the Association for Education in Journalism and Mass Communication. He has served as the AEJMC liaison and *ex officio* board member for the Radio Television News Directors Association and received a fellowship through that organization in 2000. His B.A. is from Austin College, his M.A. is from the University of Missouri and his Ph.D. is from the University of Texas at Austin.

Sources of Law and Systems of Justice

LEARNING OBJECTIVES

After reading this chapter you should know:

- How the branches of government limit each other's legal authority in crafting laws with respect to freedom of expression
- The role of judicial review in upholding acts of law or striking them down
- What courts can do when neither the acts of the legislature nor legal precedents seem to apply

- The levels of jurisdiction that courts have with respect to deciding cases and their appeals
- The manner by which regulatory agencies administer regulations
- How historical precedence contrasts with other forms of precedence
- The contrasting legal processes of civil and criminal law

FLAG BURNING AND THE FIRST AMENDMENT

The United States tolerates acts of symbolic protest—even inflammatory ones. Under the First Amendment, protestors who seek to burn a flag, a politician in effigy, or a holy book can do so unless the act poses an imminent threat to other people or property. In 2010, a Florida pastor threatened to burn the Muslim holy book, the Qur'an, in retaliation for a Muslim cleric's plans to build an Islamic center near Ground Zero where the twin towers were destroyed during the 9/11 terrorist attacks. Following extensive news media coverage, Pastor Terry Jones retreated from his symbolic act of conflagration, but others have followed through with symbolic inflammatory acts, causing distress and outrage, even resulting in court decisions in their favor that turned on the narrowest of margins in the United States.

One vote in the U.S. Supreme Court and one vote in Congress determined whether protestors who burn the flag are to be prosecuted for desecrating a national symbol. When a Texas statute in 1984 was enforced against a political protestor, Gregory Lee Johnson, the U.S. Supreme Court decided by a single-vote majority that he was within his constitutional rights. That ruling struck down similar laws in other states.

Johnson ignited a stolen U.S. flag while his cohorts spat upon it before police moved in near the site of the Republican Party's presidential convention in Dallas. At his trial, Johnson received a one-year prison sentence, but on appeal the state's highest criminal court held that his flag burning was protected speech. Symbolic patriotism had to give way to free expression, even outrageous forms of it. The Texas court stopped short of striking down the desecration statute though, which gave room for a higher court to examine the larger legal question.

The U.S. Supreme Court took up the case in order to examine the constitutional issue involved. By a 5–4 vote, it struck down the law in *Texas v. Johnson*.[1] The following year Congress acted in response and drafted the federal Flag Protection Act, but that law was struck down as well.[2] Only a constitutional amendment could stave off this judicial precedent and keep other flag-burning laws from being struck.

During the summer of 2006, Congress was asked to do just that by adding the Twenty-Eighth Amendment to the Constitution—a measure to protect the flag of the United States of America. Similar bills were routinely drafted since the *Texas v. Johnson* ruling, but all failed either to make it to a vote or to muster the super majority (two-thirds + one) needed in the U.S. Senate. In 2006, Sen. Orrin Hatch's (R-Utah) bill fell just one vote shy of the number needed.

Freedom of expression is constantly under scrutiny from the three branches of government that determine how the First Amendment will be construed. The sources of laws that govern the United States are ancient, but the way the three branches of federal government check each other is relatively modern and an understanding of their special balance begins with an understanding of their constitutional origin.

---

[1]491 U.S. 397 (1989).

[2]*United States v. Eichman*, 496 U.S. 310 (1990).

SOURCES OF LAW

Our national mythology depicts the framers of the Constitution standing as oracles in silk stockings like they appear in the National Archives mural in Washington, D.C. Upon closer inspection, however, they seem more like feisty politicians bickering over how to protect their rights of property and freedom in the messy lab of constitutional chemistry. The American charter of government was a different animal from the sort that had guided civilizations since ancient Rome. The divine authority of kings was no longer sacred since the architects in Philadelphia believed "rebellion to tyrants is obedience to God."[3] Government had to be constrained to permit breathing room for liberty and equality; as one of the wives to the framers, Abigail Adams, emphasized to her husband John Adams, "Remember the Ladies, and be more generous and favorable to them than your ancestors. Do not put such unlimited power in the hands of the Husbands. Remember all men would be tyrants if they could."[4]

There was also a sense of urgency since the Articles of Confederation failed to offer sufficient federal power or revenue to sustain the nation. The alternative was a division of three separate branches of government—**executive, legislative,** and **judicial**—to check each one's use (or abuse) of power. To George Washington's thinking, this was the key to its success, "the spirit of encroachment (that) tends to consolidate the powers of all departments in one," if unchecked creates "a real despotism." The solution, declared the commander in chief, is "reciprocal checks in the exercise of political power; by distributing it into different depositories."[5] Due to its radical nature, the new national document was prepackaged and presented to early Americans by Alexander Hamilton, James Madison, and John Jay in a series of newspaper articles known as *The Federalist* papers, which tried to convince New York readers the charter was a necessary change.

Not all of the new citizens were convinced, and the **Bill of Rights**—the first ten amendments—was crafted to ensure the Constitution's passage by protecting freedoms of religion and the press, the right to a trial by jury, and the right to bear arms, among others. Those amendments were safeguards against what Americans dreaded most

Executive branch
■ The executive branch of government has authority for execution of the laws. In the federal government, executive authority derives from the president.

Legislative branch
■ The legislative branch of government, established in Article 1 of the U.S. Constitution, has the authority to pass laws. In the federal government the legislative authority rests in congress.

---

[3]Thomas Jefferson and Benjamin Franklin used this phrase, which was coined by a British lawyer who participated in the death sentence of King Charles I in 1649. *See* Dave Kopel, *God, Man and Tyrants,* 18 Liberty 5 (2005).

[4]Letter from Abigail Adams to John Adams (Mar. 31, 1776), as documented by Founder's Library, *available at* http://www.founding.com/library/lbody.cfm?id=1276parent=54 (last visited June 7, 2006).

[5]*The Farewell Address of George Washington* 35 (Frank W. Pine ed., American Book Company 1911).

Judicial branch ■ The judicial branch of government, established in Article III of the U.S. Constitution, is the court system. In the federal government, judicial authority rests in the Supreme Court, and whatever lower federal courts congress may establish.

Bill of Rights ■ The first ten amendments to the U.S. Constitution.

about British rule—quartering of soldiers in homes, unreasonable searches and seizures, and unfair trials. Time was of the essence since James Madison warned if deliberations were postponed, "it may occasion suspicions, which, though not well founded, may tend to influence or prejudice the public mind, against our decisions," so he asked all "wise and liberal men to make such alterations as shall produce that effect" and the first ten amendments were adopted.[6]

The Bill of Rights was added to the U.S. Constitution, but the task of interpreting it became the province of the U.S. Supreme Court. Chief Justice John Marshall started holding acts of the U.S. Congress accountable to the Constitution in the landmark case of *Marbury v. Madison* (1803). Chief Justice Marshall's exercise of **judicial review** power was the culmination of legal thinking, advocated by Alexander Hamilton in *The Federalist* papers, who argued that such power must be given to the judiciary. An early example of it is found in British history, when a magistrate, Sir Edward Coke, ruled against parliamentary enforcement of a licensing rule for physicians because "no person should be a judge in his own case." Congress gave its blessing to the Supreme Court's review function in the Judiciary Act of 1789.

UP CLOSE

Party Politics in Early America

If partisan politics seems like a popular game today, consider how the founding fathers of the United States played it. To secure his party's base of power, President John Adams appointed forty-two members of his fellow Federalists to the judiciary on his last day in office. One problem: those eleventh-hour appointments did not all arrive at Secretary of State James Madison's desk on time and he refused to sign twenty-five judicial commissions.

One candidate missing a letter of appointment was William Marbury, an up-and-coming financier from Baltimore looking for his place among Maryland's aristocracy. President Adams had promised him the office of justice of the peace, but Adams's successor, President Jefferson, refused to grant those late-hour judicial commissions because they had missed the deadline. Marbury was not dissuaded; he wanted that appointment and was willing to take his case up to the U.S. Supreme Court.

If Marbury could get a **writ of mandamus**, this court order would force Secretary Madison to grant him that judge's office. What Marbury secured instead was a Supreme Court decision against him. In a unanimous 4–0 ruling, Chief Justice John Marshall delivered the ruling holding that even though Marbury acted properly in seeking a legal solution from his Court, this petition for a writ of mandamus was out of order. Even though Congress passed an act empowering such writs, Marshall held that it went beyond their constitutional authority.

In deeming such writs to be beyond congressional reach, the chief justice gave his court the authority to judge acts of Congress. This was the first time the U.S. Supreme Court had exercised its power of judicial review, but it would not be the last. As for what happened to Marbury—he did well for himself and eventually was named a director to lead one of the major banks of his day.

---

[6]James Madison, "Debate in the First Congress," June 8, 1789, as cited by Neil H. Cogan, *Contexts of the Constitution* 812 (Foundation Press 1999). Twelve amendments were proposed originally but the first two were not ratified, leaving us with the Bill of Rights we know today.

Statutory Acts

Somewhat like tributaries flowing into a river, distinct sources of law channel the government's legal authority. These sources of law are found in the **statutory law** drawn up by legislatures, city councils, and county or parish seats of government. Elected lawmakers vie in separate chambers to enact new laws at the state capital. (Nebraska stands as an exception with a single chamber.) Away from the capital, civic leaders and county officers meet in commissions and boards to draft the rules necessary to keep local governments running. Statutes adopted at the local, state, or national levels are studies in negotiation—in essence political acts forged by compromise.

An act's passage through the U.S. Congress is something like a gauntlet where each bill overcomes a chain of hurdles and hostilities before it is written into law. Proposed acts are printed in similar formats but legislative sponsors are required from both parties to escort them through committee hearings, up-and-down votes, and on to the floor for debate and decision. If the bill survives votes in both houses of Congress, a conference committee must meld the differences between the different versions and offer a measure for the president to sign. Few bills actually make it that far, and if an act does survive both legislative chambers, the president can stop it with an executive veto. When that happens, it takes at least a two-thirds majority to override such a stamp.

Hierarchy of Law

The U.S. Constitution is the "supreme law of the land," which means that all other laws must be consistent with its provisions. This is spelled out in in Article VI, paragraph 2, which is referred to as the **supremacy clause**. When Congress passed the Communications Act in 1934, for example, it drew its power from the first article of the Constitution (§ 8) that endows Congress with the authority to regulate interstate commerce. Electronic communication is a form of interstate commerce and this rationale explained how federal power could be expanded over radio stations and eventually other electronic media. In the same bill, the Federal Communications Commission was created to administrate the day-to-day regulation of broadcasting. If the FCC creates a rule in variance with either the Communications Act or the U.S. Constitution, the legal challenge to that action would test the rule's validity in accordance with "higher" forms of law.

Note that it is only invalidated *after* it has been legally challenged; sometimes laws are created and enforced for years before they're officially questioned. American cities, for example, often enact laws restricting the size and location of billboards, or the amount of noise permitted at certain times of day (these time, place, and manner rules will be discussed in a later chapter). Such a billboard rule would have to be consistent with statutes, the state constitution, or relevant federal code, in addition to the U.S. Constitution.

Approved statutes are organized into codes and indexed under various titles as subjects dealing with particular issues. For example, Title 17 of the U.S. Code covers copyright issues in thirteen chapters covering everything from music videos to

Bedrock Law: The legal authority of the U.S. government is subject to a system of checks and balances that is exercised by executive, legislative, and judicial branches.

Judicial review
■ The doctrine under which the judiciary is the final interpreter of the constitutionality of executive and legislative actions. First established in *Marbury v. Madison* (1803).

Writ of mandamus
■ Issued by courts to command lower courts or government officials to perform specific actions.

Statutory law ■ Law that is enacted into statute by a legislative body.

Bedrock Law: The U.S. Supreme Court first exercised its authority to strike down acts of Congress through its broad powers of judicial review in *Marbury v. Madison*.

Supremacy clause
■ Article VI, paragraph 2, of the U.S. Constitution mandates that federal law is supreme whenever a conflict arises between federal and state law.

royalties. Congress and state legislatures wrestle with drafts of statutes, but there is another source, the "common law," sometimes called *judge-made law,* which is an even broader form of legal authority.

THE COMMON LAW

In the 1930s, a fictional lawyer/detective, "Blackstone Kent," appeared in the pulp fiction sagas of *Amazing Detective Tales*.[7] Blackstone was the nickname for lawyers inspired by an Oxford professor, Sir William Blackstone, who analyzed old British cases and the writings of jurists to be compiled in his *Commentaries on the Law of England*.[8] American lawyers from the nation's creation forward schooled themselves on Blackstone's eighteenth-century writings, and some even enrolled in his class in England. Even Abraham Lincoln began preparing for his legal career in Illinois by borrowing six volumes of Blackstone's commentaries just to learn the **common law**.

This form of judge-made law relies on the record and reasoning of earlier cases. The key phrase indicating the legal system's reliance is **"stare decisis,"** which is Latin for "let the decision stand."[9] In other words, both the common law of England and the case law of the United States may be applied to determine how earlier court rulings would resolve the civil disputes and criminal acts at bar.[10]

There are actually two ways to view the concept of legal precedent; one is as a legal rule or authority that is consistently upheld in previous cases over time. Such a precedent becomes a "must-follow rule" if handed down by a higher court in the same jurisdiction, and if the legal circumstances are similar enough to consider it to be "on point." The second type of precedent fulfills an advisory function, which is applied from rulings in other jurisdictions dealing with similar issues. This type of precedent is persuasive when no other case is binding and the issue at hand warrants it. For example, if one state legislature decides to ban the access of minors to violent video games, lawyers for the manufacturer may argue the statute is unconstitutional based on an appeals court's ruling concerning a similar law. Until the U.S. Supreme Court rules on the question that decision might be accepted as persuasive, though nonbinding, precedent. Over time, case precedents become part of the legal tradition until a case comes along that upends that tradition and establishes a new principle. Such a decision is known as a **landmark ruling**.

Precedent is essential for any system of laws based on the notion that previous decisions allow the participants in a dispute to apprehend what legal principles

Common law ■ Law that represents the precedent set by courts in past decisions.

Stare decisis ■ The legal doctrine that judges are bound to follow the decisions of past courts, or precedent, in deciding similar cases.

Landmark rulings ■ Cases that establish new legal principles.

---

[7]"Blackstone Kent" was created by pulp fiction writer Ralph Milne Farley (Roger Sherman Hoar).

[8]William Blackstone, *Commentaries on the Law of England* 4 vols. (Stanley N. Katz intro., facsimile ed. Univ Chicago 1979).

[9]The complete Latin phrase is actually *"stare decisis et non quieta movere,"* which means "stand by the decision and don't move what has been settled."

[10]Louisiana is the nation's only civil law state, which means it rests judicial authority not on the common law of England but a civilian code based on French, Spanish, and Roman legal traditions.

apply. If a person sees that most previous decisions have gone a certain way, he or she must assume that the next decision will follow the same pattern. If that means the court is likely to decide against the litigant, they might be less likely to go to court. Imagine a system where this process does not occur. No one would know what to expect. It is up to the courts to decide which precedents must be followed and if more than one can be applied, which is done by distinguishing the legal question's material elements. Those are the factors most important in deciding who is responsible for what has happened to cause the dispute, and how it is to be resolved.

One precedent found in Blackstone's *Commentaries* on the common law dealt with the question of censorship. "The liberty of the press is indeed essential to the nature of a free state," he wrote, "but this consists in laying no previous restraints on publications, and not in freedom from censure for criminal matter when published."[11] The common law principle would accept punishment after the fact, but not beforehand where freedom of expression might be curbed.

Actions in Equity

Listen to the bailiff at the beginning of a courtroom trial and you might hear the phrase shouted, "Oyez, Oyez, Oyez . . . this court now presides in law and **equity**." Equity is actually another source of law. It does not replace legislative statutes or common law, but such judicial writs of equity speak to certain issues.[12] It fills the gap between new statutes and old cases by granting the court greater latitude on how to decide what might be the best course of action in resolving a dispute.

Judicial orders in equity fall outside legislative or common-law actions and are rendered on the basis of what is viewed as the best solution to resolve a civil complaint. Judges may choose to offer **injunctive relief,** which is the legal term used for stopping someone or some group from pursuing a particular course of action. One example is the injunction a judge may order to force a paparazzi photographer to back up a certain distance from a famous target, as one particularly aggressive photographer was required to do as a result of his relentless pursuit of Jackie Onassis.[13] Celebrity stalkers or disgruntled spouses also can be enjoined by the court from coming too near to subjects of their ardor. Equity law serves as a means to counterbalance common law because it grants the judge greater latitude to exact justice in cases where common law is not well suited to the task.

Bedrock Law: Courts are bound to legal principles established by both case precedent and statutory law.

Equity law ■
Historically, courts of equity were able to grant equitable remedies, which require the parties to perform, or refrain from, certain actions rather than simply requiring a defendant to pay monetary damages. Modern U.S. courts are a unified system, with access to both equitable and legal remedies.

Injunctive relief ■
A form of equitable remedy; but rather than commanding action, injunctive relief commands inaction, prohibiting the respondent from acting.

Bedrock Law: Equity law allows a court to create a just and fair remedy to resolve a civil dispute in circumstances where common law or statute does not apply.

---

[11]4 Blackstone, *supra* note 8, at 151, 152.

[12]Equity law can be traced to the British heritage when subjects of the crown would—lacking common-law relief — take their grievance to a special court of the chancery, where a magistrate drafted an order to prevent an anticipated harm or deal out a legal remedy.

[13]*Galella v. Onassis*, 487 F.2d 986 (2d Cir. 1973).

Executive Orders

There is another source of law, which arrives by personal order through executive actions that in a certain way resembles royal dictates. When governors issue curfews during crises, or when mayors designate special areas as free speech zones during conventions, they authorize **executive orders** that carry the force of law. The exercise of this executive authority, however, varies by individual office and the level of government. The president, for example, draws "executive power" from the Constitution that mandates he is required to faithfully execute all federal laws (art. 2, §§ 1, 3).

For more than a century, executive orders (E.O.s) were narrowly construed as the chief executive's means for directing administrative agencies. In more recent times, E.O.s have been used expansively to desegregate schools, grant civil rights, or even bar federal funding for abortions. President Harry S. Truman issued an executive order as he sought to protect national security by classifying federal documents according to levels of secrecy. Certain papers and records were so sensitive,

Executive orders ■ Issued by the president to direct the executive branch as to how it should execute the law. Many executive orders carry the force of statutory law by congressional consent.

UP CLOSE

Ordering Freedom of Access

When the United States began leading a War on Terror in 2003, national security took on added significance and executive orders were issued to restrain the public from gaining access to military records, intelligence sources, and other federal documents. Domestic spying operations for suspected terrorists were instituted in 2001 that included inspection of transnational phone calls. Certain members of Congress later questioned the constitutionality of this program and the executive orders authorizing it; one even proposed censuring the president.[a]

Former U.S. Attorney General John Ashcroft directed federal employees to release information only after they had a chance to give "full and deliberate consideration of the institutional, commercial, and personal privacy interest that could be implicated by disclosure of the information."[b] Ashcroft's position veered from his predecessor's policy, which ordered federal agencies to quickly release government documents unless foreseeable harms could be specified. President Bush late in 2005 issued an executive order to speed up public access to federal documents under the Freedom of Information (FOI) Act, but he also kept in place certain restrictions. His order did place an FOI officer in charge of each of the 89 federal agencies to handle all the requests. Executive orders and memoranda carry the force of law, but also create controversy since it means one person dictates the law without having to answer to another branch of government.

---

[a]Sen. Russ Feingold (D-Wis.) took this futile action after the National Security Agency began monitoring transnational telephone conversations. *See* Senate Press Release, "Feingold to Introduce Resolution Censuring the President, Feingold Says Congress Must Condemn the President's Violation of the Public's Trust Through Illegal Wiretapping Program," available at http://www.senate.gov/~feingold/releases/06/03/20060312 (last visited June 24, 2006).

[b]*See* Posting of U.S. DOJ Office of Information and Privacy, "New Attorney General FOIA Memorandum Issued" to http://www.usdoj.gov/foiapost (10/15/01).

he stamped them "TOP SECRET" on the cover or title page in order to place them outside the reach of the general public.

FTC-1914

Administrative Agencies

Another source of law that is even more pervasive is drawn from administrative agencies, which regulate business and media interest. Judging by the broad sweep of administrative agencies, this part of the executive branch of government seems to belong in a class by itself. While part of the executive branch, administrative agencies draft binding rules and then enforce the same and even deliberate on appeals to their agency decisions. In sum, the executive, legislative, and judicial duties are all rolled into the executive agencies of federal government.

Administrative law
■ Law that derives authority from being part of the regulations set out by executive agencies.

Such agency decisions can be challenged in a courtroom outside the federal bureaucracy. In fighting an FCC decision, for example, a plaintiff might take the petition to the U.S. Court of Appeals for the District of Columbia. The D.C. Circuit has the smallest jurisdiction of any federal court of appeals, but frequently decides important cases given its authority over federal agencies in the nation's capital.[14]

Executive branch agencies began shaping the legal terrain in the late nineteenth century after the nation's railroads invited oversight, and the Interstate Commerce Commission was formed to answer that particular need. The early twentieth century saw federal agencies sprout up around Washington, D.C., for the purpose of regulating business enterprise. The Federal Trade Commission (FTC), for example, was formed in 1914 and regulated advertising and other forms of commerce. The Federal Communications Commission (FCC) followed the Federal Radio Commission (FRC) in 1934 as a "temporary agency" charged with licensing airwaves to radio stations. The Securities and Exchange Commission (SEC) and the Federal Election Commission (FEC) also enforce rules on financial markets and campaign expenditures, and exercise periodic influence over communication media and the freedom of expression. Through the advice and consent of the Senate, the president chooses who is to direct these administrative agencies and serve as a commissioner or lead as the chair. Today, there are more rules drawn up in administrative offices affecting communication enterprise than are passed by elected officials convening on Capitol Hill.

Bedrock Law: Federal agencies have legal powers that include drafting rules, enforcing them, and deciding appeals to their enforcement.

SYSTEMS OF JUSTICE

Some might think the court system functions like a "fight club," where two sides tangle and the judge and jury simply declare the winners and losers.[15] It is closer to the truth to view it as a chess match where both sides hope to achieve their objective

---

[14]Several U.S. Supreme Court justices served there first before their confirmation, including Chief Justice John Roberts along with Associate Justices Ruth Bader Ginsburg, Antonin Scalia, and Clarence Thomas.

[15]S.L. Alexander, *Covering the Courts–A Handbook for Journalists* 39–54 (2nd ed. Rowman & Littlefield 2003).

Criminal law ■ The body of law that defines conduct prohibited and punished by the state.

Civil law ■ The body of law that regulates disputes between private parties.

Burden of proof ■ Refers to the threshold of certainty a party in court must meet to prove a matter in dispute.

Beyond a reasonable doubt ■ The burden of proof in criminal cases.

Preponderance of evidence ■ The burden of proof in civil cases.

Plaintiff ■ In a civil trial, the party bringing the action.

Damages ■ Money awarded to the plaintiff in a civil suit, to be paid by a defendant.

> **Bedrock Law:** Civil law involves rules designed to protect individuals or groups of individuals, while criminal laws are enforced to protect society at large.

by choosing the right move for their client but must obey the rules for each move they make. Courts are established to resolve these matches on behalf of defendants in criminal trials, and litigants in lawsuits who seek to resolve their differences in civil actions. Criminal laws address trespasses against society, whereas civil suits deal with complaints against groups or individuals. A criminal case might produce a civil result depending on the nature of the alleged crime. All trials play out under specific rules of procedure designed to give justice its best shot.

The difference between **criminal** and **civil law** is that in terms of criminal matters, actions are taken by the "State," which actually could be a government body at the local (municipal, county, or parish), state, or national level in order to protect all the residents. When a crime is committed, the nature of the act and the perpetrator are entitled to a presumption of innocence. Punishment then strictly follows evidentiary bounds. It can mean removal from society in the form of imprisonment or even execution. Crimes against the person, such as assault, rape, and murder are felonies where punishments are more severe than those against property, such as burglary, theft, and robbery.

A person is either found guilty or not guilty of an offense; the term *innocent* is less apt because the scope of the charges may not necessarily extend that far. All that is required in a criminal case is that the accused be cleared or convicted of the alleged act. Since there may be multiple criminal acts facing the accused at a trial, an individual is either found guilty or not guilty of each of the criminal counts, but the standards for reaching the verdict vary from case to case. The highest **burden of proof** in criminal law is to show guilt **beyond a reasonable doubt,** a standard assuring a high level of certainty. There are two lesser standards: clear and convincing evidence—a medium standard of proof—and a **preponderance of evidence,** where it is only more likely than not to be true.

In civil cases, lesser standards of proof are brought to bear because the question is not one of guilt, but one of liability, an indication of some lesser measure of fault. For example, a defendant is blamed in a lawsuit for some harm that has come to a complaining party's reputation, the **plaintiff** in the case. In order to make that plaintiff whole after the supposed harm, the court decides if the defendant caused the defamation and is thus to be held liable for the harm. The result will most often be an award of money or **damages,** but freedom or life are only held in the balance as criminal penalties. Because these charges and complaints contrast considerably, legal proceedings in criminal cases and civil actions also vary to meet the needs of justice.

CRIMINAL PROCEDURES

Criminal cases enter the courtroom through a number of portals. They may arrive as a police citation, an arrest warrant, or indictment by a grand jury for a more serious offense. Small crimes are treated as misdemeanors—as distinguished from felonies—and include such day-to-day infractions as traffic violations, disorderly conduct, shoplifting, or other minor offenses. Misdemeanor convictions produce smaller fines and shorter jail times than more serious crimes.

The crimes that are more serious threats to society, such as assaults, armed robberies, and murders are prosecuted as felonies. Felonies also encompass high-dollar crimes or criminal conspiracies, such as extortion, which is punishable by imprisonment. Naturally, felony convictions carry stiffer penalties in terms of both fines and prison terms than do misdemeanors. The charge in felony cases is made by a grand jury **indictment** that follows a hearing of witnesses presented by the prosecutor regarding the crime. The judge may reject or accept the charges contained in the indictment. If the judge accepts the indictment, the defendant will be charged with the crime.

Pre-trial Phase

Any fan of courtroom drama knows the basic elements of an arrest require that the police advise the accused of certain civil rights. This is called the **Miranda warning,** or "Mirandizing" a suspect. This requirement to apprise a suspect of their rights arose out of the 1966 case *Miranda v. Arizona.* The right to remain silent—so as not to incriminate oneself—and the right to a trial by jury with legal counsel are both guaranteed by the Constitution. Suspected criminals cannot be held for long without charges (usually twenty-four hours or less). The court sets bail so the accused can remain free in exchange for the financial promise to show up in court once the lawyers and judge are ready to proceed.

The criminal case then enters the pre-trial phase or **discovery** when attorneys review the reports of police, photographs, physical evidence, and other materials related to the crime. Lawyers look at witness statements and take their own **depositions**. The official charge of the crime is read at the **arraignment,** where the defendant has a chance to plead guilty, not guilty, or **nolo contendere** (no contest) to the criminal counts. Attorneys may make motions at the pre-trial hearing, such as ones to quash subpoenas that might produce new evidence against the defendant including the defendant's arrest record or medical history. Defense lawyers also can move to entirely dismiss the prosecution of the case.

Pre-trial hearings have a bearing on what is allowed into the court record. Evidence seized without a proper warrant can be ruled out of bounds, or inflammatory photos, documents, and depositions can be deleted from the record. The prosecution even can decide to drop charges and work out a plea agreement offering the defendant a punishment less severe than the kind the state could deal if convicted. If those negotiations fail, a trial date usually will be set for docket.

Trial Phase

The jury selection or **voir dire** (French term meaning "to speak the truth") opens the trial. The truth spoken is each juror's ability to render a fair and impartial verdict. If it seems that the prospective jurors cannot do so, three options are usually available—a **change of venue** will move the case to a distant locale, a **change of venire** will import jurors from another community, and a **continuance** will postpone the trial until a more suitable time.

Once the trial begins, lawyers for both sides either accept or refuse to seat jurors in a selection process that is also defined by the law. Attorneys can strike for cause if a prospective juror is biased or seems to be impaired in another way. If there is no

Indictment ■ A formal accusation that a person has committed a felony or serious crime. After a grand jury hearing, the grand jury issues either a true bill, in which case the person is charged, or a no bill, in which case the person is not charged.

Miranda warning ■ Requirement to apprise suspects of their rights arose out of the 1966 case *Miranda v. Arizona*.

Discovery ■ Pre-trial phase in which each party is entitled to request and gain access to evidence possessed by the other side.

Depositions ■ Out of court sworn oral testimony that is transcribed for use at trial.

Arraignment ■ A hearing where formal charges are read against a criminal defendant and the defendant is expected to enter a plea.

Nolo contendere ■ A plea entered by the defendant in a criminal proceeding, which admits neither guilt nor innocence, but does not contest the charge.

Voire dire ■ The pre-trial process of jury selection.

Change of venue ■ Moving a trial to a different geographical location.

Change of venire ■ Importing jurors from a different geographical location.

Continuance ■ Postpones proceedings until a later date.

Peremptory challenge ■ A challenge to a juror in voire dire that is not for cause. Most jurisdictions afford attorneys one or more "strikes" without giving a reason for striking the names.

Reversible error ■ Error found by an appellate court to have occurred at trial that sufficiently prejudiced the outcome to warrant reversal.

Harmless error ■ Error found by an appellate court to have occurred at trial that did not sufficiently prejudiced the outcome to warrant reversal.

Vacated ■ A vacated judgment voids a previous judgment.

clear reason why a juror should not be seated, the lawyer can raise a **peremptory challenge** and not disclose the reason; however, prospective jurors cannot be denied a seat on account of ethnicity, religion, or gender. Most jurisdictions afford attorneys one or more "strikes" without giving a reason for striking the names.

After the jury is seated, attorneys for the state and the accused present their opening statements, followed by the examination of witnesses. That gives way to statements and rebuttals from both sides, just before the judge presents the charge to the jury and hands the case over for deliberation. As noted earlier, closing arguments are made either showing or not showing guilt beyond a reasonable doubt in criminal cases. If a conviction is reached by a judge or jury, the sentencing phase will follow in a separate hearing (with relaxed rules of evidence) afforded to parties of the trial.

Post-trial Phase

If the evidence points to a guilty defendant, the verdict can be appealed, but not overturned unless there is what is called **reversible error**. Small mistakes at a trial are inevitable and are considered **harmless error** since they do not constitute reversible error. If a mistake at trial is significant, a verdict can be **vacated** or **remanded**. Setting aside a verdict does not require a new trial, but a remand does. Criminal procedure is more exacting and rigorous than civil litigation primarily because life or liberty can hang in the balance.

CIVIL PROCEDURES

Lawsuits bring individuals, political officials, or corporations to court because of some **tort** (Latin: "to distort or break") or wrong that interferes with someone's rights. The principal questions are who is at fault and who should pay for it. Knowing the actors and their roles makes it easier to figure out who will prevail in such matters. In civil court, legal rivals are called litigants, or plaintiffs and respondents. The plaintiff frames a complaint in the form of a lawsuit or petition, which he or she files against a **respondent** or **defendant**.

Pre-trial Phase

Once the lawsuit is filed in court, the respondent receives the written complaint and is supposed to answer it in a fixed period or risk losing the case by default. If the respondent thinks the plaintiff has no standing, or if there is actually no just cause of action, then that party files a **demurrer**. This is the necessary response when the facts of the case are accurate, but there is no evidence of an unlawful act that can be attributed to the respondent. Another pre-trial motion is one for **summary judgment,** where an attorney asks the judge to declare a lawsuit too weak to bring to trial.[16] Once all sides agree it would be better to remove the proceedings from the complications of a trial and come to terms, a settlement is the proper solution.

---

[16]There are other motions intended to show that there is no reason to bring a case to trial. Most lawsuits never do make it to trial, in fact, and are settled out of court.

If a civil complaint does move forward to the discovery phase, witnesses will give their depositions, sign affidavits, and answer **interrogatories**—questions pertinent to the case posed by attorneys for both sides. A party to the suit may file a legal brief, a summary of decisions supporting a favorable decision. If other parties wish to get involved, then *amicus curiae*—friend of the court briefs—will be filed. The American Civil Liberties Union, for example, often files supporting briefs when First Amendment rights are involved. The judge then decides either to try the case, dismiss it, or recommend that both sides seek alternative dispute resolution (ADR), which could mean inviting a mediator to settle the matter once and for all.

Trial Phase

If the civil lawsuit does make it to trial, the question becomes not one of guilt or innocence, but liability. No unanimous verdict is required, only a convincing majority (three-fourths or five-sixths of the jurors) to determine the outcome of the complaint. As noted, the standard is not reasonable doubt as it is in criminal cases, but simply a preponderance of the evidence.

Post-trial Phase

If the plaintiff's side prevails, financial relief can be recovered by collecting damages that are calculated three ways: **actual damages** (sometimes called **compensatory**), where an estimate is made of the dollar amount for the harm done based on loss of reputation, invasion of privacy, or some other personal hurt. Special damages are when the recovery is for out-of-pocket losses, which could include missing wages, extra expenses, downturns in profit, and the like. Also, **punitive damages** will be levied in cases where the court seeks to punish the defendant.

In cases where punitive damages are awarded, a jury might assess an exorbitant punitive figure "to send a message" to the public. Note well those headline-fetching awards are either capped in certain states, or can be drastically reduced by an appeals court if the trial jury's punitive award is "grossly disproportionate" to the actual harm done. Of course, either side may choose to appeal the decision. These procedures stand in contrast to criminal law, where lines are drawn to distinguish each offense's degree of danger to society.

COURT SYSTEM

Americans are entitled to their day in court, and there are fifty-two court systems that have been established around the country to give that to them—one for each state, the nation, and the District of Columbia. The judges who run these courts either are elected or appointed to their respective jurisdictions. At the federal level, all judges are appointed by the president and confirmed by the senate. Supreme Court appointments receive more attention because they occur so infrequently,[17]

Remanded ■ A higher appellate court may send back, or remand, a case to a lower court for some subsequent action.

Tort ■ From the Latin "break," a tort is a civil wrong that involves the breach of a duty to someone else, resulting in foreseeable harm.

Respondent ■ The responding party in a legal proceeding, particularly in appellate proceedings or proceedings initiated by petition.

Defendant ■ The accused in a criminal legal proceeding, or responding party in a civil proceeding initiated by complaint.

Demurrer ■ A motion that challenges the legal sufficiency of a claim set forth in a filing by an opposing party.

Summary judgment ■ A final judgment for one party without trial when a court finds either no material fact is in dispute, or when the law alone clearly establishes one party's claim.

---

[17]Between 1789 and 2005, the Senate has only voted 132 times on Supreme Court nominees. *See* Denis Rutkin & Maureen Bearden, *Supreme Court Nominations, 1789–2005* (Congressional Research Service 2006).

TABLE 1.1 Elements in a Criminal Case and Civil Actions

CRIMINAL CASE	CIVIL ACTIONS
FIRST: CRIME COMMITTED How large—felony or misdemeanor?	**FIRST: HARM OCCURRED** Is there a cause of action, a legal claim?
SECOND: PERSON RESPONSIBLE Criminal defendant charged or indicted	**SECOND: PERSON RESPONSIBLE** Plaintiff sues respondent/defendant
THIRD: PRE-TRIAL STAGE Discovery (police reports, evidence, eyewitness depositions) Arraignment (guilty, not guilty, nolo contendere)	**THIRD: PRE-TRIAL STAGE** Discovery (affidavits, depositions, interrogatories, legal briefs, *amicus* briefs) Motions: summary judgment Alternative dispute resolution (ADR)
FOURTH: TRIAL STAGE Delays (continuance, change of venue, change of venire) Opening statements Witnesses and cross-examinations Deliberations Verdict (guilty or not guilty)	**FOURTH: TRIAL STAGE** Opening statements Witnesses and cross-examinations Closing arguments Deliberations Verdict (liability for damages)
FIFTH: POST-TRIAL STAGE Sentencing or freedom	**FIFTH: POST-TRIAL STAGE** Assessment of damages

Interrogatories ■
Written questions pertinent to the case posed by attorneys for both sides in the discovery phase of a trial.

Actual damages ■
Also called compensatory damages, this is the monetary compensation designed to remedy the losses suffered by the plaintiff.

but the same process is followed for each appointment to federal district and circuit courts. All federal judges are appointed for life terms. Provisions exist to remove federal judges for serious breaches of duty through impeachment, but the majority of appointees serve as jurists until they retire, sometimes a mandatory age, or die in office.[18]

In some states, selecting judges may involve either election or appointment with party affiliation either known or concealed in a system that varies from state to state. Some states allow for direct election of judges by the citizens while other states use a system that provides the governor or a commission with the power to appoint the judges. Some states have a system where trial court judges are elected but appellate judges are appointed. After their first term of service, most judges can choose to stand for reelection. In instances where voters do not select judges, the governor or state commission can make a new appointment. Each state is responsible for establishing its own system.

---

[18]One public interest group calculates that 13 federal judges out of 3,027 have faced impeachment for an impeachment rate of 0.4 percent. The percentage actually removed of course is lower still: 0.2 percent. http://CourtZero.org.

Judges serve different jurisdictions based on their location and the type of cases tried or subject matter, and that also varies by state. At the federal level, the U.S. Constitution vests legal authority in "one Supreme Court," but it also authorizes Congress to ordain and establish "such inferior courts" as necessary. In 1789, Congress began that process of lower-court construction, and has been involved with the process ever since.

In first dividing up the national jurisdictions, 94 federal district courts were allocated according to population size. Each district sends its disputed decisions up to twelve circuit courts of appeal including one for the District of Columbia.[19] The federal appellate circuit courts serve at least three states. Among these geographic jurisdictions, the Ninth Circuit Court in San Francisco is the largest and some would claim the most famous. High-profile decisions such as a pledge of allegiance case (*Elk Grove Unified School District v. Endow*, 542 U.S. 1 (2004)), a cruel and unusual punishment decision (*Ewing v. California*, 538 U.S. 11 (2003)); *Locker v.* (*Andrade*, 538 U.S. 63 (2003)), and a decision affecting Holocaust survivors (*Altering v. Vatican Bank*, F.3d, 05 C.D.O.S. 3216, 9th Circ. (2005)) originated in the Ninth Circuit Court.

Punitive damages
■ This type of damage award is not intended to make the plaintiff whole, but to act as an additional deterrent to the type of conduct the defendant engaged in.

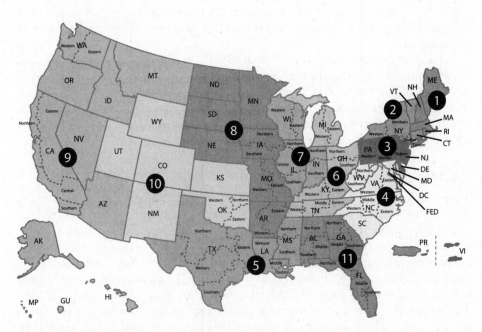

Federal Appellate Court Map of the United States
The United States as divided into federal appellate circuits. Each of the eleven circuits has multiple district courts. A twelfth appellate court is in Washington, D.C.

---

[19]The D.C. Circuit Court of Appeals is especially relevant to First Amendment law since it handles cases challenging federal agencies. The U.S. Court of Appeals for the Federal Circuit hears patent appeals or other claims against the federal government. This federal appeals court was actually the consolidation of two legal jurisdictions—the old Court of Customs and Patent Appeals and Court of Claims.

The Appeals Process

Imagine the legal system as a courthouse with three floors. On the first floor, the trial court serves to gather the facts of a dispute or an alleged crime, which makes it the court of original jurisdiction. The record of fact is drawn from depositions, eyewitness testimony, and those items that are admitted in evidence. It is on this floor that judges and juries perform their role in assessing the facts of the case. Because two parties are in contest, there is often some disagreement regarding both the facts of their dispute and the law's application. When such questions produce a disagreement of fact, the jury or judge's discretion enters in to render a decision. Once all the testimony has been heard and the necessary evidence is presented, a verdict is reached by applying the law to the evidence admitted.

If an appeal is filed, the case moves to the appellate level on the second floor for a fuller interpretation. In most but not all states, appellate court acceptance is automatic. Appellate courts will not only look at the evidence presented at trial, but how the law was applied to a particular case. In some instances, the appellate court may opt to review the factual record if the case was dismissed during the pre-trial phase or some allegation of lawyer misconduct was made. This event would call for a **de novo** review. When judicial review occurs at the appellate level, judges search for defects, for what is called reversible error. Some appellate courts may find particular pieces of evidence that should not have been allowed, or an error in procedure.

One common misconception is that an appeals court arrives at a separate verdict, but what actually occurs is the trial court's decision is either upheld or not. If the case is returned to the first floor, it is remanded or remitted, which means that the appeals court wants the lower court to reconsider its judgment based on a new interpretation or rationale. If the lower court's ruling is affirmed, the losing party has the right to pursue the matter to a court of last resort, which would be the third floor of justice.

De novo ■ From the Latin "from the beginning," when an appellate court reviews a non-jury trial record, it may conduct the review de novo, meaning to look for error in the judge's findings of fact, as well as matters of law.

Supreme Courts

In each state a high court may render the final decision. After hearing the appeals, the high court passes judgment on issues both of law and of fact. It is this tribunal that is responsible for finding and correcting the mistakes made by both the trial and lower appeals courts. The power of this panel of judges (usually identified as the state supreme court) is defined by the state constitution, but lower state courts and federal courts respect its determinant authority. A case will only move beyond this court's decision if there is a federal question involved, such as one involving the Constitution. Most state supreme courts operate on the principle of discretionary review, which means it can refuse to consider cases from a lower court if no conflict of precedent issue is involved. The same holds true at the federal level.

Nine justices sit on the bench of the U.S. Supreme Court and they serve to define and redefine the law through wide-ranging opinions that cover a broad spectrum of controversies. Although the "high court" normally serves as the final stage of an appeal of federal importance, it does act as a trial court of original jurisdiction for certain issues. For example, the U.S. Supreme Court has twice tried cases involving the state of New Mexico against the state of Texas over boundaries and water rights to the Pecos River.[20] Those trials are extraordinary; more often the Court serves as the last stop in the chain of appeals.

Granting Certiorari

Less than 5 percent of the petitions submitted to the U.S. Supreme Court are granted a hearing, which means thousands of appeals are filed each year, and less than a hundred are accepted for review. Most lawyers seek a **writ of certiorari,** which means to be informed of the case, and once that is granted, the Court will hear the appeal because it sees a significant issue is involved that will help define the law. Just because "cert. is denied," it does not mean the Court necessarily agrees with the lower court's ruling; it just means a majority of the justices[21] see nothing significant and relevant about the case to warrant any further hearings, and the lower court decision will stand.

Writ of certiorari
■ A writ the U.S. Supreme Court issued to review a lower court's decision.

In order for the U.S. Supreme Court to hear a case, four of the justices must vote to grant certiorari. The decision to grant cert. does not mean that a justice believes a lower court decision needs to be overturned, just as denial of cert. does not necessarily mean that the justices believe a lower court decision was correct. There is no requirement that justices give a reason for their decision to grant or deny certiorari, but court historians, judicial biographers, and legal scholars provide us with some insight.

One of the primary reasons justices grant cert. is in those instances where they believe that they need to provide guidance to lower courts on a particular issue. For example, if one federal appellate court decides a case one way and another jurisdiction decides a similar case differently, the Court may feel the need to reconcile the decisions. The justices may also want to make a statement about an issue to direct lower court analysis. Somewhat surprisingly, the Court might choose to avoid certain issues or decisions because they are not ripe. When the Supreme Court creates precedent it hopes that the decision will guide courts for decades to come (even centuries), so it tries to avoid decisions where shifting social conditions or changes in technology could cause a ruling to become outdated or obsolete. For the sake of consistency the Court does not want to rule in cases where it believes it might have to modify or (most drastically) reverse an earlier ruling. The Court might wait years for lower courts to explore the nuances of a particular area before weighing in on the issue. Once the subject has been allowed to ripen, it may be time for the Supreme Court to step in.

Bedrock Law: The U.S. Supreme Court accepts only a small percentage of the appeals it is asked to hear based on the significance and timing of the case.

Oral Arguments and Opinions

Attorneys for both sides are first required to file written briefs, which are followed some time later by an oral argument presented before the panel of judges. Judges may decide to interrupt oral arguments in order to interview the attorneys on the

---

[20]*New Mexico v. Texas,* 276 U.S. 558 (1928); and *Texas v. New Mexico,* 462 U.S. 554 (1983).

[21]The term *justice* is a title reserved for a state or federal Supreme Court judge.

points raised either by their verbal presentations or in their written briefs. At oral argument the justices' remarks are public and there is usually speculation about the outcome of a case based on who said what at that hearing. However, much of the debate about the case occurs behind closed doors, in the conference.

The justices will gather with no one else present, not even a secretary to take notes, to discuss the case. In fact if someone knocks at the door, it is the obligation of the junior justice (the one who has been on the Supreme Court for the least time) to answer the door. But the importance of seniority in the conference goes far beyond such trivialities. When they begin to deliberate, the Chief Justice speaks first followed by associate justices in descending order of seniority.[22]

Anyone who has ever argued knows the importance of speaking first for its value in framing the debate. When it comes time for the vote, justices vote in reverse order of seniority with the chief justice voting last. Seniority affords one more privilege: when the writing is assigned, it is the senior justice voting with the majority who assigns the writing. The justices recognize that the decisions they write will be cited for decades to come, and each one writes for posterity. They recognize the legacy they leave behind. In 1964 Justice William Brennan wrote for a unanimous Court in *New York Times Co. v. Sullivan,* a seminal case in libel law. Justice Brennan retired from the Court in 1990 and died in 1997, yet the words he wrote more than forty years ago echo today as the law of the land when it comes to libel.

A majority opinion usually means five or more justices were of like mind, and one of them is delegated the honor of explaining to the parties involved and the legal community as a whole how the Court reached its decision. Sometimes a majority of justices agree, but for different reasons, which calls for a **concurring opinion**. Here a justice will write his or her own explanation and indicate why his or her reasoning departs from the others.

There are also plurality opinions that join together several justices who agree on the rationale for a particular course of action, but their agreement does not produce any precedence. The simplest and briefest way of dispensing justice is by a **memorandum order,** which indicates the winning party but does not explain why. In such cases, the Supreme Court may be suggesting that precedent should stand and there is no special significance to that case. In some instances, a decision is rendered with an opinion, but it is not signed. This type of ruling is called a **per curiam** order, which means "by the Court" as a whole. For example, the decision in *Bush v. Gore* concerning the 2000 presidential election was a per curiam opinion. Finally, dissenting opinions give justices voting against the majority an opportunity to explain their viewpoints on the case. These dissents may

Concurring opinion ■ When justices agree with the result reached by the majority, but they think the majority's rationale is wrong, the justice may author a concurrence which agrees with the result but offers a different rationale.

Memorandum order ■ Indicates the winning party but does not explain why. In such cases, the Supreme Court may be suggesting that precedent should stand and there is no special significance to that case.

---

[22]The Chief Justice always has the position of seniority, even though he or she may have served less time on the Court than other justices.

take on greater importance over time, and even figure in future decisions. Opinions of the Court are the subject of law review articles and discussions that often have a long-term impact.

Per curiam order
■ A decision rendered with an opinion, but not signed. This type of ruling is "by the Court" as a whole.

SCHOLARSHIP IN LAW

Scholars in communication law can write from the perspective of revered judges, lawyers, or the faculty of major law schools. Their alma maters and colleagues embrace their scholarship because their writings have a chance to make a difference. A well-framed analysis of a landmark case or a powerful argument against the status quo might strike a chord resonating in the case law for years.

Ultimately, two threads wend their way through legal analysis—history and logic. U.S. Supreme Court Justice Oliver Wendell Holmes, Jr. observed, "the life of the law has not been logic; it has been experience."[23] Yet his colleague Justice Louis D. Brandeis recommended, "the logic of words should yield to the logic of realities."[24] If legal logic is a form of common sense, Justice William O. Douglas's opinion is apt, "common sense often makes good law." Thus, lawyers offer the traditions of logic and history to make their points and share in common a good deal of the law's depth, context, and perspective. These are the basic ingredients; how the legal scholar puts them into writing is the difference.

The quality of legal writing relies on several factors—the strength of the issue, the soundness of the reasoning, and the depth of analysis cobbled together by careful thought and engaging prose. Legal research begins with one cardinal rule: *Read the law; apply the law.*[25] Conventional sources of legal codes, briefs, legislative records, case reporters, and digests go a long way in addressing legal questions, according to Susan Dente Ross who calls it the formal positivist approach, and it is a time-honored regimen. The legal realists represent a different type of scholarship; they explore the character and context of important cases and the parties involved in order to understand the decisions.[26] Scholars additionally look beyond these traditional approaches to address questions using the tools of social sciences to probe the law with the tools of content analyses, survey questionnaires, and experimental design. Such research is accepted from the qualitative and empirical sciences, and has found an accepted place in the legal literature.

Research Procedures

When national laws are invoked, scholars turn to one of several sources. *The United States Statutes at Large* orders the law chronologically. For that reason lawyers turn to reference the *United States Code* with volumes organized by

---

[23]As cited in *The Common Law* (Little, Brown 1881).

[24]*See* Brandeis's opinion *DeSanto v. Pennsylvania*, as cited in Melvin I. Urofsky, *Louis D. Brandeis: Advocate Before and On the Bench*, 30 J. Sup. Ct. Hist.31-46 (2005).

[25]Susan Dente Ross, *Deciding Communication Law: Key Cases in Context* 2.1–2.2 (Lawrence Erlbaum Associates 2004).

[26]*Id.*

subject heading. For timely access, federal statutes are published as "slip pages," such as the *United States Code Service* from the Lawyers Cooperative, or West Publishing's *United States Code Annotated*. Federal statutes can also be viewed online at http://uscode.house.gov/usc.htm.

If the point of the research involves federal regulation, then either the *Federal Register* (Fed. Reg.) or *Code of Federal Regulations* (CFR) can serve as valid resources. CFR is organized by legal subjects, which are known as titles, and the Fed. Reg. is ordered by chronology. Electronic access through an administrative agency's website is yet another option. For example, http://www.fcc.gov offers indexes for finding the latest electronic media regulations. The government printing office's online address, http://www.gpo.gov, opens the necessary window to agency rules.

If the research objectives call for digging deeper into the legislative record, it could mean exploring the *Congressional Record*. Attorneys also search online at http://thomas.loc.gov for archival data. For state research, the official codebook of statutes is placed on library shelves under a number of titles, such as *Vernon's Texas Civil Statutes* or *California Codes,* but usually a search of the state government's websites yields faster results.

Case Law Sources

The Internet gives scholars their first look at both statutes and cases. Lexis-Nexis through its Academic Universe database puts readers in touch with the cases and number of commentaries. LegalTrac is the search engine where simply keying in subjects or keywords helps collect the responses to the inquiry. Three other popular search engines are Findlaw (http://www.findlaw.com), LawCrawler (http://www.lawcrawler.com), and the Meta Index for Legal Research (http://www.gsulaw.gsu.edu/metaindex/). Online indexes usually guide scholars to decisions before published versions are available. Printed rulings by the U.S. Supreme Court will appear in print in the *United States Reports* after being available online in the legal databases of Lexis-Nexis or Westlaw.

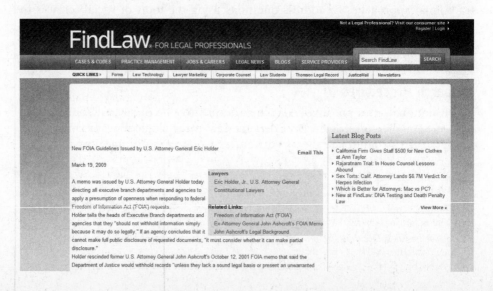

The first printed versions of the U.S. Supreme Court decisions often appear in *United States Law Week* (U.S.L.W.), along with rulings from other courts and federal agencies. The decisions from the U.S. District Court are published in *Federal Supplements* (F. Supp.), and once cases are taken up on appeal West's *Federal Reporter* prints the decision from the U.S. Circuit Courts. State appellate court decisions are grouped together by geographic region in seven different series, known as reporters, which are not necessarily intuitively organized. Oklahoma's federal cases, for example, presumably would appear in the *Southwestern Reporter* along with appellate cases from Texas; instead they are located instead in the *Pacific Reporter*.

Briefing the Case

After the law has been digested and the text of relevant cases examined, then the key decisions can be organized according to a fairly familiar format. An abstract of an important case is organized by its basic elements: citation, facts, issue, decision, explanation, ruling, concurring and dissenting opinions. For the purposes of illustration, consider the case of *Texas v. Johnson,* 491 U.S. 397 (1989). The brief begins with the citation that includes the name of the case, the volume and page numbers of the legal reporter where it is published, followed by the year it was decided. The state of Texas is the appellant and Johnson is respondent in this case. The petitioner who is appealing the lower court ruling comes first in citations, while the respondent is listed second, and "v." signifies *versus*. In *Texas v. Johnson,* the state of Texas is prosecuting a criminal law action against Gregory Lee Johnson under its Texas Penal Code [Ann. § 42.09 (a) (3)]. "U.S." is the abbreviation for the official publication, *United States Reports*; the numeral 491 represents the volume; and 397 marks the beginning page number in this legal reporter. The year 1989 is when the Supreme Court handed down its decision. *Texas v. Johnson* is also found in other publications so parallel citations may be used. The second element of the brief is the facts of the case. This is the summary given to report the key elements that led to this particular decision. This part answers the journalist's basic questions of "who, what, where, when, how, and why" in a summary that briefs with the conflict.

Facts

Gregory Lee Johnson was taking part in a protest held during the Republican National Convention in 1984. He was protesting the "Republican War Chest," which involved contributions of certain Dallas-based corporations that he believed posed the threat of nuclear war. Johnson unwrapped an American flag that was given to him by a fellow protestor and he doused it in kerosene, ignited the cloth, and with his fellow protestors shouted, "America, the red, white, and blue, we spit on you!"

Johnson was the only protestor charged with the crime, and upon conviction was sentenced to one year in prison and fined $2,000. He appealed the verdict, but the Court of Appeals for the Fifth District of Texas upheld his conviction. The court of last resort in the state, the Texas Court of Criminal Appeals, reversed Johnson's conviction holding that the State could not punish him for burning the flag under the First Amendment. The ruling was based on the reasoning that Texas could not preserve the flag as a symbol of national unity by suppressing free speech, and that flag burnings do not necessarily incite a breach of the peace.

The third part of the briefing covers the "Issue," and spells out the principal question the court was seeking to resolve. It is usually stated as a question or described in one or two declarative sentences.

Issue(s)

Does the Government have the right to ban flag burning in order to honor particular symbols or prevent a breach of peace, or do such laws violate the First Amendment's protection?

The fourth part of the case briefing abstracts the decision of the court, which usually begins with a one-word response to the question framed in the issue. It may be referred to as a ruling, holding, judgment, or sometimes disposition.

Decision

AFFIRMED. In a 5-to-4 decision, the U.S. Supreme Court affirmed the lower court's ruling by finding that Johnson's flag burning was expressive conduct, and that the governmental interest in protecting symbols of national unity did not override the First Amendment. No breach of peace occurred. Justice Brennan wrote the majority opinion with Justice Kennedy concurring. Justice Rehnquist filed the principal dissent and Justice Stevens dissented separately.

The fifth part of the brief is the explanation where the rationale for the ruling indicates how the decision relates to earlier case precedents and statutes and discusses relevant legal theory.

Explanation

The Supreme Court ruled that Texas identified two interests to justify Gregory Lee Johnson's conviction under this statute—one that it was preventing a disturbance of the peace and the other that it was protecting the national symbol of unity. The record failed to show there was any incitement to violence among the demonstrators that day, and suppressing symbolic protests was a violation of the First Amendment.

The sixth part of the brief summarizes in one or two sentences the consequences of the ruling.

Rule of Law

As a result of this ruling, the flag-burning law in Texas was struck down as unconstitutional. States cannot enforce similar laws that would punish a person for burning a flag as a means of political protest. That would mean the state is enforcing only one attitude toward the flag, which is constitutionally prohibited. Justice Brennan wrote, "We can imagine no more appropriate response to burning a flag than waving one's own. . . ."

Finally, if there are dissenting or concurring opinions of the court, they should be summarized and attributed in the seventh part.

Concurring or Dissenting Opinions

Justice Kennedy concurred, but apologized for the decision believing that the "hard fact is that sometimes we must make decisions we do not like" because it is both "poignant but fundamental that the flag protects those who hold it in contempt."

Chief Justice Rehnquist dissented and condemned the decision in historic terms, quoting Justice Holmes' aphorism that "a page of history is worth a volume of logic." He traced the flag's blood-stained history through major wars, quoting poets, and citing cases where the flag was specifically revered. He concluded that "the uniquely deep awe and respect for our flag" should not be "bundled off under the rubric of designated symbols" that the First Amendment prohibits the government from establishing.

Justice Stevens' dissent focused on the authority to prohibit certain means of expression though not the ideas. He concluded flag burning would fall in that category. "Had (Johnson) chosen to spray-paint—or perhaps convey with a motion picture project—his message of dissatisfaction on the face of the Lincoln Memorial, there would be no question about the power of the government to prohibit his means of expression."

The case briefing is helpful in understanding how the rule of law proceeds through the judicial branches of governance, which is a product of both trial and appellate courts of law. The legislative branch relies on the judiciary for its interpretation of case law and so does the executive branch for enforcement. Both the activities of the courts and their sources of authority provide worthy subjects of scholarly investigation especially since laws and legal practitioners are subject to the will of the governed.

SUMMARY

- The Supreme Court has the authority to strike down flawed laws, and in the process set precedent for the rule of law. Courts preside over equity actions and are empowered to offer injunctive relief to citizens where the common law is not clearly applicable. The lifeblood of a nation's democracy is measured by its rule of law, and American governance is a product of both the sources of law and their application to systems of justice. The sources of legal power in the legislative branch rely on the judiciary for interpretation and the executive branch for enforcement.

- The three branches of federal government limit each other's power in crafting the laws with respect to freedom of expression through a system of checks and balances between executive, legislative, and judicial branches.

- Appellate courts in the nation and the states exercise the power of judicial review and can either uphold laws or strike them down. This form of common law dates back to the landmark case of *Marbury v. Madison* where the U.S. Supreme Court seized power for itself to strike down acts of Congress if they were found to be unconstitutional on appeal. Courts are bound to follow precedent or *stare decisis*, which means "to let the decision stand." The U.S. Supreme Court accepts only a small percentage of the appeals it is asked to hear based on the significance and timing of the case.

- Courts can serve injunctions and issue other writs through equity law when neither the statutes nor the case precedents apply to the legal disputes at hand. Such cases usually do not involve any recovery for damages.

- The levels of jurisdiction that courts have with respect to deciding cases and their appeals vary by state and the particular type of case that is being heard. In all states though a legal hierarchy allows higher courts to review and examine lower court rulings. Precedent-setting cases influence the common law that guides judges in resolving disputes beyond the statutory construction.

- The contrasting legal processes of civil and criminal law involve the type of offense that is in question. While crimes against society involve harm to person or theft of property, civil disputes can boil down to legal disputes over reputation, privacy, and intellectual property rights. Instead of losing personal freedom through incarceration, civil cases usually only yield monetary settlements.

- Federal agencies have legal powers that include drafting rules, enforcing them, and deciding appeals to their administration. They usually serve by appointment from the president with the confirmation of the U.S. Senate.

- Attorneys in most states are required to stay abreast of changes in the law by continuing their education. Both the activities of the courts and their sources of authority provide worthy subjects of scholarly investigation especially since laws and legal practitioners must adapt to the dynamic circumstances of their society.

Divided Circuits?

The system of checks and balances directly influences how laws are enforced, but that varies from state to state and even judicial district according to how the laws limiting freedom of expression are upheld. And it is possible that a federal law can be struck by one appellate court but not another. Congress has been reluctant to criminalize speech, even lying, unless some fraud is involved and the lie conveyed with the motive to capitalize financially on a false claim. What happens though if someone makes a false boast—should the government step in and have people arrested for telling lies about their age or weight, or exaggerating on their résumé, if no fraud is involved?

In 2006, the U.S. Congress voted overwhelmingly to make it a crime to falsely lay claim to a record of military service worthy of commendation. The Stolen Valor Act was introduced by Sen. Kent Conrad (D-N.D.) in Congress and sailed through both houses with 27 Democrat and Republican cosponsors. President Bush gladly signed it into law and it stood without contradiction until August 2010, when the U.S. Court of Appeals for the Ninth Circuit in San Francisco declared it unconstitutional under the First Amendment.

The defendant in the case, Xavier Alvarez, had falsely claimed to have won the U.S. Marines' highest award for bravery, the Medal of Honor. Why would he make such a claim? Some liars boast of military service just to obtain free motel rooms or to purchase discount airline tickets, or gain some other personal advantage. But Alvarez was just boasting to a public meeting after winning a seat on the water district board in Pomona, California. "I'm a retired Marine of 25 years. I retired in the year 2001. Back in 1987, I was awarded the Congressional Medal of Honor. I got wounded many times by the same guy. I'm still around." There was no clear reason for Alvarez to lie in public, except perhaps to realize some personal fantasy. If that was the case, Alvarez's fantasy was a costly one. He was convicted in California of violating the Stolen Valor Act and sentenced to serve community service hours at a veteran's hospital and assessed a monetary fine of $5,000. His lawyers appealed his conviction on First Amendment grounds. In August 2010, Alvarez won his appeal before the Ninth Circuit Court of Appeals in San Francisco.[a]

The ruling in favor of Alvarez's so-called right to lie held that "First Amendment protection does not hinge on the truth of the matter expressed." Such untruths seem to harm no one, the judge speaking for a two-to-one majority ruled. But the dissenting voice on the three-judge panel felt quite a bit differently and pointed out that false statements of fact are not protected speech and the dictates of the Stolen Valor Act, which had produced convictions before the Alvarez case, was consistent with that view.

What this particular appellate court ruling did was to strike down the law's enforcement in the nine states and two U.S. territories governed by the Ninth Circuit Court of Appeals, but the Stolen Valor Act remains in effect in other states. It is not a case that represents binding precedent, but it could be considered persuasive precedent if and when appellate court judges take up similar cases prosecuted under this act and agree that the Stolen Valor Act is unconstitutional. If another appeals court upholds the law then the law will face a case of divided circuit courts. This situation invites the Supreme Court to step in and determine exactly when the First Amendment protects lies and liars, but it can only do so once a case is appealed to that level of justice for review. ∎

---

[a] *U.S. v. Alvarez,* No. 08-50345 (9th Cir. Aug. 17, 2010).

First Amendment in Principle and Practice

LEARNING OBJECTIVES

After reading this chapter you should know:

- How fear often results in pressure to curtail rights of free expression

- Thomas Emerson's four values inherent in the protection of free expression

- Who exactly is restricted by the admonition in the First Amendment

- That words are sometimes not speech but action, and actions can sometimes be considered protected free expression

- The First Amendment attempts to protect both the rights of the speaker *and* the listener, but sometimes those rights may be in conflict

- Rights of free expression are never absolute: there are multiple factors considered in determining the limits

- The language of the First Amendment is brief, but the interpretation of key phrases such as "no law," "abridging freedom," and "petition for redress of grievances" has been the subject of extensive debate—and litigation

DRAWING THE LINE

Let's begin with this understanding: the right of free expression is *not* an absolute. There are limits to what the law will allow. Perhaps the most famous example of this is the pithy quote from U.S. Supreme Court Justice Oliver Wendell Holmes. Writing in *Schenck v. United States,*[1] he stated, "The most stringent protection of free speech would not protect a man in falsely shouting fire in a theatre and causing a panic."[2] Most Americans support limiting free expression in areas where it would endanger national security, unfairly damage the reputation of individuals, or corrupt children. The difficulty lies in deciding exactly when expression does these things and how to prohibit those expressions, while still protecting other communication. In order to engage in this line-drawing exercise, it is important to understand the reasons for protecting free expression in the first place. Knowing *why* we protect expression will help us understand *what* we protect and what we don't.

We should also begin this chapter by noting that the First Amendment, while referring specifically to five freedoms (religion,[3] speech, press, assembly, and petition), is generally accepted as protecting freedom of expression. All five of those individual rights are different, and yet broadly reflect our freedom of expression.

Another revolution that shook the world came in the early twentieth century in Russia. The Bolshevik Revolution in 1917 brought Marxists to power and caused quite a stir, even in the United States. Fear that a similar revolution might occur here caused our government to suppress the free expression of splinter groups that distributed pamphlets or otherwise spoke out against our leaders or system of democracy. World War I added to the uncertainty. The U.S. Congress responded with an Espionage Act in 1917 and yet another Sedition Act in 1918. The constitutionality of the Act was upheld by the Supreme Court, and it wasn't until 1921 that the law was repealed.

Nuclear weapons certainly cause fear among many people, and the prospect that they might fall into the wrong hands understandably causes Americans concern. In 1979 *The Progressive* magazine intended to publish a kind of "how to" piece on nuclear weapons. When it came to the attention of the U.S. Justice Department, officials took action to stop the publication. Publication might still be enjoined except that another magazine published essentially the same information. Because the justification for enjoining publication no longer existed (the information was already out), the case was dismissed.

These are but three of the many examples of government attempts to suppress free expression when our nation feels threatened. Fortunately none of these perceived threats ever materialized and the suppressions were seen in retrospect as unnecessary. In the twenty-first century the United States continues to face threats, real and perceived, and free expression often hangs in the balance.

---

[1] 249 U.S. 47.

[2] *Id.* at 52.

[3] Some scholars suggest religious freedom is actually *two* rights: freedom *of* religion, known as the free exercise clause, and freedom *from* government-dictated religion, which is the establishment clause.

Free Expression versus Fear

Throughout the history of the United States, the government has restricted the right of free expression based on threats, real or imagined, to the safety and security of the government and its citizens. The ink on the Bill of Rights was barely dry when Congress first enacted the Alien and Sedition Acts of 1798.[a] The young nation had seen the revolution that occurred in France (in addition to its own) and was fearful that it might be the victim of a revolution. The Acts expired in 1801 when Thomas Jefferson became president, but it wasn't until 1964 that the Supreme Court actually stated the Sedition Act was unconstitutional.

[a]A slight exaggeration. Actually it was seven years later.

THE VALUE OF FREE EXPRESSION

Yale University Law Professor Thomas Emerson identified four values inherent in the American desire to protect freedom of expression.[4] They are as follows:

- Free expression aids in the discovery of truth.
- Free expression is necessary for democratic governance.
- Free expression helps promote a stable society.
- Free expression assures individual self-fulfillment.

Discovery of Truth

If we assume that people would prefer knowing what is true rather than what may be wrong, or even worse a lie, it is necessary for people to express their thoughts, opinions, ideas, and theories. If the only things people hear come from those in authority, the only things people will hear are those opinions that support the existing authority. Dissent will never be heard.

Marketplace of ideas ■ The justification for freedom of expression that holds that the best way to find truth is to allow conflicting ideas to compete. Typically associated with philosophers John Stuart Mill or John Milton.

In common parlance, the concept of allowing for the discovery of truth is known as the **marketplace of ideas**.[5] Imagine an open-air marketplace with stores positioned all around. Each of these shops represents someone with a different thought, opinion, or idea. People can browse the shops, searching for just what suits them. In this metaphor, if what one merchant is "selling" is too expensive or doesn't look appetizing, "buyers" can find someone else providing a satisfactory "product." Competition in the open market will result in the "buyers" making the right choices from the best vendors, forcing those with inferior "products" to either modify their wares or go out of business.

[4]T. Emerson, *The System of Freedom of Expression* (1970).

[5]*Abrams v. United States,* 250 U.S. 616 (1919). The concept appears in Justice Oliver Wendell Holmes's dissent at 630, "...the ultimate good desired is better reached by free trade in ideas—that the best test of truth is the power of the thought to get itself accepted in the competition of the market...."

The value of a marketplace of ideas has been around for centuries. One of the best-known and most-often-quoted passages is from *Areopagitica*, a work written by English poet John Milton in 1644. In arguing that the government should do away with a law requiring authors to receive prior approval before publishing their work, he asserted that free expression would provide the best course for discovering the truth:

> And though all the winds of doctrine were let loose to play upon the earth, so Truth be in the field, we do injuriously, by licensing and prohibiting, to misdoubt her strength. Let her and falsehood grapple; who ever knew Truth put to the worse, in a free and open encounter.[6]

The belief by Milton was that in a "free and open encounter," truth would win out over all other thought. People will choose what is best. This approach to the discovery of truth has been used by scholars and philosophers for centuries[7] and has been cited by the U.S. Supreme Court in dozens of cases.

UP CLOSE

John Milton's *Areopagitica*

Best known for his epic *Paradise Lost*, John Milton was born in London in 1608 and had a comfortable upbringing, including tutors and a Cambridge education. By the time he married in 1642 he was already an established author not only of poems, but also religious and political pamphlets—the seventeenth century way of speaking out on the controversies of the day. Milton's marriage to a woman half his age was in trouble early on. After just a month, Mary went home to visit her family and did not return to Milton. He then published a couple of pamphlets on divorce, advocating it as an appropriate action—rather controversial at the time. When the British Stationers, a licensed organization of printers and publishers, attempted to censor Milton's divorce writings, he responded by writing *Areopagitica*, calling for an end of censorship and advocating a marketplace of ideas. Ironically perhaps, not even Milton adopted an absolutist view of free expression. He believed there were certain forms of expression that deserved to be censored (most notably blasphemy). As it happens, John Milton married three times but never once divorced. Mary did return to him after several years but died in 1652.

---

[6]*Areopagitica* in 2 *Complete Prose Works of John Milton* 504 (D. Wolfe ed. 1975).

[7]A few well-known examples include the works of Jean-Jacques Rousseau, John Locke, and John Stuart Mill.

Of course the marketplace metaphor relies on a *fair* marketplace in order to be effective. In imagining our open-air marketplace, would our expectation of the outcome change if we knew that all the "stores" were owned by only one or two people? What if we knew some sellers had the ability to "package" their wares more attractively than their competitors? Would the consumers in the marketplace be educated enough to see through the packaging and actually analyze the product? The metaphor of the marketplace is less enticing to us if we believe that the marketplace is anything less than "fair." If certain buyers or sellers have advantages, which others do not enjoy, the likelihood that "truth" will be the "winner" in the marketplace is doubtful.

It is ironic that John Milton, often cited as a pillar of the marketplace of ideas metaphor, did not even support it in all circumstances. In fact Milton asserted that blasphemy had no right to be heard in an open marketplace and that it could most certainly be punished. Nevertheless, supporters of the marketplace of ideas believe that free expression needs to be protected in order to facilitate both the discovery of truth, and the correction of error.

Bedrock Law: The marketplace of ideas rationale for free expression argues in favor of the public's ability to choose good and truthful ideas over bad and false ones.

Democracy

The basic premise of representative government is that citizens elect their leaders. How do citizens make the decision about whom to elect? In order to make informed choices, citizens must have information about the candidates and the issues. To get this information, people must be free to express their opinions and beliefs. Without this prerequisite, the electorate cannot possibly select the best leaders. If democracy is to be at all effective, there must be a free flow of information so that the best choices can be made. Democratic government without a right of free expression is virtually useless.

Early twentieth century legal philosopher Alexander Meiklejohn asserted that the main reason for protecting free expression in our society was its key role in support of representative government.[8] The Supreme Court has repeatedly noted that **political speech** lies at the "core of the First Amendment."[9] There are several implications of such an approach, not all of them positive for proponents of free expression. If political speech is most worthy of protection, that implies that other forms of expression are less worthy of protection, or worthy of less protection. It also creates the dilemma of distinguishing whether or not expression is political, thereby deserving of the highest level of protection. Early in his career Meiklejohn asserted that only political speech was deserving of the ultimate protection, but in later writings he conceded that artistic and scientific speech certainly had the capacity to also be political speech. Certainly paintings and literary work can offer political commentary. Scientific writing about abortion or secondhand smoke surely has the potential to influence political decisions regarding such issues. If any form of

Political speech ■ Political speech is the most protected form of speech due to its key role in support of representative government.

---

[8]A. Meiklejohn, *Free Speech and Its Relation to Self Government* (1948).

[9]The Supreme Court decisions noting political speech at the "core" of the First Amendment include *Williams v. Rhodes*, 393 U.S. 23, 32 (1968); *Buckley v. Valeo*, 424 U.S. 1, 45 (1976); and *McConnell v. FEC*, 540 U.S. 93, 264 (2003).

communication has the potential of influencing political decision-making, it does no good to assert that political speech is at the core of a free expression right because all speech is potentially political. **Commercial speech** is generally placed far from the heart of the First Amendment (advertising will be covered in chapter 12), therefore less worthy of protection than political speech, yet legal battles have occurred over whether cigarette commercials raised controversial issues about smoking,[10] or if advertising for gas-guzzling automobiles was a form of political commentary in the debate over environmental issues.[11]

In spite of this, courts continue to differentiate expression when the connection to democracy is less ambiguous. On April 26, 1968, Paul Cohen walked into the Los Angeles County Courthouse wearing a jacket emblazoned with the phrase, "Fuck the Draft," to show his displeasure with the U.S. Selective Service and the American involvement in the Vietnam conflict. When California found him guilty of disturbing the peace by "offensive conduct," he appealed his case and eventually the U.S. Supreme Court found Cohen's expression protected.[12] We don't know for certain, but it's probably a safe bet that if he had been walking the corridors of the courthouse saying "fuck" over and over, the Court would be less concerned with his rights. While "offensive conduct" may be punished in California, offensive political speech is another matter. Because Cohen's speech was related to a political issue, it took on a heightened value worthy of First Amendment protection. Writing for the Court, Justice John Harlan II quoted a decision written by Justice Felix Frankfurter: "[O]ne of the prerogatives of American citizenship is the right to criticize public men and measures—and that means not only informed and responsible criticism but the freedom to speak foolishly and without moderation."[13] Cohen's choice of words may have been crude and distasteful, but the Court refused to allow him to be punished for such an indiscretion given the nature of his expression.

> **Commercial speech** ■
> Commercial speech is speech with a profit motive. The classic example of commercial speech is advertising. This type of speech is much more subject to regulation and restriction than other forms.

> **Bedrock Law:** Political expression is granted a higher order of freedom because of its value to the democratic process.

Stability of Society

To promote a stable society, individuals must have the means to complain. Allowing for dissent actually helps to quell potential problems. If individuals are restricted in their expression, their pent-up frustration could result in far more damaging action than merely dissent. Frustration and the inability to speak out are the prerequisites for an uprising. It may seem counterintuitive, but suppressing complaint and criticism can lead to greater societal damage than allowing it.

The metaphor to think of here is a pot of water on the stove. As the water temperature rises, if the lid on the pot is tightly sealed eventually the steam will build up enough pressure to blow off the lid. Instead, if the pot is allowed to "let off steam" slowly, the pot is not damaged. Our society (the pot in the metaphor) is better served by allowing the citizenry to let off steam as necessary rather than trying to prevent it.

---

[10]*Banzhaff v. FCC*, 405 F.2d 1082 (D.C. Cir. 1968), *cert. denied*, 396 U.S. 842 (1969).

[11]*Friends of the Earth v. FCC*, 449 F.2d 1164 (D.C. Cir. 1971).

[12]*Cohen v. California*, 403 U.S. 15 (1971).

[13]*Id.* at 26 (citing *Baumgartner v. United States*, 322 U.S. 665, 673–74 (1944)).

Marxist critics of our system point out another aspect of this metaphor. Allowing steam to escape means that the pot never changes. An exploding pot at least puts an end to the constant boiling. Critics would assert that rather than addressing societal problems, allowing "controlled" dissent allows those in power to maintain the status quo while never having to do anything differently.[14]

Marxist criticism aside, the right to protest in America is regarded as highly valued because it *can* lead to changes in society. Picketers spend hours carrying signs, sometimes in inclement weather and other adverse conditions, precisely because they believe their actions will result in some kind of change. The Supreme Court has protected the right of protest, recognizing the importance of picketing as a way of expressing that protest. In 1988 the Court struck down a law prohibiting picketing within 500 feet of a foreign embassy.[15] Congress had passed such a law to protect foreign diplomats from embarrassment, and also as a means to protect officials from possible security threats. The Court was less concerned with embarrassment than it was with the importance of security and asserted that security could be provided in a manner that was less restrictive of free expression.

As with every First Amendment issue, the protection is not absolute. The Supreme Court upheld a Colorado law restricting the activity of protesters within 100 feet of the entrance to a health care facility.[16] While finding that protesters still had free speech rights, the Court found that restricting their communication in this specific context did not completely eliminate their ability to express themselves, and that the distance imposed by the statute fairly balanced the protestors' rights and those of the clinic's patrons.

The Supreme Court's use of a **clear and present danger test** is a further example of this adherence to the value of free expression to protect a stable society. The Court is unwilling to protect expression that constitutes a clear and present danger to society. This will be covered in detail later, but for now it serves to illustrate the notion that free expression serves as a stabilizing force in society. If free speech is destabilizing to the point of public disruption then it is not deserving of protection. There is a bit of irony here. If the Supreme Court were to believe a crackpot was advocating violence it might not allow the government to prohibit his speech because it constitutes no clear and present danger. On the other hand, the very same advocacy presented by a more believable, charismatic speaker might be actionable under a clear and present danger analysis. Viewed in this way, the government actually is permitted to regulate speakers based on the individual's effectiveness. Ineffective speakers bear no threat to society but those who are able to whip a crowd into a frenzy may be considered a clear and present danger.[17]

Clear and present danger test ■ Speech that presents a clear and present danger is outside the protection of the First Amendment. This test was first articulated by Justice Oliver Wendell Holmes in *Schenck v. United States,* with the example of a man shouting "fire" in a crowded theatre.

Bedrock Law: Some types of communication may pose so real and imminent a danger that the courts have ruled in favor of the government's right to restrain it.

---

[14]The successful demonstrations against U.S. troops in Vietnam and the protests of the civil rights movement are used to rebut the arguments of the Marxists.

[15]*Boos v. Barry,* 485 U.S. 312 (1988).

[16]*Hill v. Colorado,* 530 U.S. 703 (2000).

[17]*See Terminiello v. Chicago,* 337 U.S. 1 (1949) that stands as an exception to this rule. A defrocked priest was arrested for stirring up a crowd outside of Chicago's Christian Veterans Hall with anti-Semitic rhetoric. However, Father Arthur Terminiello won his appeal before the U.S. Supreme Court based on the idea that sometimes free speech functions best when it causes unrest or even stirs people to anger.

Self-Fulfillment

Some contend that the true value of free expression is that it protects a basic human right. The ability to freely communicate is part of what defines us as human. Viewed in this light, freedom of expression is a fundamental right and deserving of protection whether or not it promotes some public good. The values of promoting democracy, discovering truth, and maintaining stability are all societal goods, but free expression viewed as a human right has both intrinsic and extrinsic value. The Supreme Court has stated the importance of self-fulfillment in First Amendment cases for more than 30 years.[18] There is a litany of philosophers from centuries past who have argued for the freedom of self-realization.[19]

After all, when we think about the kind of expression that *needs* to be protected, isn't it often that emotional expression that a speaker engages in when s/he is especially passionate about a topic? People who get worked up over something are often the ones who are outspoken and who may use language that offends or upsets others. In this chapter we have seen how different instances of offensive speech resulted in legal action that was appealed all the way to the U.S. Supreme Court. Such expression certainly can be political but it is also most definitely self-fulfilling. People engaged in such communication make political statements but they also make personal statements. Their expression is likely to be far more visceral than some corporation speaking only to drive up its profits or even some political figure whose speech has been massaged by a spin doctor trying to win the most votes.

So Then, Which Value Is the Important One?

Obviously this is a ridiculous question. *All* four values espoused by Emerson can be found in philosophical arguments, sociological data, and court decisions. If discovery of truth were the *only* reason for valuing free expression, then any expression that did not directly advance the cause of discovering truth would not deserve protection. A lot of advertising simply provides brand awareness rather than information and as such does not advance the discovery of truth. Advertising also might lose some protection if free speech's only purpose is to protect individual self-fulfillment, as very little advertising is motivated by the desire to express oneself.[20] If it is only necessary to uphold democracy, then political messages might be the only ones protected—and then only voices of dissent, if the object is mainly to create a stable society.

Our deeply held protection of free expression encompasses all of the values Emerson identifies. The concept of free expression is rather complex and, quite frankly, misunderstood by many Americans. Surveys have shown that more

---

[18]For example, *Police Department of Chicago v. Moseby*, 408 U.S. 92 (1972), at 95–96. "To permit the continued building of our politics and culture, and to assure self-fulfillment for each individual, our people are guaranteed the right to express any thought, free from government censorship."

[19]The list includes such famous names as Dewey, Kant, Spinoza, Hobbes, Voltaire, and Hume. *See* 1 M. Adler, *The Idea of Freedom* 171–201 (1961).

[20]One exception to this might be advocacy advertising, such as the sort encouraging some sort of social cause (safe sex/abstinence, environmental issues, etc.).

Americans can identify the five members of the cartoon Simpson family than can identify the five freedoms protected by the First Amendment.[21] Opinions about free expression change based on political climate, most notably Americans' sense of security. The First Amendment Center conducts an annual survey on the state of the First Amendment. Immediately following the terrorist attacks of September 11, 2001, survey results showed a much lower level of support for the rights of free expression but the percentages have been gradually increasing to pre–September 11 levels.[22]

Because free expression is such a complex concept, it is often frustrating for people studying the subject. Students who have spent years learning to provide the "right answers" to their teachers and professors want to be given one true answer. Unfortunately, because so many elements must be considered in the analysis of free expression, the answer must often be, "It depends." There are so many conditions that determine how far the First Amendment extends that a simple yes or no answer is often inadequate and inappropriate. In the next section we will examine a variety of factors that impact the decision about whether the expression is protected.

THE FIRST AMENDMENT RESTRICTS *GOVERNMENT* ACTION

The First Amendment ■ "Congress shall make no law respecting an establishment of religion, or prohibiting the free exercise thereof; or abridging the freedom of speech, or of the press; or the right of the people peaceably to assemble, and to petition the Government for a redress of grievances."

CONGRESS SHALL MAKE NO LAW RESPECTING AN ESTABLISH-MENT OF RELIGION, OR PROHIBITING THE FREE EXERCISE THEREOF; OR ABRIDGING THE FREEDOM OF SPEECH, OR OF THE PRESS; OR THE RIGHT OF THE PEOPLE PEACEABLY TO ASSEMBLE, AND TO PETITION THE GOVERNMENT FOR A REDRESS OF GRIEVANCES.

–The First Amendment to the U.S. Constitution, 1791

The First Amendment begins, "*Congress* shall make no law..." Through a sequence of legal decisions we have come to interpret "congress" as "government." At first it just meant the federal government but thanks to the Fourteenth Amendment,[23] the same restriction on the federal government also applies to state and local governing bodies.[24] "Government means *all* branches of government—executive, legislative, and judicial. We are told the founders used the "congress" language because the legislature was seen as the branch

---

[21]Howard Troxler, *Even Homer Can Defend Our Nation's 5 Freedoms*, St. Petersburg Times, March 5, 2006, at 1B.

[22]The latest results, as well as previous surveys dating back to 1997, can be found at http://www .firstamendmentcenter.org.

[23]Section One of the Fourteenth Amendment reads, "All persons born or naturalized in the United States, and subject to the jurisdiction thereof, are citizens of the United States and of the State in which they reside. No State shall make or enforce any law which shall abridge the privileges or immunities of citizens of the United States; nor shall any State deprive any person of life, liberty, or property, without due process of law; nor deny to any person within its jurisdiction the equal protection of the laws."

[24]The Supreme Court resolved the question in *Gitlow v. New York*, 268 U.S. 652 (1925).

responsible for making laws, but our more modern view is that when courts interpret law and executive agencies enforce law, they, too, engage in law*making*. This means that not only legislatures and police are barred from restricting free expression, but so are other government entities—like public schools and universities.

Note the adjective "public." Public schools and universities are a part of the government because they are publicly funded. There is no question that public schools and universities must comply with the First Amendment's free expression directive, but what about private schools? Are they bound to abide by the First Amendment? This is not so clear, although courts have generally taken the position that a private school's restriction of free expression would not be a violation of the First Amendment because there is no *state action* involved.[25] Private actors who restrict free expression through whatever means are generally not in violation of the First Amendment. They may be guilty of other legal infractions, but not limiting a constitutional right of free speech. For example, if your friend covers your mouth to keep you from speaking it might be considered battery (unlawful touching) but it would not violate the First Amendment. If someone does not like the same political candidate you do and tears down the sign you've placed in your yard to show your support it's probably trespassing, but it's not a violation of the First Amendment. Newspapers that refuse to publish a story, radio and television stations that refuse to air a program, and magazines that reject an advertisement might all be accused of "censorship,"[26] but unless they are government-operated they are not infringing on anyone's First Amendment rights.

> **Bedrock Law:** The First Amendment specifies "Congress," but it applies to other lawmaking bodies that serve as tax-supported representatives of government.

Words ≠ Speech

At the beginning of this chapter we quoted the words of Justice Holmes who argued that falsely shouting "fire" in a theatre would not be protected speech. The best way to understand this idea is to recognize that in this case, the speaker is not so much engaged in expression as in action. Shouting "fire" in this situation is not protected as free expression because the "speaker" isn't engaging in expression at all—the speaker is inciting a panic. The First Amendment is intended to protect expression, not action. It may seem self-evident that words are expression but that is not always the case.

This concept may be even clearer to see using the word *fire* in another context. Suppose for a moment that a gang had bound and gagged someone and pointed

---

[25]In 2000 a student was expelled from a New York private school because he maintained a website the school considered "inappropriate." The family's lawsuit in federal district court was dismissed because the school was not a government entity for First Amendment purposes. *Ubriaco v. Albertus Magnus High School,* 2000 U.S. Dist. LEXIS 10141 (2000).

[26]While the term *censorship* is sometimes used to define government restriction of expression, its colloquial use often includes other limitations that are not government action. In fact, the phrase "self-censorship," used by the Supreme Court in dozens of cases, implies that censorship can occur without state action.

their guns at the victim. Imagine that the gang leader then says, "Fire," and the gangsters shoot the victim. Would the gang leader be able to successfully defend his actions in court by claiming that he was merely exercising his right of free speech? Certainly no court would accept this argument; so, why not? The utterance was more than speech; it was action—the illegal action of murder. In this instance, "speaking" was not expression. Whenever speech is mixed in with illegal activity, it can be punished as a crime, including such deeds as sexual harassment, blackmail, perjury, conspiracy, and fraud.

On the other hand, things that appear to be actions might actually be protected expression. Protesters wearing armbands, badges, or holding signs may be uttering no words, but their "actions" have meaning, and this symbolic form of speech is protected. Again, we recognize that there are times when actions are forms of protected expression.

In the pages ahead, we will look at all expressive activities that the First Amendment shields from government intrusion, including art, dance, music, and motion pictures, as well as pickets, boycotts, and other political demonstrations. But for now, let's take a look at how even spending money can be viewed as a First Amendment activity.

When Congress was attempting to create campaign finance reform laws, the Supreme Court upheld some of the rules while finding other parts of the legislation unconstitutional.[27] The Federal Election Campaign Act of 1971 limited the amount that individuals could contribute to candidates in presidential elections, and it also limited the amount that individuals could spend on their own to express their support for candidates or the amount candidates could spend on their own campaigns. The Court upheld the limits on individual contributors claiming that it was reasonable to restrict the amount to prevent improper influence, or even the appearance of improper influence on a candidate. When it came

> **Bedrock Law:** When courts interpret freedom of expression, they also weigh the sources and support for the communication event.

to restricting how much an individual could spend on his/her own speech, though, the Court would not allow the limit to stand. "A restriction on the amount of money a person or group can spend on political communication during a campaign necessarily reduces the quantity of expression by restricting the number of issues discussed, the depth of their exploration, and the size of the audience reached. This is because virtually every means of communicating ideas in today's mass society requires the expenditure of money."[28]

Speaker Rights versus Listener Rights

Something else to consider when examining why we protect free expression is the distinction between the rights of speakers and the rights of listeners. Often the rights are complementary, and protecting one results in a benefit to the other. When we protect the rights of speakers, listeners benefit from the opportunity to

---

[27]*Buckley v. Valeo*, 424 U.S. 1 (1975).
[28]*Id.* at 19.

hear a multiplicity of views. This is the concept underlying the marketplace of ideas discussed previously. The listeners benefit when the rights of speakers are protected.

It is not always a given that protecting speakers' rights is to the benefit of listeners, most notably when listeners would prefer to be shielded from certain communications. When Paul Cohen was allowed to wear his offensive jacket into a California courthouse, it was with the recognition that others might find it distasteful. Gregory Lee Johnson's burning of the American flag was "seriously offensive" to some people. In each of these instances and in many others, the Supreme Court recognized the rights of the speakers to express themselves—even in ways that may have been objectionable to others. The Court pointed out that those offended by Cohen's jacket could "avoid further bombardment of their sensibilities simply by averting their eyes."[29]

What happens though in instances where listeners are not able to avoid offensive expression? The Court has shown more sympathy in the case of a *captive audience* than it has in situations like those in the California courthouse. In a number of instances where audiences are unable to avoid communication, their right *not* to be subjected to offensive messages may outweigh the rights of those wanting to disseminate them. The Court has stated, "The First Amendment permits the government to prohibit offensive speech as intrusive when the 'captive' audience cannot avoid the objectionable speech."[30] Of course the term *captive* is not absolute at all. The concept has changed somewhat over time. In a 1951 decision, the Supreme Court contended that street preachers take advantage of what is "in a sense, a captive audience."[31] Certainly individuals who must use the street to reach their destinations are no more captive than individuals who must conduct their business in a local courthouse. Despite the shifting concept of captivity, the courts still show a willingness to protect listeners from communications they do not wish to receive in those situations where they have less opportunity to avoid the message.

One of the reasons the U.S. Supreme Court cited for prohibiting invocations at official graduation ceremonies for public secondary schools is precisely because the audience in attendance, most notably the students, are a captive audience.[32] The Court asserted that religious invocations at Thanksgiving Day addresses were "worlds apart" from a situation that exists when students and their families are captive audiences at graduation ceremonies.

One other area where listeners' rights have outweighed the rights of speakers has been in the listeners' own homes. In *Rowan v. United States Post Office,* the Supreme Court upheld a law that allowed individuals to "block" mail they find offensive, and to require the senders of such mail to remove them from future

---

[29]*Cohen v. California, supra* note 12, at 21.

[30]*Frisby v. Shultz,* 487 U.S. 474 (1988), at 487.

[31]*Kunz v. New York,* 340 U.S. 290 (1951), at 298.

[32]*Lee v. Wiseman,* 505 U.S. 577 (1992). The larger First Amendment issue in this case was whether such an invocation constituted an "establishment of religion," as constitutionally prohibited. In its analysis, the Court also addressed the captive audience.

mailing lists.[33] Rejecting the argument that such a rule violated the free expression rights of those speakers wanting to reach their audience, the Court adhered to the ancient notion that "a man's home is his castle into which not even the king may enter."[34] The Court was unwilling to give the speaker's rights preference over the listener's rights when the listener was within his/her own home. "That we are often 'captives' outside the sanctuary of the home and subject to objectionable speech and other sound does not mean we must be captives everywhere."[35]

Thus, free expression is not an absolute, and the right is moderated by other influences and conditions. The difficulty arises in understanding all the various environmental pressures and externalities that impact free expression. It might be useful here to use an environmental example as an analogy—the weather.

Whenever someone complains about the heat, invariably someone else will add, "It's not just the heat, it's the humidity." When it's cold, meteorologists are always telling us the "wind chill factor" because just knowing the temperature is not enough to know what it feels like outside. Each of these measures affects our "comfort level."

So it is, too, with our "free expression comfort level." There are multiple factors that affect how free we are to express ourselves. Just as an 80-degree day may "feel" warmer with 100 percent humidity, an adult, nongovernment speaker (highly protected) may have his or her speech restricted on private property. Each of the indicators below reflects one of those factors. The higher up on each scale, the greater the free expression rights are. It is never enough to be at 100 percent protected on just one indicator; the level on *all* the indicators are necessary.

Bedrock Law: Weighing all the factors that could curb freedom of expression requires understanding the nature, content, and location of the communication.

While a 100-percent level on any one of the indicators may not be enough to guarantee protected expression, it is a fair bet that a zero level on any of the indicators will result in unprotected expression. Speakers have very few rights of free expression in the privacy of other people's homes regardless of what their status as speaker or the subject of their expression.

Speaker	Venue	Subject	Speech/Action
Adults	Public Parks	Politics	
Govt. Employees	Streets	Art/Science	
College Students	Public Campus	Commercial	
9–12 Students	Military Bases	Indecent	
6–8 Students	Businesses	Obscenity	
K–5 Students	Others' Homes		

| Measuring the "Climate" for Free Expression

---

[33]397 U.S. 728 (1970).
[34]*Id.* at 737.
[35]*Id.* at 738.

Reviewing the First Amendment

Now that we have been through the premises underpinning free expression in the United States, we will examine the First Amendment, paying special attention to the clauses relevant to communication law.

Who Is "Congress" *Congress* is interpreted as meaning government or anyone acting under the authority of the government. Obviously this term applies first and foremost to the U.S. Congress, but it also applies to the president of the United States and all the government-funded agencies created by the government (including the Federal Communications Commission, Federal Trade Commission, etc.). Whether the original intention of the framers was for the Bill of Rights to apply to only the federal government or to be extended to the states is moot: the Fourteenth Amendment is now understood to make the First Amendment applicable to all states. Local jurisdictions are also included, so that city government, public schools, and local police are prohibited from restricting free expression rights.

The Meaning of "No Law" *Shall make no law* translates to more than just legislation. It is considered to incorporate other government action such as law enforcement. Sometimes a law can be ruled as constitutional but the manner in which it is enforced is not. Thus, when a law or rule is enforced in such a way as to violate someone's right to free expression, it is still a First Amendment violation. In 1993, Gloria Bartnicki used her cell phone to talk with the president of a local teachers' union about the negotiations she was handling for them with a school district in Pennsylvania. The calls were intercepted by a third party, and recordings were passed among several people, including a radio talk show host, who aired a portion of the tape. Bartnicki filed a lawsuit, claiming that the interception of her telephone conversation was in violation of a portion of the Omnibus Crime Control and Safe Streets Act of 1968 dealing with wiretapping and electronic surveillance. The Supreme Court refused to hold radio show host Frederick Vopper responsible for airing a confidential telephone conversation. The ruling was *not* a finding that there was anything constitutionally wrong with the Omnibus Crime Control and Safe Streets Act. The Court ruled that applying it in this case to Vopper would result in a violation of his First Amendment rights.[36] A law that may or may not infringe on freedom of expression might be found unconstitutional as applied in a particular instance. That was the Supreme Court's response to Frederick Vopper's playing of the tape recorded phone conversation on his radio program: the law itself was constitutional, but the law as applied was unconstitutional.

Abridging Freedom *Abridging* freedom of speech can occur through a variety of means. The plain meaning of the term *abridge* is to diminish or reduce in scope. Thus, to abridge freedom of speech is to engage in any government action that

---

[36]*Bartnicki v. Vopper,* 532 U.S. 514 (2001). Specifically, the Court claimed that the unique circumstances that protected Vopper were the facts that he had no part in the illegal interception of the phone call, that he obtained the tapes legally, and that the content of the recordings was a public concern. *Id.* at 525.

diminishes free expression. Obviously laws restricting free speech would abridge this right, but so might laws or government action that discourage free expression without overtly restricting it. The Supreme Court repeatedly refers to the "chilling effect" that government actions can have on free expression. This most often occurs in situations where a law is vague and can be interpreted to apply to a wide variety of communications and/or behaviors, well beyond whatever is intended to be regulated. In these instances, the laws are considered to have a "chilling effect" on expression that would not be deemed illegal. For example, Congress passed the Communications Decency Act into law in 1996. It was an attempt to regulate content on the Internet to keep obscene and indecent material away from minors. As soon as the CDA became law it was challenged in court (more than one court, actually). The CDA was ruled to be unconstitutional for many reasons (which will be discussed more in a later chapter), but one of those reasons was the vagueness of the rules. The Court stated, "The vagueness of such a regulation raises special First Amendment concerns because of its obvious chilling effect on free speech."[37] In other words, speakers might restrict themselves from saying certain things for fear that they might subsequently be punished, when in fact the speech in which they would engage would be constitutional.

Chilling effect ■ A criticism of vague restrictions on speech which may cause speakers to restrict themselves from saying certain things for fear that they might subsequently be punished, when in fact the speech in which they would engage would be constitutional.

The first time the U.S. Supreme Court majority used the **chilling effect** argument to assert that a law was preventing expression that should otherwise be protected was in the landmark libel case of *New York Times Co. v. Sullivan*[38] (discussed extensively later in chapter 5). In unanimously finding that an Alabama libel law could not hold the *New York Times* responsible for libeling a public official without also showing that the paper had acted with a knowledge of falsity or a reckless disregard for the truth, the Court broke new ground in 1964 by prohibiting punishment of criticism of government officials, even if the criticism were later proven to be false. Those criticizing public officials must be given the "breathing room" required. Errors must be allowed, so long as they are not intentional in order to protect the robust sort of debate that is necessary. If speakers are fearful that a single misstatement can result in punishment, they might be overly cautious and avoid any commentary that is not absolutely, 100 percent provable. While some people who feel they have been maligned by the media might prefer that this be the standard, our value on free expression is too great to permit such a restriction. In the *New York Times* libel case, the Court quoted from a decision a couple of years earlier that error must be protected if the First Amendment is to have the "breathing space" it requires to survive.[39]

Compelling Speech   Interestingly, one's speech can also be abridged if compelled to speak. Being made to speak if one would prefer to remain silent is also a form of abridging free expression. The issue of compelled speech was first addressed by the Supreme Court in 1943. In the previous year, the West Virginia State Board of Education made the Pledge of Allegiance a daily requirement in its classrooms for both students and teachers. Expulsion and fines were possible for those refusing to

---

[37]*Reno v. ACLU*, 521 U.S. 844 (1997), at 871–72.
[38]376 U.S. 254 (1964).
[39]Quoting *N.A.A.C.P. v. Button*, 371 U.S. 415 (1962).

participate. A group of Jehovah's Witnesses filed suit against the law, claiming it violated their religious beliefs.[40] Somewhat surprisingly, the Court did not address the issue as much from religious grounds as from a freedom of speech perspective. In finding the requirement unconstitutional, the decision stated, "To sustain the compulsory flag salute we are required to say that a Bill of Rights which guards the individual's right to speak his own mind, left it open to public authorities to compel him to utter what is not in his mind."[41] The Court asserted that compelling speech is abridging speech, and it would be just as restricting.

Since we have already discussed the fact that money can be a form of expression and we have determined that individuals cannot be compelled to speak, does this then mean that people could refuse to pay their taxes if those tax dollars were being used to support speech with which they did not agree? In 1996, some students attending the University of Wisconsin were upset that they had to pay over $300 per year in student activity fees, largely to support student organizations. They were particularly upset that some of the money went to support student groups such as the Wisconsin Student Public Interest Research Group, a social activist group. The U.S. Supreme Court allowed the university to continue collecting and distributing fees providing it did so in a viewpoint-neutral manner (in other words, not favoring or disfavoring any groups based on their viewpoints).[42]

It was because this support for the Wisconsin student organizations was a viewpoint-neutral distribution of funds that it was constitutional, unlike the situation a few years earlier involving the California State Bar Association. The Bar is an organization that attorneys must belong to in California in order to practice law. They have no choice but to pay their dues if they want to work. Twenty-one members of the California Bar filed suit claiming that the Bar used a portion of their dues to support political and ideological causes and thus their dues were a form of compelled speech, violating their First Amendment rights. The U.S. Supreme Court decided that the Bar could not require its members to pay dues to support speech that members did not support.[43] Dues could be required of members, but that money could not then fund expressive activity.

The Court followed the precedent it had established in an earlier case dealing with labor unions and compelled speech. Michigan had authorized union representation for nonunion government employees. Rather than requiring employees to join the union, employees could opt instead to pay a "service charge" to the union. After all, nonunion government employees also benefited when the union negotiated labor contracts. Some teachers filed suit against the Detroit Board of Education, refusing to pay compulsory dues to the teachers union. Rather than invalidate the arrangement, the Court held that the portion of the service charge used to fund expression could not be required of nonunion employees. The Court had no

---

[40]Jehovah's Witnesses believe that no "graven images" should be bowed to or served, in keeping with God's commandments as set forth in the book of Exodus. For them, pledging allegiance to a flag constitutes bowing to a graven image.

[41]*West Virginia State Bd. of Ed. v. Barnette*, 319 U.S. 624 (1943), at 634.

[42]*Board of Regents v. Southworth*, 529 U.S. 217 (2000).

[43]*Keller v. State Bar of Cal.*, 496 U.S. 1 (1990).

problem with a requirement that nonunion employees had to pay for union representation, but refused to allow the union to assess nonmembers for the promotion of its ideology. Quoting Thomas Jefferson, the Court stated, "...to compel a man to furnish contributions of money for the propagation of opinions which he disbelieves is sinful and tyrannical..."[44] Unlike the University of Wisconsin case, the rules for the California Bar and Michigan school teachers were unconstitutional because the ideological speech that members' fees were funding could be distinguished from the other activities of the Bar and the union.

The Beef Promotion and Research Act of 1985 contained a provision requiring cattle farmers to pay one dollar per head on the sale or import of cattle, and that money would be used for the promotion of beef (perhaps you've heard their "Beef—It's What's for Dinner" slogan). The Livestock Marketing Association challenged the law, arguing that cattle farmers were being compelled to subsidize speech. Unlike the compelled speech cases mentioned earlier, the Supreme Court did not find this to violate the First Amendment. The critical difference in this case was the fact that the speech was *government* speech, and citizens have no First Amendment right not to fund government speech.[45] It would be a real Pandora's Box to permit taxpayers to refuse to pay a portion of their taxes anytime they claimed the government promoted policies with which the people did not agree.

Speech and Press   *Speech, or of the press* has been debated by legal scholars, including our Supreme Court justices.[46] Some commentators assert that the inclusion of speech and press rights in the First Amendment is general language freeing all forms of expression, and that the First Amendment, with its protections for speech and press along with religion, assembly, and petition, should be read as a general protection of expression. On the other hand, others have argued that because the framers chose two different words, *speech* and *press,* it must mean they viewed the rights as distinctive and distinguishable.

While recognizing the arguments for distinguishing between speech and press freedom, this book follows the perspective that the words simply include all forms of expression—print and spoken (there were no forms of electronic communication in the eighteenth century). Supreme Court decisions have suggested as much. For example, in 1972 a reporter was required to appear before a Kentucky grand jury. Paul Branzburg had reported on illegal behavior that he observed, and the grand jury wanted to investigate. He attempted to avoid testifying by claiming that the First Amendment shielded him from having to testify. In a 5–4 decision the Supreme Court ruled that it was unwilling to grant the press a "testimonial privilege that other citizens do not enjoy."[47] In 1974 the Court held that a California law that prohibited face-to-face interviews between inmates and news media did not violate the First Amendment. Inmates' free speech was not violated, but the Court also responded to the argument that the press had a First Amendment right

---

[44]*Abood v. Detroit Board of Ed.,* 431 U.S. 209 (1977), at 235.

[45]*Johanns v. Livestock Mkting. Ass'n,* 544 U.S. 550 (2005).

[46]Potter Stewart, *Or of the Press,* 26 Hastings L.J. 631 (1975).

[47]*Branzburg v. Hayes,* 408 U.S. 665 (1972), at 690.

as well. The Court held that the press's right of access to sources of information was no greater (or less) than that of the general public.[48]

After all, legal language is filled with redundancies so it's easy to imagine how terms such as *speech* and *press* are just two different manifestations of the same concept. The Federal Trade Commission may issue a "cease and desist" order if it believes someone is engaged in deceptive advertising. Why is it a cease *and* desist order? Is there a legal difference between "ceasing" and "desisting"? Probably not, but it does make the point—at least more than once.

It helps us understand the distinction between speech and action to understand the phrase "speech, or of the press" as simply the declaration that all forms of expression fall under the protection of the First Amendment. As previously stated, expression may be protected when action is not, therefore it is useful to remember that expression manifests itself in many different ways including speaking and publishing, but also wearing armbands or offensive clothing, marching, and protesting. This idea provides the segue for the next phrase to examine in the First Amendment.

Right of Assembly *Right of the people peaceably to assemble* is not a concern for most mass media fighting for their own First Amendment rights of free expression, but it is a concern for the many public interest groups seeking to stage parades, protests, and rallies in public spaces. What's more, this phrase has been interpreted to incorporate other rights in addition to just assembling in public places, most notably the right of *association*. Do Americans have the right to belong to any organization of their choice? What if those organizations are subversive? Do they have the right to join these groups secretly and keep their memberships confidential? The answers may appear easy at first, but they are complex issues.

In 1951, the NAACP opened a regional office in Alabama. At that time, Alabama had a law that required, among other things, that organizations doing business within the state must give the government a list of their members. The NAACP had never complied with the law. After five years, the state filed suit. The case made it all the way to the U.S. Supreme Court, which unanimously decided that the NAACP should not be required to provide the names of its members to the state.[49] This is a principle that has been upheld in a multitude of situations, often as a means of protecting both the organization and

[48]*Pell v. Procunier*, 417 U.S. 817 (1974).

[49]*NAACP v. Alabama*, 357 U.S. 449 (1958).

its members. The logic is that some organizations might have fewer members if they were required to make their names a matter of public record. This is easy to see with noxious groups like the Ku Klux Klan but it also might be true of other "mainstream" organizations. In the context of Alabama in the 1950s, it is easy to imagine how some people would fear that their membership in the NAACP might result in action taken against them if this association were made public. Perhaps a liberal physician might fear that conservative patients would choose another health care provider if they knew about those personal political leanings. The result would be fewer members for the organization and a denial of the physician's right to freely associate with the group.

In another registration decision, the Supreme Court held that a member of the Communist Party could not be penalized because he did not register as a member of a "subversive" group while working at a shipyard, which the government had classified as a "defense facility." The Subversive Activities Control Act of 1950 stated that it was unlawful for any member of a Communist action group to work in a defense facility. The government tried to assert that, as part of its war powers, it could pass such legislation to limit such subversive activity. The Supreme Court agreed that the government could limit subversive *activity* but to prohibit someone's employment merely because he was a *member* of a group infringed on his right of association under the First Amendment.[50] The Court was not limiting the government's ability to regulate illegal activity, but it was limiting its ability to restrict free association rights. In fact, the Supreme Court earlier upheld the Subversive Activities Control Act requirement that the Communist Party register with the government.[51]

Does an organization have the right to discriminate? Does the right of association also include the right to *exclude* members? In a rather controversial case, the Supreme Court narrowly decided that the Boy Scouts did not have to allow an avowed homosexual to be an assistant scoutmaster.[52] While generally the law prohibits discrimination based on sexual orientation, the 5–4 ruling asserted that the Boy Scouts had a constitutional right of expressive association that allowed them to exclude from their membership individuals whose presence affects the group's ability to advocate public or private viewpoints. New Jersey's public accommodation law, which prohibits discrimination, might prevent other groups from excluding members based on sexual orientation, but the Court found the Boy Scouts' position on homosexuality to be part of its values, and to require the group to accept as a member someone who directly contradicted those values was to violate the group's First Amendment right of *expressive* association, meaning the group engaged in expressive activity as a normal part of the organization.

Petitioning for Redress The petition clause completes the First Amendment, and even though it comes last in order it was foremost in the minds of the framers who noted in the Declaration of Independence the royal lack of response from the monarchy to their colonial petitions: "We have petitioned for redress in the most

---

[50]*U.S. v. Robel,* 389 U.S. 258 (1967).

[51]*Communist Party v. Subversive Activities Control Bd.,* 367 U.S. 1 (1961).

[52]*Boy Scouts of Am. v. Dale,* 530 U.S. 640 (2000).

humble terms: our repeated petitions have only been answered by repeated injury." Thomas Jefferson and his fellow revolutionists felt that the King's indifference was surely the mark of a tyrant.

It is the right to petition that gives the rest of the First Amendment its teeth, because it guarantees the people can sue the government in order to recover from the loss of civil liberties. Before the Civil War, northern abolitionists, seeking to end the South's reliance on slavery, used the petition clause to encourage Congress to pass a bill of abolition. However, this redress promised in the First Amendment's petition clause does not guarantee satisfaction with the result. It only promises public officials shall grant some access to the people they govern who have an issue. In this way, it ensures a form of public dialogue. Today, the right of petition extends to all branches of government, which is why names on a petition are often gathered to affect change in our schools, our governments, or even our taxes. The right of petition has come to mean that we are entitled to a nonviolent means of motivating our government to action.

SUMMARY

- Throughout the history of the United States, threats to national security have resulted in increased restrictions on free expression. In retrospect, most of those restrictions appear to have been unnecessary and/or excessive.

- In the United States we value free expression for four reasons: because it is necessary to the discovery of truth; because a democratic system of government requires an informed electorate; because allowing free expression promotes stability in a society; and because part of what it means to be human is to be expressive.

- The First Amendment to the U.S. Constitution is a restriction on the infringement of free speech by government, including individuals and institutions. It does not prohibit any private restrictions on expression.

- The protection of free expression includes actions that are primarily expressive in nature, such as the burning of a flag. Conversely, not all words are necessarily deserving of protection as expression, such as ordering someone's execution.

- It's easy to understand that the First Amendment protects speakers, but it goes much further. Having the right to speak also implies the right not to be forced to speak. Protecting free expression to promote democracy implies that listeners' rights also need to be protected. There is a right to hear messages as well as the right not to be forced to hear them.

- The U.S. Supreme Court has *never* held that free expression is an absolute. It must always be weighed against other rights. In determining the relative weight of free expression, courts consider factors such as the identity of the speaker, the venue, and the subject of the expression, and whether the expression is more speech or more action.

- The First Amendment, like the rest of the U.S. Constitution, is a framework rather than an explicit list of rules. It has been subject to legal interpretation for more than 200 years and, as a living document, continues to evolve.

Twenty-first-Century Terrorism

Since 2001 there has been a rapid growth of jihadist websites dedicated to recruiting terrorists and spreading terrorist ideology. Many of the websites are located within the United States, but others originate outside the country where American law does not apply. Even for websites within our borders though, it is not illegal to provide instructions for the making of an Improvised Explosive Device (IED) or to suggest that sacrificing one's life for a cause is a noble thing to do. The unsuccessful Christmas Day plot in 2009 to blow up a flight over Detroit was undertaken by a man who was recruited by a website where radical cleric Anwar al-Awlaki reached out to his followers with the message of jihad. U.S. law prohibits advocating violent overthrow of the government,[a] but these websites do not usually rise to that level.

Army Brigadier General John Custer stated that the Internet was serving as the most important means for terrorists to radicalize young people, and other sources support that assessment. Nine years after the September 11 attacks, Interpol Secretary General Robert Noble said that middle-class young people from around the world are being recruited for terrorist groups via websites that are not necessarily illegal. He estimated these radical sites had increased from 12 in 1998 to 4,500 in 2006.[b] Other sources give even higher estimates; the FBI Directorate of Intelligence in 2009 estimated 15,000 websites and web forums were actively reaching out to disaffected Americans like Zachary Chesser, 20, of Fairfax, Va., who was accused of trying to join Al-Shabaab, an Islamist militant group based in Somalia, and Michigan's Colleen LaRose ("Jihad Jane") who was put on trial for actively recruiting Islamic jihadists online.

The U.S. House of Representatives in 2010 solicited input on how to deal with the issue of terrorist recruitment via the Internet, and the consensus from just about every witness was that not much could be done about the situation. If the sites could be shut down they would just reappear at new locations, and with renewed criticism about their oppression.

So, what should be done? If terrorism is a threat, and if recruitment occurs online, should the government engage in activity to stop it? At what point does a terrorist site cross the line from making a political statement to becoming something more, and who gets to decide? If the people who operate these websites are Americans who oppose U.S. policy, should they be arrested, or do they have the right to recruit people in the name of religion? ∎

---

[a] 18 U.S.C. § 2385.

[b] *Extremist Sites Boost Terrorist Recruitment,* Breaking News, Sept. 21, 2010, http://www.breakingnews.ie/world/extremist-sites-boost-terrorist-recruitment-474455.html. Interpol is the world's largest international police organization with almost 200 participating countries.

Forums of Freedom

LEARNING OBJECTIVES

After reading this chapter you should know:

- Whether a specific location is a public or non-public forum in terms of free expression

- How the principle of viewpoint discrimination prevents enforcing certain types of laws

- How far free expression goes for students on campuses of public education

- Why some public institutions can restrict freedom of expression more than others

- That public employees are free to speak out at work on some issues but not others

- The difference between strict scrutiny and intermediate scrutiny

- What fighting words restrict in terms of imminent danger

- How the infliction of emotional or physical harm is considered unlawful when it is judged as a foreseeable event

THE UMBRELLA OF FREE EXPRESSION

It was not meant to be a joke. A nine-year-old boy stood outside the U.S. Supreme Court holding a picket sign proclaiming that "God Hates You." Others beside the youth held pointed references to their belief God was displeased with the nation for tolerating homosexual acts and abortion. The youth was the grandson of a Kansas-based minister, Rev. Fred Phelps, who along with other members of Phelps's family became symbols of religious protest at funerals for American soldiers killed in action in Iraq and Afghanistan. They were standing outside the Supreme Court building because the father of one dead soldier, whose funeral had been subjected to their protests received permission to argue his case against them before the Court.

A trial court in Virginia awarded millions of dollars in damages to Albert Snyder, the father of Lt. Corporal Matthew Snyder, an American soldier killed in a 2006 Humvee accident in the Ambar Province of Iraq. Snyder sued the Phelps family for infliction of emotional distress, invasion of privacy, and civil conspiracy after the congregation of Westboro Baptist Church stood in protest outside his son's funeral in Westminster, Maryland, and referred to his son's death on their website. The Fourth Circuit Court of Appeals dismissed the damages awarded to Snyder on First Amendment grounds, but the father was encouraged to continue the fight up to the U.S. Supreme Court by political leaders of both parties who filed *amicus curiae* (friend of the court) briefs in his favor. In 2011 the Supreme Court voted 8–1 that picketing at funerals is protected free expression. Writing for the majority, Chief Justice John Roberts stated that our national commitment to free speech requires protecting "even hurtful speech on public issues."[1]

Freedom of expression at outdoor assemblies can expand or contract like an umbrella depending on the location, the nature of such events, and the expressions. Elected officials establish rules regarding public spaces, and courts enforce legal standards for such outdoor activities as parades, protests, and pickets. Understanding the legal distinctions applied to different spaces begins by defining the legal questions according to case law. The procedural tests that apply in such cases are calculated to prevent rules that go beyond constitutional limits.[2]

THE ORIGIN OF FORUMS

Two early landmark cases spoke to the right of political and religious freedom on public grounds. A New England evangelist was arrested for preaching his gospel message in a Boston park. Rev. William Davis was convicted for preaching without a permit in the Boston Common, but he fought his case up to the nation's highest court. In 1897, Davis lost his appeal[3] after the U.S. Supreme Court

---

[1] *Snyder v. Phelps*, 2011 U.S. LEXIS 1903 (2011).

[2] *Cox v. New Hampshire*, 312 U.S. 569 (1941). Speaking for the majority in a case involving permits for parades, Chief Justice Hughes defended the application of law "only to considerations of time, place and manner so as to conserve the public convenience." *Id.* at 575–6.

[3] *Davis v. Commonwealth of Massachusetts*, 167 U.S. 43, 47 (1897).

accepted a theory of government authority comparing state control over a public forum to that of a private homeowner and his house. This rationale survived for decades until the 1930s when a decision was handed down regarding the way labor unions began to recruit workers to hand out flyers in public places.[4]

In Jersey City, New Jersey the Congress of Industrial Organizations (CIO) came in conflict with the city's chief administrator during the Great Depression. Mayor Frank Hague earned his title "Boss" Hague by ruling his city with a tight grip for more than 30 years.[5] CIO organizers began stopping passersby in Jersey City parks and announcing the new rights granted under the National Labor Relations Act (1935), and the mayor took offense. He had union representatives boarded onto boats and ferried back to New York City, but the CIO challenged his authority to take such actions under Jersey City's permit ordinance. Eventually, the U.S. Supreme Court was asked to settle the dispute. The Court identified public areas as the proper place for "assembly, communicating thought between citizens, and discussing public questions" and held in favor of the labor representatives.[6] *Hague v. CIO* (1939) formed the first rung of a legal theory suggesting public parks, streets, and sidewalks should serve as **traditional public forums.** Freedom of expression and access were to be granted at such places, and those rights were not to be abridged just because a powerful public official found them to be objectionable.

> **Bedrock Law:** Traditional public forums cannot exclude, by government license or permit, specific messages based on their viewpoint.

> **Traditional public forum** ■ Refers to public property that is open for expression and assembly, such as streets, sidewalks, and parks. Public forums have strong First Amendment protection.

STUDENT EXPRESSION LESSONS

When deciding if a speaker's location is a public forum suitable for free expression, the law looks to the prior uses of that place (and others like it). The law has viewed "streets and parks" as traditional public forums since the *Hague* case, but such places have been used by citizens to congregate and exercise their free expression rights since our nation's founding and before, in fact. However, just because expression takes place on public property does not mean that it is actually a traditional forum.

In effect, state-owned universities contain similar spaces that serve both as traditional public forums and non-public forums. Certainly a university president's office is no more a public forum than the Oval Office is. On the other hand, spaces on campus that resemble traditional parks (perhaps a university's quad) or streets (pedestrian walkways) are much more likely to be deemed public forums. If a space has been traditionally treated as a public forum, or it *resembles* space that has been traditionally treated as a public forum, free expression is likely to be protected there.

---

[4]In *Jamison v. Texas*, 318 U.S. 413 (1943), the U.S. Supreme Court explicitly rejected the Boston Common decision after Dallas city officials cited Davis to support their ban upon the distribution of handbills in city streets. The open forum concept outweighs government interest unless it is substantial.

[5]Another moniker coined for Hague was "I am the law," which were the words he used to silence a subordinate who dared to challenge his authority.

[6]*Hague v. Committee for Indus. Org.*, 307 U.S. 496, 515 (1939).

History Matters

Courts also review the history of a specific venue to determine how it is to be treated. Is a school bulletin board a public forum? The answer is, "it depends." How has that bulletin board been used prior to a case coming before the court? In a case involving whether advertisements on city buses were a public forum, Supreme Court Justice Harry Blackmun wrote, "before you could say whether a certain thing could be done in a certain place you would have to know the history of the particular place." If a public high school has a bulletin board that has been used by the English department to post notices, scholarship announcements, and other departmental business, a court is likely to ask if that particular bulletin board constitutes a public forum or if it has been strictly the decision of the English department regarding what is to be posted. On the other hand if a high school has permitted students to post their own notices, items for sale, or announcements on the bulletin board, a court would likely determine that it has become a public forum. It is not only the use and location of a public space for free expression, but it is also a matter of who is using it and who is sponsoring the communication that controls the issue—the legal question at hand.

Speaker's Impact Matters

High-school-age students, and younger, have fewer free expression rights than adult speakers enjoy. They are not without First Amendment freedoms, but their rights are not as far-reaching as those of adults. In 1965, John Tinker and Christopher Eckhardt were high school students in Des Moines, Iowa, and John's younger sister Mary Beth was in junior high. The three planned to wear black armbands to school to protest American involvement in the war in Vietnam. School officials became aware of their plans and decided to prevent the protest by creating a rule prohibiting students from wearing armbands in school. Students wearing armbands would be told to remove them, and any student who did not comply would be suspended. The three students, John, Christopher, and Mary Beth, wore their armbands to school and were sent home until they were willing to return without them.

The families of the three students filed a lawsuit in federal court. The families requested an injunction preventing the schools from enforcing the armband policy, but the district court ruled against them. The school district had persuaded the court that schools need to have the authority to maintain order, and that if the court prohibited enforcement of this rule, it would significantly damage the schools' ability to provide the necessary discipline and rigor for a good learning environment. Even though the appellate court upheld the district court's decision, the family felt strongly enough about the issue to appeal it to the U.S. Supreme Court, which agreed to hear the case. It actually presented the Court with a number of questions, including whether or not the wearing of an armband is actually a form of expression under the First Amendment.

---

[7]*Lehman v. Shaker Heights*, 418 U.S. 298 (1974), at 302.

Symbolic Speech

Through a series of decisions throughout the twentieth century, the Court has determined that actions such as wearing armbands are a type of **symbolic speech** that is entitled to protection unless there is a material, substantial disruption that would stop the educational enterprise.[8] In the case of John, Christopher, and Mary Beth, the basic reason for wearing the armbands was to make a statement. The justices had no difficulty in determining that wearing armbands was a form of constitutionally protected expression.

However, that is not the end of the argument. An expression might be otherwise protected but is actually denied protection because of some conflicting concern. In a school classroom, certainly a student cannot claim that a right of free expression entitles a student to speak at anytime about any topic. The teacher in a classroom has the authority to prevent a student from talking out of turn without being accused of denying the student's First Amendment rights. This balance between the right of students to free expression and the right of the school district to maintain its authority and classroom decorum was at the heart of the debate. The Court had adequate precedent that students do not "shed their constitutional rights to freedom of speech or expression at the schoolhouse gate."[9] The difficulty was in striking a balance with the "need for affirming the comprehensive authority of the States and of school officials, consistent with fundamental constitutional safeguards, to prescribe and control conduct in the schools."[10] As is typical in free expression cases, the Court was not faced with deciding whether some hypothetical form of expression should be protected in an abstract setting, but whether *this* specific form of expression should be protected in *this* particular setting. In this instance, armbands are political expression, and in the abstract, students have free expression rights in schools; yet, what happens when those rights conflict with the needs of the school authorities?

Symbolic speech ■ Speech is more than just words. Actions or symbols can also be considered speech protected by the First Amendment.

Disruption Test

In the *Tinker* case, the Court found in favor of the children's rights to wear the armbands to school. In balancing between the conflicting interests, the Court noted that the school district provided no evidence that the students' behavior was substantially disruptive. The Court dismissed the school district's assertion that wearing the armbands somehow intruded on the rights of other students to learn in an orderly classroom environment. The Court held that merely having the *fear* of a *possible* disturbance was not enough to warrant suppressing the free speech rights of the students. It is worth noting that the school district mentioned its desire to "avoid the controversy" that might be a result of allowing students to silently protest by wearing armbands. The Court was critical of the

Bedrock Law: The *Tinker* rule allows students freedom of expression on school grounds unless it poses a material, substantial disruption to education.

---

[8]Some of those cases are *West Virginia v. Barnette,* 319 U.S. 624 (1943); *Stromberg v. California,* 283 U.S. 359 (1931); and *Thornhill v. Alabama,* 310 U.S. 88 (1940).

[9]*Tinker v. Des Moines Sch. Dist.,* 393 U.S. 593 (1969) at 506.

[10]*Id.* at 507.

The *Tinker* test ■
Schools cannot
restrict symbolic
speech unless it
causes a substantial
material disruption.
School officials'
desire to avoid a
substantial, mate-
rial disruption. The
desire of school
officials to avoid
the unpleasantness
of an unpopular or
controversial view
is not enough,
without substantial
disruption.

fact that schools were attempting to eliminate one topic of discussion with which the school administrators were uncomfortable. The ban on armbands was an attempt to silence one form of protest while other political symbols (in the form of buttons or jewelry) would be permitted. Justice Abe Fortas wrote the land-mark language in the *Tinker* case, "it can hardly be argued that either students or teachers shed their constitutional rights to freedom of speech or expression at the schoolhouse gate."[11]

Interestingly, a dissenting opinion was filed in this case by Justice Hugo Black, who was in many other cases a strong defender of the First Amendment. It was Justice Black's position that students in schools were not entitled to defy school rules under the guise of free expression. He felt that the record showed the arm-bands *were* disruptive inasmuch as they took the students' minds off of their schoolwork. He took issue with the fact that the Court's decision supplanted the authority of school officials, instead allowing the judgment of children to rule the day. He supported the notion that "taxpayers send children to school on the prem-ise that at their age they need to learn, not teach."[12] Years later, the Court seemed to follow the reasoning of Justice Black's dissent.

Some disagree whether the *Tinker* standard was properly applied in a case years later that was prompted by a high school student's speech relying heavily on sexual innuendo. Matthew Fraser was speaking on behalf of one of his classmates, Jeff Kuhlman, who was running for a student government vice president at Bethel High School near Tacoma, Wash. Fraser, who became a debate coach at Stanford University, told the auditorium of teenagers that he knew a man "who was firm in his pants . . . Jeff is a man who will go to the very end—even the climax, for each and every one of you."[13] The court record states Bethel High School students hooted and yelled during the speech, and some mimicked sexual activities. Fraser was suspended from school for three days for this disruption but appealed his sus-pension with the support of his parents and the American Civil Liberties Union. Fraser won his case at the state level in Washington, where the *Tinker* test was applied to his favor despite the auditorium uproar at his use of vulgarities. How-ever, the Supreme Court voted 7–2 to uphold Fraser's suspension, and Chief Justice Warren Burger concluded a "high school assembly or classroom is no place for a sexually explicit monologue directed towards an unsuspecting audience of teenage students."[14]

Speaker's Medium Matters

Twenty years after the Supreme Court defended the rights of children to wear armbands to school as protected free expression, journalism students in Hazel-wood, Missouri, were about to test the limits of students' rights again. Students

---

[11]*Id.* at 506.

[12]*Id.* at 522 (Black, J., dissenting).

[13]*Bethel Sch. Dist. v. Fraser*, 478 U.S. 675 (1986).

[14]*Id.* at 686.

in the Journalism II class (which was responsible for publishing the school newspaper) at Hazelwood East High School had included two articles in the issue scheduled for publication on May 13, 1985, that the school administration found unsuitable. One article featured the accounts of three students about their experiences with pregnancy, while the other article focused on the effect of divorce on students.

It was the custom of the student paper to deliver the pages to the principal for approval prior to publication. Principal Robert Reynolds was concerned that the pregnant students might be identified (even though their names were not used), that the subject of sexual activity might not be appropriate content for some of the younger students, and that parents who were the subject of a student's quotes ought to be afforded an opportunity to reply to critical comments. Because the school year was ending, there was not enough time to simply delay publication of the newspaper to resolve his concerns. Principal Reynolds was faced with the choice of either allowing the paper to publish as submitted or prohibiting publication of the two pages containing the questionable material. He decided that the issue of *Spectrum* in question ought to be published with only four pages rather than the six pages submitted, opting to censor the offending material.

Three students went to federal district court requesting an injunction against the principal, hoping to get legal relief quickly so that the pages would be included. The court would not grant the injunction, and the students appealed. The court of appeals found in favor of the students, ruling that their First Amendment rights had been violated. The appellate decision used a *Tinker* style of analysis, concluding that the school had no evidence that the articles would be disruptive in classes or result in disorder to the environment. This time the school district appealed.

Who Controls the Channel?

In a 5–3 decision, the Supreme Court ruled that Principal Reynolds did not violate the students' First Amendment rights when he censored two pages of the newspaper. Unlike the Tinker armbands, the articles were not student-initiated speech—it was a school-owned medium. In doing so, the Court addressed a couple of different issues raised by the case. First, student newspapers are not *traditional public forums*. The Hazelwood school officials had not designated the school newspaper as a public forum, open to anyone's expression, and as such were not required to treat it as a traditional public forum. Rather, the school newspaper was produced as part of a class, and so the newspaper was a laboratory experience for the students. A faculty member oversaw the newspaper's publication as part of his teaching load, and students received academic credit for their work on it. Further, both a faculty adviser and the principal reviewed every issue prior to publication. So, while American student expression is encouraged, it is not unfettered and is subject to review. Secondly, the Court distinguished this case from *Tinker* by asserting that its legal precedent stood for the idea that a school may not suppress student expression, whereas the situation in *Hazelwood* was the question of whether the school had to defend a particular student's expression. The Court pointed out that "we hold that educators do not offend the First Amendment by exercising editorial control over the style and content of student speech in school-sponsored expressive activities so long as their actions are reasonably related to legitimate pedagogical concerns."[15]

At Hazelwood East High School, it was not just because the students were minors that the Court allowed the censorship to occur, but also because of the conditions surrounding the school paper's publication. The paper was the extension of a classroom, and as such the school was able to exercise jurisdiction over it. Although the Court did not directly say so, the students were being treated the same as if they had spoken in class without raising their hands. Their status as students in a classroom restricted their free expression.

Who Owns the Content?

Two college cases considered the reasoning of *Hazelwood* to student publications and yet achieved different solutions. In 1999, students at Kentucky State University were upset because the administration had refused to distribute their yearbooks for that year. A university administrator, Betty Gibson, felt the yearbook's theme, color, and lack of captions for photographs were unsuitable for distribution and refused to allow the students to receive their copies. This ban on their yearbook was not well received by a number of students, who felt it amounted to a form of school censorship.

A former soldier and nursing student, Charles Kincaid spoke with school officials about his concern that he paid for the yearbook and felt that his property had been illegally seized. The U.S. Court of Appeals for the Sixth Circuit (Ohio, Kentucky, Tennessee, and Michigan) took up Kincaid's case after the university won lower-court rulings where *Hazelwood* had been applied. The appeals court rejected the *Hazelwood* analysis and held the university failed to recognize the students' rights to property, ruling that it could not hold the yearbooks captive. Kentucky State University ended up having to pay the students the cost of their court battle and released the yearbooks.[16]

In 2005, the U.S. Court of Appeals for the Seventh Circuit (Indiana, Illinois, and Wisconsin) found the logic of *Hazelwood* to be more relevant. *The Innovator* at Governors State University in Illinois became controversial for its front-page criticisms of both teachers and administrators. The student editors enjoyed freedom from censorship until Dean Patricia Carter chose to withhold issues of the newspaper until the administration approved the papers, which the students considered to be in violation of the school's stated policy. The student editors went to court to seek an injunction, but an appeals court applied *Hazelwood*'s reasoning to the case to find that school-sponsored speech—even at the college level—did not necessarily represent a public forum. The Seventh Circuit Court held if a college official wishes to preview a student publication, he or she has the authority to do so and may censor it if the official deems it necessary, and that the extracurricular nature of a newspaper's publication is not a decisive factor in making the forum determination. This appellate court decision is binding precedent only within that

[15]*Hazelwood Sch. Dist. v. Kuhlmeier,* 484 U.S. 260 (1988), at 273.
[16]*Kincaid v. Gibson,* 236 F.3d 342 (6th Cir. 2001).

particular jurisdiction since the U.S. Supreme Court has yet to rule on college publications and the question of prior review, but lawyers in other jurisdictions can use reference to this decision as a nonbinding precedent.[17]

Following this decision, the legislature of Illinois and at least two other states enacted bills to allow more student control of university newspapers, which some consider to be the good news for student free expression that came out of the *Hazelwood* case.

Compatible Use of the Forum?

The theory of student expression in *Grayned v. City of Rockford* (1972), where the "time, place, and manner" phrase was coined, involved high school students convicted for violating two rules—a city anti-noise ordinance and a picketing ordinance. During the school day, African-American students in Rockford, Illinois, rallied outside classrooms loud enough for students and teachers to hear and view their activities from school windows. Protesters held picket signs on school grounds, and some classroom activities were disrupted.[18] Students protested the school's lack of fairness and racial equality in hiring teachers and counselors, and even in cheerleader tryouts.

When the case was appealed to the U.S. Supreme Court, the first African-American justice ruled against the protesters. Justice Thurgood Marshall held the nature of a public place is important, including "the pattern of its normal activities" that "dictate the kinds of regulations of time, place, and manner that are reasonable."[19] While the Court's decision upheld the enforcement of Rockford's anti-noise ordinance, the picketing rule was struck because its language unfairly discriminated against particular viewpoints. This decision formed the basis of what became known as the **compatible use doctrine.** "The crucial question is whether the manner of expression is basically incompatible with the normal activity of a particular place at a particular time."[20] Courts would have more to say on the limits of free expression in public places designated to serve other purposes.

> **Bedrock Law:** The compatible use doctrine requires that the forms of expression allowed in a public space should follow the purpose of that particular forum.

> **Compatible use doctrine** ■ Allows restriction of speech when "the manner of expression is basically incompatible with the normal activity of a particular place at a particular time." *See Grayned v. City of Rockford*, 408 U.S. 104 (1972).

Workplace Rules on Expression

While free speech is restricted to some extent in schools, it is not *as* limited as it might be in certain venues. Extrapolating from this, there are places that are even less conducive to free expression.[21] Just because property is publicly owned does

---

[17]*Hosty v. Carter*, 412 F.3d 731 (7th Cir. banc 2005).

[18]*Grayned v. City of Rockford*, 408 U.S. 104 (1972).

[19]*Id.* at 116.

[20]*Id.*

[21]*United States v. Grace*, 461 U.S. 171 (1983). The decision held that a ban on leafleting and picketing with regard to the public sidewalks beyond the Supreme Court grounds to be unconstitutional.

not mean it is an open public forum. The White House is owned by the public, yet no one has a First Amendment right to stage a sit-in in the Oval Office. Supreme Court decisions have upheld restrictions on speech in jails[22] and on military bases[23] in light of the special purposes of those governmentally controlled forums.

Freedom of speech and assembly are the tools used by labor unions in their collective bargaining struggles, which often take place near places of work. Labor groups in the United States have organized picketers for years—a practice that was once banned under British common law.[24] In the case of *Thornhill v. Alabama* (1940), the U.S. Supreme Court reviewed one union leader's arrest and conviction in order to establish that picketing was worthy of First Amendment protection.[25] During the Great Depression, Byron Thornhill was president of his local union and joined strikers outside the Brown Wood Preserving Company, where he was arrested, convicted, and fined $100. The question that came before the Court was whether his union picketing should be enjoined because of its threat to public order. The Court sided with Thornhill, since he was engaged in a communication activity "indispensable to the effective and intelligent use of the processes of popular government to shape the destiny of modern industrial society."[26]

Combining expressive actions with words became known as "speech plus," indicating that behavior can convey a message and is entitled to protection, although just how much "speech plus" can be allowed varies according to the time, place, and manner of the public expression. In Thornhill's case, the law was struck because it was overbroad.

Shopping Malls

While it might seem to make good sense that privately owned spaces are *not likely* to be considered public forums, there are instances when they actually might be. Perhaps the best example of this is the modern-day shopping mall. The entire space is privately owned, but it looks quite like the modern equivalent of public spaces. In 1968, the U.S. Supreme Court first considered whether individuals may have free expression in and around shopping centers. The Court ruled that, because the shopping area was the "functional equivalent" of publicly owned spaces, a privately owned shopping center in Pennsylvania had to allow union members to picket on its property.[27]

In 1972, the Supreme Court decided that a different group of protesters did not have a free expression right on the private property of another shopping area because, unlike the case four years earlier, their protest was unrelated to that

---

[22]*Adderly v. Florida*, 385 U.S. 39 (1966).

[23]*Greer v. Spock*, 424 U.S. 828 (1976).

[24]To the British jurists, labor strikes represented the flipside of monopoly—rather than businesses exploiting labor, it had the taint of workers conspiring against employers.

[25]*Thornhill v. Alabama*, 310 U.S. 88 (1940).

[26]*Id.* at 103.

[27]*Amalgamated Food Employees Union Local 590 v. Logan Valley Plaza*, 391 U.S. 308 (1968).

shopping center's business in Oregon.[28] After another four years, the Court again weighed in on this type of forum and ruled that the private property rights of the shopping center were as protected as free expression rights and that privately owned shopping centers were not public forums.[29] That seemed to settle the issue—almost. In 1980 (after another four-year interval), the Court ruled that free expression rights at shopping centers in California *were* protected—but not because of the U.S. Constitution. In that case, it ruled that shopping centers are public forums in California because that state's own constitution says they are.[30]

If a state decides to expand free expression rights beyond what the federal government requires, it certainly can do so. This holds true not only for the state of California but also New Jersey,[31] Colorado,[32] Washington,[33] and Massachusetts,[34] where the public forum nature of shopping centers have been recognized. On the other hand, states such as North Carolina have ruled that even handing out flyers in mall parking lots may be forbidden.[35]

Freedom of Expression for Employees

Public schools throughout the nation have imposed dress codes that repeatedly have been held to be constitutional.[36] Those same dress codes for adult-aged college students would be unlikely to stand. On the other hand, the "unique" condition of military employment has been considered a valid condition for the requirement of a dress code. An Air Force regulation prohibiting headwear indoors while on duty was enforced against an Orthodox Jewish officer who wished to wear his yarmulke. Despite his First Amendment claims, the Supreme Court ruled that the military needed great deference in matters of uniform requirements.[37] A similar requirement on a civilian would not likely be permitted.

What's more, the speaker's employment may impose additional limitations on free expression, not just the speech of students or soldiers. For example, an adult government employee may have his or her free expression limited as a condition of that employment. Intelligence agencies such as the FBI and CIA routinely require their employees to sign contracts that prohibit them from publishing anything about their agency, while employed or after, without prior approval from the

---

[28]*Lloyd Corp. v. Tanner*, 407 U.S. 551 (1972).

[29]*Hudgens v. NLRB*, 424 U.S. 507 (1976).

[30]*Pruneyard Shopping Ctr. v. Robins*, 447 U.S. 74 (1980).

[31]*New Jersey Coalition against the War in the Middle East v. JMB Realty*, 650 A.2d 757 (N.J. 1994).

[32]*Bock & Lawless-Avelar v. Westminster Mall*, 819 P.2d 55 (Colo. 1991).

[33]*Alderwood v. Washington Envtl. Council*, 96 Wash. 2d 230, 635 P.2d 108

[34]*Batchelder v. Allied Stores Int'l*, 445 N.E.2d 590 (Mass. 1983).

[35]*See Pruneyard Shopping Center v. Robins, supra* at note 30; and *State v. Felmet*, 302 N.C. 173, 273 S.E.2d 708 (1981).

[36]For example, *Harper v. Poway Unified Sch. Dist.*, 445 F.3d 1166 (9th Circ. 2006), upheld public school prohibition on T-shirts that denigrate others on the basis of sexual orientation.

[37]*Goldman v. Weinberger*, 475 U.S. 503 (1986).

agency. When a former CIA agent published a book in violation of that agreement, the U.S. Supreme Court found that his free expression right did not supersede his contractual obligations, even though the CIA conceded that no national secrets were revealed in the book.[38]

Public employees thus find their rights to expression curbed depending upon where they work and for whom. The first measure directed at free expression for government employees was passed in 1939, and it required that federal employees not become involved in political campaigns or rallies by distributing literature or making speeches at candidate rallies.[39] The U.S. Congress liberalized that law in 1993 when it gave U.S. civil servants the freedom to campaign on behalf of political candidates away from the office and hold party office. Still, it did not preclude the possibility that public employees may be punished for getting involved in certain issues that enter the public arena.

At the local school level, the case of Marvin L. Pickering is relevant. He was a teacher concerned with a school board issue in Illinois,[40] where he took it upon himself to criticize the school board in a letter to the editor of a local newspaper. As a result, he was fired from his job for acting in a manner that the board deemed "detrimental" to the school's interest. The Supreme Court rejected that contention and supported Pickering's right to participate in public debate, but just how far public employees can go is related to when, where, and what they decide to say.

What happens to a public employee who speaks out on the job about a news event? Ardith McPherson found her services no longer needed at the Harris County Constable's office in Houston, Texas, after she responded aloud to radio news of the failed attempt to assassinate President Ronald Reagan. She told a co-worker if someone tries to kill him again, she hopes they succeed. When Constable Walter Rankin heard of McPherson's statement from a third party, he had the public employee dismissed. In a 5–4 decision, the U.S. Supreme Court felt McPherson's offhand remarks demonstrated no unfit character traits on her part, and ruled in her favor.[41]

Disruptions to the Workplace

An assistant district attorney of New Orleans was accused of creating unrest in the Orleans Parish office in the 1980s. Shelia Myers was fired from her job by then District Attorney Harry Connick (father of the popular singer), and she protested her dismissal. Myers felt this action was unreasonable punishment for circulating a questionnaire critical of Connick's administration. The Court, however, upheld Myers' firing since her speech on administrative matters potentially undermined the workplace and thus was outside constitutional protection.[42]

---

[38]*Snepp v. United States,* 444 U.S. 507 (1980).

[39]An act to prevent pernicious political activities named for Senator Carl Hatch of New Mexico (5 U.S.C. §§ 7321–7326, and §§ 5001, 5008)

[40]*Pickering v. Board of Educ.,* 391 U.S. 563 (1968).

[41]*Rankin v. McPherson,* 483 U.S. 378 (1987).

[42]*Connick v. Myers,* 461 U.S. 183 (1983).

In another employee case, the remarks were found by the Court to be more harmful. A nurse at an Illinois hospital was fired after she criticized the facility's training and staffing policies. Cheryl Churchill's hospital superiors said she was acting out of spite, and her criticisms were disrupting the harmony of the hospital. When the case reached the U.S. Supreme Court, Justice Sandra Day O'Connor established a test for judging a public employee's right to free speech. This standard recognized the highest level of constitutional protection for discussion of public issues, but it also provided that employers have a legitimate interest in avoiding disruptions to workplace efficiency and morale. Ultimately, the government must prove the disruptive quality of the employee's communication outweighs their First Amendment protection. If the employer reasonably arrives at such a conclusion, then punishment or dismissal may be deemed as acceptable even when no disruption actually took place.[43]

In a 2006 decision, the Court held that a government employee who speaks out as a part of his job does not have full First Amendment protection. The reasoning was that his employer (the government) may have just cause to discipline the employee for what was said. Richard Ceballos was a deputy district attorney who criticized a sheriff's conduct in obtaining a search warrant. When Ceballos was demoted and transferred, he filed a lawsuit, which made its way all the way to the Supreme Court. The Court ruled 5–4 that the free expression of government employees is limited when they act in their official capacities. Justice Anthony Kennedy's majority opinion stated, "We hold that when public employees make statements pursuant to their official duties, the employees are not speaking as citizens for First Amendment purposes, and the Constitution does not insulate their communications from employer discipline."[44]

> **Bedrock Law:** Case law supports employer controls over employee expression if it is shown to disrupt workplace efficiency and morale.

LEVELS OF SCRUTINY

When the government passes a rule or law dealing with more than just traditional public forums, and it becomes the subject of a court dispute, then the law may be judged by a standard known as **strict scrutiny**. This means that the law's wording is held up to a sort of legal magnifying glass to see if it satisfies a compelling public interest larger than the freedom of expression guaranteed by the First Amendment.[45] If something in the actual content of a message is considered to be so inflammatory in nature that it is a danger to personal reputation, privacy, and the public order, and the rule regarding these harms is **content-based,** it must be proven valid under the U.S. Constitution. What does this mean? Its wording should take no more freedom than is necessary, and there should be no other means available to satisfy the compelling interest that the law is meant to address.

> **Strict scrutiny** ■ The highest standard of scrutiny courts apply when reviewing laws. Strict scrutiny requires the law 1) serve a compelling government interest, 2) be narrowly tailored to achieving the goal, and 3) use the least restrictive means to do so.

---

[43]*Waters v. Churchill,* 511 U.S. 661 (1994).

[44]*Garcetti v. Ceballos,* 2006 U.S. LEXIS 4341.

[45]Consider the flag-burning case, for example, where strict scrutiny was applied to the Texas law that placed Gregory Lee Johnson in custody. *Texas v. Johnson,* 491 U.S. 397, 414 (1989).

Intermediate Scrutiny

Content-based restrictions ■ Content-based restrictions do not apply equally to all speech, but only restrict certain speech content. Content-based restrictions are subject to strict scrutiny.

Forum analysis, on the other hand, typically involves **content-neutral** rules, where the government is controlling *all* communication activities without regard to any particular content in order, for instance, to protect neighborhoods from excessive noise, afford access to entrances and exits of public buildings, keep order along parade routes, and other noncommunication concerns. When courts turn their attention to content-neutral rules, they rely on a balancing test called **intermediate scrutiny** that reduces the government's burden to simply showing a *substantial* or *important* interest is involved, and the rule achieves it without suppressing any viewpoints. One example would be a draft resister's case, where a draft registration card was burned in protest.

Content-neutral restrictions ■ Content-neutral restrictions do not single out certain viewpoints; they apply equally to all speech. Content-neutral restrictions are subject to lower scrutiny than content-based restrictions.

In 1966, David Paul O'Brien was taken into custody on the steps of a Boston Courthouse. O'Brien, along with several protesters, stood before print and broadcast media and used a lighter to ignite his draft registration card, property of the government documenting draft-eligible men. The U.S. Supreme Court found that the United States had a legitimate interest in protecting such records, and O'Brien had other means of protest at his disposal.[46]

This 1968 Supreme Court decision has been cited literally dozens of times in subsequent Supreme Court decisions, and hundreds of times by state and federal lower courts. The case provides the yardstick that measures whether a time, place, or manner regulation is constitutional. When speech and nonspeech elements are both contained in some conduct, the Court says "incidental limitations" on free expression are justified. There are countless laws that regulate the size and placement of signs, or the volume of sounds, or the location of newspaper distribution boxes. The Supreme Court recognized the need for government to regulate when (time), where (place), and how (manner) expression is permitted, provided it does not exceed certain boundaries. The test asks the following questions:

Intermediate scrutiny ■ The middle level of scrutiny courts apply when reviewing laws. Intermediate scrutiny requires the law serve an important state interest in a way that is substantially related to the public interest.

- Is the law regulating expression *content-neutral*? If it is not, the time, place, and manner restriction is unconstitutional.
- Does the law further some substantial or important government interest? If the interest is minor or one the government may not enforce, the law must be invalidated.
  - Is the law regulating expression *narrowly tailored*? If the regulation restricts more expression than necessary to achieve the government's goal, it is unconstitutional.
  - Does the law leave *adequate alternative channels* of communication? Rules eliminating communication opportunities but leaving no viable alternatives will not stand.

Bedrock Law: Content neutral rules of expression such as those dealing with time, place, and manner can be challenged under a four-pronged test known as intermediate scrutiny.

The *O'Brien* test is not a "best three out of four" examination. All four conditions must be met in order for a time, place, and manner rule to be deemed constitutional.

---

[46]*United States v. O'Brien*, 391 U.S. 367 (1968).

THE OPEN FORUM TEST

We have seen how the First Amendment stretches beyond written and spoken words to encompass expressive conduct, such as wearing armbands, but the law can be used to halt communicative acts where other interests are more important, such as burning a draft card. Constitutional rules can limit the expression of students working on a school newspaper or even employees speaking out against their employer. In other words, we have seen how the forum of an expression is only part of the equation. By considering a landmark ruling in a teachers' union case in Indiana, we can construct a framework for this type of forum analysis.

The public school teachers in Perry Township were considering which collective bargaining union should represent them in negotiations over salaries, benefits, and other work-related issues. Two unions were vying for representation, but the Perry Education Association (PEA) won over the Perry Local Educators' Association's (PLEA) bid. A key stipulation of the new contract was that no other union would be granted access to the teachers' mailboxes. PLEA, upset by this provision, contested the teacher's mailboxes ban believing it to be unconstitutional. In a close vote (5–4), the U.S. Supreme Court ruled against PLEA because the majority reasoned that public employee mailboxes should not be given the status of an open forum and thereby accessible to all parties. Justice White laid down the Court's reasoning, and established the three-part test of public (or open) forums.[47]

The traditional public forum was designed to identify areas around public parks, streets, and sidewalks, and in certain parts of public buildings. The rules adopted for such places should afford safety and reasonable access to all concerned. Such places included offices, auditoriums, and pavilions where official business could be conducted without interference. Any rule limiting expression at such places would be subject to strict scrutiny, and it would place the burden on the government's shoulders to show that its interest in restricting freedom there was compelling.

Limited public forums include bulletin boards, speakers' corners on college campuses, and even student-run newspapers. This type of forum is where the compatible use doctrine is a good fit because the test for curbing speech at such forums has to show an important interest was involved, that no particular viewpoint was discriminated against, and that alternative channels were available.

Finally, Justice White recognized a third classification for **non-public forums,** which included the teachers' mailboxes in Perry, Indiana. Such places where taxpayers have invested dollars in buildings and surrounding grounds may lawfully refuse all sorts of communication activities. Added to the list of non-public forums would be military bases and prisons, which must meet a different set of priorities that at times inhibit the free flow of information. In such realms, the hierarchy of power is necessary and the First Amendment serves a secondary interest. Several cases have shown how far the government can go in regulating non-public forums to forbid free expression in terms of personal dress, religious garb and ornaments, sexually oriented materials, and even personal correspondence.[48]

Limited public forum ■ A forum that has traditionally only been open to public expression and assembly for specific limited purposes.

Non-public forum ■ A forum that has traditionally not been open for public expression and assembly.

---

[47]*Perry Educ. Ass'n v. Perry Local Educators' Ass'n,* 400 U.S. 37 (1983).

[48]*See Parker v. Levy,* 417 U.S. 733 (1974), at 743–49; *Goldman v. Department of Defense,* 475 U.S. 503 (1986); *General Media Communications v. Perry,* 952 F. Supp. 1072 (1997), and *Procunier v. Martinez,* 416 U.S. 396 (1974).

The burden of challenging restrictions at such non-public forums shifts to the petitioner, who must show the court that the rule is unreasonable and that no legitimate interest is served by restricting expression, that it is simply an arbitrary law. If there is no reasonable basis for restricting speech or other forms of communication in a non-public forum, and evidence clearly shows how certain viewpoints are discriminated against, the rule can be struck. We will see how other places recognized as non-public forums include courthouses, airport terminals, and even public sidewalks.

> **Bedrock Law:** Courts determine if a traditional (quintessential), limited (designated), or non-public forum is involved in a time, place, or manner rule to determine if a law is valid.

UP CLOSE

Free Speech Zones

One controversial area involving forums and speech plus are known as free speech zones, whose creation some have questioned on constitutional grounds. Generally, a public official or governmental body decides that protesters, political activists, or preachers should be confined to a certain place and not allowed to move unrestricted on public property. The idea of free speech zones gained favor during the late sixties and early seventies when university administrators designated corners on campus for protesting students to make their feelings known about the Vietnam War and the draft into military service. The idea has resurfaced several times since then at a number of places including political party conventions.

During the 1988 Democratic National Convention, the city of Atlanta set up free speech zones to keep protesters from interfering with the activities and movement of party delegates. At the 2004 Democratic National Convention in Boston, protesters and picketers were confined to a space behind concrete walls out of sight of the convention center. In New York City, police acted spontaneously during the Republican National Convention of 2004 to create ad hoc free speech zones by surrounding protestors on city streets and cordoning them off with police netting and tape that read "Police Line—Do Not Cross." Is such governmental action constitutional? So long as there is no evidence of viewpoint discrimination

and it survives the intermediate scrutiny test that such restrictions are subject to under the time, place, and manner analysis, then the answer is yes.

In its protection of the White House, the Secret Service designates areas that indicate how close protesters can come to the president's location. Some have argued their handling of this jurisdiction is unfair because agents grant nearer proximity to the president's supporters than they do his opponents. In 2003, the Association of Community Organizations for Reform Now (ACORN) went to court, suing the Secret Service for practicing a form of viewpoint discrimination by pushing protestors away from the president, but the agency maintained it held no regard for any onlooker's "purpose, message, or intent." A Texas couple sued the Secret Service after they were arrested in 2004 while wearing T-shirts that read "Regime Change Begins at Home" and "Love America Hate Bush" in West Virginia during a Fourth of July rally.

Free speech zones on college campuses have produced varying results in New York, Texas, and California, among other states. A judge ruled in a Texas Tech complaint that the university could designate more places but not fewer ones for free expression on campus. Penn State University liberalized its policy regarding free speech zones in 2006, and essentially declared the entire campus an open forum.

PROTESTING ON PRINCIPLE

The key to understanding the law in areas of public debate such as war, religion, and abortion is first to examine how courts either affirm the protester's rights or allow the government to discourage demonstrations based on time, place, and manner rules. In a St. Louis suburb, one lettered sign appeared in a homeowner's window protesting the War in the Persian Gulf during the first Bush administration. Margaret Gilleo's message to passersby simply read, "For Peace in the Gulf." The City of Ladue informed her of a local ordinance restricting signs to the sale of property, zoning restrictions, and safety hazards. She reminded local officials of the First Amendment and successfully defended her right to place a sign in her window. Ms. Gilleo fought her case all the way up to the U.S. Supreme Court, where she won despite the acknowledgement that cities do have a right to reduce visual clutter. Cities, however, that enforce an ordinance preventing residents from even placing signs in the windows of their own homes have probably gone too far.[49] Ms. Gilleo's victory has something to say about the importance of freedom of expression in a person's private residence in a public neighborhood.

In outdoor areas, lawsuits over residents' symbolic rights may be subject to questions of zoning restrictions and even patriotism. Billionaire developer Donald Trump in 2006 sued the city of Palm Beach, Florida, after it asked him to take down a 15-by-25-foot American flag he had unfurled at his Palm Beach club, Mar-A-Lago. The city began fining him $1,250 a day for hoisting "Old Glory" up the 80-foot flagpole in violation of a law to protect views of the beach. All fines were dropped, however, after Trump agreed to move the flag away from the ocean view and lower the pole by ten feet. In addition, Trump agreed to donate $100,000 to charities for veterans' organizations.[50]

Viewpoint Discrimination

Door-to-door salesmen and church witnesses face chilly receptions at the doorsteps in some neighborhoods if the product they're selling is religion. Religion in general figures prominently in First Amendment law and the Jehovah's Witnesses occupy a special niche in fighting for free expression whenever cities, without regard to the Constitution's protection, enforce laws that keep them from knocking or even standing on the street corner.

In the late 1930s, the U.S. Supreme Court joined several First Amendment cases from Wisconsin, California, Massachusetts, and the town of Irvington, New Jersey All four appealed convictions for either handing out leaflets on public streets or door-to-door evangelism. Three communities punished Jehovah's Witnesses when their flyers were thrown to the ground after they placed them in the hands of people on the street. Did such rules meet the Court's scrutiny test by establishing an important interest in good appearance and clean streets over free expression? Not according to this

---

[49]*City of Ladue v. Gilleo,* 512 U.S. 43 (1994).

[50]*Flag Flap between Trump, Palm Beach Ends in Settlement,* Associated Press and St. Petersburg Times, April 22, 2007, http://www.sptimes.com/2007/04/22/State/Flag_flap_between_Tru.shtml.

ruling, which held that the government should carry the burden to clean up afterward and not punish pamphleteers for what others did carelessly with their flyers.[51]

Just how far can religious advocates go in stating their beliefs in private homes and public places? Georgia lawyers in 1938 prosecuted one woman for taking religious bulletins door to door. Alma Lovell was arrested by the city of Griffin, Georgia, and fined $50 for this misdemeanor. She had defied the ordinance requiring a permit from the city manager, but refused to pay the fine after her conviction. Lovell appealed her case and challenged the law that gave Griffin's city manager wide discretionary power over who was to be licensed. Because religious circulars enjoy the same protection as other publications, Lovell won her case in the U.S. Supreme Court. Moreover, the Court made it clear such ordinances must be blind to content in order to apply the law constitutionally.[52]

In a similar situation, the Jehovah's Witnesses took on another southern town and its law requiring a book agent license fee. Again, the Court struck down an Opelika, Alabama, ordinance for handing too much discretionary power to the government by requiring permits of this religious group before witnessing. The outcome underscored how liberty of speech and the press occupy a "preferred position" in resolving such public forum disputes,[53] but would those precedents be enough to convince all cities? Evidently not, as the very next year the Supreme Court struck down a law in Pennsylvania when Jehovah's Witnesses challenged a fee for religious canvassers.[54]

Just before World War II, members of the same faith met with police officers as they marched single file down the streets of Manchester, New Hampshire. Sixty-eight members of that church were arrested for failure to obtain a permit, but this time their convictions were upheld by the Court because Justice Hughes pointed out the local law justifiably regarded "considerations of time, place and manner so as to conserve the public convenience . . . and to minimize the risk of disorder."[55] In addition, the city's license fee for such demonstrations was deemed necessary to meet the expenses of public services that the government had to provide.

The Jehovah's Witnesses' struggle to engage in religious persuasion did not close with the twentieth century. In the Village of Stratton, Ohio, in 2002, the municipal government demanded a permit before allowing neighborhood canvassers to share their faith. The Court refused the government's argument that it was only trying to prevent fraud and protect residents' privacy. Stratton had to allow the Witnesses, political speakers, and other pamphleteers free access to their neighborhoods in order to be constitutionally correct.[56] Because it was not "narrowly tailored," the Court struck the rule because it would have made it unlawful for even trick-or-treaters to make their rounds as uninvited "solicitors."

Bedrock Law: The Court has struck down laws where governments use licensing without clearly defined rules for granting or denying permits.

---

[51] *Schneider v. State*, 308 U.S. 147 (1939).

[52] *Lovell v. Griffin*, 303 U.S. 444 (1938).

[53] *Jones v. Opelika*, 316 U.S. 584 (1942).

[54] *Murdock v. Pennsylvania*, 319 U.S. 105 (1943).

[55] *Cox v. New Hampshire*, 312 U.S. 569, 576 (1941).

[56] *Watchtower Bible & Tract Soc'y of N.Y., Inc. v. Village of Stratton*, 536 U.S. 150, 122 (2002).

Pro-Life Protests

What happens when the question is not a door-to-door visit or a flyer handed out in the streets, but pickets in front of a personal residence? In the late 1980s, a Wisconsin abortion doctor sought to remove protesters outside his home in a Milwaukee suburb, where right-to-life advocates stood. The Court decided that they had effectively held the man captive in his own home and, because one's home is one's castle, the pickets had to go.[57] This decision in *Frisby v. Schultz,* based on the common law, served a key public interest—protecting residential privacy. While privacy at one's home is protected, the workplace is a different matter.

In *Madsen v. Women's Health Center, Inc.*, the U.S. Supreme Court affirmed that injunctions could limit right-to-life protests outside of an abortion clinic.[58] Protesters in this Florida case sought to dissolve an injunction ordering them to stay at least 36 feet away from the clinic's entrance. The order also banned displaying observable signs (usually graphic) with images within the sight of pregnant patients. The Court declared the restriction on graphic signs was unreasonable, but the buffer zone of 36 feet around the clinic's doors was upheld.

One approach in the state of New York was to limit the abortion protesters' access by creating a 15-foot bubble of breathing space around women entering or leaving the clinic. That moveable zone of privacy, however, was struck down in *Schenck v. Pro-Choice Network* (1997). The Court did accept the footage around the clinic's entrance—as it did in Madsen—as a no-protest zone allowing 15-foot zones free of protest around the entrance and exits.[59] However, right-to-life advocates were free to approach abortion patients on public sidewalks and had the right to loud demonstrations beyond the zone outside the clinics.

In *Hill v. Colorado* (2000), the question of maintaining a zone of privacy for abortion patients was raised again.[60] The state was trying to protect the women from unwanted intrusions by strangers seeking to counsel them against having an abortion. This time the Court upheld Colorado's law preventing protesters from coming closer than eight feet "for the purpose of passing a leaflet or handbill to, displaying a sign to, or engaging in oral protest, education or counseling with such other person." The law was passed amid an eruption of violence at abortion facilities throughout the nation.

The longest-running courtroom drama testing freedom in the context of abortion protests is the 20-year legal action pursued by the National Organization for Women (NOW) against Joseph Scheidler and his Pro-Life Action League of Chicago. The lawsuit first filed in 1986 produced a jury verdict years later that found the right-to-life activists liable for using intimidation, violence, and extortion. But in 2003 the U.S. Supreme Court in an 8–1 decision reversed that ruling.[61] The Court held pro-life groups should not be subject to an application of the

---

[57]*Frisby v. Schultz,* 487 U.S. 474 (1988).

[58]*Madsen v. Women's Health Ctr., Inc.,* 512 U.S. 753 (1994).

[59]*Schenck v. Pro-Choice Network of W.N.Y.,* 519 U.S. 357 (1997).

[60]*Hill v. Colorado,* 530 U.S. 703 (2000).

[61]*Scheidler v. National Org. for Women,* 537 U.S. 393 (2003).

UP CLOSE

Nuremberg Files

Few issues are more divisive to Americans than the controversial procedure of abortion. Some who regard it as a crime are willing to pursue acts of violence against physicians and health care workers who terminate pregnancies or counsel young women to do so. The level of protest accompanying such activities caused acts of lethal violence prompting Congress to adopt the Freedom of Access to Clinic Entrances (FACE) law, which made it a federal crime to "injure, intimidate, or interfere" with anyone seeking or providing an abortion.[a]

One group ardent in its opposition to this procedure was brought to trial in 1995 in Portland, Oregon, when Planned Parenthood sued the American Coalition of Life Activists (ACLA) for distributing "wanted" style posters with the names of doctors who had performed abortions under the heading, "Guilty of Crimes Against Humanity." The ACLA said it was offering a $5,000 reward for information leading to the arrest, conviction, and revocation of licenses for those doctors who practice abortion.

The FBI consequently advised the named physicians to take special precautions, such as wearing bulletproof vests or protecting their families from gunfire and assault. In 1997, the ACLA created a website using the title "Nuremberg Files"—to indicate that it was trying to prevent crimes against humanity by listing the names of abortion providers. Neal Horsely, a resident of Carrollton, Georgia, was identified as the website's author. Once a doctor's name appeared on the site, it would be shaded if the

person was wounded or appear with a black bar through the name if that person was murdered.

A federal jury said "The Nuremberg Files" constituted a true threat to do bodily harm, assault, or kill. The court held this graphic device of striking through names represented an incitement to violence. The ACLA maintained that its website did not constitute imminent lawless action, and that the list of murdered doctors could be found on other websites albeit not with a line struck through the names of the deceased physicians. In 1999, the ACLA lost its lawsuit and later its appeal of the $100 million verdict, but the Nuremberg Files website is still active with more than eighty names crossed out under the heading, "Alleged Abortionists and Their Accomplices."

---

[a]Freedom of Access to Clinic Entrances Act, 18 U.S.C. § 248 (a) (1).

Racketeer-Influenced and Corrupt Organizations (RICO) Act, regardless of the tactics used. In other words, the incidents cited by NOW did not amount to racketeer violence or extortion.

The lawsuit was originally pursued under the Freedom of Access to Clinic Entrances (FACE) Act. President Clinton signed that bill into law in 1994. It overwhelmingly passed Congress allowing for both criminal and civil penalties against anyone who used "force, threat of force or physical obstruction" to halt the use of reproductive health services.[62] Two lower-court cases found the FACE law constitutional.[63]

Inflicting Harms

The idea that expressive acts can and do cause personal harm—either physical or emotional—raises the question of liability against a media defendant or individual communicator. The infliction of emotional distress is one cause of action that can yield millions of dollars in damages if the courts find the media wronged them by sending out messages inflicting pain. If the media harm caused is deemed an accident, the outlet involved can still be held liable for negligence even after declaring the protection of the First Amendment, as the *Columbia Daily Tribune* learned in covering the assault on Sandra K. Hyde in Missouri.

Walking on a downtown street in August 1980, the woman was stopped after midnight by a male driver, who revealed a shotgun and ordered her to get into his Ford Mustang. Out of fear, Ms. Hyde got in the car but managed to escape at a traffic light and later reported the incident to local police. A newspaper reporter dutifully took down the details of the incident including the woman's name and address from the police blotter. Once published, the newspaper article gave Ms. Hyde's attacker all the details he needed to begin stalking and terrorizing her at her home and at her work. In order to prove negligence, Ms. Hyde had to present in logical order that the media defendant had a duty to perform and failed to perform it. That breach of duty became the proximate cause of the terrorizing that befell her. Simply stated, the reporter should have thought more carefully about what might happen once the would-be abductor read Ms. Hyde's name and address in the newspaper. She consequently endured weeks of anguish and terror because the newspaper failed to recognize its duty to protect the woman.[64] When the lower court ruled in the woman's favor, the defendants asked for another try in court, but the U.S. Supreme Court denied certiorari and let the ruling stand.

A federal appeals court also found that the publisher of a book giving detailed instructions on how to commit murder should have stopped to think about how this actually might be used by a contract killer to commit murder. Paladin Enterprises published *Hit Man, a Technical Guide for Independent Contractors,* which figured in the death of a quadriplegic boy, his mother, and a nurse assigned to care for the eight-year-old. James Perry was convicted in the triple murder as a hired assassin but it was the boy's father, Lawrence Horn, who had the financial incentive

---

[62]*See* 18 U.S.C. § 248, Freedom of Access to Clinic Entrances Act of 1994.

[63]The Fourth Circuit Court of Appeals considered Joyce Woodall's claim that the FACE law would restrain her and members of her group, Concerned Women of America, from praying in front of clinics in order to discourage women from getting abortions. The court rejected her anti-abortion arguments. *See Woodall v. Reno,* 47 F.3d 656 (4th Cir. 1995).

[64]*Hyde v. City of Columbia,* 637 S.W.2d 251, 253–55 (Mo. Ct. App.1982), *cert. denied,* 459 U.S. 1226 (1983).

of a $2 million trust fund that led to hiring the boy's killer. The book publisher sought First Amendment protection, but the court ruled the physical harms that would be inflicted by publishing a step-by-step guide on how to commit murder were foreseeable and placed the book dealer outside the realm of constitutional protection.[65]

Soldier of Fortune magazine also should have foreseen the physical harm that would occur if it published an advertisement for a contract killer, who used the words "GUN FOR HIRE" in his advertisement. Michael Savage took out two classified ads, and one of them was tied to the attempted murder of an Arkansas man, Norman Norwood, who was wounded by two contract gunmen. The magazine failed to have Norwood's suit dismissed on First Amendment grounds because reasonable jurors would find that the ad with words about the lethal weapon posed a substantial risk of harm.[66]

A second lawsuit filed against the magazine was also successful after four men were convicted of conspiracy to kill Richard Braun of Atlanta, Georgia. The prominent use of the term, "GUN FOR HIRE," again left the editorial staff of the magazine without a defense when it came to the question of whether or not it was foreseeable that the advertisement would place someone in danger of physical harm. The sons of Richard Braun won a $4.37 million judgment against *Soldier of Fortune* that was affirmed by the Eleventh Circuit Court of Appeals because the "publisher could recognize the offer of criminal activity as readily as its readers, obviously, did."[67]

Soldier of Fortune magazine eventually chose to refrain from accepting such advertisements, but it did successfully defend its publication from one lawsuit due to the oblique wording of the contract killer's advertisement. Sandra Black was killed in Bryan, Texas, by a mercenary hired by her husband, but John Hearn's advertisement did not promise, "GUN FOR HIRE," or anything that explicit. The Fifth Circuit Court of Appeals in New Orleans held that the wording of Hearns's ad was "facially innocuous" and was not reasonably discernible as a contract killer's offer leading to the murder of Ms. Black.[68]

The number of failed attempts to make media pay for the infliction of physical or emotional harms due to something published, recorded, televised, or filmed far outnumber the successful lawsuits for intentional or negligent infliction of physical or emotional distress. There are dozens of lawsuits against video game makers, rock 'n' roll legends, magazine articles, violent films, and television programs that have been dismissed after trying to affix blame on the media for some act of violence or death. Unless the plaintiff can show more than just inspiration and imitation was involved and that there was some causal instigation that produced the foreseeable harm, then the lawsuit blaming the explicit lyric, the violent video game, or gruesome murder scene will not likely be sustained.

---

[65]*Rice v. Paladin Enters.,* 940 F. Supp. 836, 839 (S.D. Md. 1996).

[66]*Norwood v. Soldier of Fortune Magazine, Inc.* 651 F. Supp. 1379 (W.D. Ark. 1987).

[67]*Braun v. Soldier of Fortune Magazine, Inc.* 968 F.2d 1110 (11th Cir. 1992), *cert. denied,* 506 U.S. 1071 (1993).

[68]*Eimann v. Soldier of Fortune Magazine, Inc.,* 880 F.2d 830, 832 (5th Cir. 1989), *cert denied,* 493 U.S. 1024 (1990).

DANGEROUS SPEECH

Whether people are speaking at school or church, their standing to express themselves does not protect words that are seen to pose a dangerous threat to others. The judicial precedent underscoring this point is "fighting words," a term coined early in World War II. The Court held, "There are certain well-defined and narrowly limited classes of speech, the prevention and punishment of which have never been thought to cause any constitutional problems. These include . . . the insulting or **'fighting words'**—which by their very utterance inflict injury or tend to incite an immediate breach of the peace."[69]

Chaplinsky v. New Hampshire (1942) stands as the early landmark for the legal doctrine of "fighting words," where it becomes necessary to discern when and where someone has gone too far with their expressions of anger or threats. Because such words lead to so little discovery of truth, the Supreme Court holds they are easily outweighed by the people's interest in peace and public order. Delineating what types of words and images inflict harm by their very nature, or when the provocation should be liable for harms committed, is a subject of considerable interest to the news media and public speakers.

Given that the speakers of inflammatory words can lead picket lines or protest marches, blast their message from loud speakers, or simply shout from street corners, the case law of fighting words is a legal puzzle worth piecing together. In 1942, a street-corner speaker railed against the constables of his day, and the case record says that Walter Chaplinsky called one city marshal a "racketeer" and a "goddamned fascist" at a time when such words might provoke volatile reactions. The U.S. Supreme Court upheld Chaplinsky's conviction for the use of threatening language against the police of Rochester, New Hampshire Justice Frank Murphy declared that "fighting words" fell outside the umbrella of the First Amendment because they either inflict injury or incite an immediate breach of the peace. Such utterances spoken in a personal, face-to-face encounter—a verbal assault—must be constrained if threatening, but what of the inflammatory rhetoric shouted out in a public place or auditorium?

A Catholic priest with a radio program from Alabama came to Chicago at the behest of a patriotic group of veterans who shared his outrage against certain political and religious factions. Father Arthur Terminiello's tirade against the Communists and Zionists drew rocks and bottles from a crowd gathered outside the auditorium where the Christian Veterans of America were meeting. The priest was arrested under a *Chaplinsky*-styled ordinance designed to preserve the peace in Chicago. He was fined a hundred dollars, but Terminiello appealed his conviction all the way to the Supreme Court. There might have been a breach of the peace, the Court held, but the duty of enforcing it did not wholly belong to the speaker, since the "function of free speech under our system of government is to invite dispute."[70] The Court struck down the Chicago ordinance as unconstitutional and Father Terminiello considered it a victory for the First Amendment.

A different set of facts defined the limits of sidewalk rhetoric when a college student provoked public wrath in response to his speech against racial oppression in Syracuse, New York. Feiner's words brought a police response to a street corner in 1949 where he was encouraging local African-Americans to attend a civil rights rally.

Fighting words ■
Speech which by its very utterance inflicts injury or tends to incite an immediate breach of the peace. *See Chaplinsky v. New Hampshire,* 315 U.S. 568, 572 (1942).

---

[69]*Chaplinsky v. New Hampshire*, 315 U.S. 568, 572 (1942).
[70]*Terminiello v. City of Chicago*, 337 U.S. 1, 4 (1949).

UP CLOSE

The Heckler's Veto

It is a strange turn of phrase—heckler's veto—but the U.S. Supreme Court uses it to show that First Amendment rights cannot be sacrificed in order to appease aggressive audiences. That is to say, the heckler's veto should *not* prevail and some risk of public unrest or verbal assault must be accepted as necessary to protect the rights of controversial speakers in public. More recently the phrase was used to refer to the Communication Decency Act provision that would allow a viewer of the Internet to veto indecent communications because someone younger than 18 was online at the time.

The Supreme Court's first use of the term was a footnote in *Brown v. Louisiana* extracted from a law professor's book on the First Amendment struggles of African-Americans.[a] The ruling in *Brown* held that blacks in Louisiana had a right to conduct a sit-in protest at a public library, where they were forbidden from using the books on the library's premises because of their skin's color. In a narrow win for civil rights protestors, the Court held the heckler's veto, which would favor the librarian who asked protestors to leave the library in order to prevent public unrest, would not be affirmed. "Participants in an orderly demonstration in a public place are not chargeable with the danger, unprovoked except by the fact of the constitutionally protected demonstration itself, that their critics might react with disorder or violence."[b]

The fear of hecklers in public convinced some local governments to charge speakers a fee for police protection, which had the effect of preventing them from making their opinions known and the U.S. Supreme Court has ruled that these speaker's fees would be unconstitutional.[c] It is not the controversial speaker but the angry hecklers who must be constrained by the government, Associate Justice William O. Douglas made clear in his *Terminiello* ruling: "freedom of speech, though not absolute, is nevertheless protected against censorship or punishment, unless shown likely to produce a clear and present danger of a serious substantive evil that rises far above public inconvenience, annoyance, or unrest."[d]

The reason Feiner's arrest was upheld in Syracuse was because police became convinced that imminent lawless action was at hand due to one heckler's threat of violence. Feiner called the police story nonsense because he said he saw no angry dissenters—only angry police who did not like his stubborn refusal to step down. The heckler's veto thus is a right *not* to be granted to angry listeners, but still the police have to decide exactly when and where imminent lawless action is about to occur in the midst of a public gathering.

[a] Harry Kalven Jr., *The Negro and the First Amendment* (Ohio State University Press 1965).
[b] *Brown v. Louisiana*, 383 U.S. 131, 133 n. 1 (1966).
[c] *Forsyth County, Ga. v. Nationalist Movement*, 505 U.S. 123, 125–26 (1992).
[d] *Terminiello v. City of Chicago*, 337 U.S. 1 (1949).

He challenged the "negroes of Syracuse" to secure their freedoms and "rise up in arms and fight for their rights." Three times, police asked him to step down from his soapbox, fearing for his safety after someone supposedly shouted, "If you don't get that son-of-a-bitch down, then I will." Feiner, a veteran attending college on the G.I. Bill, later claimed the threatening man was a fiction concocted by police in order to justify his arrest for inciting a breach of the peace under the New York statute. The Court, accepting the factual record established at his trial, upheld Feiner's conviction.[71]

[71]*Feiner v. New York*, 340 U.S. 315 (1951).

Revisiting the "Fighting Words" Doctrine

What happens when words are not spoken in anger, but written out on a jacket? Earlier we discussed Paul Robert Cohen's arrest in a Los Angeles courthouse for his statement of protest. Cohen had decorated his jacket with the words, "Fuck the Draft," a profane version of a familiar sentiment for certain draft-age men of that era. Because there were children in the public courthouse corridor where Cohen stood, the trial court found his jacket lettering outrageous and declared he maliciously and willfully disturbed the peace. There were no loud threats or noise on this occasion, just a pointed political statement that fell within view of a mother and her young son.

Cohen pursued his appeal of this conviction to the U.S. Supreme Court. He won by a one-vote margin and Justice Harlan wrote the opinion that cited two reasons for the Court's reversal of Cohen's conviction:

1. The law cannot ban particular words regardless of context.
2. Emotional expressions are worthy of First Amendment protection.

This ruling left up in the air the question of whether angry words directed against authorities would warrant protection. Anti-Vietnam War activists in Atlanta, Georgia, blocked the entrance to an army recruiting station in 1966. When police arrived to clear the door, they were threatened with epithets, "You white son-of-a-bitch, I will kill you!" Johnny C. Wilson looked at a second officer and threatened, "If you ever put your hands on me again, I'll cut you all to pieces."[72] Wilson was convicted under a Georgia law that forbade the use of "opprobrious words or abusive language" tending to cause a breach of the peace.

When Wilson's case made it to the Supreme Court, the decision in his favor acknowledged his threat seemed real enough, but the burden fell on the police to not overreact. In Justice William Brennan's opinion, the law's language was too vague and over-broad. The fighting words standard would not punish all curses and insults but only words that had "a direct tendency to cause acts of violence by the person to whom, individually, the remark is addressed."

The fighting words doctrine is troubling to many First Amendment scholars.[73] In effect, it results in punishment based on the *effectiveness* of one's communication. Someone hurling insults at another person is not necessarily engaging in fighting words until the verbal aggression becomes a threat. It may be best to think of fighting words as somewhat similar (if not analogous) to assault. Assault is not the act of striking someone (that is battery) but a "willful attempt or threat to inflict injury upon the person of another, when coupled with an apparent present ability to do so, and any intentional display of force such as it would give the victim reason to fear or expect immediate bodily harm."[74] It's the transformation of the words from expression to action (intimidation/ threat) that removes their First Amendment protection.

> **Bedrock Law:** The fighting words doctrine developed in *Chaplinsky* evolved to curb fighting words that would tend to incite an imminent threat of violence.

---

[72]*Gooding v. Wilson*, 405 U.S. 518 (1972).
[73]*See*, e.g., Burton Caine, *The Trouble with Fighting Words*: Chaplinsky v. New Hampshire *Is a Threat to the First Amendment and Should be Overturned*, 88 Marq. L. Rev. 441 (2004).
[74]*Black's Law Dictionary* 114 6th ed. (1990).

Modern Hate Crime Controls

Hate speech is a global concern, and it has been the subject of laws against insults or jokes based on race, gender, ethnic status, religion, or sexual orientation. Countries such as Canada and France have criminalized speech leading to discrimination, hatred, or violence based on race and religion. The United States has a different tradition in this area, but two scholars have led the battle for stronger ordinances against hate speech. Richard Delgado argued for a civil solution, claiming that victims of racist words are entitled to sue for the psychological, sociological, and political harms of hateful insults. He contends that such language injures one's dignity and self-respect, and communicates a toxic message that deserves damages for recovery.[75]

Another scholar, Mari J. Matsuda, saw the government's failure to punish racial epithets as part of the problem because she felt that this tolerance in the United States was tantamount to supporting it. Matsuda cited a United Nations resolution calling for the countries of the world to declare illegal ideas based on "racial superiority or hatred, [and] incitement to racial discrimination."[76]

There is common ground in this area of hate speech with American defamation law as it pertains to groups. In 1952, the state of Illinois employed its version of group libel against the president of the so-called White Circle League, Paul Beauharnais. He conducted a leaflet attack against African-Americans moving to Chicago at a time when such migrations were common. Beauharnais's leaflets warned of the "southern negro's" propensity for "rapes, robberies, knives, guns, and marijuana." He was prosecuted and convicted under an Illinois law making it unlawful to exhibit a publication which attributes "depravity, criminality, unchastity, or lack of virtue" to a particular class of citizens based on their race, color, creed, or religion.[77] His conviction was upheld by the U.S. Supreme Court, but by only one vote. Justice Hugo Black led the four dissenters, who called the concept of group libel antithetical to American freedom and said this affirmation of the Illinois statute might further curb freedom of expression. It is for this reason that the *Beauharnais* decision is viewed as an oddity rather than a landmark precedent.

Twenty-five years later in the Skokie suburb of Chicago, it was not the White Circle League but the neo-Nazis who were the subject of First Amendment law. They held marches and staged rallies in largely Jewish neighborhoods, where lawsuits were filed to stop them based on the "fighting words" doctrine of *Chaplinsky*. That action failed because the Seventh Circuit Court of Appeals ruled "peaceful demonstrations cannot be totally precluded solely because the display of the swastika may provoke a violent reaction by those who view it. . . . A speaker who gives prior notice of his message has not compelled a confrontation with those who voluntarily listen." This became known as the heckler's veto.[78]

---

[75]Richard Delgado, *Words that Wound: A Tort Action for Racial Insults, Epithets, and Name-Calling,* 17 Harv. C.R.-C.L. L. Rev. 133 (1982).

[76]Mari J. Matsuda, *Public Responses to Racist Speech: Considering the Victim's Story,* 87 Mich. L. Rev2320 (1988–1989).

[77]*Beauharnais v. Illinois,* 343 U.S. 250 (1952).

[78]*Collin v. Smith,* 447 F. Supp. 676 (N.D. Ill.1978), *aff'd,* 578 F.2d 1197 (1978), *cert. denied,* 439 U.S. 916 (1978).

Flames of Racism

By 1992, hate crime legislation had been adopted in all but four states of the nation. Most of these laws followed a model established by the Anti-Defamation League of B'nai B'rith calling for both criminal sanctions and civil penalties. One case made its way to the U.S. Supreme Court to test the validity of such ordinances. In this area, *R.A.V. v. St. Paul* (1992) is the landmark case, distinguished by the juvenile defendant's initials concealing his identity. "R.A.V." actually stands for Robert A. Viktora, who at the time was a teenager convicted of burning a cross inside the fenced yard of Russ and Laura Jones, an African-American couple living in St. Paul, Minnesota.[79] The incident violated a city bias ordinance that prohibited "any symbol, object or graffiti including burning a cross or placing a Nazi swastika, which one knows arouses anger, alarm or resentment in others on the basis of race, color, creed, religion or gender."[80]

The Minnesota Supreme Court upheld one bias-motivated crime rule, applying the doctrine created in *Chaplinsky*. When the case reached the U.S. Supreme Court, the majority opinion was unanimous in overturning an ordinance against hate speech, but justices debated the proper rationale for doing so. The majority claimed any law is unconstitutional if it singles out "bias-motivated" expressions for punishment. The decision ruled against the city ordinance because it prohibited only fighting words based on "race, color, creed, religion, or gender," while permitting hate speech motivated by other factors such as political party, union membership, or homosexuality. "The First Amendment," Justice Antonin Scalia wrote, "does not permit St. Paul to impose special prohibitions on those speakers who express views on disfavored subjects." The resounding metaphor in his opinion alluded to the freedom to speak inflammatory words even if only as symbolic expression. "Burning a cross in someone's yard is reprehensible," he said. "But St. Paul has sufficient means at its disposal to control such behavior without adding the First Amendment to the fire."[81]

The St. Paul decision echoed an earlier judgment in *Brandenburg v. Ohio* from 1969. A Klansman in that case was tried under the state's criminal syndicalism act, which held it to be an offense to advocate violence for political reform. The indicting phrase against Brandenburg was filled with hateful prejudice: "might have to be some revengeance taken, if our President, our Congress, our Supreme Court continues to suppress the white, Caucasian race."[82] In *R.A.V. v. St. Paul,* the Court found that hate speech cannot be banned, but when an act of violence is motivated by prejudice based on race, religion, gender, or other personal traits, the First Amendment obviously does not protect the violent act. However, Brandenburg did not have present the means to make good on his words of implied violence.

---

[79]Viktora actually changed the spelling of his name to include a "K" for the Ku Klux Klan (KKK), and was represented by the normally liberal ACLU. He was subsequently prosecuted for criminal trespass and was convicted.

[80]*R.A.V. v. St. Paul,* 505 U.S. 377 (1992).

[81]*Id.,* at 396.

[82]*Brandenburg v. Ohio,* 395 U.S. 444 (1969).

Neither did an eighteen-year-old protester during the Vietnam era, who rallied against the draft at the Washington Monument as the Vietnam War escalated in 1966. He swore in public that if he was ever inducted into the Army, and a gun was placed in his hands, "the first man I want to get in my sights is L.B.J." (President Johnson). Even though the law forbids any threat against the life of the president, the Court held that the protester was using a form of "crude political hyperbole," which did not constitute a knowing and willful threat on the president's life. This legal standard defines a "true threat" as a message that must be uttered with the expressed aim of striking fear in the persons named and with the means for making good the threat.[83]

In some cases, the state may choose to further penalize a threat if it culminates in a violent assault motivated by prejudice and hatred. In 1993, the vicious beating of a 14-year-old white youth resulted in a unanimous Supreme Court decision against his assailants. The attack by several black youths, who had just seen the movie *Mississippi Burning,* called into question penalty enhancements for hate crimes. When 19-year-old Todd Mitchell asked his friends, "Do you feel all hyped up to move on some white people?" he was looking at a 14-year-old youth across the street. "There goes a white boy. Go get him." The victim spent days in a coma but survived the attack. Mitchell was convicted of aggravated battery, but his sentence was increased under a state hate crime law. Writing the decision upholding the enhanced penalty for the Supreme Court, Chief Justice William Rehnquist concluded, "A physical assault is not by any stretch of the imagination expressive conduct protected by the First Amendment."[84]

The Court returned to the question of cross burning in 2003 to determine if it was an expression of free speech or an act of intimidation beyond First Amendment protection. The state of Virginia's ban reached the U.S. Supreme Court with two cases involving cross burning. The first incident occurred in May 1998 when two Virginia Beach teenagers tried to ignite a cross in the front yard of James Jubilee, an African-American neighbor living with a Caucasian wife.[85] That case was joined with a second one where a Pennsylvania Klansman drove to Carrol County, Virginia, in 1998 to celebrate his white supremacist views with a "cross lighting." Barry Elton Black led the Klan rally on private property with the consent of its owner. The Klansmen marched around the burning cross while a neighbor and motorists traveling a nearby highway observed the spectacle.

The state law in Virginia held that it was a felony for "any person . . . with the intent of intimidating any person or group of persons to burn, or cause to be burned, a cross on the property of another, a highway or other public place." The Virginia law further held "any such burning of a cross shall be prima facie evidence of an intent to intimidate a person or group of persons." The Virginia Supreme Court

---

[83] *Watts v. United States,* 394 U.S. 705 (1969).

[84] *Wisconsin v. Mitchell,* 508 U.S. 476 (1993). The Court subsequently held that if there is a sentence enhancement for hate crimes, that extra sentence must be imposed by the jury and not by the judge.

[85] *Virginia v. Black,* 538 U.S. 343 (2003). In the Virginia Beach incident, one of the defendants, Elliot, said he wanted to get back at Jubilee for complaining about his backyard shooting practice. The crude cross he planted on Jubilee's front lawn failed to burn, despite repeated efforts at incineration.

ruled that it was unconstitutional on its face because it discriminated on the basis of viewpoint and cited as its precedent *R.A.V. v. St. Paul, supra,* however; the Commonwealth's attorney appealed to the U.S. Supreme Court, which granted review.

The Court upheld the constitutionality of the portion of the Virginia statute banning the burning of a cross with intent to intimidate because it represented a true threat, wrote Justice O'Connor. She concluded for the majority that the First Amendment permitted Virginia to outlaw cross incineration only if it was conducted with this intent, since it is a particularly virulent form of intimidation. In a nutshell, the Court held some cross burnings are protected by the First Amendment; however, Justice Thomas dissented, believing cross burnings to be threatening conduct, and not speech, making it unworthy of this First Amendment defense.

In some states, such as Maryland, New Jersey, and South Carolina, laws prohibiting cross burnings have been struck down. In the *People of the State of California v. Metzger,* it was successfully argued that the court must decide what is the true intent and the likely and apparent effect of the cross burning. If done as a political statement it will be protected; but if it actually is meant to intimidate, then the First Amendment gives way to the right of the people to be free from fear and oppression.

SUMMARY

- It is not only the use and location of a public space that determines the level of expression allowed, but also who is using it and who is sponsoring the forum that can control the legal issue at hand. Public parks, streets, and sidewalks are typically regarded as traditional public forums, and the level of access and free expression are usually greater at such places. Rights of personal expression at those forums are not to be abridged even when a powerful official considers them to be objectionable, unless they are obscene or the expressions are a prelude to imminent lawless action. However, just because property is publicly owned does not mean it is necessarily an open public forum and, even though privately owned spaces are *not likely* to be considered public forums, there are instances when they actually should be. Shopping mall areas, for example, are defined as a public forum in certain states.

- The privilege of a citizen of the United States to use the streets and parks for the communication of views on national questions may be regulated in the interest of all; this privilege is not absolute, but relative, and must be exercised in subordination to the general comfort and convenience, and in consonance with peace and good order; but it must not, in the guise of regulation, be abridged or denied. The legal theory of time, place, and manner does allow local governments to enforce rules that control expression in public places, so long as particular viewpoints are not banned and others accepted in those areas.

- The difficulty in striking a balance between the need to support the authority of teachers and school officials, while still affording students limited rights of free expression consistent with fundamental constitutional rights requires a test. In balancing the conflicting interests, the court notes if the school district is enforcing rules to prevent student behavior that is substantially disruptive, it is operating within the law. This is known as the *Tinker* rule; however, the law also recognizes a difference between student-generated speech and school-sponsored speech, affording greater latitude to official censorship of school newspapers, which is known as the *Hazelwood* test.

- Public employees find their rights to expression curbed depending upon where they work and for whom; and, just how far public employees can go with their language is related to when they speak, where they speak, and what they decide to say. The Court held that a government employee who speaks out as a part of his job does not have full First Amendment protection. The reasoning was that his employer (the government) may have just cause to discipline the employee for what was said. The free expression of government employees is limited when they act in their official capacities.

- In order for any rule that threatens free speech to stand, it must survive either a strict scrutiny test where the burden is on the government to identify the compelling public interest that prompts the state to pass a law affecting the freedom of its citizens, or an intermediate scrutiny test, where an important level of public interest must be identified. The procedural tests defined by levels of scrutiny suggest how far First Amendment freedoms will be defended. In order to determine if the government's rules are constitutionally permissible, the court applies a test of intermediate scrutiny, which means that an important public interest is served by the rules—although not necessarily a compelling one—the rules are narrowly tailored to serve that interest, and alternative channels of communication are available to speakers.

- The Supreme Court at first declared that "fighting words" fell outside the umbrella of the First Amendment because they either inflict injury or incite an immediate breach of the peace and were among the "well-defined and narrowly limited classes of speech" which the law can prevent. However, the fighting words doctrine began to raise constitutional problems. In subsequent cases involving profane epithets against the draft and untenable Ku Klux Klan threats against the government, the Court made clear that offensive language would be protected unless it represented a true threat, wherein there was any intentional display of force, which would give the victim reason to fear or expect immediate bodily harm. It's the transformation of the words from expression to action (intimidation/threat) that removes their First Amendment protection.

- Hate speech cannot be banned, but when an act of violence is motivated by prejudice based on race, religion, gender, or other personal traits, the First Amendment does not protect the violent act. Greater latitude is given to political expressions, but if the aggressive words or acts are meant to intimidate, then the First Amendment gives way to the right of the people to be free from fear and oppression. The Constitution allows people to say hurtful things, but words that provoke anger do not always inform; and when they "set fire to reason" and begin to provoke acts of violence, then state governments, cities, and even campuses have the right to regulate that type of language.

Student Websites—How Far Can They Go?

It would seem that what a high school student chooses to do with his or her personal computer at home is a personal concern and not any business of teachers or principals. That is true, unless the student decides to start making comments that might go beyond offensive or rude statements about school friends, rivals, or instructors. In King County, Washington, the Kent School District imposed a policy that was designed to protect students from harassment but was found offensive to the First Amendment. Officials tried to prohibit "inappropriate, harassing, offensive, or abusive" behavior online.

One student, Nick Emmitt, constructed a website titled the "Unofficial Kent Lake High Home Page," where he invited his fellow students to vote for the one student or teacher they would most like to see die. After Emmitt was suspended for this form of cyber-aggression, he sued and the court ruled in his favor because his personal computer was "entirely outside the school's supervision or control."[a] In a similar fashion, a federal court in Pittsburgh struck down a policy that targeted "inappropriate, harassing, offensive, or abusive behavior" among students after a volleyball player posted four messages on an Internet bulletin board that were critical of certain teachers at the school and he was punished by being taken off the team. He was reinstated on the volleyball team because a material disruption interfering with the school day due to his Internet expressions could not be substantiated. The question became a bit trickier in Missouri, when a classmate of one website user showed the teacher during the school day the nasty comments made about the instructor online. Recognizing the *Tinker* rule regarding material disruption applied, the court held that these critical comments were more unpleasant and offensive than they were materially disruptive, and the student prevailed in that case.[b]

The National School Boards Association says that student websites can, at their mildest, simply reflect immaturity with "offensive, obnoxious and insulting comments;" but at their worst, they might pose outright or veiled threats to person or property. It is this latter category that the Supreme Court of Pennsylvania was dealing with in a case where a student's off-campus website featured a teacher's decapitated head dripping with blood with an invitation for visitors to donate $20 to hire a hit man, apparently to fulfill this image's not-so-veiled threat. The court held that, even though the student created his website off campus, it was aimed at school personnel and was even accessed online at school by the perpetrator. As a result, the student's punishment for this form of aggression was upheld by the state supreme court after the *Tinker* test was applied, but how it will figure in future cases in other states depends as much on their statutes as it does on the case law. ■

[a] *Emmett v. Kent Sch. Dist.*, 92 F. Supp. 2d 1088 (W.D. Wash. 2000).
[b] *Beussink v. Woodland Sch. Dist.*, 30 F. Supp. 2d 1175 (E.D. Mo. 1998).

Sedition and Censorship

LEARNING OBJECTIVES

After reading this chapter you should know:

- If government censorship is prohibited in the United States

- Why the Supreme Court had to act to bring the First Amendment to the States

- What principles of freedom of expression guide lawmakers and judges

- The differences between a bad tendency and a clear and present danger

- What type of legal tools have been used to control the media in the United States

- How historical restraints have been used to silence political dissenters

- What forms of prior restraint the government uses to control speech

- Whether or not ordinary citizens give up their First Amendment rights at work

CRACKDOWN ON DISSENT

When we hear terms like **sedition** or **treason,** it can conjure up visions of British redcoats or powdered wig magistrates, but these are contemporary crimes,[1] and enforcement against them after the terrorist attacks on September 11, 2001, addressed issues of national security, censorship, and the limits of free expression. A clinical nurse working for the Veterans Administration in New Mexico encountered a modern definition in 2006. Ms. Laura Berg of Albuquerque found her office computer seized by federal agents and learned from a Human Resource manager the confiscation from her office was because "the Agency is bound by law to investigate and pursue any act which potentially represents *sedition.*"

The nurse had drafted a letter criticizing President George W. Bush's response to Hurricane Katrina and the invasion of Iraq and mailed it to a weekly newspaper. "As a VA nurse working with returning vets," she wrote, "I know the public has no sense of the additional devastating human and financial costs of post-traumatic stress disorder." Berg urged readers to "act forcefully to remove a government administration playing games of smoke and mirrors and vicious deceit."[2]

Was this letter a case of sedition? Two months later the government advised Ms. Berg that her story checked out—she actually had not been using her office computer to express her disapproval of actions by the federal government. No one seemed quite sure why she was even suspected of sedition, and her lawyer's request for an official apology went ignored. The *Albuquerque Tribune* asked Berg about her views but she declined comment. The *Tribune*'s managing editor concluded the government "shut her up for speaking her mind. When you add up threats to the republic and our constitutional liberties, who's sliding faster toward sedition?"[3] The question of censorship and sedition is a longstanding one in United States' history and the national commitment to the First Amendment is tested at times when public officials find political speech to be seditious.

Censorship is usually defined as an act of government to prevent expressions of speech or publications which may be considered objectionable or harmful to some group of people, but the reasoning behind censorship shifts depending on who has the power to exercise control over communications.

Sedition ■ The common law crime of advocating and intending to bring about harm to the government.

Treason ■ Generally, the crime of betraying your sovereign nation. In United States law, treason is levying war against the United States or giving aid and comfort to its enemies.

Censorship ■ An act of government to prevent expressions of speech or publications.

SEEDS OF SEDITION

During the three centuries of British rule that led to the signing of the Declaration of Independence, the Crown held trials for seditious libelers, to punish those who wrote or spoke ill of either church or state. The royal throne exercised control by licensing printers and demanding their bonds be forfeited if ever their prints generated unrest. That tradition for punishing truth tellers crossed the ocean despite the fact the American colonists grew bolder in promoting their subversive views in print.

---

[1]*See* 18 U.S.C. §§ 2381–2390, "Treason, Sedition, and Subversive Activities."

[2]*ACLU of New Mexico Defends VA Employee Accused of "Sedition" over Criticism of Bush Administration,* Jan. 31, 2006, http://www.aclu.org/freespeech/gen2403prs2060121.html.

[3]Kate Nelson, *Mere Mention of Violent Talk Brings Silence,* Albuquerque Tribune, Feb. 11, 2006. http://www.abqtrib.com/albq/nw_columnists/article/0,2564,ALBQ_19856_4459578,00.html.

Power and the press went hand in hand for those who ruled with a scepter and saw the need for this type of censorship whenever their authority was threatened. King Henry VIII insisted on licensing printers to keep his critics from circulating pamphlets in the early sixteenth century. Acting as both head of church and state, he consolidated his powers by proclaiming how he would censor all "errors and seditious opinions," forbidding heretics from encouraging puritanical revolt.

King Henry seized power over all printed materials he deemed mistaken—either political or ecclesiastical.[4] The press could still sway the people, but it was at his behest. Gold was the incentive for printers who accepted royal contracts. The company of printers known as the *Stationers* was organized to serve those interests, and they handed over unlicensed renegades to the Court of High Commission for criminal prosecution and trial in the Court of the Star Chamber. At this point truth was no defense for defaming a public official, since such reports were by nature inflammatory, causing "not only the breach of the peace, but also the scandal of government. . . ."[5] A conviction for this crime carried severe consequences. For merely publishing a book favoring the right to rebel against a despotic ruler, printer William Twin in 1663 was sentenced to a cruel death, to be "emasculated, disemboweled, quartered, and beheaded. . . ."[6]

English printers were not always submissive to this form of control by licensing. When the blind poet John Milton's treatise on divorce failed to please the throne, he responded with an argument for a "marketplace of ideas" approach to free expression (*see* chapter 2). Milton felt it was important to allow for a struggle in "a free and open encounter" between truth and falsity because truth would ultimately prevail, and thus licensing should end. Milton's position was not the only wisdom of the day; however, pamphleteer Richard Baxter felt quite the contrary. Giving all men the right "to speak both in presse and pulpit" as they please would cause trouble because "if ten mens voices be louder than one, would the noyse of errour drown the voice of truth."[7]

The licensing law of Britain was curtailed in 1695 and, over the next 25 years, government censorship grew less severe until treason was reconceived of as a crime of more than just words—it was one that required action. In its place came the lesser crime of **seditious libel**, rebellious speech to be punished by whippings, fines, or imprisonment.[8]

Seditious libel ■
The common law crime of punishing speech harmful to the government.

Bedrock Law: The theory behind freedom of the press is that truth ultimately prevails in a free marketplace of ideas.

---

[4]Frederick S. Siebert, *Freedom of the Press in England, 1476–1776* (Univ. of Ill. Press 1952).

[5]2 Sir James Fitzjames Stephen, *A History of the Criminal Law of England* 304–05 (London, 1883), quoted by Leonard W. Levy, *Emergence of a Free Press* 7 (Oxford Univ. Press 1985).

[6]*See* Levy's abstraction of *Rex v. Twyn* as recorded by 6 Thomas Bayly Howell, *State Trials* 513, 536, 1663, in *Emergence of a Free Press, supra* note 5 9.

[7]Richard Baxter, *Aphorisms of Justification* (1649), "To the Reader," as quoted in William Haller, *Liberty and Reformation in the Puritan Revolution* 171–72 (Columbia Univ. Press 1955).

[8]Today, we think of the term "libel" as someone harming a person in reputation only, but the broader term of libels (little books) once specified several crimes, including obscenity, blasphemy against religion, criticism of the government, or slandering private persons.

The American Experience

The idea of voting for lawmakers to serve the will of the people was something early Americans, subjects of the Crown, could not envision at first, and the prospect of a system of checks and balances in government was unimaginable. So, the idea of freedom of expression was not taken to mean a lack of government controls, only that censorship or **prior restraint** had to be handled through a colonial system of British licensing. Benjamin Franklin's older brother James exploited that system until he was arrested for his humor lampooning the actions of the state legislature of Massachusetts in his unlicensed *New England Courant*.[9]

What raised the colonial government's ire was his tongue-in-cheek dig at Massachusetts' lack of competency in arresting coastal pirates, who might be rounded up "sometime this month, wind and weather permitting."[10] This bit of sarcastic wit cost Franklin his freedom. Placed under confinement in his quarters and forbidden from printing any pamphlet or paper lest he disturb the public peace after his release, Franklin simply named his younger brother Benjamin as the publisher of the *Courant*. The royal officers were not amused by that move and James again was brought up on charges, but the grand jury signed a **"bill ignoramus"**[11] and set him free in 1723.

For both English and colonial Americans, the innovative idea that liberty of the press actually meant punishing harmful expressions *after the fact* became clearer in 1769, when Sir William Blackstone's common-law commentary on Crown libels held that "*liberty of the press* is indeed essential to the nature of a free state; but this consists in laying no *previous* restraints upon publications, and not in freedom from censure for criminal matter when published."[12] Blackstone's broad stroke painted the terms of what could be punished after the fact, "but if he publishes what is improper, mischievous, or illegal, he must take the consequences of his own temerity."[13]

The danger in uttering or publishing words of sedition meant that suspects would be prosecuted because of their danger to peace and public order. The famous trial of a German immigrant who printed criticisms of the colonial governor of New York was a seminal event to test this line of reasoning. John Peter Zenger's contributors blistered William Cosby for a variety of misdeeds in Zenger's *New York Weekly Journal*. The printer was tried for seditious libel, but the jury

Prior restraint ■
A form of censorship in which the government, in advance of publication, orders a publisher not to publish certain material.

Bill ignoramus ■
When a grand jury does not find enough evidence to charge a crime, it returns a no bill, or bill ignoramus, instead of a true bill. *See also* grand jury, true bill.

---

[9]Legal historian Leonard Levy noted that "the most suppressive body by far, surpassing even the prerogative court of the (royal) governor-and-Council, was that acclaimed bastion of the people's liberties: the popularly elected Assembly." Leonard W. Levy, *Legacy of Suppression: Freedom of Speech and Press in Early American History* 20 (Harvard Univ. Press 1960).

[10]*Id.* at 36–37.

[11]A bill ignoramus was an indication that the jury refused to find him guilty. Technically the jury was unable to find him not guilty because he had, in fact, published the statements and they were not being asked to judge whether the statements were libelous. It was a legal trick to keep from having to find him guilty.

[12]4 Sir William Blackstone, *Commentaries on the Laws of England* 151–52 (London 1765–1769), as cited by Levy in *Legacy of Suppression, supra* note 9 at 14.

[13]*Id.* at 14.

A Great Noise in the World

When the German-born printer John Peter Zenger was arrested in 1734, he had spent less than 25 years on American soil, but had willingly challenged ruling Tories, and his trial produced "a great noise in the world" because his paper had scandalized a public official. Governor William Cosby was Zenger's principal target after Cosby began seizing lands from American colonists and gifting the property to friends and supporters. In addition to these royal acts, Cosby appointed loyal followers to lifetime commissions at salaries so high the New York General Assembly had them overturned. When the governor read in Zenger's *New York Weekly Journal* about his rigged elections, his failure to deal properly with Indian tribes, his "petty fogging knaves" and "scoundrel rascals," and basically how he had failed to govern properly, he was moved to act.

For eight months, Zenger was held behind bars while his wife, Anna, cranked out editions of the newspaper. A Philadelphia attorney, Andrew Hamilton, argued the case on Zenger's behalf and persuaded the jurors to consider it no crime when a journalist is "exposing and opposing arbitrary power in this part of the world at least by speaking and writing the truth."[a] As with Franklin, the jury simply refused to find him guilty and even though Zenger's acquittal received widespread publicity and moved public sentiment against government censorship, it did not bring the curtain down on seditious libel. However, the acquittal caused colonial America to consider carefully Hamilton's main point about defending truthful reporting.

---

[a] James Alexander, *A Brief Narrative of the Case and Trial of John Peter Zenger* (reprint ed. Harvard Univ. Press 1972) (1736).

freed Zenger while his case made news all across Britain: in the colonies, truth was accepted as a defense against sedition.

Alien and Sedition Acts

The nation's second president, John Adams, addressed the question of sedition with repressive legislation that Congress enacted after the War for Independence. President Adams was a Federalist, and he feared the Democratic-Republicans supporting his rival Thomas Jefferson would favor France's revolution and its reign of Jacobin terror against public leaders, including his own party. The Alien and Sedition Acts of 1798 were actually three laws expanding the period of residence prior to naturalization and these acts gave the president extraordinary powers to detain and deport noncitizen residents of the United States. Significantly, the Sedition Act forbade false, scandalous, and malicious publications against Adams, the Congress, and the national government.

Prosecutors of the president's party brought 14 prosecutions under this law, including counts against editors of eight Democratic-Republican newspapers. Matthew Lyon, a popular editor and member of Congress, was jailed, and that act moved public sentiment against this law and Adams administration. The sedition law led to Adams's defeat in 1800 and it expired the following year. President Jefferson pardoned all persons convicted under it, and Congress eventually repaid most of the fines. Yet a different form of repression emerged when the nation's "peculiar institution" of slavery fell into disfavor.

SEDITION DURING TIMES OF WAR

Governments in a democracy rely on the consent of the governed, which calls for open debate on policies that shape the national destiny and character. During times of war, when citizens are called upon to risk and sacrifice their lives to achieve the government's goals, the debate can become defiant to the point of insurrection. Should free expression be curtailed during such times of violent conflict or should the government tolerate virulent strains of dissent? This question is of particular interest during major conflicts in American history.

In the period leading up to the Civil War, particularly in the South, laws were drafted directed against the opponents of slavery—especially the abolitionist press. The Confederacy attempted to keep slavery alive by muffling those who opposed it. In 1836, Congress adopted restraining rules to stop antislavery proposals from reaching the floor, but repealed them eight years later in order to allow for debate on the divisive issue. Union officers stopped the presses for three days at the *Chicago Times* for disloyal expressions, while southern legislatures drafted laws to silence the opponents of slavery. These acts lasted until the Civil War ended and were then struck down. The most important consequence for free expression was the adoption of the Fourteenth Amendment of the U.S. Constitution that essentially federalized the First Amendment for the nation. It played a special part in the twentieth century and in the "war to end all wars."

THE ESPIONAGE AND SEDITION CASES

After the United States entered World War I, the Espionage Act of 1917 was approved by Congress and signed by President Woodrow Wilson. It dealt primarily with espionage, but parts of the bill were aimed at dissent to the war. Congress drafted this law to stop spies from undermining the nation's aims through sabotage or by uncovering military secrets. Eventually zealous politicians expanded it to condemn dissent. "When the United States is at war," the law read, whoever shall willfully obstruct or attempt to stop the recruiting or enlistment service of the United States with "language intended to incite, provoke, or encourage resistance to the United States" should be punished by a fine of up to $10,000 and a prison stay of up to 20 years.[14]

In 1918, the Sedition Act, an amendment to the Espionage Act, also made it a crime through oral or written means for one to attempt to cause contempt and scorn for the U.S. government. Federal prosecutors brought about two thousand people to

---

[14]40 *Statutes at Large* 553–54 (1918).

trial and secured around 900 convictions, but implementation of the Act did not stop there. In its zeal to protect the U.S. war effort, the Post Office censored thousands of newspapers, books, and pamphlets under that same act. Entire issues of magazines went undelivered if pages appeared to cross the line into seditious territory.

The *Schenck* Case

The first twentieth-century landmark decision from the U.S. Supreme Court concerning sedition during World War I was the ruling against Charles T. Schenck for what he had done as general secretary of the American Socialist party in Philadelphia. He printed 15,000 leaflets that decried U.S. involvement in World War I and handed them out to young men of draft age questioning their participation in what his party considered to be a cold-blooded and ruthless venture designed to fatten Wall Street purses. Schenck's propaganda urged young men of draft age to "Assert your rights—Do not submit to intimidation." This outspoken socialist and one of his fellow party officers were arrested, tried, and convicted of obstructing the war effort. The U.S. Supreme Court took the *Schenck* case on appeal and handed down the ruling in 1919.

Writing the unanimous decision, Justice Oliver Wendell Holmes coined a phrase that would echo in First Amendment case law for years to come. The question was would "the words create a clear and present danger that they will bring about substantive evils Congress has a right to prevent?"[15] Clearly, that test was not the one applied to Schenck's case; instead the Court held his printed dissent up to a magnifying glass of reasonableness—or bad tendency—the standard that only required prosecutors to show how Schenck's words were *intended* to put readers in a mind of revolt toward the war. Whether or not someone even protested after reading a leaflet was of less concern. After this ruling, Justice Holmes' clear and present danger test became well known, but not well tried, as federal agents continued to lock up dissidents. "When a nation is at war many things that might be said in time of peace are such a hindrance to its effort that their utterance will not be endured," and that was the law of the land.[16]

Holmes
clearl present
danger p̄
Schenck Case

Abrams v. United States

The United States embarked on a serious phase of suppression during and immediately after World War I. The intolerance of public dissent while American soldiers were being killed overseas brought a group of Jewish immigrants from Russia to trial in New York City. President Wilson had dispatched the military to fight on the Russian front, which concerned Jacob Abrams and his friends, who secretly printed out flyers they hoped would keep American-made bullets from striking fellow Russians. It was unlikely such leaflets printed in English and Yiddish had any significant impact on the U.S. war effort or its armament factories.

---

[15]*Schenck v. United States*, 249 U.S. 47, 51 (1919).
[16]*Id.* at 52.

► **UP CLOSE**

The American Civil Liberties Union

It is difficult to imagine how much violence Americans have encountered due to national fevers of war and labor unrest, but in the Roaring Twenties dissent literally exploded. A box blew up in 1920 on the doorstep of the U.S. Attorney General A. Mitchell Palmer, the man behind the nation's crusade to bring "Bolsheviks" to justice in the United States. At Palmer's behest, federal agents rounded up more than 5,000 people, in thirty-three American cities, suspected of siding with the wrong side of the Russian uprisings during World War I. He vigorously applied espionage and sedition laws to deport hundreds of residents without trial.

These deportees included famed anarchist Emma Goldman, who was shipped back to the Soviet Union along with hundreds of others. Not one of the nonconforming immigrants, who were deprived of their freedom after two months of aggressive law enforcement, was charged with the fateful bombing at Palmer's Washington townhouse; however the ruthless

means for dealing with suspect newcomers did create a special interest group. A small band of eastern intellectuals, headed by Roger Baldwin, channeled their rage with the Justice Department's tactics by forming a watchdog group in 1920 that became the American Civil Liberties Union.

Among the co-founders of the ACLU was Elizabeth Gurley Flynn, a New England activist, who made speeches as a teenager on behalf of the Industrial Workers of the World (IWW, "Wobblies"). She rose as an early feminist in the United States and was appointed to serve on the ACLU Board. However, her tenure came to an abrupt end after it became known that she was a member of the Communist Party. The ACLU refused to seat supporters of any form of totalitarian government. Flynn would later go to jail for her political leanings; but after her death, the ACLU voted to restore her membership based on her important contributions to women's rights.

The flyer's headline read, "The hypocrisy of the United States and allies." Jacob Abrams and his girlfriend, Molly Steiner,—along with three others—were found guilty of violating the Espionage Act of 1917. They fought their convictions before the U.S. Supreme Court, but the legal rule guiding the Court was again the "bad tendency" test, which convicted protestors who opposed the war effort regardless of the real threat posed. In *Abrams v. United States*, the rumblings of a movement toward a more liberal, speech-protective test could be heard.

Justices Holmes and Brandeis broke from the majority with a dissenting opinion stating the "silly leaflet" of "poor and puny anonymities" posed no real threat to American efforts, and thus failed to present a "clear and present danger" that the government should be justified in trying to suppress. Summoning Milton's proverb, "the best test of truth is competition of the market," Holmes urged his brethren to more seriously commit to freedom of speech and regretted he could not "put into more impressive words my belief that the defendants have been deprived rights under the Constitution of the United States."[17]

---

[17]*Abrams v. United States*, 250 U.S. 616 (1919).

Criminal syndicalism ■ Violent insurrection and anti-government protests.

Bad tendency test ■ A standard which allows government to criminalize speech if it has a bad tendency to contribute to collapse of the government. *See Patterson v. Colorado; Gitlow v. New York.* Contrast with Clear and present danger test, which allows less restriction of speech.

BAD TENDENCY OR CLEAR AND PRESENT DANGER?

"Socialism Is the Answer," was the title of the speech Eugene Debs gave in Canton, Ohio, but the sticking point of his message shot out in one sentence against soldiering under the U.S. flag. "I might not be able to say all that I think, but you need to know that you are fit for something better than slavery and cannon fodder."[18] Even though Debs's speech was only mildly provocative in terms of its antiwar message, the Court applied its bad **tendency test** to seal his conviction and ten-year sentence in a Georgia federal prison. What that meant was his speech did not necessarily represent a clear and present danger to others, but it might produce a bad result. Undaunted, the 65-year-old Debs ran for president while serving time in a Georgia prison for seditious speech. One federal judge, Charles Amidon, felt the reactionary mood of jurors who were hearing such cases during World War I: "[Jurors] looked back into my eyes with the savagery of wild animals, saying by their manner, 'Away with the twiddling, let us get at them.'"[19] State legislatures followed the 1918 Sedition Act with laws against **criminal syndicalism**, another name for violent insurrection and anti-government protests. These laws were aimed at European immigrants to whom the fashionable doctrines of Karl Marx were attractive even before their arrival in the United States. New York adopted its criminal syndicalism law in 1902.

Gitlow v. New York

Under that New York statute, a leftist landed in jail. Benjamin Gitlow brought his conviction before the U.S. Supreme Court in 1925. He was one of the founders of the Communist Party USA, who distributed the *Left Wing Manifesto* urging socialism by class action in any form. Gitlow called for a nonviolent protest to cancel the draft, which he compared to a type of "involuntary servitude," banned by the Thirteenth Amendment. While the Court agreed with Gitlow's lawyer that due process placed New York under the watchful care of the First Amendment, Gitlow's conviction was affirmed. Again there was dissent from two justices who thought it best to apply a **clear and present danger test**. Holmes and Brandeis felt the conviction should be reversed and argued in support of Gitlow's freedom of speech. There exists only a slight difference between an opinion and an incitement that would change the fate for Gitlow, wrote Justice Holmes. "The only difference

---

[18]*Debs v. United States,* 249 U.S. 211, 214 (1919).

[19]Geoffrey R. Stone, *Civility and Dissent during Wartime,* Human Rights Magazine, Winter 2006, at 4.

Doctrine of Incorporation

At first reading of the Bill of Rights, one thing becomes clear—it is designed for federal lawmakers. "Congress shall make no law" the First Amendment begins, but does that mean state governments can abridge freedoms of speech, press, religion, or assembly? In the early nineteenth century, the answer was a resounding "Yes" from the Supreme Court. In the case of *Barron v. Mayor of Baltimore,* Chief Justice John Marshall ruled that the first ten amendments to the U.S. Constitution "contain no expression indicating an intention to apply them to the State governments."[a]

John Barron's case was about the money he felt the city owed him as a wharf owner in the Baltimore harbor, where he had lost thousands of dollars in shipping business because the city had been dumping mounds of dirt from road construction in the water near his wharf. Barron asked the high court to honor the Fifth Amendment's guarantee that it would not take private property for public use without justly compensating the owner. The U.S. Supreme Court, however, ruled that constitutional amendment applied only to the federal government in Washington, D.C., and not the one in Baltimore, Maryland.

After the Civil War ended, the Fourteenth Amendment ending slavery added rights for all citizens to the Constitution. It also provided a means for the Court to incorporate the Bill of Rights into the states. The Court began to take very finite steps in that direction, but strictly limited incorporation to clauses that were applicable to particular cases and not entire amendments. The *Gitlow* case, for example, incorporated only freedom of speech while other clauses of the First Amendment were dealt with in subsequent cases. The freedom of the press clause was incorporated for the states in the 1931 case of *Near v. Minnesota,* discussed later in this chapter. Interestingly, Justice Hugo Black disagreed with this piecemeal approach to incorporation and argued that the first eight amendments should be applied to the states all at once. However, Justice Black's view failed to persuade his fellow justices, who chose selective incorporation instead.

[a]*Barron v. Mayor of Baltimore,* 32 U.S. 243, 250 (1833).

---

between the expression of an opinion and an incitement in the narrower sense is the speaker's enthusiasm for the result."[20]

Whitney v. California

How much enthusiasm for such cases would there be on the high court when a person of prominence was named in criminal syndicalism charges? California's 1919 law defined the crime as teaching or advocating any doctrine of violence, sabotage, or destruction in order to effect political change—or belonging to a group that does. Anita Whitney was a member of a prominent family in Alameda County, Cal., and was active in the local Oakland branch of the Socialist Party, which in turn switched its allegiance to the Communist Labor Party (CLP).

Clear and present danger test ■ A standard applied by courts that allows government to criminalize speech only if it presents a clear and present danger. *See Schenk v. United States,* Homes, J., dissenting. Contrast with the bad tendency test, which allows more restriction of speech.

---

[20]*Gitlow v. New York,* 268 U.S. 652, 673 (1925).

Whitney testified she never intended to violate any law, or serve as "an instrument of terrorism or violence," but the Court saw that she participated in the inauguration of the CLP in California and affirmed her conviction. In the concurring opinion fashioned by Justice Louis D. Brandeis, a fuller interpretation of the clear and present danger test is recommended. "No danger flowing from speech can be deemed clear and present," Justice Brandeis allowed, "unless the incidence of evil apprehended is so imminent that it may befall before this opportunity for full discussion."[21] Whitney was "to be punished, not for attempt, incitement or conspiracy, but a step in preparation, which, if it threatens the public order at all, does so only remotely."[22] Justice Holmes advocated it should also include a "time to answer" standard. That is, no threat should be considered imminent if participants were given time to disagree and react against the expressions of political force. Legislatures should not punish any offensive ideas of political protest, but first define just what danger they posed to the state.

THE SMITH ACT

As Axis forces in Europe and Japan began to consolidate their military might, another U.S. law targeting sedition was proposed by a Virginia congressman, Rep. Howard W. Smith, which called for the alien registration of noncitizen adults in the United States. The law made it a crime for any foreign citizen or American to teach or advocate "destroying any government in the United States by force or violence" and would criminalize joining any group that had that form of insurrection in mind. President Roosevelt signed it into law in 1940 and the "Smith Act" became a tool for ferreting out dissidents, including members of the Socialist Worker's Party, pro-Nazi groups opposed to American involvement in World War II, and leaders of the Communist Party USA.

Dennis v. United States

It was the red-baiting era of the 1950s that helped produce the convictions of twelve Communists, and one of them was Eugene Dennis, secretary general of the Communist Party USA, who also had been a member of the Industrial Workers of the World—nicknamed the "Wobblies" in California. Dennis's name was a pseudonym for Francis Xavier Waldron, who had spent several years in the Soviet Union and was believed to have been a source of Russian intelligence during World War II. He was arrested with eleven other party leaders in 1948 and, for months, the nation followed with proceedings against him, where evidence included passages of the *Daily Worker* newspaper and the *Communist Manifesto*. The prosecution had to prove that, even though Dennis and the others had not actually called for the violent overthrow of the United States in public, they had done so privately. Under the Smith Act, Communists were to be convicted for advocating the forcible overthrow of the United States.

---

[21]*Whitney v. California*, 274 U.S. 357, 377 (1927).
[22]*Id.* at 373.

The government won its case against the Wobblies, and the U.S. Supreme Court upheld their convictions by a 6–2 vote, although Chief Justice Fred Vinson said, "an attempt to overthrow the Government by force, even though doomed from the outset because of the inadequate numbers or power of the revolutionists, is a sufficient event for Congress to prevent."[23] Justice Hugo Black wrote a stirring dissent that concluded, "No matter how it is worded, this is a virulent form of prior censorship of speech and press, which I believe the First Amendment forbids." To Justice Black, the First Amendment does not permit the Supreme Court to suppress freedom of speech based on their notions of "reasonableness." "Such a doctrine waters down the First Amendment so that it amounts to little more than an admonition to Congress (and) so construed is not likely to protect any but those safe or orthodox views which rarely need its protection. . . ."[24]

Yates v. United States

Over the next few years, dozens of Communists were prosecuted, until the Supreme Court decided to take another look at the Smith Act. Following the death of Joseph Stalin, the end of the Korean conflict, and the censure of anti-communist Sen. Joseph McCarthy, the Supreme Court chose to revisit the Smith Act in the case of *Yates v. United States*.[25] The legal question to be decided for California heiress, Oleta Yates, was, could the law be used against her and 13 other Communists for simply advocating the future overthrow of the United States as an abstract idea rather than an imminent threat? The majority ruled that teaching an ideal was not the equivalent of planning its implementation and consequently deserved constitutional protection. The Court, however, did not strike down the Smith Act, only removed its sting and left it standing.

Brandenburg v. Ohio

In the midst of the landmark Communist prosecutions, a radical leader from the other side of the political spectrum entered. In 1967, Clarence Brandenburg was tried under Ohio's criminal syndicalism law for advocating "revengence" against U.S. politicians and judges for their civil rights activities on behalf of African-American citizens.[26] Brandenburg was a Klansman, who made the televised charges while rallying white supremacists to his cause. The court applied the "clear danger" test advocated almost a half-century earlier by Justice Holmes. As a result, the government would only penalize direct incitement to imminent lawless action, and invalidated state sedition laws.

Bedrock Law: The *Brandenburg* case established that only direct incitement to imminent lawless action would invalidate the First Amendment's protection for political speech.

---

[23]*Dennis v. United States*, 341 U.S. 494, 509 (1951).

[24]*Id.* at 508.

[25]*Yates v. United States*, 354 U.S. 298 (1957).

[26]*Brandenburg v. Ohio*, 395 U.S. 444 (1969).

THEORIES OF PRIOR RESTRAINT

Some powers seek to silence dissent even before it enters the public arena. This form of censorship, previously discussed as prior restraint, also can assume the form of licensing, taxation, or even seizing the actual machinery of communication. By whatever means, it is clearly the evil the First Amendment was designed to prevent. The modern use of the term *prior restraint* calls for careful denotation to prevent its confusion with more random encroachments on free expression. Strictly speaking, prior restraint means government oversight of expression in a systematic manner, not simply targeting single messengers or their messages. Second, it empowers by means of government appointment third-party gatekeepers who can replace the communicator's discretion with personal tastes. Finally, prior restrainers do their work before the communication reaches the public, not during or afterward.

Because prior restraint is the most abhorrent form of government intervention, the courts require strict scrutiny as the test of constitutional validity. Strict scrutiny places a high burden on the government. There must be a compelling public interest at stake for the law to stand. The courts might allow prior restraint only if national security concerns are at stake, but not for lesser interests such as aesthetics or inconvenience. Given these rigors, it is easy to see how seldom such a system might work and yet, there are cases.

Twentieth-Century Landmarks

Historians of First Amendment law search for the trail of binding precedents at the point where Sir Blackstone's sentiments against "previous restraints" of expression clearly emerge in the judicial record. A major twentieth-century gate is marked by the criminal prosecution of a northern scandal sheet known as the *Saturday Press,* which rose to the U.S. Supreme Court's attention in 1931. Sensational journalists Jay M. Near and his partner in print, Howard Guilford, a former mayoral candidate, were the twin editorial forces roiling the political powers of Minneapolis and St. Paul in the Roaring Twenties. Once deemed a nuisance, a court could issue an injunction against future publication or distribution.

After Near and Guilford lost in Minnesota's legal system, Near alone took his case to the U.S. Supreme Court, which applied the **doctrine of incorporation** citing the freedom of press in the First Amendment.[27] Covering state law with First Amendment freedoms meant striking down Minnesota's Public Nuisance law of 1925. Because the law punished the press prior to publication, Chief Justice Charles Evans Hughes and four of his brethren rejected it as flawed. Justice Hughes' landmark opinion left the door open for government oversight. The press could be suppressed under certain conditions—national security for example, "the sailing dates of transports or the number and location of troops" could be restrained.[28] In his

Incorporation doctrine ■ Neither the U.S. Constitution nor its amendments apply to the states as a whole. However, once specific parts of the Constitution are individually incorporated into the 14th Amendment by the Court, they become applicable to states through the 14th Amendment's limitation on state action.

---

[27]As noted in the "Doctrine of Incorporation" feature, selective incorporation applied the Bill of Rights to the States as a part of the Fourteenth Amendment, which specifies due process for all Americans regardless of their state of residence.

[28]*Near v. Minnesota,* 283 US 697, 716 (1931).

opinion, government had a right to censor expressions that incited acts of violence or generated obscenity. Moreover, "the constitutional guaranty of free speech does not protect a man from an injunction against uttering words that may have all the effect of force."[29]

Near v. Minnesota did not absolutely sustain the British common law, but it did make clear that prior restraint is the exception to the rule, and it usually involves some visible danger. "The fact that the liberty of the press may be abused by miscreant purveyors of scandal does not make any the less necessary the immunity of the press from previous restraint in dealing with official misconduct. Subsequent punishment for such abuses as may exist is the appropriate remedy, consistent with constitutional privilege."[30]

The *Near* case was a close victory for freedom of the press, with four dissenting justices holding to the belief that it was a valid interest of society to prevent publications that smack of hatred and prejudice and allege official misconduct without adequate proof. The majority opinion made clear that protection from prior restraint is not unlimited in the United States. Citing an earlier

---

▶ UP CLOSE

Anti-Semitism in Print

The typewriters of the *Saturday Press* were raking muck against city and county politicians, including the chief of police, whom Near and Guilford accused of taking graft from high-rolling bootleggers and gamblers they smeared as a Jewish mafia. The two scandalmongers were arrested under Minnesota's gag law, which forbade "malicious, scandalous, or defamatory" content from being published in the state. One passage reveals the anti-Semitic flavor of their journalism: "It is Jew thugs who have pulled practically every robbery in this city. . . . Practically every vendor of vile hooch, every owner of a moonshine still, every snake-faced gangster and embryonic yegg in the Twin Cities is a Jew . . . ninety percent of the crimes committed against society in this city are committed by Jew gangsters."[a]

In 1927, the *Saturday Press* was padlocked after nine editions, and Near and Guilford were threatened with arrest if they tried to print out more editions. Before their presses could roll again, they faced the high hurdle of convincing a court their notorious scandal sheet had been cleansed of its polluted prose. This action "put the publisher under an effective censorship" through the "suppression of the offending newspaper."[b] Instead, the two men chose to slug it out in the Minnesota court system, which handily dealt them defeats all the way up to the Supreme Court.

---

[a] *Near v. Minnesota*, 283 US 697, 738 (1931).
[b] *Id.* at 697.

---

[29] *Id.* at 716.
[30] *Id.* at 697.

landmark, "When a nation is at war many things that might be said in time of peace are such a hindrance to its effort that their utterance will not be endured. . . ."[31] On similar grounds, the decency and security of community life may be enforced against obscene publications, incitements to violence, and advocacy of the violent overthrow of the government.

A Taxing Question

While the Supreme Court restricted the use of direct censorship to chill the speech of dissenters and rabble-rousers, the numbing threat of taxation against news media in states where the press was a problem for the high and mighty did the same disservice. During the Great Depression, rural residents of Louisiana were mesmerized by the animated speeches of the "Kingfish," Governor Huey P. Long. However, the populist Democrat did not hold all of Louisiana under his spell, and so he decided to relieve his exasperation with Louisiana's adversarial press by imposing a "license tax" of 2 percent for all newspapers with a circulation of 20,000 or more. The governor quipped it was "two pennies per lie," and levied it against 13 daily newspapers, including the *New Orleans Times-Picayune,* well known for its criticisms of Long's administration.

The case of *Grosjean v. American Press Co.* brought the tax question before the U.S. Supreme Court, and sealed for posterity the name of Alice Lee Grosjean, the governor's former secretary and alleged mistress, who was responsible for collecting the newspaper tax.[32] In a unanimous opinion against Louisiana's politically charged revenue scheme, the Court recalled how British rulers used similar means to silence dissent, and how much of the nation's founding was owed to outrage against onerous taxes and despots who levied them. Justice George Sutherland's opinion underscored how "well known and odious" censorship was through financial means, and that to allow the press to be fettered is to "fetter ourselves." Thus, Louisiana's press tax was an impermissible violation of the First Amendment. As a historical footnote, by the time this case reached the Court, the controversial Long had been assassinated by one of his rivals' sons in the state capitol.

The threat of politicians taming the news media by taxing them into submission was not buried in the bayous but sprang to life anew in the laws of Arkansas and Minnesota. The Commissioner of Revenue in 1974 began levying a "use tax" on Minnesota publications that spent major sums of money on paper and ink—more than $100,000 worth per year. Such a tax tightened government controls on eleven publishers, including the state's largest circulation daily, *The Minneapolis Star-Tribune.*

That one company paid roughly two-thirds of the revenue garnered by this print and ink tax. After the U.S. Supreme Court heard the newspaper's complaint, it became clear the state was saddling an unequal share of the burden on the paper's shoulders. In Justice Sandra Day O'Connor's opinion that "differential

---

[31]*Schenck v. United States, supra* note [[15]], at 51.

[32]*Grosjean v. American Press Co.,* 297 U.S. 233 (1936).

treatment, unless justified by some special characteristic of the press, suggests that the goal of the regulation is not unrelated to suppression of expression, and such a goal is presumptively unconstitutional."[33]

The "intimidation-by-taxes" episode concluded in Minnesota, but magazine owners in Arkansas felt the squeeze on their pocketbooks when the legislature decided to separate general-interest magazines from newspapers, religious periodicals, and sports journals. In *Arkansas Writer's Project, Inc. v. Ragland,* the government of Arkansas felt the brunt of justice from Associate Justice Marshall who found the state's discriminatory tax on general-interest magazines "disturbing" and "particularly repugnant to First Amendment principles."[34]

> **Bedrock Law:** Government attempts to exercise control over the press through discriminatory taxes have been regarded as unconstitutional prior restraints.

PRIOR RESTRAINT BY INJUNCTION

When a court commands someone to act in order to preserve justice through a document called a writ, that individual is bound by law to either perform a duty or refrain from some activity. This order is called an **injunction** because it enjoins the person from acting contrary to good conscience, and sometimes an injunction can be an effective means for restraining publication, including messages about the spread of weapons of mass destruction, racial fear, or the reasons a nation has gone to war.

> **Injunction** ■ A form of equitable remedy which requires a party to refrain from doing things specified in the injunction.

Pentagon Papers Case

In 1971, a secret Pentagon study fell into the hands of reporters at the *New York Times* and the *Washington Post* through an ardent anti-Communist and Harvard-trained economist, Dr. Daniel Ellsberg. Ellsberg was convinced the American war effort in Southeast Asia was futile, and the public needed to know why Americans were sent to die there, by revealing "the Pentagon Papers." Photocopies were made of the 47-volume Defense Department study of the historic evolution of Vietnam involvement, "History of the United States Decision-Making Process on Vietnam Policy."

For several months, *Times* reporter Neil Sheehan and his colleagues pored over thousands of pages. When it was time to go to press, the *New York Times* headlined their initial feature, "Vietnam Archive: Pentagon Study Traces 3 Decades of Growing U.S. Involvement." Within two days, U.S. Attorney General John Mitchell telegrammed the *Times* urging it to cease printing that series immediately because of the harm it posed to our military presence.

When the *Times* refused to stop the presses, the Department of Justice found a federal judge, Murray I. Gurfein, to issue a temporary restraining order, or "TRO." Judge Gurfein was serving his first day as a federal judge when he enjoined the *Times*. The *Washington Post* stepped into the breach to publish its portions of the secret report, but the U.S. attorney general quickly secured a second injunction against the *Post*.

---

[33]*Minneapolis Star Tribune Co. v. Minnesota Comm'r of Revenue,* 460 U.S. 575, 581–585 (1983).
[34]*Arkansas Writer's Project, Inc. v. Ragland,* 481 U.S. 221, 230 (1989).

Appeals for the *Times* and *Post* quickly moved up through the courts to the U.S. Supreme Court, which responded with unusual efficiency handing down a decision within two weeks. The outcome was a press victory of sorts. The Court's 6–3 decision was written without a majority opinion (five justices could not agree), but each justice gave a brief explanation of his opinion. The per curium opinion cited earlier precedents, including the one that found any prior restraint on publication bears "a heavy presumption against its constitutional validity."[35] Not only did the newspaper continue its work on the series but won a Pulitzer Prize for public service for its articles.[36]

Three Justices, Chief Justice Warren Burger, John Harlan, and Harry Blackmun dissented, citing concerns about foreign relations and national security that would be caused by the publication of these documents. Blackmun gave a stern warning, outlining the possible consequences if this grant of freedom unfolded into remorse: "If, with the Court's action today, these newspapers proceed to publish the critical documents and there results there from the death of soldiers, the destruction of alliances, the greatly increased difficulty of negotiation with our enemies, the inability of our diplomats to negotiate, to which list I might add the factors of prolongation of the war . . . then the nation's people will know where the responsibility for these sad consequences rests."[37]

Three justices complained they did not have enough time to properly consider the legal questions. Justices Black and Douglas believed that federally imposed prior restraints on the press were unconstitutional—period. While four of their colleagues disagreed with that absolutist position, they felt in this case the government failed to meet the test. Simply put, the government failed to prove publication would pose "direct, immediate and irreparable harm" to the people. The disposition of the case was a victory for the First Amendment, but the only guidance it gave was that the requisite test of prior restraint had not been met.

> **Bedrock Law:** Censorship of the news media in order to protect national security must meet a heavy burden of proof that includes direct harm to the people.

Banning the Bomb

Another judicial controversy centered on a political digest, *The Progressive*, founded by famed socialist, Robert M. LaFollett. In 1979, *The Progressive* published a story about the creation of the hydrogen bomb, "The H-Bomb Secret: How We Got It, Why We're Telling It." The article was the work of a freelance journalist, Howard Morland, who relied on interviews, encyclopedia texts, and guesswork to draft his special feature.

Morland claimed a college student at the University of Alabama gave him a glimpse of the H-bomb secret during a class lecture in 1978. After following up on key terms in the student's comments and consulting two encyclopedias, Morland traveled to factories that produced H-bomb parts and conducted more interviews with experts in the field.

---

[35] *Bantam Books v. Sullivan,* 372 U.S. 58, 70 (1963).

[36] *New York Times Co. v. United States,* 403 U.S. 713 (1971).

[37] *Id.*

After Morland's piece was written, *Progressive's* editor wanted the facts checked, and he sent Morland's draft to experts for verification. Soon, the article ended up in government hands; the Department of Justice recognized a bombshell when they saw one. In its Atomic Energy Act (Sec. 2274), the U.S. Congress had banned anyone from "communicating, transmitting or disclosing any restricted data," which was defined as data about the "design, manufacture, or utilization of atomic weapons."[38]

Morland and the magazine maintained all of their information came from public sources, and practically any citizen willing to do the research would get the same results just by going to the Department of Energy and federal libraries. The U.S. attorneys disagreed and argued that he had disclosed crucial details yet unseen by the general public. Federal prosecutors further cited national security as the reason for the prior restraint because *The Progressive's* article posed "immediate, direct and irreparable harm to the interests of the United States."

The judge in the case could see "no plausible reason why the public needs to know the details about bomb construction to carry on an informed debate on the issue."[39] Judge Warren's approach seemed out of line with constitutional philosophy. Why should it be the judge's decision as to whether the public "needs to know" something to determine whether it deserves protection? First Amendment rights are not based on the "need" for speech; otherwise our communication would be without protection. The clear and present danger test could have been applied to this case but was not.

The substantive evil that Congress has the right to prevent was huge (nuclear proliferation and perhaps annihilation), but the danger was far from clear (obvious) or present (immediate). It is almost as if the judge allowed a lesser level of present-ness and clarity because the evil was so significant, but the government was thrown a curve ball when a similar article on H-bomb construction appeared in the *Press Connection,* and the case became moot.[40] The government dropped its charges, but *The Progressive* went to press with the Morland piece, months after its scheduled release–even though the author admitted his blueprint was inaccurate and he needed to print a corrected version. The upshot is that no unconstitutional prior restraint occurred when the court stopped the press in view of the federal law defining this violation. The *Progressive* case was a classic example of "balancing," where freedom of the press is held in balance with the public interest.

Free Speech for Spies?

While pulling the plug on news media coverage is an unlikely solution for national security measures, government employees, especially those with tenure at the Central Intelligence Agency, could be swiftly censored. Victor Marchetti wrote a novel, *The Rope Dancer,* based on his CIA experiences after he exited

---

[38]*See* 42 U.S.C. § 2274.

[39]*United States v. Progressive*, 467 F. Supp. 990 (W.D. Wis. 1979).

[40]*United States v. Progressive, dismissed without opinion*, 610 F.2d 819 (7th Cir. 1979).

the agency in 1969. It caused little difficulty, but his second book, *The CIA and the Cult of Intelligence,* was nonfiction and alarmed his former agency employers in hundreds of passages. The agency asked him to delete all of them, but he resisted until a compromise was achieved where Marchetti excised only classified material.

In Marchetti's words, "democratic governments fighting totalitarian enemies run the risk of imitating their methods and thereby destroying democracy." He charged the CIA with contriving political fictions for a believing public, which "has posed a particular threat to the right of Americans to be informed for the present and future by an objective knowledge of the past."[41]

When another ex-CIA employee began to write of secret matters, the U.S. government's response to reporters became clear. Frank Snepp served as an agent in Vietnam, but he exited Saigon with a burden of guilt for the suffering of the South Vietnamese. As all operatives in that sector were asked to do, he signed a secrecy order and he cleaned out his desk. He then chose to ignore it once he began writing about his life in Vietnam for publication. After *Decent Interval* went to press, Snepp's attorneys argued his federal contract violated his constitutional rights; a trial judge disagreed and called upon Snepp to place all of his book profits in a trust fund for his former employer.

The ex-CIA analyst-turned-author appealed to the U.S. Supreme Court, which showed little sympathy for his claim. Upholding the federal district court's ruling based on his breach of contract, the Court enjoined him from future writings about his days at the CIA. The ruling said that Snepp signed away those rights when he first joined the agency and again when he left it in 1976.[42]

> **Bedrock Law:** By virtue of secrecy agreements, Americans can cede their right of free speech on the basis of contractual terms of employment.

Panic-Peddling Flyers

A dispute in a Chicago suburb brought up another important area of prior restraint—one involving private citizens and business interests. This case pitted a community of citizens in a Chicago suburb against a disreputable practice in real estate sales. *Organization for a Better Austin v. Keefe* decided the case of a real estate broker who tried to stop a neighborhood civic group from handing out pamphlets against him.[43] This group had noticed that certain unethical realtors would come into neighborhoods, spread the word that "negroes" were moving there, and then buy up white-owned homes cheaply in the ensuing panic and resell them at a healthy profit to either blacks or whites. This organization received pledges to halt the practice from most real estate firms, but not from Jerome Keefe. So, they printed leaflets describing him as "panic peddler." Keefe went to court and

---

[41]Victor Marchetti, *Propaganda and Disinformation: How the CIA Manufactures History,* 9 J. Hist. Rev. 305 (1989).

[42]*Snepp v. United States,* 444 U.S. 507 (1980).

[43]*Organization for a Better Austin v. Keefe,* 402 U.S. 415 (1971).

UP CLOSE

Judicial Temperament

Even Supreme Court justices might find themselves embroiled in prior restraint controversy. When Supreme Court Justice Antonin Scalia spoke at a private high school in Mississippi, reporters for the local newspaper and the wire service wanted to capture his words on cassette tapes. The problem was that no one advised local news media that Justice Scalia kept a strict policy preventing electronic recordings of his remarks. In deference to that practice, a deputy federal marshal seized and destroyed the reporters' tape recordings.

Both the *Hattiesburg American* and the Associated Press sued the U.S. Marshall Service in 2004, claiming that it had violated their constitutional right "to publish news without pre-publication interference." Before that case came to trial, however, the parties settled their differences, and the U.S. Marshall Service adopted a new policy where they promised not to interfere with the "photography, audio taping, and videotaping of the event except when the personal security and safety of the federal judiciary is believed to be in jeopardy." As a personal footnote, Justice Scalia later announced he had revised his thinking about preventing electronic recordings of his speeches and agreed to allow it, but only for the print media.[a] The broadcasters would continue to enjoy second-class status at his speaking engagements.

---

[a] *The Hattiesburg American v. United States Marshall Service,* No. 3:04-CV-344LN (S.D. Miss. May 10, 2004).

obtained an injunction that prohibited further distribution of the leaflets labeling him as such.

In May 1971, the U.S. Supreme Court dissolved the injunction. Chief Justice Warren Burger ruled that Keefe's argument about the pamphlets aiming to get him to sign the no-blockbuster rule was immaterial. "So long as the means are peaceful, the communication need not meet standards of acceptability." The decision against *Keefe* underscored the Court's position taken in *Near* regarding prior restraint.

RESTRAINT IN AN AGE OF TERRORISM

It would be a mistake to say seditious libel ended with the freedom granted to Clarence Brandenburg, since the United States found itself in the midst of a War on Terror following the attacks of September 11, 2001. Federal prosecutors looked for legal means to guard the nation from the Islamic extremists, such as the ones who bombed the World Trade Center earlier, in 1993. Ramzi Yousef of Kuwait and Sheikh Omar Abdel Rahman, a leader of an Egyptian Muslim group devoted to terrorist acts, along with eight others, were convicted of violating the seditious conspiracy act which made it a crime to seek the violent overthrow of the U.S. government. Youssef Adel Rahman and others acted upon their words, and the clearly present danger they caused produced the deaths of six New Yorkers while wounding more than a thousand others.

After the September 11 attacks, President George W. Bush announced that the nation was at war, and soon thereafter, his administration asked broadcasters to resist telecasting the videotaped statements of al Qaeda leader Osama bin Laden that were being transmitted by Arab broadcasting stations. The American networks opted to comply and so the government's power in this regard was never tested. Yet, some columnists criticized this informal means of prior restraint based on the notion that Bin Laden would somehow use such a means to send coded messages to his followers. Other more intrusive measures alarmed Americans.

Reacting to some of the president's initiatives, the township of Brewster, Massachusetts, summoned its revolutionary history to a town meeting where the subject was the counter-terrorist **USA PATRIOT Act.** Because U.S. law enforcement agents, not local governments, enforced the PATRIOT Act's search, seizure, and detention provisions, the town-hall opposition reflected an alliance of people opposing the administration's policies that would pose a chilling effect to anti-war research or communications. The U.S. Department of Justice argued that such alarm over the USA PATRIOT Act was unfounded. Federal law enforcement officials rarely, if ever, applied its most controversial provisions, which would involve secretly subpoenaing library records, or "sneak-and-peek" warrants allowing investigators to conduct a secret search.

PATRIOT Act (USA PATRIOT Act) ■ Uniting and Strengthening America by Providing Appropriate Tools Required to Intercept and Obstruct Terrorism Act of 2001.

Hezbollah Television

The federal government did move, in one instance, to prosecute subversive television content. In 2006, federal agents appeared at the office of a satellite television system in New York to arrest the owner for one particular channel that was sold to viewers in Brooklyn. Javed Iqbal was taken into custody for dealing with a Hezbollah-operated TV channel known as al-Manar. The 42-year-old Pakistani immigrant and owner of HDTV Ltd. was prosecuted under the International Emergency Economic Powers Act—a law that made it a federal crime to deal financially with terrorist groups. The U.S. government labeled the channel, al-Manar, a "Designated Global Terrorist," believing that its sources of revenue were used to fund terrorist activities. Iqbal pleaded guilty in 2008 to providing material support through Hezbollah television in exchange for thousands of dollars in payment. One consequence of Iqbal's case was the loss of televised reports for New York of the opinions espoused by Hezbollah, the Shiite Muslim group then at war with Israel in Lebanon.

Coffin Coverage

A decade earlier, the news media protested a federal policy that amounted to visual prior restraint. During the first Persian Gulf War, the U.S. Defense Department prohibited recording images, by photography or television video cameras, of flag-draped coffins carrying the bodies of slain servicemen home to Dover Air Force Base, to the nation's largest mortuary. Several media organizations led by JB Pictures protested the government-imposed ban, and appealed the case to the U.S. Court of Appeals for the District of Columbia.[44] This policy of prior restraint on news coverage was sanctioned by invasion of privacy claims, despite the fact this argument presumed viewers could identify individual soldiers residing in their flag-draped coffins. News media were not to be allowed to convey scenes of war's grim toll.

ARGUMENTS FOR FREE EXPRESSION

Philosophers of the age of enlightenment would argue that freedom of expression is a natural right, or as John Locke, who greatly influenced Thomas Jefferson's thinking, would have stated, "life, health, liberty, or possessions" are inalienable rights. Of course, the question arises when liberties lead to irresponsible or abusive actions. Then philosophers such as Jean Jacques Rousseau turn to our social obligations and balance Locke's freedom-based thesis. Rousseau defended popular sovereignty in terms of a **social contract** (*Du contrat social*) requiring free citizens to keep in mind the greater good of society in their acts and words of liberty. Such theories were familiar to the framers and help Americans today understand how government-imposed control over expression portends more harm than good. Of course in 1791, that was a radical idea.

Social contract ■
A concept in political philosophy first proposed by Jean-Jacques Rousseau, which justifies the power of the sovereign ruler by the existence of a social contract between free subjects, who voluntarily and mutually submit to the sovereign authority for the good of all.

Sentiments of free expression did not spring forth solely from Professor Blackstone's hand, but owed some inspiration to the thinkers of Athens, Rome, and even philosophers of the Middle Ages. In Demosthenes' mind, "the privation of free speech" would produce unwise governance. The plays of Euripides showed how proudly Athenians felt about their birthright to speak freely in public. The philosopher, Benedict Spinoza in 1670, observed "in a free state every man may think what he likes, and say what he thinks," and Niccolo Machiavelli characterized the Renaissance's gift as giving us the right to "think all things, speak all things, write all things," and yet he later warned that princes should be "talked of with Reserve and Respect."[45]

With somewhat less deference to royalty, American constitutional framers began to consider what the First Amendment should mean to them. That debate over whether greater libertarian thought was encoded in the Bill of Rights, or whether the constitutional authors simply wished to extend Blackstone's common-law advice against prior censorship, persists to this day. Legal historian Leonard Levy concluded that even the founding fathers prosecuted government criticism, and "the Bill of Rights was more the chance product of political expediency on all sides than of principled commitment to personal liberties."[46] Others believe the type of expansive freedoms enjoyed today would not surprise early Americans,

[44]*JB Pictures v. Department of Defense,* 86 F.3d 236 (D.C. Cir. 1996).

[45]Levy, *supra* note 5, at 88, 89, quoting 2 Thomas Erskine May, *The Constitutional History of England* 102 n.1 (1880), and *Theologico-Political Treatise,* in 1 *The Chief Words of Benedict de Spinoza* 258 (R.H.M Elwes trans., London 1883).

[46]*Id.* at vii.

even though they had seen citizens pilloried for failing to attend church and for uttering curses in public.[47]

The First Amendment air we breathe today is a far different blend than the winds of 1791. In the eighteenth century the framers debated the question of slavery, but it was too divisive an issue, so it was left out of the original Constitution. It took a civil war and amendments in the nineteenth century to address the issue. Sometimes, "intent of the framers" arguments may be helpful in understanding documents; yet, scholars who view the Constitution as a living document do not consider interpretations from centuries ago as necessarily determinative.

Arguments against censorship are well known and society has an interest in protecting citizens from chicanery, but the government's reliance on prior restraint is the last resort. One principle that guards against prior restraint by the government stems from the belief that more, not less, speech is best suited to advance society's interests. The people's right to know depends on it, and the idea of limited government carries with it the requirement that citizens be informed of errors, in order to correct their elected leaders. Consequently, government can ill afford to silence its critics, especially if it means forbidding them to share their insights and solutions.

Beyond the arena of political interest, freedom of speech and thought is critically essential for the successful search for truth. Scientists of an earlier age understood how harshly ecclesiastics punished unbelievers for simply observing the sun occupies the center of the solar system, or that the earth is a round sphere and not a flat surface.

Prior restraint tends to curb the power of unpopular sentiments. The mere act of reviewing ideas before they enter the marketplace imposes a delay that dilutes their strength. Once the authority of prior restraint is removed, and the censorial role is relieved, society can afford a judicious, public hearing of controversy. The forty-five words of the First Amendment are thus essential to protecting minority viewpoints from those who stand in dissent of popular opinion.

SUMMARY

- Government censorship today is not forbidden, but it must surmount a high hurdle usually when arguments of national security are involved. Ever since the *Brandenburg* case, the rationale of government has been to prevent imminent lawless action, such as the planned forcible overthrow of the government.

- In 1833, the Supreme Court ruled that the Bill of Rights did not apply to state governments since nothing in the language of the first ten amendments suggested otherwise. It was not until after the Fourteenth Amendment was adopted, following the Civil War, that the Supreme Court adopted a selective

---

[47]A vocal opponent of the Levy philosophy has been Jeffery A. Smith. *See Printers and Press Freedom* (1988).

incorporation approach and began to apply various clauses of each amendment to the states as a matter of case law. The free speech clause of the First Amendment was incorporated in the case of *Gitlow v. New York,* and the free press clause came later in *Near v. Minnesota.*

- The theory behind freedom of the press is that truth ultimately prevails in a free marketplace of ideas. This naturally leads into the conviction that the best antidote to bad speech is better speech to correct it. Democracies rely on an informed electorate so it is imperative that citizens be informed of errors in policy and political judgment, in order to have an impact on the outcome of laws and elections.

- The bad tendency test simply meant that seditious speech posed no real threat to American security interests, but that it was intended to put hearers or readers in mind of revolt toward the government. The Supreme Court developed its bad tendency test during the twentieth century, when immigrants and left-leaning radicals were viewed as threat to the federal government, particularly during times of war. Justices Holmes and Brandeis argued in dissent that the Constitution protected defiant and rebellious speech. A clear and present danger meant that there was both the means and opportunity for real violence and the forcible overthrow of the agents of government.

- Governments have attempted to exercise control over the press through discriminatory taxes, which are also considered unconstitutional prior restraints, but the most common legal tool used to censor free expression is a court-ordered injunction.

- Governments have used a number of means to hold critics in check. The power of government licensing was used in ancient times to prevent outlandish publications from reaching the public, and prosecutions for seditious libel were used to silence political dissent in Great Britain and the United States. These laws have failed to stand in the face of those willing to go to jail for unjust laws and fight in court for the right to reveal unpleasant truths or poke fun at public officials.

- Various types of legal controls used against government critics include the injunction to stop communication before it is actually published such as the court order used to prevent books or newspapers. Another means of stopping speech before it occurs is by simply refusing to grant access, as the government has done in times of war. There is a larger principle raised by twentieth-century landmark cases—that one of the temptations of power is to control speech and publications, but service to freedom requires a price be paid for it, because the government will often attempt to suppress more information than is necessary.

- By virtue of secrecy and confidentiality agreements, Americans can cede their right of free speech on the basis of contractual terms of employment.

What Is Treason?

By law, treason is defined as acts of subversion and espionage against one's country of citizenship. In the United States, it is a prominent crime spelled out in the Constitution.[a] Treason against the United States means siding with the nation's enemies, including giving them aid and comfort. Whoever is found guilty of treason, according to the federal law passed by Congress, "shall suffer death, or shall be imprisoned not less than five years and fined under this title but not less than $10,000; and shall be incapable of holding any office under the United States."[b]

Since World War II, only two Americans have been charged with treason, but one of them is still at large. The most recent conviction came in 1952 when Tomoya Kawakita of Calexico, Cal., was tried for brutally holding American prisoners captive in Kyoto, Japan, during World War II. Kawakita was sentenced to life in prison and served time at Alcatraz federal penitentiary until President Kennedy pardoned him in 1963.

The second American charged with treason is Adam Gadahn (born Adam Pearlman), a Californian who was raised in a Christian household but converted to Islam at the age of seventeen. He became known as "Azzam the American" after his enlistment to the cause of Islamic jihadists in Afghanistan, and he evidently helped Osama bin Laden produce videos for dissemination over al-Jazeera. On the fourth anniversary of September 11, 2001, ABC News telecast a video containing violent threats emanating from the concealed face of man whom U.S. intelligence officers identified as Gadahn. Not only did he praise slitting the throats of infidels, but also predicted future terrorist assaults in California and Australia. His recruitment film, *Knowledge Is for Acting Upon — The Manhattan Raid,* celebrated al Qaeda's attacks in 2001 and featured pre-attack videos of the 9/11 hijackers with captions in English and Arabic.

In 2006, Adam Gadahn was indicted by a federal grand jury in southern California for the capital crime of treason based on evidence presented by the FBI that indicated he had aided an enemy of the United States. Following that indictment came multiple reports of Azzam's death or capture in Pakistan, all of which were later discovered to be false. Not long after another false report of Gadahn's arrest in 2010, a videotape was released urging Muslims serving in the U.S. military to follow the example of U.S. Army Major Nidal Malik Hasan, who opened fire on soldiers at Fort Hood killing thirteen soldiers and wounding thirty-two others. Adam Gadahn's trial for treason against the United States awaits his arrest and return to American soil. ∎

---

[a]Art. III Sec. 3: "Treason against the United States, shall consist only in levying War against them, or in adhering to their Enemies, giving them Aid and Comfort. No Person shall be convicted of Treason unless on the Testimony of two Witnesses to the same overt Act, or on Confession in open Court. The Congress shall have power to declare the Punishment of Treason, but no Attainder of Treason shall work Corruption of Blood, or Forfeiture except during the Life of the Person attainted."
[b]18 U.S.C. § 2381.

Libel

The New York Times.

NEW YORK, TUESDAY, MARCH 29, 1960.

Heed Their Rising Voices

"The growing movement of peaceful mass demonstrations by Negroes is something new in the South, something understandable.... Let Congress heed their rising voices, for they will be heard."

—New York Times editorial
Saturday, March 19, 1960

LEARNING OBJECTIVES

After reading this chapter you should know:

- Whether defamation, slander, and libel are basically the same or totally different from each other
- The distinction between criminal and civil libel
- Who has to prove what to win a lawsuit
- Why public figures have a harder time winning libel suits than private figures
- That media reporting someone else's libelous statement aren't immune from libel suits
- The good and bad news about "truth" as a defense in a libel suit
- The defenses for media sued for libel

Your Help Is Urgently Needed . . . NOW!!

COMMITTEE TO DEFEND MARTIN LUTHER KING AND THE STRUGGLE FOR FREEDOM IN THE SOUTH
312 West 125th Street, New York 27, N. Y. UNiversity 6-1700

On March 29, 1960, a full-page ad appeared in the *New York Times* requesting donations to the "Committee to Defend Martin Luther King and the Struggle for Freedom in the South." Written more like a news story than a traditional advertisement, the ad had a headline that read "Heed Their Rising Voices." The ad claimed to describe the plight of African-American students in the southern United States and the denial of rights suffered by black people. It appealed for donations to support the students, the right to vote, and Dr. King's legal defense in Montgomery, Ala., on charges of perjury. The ad was then "signed" as a petition might be by 64 prominent citizens.[1]

At the time, L.B. Sullivan was one of three elected commissioners of the city of Montgomery and part of his responsibility included supervision of the police department. He claimed that the advertisement libeled him. **Libel,** at that time in Alabama, was defined as making untrue statements about an individual that damaged his reputation. Although Sullivan was never named in the advertisement, he was able to provide witnesses who asserted that when they read the ad, they inferred from it that Sullivan was responsible. He claimed his reputation was damaged because portions of the advertisement read as follows:

> after students sang "My Country, 'Tis of Thee" on the State Capitol steps, their leaders were expelled from school, and truckloads of police armed with shotguns and tear-gas ringed the Alabama State College Campus. When the entire student body protested to state authorities by refusing to re-register, their dining hall was padlocked in an attempt to starve them into submission. . . . Again and again the Southern violators have answered Dr. King's peaceful protests with intimidation and violence. They have bombed his home almost killing his wife and child. They have assaulted his person. They have arrested him seven times—for "speeding," "loitering" and similar "offenses." And now they have charged him with "perjury"— a *felony* under which they could imprison him for *ten years*.[2]

Some of the statements made in the advertisement were incorrect. The students sang the national anthem rather than "My Country 'Tis of Thee." The student leaders were not expelled for their protest at the Capitol but instead because of a lunch-counter demonstration on another day. Student protests did not include a refusal to register for a semester but a single day's boycott of classes. The dining hall was never padlocked and the only students prohibited from eating there were those who lacked the requisite meal cards. Although the police had been dispatched to the campus, they had never "ringed" it. Dr. King had been arrested only four times rather than seven.

The Alabama courts awarded L.B. Sullivan a libel judgment against the *New York Times.* Under the applicable Alabama laws at the time, Sullivan had been libeled because the *Times* had published false information about him, which damaged his reputation. In 1960, that was the end of the argument. The newspaper appealed the

Libel ■ Traditionally, libel was thought of as printed defamation, as opposed to spoken, which is slander. Libelous statements are untrue and cause harm.

---

[1]While not part of the discussion of media law, the context of era needs to be noted. This was a case of a northern metropolitan newspaper seen as sympathetic to the rights of minorities fighting a legal battle against a southern government official at a time when the fight for civil rights was extremely heated. Vitriol and violence were widespread. Some suggest that the case was about a lot more than just libel. For a detailed account, read Anthony Lewis's thorough examination, *Make No Law: The Sullivan Case and the First Amendment* (1992).

[2]*New York Times Co. v. Sullivan,* 376 U.S. 254, 257–58 (1964) (emphasis in original).

decision to the U.S. Supreme Court and in 1964 the Court unanimously overturned the Alabama courts and found that the *Times* had not libeled Sullivan.[3] The rationale was that the Alabama law did not do enough to protect First Amendment rights (the Court called it "constitutionally deficient") if it allowed public officials to win libel suits against critics of their official conduct.[4] The case was groundbreaking for many reasons. It assailed the notion that speech appearing in an advertisement is not entitled to First Amendment protection (as discussed in chapter 12). But most importantly the decision by Justice William Brennan reaffirmed the notion that free expression must protect the ability of people to criticize their government and government officials. "[D]ebate on public issues should be uninhibited, robust, and wide-open, and . . . it may well include vehement, caustic, and sometimes unpleasantly sharp attacks on government and public officials."[5] Brennan went on to assert that in free debate, erroneous statements were inevitable, but that some errors must be tolerated if free expression is to have the "breathing space" necessary.

> Allowance of the defense of truth, with the burden of proving it on the defendant, does not mean that only false speech will be deterred. Even courts accepting this defense as an adequate safeguard have recognized the difficulties of adducing legal proofs that the alleged libel was true in all its factual particulars. Under such a rule, would-be critics of official conduct may be deterred from voicing their criticism, even though it is believed to be true and even though it is in fact true, because of doubt whether it can be proved in court or fear of the expense of having to do so. They tend to make only statements which "steer far wider of the unlawful zone."[6]

Actual malice ■
The requirement in cases of libel against public officials that the publisher acted with knowledge of falsity or a reckless disregard for the truth.

Obviously the Court did not want to rule that any false, damaging statements made about public officials would be completely protected either. What was needed was some sort of compromise position that allowed the kind of "breathing space" Brennan argued for while still allowing libel suits in the most egregious situations.

The solution was to create a new standard. In libel cases with public officials as plaintiffs, there would have to be **actual malice** in order for the plaintiff to win the suit. *Actual malice* was defined by the Court as the knowledge of falsity or a reckless disregard for the truth. In other words, inaccurate statements like those made about L.B. Sullivan, where the defendant did not know the statements to be false, nor *should* have known that they were false, would not result in libel.[7] This became a major principle in libel law, and *New York Times Co. v. Sullivan* has been the bedrock case for more than 40 years.[8]

Bedrock Law: *New York Times Co. v. Sullivan* established the principle of **actual malice**, increasing the burden of proof necessary for public officials to win a libel suit. Media have a "right to be wrong" about public officials as long as there is no knowledge of falsity or reckless disregard for the truth.

---

[3]*Id.*

[4]*Id.* at 264.

[5]*Id.* at 270.

[6]*Id.* at 279 (citations omitted).

[7]Concurring opinions written by Justices Black and Goldberg and joined by Douglas asserted that any criticism of government officials should be constitutionally protected without creating an actual malice standard. *Id.* at 293–305.

[8]*Shepard's Citations* is an index (available electronically) that tracks court decisions. Searching for references to a particular case is referred to by the legal community as "Shepardizing." Shepardizing New York Times Co. v. Sullivan results in more than 1,000 citations.

DEFINING LIBEL

Libel is actually one form of **defamation,** which is defined as "holding up of a person to ridicule, scorn or contempt in a respectable and considerable part of the community."[9] Libel and **slander** are both forms of defamation. Once, libel meant defamation that was printed and slander meant defamation that was spoken. The intent was to have a tort that treated more severely widely distributed defamations in print than those spoken harms that were considered less damaging. With the advent of broadcasting, however, spoken defamations could be just as widely distributed as written ones, so the distinction wasn't quite as clear. Some jurisdictions even went as far as to create a new category, "defamacast," to describe defamatory broadcasts as something that were ephemeral like speech but with a wider audience.[10] The major distinction between these terms is the amount of damage caused and therefore the amount of recovery allowed in a successful suit. Slander was defamation that caused limited damage while libel was defamation with more potential impact. For our purposes, the terms *libel* and *defamation* are interchangeable.

Other torts may protect individuals even after they've died (such as the right of publicity or protections against misappropriation, discussed in chapter 6), but not defamation. Common law has long established that one must be living to file a libel suit, although some states, such as Louisiana, still have provisions for protecting the reputations of the deceased on their books. Aggrieved family members cannot file a claim for defamation in order to protect the reputation of their departed relatives. Precedent also has established that damaging the reputation of the deceased does not harm the reputation of surviving family members.[11] There is no "guilt by association" and one may not sue for libel on behalf of someone else.

On the other hand, a legal entity such as a business or organization can pursue a libel suit if its reputation has been damaged. Product disparagement is a form of "trade libel," where instead of an individual a product has had its good name tarnished. In a rather high profile case a few years ago, Oprah Winfrey was unsuccessfully sued by cattle raisers in Texas who claimed that her nationally syndicated television talk show violated the Texas False Disparagement of Perishable Food Products Act by implying that consumption of Texas beef might lead to mad cow disease.[12] The law might have held Oprah responsible but the Fifth Circuit Court of Appeals determined no knowingly false statements were made.

While businesses and organizations may sue for libel, government entities may not. A government official who is defamed has the ability to sue for libel as an individual whose reputation has been damaged, but a local, state, or federal governmental body may not sue for libel.[13]

---

[9]*Black's Law Dictionary* 417 6th ed. (1990).

[10]The term *defamacast* first appeared in a court decision in Georgia, *American Broadcasting-Paramount Theatres v. Simpson,* 126 S.E.2d 873 (Ga. Ct. App 1962). For a thorough history, *see* L.L. Wood, *The Case of David v Goliath:* Jewell v. NBC *and the Basics of Defamacast in Georgia,* 7 Fordham Intell. Prop. & Media Ent. L.J. 673 (1997).

[11]*Rose et al. v. Daily Mirror,* 20 N.Y.S.2d 315 (N.Y. App. Div. 1940).

[12]*Engler v. Winfrey,* 201 F.3d 680 (5th Cir. 2000).

[13]*Rosenblatt v. Baer,* 383 U.S. 75 (1966).

CIVIL VERSUS CRIMINAL LIBEL

Simply stated, civil cases are those where one individual sues another while criminal cases are government lawsuits brought against individuals for the commission of crimes. Once upon a time libel was seen as a crime and there were criminal prosecutions for it, but today most legal scholars view defamation as strictly a civil issue. We could provide a lengthy history of cases, but it would only serve to make a short story long. Most states have eliminated antiquated laws on their books recognizing **criminal libel,** but in the minority of states that have such a statute, none have had a successful prosecution since L.B. Sullivan lost his case before the U.S. Supreme Court. Though never explicitly eliminated by that ruling and we can never say "never," the Court raised the ante for any state trying to prosecute a criminal libel. The result: no prosecutions for half a century.

Criminal libel ■ An antiquated crime in which a publisher could be charged with defamation by the government. In modern United States jurisprudence, the crime of criminal libel does not exist.

MAKING A CASE FOR LIBEL

The most practical way to approach defamation at this point is to discuss the six requirements a plaintiff must meet in order to have a legally sufficient case for libel. As is the case in any civil suit, the plaintiff has the burden of showing that any of a number of conditions have occurred to cause harm, and the defendant has the opportunity to refute any of these claims. Later we will examine possible defenses, but if the plaintiff can't show these six elements are present, the defendant has no need to defend itself.

6 REQ. FOR LIBEL CASE.

1. Identification

It's fairly obvious that someone cannot win a libel suit unless that person has been identified, but—believe it or not—this condition is not always easily decided. In L.B. Sullivan's case, his name was never mentioned. Was he identified for the purposes of a libel suit? The Alabama courts said he was, and the U.S. Supreme Court never challenged this belief.

That's primarily because people can be identified in a number of ways other than just by the use of their name. A photograph might identify a person although if it is blurred it may not. A description might also identify a person if enough characteristics are included. L.B. Sullivan was identified for the purposes of a libel suit by his job responsibilities. If there is enough context provided to identify a particular individual, then that's all that matters. How does anyone know? With Mr. Sullivan as with many other libel plaintiffs, courts will answer the **identification** question by having witnesses testify as to whether they believed that the defamatory statements were made about the plaintiff.

Individuals might be identified even if the speaker had not intended to identify them, or actually was referring to someone else. This might happen either because the speaker misidentified someone, was not specific enough in the details of the identification, or ended up identifying a real person while intending to create a fictional character. Misidentification is usually just the case of a simple error. If Mary Doe is arrested for driving under the influence and a newspaper prints that Mary *Dow* was arrested, the misidentified Mary was identified for the purposes of a libel

Identification ■ In libel law, plaintiffs must show that they were identifiable from the libelous material.

suit. Whether Mary Dow will be able to win the suit depends largely on the other criteria outlined in this chapter, but certainly she will be able to claim that she was identified.

Leaving out personal data might result in more people being identified than the speaker intended. When Mary Doe is arrested for driving under the influence, a newspaper printing that information might actually alarm *several* Mary Does if it prints nothing more than the first and last name. That's why media usually use a middle initial, age, address, and/or a photo. There might be more than one Mary Doe in town, but there's probably only one Mary E. Doe, who lives at 123 Fourth Street.

Sometimes authors writing works of fiction come dangerously close to identifying real people. If a fictional character is interpreted by a substantial number of people to be one specific real person then that individual may claim that harm was done. In 1991, *Seventeen* magazine published a piece clearly labeled as fiction, containing a character named "Bryson" who was labeled as a slut. The author had known someone with that surname who was successfully able to assert that she had been identified. The fact that the work was fiction did not change the potential damage to her reputation.[14]

> **Bedrock Law:** In libel claims, names are not necessary in order to prove identification because context, circumstance, or association can reveal the real person.

Is an individual identified if defamatory statements are made about a group? The answer to that question often depends on the size of the group. Libel is a tort that relates to the damage that occurs to an *individual's reputation* (or a corporation's reputation, since the law sometimes treats corporations as individuals). If a newspaper published a story that members of a local club were engaged in illegal activity, then individual members of the group might be able to claim they were defamed if there were only ten members. But if the club consisted of one hundred members, the court might hold no one person was identified. Still if the club had only ten members, *each plaintiff* would have to bring in witnesses who could testify they believed the defamation was about that person.

If one hundred people is too large a group for any individual to claim identification, the obvious question becomes just how large the group can be in order for an individual to be identified. Unfortunately there is no definite number: all we have is the common law arising from previous cases. And because these rulings come from different states, they don't necessarily provide guidance for other decisions.

In New York in 1952, a group of twenty-five Neiman-Marcus salesmen were able to claim they were identified when a book charged "most" of the menswear department staff were "fairies."[15] On the other hand, 21 police officers in Massachusetts were considered to be too large a group for any one person to be identified in 1977 when a newspaper column stated that an officer had to call for help after locking himself in the back of a police cruiser with a female companion.[16]

[14]*Bryson v. News America Publ'ns*, 174 Ill. 2d 77 (Ill. 1996).

[15]*Neiman-Marcus Co. v. Laitt*, 13 F.R.D. 311 (S.D. N.Y. 1952).

[16]*Arcand v. Evening Call*, 567 F.2d 1163 (1st Cir. 1977).

Certainly there are differences in the cases—the book claimed *most* of the salesmen were effeminate while the newspaper column only claimed *one* of the officers was trapped in the vehicle.

The largest group known to have been successful in asserting identification for the purposes of a libel suit was the University of Oklahoma football team, a group of about 60 young men. In 1962, *True* magazine asserted that some team members used illegal drugs. One player sued for libel and the Oklahoma Supreme Court upheld his claim on the premise that he individually had been damaged.[17]

While not exactly a cornerstone of law, we would place sixty members at the extreme end of acceptability. Yet because we have a case where identification was successfully asserted with a group that size, we must acknowledge other groups of sixty *might* be able to claim identification. It's fairly safe to say any more than that number is out of the question. It's also fairly safe to assert that smaller groups—fewer than twenty people—will be able to claim each member has been identified. The conflicting decisions have come about with groups between twenty and sixty, where it's difficult to predict what a court would definitely decide one way or another.

2. Defamatory Language

It might seem almost silly to say that defamation can only occur in situations where **defamatory language** is used, but as with identification this criterion is not always easy to meet. A prisoner once tried to contend that being labeled an FBI informant was defamatory. Defamatory language has to result in damage to one's reputation, and among prisoners it indeed would be harmful to be considered an informant (maybe even dangerous). A Delaware court ruled that the language was not defamatory because "it does not label one with unlawful or improper conduct."[18] Recognizing that the label might in fact damage the plaintiff's reputation in prison, the court explained that the public contempt or ridicule resulting from defamatory language must be in the minds of "right thinking persons."

Some courts have gone so far as to label certain individuals as "libel-proof" because their reputations are so tarnished there is nothing left to protect. As one federal court put it, "An individual who engages in certain anti-social or criminal behavior and suffers a diminished reputation may be 'libel proof' as a matter of law, as it relates to that specific behavior."[19]

Simple name-calling is not necessarily defamatory language. If the name you call someone is "murderer," that in fact would be defamatory because it is a claim about a person that would be damaging to one's reputation. On the other hand, calling someone "butt-head" would not be considered libel. It might be embarrassing and it could cause the person to feel bad, but the tort of defamation does not exist to protect

Defamatory language ■ In libel law, the plaintiff must show that the libelous material was defamatory, meaning it asserts an untrue fact that would cause harm to the plaintiff's reputation in the mind of "right thinking persons."

---

[17]*Fawcett Publ'ns v. Morris*, 377 P.2d 42 (Okla. 1962).

[18]*Saunders v. WHYY*, 382 A.2d 257 (Del. 1978).

[19]*Wynberg v. National Enquirer*, 564 F. Supp. 924, 928 (C.D. Cal. 1982).

UP CLOSE

Celebrity Justice?

Americans often learn of libel claims when celebrities sue the media over some gossip. When Britney Spears saw her name in an article, "Hot Stuff," published by *US Weekly,* she took offense because it reported how she and her then-husband Kevin Federline made a sex tape. Once she sued the magazine in Superior Court in Los Angeles, Spears soon discovered libel law was not on her side. In dismissing her complaint the judge noted how Spears "put her modern sexuality squarely, and profitably, before the public eye," and hence defamation could hardly result from a report about how she and her husband videotaped themselves engaging in consensual sex.[a]

Some celebrities become the targets of libel actions themselves and may choose to settle before their case ever makes it to trial. A popular NFL football player found his recollections on college locker room activities subject to libel action. In the pages of *Manning: A Father, His Sons and a Football Legacy* about famed Indianapolis Colts quarterback Peyton Manning, a female physical trainer is accused of having a "vulgar mouth." Jamie Ann Naughright received a $300,000 settlement from the University of Tennessee over allegations of sexual harassment that involved a locker room "mooning." When the Manning book was published, Naughright learned of the words against her and sued for libel. In 2003, the Mannings settled with the personal trainer in confidential terms rather than face a public trial over what took place in a college locker room years ago.[b]

Not all celebrity lawsuits make it to trial, but one famous decision resulted in a major victory against tabloid journalism for Carol Burnett. The actress and comedienne was falsely accused by the *National Enquirer* of drunken behavior while in the company of former Secretary of State Henry Kissinger, and a California jury awarded her a $1.6 million decision against the tabloid newspaper (reduced by the judge to half the amount). Burnett's parents had struggled with alcoholism, and she was determined to fight the defamatory report on principle. On appeal the judgment was reduced to $200,000. Burnett was given the option of accepting the settlement, appealing the decision, or agreeing to a settlement out of court, which is what she opted to do. She then donated a large portion of the undisclosed settlement to train college journalists in law and ethics.

So why don't more celebrities sue the tabloids more often? There is a legal answer and a business answer. Legally, celebrities are public figures who must prove actual malice: a higher fault standard than just proving falsity (which they must also prove). From a business perspective, filing a lawsuit just serves to bring more attention to the original defamatory remark. If a celebrity sues for an allegedly defamatory remark, something that appeared one time in a tabloid could potentially be reported by dozens of national media outlets. Some celebrities decide the best business decision is to ignore it.

---

[a]L. Van Gelder, "Britney Spears Files for Divorce," *N.Y. Times* page E-2, (Nov. 8, 2006).
[b]ESPN.com News Services, *Lawsuit Settled; Terms Confidential,* Dec. 25, 2003, http://sports.espn.go.com/nfl/news/story?id=169408.

Bedrock Law: In order to be considered libelous, the statement has to be an assertion of fact and not mere opinion or humor.

feelings—it protects reputation. For the same reason most sketch comedy that makes fun of someone is probably not defamatory language because the people watching it know it is not a factual claim about the person being spoofed but simply humor intended as entertainment. Certainly some humor has the potential to be libelous if it makes false factual claims about a person that are damaging to reputation, but the vast majority of comedy is not taken that seriously.

Yet to be decided is whether comments made on humorous news programs are seen as statements of fact or just comedy. With the proliferation of shows such as *The Daily Show* and *The Colbert Report* we may see a plaintiff claim that a comedy routine is actually an assertion of fact.

It is easy to see some language as defamatory. If you claim that someone has broken the law as a crook, thief, or murderer, then those words might be deemed libelous. Language that casts aspersions on someone's sexual morality is defamatory, so terms such as *slut, whore, prostitute,* and *adulterer* must be used with extreme caution. It's also defamatory to call people incompetent in their profession. Stating that a doctor is a quack or a lawyer is an ambulance-chaser would be defamatory.

While people who have diseases may have not have engaged in unlawful or improper conduct, wrongfully stating that someone has a stigmatized ailment is defamatory. Venereal diseases easily fit into this category, as does AIDS. While that disease may be contracted in ways not involving sexual activity (such as a hypodermic needle puncture) the stigma surrounding AIDS warrants falsely labeling someone with the disease to be generally considered libelous.

In the past much was made of the distinction between **libel per se** and **libel per quod**. Libel per se (Latin for "through itself") consists of those words which in and of themselves are so damaging as to be considered defamatory. Libel per quod (Latin for "by reason of which") encompasses the sorts of defamatory phrases that require contextualization in order to identify the harm. The surrounding language must be examined to determine its meaning. In years past the distinction would be significant in the amount awarded to a successful plaintiff in a suit, but no longer. The U.S. Supreme Court's 1974 decision in *Gertz v. Welch* minimized this distinction,[20] making it unnecessary because courts in a libel case will examine the entire context of the communication.[21]

Certainly there are some words that are more likely to create defamatory impressions than others, but courts first have to determine whether the language actually is defamatory, or merely hyperbole. Calling someone a murderer is very likely to be defamatory, but the word *crazy* is not so easily settled. If a speaker has actually claimed that an individual is mentally incompetent, that language would be defamatory. Oftentimes speakers will use the word *crazy* in a milder sense, not to mean mentally incompetent at all, but as if to say unconventional or divergent. If a sports commentator calls another prognosticator crazy for choosing a particular team to win the championship, it's highly unlikely that description would be deemed libelous.

Determining whether language is defamatory usually requires more than just examining specific words; it requires evaluating the context in which the comments have been made. There have been lists created of "red flag" words[22]

Libel per se ■
Consists of those words which in and of themselves are so damaging as to be considered defamatory, meaning use of the words is prima fascia evidence of defamatory language.

Libel per qoud ■
Consists of words or phrases that require contextualization in order to identify the harm.

---

[20]418 U.S. 323 (1974).

[21]At least six states have explicitly asserted that they do not distinguish between defamation per se and per quod: Arizona, Arkansas, Mississippi, Missouri, Oregon, and Tennessee.

[22]*See,* for example, Bruce Sanford, *Libel and Privacy* 4.13 (2006).

> **Bedrock Law:** The context and construction of the offending words used must be examined in order to determine whether libel has occurred.

often considered defamatory, but such lists are still subject to contextualization. For example, libel scholar Bruce Sanford lists "addict" as one such word, but the term might be used humorously to refer to someone who spends too much time watching TV or loves to go shopping.[23] Analysis of whether language is defamatory necessarily includes its context.

Some states recognize that words may have more than one meaning and are willing to give speakers a benefit of the doubt. **Innocent construction rules** are prescriptions to courts that they can decide defamation cases in favor of defendants in those instances where language can be interpreted in more than one way. Ohio has recognized this rule in the past.[24] Illinois continues to recognize innocent construction as justification.[25]

Innocent construction rule ■ A rule some courts use to interpret allegedly libelous statements that might have multiple interpretations according to the most innocent interpretation, or the one that most favors the defendant.

3. Falsity

A defendant cannot be found liable for defamation unless his or her statement was false. True statements that damage someone's reputation do not fit our legal definition of libel. Centuries ago this was not the case. Before the United States broke from England, making negative statements about the king or his designee was considered defamatory, whether or not the words were true. In fact, a true critical statement was considered more damaging to the crown's reputation since it represented a greater threat to royal authority. That view began to change, however, after the famous trial of John Peter Zenger in 1734 (as described in chapter 4) in which his defense lawyer asserted that publishing the truth should not result in punishment. In the twenty-first century, this is now bedrock law: truth is not libelous.

Without delving too deeply into philosophy, we ought to at least question what truth is, and how we know it once we've found it. It's obvious that if someone has been found guilty of murder, calling the person a murderer is truth. But what if we call a person a crook? If an adult stole a package of gum when he was 12 years old, would it be acceptable to call that person a crook? One might argue that technically someone who has stolen anything at any time is a crook, but that might not be how a jury would interpret the word. Similarly, is someone who has had multiple sexual partners "promiscuous"? If those partners were simultaneous many might say that would be promiscuity, but if a person engaged in serial monogamy (only one sexual partner at a time in a committed relationship), "promiscuous" might be considered a false statement of fact. Of course all of this is subject to interpretation by a court.

Some people seem to operate under the misconception that you can say anything you want about a person if you qualify it with the word *alleged*. Calling a

---

[23]In fairness to Mr. Sanford, he points out that the red flag words "often" are defamatory rather than "always," and that the point remains there is no definitive list.

[24]*Yeager v. Teamsters Local 20*, 6 Ohio St. 3d 369 (1983).

[25]*Tuite v. Corbitt*, 2006 Ill. Lexis 1668 (Ill. 2006).

person an "alleged murderer" may be just as defamatory as only calling the person a murderer, if it isn't true. If police have arrested and charged an individual with murder, that person is, in fact, alleged to have committed the crime, and it would be accurate to call the person an alleged murderer. But, if a person is suspected of murder and no charges have been filed, then calling that person an alleged murderer is libelous.

In order to be defamatory, a statement must be false but what about a statement of opinion that is not provably true or false? To call someone the "worst singer ever" or "the clumsiest dancer" is obviously a subjective judgment. No one would be able to prove whether such statements were true. Opinions are not statements of fact. As with "alleged," though, it is not enough to qualify a statement of fact by simply prefacing it with "I think" or "I believe" in an attempt to make it sound like an opinion. For example, "I think the mayor is a crook" is a statement of fact even though it is framed as an opinion. Whether the mayor is or is not a crook can be proven true or false. It does not convert the statement of fact to an opinion simply by inserting "I think" in front of it. In order to make a claim that a statement is not false because it is opinion requires that the entire statement be a subjective judgment, including the "sting" of the allegation.

What's more, it is not enough to simply quote someone else's defamatory statement with attribution and claim that it is true. As is the case for the phrase "I think," the phrase "according to" will not necessarily protect a speaker from a libel suit either. For example, if John Smith calls the mayor a crook and the local newspaper reports, "The mayor is a crook, according to John Smith," it is not enough for the newspaper to defend itself by proving that John Smith did in fact make that claim, therefore it is true. It has long been established that the republication of a libel is also libel.[26] It can, in fact, constitute even greater damage than the original defamatory statement. In the example above, if John Smith makes his defamatory statement at a press conference where only a dozen people are present, and the newspaper read by thousands republishes the defamation, the republication is far more damaging than the original statement.

There is precedent to suggest that some venues are more likely to present statements of opinion than others and consequently deserve more liberty. The quintessential example is the editorial page of a newspaper. Editorials comprise opinions from people connected to the newspaper. Most newspaper readers distinguish between what they find on the front page (generally considered "hard news") versus what they find on the editorial page, which is opinion and interpretation. The fact that a statement is made in a venue recognized as a resource for opinions might help a plaintiff assert that a statement was subjective rather than factual, but it does not in and of itself automatically make the offending words an opinion.

Falsity ■ In libel law, a defendant cannot be found liable for defamation unless his/her statement was false.

Bedrock Law: In libel claims, the person or entity quoting false words that harm a reputation can be held just as accountable for defamation as the person making the original statement.

---

[26]Injury to a fair reputation by the repetition of a libel and the mention of the name of the earlier libeler is indefensible. *Palmer v. Mahin,* 120 F. 737 (8th Cir. 1903) citing *Times Pub. Co. v. Carlisle,* 94 Fed. 762 (8th Cir. 1899).

4. Publication

In order to damage someone's reputation, a defamatory remark must be made public. For purposes of a libel claim, the term **publication** refers to any dissemination of a defamatory statement, not strictly in print. If someone makes a defamatory remark in a speech, it has been "published" whether or not it is ever printed anywhere else. In fact, if you were to make a defamatory remark to just one other person that conversation would be considered publication, although the amount of damages might be small (we will discuss damages later).

What is *not* publication is when one person makes a damaging statement about a person *to* that person—and no third party has received the communication. If a professor accuses a student of cheating in a private meeting in the professor's office, the student may feel hurt but that would not be defamation. The professor has done nothing to damage the student's reputation to anyone else. If the student then leaves the office and tells a friend about the accusation, the professor has not defamed the student because the professor never published the remark to a third party—the student did.

Publication to a third party is usually intentional but can sometimes occur by accident. The student accused in the professor's office of cheating might be defamed because another student waiting outside the office overheard the conversation. The defamatory remarks were published to a third party, so would the professor be legally responsible or liable? That depends upon the circumstances. If the professor were speaking with the office door open, in a loud voice, he or she should have known that someone else could have heard. If, on the other hand, the door were closed and the professor was speaking softly but a nosy person had pressed an ear to the door and was able to hear the conversation, the accidental publication could not be blamed on the professor.

L.B. Sullivan filed his libel suit against the *New York Times* even though the newspaper did not create the advertisement that contained the defamatory content. Is a medium responsible for all the content that appears in it, whether the medium exercised any editorial control or not? If a book contains a defamatory passage, can the Barnes & Noble Bookstore chain be held responsible for republishing the libel? What about an Internet service provider (ISP) that makes a bulletin board available for comments and one of its members posts a libelous remark? The answer is tied to the amount of content control exercised. The *New York Times* could be considered responsible for advertisements in its publication because, even though it did not *create* the content—it exercised *control* over the content. The *Times* sometimes rejects ads, which serves as evidence that advertisements making the paper have met some minimum expectation.[27] Bookstores and web bulletin boards do not reject content and as such are not responsible for the content they provide. They serve as passive conduits for the communication. This protection is not forfeited if, on occasion, a specific book or posting is rejected because it is considered to be offensive. Prior to 1996 we had common law from a few court cases, but the Telecommunications Act of 1996 codified protection for

---

[27]It is worth mentioning that in the *Sullivan* case, the *Times* was not held responsible in part because the paper had no reason to doubt the accuracy of the content in the ad.

ISPs, which merely make the conduit of communication available rather than serve as publishers of defamatory content.[28]

Sometimes the actual date of publication of the defamatory statement becomes important. Most states have a *statute of limitations* on a libel claim requiring that a plaintiff file suit within a certain length of time from the date of publication. Usually the time limit is one[29] or two[30] years, with a handful of states extending liability up to three[31] years. The publication date for a newspaper is fairly easily identified, but other media's publication dates are not always so clear. The publication date stamped on the front of a magazine is often later than the actual date of publication. Newsweeklies such as *Time* and *Newsweek* appear on the newsstand days before the date on their covers, and *Reader's Digest* appears weeks before the month dated on its cover. Courts generally operate under the assumption that publication occurs on the date when the defamatory content is available to most readers—by mail or on the newsstand.

Online defamation creates a new problem, however. Unlike a newspaper, a web posting is not as ephemeral. Archives of blogs and postings can be easily accessed. One might argue that a defamatory statement posted on January 1 might have been published on January 1, but is also republished every time someone accesses the archive, weeks or months later. Conceivably this would extend the statute of limitations on such libels indefinitely. A federal district court ruled that online libel should be treated the same as newspapers and the statute of limitations should expire one year after the date of the original publication.[32] The irony in this particular case is that the alleged defamatory remark was made in a newspaper column for which the statute of limitations had already expired. Judge David Godbey saw "no rational reason for distinguishing between the Internet and other forms of traditional mass media." The fact that the archives were accessible electronically was considered analogous to visiting the newspaper's print or microfilm archives at the local library. This case may not be binding precedent in other jurisdictions but certainly provides guidance in this emerging area of law.

It is generally accepted that re-accessing a once-published defamatory statement is not a republication. People read old copies of books, newspapers, and magazines in libraries and that is not seen as republication of a libel. Actually quoting a published libelous remark in a *new* publication, however, would start the statute of limitations "clock" ticking again at the date of republication. For example, if a newspaper mistakenly reports that the mayor is a murderer, the statute of limitations would expire after a year or two in most states. If a television talk show host reads the statement from the paper two years later, the statute of limitations would have run out for a suit against the newspaper, but a new libel would have occurred and a new statute of limitations would apply to that televised defamatory remark.

---

[28]47 U.S.C. § 230.

[29]California and Louisiana, for example.

[30]Florida and Indiana, for example.

[31]This group includes New Hampshire and New Mexico.

[32]Jonathan Rhein, *Federal Judge Rules Statutory One-Year Libel Limit Applies Online,* Jurist, Oct. 18, 2006, http://jurist.law.pitt.edu/paperchase/2006/10/federal-judge-rules-statutory-one-year.php.

Blogging Perils

The temptation to vent online has proven costly for more than one blogger in court, and there are dozens of cases where blogging and libel have intersected. In Georgia, David Milum made the target of his online rage a former district attorney, who had become a partner in a general practice law firm. The libelous words Milum used to blog against Rafe Banks III accused him of drug dealing and bribery. It took a jury about six hours to decide that Milum had libeled his former attorney to the tune of $50,000 in damages.

A Louisiana evacuee of Hurricane Katrina posted defamatory messages against the operator of a Florida website that helps parents screen boarding schools. The target of that posting, Sue Scheff, was awarded $11.3 million dollars in damages when the defendant failed to appear in court to contest her libel suit. The defendant, Carrie Bock, who had migrated to Texas, filed a motion to set aside the defamation judgment against her.

In Texas, a San Antonio high school assistant principal took legal exception to two students for allegations about her sexual orientation that were posted on her MySpace.com page. Meanwhile in Miami, the host of the website, DontDateHimGirl.com, faced a libel suit after some of her readers posted comments about a criminal defense lawyer's sexuality and personal health.

Professor Christine Corcos is the editor of Media Law Prof Blog and believes bloggers need to beware of the difference between statements of fact and opinion especially when other people's reputations are involved. There is no question libeling someone online can result in damages for defamation.[a]

[a]Nora Lockwood Tooher, *Lawsuits Aim at Libelous Bloggers,* St. Paul Legal Ledger, Nov. 2, 2006, http://www.accessmylibrary.com/coms2 /summary_0286_23801253_ITM.

5. Fault

Even if a plaintiff identifies a defendant, uses defamatory language, makes a statement of fact that is provably false, publishes that statement to a third party, and causes injury to the defendant, a court may not find the plaintiff liable for defamation. Since L.B. Sullivan's case went to the U.S. Supreme Court in 1964, courts have been required to consider one more element in determining that libel has occurred—whether the plaintiff's case has demonstrated the appropriate degree of fault.

One reason why Justice Brennan's majority opinion in *New York Times Co. v. Sullivan* is critical to our understanding is that it established that a public official who is a plaintiff in a libel suit must show that the defendant published with actual malice, defined as knowledge of falsity or a reckless disregard for the truth. Prior to that time Alabama (as many other states) operated on the principle of strict liability: a speaker was strictly responsible for damage caused by his or her expression. The U.S. Supreme Court changed all of that in 1964 by reasoning that free expression about public officials needs more "breathing space" than strict liability provides. Speakers need to be protected from lawsuits for honest mistakes; otherwise a great deal of discussion will be stifled. In the interest of the marketplace of ideas, this is never a good thing.

Despite the fact that *malice* is the second word in the term *actual malice,* the two terms are not the same. When one generally speaks of malice it suggests ill will or the desire to cause harm. In libel law, actual malice is not related to this. As stated previously, actual malice is knowledge of falsity or reckless disregard for truth. While someone who has malice might act with actual malice, do not be confused: there is no "ill will" test for defamation.

The Supreme Court's 1964 decision was specifically couched in the context of L.B. Sullivan's public role as a commissioner with civic responsibility. Commentary about the job he was doing was certainly appropriate for the marketplace of ideas. The decision can be seen as a logical extension of the centuries-old tradition that the government ought not to be able to silence its critics by punishing them directly or indirectly for publishing criticism.

It's important to note that the actual malice standard of fault established in *New York Times Co. v. Sullivan* does not make it impossible for public officials to win libel suits, as the following case illustrates. Just a few years after the *New York Times* decision, the Supreme Court was afforded a rare opportunity to hold two cases side by side and demonstrate how one defendant had shown actual malice in a libel suit and another plaintiff had not.

In *Curtis Publishing v. Butts,*[33] an athletic director was defamed when the *Saturday Evening Post* magazine ran an article alleging he had "fixed" a football game between his school, the University of Georgia, and the University of Alabama. In *Associated Press v. Walker,*[34] the wire service was not guilty of actual malice when it ran a story alleging that a retired army official had led a mob of angry protestors over the desegregation of the University of Mississippi. Here are some of the relevant differences that help to demonstrate just what might be considered actual malice:

- *Consider the source:* In the *Associated Press* case, the source of information was one of the Associated Press's own reporters, who should certainly be considered trustworthy. In the *Curtis Publishing* case, the source of the story was a tip that came out of the blue from a convicted check forger.
- *Deadline pressure:* The Associated Press is a news cooperative that provides news feeds to its thousands of affiliates. As such, someone is always on deadline. The *Saturday Evening Post* used to be a weekly publication, meaning that seven days would pass between deadlines. While having less time should never be seen as an excuse for libel, the Court recognized that it might be more understandable that the Associated Press had less time to check the story.

---

[33]388 U.S. 130 (1967).
[34]*Id.*

- *Believability:* In the early 1960s it was certainly possible that the retired soldier had led a mob given General Edwin Walker's record of outspoken opposition to integration. Other news stories about the subject lent credence to the possibility that it happened as reported. No one at the AP even questioned it. On the other hand there had never been any allegations of wrongdoing made against the University of Georgia Athletic Director Wally Butts. This one and only allegation came from a claim that the informant overheard a telephone conversation between Butts and the opposing coach, Paul "Bear" Bryant, when some phone wires got crossed. Despite the fact that the *Saturday Evening Post* was told before publication that the story was untrue, it did not attempt to verify its substance.
- *Incentives:* By "breaking" a story, the Associated Press was unlikely to profit. New members join the cooperative to get world and national news. The General Walker story would not likely be reported in order to attract new members. On the other hand, the *Saturday Evening Post* "was anxious to change its image by instituting a policy of 'sophisticated muckraking.'"[35] A major exposé could easily lead to an increase in sales for that issue.

Categorizing Plaintiffs

Whether a plaintiff is determined to be a public or private figure can mean the difference in who wins in a libel suit. Plaintiffs who are ruled to be public figures have the significantly higher bar of actual malice to hurdle: they must prove the defendant had knowledge of falsity or a reckless disregard for the truth. Although the Supreme Court created the standard for public figures, it left to the states the determination of which standard to apply to private figure plaintiffs.[36] A private citizen in most jurisdictions must prove only that the defendant was negligent or behaved in an unprofessional way.[37] Negligence in the law is generally defined as a failure to exercise reasonable care. "Reasonable care" is further defined as what an average member of that community would have done. Thus, a journalist who is negligent is one who does not exercise the amount of care (fact-checking, etc.) that the average professional would do.

Negligence ■
Breach of a duty that results in reasonably foreseeable harm.

One other critically important point comes to us from the *Curtis Publishing* and *Associated Press* cases. In the earlier *New York Times* ruling, actual malice was applied to public officials. But it isn't just public officials who may invite critical commentary that needs "breathing space." Is a retired general a public official? What about an athletic director? It is somewhat limiting to restrict the discussion just to those publicly elected individuals or government employees who wield decision-making power. Other people might also belong to a certain class of citizens who are routinely subjected to public scrutiny, and also should have to show actual malice in a libel suit.

---

[35]*Id.* at 158.

[36]*Gertz v. Welch, supra* note 20, at 333.

[37]Some jurisdictions actually require the more difficult actual malice as the fault standard for all libel plaintiffs. In Indiana, even private figure plaintiffs must show actual malice in cases of public concern. *Journal-Gazette v. Bandidos,* 712 N.E.2d 446 (Ind. 1999).

In the cases following its 1964 decision, the Court expanded beyond the notion of "public officials" to a more inclusive category of "public figures." Public officials are a subset of public figures, but the question is who else should be included. A high-profile athlete or coach may not be a public official but would certainly be a public figure. The Court stated "a 'public figure' who is not a public official may also recover damages for a defamatory falsehood whose substance makes substantial danger to reputation apparent, on a showing of highly unreasonable conduct constituting an extreme departure from the standards of investigation and reporting ordinarily adhered to by responsible publishers."[38]

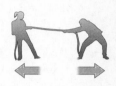

The rationale for expanding the protection of speakers is easy to understand. The tort of defamation is intended to protect one's reputation, but the free expression rights of others cannot be ignored.

One argument is that certain issues are much more likely to be the subject of public discussion and thus need more "breathing space." Another position is recognition that a lawsuit is not the only way to restore one's reputation. In fact, if an individual has the opportunity to publicly refute a false claim, that statement may do more to restore his or her reputation than a lawsuit would accomplish. This explains the reasoning for requiring public figures to meet the fault requirement of showing actual malice. A major motion picture star may not be a public official, but as a public figure that star would have instant access to mass media. When he or she is defamed, a simple phone call from a publicist would get that star an interview with major media outlets. If most "private figures" were to call a press conference they would likely find themselves standing alone in a room with no one to hear their side of the story.

Public figures are those people who can command public attention instantly. There is not a standard list of public figures or a failsafe test that can be applied, but generally speaking public figures are those who would be readily recognizable by a significant segment of the population. Such terms are open to interpretation: "readily recognizable" and "significant segment" are certainly subjective judgments—exactly the sort that a judge or jury would have to decide in a defamation suit.

One other category of public figure exists—the **limited purpose public figure.** These are the sorts of people who voluntarily inject themselves into a matter of public controversy in an attempt to influence the outcome. Imagine someone who is not a public official or a public figure who speaks out at public rallies, demonstrations, and maybe even petitions city hall about a new zoning proposal. Certainly free speech principles would favor the same sort of breathing room if defamation occurs when commenting in this instance.

The limited purpose public figure is a concept that the Supreme Court arrived at through "trial and error" (pun intended). In a 1971 case, the Court expanded the actual malice standard so that it would apply anytime the case involved a matter of public interest or concern.[39] One of the problems with such an approach was that it made actual malice the applicable standard for nearly every case involving a media

Limited purpose public figure ■ In libel law, plaintiffs that are not otherwise public figures might be considered to be if they have gained notoriety by voluntarily injecting themselves into a matter of public controversy in an attempt to influence the outcome.

---

[38]*Curtis Publishing v. Butts, supra* note 33, at 155.
[39]*Rosenbloom v. Metromedia,* 403 U.S. 29 (1971).

defendant. After all, if anything leading to a defamation suit had been in the newspaper or on television, wouldn't it by definition have to be a matter of public interest or concern? Media coverage would instantly make it a matter of public interest, but three years later the Supreme Court reversed itself.[40] Instead of the general application of actual malice anytime there is a matter of public concern, the approach was narrowed to include only those people who *voluntarily* enter the "vortex" of a public controversy in an attempt to influence it. Under the current scheme, it's hard to imagine anyone who becomes a public figure without knowing it.

Through this litany of cases post-1964, the Supreme Court has determined the actual malice fault standard must be shown in defamation cases involving the following plaintiffs:

- Public officials—or those government officials responsible for exercising authority or discretion in the affairs of state. Obviously any elected official qualifies here. As the Supreme Court has pointed out, anyone who decides to seek government office must expect close scrutiny, and not just in the affairs of government. For that reason, candidates for public office, although not yet elected, still invite the same level of scrutiny as public officials and can be considered equivalent. Their activities outside the duties of the elected office provide insight into the individual's character and as such are part of the public's interest in the fitness of that elected official.[41]

- Unelected government employees, depending on the duties involved. It's unlikely a court would find a state-paid janitor to be a public figure. On the other hand, police officers will likely be determined to be public officials by virtue of the work that they do. The more authority over the public, or greater discretion in public policy, the more likely a government employee will be classified as a public official. Those responsible for large sums of money or the public health and safety will always be public officials for the purposes of a libel suit.

- All-purpose public figures—or the world-famous people of our society, the ones who are easily recognizable by almost everyone. Just imagine someone who would be the subject of a *People* magazine story or gossip piece and you have *likely* identified this group but you can't be sure. As one Supreme Court ruling held, an individual might be mentioned in a gossip column and still not be a public figure. A member of Palm Beach society who was involved in a divorce proceeding was mentioned in a *Time* magazine piece. Although the publication tried to argue that Mary Alice Firestone's status among the upper crust and her marriage to a member of a prominent family made her a public figure, the Court majority determined that she did not have a role of "especial prominence in the affairs of society."[42] The fact that a national magazine chose to report on her divorce did not automatically transform her to an all-purpose public figure. Certainly *Time*'s case might have been bolstered had dozens of

---

[40]*Gertz v. Welch, supra* note 20.

[41]*Garrison v Louisiana*, 379 U.S. 64 (1964).

[42]*Time v. Firestone*, 424 U.S. 448, 453 (1976).

national publications reported on Mrs. Firestone, but that had not been the case. Some people might be celebrities in their own communities but not on a national scale, and these people would be all-purpose public figures in a libel suit involving local publication whereas they might not be public figures nationally. Consider a highly paid NFL lineman. Most do not get much publicity outside their own communities, yet their appearance at a local event can bring out hundreds of fans. Mary Alice Firestone may have been a local all-purpose public figure but not a national one.

- Limited purpose public figures. According to the Supreme Court, this occurs when "an individual voluntarily injects himself or is drawn into a particular public controversy and thereby becomes a public figure for a limited range of issues."[43] This category consists of several qualifiers: first, there must be a *public controversy.* A person cannot become a public figure simply by walking down the street and being photographed by a newspaper. Even if the person walking down the street were photographed because of a newsworthy event (perhaps a car accident), there would be no public controversy and the individual would not be a limited purpose public figure. The Supreme Court ruled that a person who engages in criminal activity is not automatically a public figure, not even a limited purpose public figure, without some voluntary action to gain publicity or influence a controversy.[44] Second, the individual must *voluntarily enter the controversy or be drawn into it.* Sometimes this occurs when an individual tries to sway public opinion as an advocate for a certain perspective. Someone arguing against the construction of a nuclear power plant would certainly become a limited purpose public figure as he or she spoke at public meetings, or held protest rallies, or got quoted in media coverage about the plant. That person had voluntarily entered the controversy. Voluntarily entering a controversy may not mean a conscious decision by the individual but is still purposeful. Some limited purpose public figures are drawn into a controversy by virtue of their actions or status. A court ruled that a woman F-14 combat fighter pilot became a limited purpose public figure because of the controversy surrounding the status of women in combat positions.[45] An organization that deals with at-risk teenagers was ruled to be a limited purpose public figure.[46] A for-profit probation and counseling company was a limited purpose public figure.[47] In each of these cases, though, the third qualifier was also met: the libel must be related to the public figure nature of the individual. A limited purpose public figure is only a public figure for a *limited range of issues.* A woman fighter pilot might be determined to be a limited purpose public figure in relation to the controversy of women in combat roles, but she would not be a public figure in a news story about women pilots—a much less controversial issue.

---

[43]*Gertz v. Welch, supra* note 20, at 351.

[44]*Wolston v. Reader's Digest,* 443 U.S. 157 (1979).

[45]*Lohrenz v. Donnelly,* 350 F.3d 1272 (2003).

[46]*Worldwide Ass'n of Specialty Programs v. PURE,* 450 F.3d 1132 (10th Cir. 2006).

[47]*West v. Media Gen.,* 120 Fed. Appx. 601 (6th Cir. 2005).

■ Private figures. This is simply determined by process of elimination. If a person is not a public official, not an all-purpose public figure, and not a limited purpose public figure, then that individual must be a private figure. As mentioned earlier, a plaintiff who is characterized as a private figure stands a much greater chance of winning a libel suit in most jurisdictions because the fault standard the plaintiff must prove is significantly lower. Regardless of the fault standard, in almost all cases involving media defendants it is the plaintiff who bears the burden of proving the falsity of the allegedly defamatory remarks.

6. Damages

In order for a plaintiff to win a suit for defamation, he or she must have had his or her reputation damaged in some way. Sometimes damages can be demonstrated easily but other times it can prove to be much more difficult. If a media report falsely accuses someone of infidelity and that person's spouse leaves as a result, there is a fairly obvious example of damage. If a contractor loses a bid because of a false media report of corruption by the contractor, it's easy to see the damage done. But what about instances where someone's friends become less friendly, or future business deals go unrealized? It's far more difficult to characterize the injury under those circumstances.

There may be situations where all the other conditions of libel are met, but without a showing of damage the court will not find libel to have occurred. Prior to *New York Times Co. v. Sullivan,* damages were often presumed to have occurred if the other conditions for libel were met.

When a libel plaintiff wins, a court chooses between different types of damages: actual, presumed, special, and punitive may be recovered through libel judgments. **Actual damage** is the category that accounts for compensatory awards. Courts compensating individuals for real damages, whether physical or emotional, must award actual damages. Presumed damages are just as the name implies, thought to have occurred if the other criteria for libel apply. Actual damages are similar, but are based on real injuries, including emotional sufferings of the plaintiff as well as his or her financial hurt.

The level of documentation required for special damages is more specific than actual or presumed awards; it often requires precise figures for wages lost or business sacrificed. These awards are generally smaller than **punitive damages** discussed above in regard to retractions. Punitive damages are just as the name implies: an attempt to punish the defendant for wrongdoing, perhaps deterring the defendant or anyone else from ever committing such an act. Because punitive damage awards can be in the millions of dollars, courts will not award punitive damages to private figures in libel suits unless they can prove the higher fault standard of actual malice. In other words some states may allow private figures to win libel suits by simply proving negligence, but the only amount they can recover is for actual damages.

One of the largest awards ever granted in a libel suit was a $222 million verdict in *MMAR Group v. Dow Jones.*[48] The *Wall Street Journal* was sued for libel

Actual damages ■ Also called compensatory damages, this is the monetary compensation designed to remedy the losses suffered by the plaintiff.

Punitive damages ■ This type of damage award is not intended to make the plaintiff whole, but to act as an additional deterrent to the type of conduct the plaintiff engaged in.

---

[48]187 F.R.D. 282 (S.D. Tex. 1999).

by a Texas securities firm for statements made about the firm's dealings with a retirement account. MMAR subsequently went out of business. The judgment included $22 million in compensatory damages and $200 million in punitive damages. Dow Jones appealed the decision and a federal appeals court ordered a new trial and remanded the case. The plaintiff dropped the suit before it was retried. A multimillion dollar libel verdict at the trial court resulted in no payment by the defendant.

In another case, *Penthouse* magazine publisher Robert Guccione and *Hustler* magazine publisher Larry Flynt entered into what a federal judge referred to as a "grudge match." The two pornography publishers were known not to get along, but Guccione sued for libel when Flynt's publication accused Guccione of having a live-in girlfriend while still married. Guccione won at trial and was awarded $1 nominal damages[49] and $1.6 million in punitive damages. On appeal the federal circuit court reversed the judgment because the defamatory statement was "substantially true" and that the plaintiff was "libel-proof" with regard to claims of adultery.[50]

In the process of legal wrangling, sometimes cases are settled before they go to trial, but sometimes they can be settled even after a jury has issued a verdict. A defendant who loses at the trial court often appeals and during the time between the trial and the appeal, the two litigants may settle out of court. When they do, it is often a condition of the settlement that neither party reveals the exact terms of the agreement. Texas District Attorney Vic Feazell was the subject of an eleven-part series on WFAA-TV, where he was accused of being lax in prosecuting drug cases and perhaps taking bribes. A jury in his home of McLennan County found in favor of Feazell in 1991. He was awarded $17 million in compensatory damages and $41 million in punitive damages. The station's owners (Belo Corp.) planned to appeal but a settlement was reached prior to appeal.

OTHER DEFENSES

We begin this section with "other" defenses because the first line of defense in a libel suit is to disprove any of the six elements that must be shown by the plaintiff. If a defendant can verify the truth of the offending statement, the defendant may get the case dismissed even before it gets to trial. In a majority of cases where plaintiffs bring suit against a media defendant for libel the case never does make it to trial, sometimes because there is an out-of-court settlement but often because the case is dismissed on **summary judgment**. A judge will dismiss a case on summary if it is obvious it has no chance for success. Suppose a person wants to file a libel suit against a newspaper because an article correctly reports that person's arrest for driving under the influence. Should the newspaper have to spend thousands of

Summary judgment ■ A final judgment for one party without trial when a court finds either no material fact is in dispute, or when the law alone clearly establishes one party's claim.

---

[49]Nominal damages are awarded in cases where the court wants to recognize the "winner" of a lawsuit who has not sustained any actual damage. The district court had to award at least some nominal award in order to be able to assess punitive damage.

[50]*Guccione v. Hustler*, 800 F.2d 298 (2d Cir. 1986), *cert. denied*, 479 U.S. 1091 (1987).

dollars in legal fees defending itself, or should the state spend thousands of dollars conducting a meaningless trial? Remember in our system of jurisprudence, anyone can file a legal claim against anyone else.

Privilege

Privilege ■ In libel law, privilege is an affirmative defense in which the defendant asserts a justification for having defamed the plaintiff.

One defense against a claim of libel is the assertion that the defendant had the right to defame the plaintiff. Certain people in certain conditions enjoy a **privilege**. All three branches of government hold such a form of privilege, both at the state and federal levels. Members of Congress enjoy a privilege when carrying out the duties of their office. The rationale for this right is easy to understand. Imagine that Congress is considering funding a major construction project. Imagine also that one of the contractors under consideration has a checkered past in fulfilling government deals. Should members of Congress have to worry about the potential for a libel suit if they debate the suitability of that contractor's past? In order to prevent situations like this one, the law protects legislators in their deliberations by providing them with an absolute privilege that their remarks will not be subject to libel suits.

The judicial branch provides a privilege for itself as well. Rather than facing the possibility that a witness should have to defend himself in a subsequent lawsuit, individuals testifying in a court of law have an absolute privilege for the purposes of a libel claim.[51] The law has decided a privilege should exist for courtroom arguments and testimony in order to preempt subsequent suits for libel and protect the witnesses, litigants, and other trial participants even though the opinion defense or the claim that the statements did not rise to the necessary level of fault (even if false) might do the same.[52]

Executive branch privileges are the most obvious in law enforcement. Certainly no one wants to hamper police officers with the fear that an arrest they make might result in a libel suit. The administrative paperwork generated when police write up their reports is also absolutely protected.

It's important to understand that the privileges for the legislative, judicial, and executive branches are based on the need for each branch to do its job. They do not attach to the people outside of the context of that governmental duty. A witness who has a privilege to speak freely in trial does not have the same freedom when speaking outside of the courtroom to journalists. The police officer writing an arrest report is protected, but not in a conversation later among friends. In 1979, the Supreme Court stated that a U.S. Senator did not have an absolute privilege when he chose to make remarks about a researcher away from the floor of the Senate. Sen. William Proxmire had an absolute privilege when conducting his business on the floor of the Senate, and he was protected when he implied that a college researcher was wasting government money with the sort of research he conducted.

---

[51]For example, Tennessee provides an absolute privilege. *Independent Life Ins. Co. v. Rodgers*, 55 S.W.2d 767 (Tenn. 1933).

[52]V. Veeder, *Absolute Immunity in Defamation: Judicial Proceedings*, 9 Colum. L. Rev. 463 (1909).

But when he stepped off the Senate floor, he did not enjoy the same protection in a press conference or a newsletter when he announced the awarding of his "Golden Fleece" Award to the researcher.[53]

Engaging in the legislative, executive, and judicial enterprises provides participants with an **absolute privilege,** but it also provides those reporting on that activity with a **qualified privilege.** A police officer has an absolute privilege in writing up an arrest report, and if any information happens to be false and damaging to someone's reputation, the officer is protected from a lawsuit. If a reporter writes a news story based on that arrest report, the journalist shares in that privilege as well, although the privilege is qualified: it only applies if the reporter's account of the privileged communication is accurate. Some jurisdictions expand the qualification beyond just accurate to "fair and accurate." For example, a Louisiana statute asserted that a qualified privilege existed "where the publication or expression is a fair and true report of any judicial, legislative, or other public or official proceeding, or of any statement, speech, argument, or debate in the course of the same."[54] Regardless of whether or not the rule is codified, it is safe to assume that reporting on any absolutely privileged communication by the legislative, executive, or judicial branch of state or federal government will be protected from a libel suit provided that the reporting is done professionally and responsibly.

Fair Comment

Similar to protecting opinion because it is not a false statement of fact, the doctrine of fair comment protects media commentary about those sorts of things typically featured in newspapers and television reviews. Reviews of all sorts are protected in this way: critics review books, movies, plays, and restaurants and their reviews are provided as guidance to the public. Make no mistake about it—a bad review can cost a publisher or restaurateur a lot of revenue. Still, in balancing the rights of the speaker and the rights of the performer, the law has tilted in favor of the rights of speakers, *provided* the commentary is relevant to that subject matter which is deserving of comment.

In other words statements about whether a performance was good or bad are protected as fair comment but a false statement about the performer's sexual orientation could be defamatory. In a restaurant review, the doctrine of fair comment would protect criticism of the food, personality of the wait staff, décor, and anything else affecting the dining experience, but the privilege would not protect a speaker who made false statements about the owner's criminal record.

The Supreme Court provides this definition of fair comment:

> [D]ue to concerns that unduly burdensome defamation laws could stifle valuable public debate, the privilege of "fair comment" was incorporated into the common

Absolute privilege
■ In libel law, absolute privilege means a privileged statement can never be the basis for a libel cause of action. An example is the absolute privilege given to legislators in their formal deliberations.

Qualified privilege
■ In libel law, qualified privilege means a privileged statement may or may not be the basis for a libel cause of action, based on the specific facts. An example is the qualified privilege given to journalists to fairly and accurately report the contents of a police report, even if it contains harmful untruths.

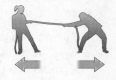

---

[53]*Hutchinson v. Proxmire,* 443 U.S. 111 (1979). Senator Proxmire awarded "golden fleece" awards monthly to what he characterized as wasteful government spending, i.e., "fleecing" the public.

[54]La. Rev. Stat., 1962 Cum. Supp., Tit. 14 § 49, as cited in *Garrison v. Louisiana,* 379 U.S. 64 (1964).

law as an affirmative defense to an action for defamation. "The principle of 'fair comment' afforded legal immunity for the honest expression of opinion on matters of legitimate public interest when based upon a true or privileged statement of fact." As this statement implies, comment was generally privileged when it concerned a matter of public concern, was based upon true or privileged facts, represented the actual opinion of the speaker, and was not made solely for the purpose of causing harm." According to the majority rule, the privilege of fair comment applied only to an expression of opinion and not to a false statement of fact, whether it was expressly stated or implied from an expression of opinion." Thus under the common law, the privilege of "fair comment" was the device employed to strike the appropriate balance between the need for vigorous public discourse and the need to redress injury to citizens wrought by invidious or irresponsible speech.[55]

Thus the fair comment defense protects speakers who provide commentary and criticism as long the opinions are related to topics appropriate for public comment and are not made with malicious intentions.

▌ UP CLOSE

Vaudeville Fair Comment

More than a century ago a newspaper in an Iowa town wrote a review of a vaudeville act, the Cherry Sisters. Although the language is somewhat different from current use, it's hard to imagine a more stinging commentary. The reviewer for the *Odebolt Chronicle* wrote:

> Effie is an old jade of 50 summers, Jessie a frisky filly of 40, and Addie, the flower of the family, a capering monstrosity of 35. Their long skinny arms, equipped with talons at the extremities, swung mechanically, and anon waived frantically at the suffering audience. The mouths of their rancid features opened like caverns, and sounds like the wailings of damned souls issued there from. They pranced around the stage with a motion that suggested a cross between the danse du ventre and fox trot,—strange creatures with painted faces and hideous mien. Effie is spavined, Addie is stringhalt, and Jessie, the only one who showed her stockings, has legs with calves as classic in their outlines as the curves of a broom handle.[a]

The Cherry Sisters sued for libel but the Iowa Supreme Court dismissed the case, stating that even a century ago "it is well settled that the editor of a newspaper has the right to freely criticize any and every kind of public performance, provided that in doing so he is not actuated by malice."[b] Disparaging comments about the ages and appearance of the performers were protected because they are part of the entertainment.

---

[a]*Cherry v. Des Moines Leader*, 114 Iowa 298 (Iowa 1901).
[b]*Id.* at 301. It is important to note that the "malice" spoken of in this 1901 case is not the notion of "actual malice" as defined by Justice Brennan but the traditional definition of malice, which is to mean "ill will."

---

[55]*Milkovich v. Lorain Journal*, 497 U.S. 1, 13–14 (1990) (citations omitted).

Neutral Reportage

Some jurisdictions recognize a **neutral reportage** defense,[56] but many have not taken a position and some have even gone as far as to outright reject it.[57] Simply stated, a neutral reportage defense asserts that so long as a medium accurately recounts all sides of an argument it acts as a neutral conveyance of information. If in the course of its neutral reporting a medium recounts the defamatory remarks of one of the participants in the debate, the neutral reportage defense argues the medium should not be responsible.

While a defense in some jurisdictions, no media professional ought to count on this defense in a libel suit. It might be worth inclusion as part of a defense strategy but has not enjoyed enough judicial support to warrant complete confidence. In the only case to reach the U.S. Supreme Court containing the term *neutral reportage,* the Court did not address the defense because of a procedural matter: the medium did not include the assertion in its writ of certiorari to the Court.[58]

Neutral reportage
■ In some jurisdictions, this is recognized as a defense to libel which asserts that, so long as a medium accurately recounts all sides of an argument, it acts as a neutral conveyor of information and should not be responsible.

Retractions

If a medium realizes that it has made a mistake and attempts to correct it, will that protect them from a libel suit? No, but it may have an effect on the award the plaintiff receives. The whole purpose of libel law is to protect the reputation of individuals. If a correction or retraction is published it can be argued that less damage has occurred. It is also arguable that anyone willing to publish a retraction has demonstrated professional responsibility—something lacking in anyone who has a "reckless disregard for the truth." At the very least in some states, printing a retraction that fits predetermined criteria[59] will prevent a plaintiff from recovering punitive damages (often the most costly).[60] On the other hand, some view retractions or corrections as admissions of guilt. If a medium publishes a retraction, isn't it admitting that it was wrong? Legal advisors are very cautious about blanket recommendations to publish retractions.

One other factor that comes into play is libel insurance. Most news media carry some form of libel insurance as a standard cost of doing business. Typically these policies grant the insurance company the right to insist on certain behavior by the news medium if they are sued, and one of those behaviors might be publishing a retraction to avoid what are known as punitive damages (discussed later). Refusing to comply relieves the insurance company of having to pay any punitive damage award, thus coercing the medium to go along with the insurer's recommendation.

---

[56]Including New York and Utah.

[57]Including Pennsylvania.

[58]*Harte-Hanks Communication v. Connaughton,* 491 U.S. 657, 660 n.1 (1989).

[59]For example, Alabama's retraction statute states that a retraction must be demanded at least five days before a lawsuit is filed. The medium then has five days to publish a "full and fair retraction in a place as prominent and public as the original charge." Ala. Code § 6-5-186.

[60]Alabama, Florida, Georgia, Kentucky. Mississippi, North Carolina, Oklahoma, and Tennessee all prohibit the awarding of punitive damages if a suitable retraction is published.

THE PROCESS OF LIBEL

An extensive national study of libel plaintiffs and media defendants was conducted in the 1980s by a group of University of Iowa professors. Their interviews revealed many critical issues. They found that the majority of libel plaintiffs' first reaction to the stories that bothered them was to contact the offending medium, not to contact a lawyer. It was after they were met with unwavering claims that "we stand by our story" and an unresponsive attitude that they turned to a legal remedy.

Most often a plaintiff will use an attorney whom the plaintiff knows and may have hired for other legal purposes: taxes, real estate transactions, etc. These attorneys are not likely to spend much time litigating cases with First Amendment issues and as such are less prepared for the issues, whereas media corporations are likely to retain counsel that is well-versed in media law and are not litigating their first-ever libel case.

Many libel cases never make it as far as a trial because a judge will dismiss the case on summary judgment, or perhaps because the parties settle out of court. In that minority of cases that makes it to trial, juries are often very sympathetic to the plaintiff. The plaintiff is this poor soul who can show how he or she has been harmed. On the other hand the defendant is often part of a deep-pocketed media conglomerate. The defense must try to argue against a judgment based on First Amendment principles, and has no sad soul to parade before the jurors to claim the harm suffered. In a clash between personal harm and ephemeral First Amendment values, juries often side with the plaintiff.

But on appeal the tables are turned. No longer is the decision left to untrained jurors but rather appellate judges well schooled in the nuances of constitutional law. The majority of libel judgments in favor of the plaintiff are reversed or reduced on appeal. Instead of being influenced by pity for the plaintiff, professional jurists understand the importance of free expression in our society and the history of providing "breathing space" so that expression may be free.

So, if the majority of libel suits against media never go to trial, and the majority of those that do eventually are decided in favor of the defendants, why are so many media outlets so concerned about libel? Isn't it much ado about nothing? Like so many other dangers, it's the mere *threat* of a libel suit that causes such concern. Even suits against media outlets that are unsuccessful have very real legal costs, not to mention the threat to credibility when news stories report on the initial filing of the suit. A terrorist attack on an airplane is a very remote possibility, yet a great deal of time and effort is invested in preventing such attacks. Libel and terrorism are not analogous, yet each is avoided by constant diligence.

SUMMARY

- Defamation is the broad term encompassing both libel and slander. All are false statements about a person or company that cause damage. Slander generally refers to defamation that is not widely distributed (such as spoken defamation) but the line is not clear.

- Although criminal libel is still on the books in some states, no legal scholar believes a suit for criminal defamation could ever be successful in the twenty-first century. Criminal defamation suits used to be filed when defamation occurred against the government or a government official. A government official might be able to win a civil lawsuit but not a criminal suit.

- The burden of proof in a defamation suit lies squarely with the plaintiff, who must prove identification, use of defamatory language, falsity of the statement, publication to a third party, and appropriate level of fault (actual malice or negligence). In addition to asserting a legal defense, a defendant can try to win a defamation suit by refuting any of the elements presented by the plaintiff.

- Because public figures are more open to public scrutiny, and because of their ability to be heard when they respond to adverse publicity, the level of fault they must prove in a defamation case is higher than it is for private figures.

- Public figures must prove that the defamatory statement was made with actual malice, which is defined as a knowledge of falsity or a reckless disregard for the truth. Some jurisdictions also hold private figures to the actual malice standard, but the Supreme Court has allowed states to apply the lower negligence standard, which requires only a showing that the defamer did not exercise reasonable care.

- The republication of a libel is a libel. It is not a defense to simply repeat someone else's defamatory statement and then claim no responsibility.

- Because a statement must be false in order to be defamatory, truth is a rock-solid defense in a defamation suit. Professional communicators are wise to make certain of the truth of any potentially damaging message, but sometimes proving truth is not as easy as it seems.

- Defendants can defend themselves against libel suits by proving they had a protected privilege to libel (such as an accurate report of a government meeting), or were entitled to provide fair comment (such as in a review of a book or movie). Because opinion is not provably true or false, *pure* statements of opinion are protected, although statements of fact disguised as opinion (such as saying "I believe . . .") are not protected.

Libel Forum Shopping

"Forum shopping" is a well-known term in legal circles. It implies that plaintiffs may look around for a jurisdiction with the most favorable laws before filing a lawsuit. Often libel plaintiffs will file suit in state court rather than federal court, expecting that their claims will receive a more favorable hearing from a local jury. L.B. Sullivan might have elected to file his lawsuit against the *New York Times* in federal court but elected instead to sue in the Alabama state courts. In libel cases involving mass media that have wide dissemination, a plaintiff could possibly file suit in a number of places: not just anywhere, but in any number of states where there are at least "minimum contacts" between the defendant and the jurisdiction. A plaintiff living in Alaska who feels wronged by ABC News might be able to file a claim in Alaska, but could conceivably file in New York (where ABC News is headquartered) or California (where parent company Disney is located) if the plaintiff is able to show damage in those places.[a] Shirley Jones, the actress who played the mom on the 1970s TV show *The Partridge Family,* sued the *National Enquirer,* an editor, and reporter for libel in a story the tabloid ran alleging Jones was drunk. The *Enquirer*'s offices are in Florida but Jones lived in California, which is where she filed suit. The editor and reporter argued that they should not have to travel across country to defend themselves and that Jones should have to file the suit in Florida. They claimed that requiring defendants to travel long distances to defend themselves would have a "chilling effect" on free expression. The Supreme Court disagreed. The *Enquirer* had a circulation of 600,000 issues weekly in California and since Jones lived and worked in California she cared more about protecting her reputation there than in Florida.[b] Libel defendants cannot preempt suits in other venues just because they may be inconvenienced. While that's good news for plaintiffs, libel defendants whose communications are widely distributed might be required to spend lots of money defending themselves in distant lawsuits.

It's not just a matter of forum shopping within the United States, but outside of it, that has a number of First Amendment defenders concerned. Americans whose published works are disseminated internationally have to worry about being sued in other countries, under laws that are less protective of free speech than U.S. law. In 2003 Dr. Rachel Ehrenfeld published *Funding Evil: How Terrorism Is Financed and How to Stop It.* The book claimed that various groups and organizations funnel money to overseas organizations to support terrorists. A Saudi businessman was upset over allegations that he and his sons were aiding terrorism by fundraising. The book was published in the United States, Sheikh Khalid bin Mahfouz lived in Saudi Arabia, but he filed suit in England. The Sheikh was able to file suit in the United Kingdom because a mere 23 copies of the book had been sold there. He claimed that it was important for him to defend his reputation in the UK, where he owned property and had business dealings. Ehrenfeld refused to appear in British court to defend herself and lost the suit by default. In 2005 a British judge ordered Ehrenfeld to publish an apology and retraction, which she has never done. Instead she filed a suit against the Sheikh in the United States asserting that her book was not defamatory and that any British decision should not be enforceable in the United States because of her First Amendment protection. Both the trial court and appellate court ruled that they lacked jurisdiction to decide the case.

Should there be restrictions on where libel plaintiffs can file suits? Is it enough to assert that "minimum contacts" exist to allow a suit to go forward anywhere the plaintiff chooses, or should laws require that libel suits be filed either in the home state of the plaintiff or defendant? In an Internet world, media located in one state can be seen and heard in other places. Should a small-town newspaper or radio station have to defend itself in a libel suit filed in another state? Should those media outlets have to defend themselves overseas? ■

---

[a]Plaintiffs *cannot* file suits in multiple jurisdictions for the same case. They must choose one.
[b]*Calder v. Jones,* 465 U.S. 783 (1984).

The Right to Privacy

LEARNING OBJECTIVES

After reading this chapter you should know:

- How illegal recordings can violate privacy, but still be broadcast
- Where in the Constitution the Supreme Court has found rights that spell out privacy
- Four causes of action under privacy law, and how each one is used
- How to draw the line around areas of law where there is a reasonable expectation of privacy
- The elements needed to show that privacy is violated by intrusion

- How the commercial appropriation right is actually about a person's ownership
- The circumstances when a celebrity's right of publicity is violated
- The circumstances when the publicity of private facts leads to liability for damages
- How false light claims are actually more about reputation than privacy

CELL PHONE PRIVACY OR PIRACY?

The First Amendment generally protects the dissemination of accurate, newsworthy information, but what happens when the news content is seized illegally—will the right to free expression be upheld? In the spring of 1993 Gloria Bartnicki was surprised to hear her voice on the radio, which was airing an intercepted cell-phone conversation between Bartniki and a teacher's union leader. Ms. Bartnicki was the chief negotiator for the teacher's union of the Wyoming Valley West School District near Scranton and Wilkes-Barre, Pennsylvania and her conversation with the president of the local teacher's union, Anthony Kane Jr., had taken a dark turn. "If they're not going to move for 3 percent," Kane was heard to say, "we're gonna have to go to their, their homes . . . to blow off their front porches, we'll have to do some work on some of those guys."

Not the sort of conversation anyone would want to air on the radio. Bartnicki and Kane felt that their right to privacy had been violated and sued radio stations WILK and WGBI and certain personnel involved with airing the tape. But who actually pirated the cell phone conversation, no one seemed to know. The package containing the tape was delivered anonymously to a local taxpayer's group, whose president brought it to radio announcer Frederick Vopper, who put it on the air during a news segment.

The key question raised was whether the wiretapping prohibition gave Bartnicki and Kane the right to recover for privacy invasion, or whether the First Amendment protected the radio station and the taxpayer's group from such damages. *Barnicki v. Vopper* made it up to the U.S. Supreme Court, which recognized that this broadcast cell phone exchange was in violation of the Electronic Communications Privacy Act (ECPA),[1] but Vopper was within his rights to make on-air disclosure of what reasonably could be expected to be a newsworthy, albeit private, conversation. The narrow 5–4 victory refined the scope of privacy and the sort of lawsuits that would not recover damages under the First Amendment.[2]

DEFINING THE RIGHT TO PRIVACY

Critical issues from hidden microphones to hidden details about one's personal life inform the law books and case decisions on privacy. This right to be let alone can mean protection from unwanted intrusion by photography or from public disclosure of personal details. Statutes requiring financial or medical records to be kept confidential are part of privacy law, but does the First Amendment give access into those areas that reasonably involve public issues? Internet disclosure of personal and private information for business transactions is often necessary, but when deceptive ploys are used online, does the law makes a distinction for the sake of privacy? Social networks online and other media invite personal exposure through twittering, Facebook pages, reality talk shows, and cell phone conversations. When public disclosure leaves someone embarrassed, humiliated, or worse, what

---

[1]*See* 18 U.S.C. § 2510.
[2]*Bartnicki v. Vopper,* 532 U.S. 514 (2001).

recourse is there to recover under the law? The answers vary from state to state, so it helps to first understand certain legal principles.

Constitutional Privacy   1, 3, 4, 5, 9, 10th Amend

There is no explicit mention of privacy in the U.S. Constitution, but the U.S. Supreme Court has discovered a constitutional **penumbra** enlightening this right.[3] A penumbra is an aura of light shining through a filter like a glistening sunset, as if through a partial shadow above the horizon. Only in this case the light is filtered through the Bill of Rights, and several amendments have been combined to create this right of privacy. They are linked to historical antecedents, such as British philosopher John Locke's ideas about the government's duty to protect life, liberty, and property. They include the First Amendment's right of association, and the Fourth Amendment's protection against unreasonable search and seizure,[4] which flows the British common-law tradition of protecting one's home as one's castle. There is the right to preserve the sanctity of one's home against quartering soldiers prescribed in the Third Amendment, and the Fifth Amendment's privilege guards against self-incrimination, which implies privacy protection for personal information. The Ninth Amendment's overarching protection of all other rights to be retained by the people is associated with privacy, and the Tenth Amendment grants any power not delegated to the U.S. Congress to each state's constitution and jurisprudence.

State Laws Vary

Ten state constitutions guarantee a right to privacy apart from the federal penumbra: Alaska, California, Florida, Hawaii, Illinois, Louisiana, Montana, South Carolina, Texas, and Washington. Article II, Section 10 of the state of Montana's constitution reads, "The right of individual privacy is essential to the well-being of a free society and shall not be infringed without the showing of a compelling state interest." In the Bill of Rights of the state of Illinois, the people "have the right to be secure in their persons, houses, papers and other possessions against unreasonable searches, seizures, invasions of privacy or interceptions of communications by eavesdropping devices or other means."[5] Some interesting variations include Florida's version that rejects the tort of false light invasion, which is similar to Colorado and Minnesota in that regard while New York's law that only recognizes the privacy right of commercial appropriation. Other states have added privacy

Penumbra (right of privacy) ■ A penumbra is an aura of light shining through a filter like a glistening sunset, as if through a partial shadow above the horizon. Although the Constitution does not explicitly contain a right to privacy, courts have recognized a penumbra of the right emanating from the 1st, 3rd, 4th, 5th, 9th, and 10th Amendments.

Right of privacy ■ Privacy rights include the broad categories of rights that flow from the right to be personally autonomous and the right to be left alone. Although the U.S. Constitution does not explicitly contain a right to privacy, courts have recognized a penumbra of the right emanating from the 1st, 3rd, 4th, 5th, 9th, and 10th Amendments.

---

[3]In *Griswold v. Connecticut*, the U.S. Supreme Court ruled the "First Amendment has a penumbra where privacy is protected from governmental intrusion" 381 U.S. 479, 482 (1965). The traditional use of the term was the partial shadow during an eclipse. It is neither a full shadow (*umbra* in Latin) nor fully lit.

[4]The Fourth Amendment provides the following protection: "The right of the people to be secure in their persons, houses, papers, and effects against unreasonable searches and seizures shall not be violated, and no warrants shall issue, but upon probable cause supported by oath or affirmation, and particularly describing the place to be searched and the persons or things to be searched."

[5]Constitution of the State of Illinois, Bill of Rights, Article I, Sec. 6, "Searches, Seizures, Privacy and Interceptions."

Bedrock Law: The right to privacy is recognized by most states in statute, case history, or constitutional mandate, although the legal provisions vary from state to state.

rights to their statutes and court cases so that citizens can protect their privacy by seeking damages or criminal action.

Original Scholarship on Privacy

The decade before the dawn of the twentieth century, a future justice of the Supreme Court and his friend famously argued in the *Harvard Law Review* that the government should uphold its interest in privacy by shielding citizens from gossip-hungry news reporters. Samuel D. Warren and Brandeis based their argument for a legal protection of privacy on what they saw as a need to protect personal dignity.

Boston's muckraking reporters had provoked Warren by covering his family's parties and social events just to fill up their gossip columns. The spread of salacious details about Boston's Brahmin was affecting Warren's sense of morality and decency. "Triviality destroys at once robustness of thought and delicacy of feelings," he wrote, sensing this type of media attention detracts from loftier pursuits by "appealing to the weak side of human nature which is never wholly cast down by the misfortunes and frailties of our neighbors, no one can be surprised that it (newspaper gossip) usurps the place we give interest in brains capable of other things."[6]

By contemporary standards, Boston's yellow journalists were probably less intrusive than today's paparazzi, although the desire to be free from snooping photographers and reporters continues to be felt 120 years later. Judging by the nature of the sort of **intrusions** involved, Warren and Brandeis offered a legal theory that would challenge sensational journalism even today. Their article adopted a principle from the common law that made protection of personal dignity and property quite comparable.

Intrusion ■ This privacy tort protects people from intrusion into their private space and their private data. Since the right protects against intrusion, publication is not required.

Public disclosure of embarrassing private facts ■ Protects people against publication of private facts about them that are not newsworthy and are so intimate as to outrage the public's sense of decency.

Privacy Defined

Personally Autonomous/Ind. J Constraint to Be Left Alone

In legal terms, privacy is actually defined in one of two ways—the right to be personally autonomous and independent without constraint, and the right to be let alone. This distinct reasoning springs from the idea that not only property should be protected, but individual solitude as well, so long as it occurs where there is a reasonable expectation of privacy. As a result, communicators find themselves facing legal difficulties when an individual's seclusion is violated, or when their private affairs are publicized and the recovery of damages hangs in the balance.[7]

The liability for violating privacy varies from state to state, but the RESTATEMENT (SECOND) OF TORTS defines four causes of action.[8] Professor William T. Prosser, then dean of the University of California, Berkeley College of Law, redefined the subject through his legal research in 1960.[9] After reviewing hundreds of claims and cases, he specified the four torts of privacy defined generally as (a) **intrusion** upon personal solitude; (b) **public disclosure of embarrassing private**

---

[6]S.D. Warren & L. Brandeis, *The Right to Privacy*, 4 Harv. L. Rev. 193 (1890).

[7]RESTATEMENT (SECOND) OF TORTS § 652 (1977).

[8]RESTATEMENT (SECOND) OF TORTS § 822 (1974)

[9]W. Prosser, *Privacy*, 48 Cal. L. Rev. 383 (1960).

facts; (c) **appropriation** of one's name or image for commercial gain; and (d) shining a **false light** on one's public identity.[10] Students of privacy law would be well served to think of these actions as four completely separate torts rather than just one. Conditions vary for each cause, as do the possible defenses, so it is good to clearly define the elements of one tort from another.

INTRUSION "Newsgathering Tort"

Privacy intrusion is sometimes called the "newsgathering tort" because it so often concerns hidden cameras and microphones. The offense occurs at the point where the information—visual or verbal—is collected, not necessarily when it is published. In fact, the privacy tort of intrusion requires no further broadcast or publication in order to recover for damages. It is defined as the intentional personal invasion of one's seclusion or solitude. The plaintiff must show that the journalist violated a reasonable expectation of privacy by taking pictures secretly or surreptitiously recording personal statements. If someone is upset enough to file a complaint based on intrusion, he or she either believes no consent was granted, or that the intruder took extra liberties—perhaps even used false pretenses for the encroachment.

Visual Intrusions

Invasions beyond those perpetrated by the news media can be called intrusion. These claims are often grouped according to elements of **trespass,** secret or surprise surveillance, or just plain **fraud**. What happens when nosey neighbors, for example, videotape a person's home? If public agents or private detectives eavesdrop, wiretap, and use surveillance to uncover secrets, can a valid complaint of intrusion be made? The elements of intrusion are tied to certain principles of privacy.

Lawsuits filed over unwanted photography or videotaping must show a reasonable expectation of privacy for the cause of action to be upheld. The location of the supposed intrusion is consequently deemed important to the claim. Prosser held that "on the public street, or in any other public place, the plaintiff has no right to be alone . . . and it is no invasion of his privacy to do no more than follow him about. Neither is it such an invasion to take his photograph in such a place, since this amounts to nothing more than making a record. . . ."[11]

Is Surreptitious Recording an Intrusion?

Two questions come to mind. If it is a common practice for journalists to record conversations, can they do so without the knowledge of the individual being recorded? And if intrusion is based in large part on an expectation of privacy, then what of those circumstances where someone is recorded without knowing it?

Appropriation ■ This privacy tort protects people from having their likenesses used for commercial gain without their consent. *See* right to publicity.

False light ■ An invasion of privacy claim where the plaintiff must show that the defendant's publication, with actual malice, placed him or her in a false light that would be highly offensive to a reasonable person. A false light cause of action is not recognized in all jurisdictions. Often the same set of facts that give rise to defamation claims can provide the basis for a false light claim.

Trespass ■ A common law tort that protects people against interference with their person, land, and possessions. Often the same set of facts that is the basis for an intrusion claim is also the basis for a trespass claim.

Fraud ■ An intentional material misrepresentation of fact by the defendant that the plaintiff relies on to his or her detriment.

---

[10]The RESTATEMENT (SECOND) OF TORTS lists the four claims of privacy: (1) intrusion upon seclusion; (2) appropriation of name or likeness; (3) publicity for private facts; and (4) placing people in a false light in § 652A, at 376.

[11]Prosser, *supra* note 10, at 391–92.

ACORN and Hidden Recordings

In its heyday, ACORN, the Association of Community Organizations for Reform Now, billed itself as the nation's largest advocacy group for the poor. It was formed in the 1970s by ex-student radicals who pursued the lofty mission of helping the nation's poor improve their neighborhoods, schools, and salaries through securing community development funds from private lenders and federal institutions.

In 2009, a hidden-camera video sounded the death knell for the multimillion-dollar community service organization. A couple disguised as a pimp and prostitute, James O'Keefe III and Hannah Giles, showed up in ACORN's Baltimore offices secretly recording all they heard and saw, which included staffers dispensing tax advice to help the pair fulfill a fictitious plan of importing Latin American teens for an illegal sex trade.

The secret video conversation was posted by Andrew Breitbart, a conservative blogger in California on his biggovernment.com website. It soon went viral and showed up on the major news networks creating much undesirable publicity for ACORN. Congress began to pull back on its funding of ACORN projects, and their offices lost support in communities around the country. In response, ACORN's two Baltimore employees, fired for dispensing misbegotten advice, sued Breitbart and his investigative journalists for illegally obtaining the audio portion of the video under Maryland's statute known as the Linda Tripp law.[a] After the hidden-camera operation, ACORN announced it was disbanding its operations due to failing revenues, and the lawsuit against O'Keefe, Giles, and Breitbart.com LLC was dismissed by a state court after the plaintiffs failed to serve their complaint on the defendants within Maryland's 120-day limit.

---

[a]The statute was named for the woman who secretly recorded her telephone conversations with Monica Lewinsky as she confided intimate details of her sexual liaison with then-President Bill Clinton. The Linda Tripp law required that both parties acknowledge consent for recording their private conversations. It placed Maryland among 12 states that have such a law along with California, Connecticut, Delaware, Florida, Massachusetts, Michigan, Montana, New Hampshire, Oregon, Pennsylvania, and Washington. Most states follow what is called the single-party consent rule, which allows one of the conversation's participants to record without the other party's awareness or consent. Along the same lines, thirteen states (Alabama, Arkansas, California, Delaware, Georgia, Hawaii, Kansas, Maine, Michigan, Minnesota, New Hampshire, South Dakota, and Utah) have banned the use of hidden video cameras to capture still or moving images of individuals in private circumstances.

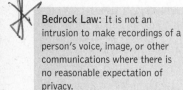

Bedrock Law: It is not an intrusion to make recordings of a person's voice, image, or other communications where there is no reasonable expectation of privacy.

Twelve states consider it to be an invasion of privacy to record a conversation unless both parties are aware of it.[12] This right would apply whether the conversation occurs face to face or over the telephone. The rules generally do not apply to public settings, such as when one delivers a speech. In most other states, it is legal for people to secretly record their own conversations. Of course recording a conversation where *neither* party is aware is a different situation and could be defined as wiretapping, which strict federal laws control. Only in specific law enforcement situations would this type of eavesdropping be allowed. The tort of intrusion does serve to give private citizens a sense of security if they can show that a reasonable expectation of privacy existed in such circumstances.

---

[12]Reporters Committee for Freedom of the Press, *The First Amendment Handbook*, http://www.rcfp.org/handbook/c03p01.html.

Food Lion Case

In 1992, the Food Lion chain of grocery stores was brought under the national spotlight by television coverage that would not exactly bring shoppers to its counters or help its efforts to build Food Lion stores in others states as planned. The chain's unwitting employ of ABC News reporters posing as food handlers resulted in an exposé on network television. In response, the corporate lawyers chose to sue ABC News and its *PrimeTime Live* producers for trespassing and fraud.

The story began when ABC's journalists learned there might be unsanitary practices at the grocery store chain and sent two undercover reporters to secure jobs as Food Lion employees and videotape food-handling practices with cameras hidden in their wigs and recorders in their clothes. They found fish packages redated for sale after passing the expiration date, expired chickens basted with barbecue sauce to mask their smell, and expired beef mixed with fresh cuts for sale to unwary consumers. Food Lion was not happy with the *PrimeTime Live* report and responded by claiming that the network employees fraudulently misrepresented themselves, trespassed on private property, and videotaped non-public areas of the store disclosing internal corporate information. In this sense, Food Lion sidestepped the traditional privacy tort of intrusion as a legal strategy presumably due to its news media–friendly provisions.

Taking this tack, Food Lion initially won a $5.5 million judgment in 1997, but those damages were later reduced to $316,000 and then overturned by a federal appeals court in Richmond, Va. The court held that even though ABC was wrong to get the story through those means, the grocery store chain had not shown substantial injury due to *PrimeTime Live,* and a nominal one-dollar recovery of damages was awarded.

Public versus Private Property

Legal guidance on privacy compares the capture of a photograph to a written description that anyone present could gather of a person. Yet this description by Prosser does not quite encompass the impact of a disseminated photograph, which is hardly comparable to a written description, especially in the digital age when manipulation can enhance the image and the Internet can transmit it in mere seconds.

Writing for the *Journal of Intellectual Property Law,* Jim Coleman imagined that a photographic stalker could pursue a ballet instructor in leotards, capture daily images and details of her life from public vantage points, and then circulate it around with little regard for her personal privacy.[13] Despite the fact that it happened in public, the stalker could manipulate and transmit the image in a variety of digital poses and descriptions that might well affect her feelings of safety, security, and personal dignity. Should this type of activity be free of legal constraint just because it took place on public property?

---

[13]Jim Barr Coleman, *Digital Photography and the Internet, Rethinking Privacy Law,* 13 J. Intell. Prop. L. 205 (2005).

Bedrock Law: The right to privacy allows individuals to file claims when intrusive images are used without consent and there is a reasonable expectation of privacy.

"Reasonable expectation of privacy," as noted, is the guiding phrase courts use in deciding cases of intrusion, and so the distinction between public and private property would be pertinent, correct? Not necessarily. A state-supported university is "public property" in that it is publicly owned, but a student using a public restroom at a public university still has a reasonable expectation of privacy. Conversely, people sitting on the front lawn of their homes, easily visible to passersby, are on private property, but have yielded their reasonable expectation of privacy.

Privacy and the Paparazzi

In 1985, helicopters flew over Madonna's wedding to Sean Penn at her Malibu home and captured photos that were sold to tabloids. Visual stories like Madonna's wedding abounded until a progressive statute was passed in California that prohibited "technologically advanced" methods of eavesdropping on celebrities or crime victims engaged in some personal or family activity.[14]

California led the nation in enacting several anti-paparazzi acts beginning in 1999 following the tragic death of Princess Diana, who was killed in a limousine crash during a high-speed chase while eluding photographers on motorcycles.[15] Basically, the law made it a crime to trespass on a celebrity's solitude in order to capture images or recordings where there is a reasonable expectation of privacy. But it didn't go quite far enough, declared Gov. Arnold Schwarzenegger, who knew personally how celebrities being aggressively pursued by desperate photographers felt. In 2005, the governor signed a "stalkerazzi" amendment that gave celebrities a chance to collect treble damages and collect any of the profits paparazzi had netted by such intrusive acts of photography.

The state made it even tougher in 2009 by amending the law in order to permit lawsuits against the media outlets that buy the photographs from the paparazzi. This action came after film and television star Jennifer Aniston was photographed sunbathing topless in her back yard by photographer Peter Brandt. Aniston filed suit for intrusion based on the contention that she was not visible to the public. Brandt asserted his photos were nothing more than what the neighbors might have seen. The disagreement turned on her expectation of privacy, but the case was settled out of court.

---

[14]*California Law Shutters Paparazzi's Profit*, St. Louis Post-Dispatch, Oct. 2, 1998, A14.
[15]*See* Cal. Civil Code § 1708.8.

Brandt said Aniston dropped the suit provided that he would never publish the pictures.[16] Aniston then led the fight for a new bill that meant not only can paparazzi like Brandt be sued, but civil penalties of up to $50,000 would be permitted against media outlets, which pay for and make use of celebrity images they knew were not obtained properly.

The undisputed godfather of the American paparazzi is a native of the Bronx, N.Y., and is a photojournalism graduate of the Art Center College of Design in Los Angeles. Ron Galella gained quite a reputation for his aggressive pursuit of the Kennedy family and Jacqueline Kennedy Onassis in particular. The former U.S. Air Force photographer in Korea has been beaten up, suffered lost teeth, a broken jaw, and generally roughed up in pursuit of celebrity images. More significantly, he was the subject of litigation that established the line at which intrusion can become harassment.

After President John F. Kennedy's assassination in 1963, his wife and young children became a frequent subject for paparazzi. In the lawsuit against Galella, no contention was made that the family was in a private place but instead Galella's actions were alleged to be so disturbing as to frighten the children. In one incident, he was said to have jumped out from behind the shrubs to snap a surprise photo of John Jr. riding his bicycle in Central Park, causing Secret Service agents some measure of concern. A federal court required him to maintain a distance from the family members.[17] It also refused to allow Galella to use the First Amendment as a shield for what it considered to be harassment.[18] Because he had violated a restraining order, the court subsequently barred him from taking pictures of Onassis and her family.

With or without a guiding statute, most courts find that an intrusion has occurred when "extraordinary" means are used to see or hear or see an individual. If a photographer walking on the sidewalk past someone's house takes a picture that shows no more than anyone walking along the sidewalk would see, there is probably no intrusion. But if the photographer uses a large telephoto lens to shoot a sunbather who normally would not be seen from the sidewalk, then presumably intrusion has occurred. A case from Seattle indicates how courts seek to tell the difference.

KING-TV was capturing video of a pharmacist outside his store window while he was on the phone. He sued after the station aired a news story about suspicious practices at his place of work. The court held that in order for such videotaping to be intrusive, it must be of something that the general public would not be able to normally view. In this instance there was nothing concealed, and no extraordinary effort necessary to capture the footage. Nothing offensive or objectionable about what KING-TV did in pursuit of its video images for this story was observed and the station was free from any penalty. The pharmacist, however, was later convicted for criminal charges.[19]

---

[16]*Names and Faces,* Washington Post, Sept. 4, 2006, C3.

[17]Originally set as 50 yards from Jacqueline Kennedy Onassis and 75 yards from the children, reduced to 25 feet and 30 feet respectively on appeal. *Galella v. Onassis,* 487 F.2d 986 (2d Cir. 1973).

[18]*Id.*

[19]*Mark v. King Broadcasting Co.,* 618 P.2d 512 (Wash. Ct. App. 1980).

The news media are perhaps more susceptible to lawsuits on private property. A California plumber practiced medicine in his home but prevailed in his privacy lawsuit against a national magazine. *Life* magazine ran a story about his private practice based on the notes and recordings of an investigative reporter who posed as a patient in A.A. Dietemann's home. The photographer and reporter used a ruse to gain access to his home for a physical examination by claiming to need the plumber's medicinal powers of herbs and minerals. The unlicensed amateur doctor diagnosed a lump in the reporter's breast and attributed it to eating rancid butter. While Dietemann was later convicted for fraud, he did manage to win his case based on this intrusion. The court agreed he deserved privacy in his home, and noted the false pretenses the *Life* reporters used to intrude on his premises by posing as prospective patients.[20]

There are other instances when newsgathering techniques involving illegal activities can spell trouble for reporters and photographers, even if they are not directly involved. A Texas TV reporter was implicated for illegally intercepting cordless phone conversations concerning a Dallas school board trustee. The reporter was not actually doing the recording, but the court took note of his contacts with the neighbor who was responsible for the illegal intercept of cordless phone conversations from the home.[21]

In another case that indicates where the line is drawn for surreptitious reporting techniques, ABC News secretly recorded workplace conversations of two "tele-psychics," who operated a call-in service for those seeking their fortunes told by phone. The ABC News employee recorded their workplace conversations with a hidden video camcorder to devastating effect, and after the *PrimeTime Live* piece aired the tele-psychics sued for intrusion. The case turned on whether they had a reasonable expectation of privacy in their workplace.[22] The California Supreme Court agreed that intrusion had occurred based on the analysis of their workspace. Advocates of a free press found the ruling troubling since it would seem to establish a zones of privacy rationale that would allow for differing expectation of privacy depending on the workplace.

Two famous Washington, D.C., columnists, Drew Pearson and Jack Anderson, became the recipients of illegally obtained documents from a senator's office. The senator involved, Thomas Dodd of Connecticut, was accused of repurposing campaign funds to his personal use based on documents obtained by his former employees. Sen. Dodd was later defeated in his bid for reelection, but his son, Christopher Dodd, was elected to that office. The court found Pearson and his employees had not participated in any illegal activity and thus no intrusion had occurred.[23] When surreptitious means are used to gather news and the subjects of the coverage file an intrusion complaint, courts inquire to what extent the reporters engaged in unlawful activity to get at the story.

---

[20]*Dietemann v. Time*, 449 F.2d 245 (9th Cir. 1971).

[21]*Peavy v. WFAA-TV, Inc.*, 221 F.3d 158 (5th Cir. 2000), *cert. denied*, 531 U.S. 1051 (2001). The federal wiretap law had been amended to include cordless phone conversations in the home, which the station did not realize when the investigative coverage began.

[22]*Sanders v. American Broadcasting Cos.*, 20 Cal. 4th 907, 85 Cal. Rptr. 2d 909, 978 P.2d 67 (1999).

[23]*Pearson v. Dodd*, 410 F.2d 701 (D.C. Cir.), *cert. denied*, 395 U.S. 947 (1969).

In Illinois, residents grew weary of a neighbor's video camera panning back and forward taking pictures of their home in a search for possible violations of neighborhood rules imposed by the Highland Park community. While the appeals court agreed that scrutinizing for infractions via camcorder certainly could be annoying, it did not amount to an intrusion under that state's tort law.[24] Interference with someone's "solitude or seclusion" defines the tort of intrusion, but it must be judged "highly offensive" to a reasonable person.[25]

> **Bedrock Law:** A cause of action for privacy invasion exists in public places if the intrusion is found to be highly offensive and unreasonable.

Data Snooping

The right of an individual to be free from the intrusion of governmental surveillance can be constructed from the Fourth Amendment freedom that protects Americans from unreasonable search and seizure. The National Security Administration (NSA) began eavesdropping on international phone calls and e-mails following the terrorist attacks of September 11, 2001. In one memorandum and order, a federal judge struck down the NSA's program as unconstitutional. Relying on the 1967 decision in *Katz v. United States,* the Court held that eavesdropping on private phone conversations needed prior judicial sanction, and Associate Justice Potter Stewart felt that searches conducted without prior approval by a judge or magistrate were unreasonable per se, under the Fourth Amendment.[26] This was not the end of the government eavesdropping program. The U.S. government successfully fought back for the right to eavesdrop on telephone calls between American citizens and foreign nationals abroad as a tool in the effort to combat foreign terrorists.[27]

Digital Privacy

Intrusion laws have been enacted to curb wiretapping and to prevent the collection of personal medical data. The U.S. Supreme Court recognized the collection of such details could be a threat to privacy when it upheld a New York state law that required doctors to send prescription records for harmful drugs to a state agency.[28] Another question raised about privacy is whether it can be sacrificed once a citizen has taken the initiative of disclosing personal information to a third party, or perhaps to a public agency in order to obtain goods and services. This assumption of risk carries with it the notion that once a person's privacy is compromised, it cannot be recovered again, but differences of opinion arise on that count.

---

[24]Steven P. Garmisa, Neighbors' Video Surveillance May Be Annoying But Not Tortious, Chicago Daily Law Bulletin, 23 June 2005, p. 1.

[25]*See* RESTATEMENT (SECOND) OF TORTS § 652B (1977).

[26]*Katz v. United States,* 389 U.S. 347 (1967).

[27]FISA Amendments Act, 50 U.S.C. § 1801, in *Amnesty Int'l v. McConnell,* 2009 WL 2569138 (S.D. N.Y. 2009).

[28]*Whalen v. Roe,* 429 U.S. 589, 605 (1977).

UP CLOSE

One Nation Under Surveillance?

In Arabic, the phrase means "the place," but to Americans "al Qaeda" suggests the frightful images of September 11, 2001, and a brand of fiery terror that leaves onlookers in stunned silence. Just what would it take to prevent a repeated strike at innocent lives? Part of the government's answer was found in a program launched by the U.S. National Security Agency that employed tools of electronic surveillance. By tapping phones and intercepting e-mails, the federal government began unraveling terrorist cells bent on further destruction in the United States.

There was a problem though—a federal law prohibited this sort of electronic eavesdropping without an order from the Foreign Intelligence Surveillance Court (FISC). This special court was created by the Foreign Intelligence Surveillance Act of 1978 and served as a means to handle requests for surveillance warrants for uncovering intelligence agents working inside the United States.[a] FISC was willing to honor the surveillance requests at first, but in 2005 Attorney General Alberto Gonzales declared that it was no longer necessary to seek FISC approval in order to collect foreign intelligence under the Authorization for Use of Military Force (AUMF), the law empowering the United States to invade Iraq.

The government's chief lawyer assured Americans no surveillance of foreign phone calls or e-mails was authorized by the executive branch without a reasonable basis for believing al Qaeda was involved. Not everyone was satisfied with the approach, and a number of lawyers, politicians, and scholars agreed that this form of electronic surveillance went too far. They persuaded the Department of Justice to back away from it until new legislation could be drafted.

That new law passed in 2007. "The Protect America Act" gave the White House the power it needed to listen in on overseas phone calls and intercept personal e-mails if there was good reason to believe al Qaeda was involved. It was not a permanent law though, but one with a six-month sunset provision attached. Congress would have to take another look to see if it had properly balanced the concerns for civil liberties with the threat against national security.[b]

[a]*See* 50 U.S.C. § 1566 ("FISA" Public Law 95-511, 92 Stat. 1783, enacted Oct. 25, 1978).
[b]*See* No. 08-01, *In re Directives Pursuant to Sec. 105B of the Foreign Intelligence Surveillance Act on petition for Review of a Decision of the United States Foreign Intelligence Surveillance Court* (2008).

The business lobby in the United States argued for years that personal financial information should be easily accessed for the free enterprise system to function properly, and consequently marketing information about individuals is easily transferred from company to company with few legal barriers over privacy concerns. A federal law enacted in 1986, the Electronic Communications Privacy Act

(ECPA) began to establish some privacy safeguards for online communications.[29] It made illegal eavesdropping on e-mail transmissions unless it was by an employer who had professional oversight of the employee's computer and the Internet access at the workplace. In addition, "hackers" who tried to access files or documents on anyone's computer—employee or not—could be convicted of a federal crime if they intruded without permission.

In 1998, Congress moved to protect children's privacy by enacting a law concerning computer intrusions for times when the kids were playing online video games and visiting websites. The Children's Online Privacy Protection Act of 1998 gave the Federal Trade Commission power to prevent websites from indiscriminately collecting data from those youngsters under the age of 13 without parental permission.[30]

COMMERCIAL APPROPRIATION

In the eyes of the law, appropriation has been taken to mean the use of another person's name, likeness, or image without permission for commercial gain. It is often described legally as "misappropriation."[31] As a legal principle, this area of law is traced to upstate New York and an incident involving a pretty face, a sack of flour, and brand advertising that took place at the turn of the twentieth century. In Albany, N.Y., young Abigail Roberson awoke one day to discover her face displayed on thousands of posters around the town advertising Franklin Mills Flour above the slogan "The Flour of the Family." Her parents said she suffered severe embarrassment and humiliation due to the unwanted publicity. Ms. Roberson sued the flour company asserting her common-law right of privacy.

The New York court acknowledged the young woman indeed had suffered but was not entirely sympathetic to her claim since the law offered little in the way of a remedy. The decision speculated on how another person actually might enjoy the free publicity. Ultimately, the young woman's case failed for a lack of legal standing in New York because the so-called right of privacy had "not yet found an abiding place in our jurisprudence."[32] Ms. Roberson's disappointment, however, had a salutary effect. The publicity emanating over her anguish from the advertising convinced state legislators that New York citizens had a right to privacy, and that it should be coded into law.[33] Less than a decade later, a state court handed down the first judicial opinion protecting individuals from use of their pictures and testimonials for advertising purposes.

---

[29]*See* 18 U.S.C. Ch. 119, "Wire and Electronic Communications Interceptions and Interception of Oral Communications."

[30]See Title XIII, "Children's Online Privacy Protection Act," §§ 1301–1306. Also, 15 U.S.C. § 6501.

[31]Louisiana has based the tort of misappropriation upon both its constitutional Article I, Section 5, of the Constitution of 1974 (privacy) and the general tort article of the Louisiana Civil Code, Article 2315.

[32]*Roberson v. Rochester Folding Box Co.*, 171 N.Y. 538, 64 N.E. 442 (1902).

[33]As a result of the *Roberson* case, New York drafted §§ 50 and 51 in its civil code to protect citizens from unauthorized use of their name or likeness for commercial advertising or profit.

The photograph of Paolo Pavesich appeared in a newspaper advertisement for New England Life Insurance, and the Georgia Supreme Court ruled that the insurance company was liable for damages.[34] Pavesich was not a customer of the insurance company nor had he consented to the use of his image, but his picture appeared in the *Atlanta Constitution* with a caption falsely indicating he was a customer next to an unhealthy individual who ostensibly did not buy insurance. In this 1905 ruling, the Georgia Supreme Court validated an individual's cause of action against this company using Pasevich's name and picture without permission to construct a false testimonial. In the RESTATEMENT (SECOND) OF TORTS, "one who appropriates to his own use or benefit the name or likeness of another is subject to liability to the other for invasion of privacy." The main point of proof in such claims is that the plaintiff's likeness or name was used for commercial purposes.[35] What this cause does not substantiate are claims for appearing in background images of a television story, as one nude dancer discovered in *Puckett v. American Broadcasting Companies, Inc.*[36]

Bedrock Law: Commercial appropriation protects a person's name, image, and likeness or voice for advertising purposes without permission.

Right to Publicity

Right of publicity ■ Protects famous people who wish to protect their likeness, voice, or image from others exploiting it for commercial gain. *See* appropriation.

The **right of publicity** is a parallel claim to commercial (mis)appropriation and it gives famous people the right to control and profit from their likeness or name, in other words, their identity, without fearing others using it to their undeserved benefit. This tort recognizes valid claims from individuals who realize a loss of commercial value resulting from the unauthorized, usually promotional display of their image and/or name in public.

This concept is usually traced to a lawsuit in the early 1950s between two baseball trading card companies. Topps Chewing Gum of Brooklyn, N.Y., and Haelen Laboratories were competing to sign starring major league baseball players to an exclusive contract for their images. A federal appellate judge coined the term *right to publicity* in this case and the majority opinion recognized each player had a common-law right of property that could be transferred to another party and also legally protected from any future unauthorized use. Since that time, twenty-eight states have recognized the right of publicity by either court ruling or explicit statute. Interpretations vary in their particulars, such as whether or not descendants inherit this right to publicity, but the right remains intact.

The right of publicity in California was subjected to what became known as the *Comedy III* test, which held that when an artist's work is "manifestly subordinated to the overall goal of creating a conventional portrait of a celebrity . . . then the artist's right of free expression is outweighed by the right of publicity."[37] In the

---

[34]*Pavesich v. New England Life Ins. Co.*, 50 S.E. 68 (Ga. 1905).

[35]*See* RESTATEMENT (SECOND) OF TORTS § 652C (1977).

[36]*Puckett v. American Broadcasting Cos.*, 917 F.2d 1305, 18 Media L. Rep. 1429 (6th Cir. 1990).

[37]*See Comedy III Prods., Inc. v. Gary Saderup, Inc.*, 25 Cal. 4th 387, 106 Cal. Rptr. 2d 126, 21 P.3d 797 (2001).

Hey, Is That You I Saw in My Video Game?

The National Collegiate Athletic Association (NCAA) considers college athletes "amateurs," since they are given no salary to speak of, although some earn impressive sums for their colleges and universities, especially if they're lucky enough to be playing for NCAA teams frequently showcased on national television. The NCAA also enjoys tax-exempt status, and its licensing contracts are member schools, but it does not license individual student-athlete likenesses or stand in the way of former student-athletes doing so themselves. Their expected compensation is a full scholarship with room, board, tuition, and fees, which can be royal treatment in dormitory rooms, cafeterias, and workout facilities on certain big-competitive athletic campuses, but are they entitled to more?

What happens to these student athletes after graduation may turn out to be a different story. Most do not enjoy profitable careers in professional sports after graduation, and some find themselves struggling as car salesmen, bartenders, or even unemployed. Is it not understandable that after graduation they might feel something is to owed to them if their old uniformed college image is used to sell a video game, depicting them to the T in terms of their height,

weight, build, even the number on their jersey, and home state?

Electronic Arts is a multibillion dollar video game enterprise that licenses its product to the NCAA, which in turn receives an undisclosed amount of money for licenses. A class action lawsuit filed by attorneys for a former basketball star at U.C.L.A., Ed O'Bannon, and eleven former college athletes demanded the use of their images and likenesses in video games, TV commercials, and sportswear be compensated. In 2010, a San Francisco judge opened the licensing contracts to the legal process known as discovery.

In a separate legal action, former Nebraska quarterback Sam Keller sued EA Sports and the NCAA for allowing video game makers to continue the so-called identity theft. Hall of Famers Jim Brown and Herb Adderly signed on to Keller's cause of action. It seems in both cases the question boils down to whether video games are viewed as transformative expressions subject to First Amendment expression or not. Creative artists owe their subjects compensation under the right to publicity if all that is involved is the commercial promotion of their likeness.

Comedy III case, the artist, Gary Saderup, depicted the Three Stooges through the medium of charcoal drawings, and the court found that essentially the value of his work came only from the fame of the Stooges of Larry, Moe, and Curly.

The *Comedy III* test was essentially a measuring test to see if enough transformative elements were involved to warrant First Amendment protection. If the works were simply substitutes for conventional depictions of the celebrity or celebrities, then the right of publicity was upheld. The transformative elements that find First Amendment protection for the artist counterbalance that right though parody, or other original, creative factors measured in the balance. Some courts have fashioned it a balancing test for the right of publicity pitting the commercial elements against the artistic elements. If the court sees more artistic creativity than commercial purpose, the victory goes to the artist and not the celebrity who claims it was his or her likeness at stake.[38]

---

[38] *See Doe v. McFarlane,* 207 S.W.3d 52, 34 M.L.R. 2057 (Mo. Ct. App. 2006).

In a landmark Ohio case, the U.S. Supreme Court ruled on whether a freelance photographer who filmed a human cannonball act for a local television station's newscast had encroached on this circus performer's right of publicity. The clip lasted only 15 seconds, but it was the entire act and Hugo Zacchini felt that his marketability had been harmed by the nonconsensual publicity. He specifically asked the TV crew not to record or broadcast his entire act.

There is obviously a difference between the right to privacy and the right to publicity. In the case of Abigail Roberson, there was no desire to become famous from commercial advertising or other means. In Zacchini's case, the right to privacy was defined by his choice of profession and the issue revolved around his right to publicity in order to control television coverage of his act, not by his desire to be left alone.

In supporting the local TV station's defense, the Ohio Supreme Court took its cue from another privacy landmark, *Time, Inc. v. Hill*,[39] albeit noting a difference existed in the false light nature of that claim.[40] Regardless, the plaintiffs did not prevail due to the newsworthiness surrounding the Hill family's hostage ordeal. Similarly, there is an exception for the use of a famous name or image in a news context, which may prevent a celebrity from claiming a right to publicity while trying to halt an unauthorized biography or docudrama that draws upon their fame in the public's eyes.

On the other hand, the U.S. Supreme Court compared Zacchini's arguments in favor of controlling his personal publicity to be consistent with the goals of patent and copyright laws that reward personal creativity for commercial gain.[41] Once viewers had a chance to see the human cannonball's act on television, there was less incentive for them to consider Zacchini's act as worthy of the price of admission to see him perform in person, which deprived him of a portion of his income. For that reason, the Court upheld his claim against the TV station's parent company, Scripps-Howard Broadcasting Co.

Even the unauthorized use of a celebrity's image in an advertisement will not be actionable if the use honestly illustrates the nature of a product. For example, an actress sued and lost her claim of right to publicity when a photograph of her that was taken for an article about her was later republished. The court held it was incidental to the advertisement and ruled against claim.[42]

Celebrity Publicity Rights

A celebrity likeness complaint was at the center of a famous commercial action against Procter & Gamble, Inc. This right to publicity lawsuit filed in 1992 emanated from a television commercial where a lookalike actor played the role of New Orleans chef Paul Prudhomme. It was part of a series of commercials featuring famous restaurateurs who appear to be switching from fresh brewed to instant

---

[39]*Time, Inc. v. Hill*, 385 U.S. 374 (1967).

[40]This cause of action falls under the tort of false light invasion of privacy.

[41]*Zacchini v. Scripps-Howard Broadcasting Co.*, 433 U.S. 162 (1977).

[42]*Booth v. Curtis Publishing Co.*, 223 N.Y.S.2d 737 (App. Div. 1962), *aff'd*, 182 N.E.2d 812 (N.Y. 1962).

coffee served by Folger's. Chef Prudhomme charged that Folger's parent corporation, Procter & Gamble, had capitalized on his fame without his consent.[43]

The TV spot featured an actor who bore a "striking resemblance" to Prudhomme including the "actor's portly build, dark hair and full dark beard, facial features, and apparel including a white cap and bandana."[44] Procter & Gamble defended its advertisement since the commercial identified the actor, a Paul Prudhomme lookalike. The coffee company further maintained the New Orleans chef had no standing as a celebrity necessary to pursue the right to publicity since Louisiana had yet to incorporate this element into its privacy law.[45] The parties ultimately settled out of court.

In this area, privacy lawsuits usually involve more than just a name used to sustain the misappropriation and right to publicity claim. It usually features the person's identity and according to legal scholar, Dorothy Bowles, "no cause of action exists for an individual who happens to have the same name as another person who consented to have the name used in a commercial sense."[46]

Some confusion persists in this area due to the fact that it is not always easy to define when someone's persona begins clearly to take shape. Two cases, one involving Vanna White's commercial interests and the other Muhammad Ali's image, are good examples. In the former case, a robot appearing in a dress with a blonde wig seemed to move like a game show host to promote Samsung products. In the 1992 case of *White v. Samsung, Inc.*, the likeness was judged to be similar enough to bring to mind the game show hostess Vanna White. The court ruled in Ms. White's favor because this type of advertisement was an unfair infringement on her right to publicity.[47]

The case of *Muhammad Ali v. Playgirl* magazine involved nothing more than a silhouette drawing and a banner title, "The Greatest," accompanied by some verses about an unnamed boxer. Again, the court ruled that even though it was not his true likeness it was close enough. Ali had a right of publicity that should not be taken without his permission.[48]

The fundamental justification for the right of publicity tort is based on the need to protect famous people from others unjustly enriching themselves by trading on the celebrity persona or image, and the effort that went into cultivating that image. In this sense, the law presumes that such fame is based more on hard work than good fortune. Appropriation of the commercial value of a person's identity defines the harm of "one who appropriates the commercial value of one's identity by using without consent the person's name likeness or other indicia of identity for purposes of trade. . . ."[49] Put simply, the harvest of publicity belongs to the laborer and not to the poachers.

---

[43]*Prudhomme v. Procter & Gamble Mfg. Co.*, 800 F. Supp 390, 396 (E.D. La. 1992).

[44]*Id.* at 394.

[45]The claim to publicity used by celebrities who have sought publicity for the purpose of their careers is not based on privacy injury, but rather the lost value of their publicity.

[46]Dorothy A. Bowles, *Media Law in Tennessee* 63 (3rd ed. New Forums Press 2002).

[47]*White v. Samsung Electronics, Inc.*, 971 F.2d 1395, 1398 (9th Cir. 1992).

[48]*Ali v. Playgirl*, 447 F. Supp. 723 (S.D. N.Y. 1978).

[49]RESTATEMENT (THIRD) OF UNFAIR COMPETITION 46 cmts. (1995).

Celebrity Impersonators

There is a key distinction between celebrity impersonation and celebrity parody. In an Elvis tribute show, for example, fans expect to see a recreation—the closest thing they can find to one of Elvis's old performances. Anyone who performs an Elvis tribute concert has an obligation to the Elvis Presley Enterprises (EPE) at Graceland, but what about impressionists who make a living by mimicking such celebrities—do they owe anyone for their creations? In the case of impressionists, the audience is more engaged by the versatile talent of the performer, and such parodies are viewed as a form of commentary with "transformative value" that is protected from right of publicity claims.

The Ford Motor Company's advertisers had a fancy to use the song "Do You Want to Dance" in its commercials for Ford cars. It would only be fair for the ad agency to pay the author of the song for its use in a TV commercial (a copyright issue), but the advertisers specifically wanted Bette Midler's very popular rendition of it. Her manager flatly refused the company's request principally because she did not want to do advertising. Undaunted, the Young & Rubicam Agency hired one of Midler's former back-up singers to "sound as much as possible like the Bette Midler record."[50] A federal court found that the singer's voice was distinctive enough that an imitation of it was an appropriation of her image or likeness and violated the right of publicity to the tune of $400,000 in damages.[51]

Privacy after Death?

Certain rights expire when a person dies, for example, defamation. A dead person does not have a right to maintain a good reputation, in spite of the impact this might have upon the heirs. On the other hand, the right of publicity for dead celebrities has been recognized by a number of courts, and more than half of the states have even codified the protection.

In 1984, Tennessee adopted its Personal Rights Protection Act,[52] which became known in some quarters as the "Elvis Law" as it was designed to protect Elvis Presley's estate from commercial exploitation after his former manager, Col. Tom Parker, sold his interest in the estate thereby prompting Elvis Presley Enterprises (EPE) to lobby for a state law ensuring the heirs have a right to deceased celebrities' images. This law was the protection afforded in Tennessee; similar laws vary from state to state.

California passed its first personal rights protection law in 1984. For decades, royalties were paid for the use of images or likenesses of celebrities such as Marilyn Monroe. In 2007, photographers challenged the law, which provided the rights to photos they had taken of the star to Anna Strasberg, the widow of Monroe's acting coach, to whom she bequeathed her "residual estate."[53] A federal court ruled that anyone who died before the law went into effect could not have willed rights that

---

[50]*Midler v. Ford Motor Co.*, 849 F.2d 460, 461 (9th Circ. 1988).

[51]*Id.*

[52]Tenn. Code Title 47, Chapter 25, Part II (1984).

[53]Residual estate refers to anything not specifically listed in the will.

didn't yet exist.[54] The court didn't question that rights of publicity exist beyond a celebrity's death but rather that a nonfamily member could not claim to hold those rights, which were unspecified in her will. California State Senator Sheila Kuehl soon thereafter introduced a bill in the state legislature to make the publicity rights retroactive, so the same protection exists for those who died prior to the 1984 legislation.

Entire enterprises have been fueled by the earning power of deceased celebrities. Each year *Forbes* publishes its list of "Top Earning Dead Celebrities." In 2010, Michael Jackson displaced Elvis Presley as the top earner on the list. Presley and Jackson, as well John Lennon (5th) and Richard Rogers (10th) reap residual income from their music sales, but the estates of Albert Einstein (8th) and Steve McQueen (11th) depend on their celebrity image or likeness to earn profits on everything from T-shirts to posters. One company, CMG Worldwide, protects the rights not only of entertainers such as Marilyn Monroe but also musicians like Benny Goodman, athletes like Lou Gehrig, and even public figures like Amelia Earhart. The law protects the commercial value of a famous person's identity even after death by recognizing a cause of action for anyone who uses their name likeness or other elements of their identity without consent for commercial gain.

> **Bedrock Law:** The right of publicity protects famous people who wish to protect their likeness, voice or image from others exploiting it for commercial gain.

PUBLIC DISCLOSURE OF PRIVATE FACTS

There is one claim to privacy, the U.S. Supreme Court has noted, that most directly confronts the First Amendment right to report the news truthfully and accurately.[55] It is when an ordinary person desires to keep his or her personal life private and has taken offense at what has been published about him or her. The person can then hold the reporter liable by proving two things—the truthful facts conveyed about him or her were highly offensive, and they were of no legitimate public concern. This last requirement gives courts the right to question the news media's judgment, but they seldom do.

A claim of private facts was thought to only apply to private places until 1964 when the U.S. Supreme Court rewrote the law after an embarrassing moment at a carnival. One of the fairgoers was stunned to see her blushing embarrassment published in the pages of the local press. The decision ruled in favor of an Alabama woman, Flora Bell Graham, who was exiting a funhouse ride when jet blasts of air blew up her skirt while a newspaper photographer snapped her picture. After Ms. Graham's indiscreet pose appeared in *The Daily Times Democrat,* she sued and won on the claim of intrusion.[56] In its ruling, the Alabama Supreme Court created a rule that took into account how it's possible to be put in a public place and have your status involuntarily altered in such a way that it is "embarrassing to an ordinary person of reasonable sensitivity. . . ." Ms. Graham's carnival predicament was not of legitimate public interest, but other cases are harder to determine especially if a medical marvel is involved.

---

[54]*Shaw Family Archives v. CMG Worldwide,* 486 F. Supp. 2d 309 (S.D. N.Y. 2007).

[55]*Cox v. Cohn,* 420 U.S. 469 (1975). Some legal volumes refer to the tort as the publication of embarrassing private facts.

[56]*Daily Times Democrat v. Graham,* 276 Ala. 380, 162 So. 2d 474 (1964).

One case became known as the story of the "Starving Glutton" in Kansas City, which in 1939 appeared in *Time* magazine. A wire service photographer captured without permission a hospital room picture of Mrs. Dorothy Barber, a Kansas City patient inflicted with a rare disease that caused her to eat constantly and still lose weight. A woman who "eats for ten" and still drops pounds might be a newsworthy item, which would prevent a successful lawsuit under the private facts theory. But that was not the conclusion reached by a Missouri court when Mrs. Barber sued and won $3,000 in damages because her personality and image became the focus of the coverage, and not the newsworthy disease.[57] Entered into evidence was Mrs. Barber's vulnerable state in her hospital room, where she was subjected to a barrage of reporters and photographers.

Another historic case of privacy invasion by news reporters was argued on behalf of William James Sidis, a mathematically talented teenager who graduated from Harvard University in 1916 before his peers had even finished their high school education. His early prowess and lectures on mathematics became the subject of a whirlwind of publicity when he was a teenager, but years later his adult life failed to realize the anticipated fame and fortune. When the *New Yorker* magazine decided to spotlight that sad fact under a caption that read "April Fool," Sidis sued for damages because of the unwanted publicity that robbed him of personal dignity. The U.S. Court of Appeals did not consider the article offensive enough to award him damages and speculated that even though Sidis may have desired to live a private life after his early experience with glowing news coverage, he was no longer entitled to be left alone. Besides the magazine had not crossed any lines of truthfulness in reporting his story.[58]

What amounts to highly offensive content and a lack of newsworthiness? A personality profile from the 1970s shows how the legal criteria were applied in one magazine's personality feature. The body surfer's name was Mike Virgil, and he had agreed to cooperate with *Sports Illustrated* on a story delving into his rather unusual lifestyle that included gang fights, eating spiders, putting out cigarettes in his mouth, and diving down stairs to impress onlookers. Virgil's story was published in an era before reality shows had made such antics seem acceptable on American television, and the body surfer was truly embarrassed. *Sports Illustrated* maintained it was an honest depiction of him that was neither highly offensive nor lacking in news value based on the private facts tort. Even when an appeals court ordered a retrial, Virgil's claim failed on both tests. The court found his story was newsworthy and the publication had not been excessively sensational or morbid in its reporting.[59]

Sex and Violence Cases

Those early decisions were resolved in favor of the news media's judgment, but in cases where reporters uncover someone's personal illness, hospitalization, or public exposure of private anatomy, the plaintiff will hold the higher ground if the offense

---

[57]*Barber v. Time, Inc.*, 348 Mo. 1199, 1203, 159 S.W. 2d 291, 293 (1942).

[58]*Sidis v. F-R Publishing Corp.*, 113 F. 2d 806 (2d Cir. 1940).

[59]*Virgil v. Time, Inc.* 424 F. Supp. 1286, 1289 (S.D. Cal. 1976).

is high enough. Further complicating this cause of action are local sensitivities though, where a highly offensive account in one place and time might seem far less so in another.

The legal defenses common to the private facts tort extend beyond the public's interest in the information. They include personal consent, and the existence of public records to verify the information involved, which would make it no longer private. The identity of a juvenile, for example, would not be considered actionable if the information were taken from a public record even though a law prohibited such a disclosure. Two cases stand out as instructive when courts encounter sensitive areas of law dealing with private facts involving juveniles and victims of sexual crimes. In *Smith v. Daily Mail Publishing Co.*, two newspapers were prosecuted for violating a West Virginia statute that prohibited naming a juvenile charged with a crime without prior approval—in this case a shooting death at a junior high school.[60] The Supreme Court held West Virginia could not forbid such truthful publications unless it could show a substantial state interest that such an abridgement of press freedom would serve. Writing for the majority, Chief Justice Burger in his majority opinion noted state actions to "punish the publication of truthful information seldom can satisfy constitutional standards."[61]

What could be more emotionally distressing for a parent than losing their child to a criminal act, and then discovering the lasting impression of their daughter left on local television would be as a victim of rape and murder? In the case of *Cox Broadcasting Corp. v. Cohn*, the U.S. Supreme Court had to determine if an Atlanta television station had run afoul in its coverage of a 17-year-old girl's death, and identifying her by name.[62] The victim's father sued the owners of WTSB-TV for invading his zone of privacy, and the Court had to draw the constitutional lines for such privacy lawsuits. News media joined with Cox Communications and filed *amicus curiae* briefs asking the Court to ensure the principle of reporting truthfully facts obtained from open judicial records was protected since the television reporter encountered the woman's name in a court indictment open to public inspection. The high court was aware that Georgia had a law preventing the naming of rape victims, but established the principle in Justice White's ruling there would be no standing to sue under these circumstances.

> We are reluctant to embark on a course that would make public records generally available to the media but forbid their publication if offensive to the sensibilities of the supposed reasonable man. Such a rule would make it very difficult for the media to inform citizens about the public business and yet stay within the law. The rule would invite timidity and self-censorship and very likely lead to the suppression of many items that would otherwise be published and that should be made available to the public. At the very least, the First and Fourteenth Amendments will not allow exposing the press to liability for truthfully publishing information released to the public in official court records.[63]

---

[60]443 U.S. 97 (1979).

[61]*Id.* at 102.

[62]420 U.S. 469 (1975).

[63]*Id.* at 494–95.

The *Florida Star* case

A Florida woman was raped and a newspaper reporter in training discovered her name in a county sheriff's report that was made available to everyone in the pressroom. After the newspaper mistakenly published the brief account of her attack with the victim's name, she began receiving threatening phone calls. The woman identified only as B.J.F. sued the newspaper for making the facts of her assault a familiar item to her community and well beyond it. There was a Florida statute preventing such disclosures, and the newspaper admitted it even had a policy of its own against that type of coverage, but the use of the woman's name was inadvertent. The victim sued and testified that she felt twice victimized by the news coverage. B.J.F. won at the state court level, but encountered a different hearing when her case reached the U.S. Supreme Court.

The majority opinion by Associate Justice Thurgood Marshall was based on a different precedent. The Court reviewed three earlier decisions that could be applied to the Florida case, and then discussed which one was the correct precedent.[64] Since the newspaper obtained truthful information from sheriff's officials about a matter of public significance, should the press be punished for what amounted to a government mistake? Furthermore, the state law mentioned mass communication outlets, and failed to determine how "smalltime disseminators" could do even more damage with such a disclosure, depending upon their interpersonal contacts.[65] The Court also noted flaws in the Florida statute since it overlooked the standard of highly offensive content as well as the possibility of prior disclosure by other sources. Taken together, these facts did not bode well for B.J.F., who did not prevail in her lawsuit despite the fact there was a law against the disclosure of rape victims' names in Florida. This time the private facts came from an official public source, and the news media was not held liable.

> **Bedrock Law:** It is not publication of a private fact if the fact has been made public, or if it is part of the public record. That which is public cannot be made private.

Embarrassing private facts that are deemed newsworthy will not yield the recovery of damages in most circumstances, but particularly if a crime is involved. This hurdle of public interest was easily overcome in *Cinel v. Connick*.[66] A Roman Catholic priest, Dino Cinel of St. Rita's Catholic Church, found himself at the center of a sex scandal in 1988. One of his fellow priests discovered in his room at the rectory an assortment of gay paraphernalia, including a videotape of a priest engaged in sexual activity. The church handed over the materials to the Orleans Parish District Attorney's office for prosecution, but a copy of the homemade videotape also found its way to the news media. Two television news programs,

---

[64]The Court did not agree with the reliance upon *Cox v. Cohn* because even though both cases dealt with disclosure of a rape victim's name, the *Cohn* case involved a pending trial and the "important role the press plays in subjecting trials to public scrutiny and thereby helping guarantee their fairness." The decision in the *Florida Star* case rested instead on the *Daily Mail* case. Basically, the reason given for the ruling in the newspaper's favor was that upholding the law would cause some "timidity and self-censorship" by placing newspaper reporters in the position of trying to guess each time a public document is made available whether they can use the facts revealed.

[65]*The Florida Star v. B.J.F.*, 491 U.S. 524 (1989).

[66]15 F. 3d 1338 (5th Cir. 1994).

▶ UP CLOSE

HIPAA Rules

The Health Insurance Portability and Accountability Act (HIPAA) was a law co-sponsored by Sen. Edward Kennedy (D-Mass.) and Sen. Nancy Kassebaum (R-Kan.) as a means for protecting health insurance coverage for Americans who lose their jobs or have to move and could benefit from electronic data exchange in the health care system.[a] The law was amended in 2003, however, to create a zone of privacy for "Protected Health Information" or PHI. This confidential information includes health status and payment for health care and has been liberally interpreted to mean almost any part of a person's medical record.

This rule requires certain health care providers take steps to ensure the confidentiality of communications with patients, which is Americans are asked to sign a document when they visit their personal physician regarding the medical information they want to keep confidential.

What was not foreseen was the chilling effect this new rule would have on breaking news coverage in cases where emergency health care information was involved. Journalists found their ability to accurately report on fires, accidents and disasters frustrated by HIPAA. For example, a Chicago porch collapse that

harmed and killed local citizens received only sketchy coverage because the news media had no way of conveying the victims' names or those who had been injured in the collapse.[b]

Then-president of the Radio-Television News Directors Association (RTNDA), Barbara Cochran, testified before the National Committee on Vital and Health Statistics that the privacy rule under HIPAA had impeded newsgathering efforts, "particularly in times of emergency, disaster, and other events of high public interest."[c] The unintended consequence of this law, Cochran noted, was to have the government drop a "blanket of secrecy" over events of public interest, where victims of crime or disasters were being treated in the hospital while friends and family worried over their status or even their whereabouts. She noted misinterpretations of the privacy rule had kept reporters from uncovering corruption and mismanagement at hospitals and other publicly funded health care facilities. The rule even influenced sports coverage with some universities announcing that because of HIPAA's privacy provision, the athletic department would no longer release information about the injuries of college athletes.

[a]HIPAA, Pub. L. No. 104-191 (1996).
[b]See Andrew M. Mar & Allison Page Howard, *HIPAA and Newsgathering*, The First Amendment Center, http://www.firstamendmentcenter.org/Press/topic.aspx?topic=hipaa_news.
[c]See Proceedings of Department of Health and Human Services, National Committee on Vital and Health Statistics, Subcommittee on Privacy and Confidentiality, 14 July 2004, http://www.ncvhs.hhs.gov/040714tr.htm.

including one featuring Geraldo Rivera, *Now It Can Be Told,* used the video to tell of the salacious activities and broadcast certain scenes from it.

The priest sued for this public disclosure of his private life and sought to recover damages from both the District Attorney of Orleans Parish and the news media outlets involved. The court agreed the scenes broadcast were embarrassing and normally constituted a private activity, but it also held that Cinel's predicament was a matter of legitimate public interest relating to criminal conduct.[67]

---

[67]The former priest could be prosecuted for violating the state's sodomy statute, La. Rev. Stat. Sec. 14:89 (West 1989).

The U.S. Court of Appeals for the Fifth Circuit cited decisions in support of this conclusion, including *Ross v. Midwest Communications, Inc.*, where "judges, acting with the benefit of hindsight, must resist the temptation to edit journalists aggressively."[68] The *Cinel* case underscored the legal principle that even though embarrassing private facts are offensive, the reasonableness of public disclosure by the news media will be sustained without any recovery of damages if the material is deemed newsworthy and involves the possible commission of a crime.

When a 30-year-old woman was attacked in a Baton Rouge Laundromat in 1983, she objected to the publicity surrounding her assault and sued both the newspaper and the police department for their accounts of the incident. Sandra K. (Sandy) Batts was unloading her laundry when she suddenly found herself struggling in the clutches of a young and "very short" male. Ms. Batts bit her assailant's hand, and he then took aim with a small caliber pistol and shot her in the shoulder. She escaped serious injury, but was mortified to see her ordeal reported in the newspaper's evening edition.[69] She sued, but because the assault's occurrence in a public laundry facility made it a newsworthy event lawfully obtained from police records, the suit did not prevail.

FALSE LIGHT INVASION OF PRIVACY

One of the more intriguing areas of privacy law involves false light publicity, which is sometimes linked with defamation lawsuits. Although not recognized by all states, false light actions can in some ways resemble defamation claims. Both civil actions require a showing of publication and identification. That means plaintiffs must bring evidence indicating they were clearly identified by some form of media content. The important difference is that plaintiffs need not prove their reputation was harmed.

A false light infraction usually occurs when undesirable media attention places someone in the public eye in an inaccurate and untrue light, and in a way that would be considered "highly offensive to a reasonable person." This distortion can be either the result of an embellishment of the truth or maybe just the inaccuracy of a few key details. Similar to libel claims, it also may require from the plaintiff a showing of actual malice. If the defendant acted with "reckless disregard as to the falsity of the publicized matter and the false light in which it was placed," then damages could be the result.[70]

Journalistic Embellishment

Whenever a journalist stretches the truth in a narrative, for example, so that it is enhanced to the extent that it brings about personal offense, the U.S. Supreme Court could find that a valid claim exists. Screenwriter Joe Eszterhas[71] early in his

---

[68]870 F. 2d 271, 275 (5th Cir. 1989).

[69]*Batts v. City of Baton Rouge*, 501 So. 2d 302 (La Ct. App. 1986), *writ denied*, 503 So. 2d 482 (1987).

[70]RESTATEMENT (SECOND) OF TORTS § 652E (1977).

[71]Eszterhaz, who later became famous for scripting *Flashdance* and the *Basic Instinct* movies, argued his case before the Court.

career worked as a reporter for the *Cleveland Plain Dealer* and was assigned to cover a story about the rush-hour collapse of the Silver Bridge on the Ohio River that took the lives of at least 44 people in 1967.

Among those suffering from this accident months after the fact was Mrs. Margaret Cantrell, who lost her husband when the weight of the cars caused the bridge to buckle and bend into the water. Eszterhas appeared at her home for an interview eight months after the tragedy to complete his follow-up on the story, but Mrs. Cantrell was away from the house at that time. Some of her children were present, however, so Eszterhas decided to use their descriptions along with his own contrived and fanciful images of their mother, whom he described as a "proud woman," who "wears the same mask of non-expression she wore at the funeral."

After the story was published, Mrs. Cantrell was taken back by this fictionalized portrayal. Her feeling of violation led to a famous suit for false light invasion of privacy that produced a $60,000 judgment for damages. The case made it the U.S. Supreme Court that ruled Eszterhaz knowingly included falsehoods in his article, "Legacy of the Silver Bridge," in *The Plain Dealer* of Cleveland about the widow of Melvin Cantrell, including inaccuracies that Mrs. Cantrell had refused money from townspeople and her family was living in dirty and dilapidated conditions.[72]

Actual Malice Test

The defense failed to protect the *Plain Dealer's* publisher. The opposite appeared to be the case in an earlier landmark ruling when James J. Hill's legal counsel sued *Life* magazine's publisher, Time, Inc. *Life* had run a sensational story about three escaped convicts who held the Hill family hostage in their home for 19 hours, and yet eventually released them physically unharmed. Two of the three criminals later died in a shootout. Novelist Joseph Hays later investigated the crime in order to publish a book about the night of terror. It subsequently was produced as both a film and Broadway loosely related to the real-life scenarios portrayed by Hays in his book, *The Desperate Hours.*

When actors from a Broadway play appeared in Hill's former house in suburban Philadelphia (the family had moved to Connecticut soon after the nightmarish ordeal), a photographer captured the actors in poses suggestive of the Broadway play's fictionalized scenes. Hill sued because of those false portrayals of violence that were supposedly inflicted on the "Hilliard" family.[73] The Court ruled against the Hill family's false light claims. It drew upon the actual malice test that meant false light cases involving matters of public interest must be guided by the same logic that was applied in *New York Times Co. v. Sullivan.*[74] That is, the plaintiff must show that the false report was published with knowledge of its falsity or with reckless disregard of the truth. The Hills had not achieved this level of proof.

False light invasions of privacy may involve the videotaping of sequences taken out of context sometimes to the embarrassment of extras appearing in a

---

[72]*Cantrell v. Forest City Publishing Co.,* 419 U.S. 245 (1974).

[73]*Time, Inc. v. Hill,* 385 U.S. 374 (1967).

[74]*New York Times Co. v. Sullivan,* 376 U.S. 254 (1964).

made-for-television movie. Volunteers for the Easter Seal Society of New Orleans agreed to stage a Mardi-Gras style parade and Dixieland celebration for the television cameras of the local PBS station. The goal was to help raise money, and a 17-minute videotape was produced and broadcast nationally as part of the Easter Seal Telethon. Afterward, WYES-TV kept the field tapes on file and used sequences to add color to programs such as the Dixieland Jazz series that the PBS station later broadcast. Trouble appeared in the form of a filmmaker who wanted to repurpose the Mardi Gras scenes for his project.

WYES-TV's director of broadcasting agreed to the request from the Canadian producer asking for stock footage of a Mardi Gras parade unaware that he planned to use portions of the staged Mardi Gras scenes as backdrop for a soft-core pornography film entitled *Candy, the Stripper*. The Playboy film focused on sex and drugs causing no small embarrassment for the Easter Seal Society for Crippled Children and Adults. Because the parade scenes were used only as a backdrop, and there was no embellishment or distortion involved, the court ruled there was no false light portrayal.[75]

> **Bedrock Law:** False light claims require a showing of distortion or embellishment of the truth that is not necessarily defamatory but highly offensive.

SUMMARY

- The U.S. Supreme Court recognizes unauthorized wiretapping by a third party is an invasive and unlawful act, but it holds no liability for communicators who had nothing to do with the illegal wiretapping but convey the intercepted messages of public interest.

- In the Bill of Right guarantees of association, due process, freedom from self-incrimination, unreasonable search or seizure, peacetime prohibition of soldiers quartering in homes, the Supreme Court found a constitutional basis for privacy.

- Causes of action for privacy rights include intrusion upon personal solitude; public disclosure of private facts; commercial appropriation of one's image or identity; and placing someone under a false light.

- Zones of privacy specified in claims of intrusion typically cover newsgathering techniques, where journalists record images, sounds, and voices without consent.

- Intrusion claims prevail when private property is involved and the means of intrusion—the newsgathering technique—is highly offensive.

- Personal ownership of one's identity including name, likeness, sound, or image is protected from others making a profit by it without consent.

- A celebrity's right of publicity is violated when another's use of likeness or image enhances their product without any transformative value involved or newsworthy interest.

- Ordinary people incensed about the unnecessary exposure of their personal life in the media can recover for damages when the truthful facts conveyed about them are highly offensive and of no legitimate public concern.

- False light claims are the least recognized of the privacy rights. Similar to libel, evidence of publication, identification, and falsity is required, usually with actual malice. Instead of harm to reputation though, it covers highly offensive, embarrassing errors.

---

[75]*Easter Seal Soc'y for Crippled Children & Adults of La., Inc. v. Playboy Enters.*, 530 So. 2d 643 (La. Ct. App. 1988), *writ denied*, 532 So. 2d 1390 (1988).

The Hurt Locker

Hollywood's big night of star-studded glamour, the Academy Awards, is seldom lacking in controversy. In 2010, the 82nd night at the Oscars proved to be no exception. *The Hurt Locker* was a big winner with six Oscars including Best Picture and Best Director, but it was also the subject of a lawsuit based on its portrayal of a master sergeant, who dangerously defused bombs during the War in Iraq. In the film, the soldier is named Sgt. Will James, but in the eyes of a Clarksville, Tennessee, veteran, the story is actually about him, Sgt. Jeffrey S. Sarver.

Journalist Marc Boal interviewed Sarver in 2004 for a *Playboy* magazine article titled, "The Man in the Bomb Suit." When Boal converted his magazine piece to a movie screenplay, he described it as a fictional work based on the lives of several soldiers. Sarver saw it as his story, used without consent and without any profit. He sued on six counts, including invasion of privacy and misappropriation of his name and likeness. He asked for a total of $450,000 in damages.

The legal question boils down to Sarver's theory that he is owed a right to publicity for a work alleged to be a fictional composite. Hollywood screenwriters do seek releases for an individual's life story, but Boal made no such arrangement with Sarver in order to take liberties with his story and others he used in producing the movie. His defense could be the transformative nature of creating a feature screenplay is essentially a work of fiction that goes well beyond a simple television commercial or product advertisement that draws upon a personal likeness for its success. ■

Obscenity and Indecency

LEARNING OBJECTIVES

After reading this chapter you should know:

- The definition of obscenity by both its historic and modern terms

- How to apply the three-pronged test the Supreme Court uses to determine what is obscene or what is just offensive

- The legal distinction between the sale and marketing of pornography and the personal ownership of it

- How to judge the different standards for obscenity based on the age of the consumer

- The law's regard for child pornography is not necessarily obscenity

- How to identify the solution used to restrict access of pornography in public libraries

- Where to draw the line on erotic dancing deserving First Amendment protection

- The difference between indecency and obscenity and how legal limits vary by media channel

- The laws enacted to deal with sexual and violent content in video games

SEVEN DIRTY WORDS

When iconic comedian George Carlin was posthumously awarded the 11th Annual Mark Twain Prize for American Humor in November 2008 at the Kennedy Center for the Performing Arts in Washington, D.C., humorist Bill Maher introduced the event saying, "Well, what can you say about George Carlin that hasn't already been argued before the Supreme Court?"

Indeed, the once buttoned-down, family-friendly comedian whose act was a popular staple of 1960s television variety and talk shows reinvented himself in the early 1970s. He emerged from his metamorphosis a long-haired, iconoclastic, self-described class clown whose profane satirical witticisms cast searing commentary on societal foibles and human failings.

It was a track from a 1973 comedy album after that transformation that led to the landmark Supreme Court case, *Federal Communications Comm'n v. Pacifica Found.*[1] Rife with profane language, the 12-minute track, an expansion of Carlin's earlier bit titled, "Seven Words You Can Never Say on Television," was broadcast on New York radio station WBAI-FM at 2:00 in the afternoon. A father, driving a car with his young son, complained to the **Federal Communications Commission** about the content of the radio program and the agency, in response, sent the station's owner a letter of reprimand, alleging that the station violated FCC prohibitions against transmitting indecent material.

Pacifica Foundation appealed and the U.S. Court of Appeals for the District of Columbia concluded in 1975 that the FCC's order constituted censorship and reversed the Commission's finding. The FCC appealed; in 1978 the Supreme Court ruled 5–4 that Carlin's routine was "indecent" and gave the FCC broad authority to both prohibit such broadcasts during times when children might be awake and to shield children and sensitive adults from "patently offensive material.

The case cemented the government's role in regulating broadcast speech; the justices distinguished radio and television from print media, citing the sometimes inescapable omnipresence of broadcast media. The same language that may be acceptable in print might be considered offensive if heard or seen broadcast because of the ubiquity of the electronic media and the lack of control over its consumption in a public space, the justices said.

This tension between what is the right time, place, and manner to display or perform such material—and to what audience—ironically played out on stage during the 2008 Mark Twain Prize tribute to George Carlin at the Kennedy Center, which was later broadcast nationwide on Public Broadcasting System television stations.

During the tribute show, producers showed a video clip of a 1978 HBO cable television network presentation of Carlin's now-infamous "Seven Words You Can Never Say on Television" bit. The routine builds up layers of word play delineating all the descriptive words and phrases people use to politely describe the language in question. At the punch line when Carlin ticks off each of the words in rapid succession, producers censored each of the words with bleeps.

Federal Communications Commission (FCC) ■ A United States government agency, established by the Communications Act of 1934, that regulates interstate and international communications by radio, television, wire, satellite and cable.

---

[1] 438 U.S. 726 (1978).

Acerbic comedian Lewis Black followed the video presentation to give his tribute to the late Carlin adlibbing a comment about the irony in bleeping Carlin's routine at his own tribute. "I hadn't seen that clip, previously," Black said. "And that they bleeped it is really. . . . I mean seriously. To bleep it over TV I kind of get . . . but here? In front of a room filled with adults? I was going to try not to be irritated tonight." Modern communication law attempts to balance the rights of those who want to consume sexually explicit or "adult" media content with the rights of those who want to be shielded from it, and the question is as ancient as modern civilization.

UNRESOLVED QUESTIONS OF CONTENT AND CONTEXT

When lawmakers craft statutes and rules imposing punishments for communicating what is perceived to be either obscene or merely indecent, they intrude upon freedom of expression, and the constitutional tension that causes gives rise to a contradictory record of laws and cases. Forty states outlaw some form of pornography, and even though a handful of states have no viable statute to enforce, they do have cities enforcing ordinances against it. Traced to its roots, *pornography* is derived from the Greek words for prostitute, *porne,* and depiction, *graphos,* but the law goes quite a bit further in defining it as a crime.

In George Orwell's *1984,* pornography was promoted covertly by the government as a means for gaining control over the masses. This futuristic fantasy suggested a steady diet of pornography would make working-class masses, known as the "proles," indifferent to public injustice and submissive to Big Brother's control. In the digital age of instantaneous communication where pornography is as accessible as e-mail and instances of sexual addiction abound, Orwell's futuristic fantasy seems frighteningly real to some. Still to others the excitement over explicit sexual expression is at best much ado about nothing, or at worst a genuine threat to personal freedom.

Regardless of its form of expression—in books, movies, photographs, or animation—when erotic communication is no longer safeguarded as protected speech then how it is defined and conveyed becomes especially relevant. American broadcasters know, for instance, Title 18 of the U.S. Code actually prohibits the airing of "any obscene, indecent or profane language by means of radio communication," and the FCC further guards against repeated vulgar references to sexual or excretory functions calculated to shock or titillate the audience.[2] These companion areas of law—obscenity and indecency—warrant attention in order to understand the law and legacy of protecting Americans from erotic materials.

Colonial Controls

The United States adopted from its British heritage the moral concern that erotic literature posed a threat to public decency. An early British novel titled

---

[2]In deference to the late George Carlin, there was never a list of "seven dirty words" in FCC regulations as expressly defined and prohibited as he alleged.

Memoirs of a Woman of Pleasure narrates Fanny Hill's journey introducing this rural orphan to encounters with homosexuality, masturbation, flagellation, group sex, and other erotic affairs. Published in two eighteenth-century installments, it earned criminal prosecutions for Fanny Hill's author, John Cleland, his publisher and printer—all of whom chose to renounce the book rather than suffer a prison term. Such notoriety creates the fragrance of forbidden fruit and Fanny Hill's narrative attracted attention long after the British courts disposed of it.

The legal theory designed to protect ordinary readers from obscenity is based on the premise it tends to "corrupt their minds" and create a "loss of affection for decency and morality." Inscribing legal reasoning on this theme was Francis Ludlow Holt, a British common-law authority, who viewed obscenity as a "libel against morality and the law of nature."[3] It was outlawed because the royal monarchy and her subjects had a justified interest in ridding Britain of threats to public morality, decency, and good manners. In the former colonies of America, sexually explicit publications and artwork were met at American docksides where the imports would be offloaded until a federal agent was assigned to stop them from entering. The **Tariff Act of 1842** banned the "importation of all indecent and obscene prints, paintings, lithographs, engravings and transparencies," and gave government the authority to dispose of pornographic cargo from France or other foreign ports.[4]

> **Tariff Act of 1842** ■ Banned the importation of all indecent and obscene prints, paintings, lithographs, engravings, and transparencies, and gave government the authority to dispose of pornographic cargo from France or other foreign ports.

Once ashore, communities kept citizens safe from immoral influences by enforcing local ordinances and statutes against possession. Philadelphia authorities policing the city of brotherly love found a tavernkeeper by the name of Jesse Sharpless sharing his "lewd, wicked, scandalous, infamous, and obscene painting, representing a man in an obscene, impudent, and indecent posture with a woman" with a few of his friends.[5] The tavernkeeper and his co-defendants appealed their convictions on obscenity charges to Pennsylvania's Supreme Court. The justices were unsympathetic to Sharpless's appeal and upheld his conviction while stressing their duty "to punish not only open violations of decency and morality, but also whatever secretly tends to undermine the principles of society."[6]

Lord John Campbell, a British parliamentary leader and son of an Anglican minister, compared merchandising pornography to the open sale of poison. He proposed a bill to empower police officers to seize and destroy sexually explicit materials on London's street corners. Lord Campbell accomplished his legislative aim in 1857 with the Obscene Publications Act, a law that left obscenity undefined but gave government the power to seize suspect materials and bring seller(s) to trial.

> **Bedrock Law:** Obscenity is viewed as a crime against public morality that was prosecuted for both possession and commerce of pornographic content.

---

[3]Francis Ludlow Holt, *Of Libels against Morality and the Law of Nature, in* The Law of Libel (J. Butterworth & Son 1816).

[4]Donna I. Dennis, *Obscenity Law and Its Consequences in Mid-Nineteenth Century America,* 16 *Colum. J. Gener & L.* 43 (2007).

[5]*Commonwealth v. Sharpless*, 2 Serg & R. 91 (Sup. Ct. Penn. 1815).

[6]*Id.*, at 14.

The question of how to legally define obscenity was answered in 1868 before British magistrate Benjamin Hicklin, who was appointed to judge a protestant pamphlet critical of the Catholic Church. The defendant on trial was Henry Scott, who had drawn a bead on the Catholic practice of confessing personal sins to a priest. His pamphlet, *The Confessional Unmasked*, recounted sins that might stir impure thoughts in an unsuspecting reader and so his writing was deemed obscene.

> **Bedrock Law:** The *Hicklin* rule allowed the prosecution of obscenity based on any part of an explicit work's influence on the most susceptible mind.

Lord Chief Justice Cockburn upheld Scott's conviction despite his lack of intention to commit the crime simply because the "tendency of the matter charged as obscenity is to deprave and corrupt those whose minds are open to such influences."[7] The *Hicklin* rule formed two parts of obscenity's legal definition dealing with its harmful effects and its partiality. If any passage from a sexually explicit work tends to arouse libidinous feelings in a susceptible mind then the entire work would be judged as obscene. This *Hicklin* rule took root in the United States where courts declared entire books as obscene based on the offense of any sexually charged passages.

> *Hicklin* rule ■ This early standard finds obscenity if any part of an explicit work influences the most susceptible mind. *See Regina v. Hicklin* (1868), LR 3 QB 360.

Comstockery

American history's most famous postal clerk once served as a Union soldier in the Civil War and afterward led the charge against obscenity during President Ulysses S. Grant's administration. Anthony Comstock personally lobbied Congress to allow federal inspectors to declare foreign materials obscene as they entered the country and is credited with an anti-obscenity law passed to that effect in 1873. Once given the authority to seize all erotic imports from French postcards to nude paintings and explicit novels, Comstock was zealous to a fault—so much so that his name came to signify reactionary excess to erotica: **Comstockery.**

> Comstockery ■ Named after zealous advocate of Victorian morality Anthony Comstock, Comstockery is advocacy of censorship on the basis of perceived immorality.

With the aid of the Young Men's Christian Association, Comstock founded the New York Society for the Suppression of Vice in 1873. His morality group had emblazoned on their emblem a book-burning scene, and Comstock personally boasted of igniting tons of sordid books and photos in just that fashion. He sought to have New York district attorneys place high on their list of public priorities the prosecution of pornography. Taken together, Hicklin's rule and Comstock's act characterized the American treatment of pornography that prevailed into the dawn of the twentieth century.[8]

Early Twentieth-Century Changes

The society of the righteous began to lose some of its moral high ground in a case that held explicit works should be taken as whole and not merely judged in part. Regarding the literary talents of Theophile Gautier, a New York court placed his writings on trial in 1923 and a judge was asked to ban the *Mademoiselle de*

---

[7]*Regina v. Hicklin,* LR 3 QB 360 (1868), *in* English Common Law.

[8]The New York Society for the Suppression of Vice also targeted contraceptive materials and devices in their campaign against immorality.

Maupin. The judge found it contained "passages of purity and beauty" along with those "undoubtedly vulgar and indecent," but magnifying parts out of context would diminish passages by "Aristophanes or Chaucer or Boccaccio or even from the Bible." The court in New York found *Mademoiselle de Maupin* was not obscene when "considered broadly as a whole."[9] This decision resounded a decade later when a major publishing house actually sought to bring a novel by James Joyce to trial.

Literary Test Case

Readers who disembarked from Ireland with their copies of James Joyce's *Ulysses* attracted little attention from U.S. customs agents until Random House called attention to the book's questionable content. The publisher owned the rights to *Ulysses* and wanted it seized for the purposes of a test case in obscenity, which Random House felt was necessary to secure its future sales without fear of future prosecutions.

In the trial court's opinion, Joyce's subject matter, which included a voyeuristic scene of masturbation, was vulgar and offensive but did not inflame readers to lascivious thoughts. Judge Woolsey's ruling, which was affirmed by a three-judge federal panel, exonerated James Joyce's stream-of-consciousness novel and the publicity celebrating this decision began to move public opinion toward a more comprehensive approach to obscenity and away from gauging works on the basis of those passages that would provoke the least sophisticated readers.[10]

Roth-Memoirs Test

The U.S. Supreme Court adopted a new approach to obscenity in 1957 after joining together appeals from federal and state courts; one prohibiting the mailing of books such as *American Aphrodite* for which Samuel Roth was convicted, and the possession of obscenity that found David Alberts guilty with his mail-order business in Los Angeles. In joining the cases, the high court reached a decision that guided judges on how to separate obscenity from acceptable forms of sexual content.

Justice Brennan spoke for the majority and focused his thoughts first on the "average person," not a person of sensitive sexual interests or with aversions to apply **contemporary community standards** in order to determine if the allegedly obscene content posed a **dominant theme** taken as a whole that would appeal to **prurient interest** that was **patently offensive.**[11] In the Court's opinion, pornographic material should only be criminalized if it is "utterly without redeeming social importance," and thus undeserving of the First Amendment's safeguards.[12]

While the Supreme Court upheld the convictions for both Roth and Alberts, it prompted dissents from Justices Hugo Black and William O. Douglas, who were

Contemporary community standards ■ Jurors apply contemporary community standards to determine what is obscene. This rule localizes the definition of obscenity, and was first adopted by the United States Supreme Court in 1957 in *Roth v. United States,* 354 U.S. 476 (1957).

Dominant theme ■ According to the first prong of the *Miller* test, a work is only obscene if its dominant theme taken as a whole appeals to the prurient interest. For example, a specific sexual scene in a movie can't be taken alone without considering the rest of the film. *See Miller v. California,* 413 U.S. 15 (1973).

Prurient interest ■ Shameful or morbid interest in nudity, sex, or excretion. *See Roth v. United States,* 354 U.S. 476 (1957).

Patently offensive ■ According to the second prong of the *Miller* test, obscene material must be patently offensive based on contemporary community standards. *See Miller v. California,* 413 U.S. 15 (1973).

---

[9]*Halsey v. New York Soc'y for the Suppression of Vice,* 234 N.Y. 1, 136 N.E. 219 (1922).

[10]*United States v. One Book Called "Ulysses,"* 5 F. Supp. 182 (S.D. N.Y. 1933), *aff'd,* 72 F. 2d 705 (2d Cir. 1934).

[11]*Roth v. United States,* 354 U.S. 476, 489 (1957).

[12]*Id.* at 484-5.

troubled by its First Amendment implications. The antisocial behavior involved only "morbid and shameful" lust, according to Justice Douglas and "the arousing of sexual thoughts and desires happens every day in normal life in dozens of ways."[13] At the lower court level, the presiding judge found that "punishment is apparently inflicted for provoking, in (normal, average adults), undesirable sexual thoughts, feelings, or desire—not overt dangerous or anti-social conduct, either actual or probable."[14]

Recall authorities in Massachusetts were incensed by Fanny Hill's tale in 1821, and yet 145 years later her exploits still managed to produce a criminal conviction. *John Cleland's Memoirs of a Woman of Pleasure* was reprinted by Putnam Books in 1963, and true to the tradition of British magistrates, Cleland's book was banned in Boston.[15] In the context of an American sexual revolution in full flower, Fanny Hill's exploits no longer held their shock value at the Supreme Court level, and the result was a landmark reversal in 1966 for what became known as the *Memoirs* case that added a prong to the test of obscenity based on an erotic work's value to society.[16]

Sexual Orientation and Perversion

In *Manual Enters., Inc. v. Day*, what might have been described as gay pornography in 1962—mail-order magazines—was judged not to be obscene for lack of evidence that photos of nude male models were patently offensive, and an affront to contemporary, community standards. The magazines with titles such as *Grecian Guild Pictorial* and *Trim* "cannot fairly be regarded as more objectionable than many portrayals of the female nude that society tolerates," concluded Justice Harlan.[17]

When the Court took up the question of the pain-inflicting practices of sadomasochism in 1966, the appeal on behalf of a Manhattan bookseller Edward Mishkin set obscenity's parameters in terms of perverse sexual contact. Mishkin's conviction was affirmed for selling paperbacks that dealt with the fetish of humiliation and included such titles as *Cult of the Spankers, Bound in Rubber,* and *Screaming Flesh*.[18] In his appeal, the defense reasoned this genre of pornography would not possibly fit the "average person" test because only a fetishist would find sadomasochism attractive, and thus the *Roth-Memoirs* standard did not apply. In the majority opinion, Justice Brennan dismissed such tortured reasoning and held brutal depictions of sex are utterly without redeeming social value, patently offensive, and of sufficient prurient interest to be condemned as obscene.

---

[13]Id, at 509.

[14]*United States v. Roth*, 237 F. 2d 796 (2d. Cir. 1956).

[15]As a colony, Massachusetts in 1711 banned "wicked, profane, impure, filthy and obscene songs, composures, writings or print." *See* D.A.J. Richards, *Free Speech and Obscenity Law: Toward a Moral Theory of the First Amendment*, 123 U. Pa. L. Rev. 1 (1974).

[16]*Memoirs v. Massachusetts,* 383 U.S. 413 (1966).

[17]370 U.S. 478, 490 (1962).

[18]*Mishkin v. New York*, 383 U.S. 502 (1966).

Pandering Erotic Works

Beyond the three-pronged standard of the *Roth-Memoirs* test arose another question about the marketing of pornography, which involved a veteran journalist. Ralph Ginzburg had on his résumé career stints with the *Washington Times Herald,* NBC, *Reader's Digest,* and *Esquire Magazine,* but he also promoted erotic literature and was brought before a judge on charges of pandering. As part of his marketing promotion, Ginzburg gained mailing privileges from municipal addresses with double entendres (Blue Ball, Pa.; Middlesex, N.J.). Three of his publications—*The Housewife's Handbook on Selective Promiscuity*; a magazine, *Eros*; and a newsletter, *Liaison*—were placed in evidence at his trial. Ginzburg's promotions emphasizing the erotic nature of his mail order merchandise earned him a conviction for pandering to prurient interests. By a 5–4 majority, Ginzburg's case affirmed the constitutionality of convicting those who choose to advertise pornography as well as those who sell it. In the dissenting opinion of Justice Black, the ruling ill served justice because neither Ginzburg nor anyone else could have known the material involved was criminal reading.[19] If a defendant lacks "scienter," a guilty knowledge of his crime, an appeals court can consider that as possible grounds for acquittal.

Bedrock Law: Criminal prosecution of pandering—advertising and marketing—pornography has not been found to be unconstitutional by the U.S. Supreme Court.

Variable Obscenity

From the earliest laws against obscenity there are references to the goal of protecting youth from the effects of harmful sexual content digested prematurely. Outlawing the marketing of erotic materials to minors led to a legal principle known as **variable obscenity,** which means the harm of the explicit material varies according to the consumer's level of maturity. It was first accepted as a standard in 1968 when the U.S. Supreme Court affirmed a New York statute preventing the sale of nude magazines to consumers 17 years old or younger.

A 16-year-old had purchased two centerfold style publications depicting female nudity from a store in Long Island, operated by Sam Ginsberg, who was convicted of selling an erotic magazine which "which taken as a whole, is harmful to minors."[20] The revealing photos were not put to the test of obscenity, because the Court supported the state of New York's constitutional right to limit the access by minors to sexually graphic material without such proof. In terms of legal precedent, what the convictions of Ralph Ginzburg, the journalist, and Sam Ginsberg, the storekeeper, have in common (besides the sound of their last names) is that both convictions dealt not with what the publications expressed in terms of content but how they were advertised and sold to consumers. Courts also looked at what content should be described as erotic but not obscene.

Variable obscenity
■ According to the doctrine of variable obscenity, the harm of the explicit material varies according to the consumer's level of maturity. Under this principle, the sale of erotic though not necessarily obscene materials to minors can be prohibited.

Bedrock Law: Under the principle of variable obscenity, the sale of erotic though not necessarily obscene materials to minors can be prohibited.

[19]*Ginzburg v. United States,* 383 U.S. 463, 476 (1966).
[20]*Ginsberg v. New York,* 390 U.S. 629, 633 (1968).

Playboy magazine's success spawned imitators during the 1960s, and state prosecutors were encouraged to bring those magazines and their merchants to trial. In *Redrup v. New York,* the Supreme Court joined three obscenity appeals for selling centerfold-style magazines and pulp fiction novels in Arkansas, Kentucky, and New York City. The case's namesake, Robert Redrup (a Times Square newsstand merchant) sold William Hamling's *Lust Pool* and *Shame Agent* to law enforcement officers. The decision in *Redrup* reversed all three convictions by applying the *Roth-Memoirs* test that required proving the erotic publications were patently offensive to contemporary, community standards and utterly without redeeming social value.[21] On one hand, the majority in *Redrup* did not find featuring nude women to be necessarily obscene, but selling the magazines and books to minors, or advertising and displaying them in an indecent manner could be prosecuted as offenses. The marketing by mail of sexually oriented literature produced a landmark decision in 1973 that continues to guide jurisprudence in the area of obscenity.

MILLER V. CALIFORNIA

U.S. Supreme Court decisions usually avoid naming the parties complaining of the alleged obscenity, acknowledging the embarrassment and harm already done by the content. An unidentified restaurant owner in Long Beach, Cal., opened up the mail in his mother's presence to find graphic pictures advertising books with titles such as *Man-Woman, Intercourse, An Illustrated History of Pornography* and *Sex Orgies Illustrated,* all bulk-mailed by Marvin Miller. Miller was convicted of a misdemeanor under a California law prohibiting the distribution through the mail of knowingly obscene materials. His conviction was upheld in California, but he appealed to the U.S. Supreme Court.

Chief Justice Warren Burger wrote the majority opinion and called Marvin Miller's marketing strategy an "aggressive sales action," agreeing that California was within its constitutional rights to convict anyone who dealt in public with materials containing "prurient, patently offensive depiction or description of sexual conduct" absent of "serious literary, artistic, political or scientific value to merit First Amendment protection."[22] The obscenity standard in *Miller v. California* added the SLAPS test (lacking serious, literary, artistic, political, or scientific value) and relieved prosecutors of having to prove the all-encompassing negative proposition of "utterly without redeeming social value." Affirming all three questions meant a pornographer or panderer could be tried on obscenity charges without offending the U.S. Constitution. The bottom line for Miller was that "hard-core pornography" fit the description of obscenity, and no protection such as that afforded political debate would be granted because that "demeans the grand conception of the First Amendment and its high purposes in the historic struggle for freedom."[23]

Miller test ■ A three-prong test under which material is obscene if the average person applying contemporary community standards would find the dominant theme of the work taken as a whole 1) appeals to the prurient interest, 2) depicts patently offensive sexual conduct, and 3) if a reasonable person would find the work lacks serious literary, artistic, political, or scientific value. *See Miller v. California,* 413 U.S. 15 (1973).

---

[21]*Redrup v. New York,* 386 U.S. 767 (1967).
[22]*Miller v. California,* 413 U.S. 15, 23–24 (1973).
[23]*California v. Miller,* 413 U.S. 15, 24, 34 (1973).

This established a three-prong test for obscenity based on questions concerning the values of the content, the community, and the consumer.

1. *Would the average person applying contemporary, community standards find the work, taken as a whole, appeals to prurient interest?*
2. *Does it depict or describe in a patently offensive way sexual conduct as defined by applicable state law?*
3. *Does the work, taken as a whole, lack serious literary, artistic, political, or scientific value?*

❚ The *Miller* landmark

Privacy and Pornography

The same year *Miller* was decided, the Supreme Court considered if adult movie theaters deserved constitutional protection because consenting adults had a right to privacy in viewing cinema fare based on an earlier precedent. In *Stanley v. Georgia,* the Court ruled in the case of Robert Eli Stanley that his personal pornography stash was of no interest to law enforcement officers in Georgia. The case involved the discovery of 8-mm reels of pornographic film that police seized in the midst of a search for gambling evidence.[24] Stanley was prosecuted for possession of the pornography although it was neither covered nor anticipated by the search warrant for the gambling evidence.

A majority of the justices said that the commercial exhibition of movies is incomparable to the privacy of one's home. The Court held in a 5–4 ruling other social interests were involved in this cinema theater case. The two films, *Magic Mirror* and *It All Comes Out in the End,* appearing in 1971 at the Paris Adult Theatre I were in fact "hard-core pornography" that the state of Georgia had a right to prohibit. The ruling held other social interests were involved including the protection of a community's quality of life for families, social decency, public safety, and the "social interest in order and morality."[25]

> **Bedrock Law:** If material is determined to be obscene, laws can prohibit its creation, sale, performance, importation, or mailing—even by consenting adults—but not its possession.

Community Standards

The question of community standards came before the Supreme Court in the 1964 case of *Jacobellis v. Ohio* that dealt with a French motion picture's alleged obscenity due to its prominent theme of adultery. The case became famous for Justice Potter Stewart's out-of-context statement about obscenity, "I know it when I see it," but is more fully understood as "I shall not today attempt further

---

[24]*Stanley v. Georgia,* 394 U.S. 557 (1969).
[25]*Paris Adult Theatre I v. Slaton,* 413 U.S. 49 (1973).

to define the kinds of material I understand to be embraced within that shorthand description (of obscenity); and perhaps I could never succeed in intelligibly doing so. *But I know it when I see it,* and the motion picture in this case is not that."[26]

Justice Stewart was referring to the case against Nico Jacobellis who showed Louis Malle's *Les Amants* (The Lovers) at his cinema in Cleveland Heights, Ohio. This film was a celebration of extramarital affairs but lacked the graphic features of hard-core pornography. The justices struggled in *Jacobellis* with the idea of a local standard for obscenity since the idea of community in a federal case could mean society in general. The *Miller* standard moved the law back to the state's purview the task of defining contemporary, community standards.

Jenkins v. Georgia   If a southern jury accurately reflects community standards, a minimum standard for obscene content requires that it must rise above nudity. The Supreme Court felt that a person of average sexual sensitivities in Albany, Ga., would not find patently offensive the acclaimed Mike Nichols film *Carnal Knowledge* starring Jack Nicholson, Candice Bergen, and Ann-Margaret. Georgia's application of contemporary, community standards missed the mark in this case. Jenkins, the cinema manager in Albany, was convicted of obscenity charges by a local jury for projecting a film that showed some nudity and depicted "ultimate sexual acts," but contained not enough graphic material to be deemed obscene. Justice Rehnquist noted in his majority opinion that "nudity alone is not enough to make material legally obscene," and *Carnal Knowledge* was not the type of hard-core pornography that the *Miller* test would uphold.[27]

Social Values   If the alleged obscenity is to be judged by contemporary, community standards then should not its value to society be judged by the same standard? Under the third prong of the *Miller* test, the SLAPS test would measure a work's potential value to society that would offset the potential harm inflicted. In an appeal supported by the American Civil Liberties Union, Richard Pope and Charles Morrison fought their conviction for selling magazines to police at an adult bookstore in Rockford, Ill. Pope and Morrison's attorneys argued the jury was ill equipped to judge the literary, artistic, political, and scientific value of the magazines. Justice White agreed it was not about contemporary, community standards, but "whether a reasonable person would find such value in the material, taken as a whole."[28] In other words, the social value test under SLAPS would not be a local standard. Pope and Morrison's clarification of national values under this standard did little to win their freedom though since the magazines were found to be lacking serious literary, artistic, political, and scientific value anyway.

> Bedrock Law: Contemporary, community standards are determined by average persons from the local community (such as would be found on a jury) but serious literary, artistic, political, or scientific value is determined by experts.

---

[26]378 U.S. 184, 197 (1964).

[27]*Jenkins v. Georgia,* 418 U.S. 153 (1974).

[28]*Pope v. Illinois,* 481 U.S. 497 (1987).

CHILD PORNOGRAPHY

There is one area of law where the *Miller* test for obscenity does not apply—child pornography. The landmark case in 1982 involved Manhattan bookstore owners Paul Ferber and Tim Quinn who sold to undercover police films of adolescent boys masturbating. In this instance, the U.S. Supreme Court gave a variety of reasons why child pornography represented so great an evil to society that no judge need weigh the explicit material's danger or worth as *Miller* would have directed in obscenity trials. The physical and psychological harm of sexually exploiting children, the lasting record of the crime scarring them, the economic incentives, the negligible artistic value, and the Court's record against it were enough for the justices unanimously to favor censorship for child pornography in Ferber's case.[29] Thus, the Supreme Court created a category of speech, **child pornography,** that is without any constitutional protection.

Child pornography
■ Material depicting sexually explicit acts involving a minor. On its face, this class of material has no constitutional protection.

Ferber dealt only with the merchandising of child pornography, but the Court later upheld a ban on even its possession in *Osborne v. Ohio*.[30] In Columbus, Ohio, Clyde Osborne received the mail-order pictures he had asked of 14-year-old boys in sexually explicit poses that caught the attention of the postal inspector, who in turn notified local police. Officers searched Osborne's home, seized the children's pictures, and charged him under an Ohio law prohibiting individuals from possessing nude pictures, not of their own children, but others without any consent from the parents. In light of the *Ferber* decision that effectively outlawed child pornography without proving its obscenity, the Ohio law charged as criminal the mere possession of child pornography and the Court affirmed Osborne's conviction.

Bedrock Law: Child pornography is considered illegal without requiring any application of the *Miller* test.

Congressional Acts

For over three decades, Congress has worked to ban child pornography at the national level. In a number of laws passed during the 1980s and 1990s, U.S. lawmakers took steps to curtail child pornography. In 1986, the advertising of child pornography was outlawed, and Congress created a civil cause of action for children to recover damages for personal injuries sustained by their appearance in child pornography. The Child Protection and Obscenity Enforcement Act of 1988 made it a crime to use a computer to transport, distribute, or receive child pornography. In 1990 it became a crime to possess visual depictions of minors engaged in sexually explicit behavior. In 1996, a law was passed to ban the use of minors in sexually explicit roles, and targeted computer-generated images of child pornography. The Child Pornography Prevention Act (CPPA) became the subject of a Supreme Court case pitting the U.S. attorney general against the Free Speech Coalition and the American Civil Liberties Union.

Child Pornography Prevention Act Child pornography was given its special status under the law of obscenity to protect minors from exploitation, but what happens

---

[29]*New York v. Ferber,* 458 U.S. 747 (1982).
[30]495 U.S. 103 (1990).

if no actual children were involved in the creation of sexually explicit content? A challenge to CPPA was issued by what amounted to a trade group for California's "adult entertainment industry," which included artists specializing in nudes and a photographer whose work was dedicated to erotic subject matter. The trade group Ashcroft v. Free Speech Coalition objected to the law's prohibition against "any visual depiction, including any photograph, film, video, picture, or computer-generated image" of what would be taken to be sexually explicit conduct. In addition, the 1996 law targeted pandering by banning "any sexually explicit image that was advertised, promoted, presented, described, or distributed" as child pornography.[31]

Because child pornography fell outside the *Miller* test for obscenity, the CPPA conceivably could prohibit all visual images of pre-adult teenagers engaged in sexual activity without taking into account the possible literary and artistic merits. This created the astounding scenario that the law would possibly ban digital transmission of *Romeo and Juliet* given the lack of a SLAPS test, and because nowhere did it call for judging offensive works in their entirety; a "single explicit scene" was all that was necessary to produce criminal consequences.

The ruling held the government would first have to show how CPPA would protect real children from exploitation, and not just suppose the sexually explicit content's connection to aberrant behavior. The dissenting opinions pointed out that CPPA outlawed computer-generated images, virtually indistinguishable from real children, and the incitement harms found in such visual imagery—real or virtual—could help child molesters to seduce children.

Communications Decency Act The Communications Decency Act (CDA) added another safeguard against child pornography to punish anyone who used the Internet to reach a minor with obscene materials or content featuring "sexual or excretory activities or organs" that would be deemed "patently offensive as measured by contemporary community standards." These last words approximated regulations the FCC used to bar radio and television stations from broadcasting indecent content. Had this act been given to enforcement, it would prevent a good deal of content on the Internet, perhaps even George Carlin's famous monologue.

The bill was signed in February 1996, and within four months of its passage a panel of federal judges in Philadelphia called it to a halt, striking down the words that were designed to shield minors from pornography.[32] The CDA's death knell followed in the landmark case of *Reno v. American Civil Liberties Union*.[33] The government attempted to defend its position by comparing indecency on the Internet to selling erotic magazines to minors (*Ginsberg v. New York*[34]), profane monologues on daytime radio (*Federal Communications Comm'n v. Pacifica Found.*[35]), or zoning adult cinema theaters (*Renton v. Playtime Theaters*[36]). The Supreme

---

[31]535 U.S. 234 (2002).

[32]Title 47:5, II, I § 230.

[33]521 U.S. 844 (1997).

[34]*Ginsberg v. New York, supra* note 20.

[35]*Federal Communications Comm'n v. Pacifica Found., supra* note 1.

[36]475 U.S. 41 (1986).

Court held that the CDA was overly vague and too blunt an instrument to achieve the goal of denying minors access to "potentially harmful speech," since it would suppress a wide swath of online communication that adults were constitutionally entitled to share.

Child Online Protection Act   In 1998, Congress tried again to protect minors through the Child Online Protection Act (COPA) that would block online sites from giving children access to sexually explicit materials. The punishment for conviction would be up to six months in prison and a $50,000 fine, but the law was never enforced. In 2007, a federal judge found COPA would not survive the strict scrutiny test because there were less restrictive means for handling the problem of young people accessing online pornography. For example, installing software filters would block the content at the receiver's end. Critics of COPA noted that after nine years elapsed the Act had fallen behind the Internet's developments. It contained no provisions to deal with e-mail attachments, streaming video images, social networking sites, and only could be enforced in the United States, which left foreign sources free to send explicit material to children. Consequently, the law was deemed flawed in both its technical and legal aspects.

Children's Internet Protection Act   A parent in Livermore, Cal., was distressed in 1998 to discover her child had used the Internet at the local library to download pornographic images. She filed a lawsuit to have the library install gatekeeping software to prevent such access to minors from occurring again.[37] Her lawsuit did not prevail, but Congress eventually decided her case and others like it warranted a new law. Sen. John McCain (R-Ariz.) drafted a bill that would protect children from accessing explicit materials available online by curtailing federal funding for libraries that had failed to install filtering technology in order to prevent access to explicit images that might be "harmful to minors."

Once it became law, the American Library Association challenged the Children's Internet Protection Act (CIPA), and a federal panel ruled that it was unconstitutional, and the argument that a library stands as public forum was used to declare its invalidity. The U.S. Supreme Court took up the case of *United States v. America Library Ass'n* in 2003, and ruled 6–3 that the law should be reinstated because libraries still had the freedom to offer unfiltered access to the Internet by simply refusing to accept federal funding. The court rejected the public forum analysis because a library is not bound to "create a public forum for Web publishers . . . any more than it collects books in order to provide a public forum for the authors of the books to speak."[38]

PROTECT Act   Congress continued its legislative agenda to protect children from sexual exploitation in 2003 when it adopted the "Prosecutorial Remedies and

---

[37]*Kathleen R. v. City of Livermore,* Appeal to the Court of Appeal to the State of California, First Appellate District, Div. 4, Appeal No. A086349.

[38]539 U.S. 134 (2003).

Other Tools to end the Exploitation of Children Today"(PROTECT Act).[39] This law reworded the ban on computer-generated child pornography by prohibiting a "computer-generated image that is, or appears virtually indistinguishable from that of a minor engaging in sexually explicit conduct."[40] It also brought the *Miller* test to bear in terms of examining sexually explicit depictions of minors, if found to be outside the bounds of actual child pornography. The new law was challenged in *United States v. Williams*[41], but the majority opinion of the Supreme Court found that the PROTECT law was not unconstitutionally overbroad.

CINEMA CENSORSHIP

Perhaps nowhere is the changing definition of what is patently offensive sexual content more visible than in the American cinema. Consider that in 1896 Thomas Edison's silent short of a mustachioed man (John Rice) caressing a woman's face (May Irwin) and kissing in medium close-up was considered a threat to public morality that prompted cries for censorship.[42] Fast-forward to the twenty-first century when explicit sex scenes in the American cinema are so common they are no longer remarkable.

Early in the twentieth century, the U.S. Supreme Court was struck more by the cinema's potential for evil than by its value as a medium of public discourse. Mutual Film Corp. challenged the State of Ohio's censorship board, the Industrial Commission, created in 1913 with the authority "to reject, upon any whim or caprice, any film which may be presented." The U.S. Supreme Court in 1915 was unmoved by Mutual Film's argument and held that censorship boards were not in violation of the Constitution because films were no more vehicles for expressing worthy ideas than a circus or a theater, and in fact were potentially more dangerous. The decision emphasized the power of film to educate and amuse the audience, which made the medium even more "insidious" if they veered from good intentions. The decision further noted that films also had the capacity for appealing to "prurient interest," which did not belong in public.[43]

The *Miracle* Case

Three decades and two world wars later, Americans had seen a lot more movies—good, bad, and indifferent—and endured the harms they posed. When the Supreme Court in 1952 decided to hear the arguments challenging New York's decision to ban *The Miracle*, local censorship boards still held sway across the nation. The issue involved Roberto Rossellini's film that commented satirically on the biblical

---

[39]Pub. L. 108-21, 117 Stat. 650 (2003).

[40]Amended by 1466A of 18 U.S.C. § 2256(8)(B).

[41]553 U.S. 285 (2008).

[42]Tim Dirks, Best and Most Memorable Film Kisses of All Time, from "The 'Greatest' and 'Best' in Cinematic History," http://www.filmsite.org (last visited 13 July 2010).

[43]236 U.S. 230 (1915).

representation of Christ's birth. It depicts a bearded stranger portrayed by Federico Fellini seducing a deluded peasant girl, who (not knowing the consequences of her sexual intercourse) mistakenly believes a miraculous child has been given to her. The Roman Catholic Legion of Decency called the film a "sacrilegious and blasphemous mockery," and sought to have it declared obscene. The New York Board of Regents based its decision on state law that stipulated a film should not be permitted an exhibition in New York if it was "obscene, indecent, immoral, inhuman, sacrilegious, or is of such a character that its exhibition would tend to corrupt morals or incite to crime." The film's distributor Joseph Burstyn waged a personal fight with his own funds to overcome this censorship that produced a landmark decision in his favor against Lewis A. Wilson, the New York Commissioner of Education. In the Court's ruling, Justice Tom Clark emphasized the power of motion pictures to convey important ideas. "They may affect public attitudes and behavior in a variety of ways, ranging from direct espousal of a political or social doctrine to the subtle shaping of thought which characterizes all artistic expression."[44] Thus, filmmakers joined newspapers in their enjoyment of constitutional protection.

Times Film Corp. Case

While the *Miracle* case was the seedling that gave growth to First Amendment shade for films, unfazed censorship boards carried on their regimes of virtue by restricting community access to movies deemed detrimental to the public good. In Chicago, police censors were employed to require distributors to submit their film stock reels for review prior to public screenings. Not all were happy to oblige. Times Film Corp., famous for its Charlie Chaplin releases, paid a fee for the right to show *Don Juan,* but defiantly refused to submit the nonpornographic film for police scrutiny. The U.S. Supreme Court took up the case of *Times Film Corp. v. Chicago,* but restrained itself to hold in favor of the city in a 5–4 ruling that simply meant that Chicago's authority to exercise prior review did not in all circumstances violate the First and Fourteenth Amendments of the Constitution.[45] The film corporation's mistake was to rush past the city's censorship standards, and level a "broadside attack" against its right to preview films prior to their release. Chalk up a win for Chicago's censors. A few years later the First Amendment advocates against film censorship would seize the correct weapon.

Freedman Rules

A Baltimore theater manager, Ronald Freedman, took it upon himself to challenge the film censorship practices in his state. Maryland's law required a license fee and approval by a board of censors before a film's commercial release, and Freedman complied up to a point. In 1962, he signaled his intention to pay the fee but withhold his film about the Irish Revolution, *Revenge at Daybreak,* from prior

---

[44]*Burstyn, Inc. v. Wilson,* 343 U.S. 495 (1952).

[45]*Film Corp. v. City of Chicago,* 365 U.S. 43 (1961).

review. Freedman was convicted of violating that code in 1962, but in defying Maryland's statute, he challenged the code that was used to censor films in Maryland.[46] Freedman's attorney, Felix Bilgrey, argued that the government should shoulder the burden of proof to show a movie was legally objectionable and reach a verdict in a timely manner to prevent unfair competition. The Supreme Court took the case and agreed the government should bear the burden of proof of showing the need for censorship, give prompt judicial review, and do so soon enough to provide for release prior to commercial competition. Justice Brennan's opinion effectively discouraged state and city governments from practicing film censorship, although the right-of-prior review was affirmed so long as local jurisdictions reached a timely decision and showed how the film was offensive enough to be refused a license.

RATINGS SYSTEM

From Hollywood's viewpoint, Justice Brennan's opinion in the *Freedman* case came as a relief since the cinema industry had been embroiled in controversy since the 1920s when the less-than-exemplary lives of Hollywood celebrities first became the subject of tabloid news coverage. The public outcry from religious groups was more intense in that studio film era, which convinced the industry it would need to form a producers and distributors association to preempt Congress from acting against the industry.

The Motion Pictures Producers and Distributors Association (MPPDA, later the Motion Pictures Producers Association, MPPA) was formed in 1922 with the belief that **voluntary self-regulation** was preferable to congressional oversight. A former U.S. Postmaster General and Republican lawyer, Will H. Hays, was selected to head the MPPDA, and devise a formula for avoiding trouble with religious groups by adopting a moral code that essentially was a list of dos and don'ts for Hollywood to follow in their film productions. Hays's name soon became synonymous with self-censorship, and in 1930 he founded a Studio Relations Committee (SRC) to help ensure compliance with his code of cinema conduct. Even though his committee lacked any real enforcement authority in Hollywood, its influence was certainly felt.[47]

Voluntary self-regulation ■ Industry forming sets of rules and regulations for itself without government oversight or enforcement.

Legion of Decency

The influence of motion pictures continued to rise with the introduction of synchronous sound tracks in 1927, and with that popularity came renewed pressure for restraint in both subject matter and scenarios depicted on screen. Religious activist groups such as the Legion of Decency wanted more than just the avoidance of taboo subjects in cinema theaters; they wished to see moral advocacy that would

---

[46]*Freedman v. Maryland*, 380 U.S. 51 (1965).

[47]The code's standards banned references to sexual hygiene and venereal diseases and forbade any obscenity by "word, gesture, reference, song, joke, or by suggestion (even when likely to be understood only by part of the audience). . . ."

build character and called upon a Jesuit priest to contribute to the cause with a code for the MPPDA to formally adopt, which it did in 1930.

Audience tastes began to erode the efforts of film censorship as Hollywood exploited sensational themes of sex and violence, causing further dismay among conservatives. In 1934, the Hays Code adopted its own administration, the Production Code Administration (PCA) that would require all films to obtain a certificate of approval prior to their release. No governmental body could enforce the code, but Hollywood studios were too intimidated by the threat of federal action to ignore it, plus it was credited with discouraging the spread of censorship boards that interfered with local film releases.

The same year, Joseph Breen was appointed to head the PCA but his tenure was marked by unfavorable responses from film industry professionals who noticed that his script reviews brought with them specific changes to dialog, scenes, and even characters. It was said that Breen was the one who even had cartoon character Betty Boop change her dress from that of a flapper to a housewife's modest skirt.

Production Code's Demise

The Production Code faced more challenges from foreign directors, such as Otto Preminger, who introduced banned themes in his movies after the *Miracle* case such as drug abuse in *The Man with the Golden Arm* (1955) and rape in *The Anatomy of a Murder* (1959). After the *Miracle* decision, some directors simply chose to release their films without a certificate of approval, including Alfred Hitchcock and Billy Wilder, while others fought for the certificate but negotiated over requested changes.

The most famous of these final cut negotiations came in response to Sidney Lumet's *The Pawnbroker*, which was the first American film to show bare breasts and still win approval from the industry group. Film historians note that this 1964 retreat by the Production Code from the defense of its rigorous stance against nudity spelled the beginning of the end for the code's self-censorship. After a former presidential aide to Lyndon Johnson, Jack Valenti, became president of the MPAA, he first tried to edit from the script of *Who's Afraid of Virginia Woolf* words like "screw" and "hump the hostess," with mixed results. He decided instead to classify the movie "SMA," which indicated that it was "Suggested for Mature Audiences," for its release.

Thus began the MPAA's move away from censorship and toward a voluntary ratings classification system in 1968 based on the age of suitable audience members (G, M, R, X) that would serve to warn families of the nature of a film's violent and sexual content without attempting to change any Hollywood scripts and further upsetting Hollywood producers or directors.

The Classification and Ratings Administration (CARA) of the MPPA handles the task of evaluating the content of 800–900 motion pictures each year for language, violence, nudity, and sexual situations unsuited for children. The ratings board is comprised of parents, between eight and thirteen who have no prior film industry experience and typically remain anonymous in order to avoid outside pressure from filmmakers. The MPAA also evaluates movie advertising including

▶ UP CLOSE

What the Ratings Mean

The movie rating system offers parents three factors for judging a film's content. One of five ratings is chosen by the board to suggest the level of caution a parent should use in determining whether it is appropriate for their children. The first element is the rating: A G-rated movie, for example, indicates a motion picture is suitable for general audiences. Second, the definition explains more fully what the abbreviated rating means. A G rating, for example, means "all ages admitted." The third rating element, the descriptor explains that a G-rated film has nothing in the way of "theme, language, nudity, sex, violence, or other matters" deemed unsuitable for children. The MPAA cautions that a G rating does not indicate either a certificate of approval or that it is a children's motion picture.

The other four ratings are

- *PG, Parental Guidance Suggested, Some Material May Not Be Suitable for Children:* "There may be some profanity and some depictions of violence or brief nudity. But these elements are not deemed so intense as to require that parents may be strongly cautioned . . . there is not drug use content in a PG-rated motion picture."
- *PG-13, Parents Strongly Cautioned, Some Material May Be Inappropriate for Children Under 13:* "A PG-13 motion

picture may go beyond the PG rating in theme, violence, nudity, sensuality, language, adult activities or other elements, but does not reach the restricted R category," according to the MPAA.

- *R, Restricted, Under 17 Requires Accompanying Parent or Adult Guardian:* "An R-rated motion picture, in the view of the Rating Board, contains some adult material . . . adult themes, adult activity, hard language, intense or persistent violence, sexually-oriented nudity, drug abuse, or other elements, so that parents are counseled to take this rating very seriously."
- *NC-17, No One 17 and Under Admitted:* An NC-17 rating means "most parents would consider patently too adult for their children 17 and under . . . (it) can be based on violence, sex, aberrational behavior, drug abuse or any other element that most parents would consider too strong and therefore off-limits for viewing by their children."[a]

It bears repeating that motion picture ratings are **voluntary self-regulation**. Filmmakers are not obligated to submit their films for rating, nor are theatre owners obligated to deny admission because a patron is too young based on a rating.

[a]*See* http://www.mpaa.org/ratings/what-each-rating-means.

thousands of billboards, print, and Internet advertisements along with radio and television spots. The promotions must be suitable for the movie's target audience and not cross the line in certain areas, such as showing dismemberments, cruelty to children, extreme acts of violence, or sexual suggestiveness.

FEMINIST MYSTIQUE

Pornography is predominantly a male preoccupation, but its more virulent themes degrade women as sex objects while glorifying male dominance over them. That fact provoked the ire of feminist leaders and activists, who convinced the city of

Indianapolis that it was a civil right for women to be free of sexual debasement in images and words. In Indianapolis, pornography discriminating against women (and some men) in its violent portrayals of assault, humiliation, bondage, bestiality, or servility and submission became illegal. The city also included in its definition of criminal pornography the same content where men, children, or transsexuals were depicted. The American Booksellers called into question the constitutionality of the anti-pornography ordinance and had it struck on the grounds of viewpoint discrimination since the city defined pornography in its portrayal of women and the government has "no power to restrict expression because of its message (or) ideas."[48]

Nude Dancing

Erotic dancing has been a provocative art form since ancient Egypt when undulating and alluring movements exposing a dancer's navel fascinated pharaohs. The question of whether its more revealing variations in the United States rose to the level of First Amendment protection was addressed in 1972. California's ABC (Alcohol Beverage Control) board was concerned with nightclubs that served drinks and featured topless and bottomless dancers might produce secondary effects, such as prostitution and drug use. The U.S. Supreme Court upheld California's right to prohibit such sexual acts where alcohol was served, noting the Twenty-First Amendment gave the state wide authority to control such establishments. It noted, however, nude dancing did fall within the "limits of the constitutional protection of freedom of expression."[49] Dissenting Justice Thurgood Marshall cast doubt on the state's secondary effects argument, however, arguing that nude dancing must be properly identified as obscene before it loses First Amendment protection.

The subject came up again in upstate New York when city fathers of North Hempstead decided to prohibit local dancers, waitresses, and barmaids from exposing their breasts. The Supreme Court held government had gone too far in its righteous zeal.[50] The difference was that this anti-nudity ordinance went beyond the regulation of alcohol-serving establishments to basically prohibit nudity in any and all public places. It conceivably could interfere with dance ballets or other artistic performances. These two decisions persistently raised questions in subsequent cases from New Jersey, Indiana, Ohio, Washington, and Pennsylvania.

The city of Mt. Ephraim, N.J., chose to restrict the practice of coin-operated nude dancing in adult bookstores by placing this nonliterary expression beyond the city limits through zoning restrictions. Mt. Ephraim argued it was simply concerned with the attendant problems of sanitation, parking, and police protection, but had not imposed the same restrictions on other live-entertainment venues. This particular regulation was simply a ban on nude dancing, which ban was held to be

---

[48]*American Booksellers v. Hudnut*, 771 F.2d 323 (7th Cir. 1985).

[49]*California v. LaRue*, 409 U.S. 109 (1972).

[50]*Doran v. New Salem*, 422 U.S. 922 (1965).

UP CLOSE

The Show Me Less State

Ever since the turn of the twentieth century, Missouri's motto has been the "Show Me State," after Congressman Willard D. Vandiver declared, "frothy eloquence neither convinces nor satisfies me. I am from Missouri. You have got to show me." The legislature of Missouri, however, informed its adult entertainment industry that it would prefer that dancers show customers *less*, at least in nightclubs. What made its law remarkable was its breadth and depth. Not only did it ban total nudity, but it prohibited females from showing breasts uncovered along a horizontal swath from the top of the areola to the lower portion of the breast, and also prohibited the exposure of either anal cleft or cleavage. It further prevented dancers from coming closer than six feet to patrons; touching either them or their clothing was prohibited, ending the lap or booth dances.

Besides making it a crime for either male or female dancers to go beyond seminudity in their artistic expression it outlawed alcoholic consumption and forced the strip clubs to close at midnight. Missouri further elected to ban strip clubs locating within 1,000 feet of churches, schools, parks, or residential areas. Adult entertainment proponents argued the government was using a moral club to clobber a healthy part of its economy, the adult entertainment industry. A similar law was struck down in Missouri in 2005 and opponents say the new law will suffer the same fate.

unconstitutional.[51] Nude dancing could be zoned out of neighborhoods, but not zoned out of existence.

In the Supreme Court's 1991 attempt to resolve the conflict in *Barnes v. Glen Theater*, the justices had to untangle a rule requiring thongs and pasties for the dancers in establishments that serve alcoholic beverages. This case challenged the state law on public decency that prohibited nudity in public places including bars and other drinking establishments, but what about requiring dancers to wear g-strings and pasties? The Supreme Court found this requirement a "minimal restriction" with plenty of expressive epidermis left over "to convey the dancer's erotic message."[52] A similar result was reached in *Erie v. Pap's A.M.*, where even though nude dancing falls in the outer perimeter of First Amendment protection, erotic dancers could be required to wear pasties and a g-string rather than dance completely nude.[53]

Bedrock Law: Erotic dancing has been deemed a form of expression entitled to some First Amendment protection.

BROADCAST AND CABLE INDECENCY

Just as in other forms of expression, obscenity on the airwaves is always against the law, and the three-pronged test refined in *Miller v. California* applies. Indecent content defined as patently offensive language or material as measured by contem-

---

[51]*Schad v. Mt. Ephraim*, 452 U.S. 61 (1981).

[52]*Barnes v. Glen Theater*, 501 U.S. 560 (1991).

[53]529 U.S. 277 (2000).

porary, community standards regarding sexual or excretory activities or organs, does not rise (or sink) to the level of obscenity. Given its First Amendment protection, indecency cannot be swept off the air completely but the FCC restricts airing such content to times when children presumably are asleep and away from broadcast channels. This safe harbor is legally defined as the hours between ten at night and six in the morning. The definition of profanity is a bit vague and includes "language so grossly offensive to members of the public who actually hear it as to amount to a nuisance," but is safe for broadcast utterance at night.[54]

Documented complaints from the public are what spur the FCC to action when it comes to sanctioning profane, indecent, or obscene material on the air. The staff in Washington, D.C., is assigned to review the complaints of broadcast programming in order to determine if these laws have been broken. A detailed context of the offensive expression is important in determining if a violation has occurred, which is why the station call letters, location, date, and time of the broadcast are essential, and a tape or transcript of the offense is considered helpful in order to resolve the question. When the FCC reviews a violation that has generated enough attention to warrant government action, the FCC staff begins its inquiry with a letter to the broadcast station. The agency can also send a letter of dismissal to the complaining party explaining why the material is either legal or why the description of the offense is insufficient to determine if a violation has occurred.

The complaining citizen (or citizens) has a right of appeal if the FCC denies the complaint, but the complainant has the option of filing a petition for reconsideration or can appeal to the full Commission. A notice of apparent liability (NAL) is what the FCC issues the station when it determines a patently offensive broadcast involving profanity or indecency has occurred in violation of the law. This preliminary finding of the NAL can be reduced, rescinded, or affirmed before the terms of punishment for the station are levied. Critics say the agency is too backlogged to even begin to fulfill that legal mandate. The Parents Television Council reports that more than a million complaints await FCC review, and the agency is so far behind that the complaints over five years old are discarded.

Cable Television

Parental concern with cable television pornography spurred congressional action after a Florida mother was stunned to find her seven- and eight-year-old children watching sex scenes on the Spice Channel one afternoon. One part of the Communications Decency Act required that cable operators selling adult channels with erotic programming install the necessary filters to scramble or block the programming from reaching households which did not wish to subscribe to them, including families with children, or limit their program schedule to overnight hours. That part of the CDA, § 505, was held to be in violation of the First Amendment because it was not the least restrictive means of achieving the government's goal.[55]

---

[54]*See* "FCC Consumer Facts," http://www.fcc.gov/cgb/consumerfacts/obscene.html.

[55]*United States v. Playboy Entertainment Group,* 529 U.S. 803 (2000). Section 505 is found in Title V of the Communications Decency Act of 1996 (CDA).

Cable operators already were bound once a customer made the request to completely block any channel without charge. The trial judge said giving customers adequate notice of that alternative would be a less-restrictive rule than barring all adult-oriented cable fare during the day. Parents simply had to call the cable company and have them block the channel or buy digital devices to block it.

Fleeting Exposures and Expletives

Some called it the Golden Globes rule, which followed by almost three decades the *Pacifica* decision against George Carlin's filthy words monologue. The controversy sparked afresh during the Golden Globes Award ceremony on NBC network television stations when jubilant rock singer Bono exulted with the f-word for winning the best original song award for "The Hands That Build America," featured in the film *Gangs of New York*. "This is really, really, fucking brilliant," exclaimed the Irish singer on live television. The FCC recognized that even though Bono's use of the f-word was not expressive of sexual or excretory activity it did inherently have a sexual connotation, although no fine was levied against NBC in this particular case. What the case did accomplish was a policy shift that held fleeting expletives could be legally penalized. Fox Television was the first network to feel the sting of the stricter enforcement of unguarded profanity on the air.

Fox v. FCC

Sometimes a prior notice warning viewers of explicit content is not an option especially when television is covering live events. When pop singer Cher and actor Nicole Ritchie used "f and s bombs" from the podium at Billboard's 2002–03 Music Awards, the explosive profanity on Fox's airwaves surprised viewers. The first-blow theory the FCC uses to justify its strict measures against indecency is based on the notion that without warning an ugly word or indecent comment can enter the home and strike a child's eyes or ears to the detriment of the family's welfare.

In *Fox v. FCC*, the U.S. Supreme Court ruled that so-called fleeting expletives taking place in the context of awards shows or on reality television can be sanctioned with fines. This was the first time since the *Federal Communications Comm'n v. Pacifica Found.* case in 1978 that the high court found the whole issue of indecency worthy of its attention. A lower court thought the new approach was an arbitrary and capricious departure from the agency's longstanding policy, and refused to affirm it. By a 5–4 majority, the Court agreed that it was acceptable for the FCC to penalize the networks, but six justices felt compelled to write individual opinions indicating just how divisive policing profanity and punishing the use of "f-bombs" and "s-words" on the air had become.

Justice Scalia writing for the majority concluded that although the FCC policy shifted under President George W. Bush's administration to take a tougher stance with regard to profanity, the agency was still acting within its congressional mandate to guard the airwaves from indiscrete use of profane terms as expletives and not just as literal descriptors of sexual or excretory functions.[56] In other words, the argument that the FCC was "arbitrary" or "capricious" in changing its policy proved unconvincing to the majority, but the dissenting justices felt that isolated and fleeting expletives should not be penalized out of context.

American broadcasters felt that this ruling against fleeting expletives chilled their free speech and threatened the future programming of live television in general. The Supreme Court affirmed the FCC's policy on procedural grounds but then returned the case to the New York–based Second Circuit Court of Appeals to consider the constitutional arguments involved.

In 2010, Judge Rosemary Pooler wrote for a three-judge panel holding that the FCC had acted unconstitutionally to punish broadcasters for fleeting profanities, which celebrities blurt out during live programming. Her opinion held the Commission's policy was chilling to free speech because broadcasters had no way of knowing when references to sexual and excretory habits and the like crossed the line into indecency. The indecency regulation promoted self-censorship, and so it was struck but the Court said an alternative rule on indecency could be drafted by the FCC.

Nipplegate

Most American football fans can hardly remember last year's Super Bowl, much less what happened in years previous, but what happened in the Super Bowl of 2004 appears indelibly etched in the national consciousness. Justin Timberlake and Janet Jackson were performing during the halftime show when a "wardrobe malfunction" exposed for a fraction of a second the singer's right breast.

It was a fleeting exposure, but it excited the American public enough to complain en masse to the Federal Communications Commission, which in turn levied a forfeiture of $550,000 for violating the indecency rule with the national network broadcast. For years after the fleeting halftime glimpse of Ms. Jackson's breast, lawyers fought over the FCC's extraordinary fine until a three-judge panel of the Third Circuit Court of Appeals ruled in favor of CBS in 2008. The FCC did not give broadcasters enough prior notice that it would more strictly enforce its policy against fleeting nudity during the daytime hours of television.

The federal panel also took issue with the idea that the stations were to blame for the artistic excesses of Jackson and Timberlake. (He actually was the one who sang the lyric, "Gonna have you have naked by the end of this song," and pulled at her breastplate to cause the malfunction, yet escaped much of the criticism afterward.)

The FCC underscored the fact that this fleeting image of a breast was not to be held exempt from its prohibition against indecency, and there was in fact no departure from standing policy at the FCC to fine CBS for its negligence that it was obligated to explain before the 2004 Super Bowl. The U.S. Supreme Court set aside the

---

[56]*FCC v. Fox Television Stations,* 556 U.S. 1, 129 S. Ct. 1800 (2009).

Third Circuit Court's ruling in 2009, and asked that it reexamine its jurisprudence in the case, leaving open the possibility that this appellate court could rule in favor of CBS.

Broadcast Indecency Act

The infamous wardrobe malfunction heightened public concern with broadcast decency and the FCC began to step up its enforcement of indecency infractions. President Bush took one step further and signed into law the Broadcast Decency Enforcement Act the following year that was sponsored by a former broadcaster, Sen. Sam Brownback (R-Kan.).[57] This law established a sizeable increase in the fine for such violations giving the Commission the authority to require $325,000 per station for each violation of the rules, a tenfold increase of the original maximum forfeiture required for indecency on the air.

Dial-a-Porn Law

Congress acted to ban indecent and obscene commercial phone messages in 1988 by amending the Communications Act of 1934. This law effectively put out of business dial-a-porn operators who would sexually titillate callers with their conversation, which was the stock in trade of Sable Communications of California. A district court judge upheld the ban for obscene messages, but not for indecent conversations. The U.S. Supreme Court followed suit and held that so long as the conversations were merely indecent rather than obscene, the First Amendment protected the commercial communication.[58]

INDECENT VIOLENCE

Ever since the Columbine massacre of 1999 when teenagers Eric Harris and Dylan Klebold, who were obsessed with the video game "Doom," undertook lethal rampage killing twelve students and one teacher in Colorado, there has been public concern with video game violence. From Europe to Asia, from the United States to the United Kingdom, dozens of violent and lethal acts have been linked to the inspiration of video games with names like "Grand Theft Auto," "Mortal Kombat," "Warcraft," "Manhunt," and "Halo," just to name a

---

[57]Pub. L. No. 109-235 (2005).

[58]*Sable Communications v. FCC*, 492 U.S. 115, 126 (1989).

few. Whenever a spectacular act of violence occurs and authorities recognize a link to someone's obsession with violent video games, it provokes public dismay and renewed pressure for law enforcement.

The U.S. Congress first called hearings on the issue in 1992–1993 to discuss possible solutions to the violent influence of gaming. The entertainment software industry was encouraged to devise some sort of rating system to restrict the sale of violent video games to minors. Video game manufacturers such as Sega Inc. and 3-DO formed their own rating groups in response to the congressional hearings, but they were eventually phased out and replaced by the Entertainment Software Rating Board (ESRB) that was approved by Congress in 1994.

Video Game Ratings

The ESRB initially established five levels of game suitability based on levels of maturity beginning with "Early Childhood," "Kids-to-Adults" (replaced in 1998 with "Everyone"), "Teen," "Mature," and "Adults Only." Later precise ages were added to the labels, including "10+" for "Everyone." Critics have charged the ESRB has not been sensitive enough in certain game ratings, and too quick to award the M rating for Mature, when the video game violence deserved an "Adults Only" (AO) label. Some games have gone back into production to temper their content and achieve an M rather than an AO rating. For example, one game titled "Mass Effect" contained two sexual scenes, but was awarded an M rating that created some controversy among conservative critics. The ESRB points out video game producers do not qualify as video game raters, who instead come from various sectors of society including educators, parents, and professionals but not the interactive entertainment industry.

In 2005, the California legislature decided to put some teeth in its video gaming ratings by enacting a law that would punish retailers who would rent and sell video games without checking on the purchaser's age to see if they were old enough to fit the requirements of an M or AO rating. The law was quickly challenged by the video game industry that succeeded in having it overturned, even though Gov. Schwarzenegger appealed to the federal district court for the Ninth Circuit and lost there as well. California defended its action on First Amendment grounds arguing violent games are comparable to sexually indecent materials that the Court has held can be legally restricted from sale to minors. At least a half dozen other states have passed similar laws that were struck down on First Amendment grounds, but in 2010 the U.S. Supreme Court agreed to hear the case of *Schwarzenegger v. Entertainment Merchants Ass'n*.

SUMMARY

- The British common law considered sexually provocative literature a guilty pleasure worthy of punishment, and an English magistrate's ruling in 1868 was adopted as the *Hicklin* Rule in the United States. It defined material that has a tendency to "deprave and corrupt those whose minds are open to such influences" as obscene, and Americans came to judge as criminal those creative works that were in whole or in part a sexual enticement for the most susceptible people.

- The U.S. Supreme Court began to look anew at the crime of obscenity, including marketing and owning it, not just by scrutinizing offensive passages but by judging the work in its entirety. In the landmark case of *Miller v. California* following the predecessors of *Roth* and *Memoirs,* the high court crafted a test that required suspect material appeal to the prurient interest and by contemporary, community standards be patently offensive to an average person, not a person of extreme sexual interests or aversions, and that it further be shown to be without serious literary, artistic, political, or scientific value.

- The laws against obscenity cover not only owning sexually offensive material, but also advertising and marketing it, which is known as pandering. Landmark cases involving the mail-order sale of pornography have shaped both the U.S. law's definition and approach to obscenity, which was further challenged by the Internet's wide distribution of pornography.

- Under the principle of variable obscenity, government can criminally punish the sale or distribution of pornography to minors—young people under the age of eighteen years old—that has not been declared as obscene under the *Miller* test.

- Child pornography is considered to be of such significant harm to minors that Congress and the courts have criminalized its possession and sale without requiring that it be judged by the standards of the *Miller* test, which would involve a showing of patently offensive content to an average person without any serious social value.

- Congress has passed several laws to restrict the access of Internet pornography, and some of which have been struck as unconstitutional if they encroach upon the free expression of adults who wish to exchange ideas about sexual activities online. In 2003, the Supreme Court upheld the Children's Internet Protection Act that requires public libraries to block access to online pornography that would be harmful viewing for children or offensive to other patrons. The Court held that a public forum analysis did not apply in this instance, and libraries that felt filters for pornography infringed on free expression could simply refuse federal funds in order to overcome the law's effect.

- Nude dancing in local bars and night clubs is given some First Amendment breathing room, but the mixed set of rulings in this area also upholds the government's right to deal differently with drinking establishments, and address the secondary effects of crime, prostitution, and drug abuse in its local ordinances.

- U.S. law recognizes different standards based on the different media channels used. Cinema was subjected to censorship boards, but that gave way to a classification system. Broadcasting stations are forbidden from airing profane or indecent content at certain hours of the day, which is defined as "language or material that, in context, depicts or describes, in terms patently offensive as measured by contemporary community standards for the broadcast medium, sexual or excretory organs or activities." This definition of indecency has been called into question by a New York appeals court that struck it down as vague.

- Several states have recognized the potential harm of selling sexual and violent content in video games to young people and enacted laws to prevent it, but several statutes have been overturned as unconstitutional. The state of California has petitioned the U.S. Supreme Court to have its law on this subject reinstated.

Sexting

The age of the mobile phone has introduced new forms of communication and news means of conveying ardor for young people. The term *sexting* is used to indicate the sharing of sexually explicit images and words between mobile phone users. This form of communication became popular among teens around 2005 but raised a legal problem for countries where child pornography laws forbid explicit sexual images of minors. Charges of child pornography—both the distribution and possession of it—have been filed against adults and minors who are holding mobile phones containing sexually explicit words and images. In Opelousas, La., a high school teacher pleaded guilty to federal child pornography charges after receiving a fifteen-year-old student's personal nude photos sent by mobile phone. The felony count carried with it a prison term of from five-to-twenty years and a possible fine of $250,000.

More common are incidents that involve teenagers sharing personal nude photos, which calls into question whether felony prosecution is contrary to the intent of the law. The National Campaign to Prevent Teen and Unplanned Pregnancy estimated 20 percent of young people between thirteen and twenty-six years old have shared nude or semi-nude pictures of themselves by mobile phone, and an even greater percentage had sent sexually explicit messages by mobile phone.[a] Other sources doubt the scope of the phenomenon is quite so widespread, but agree that it calls into question the jurisprudence of prosecuting felony charges of child pornography against "sexting" teens.

The American Civil Liberties Union in 2009 filed a lawsuit in Pennsylvania against a district attorney who threatened to proceed with the prosecution of several teenage girls on child pornography charges if they did not enter a counseling program. The girls shared by mobile phone their personal semi-nude photos in bras and bath towels. High school officials in Tunkhannock, Pa., confiscated the pictures from student cell phones and fourteen girls entered a counseling program while three others refused. Prosecutor George Skumanick threatened the holdouts but was enjoined from proceeding with child pornography charges against them by the Third Circuit Court of Appeals. Still, the question of whether such legal actions constituted a correct application of the law remained.[b] Writing for the American Bar Association, Hannah Geyer recommended a *Romeo and Juliet* exception should be enacted for juveniles of about the same age who sext each other without fear of criminal prosecution, particularly for child pornography.[c] ■

---

[a] The National Campaign to Prevent Teen and Unplanned Pregnancy, *Sex and Tech: Results from a Survey of Teens and Young Adults* 11 (2008).

[b] *Miller v. Skumanick*, 605 F. Supp. 2d 634, 637 (M.D. Pa. 2009).

[c] Hannah Geyer, *Sexting—The Ineffectiveness of Child Pornography Laws*, Juvenile Justice e-Newsletter (June 2009), http://www.abanet.org/crimjust /juvjust/newsletterjune09/june09/sexting.htm.

Media and Courts

LEARNING OBJECTIVES

After reading this chapter you should know:

- How pretrial publicity could possibly impact the fair trial rights of someone on trial

- How the Court attempts to strike a balance between the fair trial rights of the accused and the free press rights of the media

- How contempt of court can be used by judges to get what they want

- What "gag orders" are and whether they can be used to silence the media

- How the judiciary attempts to compel reporters to testify in court or before grand juries

- What shield laws are and the sorts of protections they afford

- The rules governing warrants and subpoenas for information held by news media

- Whether cameras are allowed in courts and who decides based on what criteria

- If courtrooms can be closed to observers

THE TRIAL OF THE CENTURY ... AT THE TIME

In the early hours of July 4, 1954, Marilyn Sheppard was brutally murdered in her Bay Village, Ohio, home. Her husband Sam claimed that an intruder attacked his wife while he slept on the couch downstairs. He asserted that he awoke to the sounds of the attack but when he entered the room he was hit from behind. He tried to pursue someone escaping from the house but was unsuccessful. Sam called neighbors who came over, then called the police in their Cleveland suburb.

The murder case was big news and for the next month, Cleveland media ran a story every day (whether or not there were new developments in the case). At first the news stories were sympathetic to the 30-year-old doctor who, along with his father and two brothers (all doctors), worked at Bay View Hospital in Bay Village. However, suspicion quickly turned away from the intruder Sam claimed to have pursued and attention was focused on him. From the outset there was reason to suspect him but the Bay View police resisted suggestions by the Cleveland police to arrest him. The investigation had all sorts of problems: the morning of the murder, the Sheppard home was filled with people, including neighbors, who had unlimited access to a crime scene while the police were trying to collect evidence, much of which was contaminated by the fingerprints of others. "Dr. Sam" (as he was known in Bay View) was whisked from the murder scene to the hospital the morning of the crime. It was days after the crime before authorities were able to question him to any extent.

The case contained all sorts of twists and turns: a woman who claimed to have had an affair with Dr. Sam, suspicions that the mayor of Bay View (the neighbor Dr. Sam first called) may have been the murderer, and others. No wonder two television series and a motion picture were *loosely* based on the case.[1]

Sam Sheppard was arrested July 30 and his trial in Cuyahoga County, Ohio, Court of Common Pleas began in mid-October, just weeks before presiding judge Edward J. Blythin would have to face reelection. The chief prosecutor in the case was also a judgeship candidate. Reporters from across the country wanted to cover the trial, so Blythin accommodated some of them by seating them behind the bar— the area reserved for trial participants. The judge rejected motions to postpone the trial or move it to another location due to the excessive publicity. Jurors were selected, and their names and addresses appeared in the paper. The jury was finally sequestered for deliberations after six weeks of hearing testimony (but they were still permitted to make phone calls). Shortly before Christmas 1954, Dr. Sam Sheppard was found guilty of second degree murder. His attorney began immediate efforts to appeal or have the case reheard. Ohio appellate and supreme courts affirmed his conviction.

The sequence of events after the trial was almost as bizarre as those during it. Less than two weeks after the conviction, Dr. Sam's mother committed suicide. His father died from a hemorrhaging ulcer 11 days later. Ten years after his conviction a judge ordered him released from prison, citing five violations of Sheppard's constitutional rights. Three days later he married a wealthy German divorcee he

---

[1]*The Fugitive* television show of the 1960s starring David Janssen, the short-lived TV series in 2000 starring Tim Daly, and the 1993 movie starring Harrison Ford were all *loosely* based on the story of Dr. Sam Sheppard.

The Supreme Court's *Sheppard* Decision

The following is taken directly from Justice Clark's opinion for the Court:

> A responsible press has always been regarded as the handmaiden of effective judicial administration, especially in the criminal field. Its function in this regard is documented by an impressive record of service over several centuries. The press does not simply publish information about trials but guards against the miscarriage of justice by subjecting the police, prosecutors, and judicial processes to extensive public scrutiny and criticism. This Court has, therefore, been unwilling to place any direct limitations on the freedom traditionally exercised by the news media for "what transpires in the court room is public property." The "unqualified prohibitions laid down by the framers were intended to give to liberty of the press . . . the broadest scope that could be countenanced in an orderly society." . . . And where there was 'no threat or menace to the integrity of the trial,' we have consistently required that the press have a free hand, even though we sometimes deplored its sensationalism. . . .[a]

Then citing an earlier decision, he added

> [W]e believe that the arrangements made by the judge with the news media caused Sheppard to be deprived of that "judicial serenity and calm to which [he] was entitled."[b] The fact is that bedlam reigned at the courthouse during the trial and newsmen took over practically the entire courtroom, hounding most of the participants in the trial, especially Sheppard. At a temporary table within a few feet of the jury box and counsel table sat some 20 reporters staring at Sheppard and taking notes. The erection of a press table for reporters inside the bar is unprecedented. The bar of the court is reserved for counsel, providing them a safe place in which to keep papers and exhibits, and to confer privately with client and co-counsel. It is designed to protect the witness and the jury from any distractions, intrusions or influences, and to permit bench discussions of the judge's rulings away from the hearing of the public and the jury.
>
> Having assigned almost all of the available seats in the courtroom to the news media the judge lost his ability to supervise that environment. The movement of the reporters in and out of the courtroom caused frequent confusion and disruption of the trial. And the record reveals constant commotion within the bar. Moreover, the judge gave the throng of newsmen gathered in the corridors of the courthouse absolute free rein. Participants in the trial, including the jury, were forced to run a gantlet of reporters and photographers each time they entered or left the courtroom.
>
> The total lack of consideration for the privacy of the jury was demonstrated by the assignment to a broadcasting station of space next to the jury room on the floor above the courtroom, as well as the fact that jurors were allowed to make telephone calls during their five-day deliberation.[c]

---

[a] *Sheppard v. Maxwell*, 384 U.S. 333, 350 (1966) (citations omitted).
[b] *Id.* at 355 (citations omitted).
[c] *Id.* at 355 (citations omitted).

had been corresponding with from prison for seven years. In 1965, an appeals court reinstated his conviction.

The U.S. Supreme Court had been petitioned to hear the Sheppard case in 1956 but turned it down. Given a second opportunity, the Court chose differently and Dr. Sam's case was heard in 1966. The Court was asked to determine whether Sheppard was denied a fair trial as a result of all the publicity and attention. The Court even referred to the "editorial artillery"[2] the local news media brought out in an effort to pin the crime on Sheppard. Five volumes of Cleveland newspaper clippings from before the conviction were provided. In spite of this the Court's strongest criticism was not of the news media but of the judicial officers.

Justice Tom Clark wrote the opinion for an 8–1 decision which strongly took to task Judge Blythin's lack of action to protect the due process rights of the accused. The Court remanded the case, and in a new trial in 1966 Dr. Sam Sheppard was acquitted.

6th Amendment (Fair Trial)

PRE-TRIAL PUBLICITY

The Sixth Amendment states: "In all criminal prosecutions, the accused shall enjoy the right to a speedy and public trial, by an impartial jury of the State and district where in the crime shall have been committed, which district shall have been previously ascertained by law, and to be informed of the nature and cause of the accusation; to be confronted with the witnesses against him; to have compulsory process for obtaining witnesses in his favor, and to have the Assistance of Counsel for his defence."

Burr - 1807 Trial

The amendment guarantees our constitutional right to a fair trial, which requires an **impartial jury, but it does not require an ignorant jury.** It is not just a modern phenomenon that celebrities like O.J. Simpson and Robert Blake must stand trial before jurors who have already heard some information (right or wrong) about the case. For hundreds of years there has been a great deal of pre-trial publicity surrounding notorious trials and the jurors very likely already knew something about the case before the trial began. Former U.S. Vice President Aaron Burr was tried for treason in 1807 with a great deal of publicity surrounding the case, and Supreme Court Chief Justice John Marshall stated that simply being exposed to pre-trial publicity did not necessarily prejudice a juror.[3]

Right to impartial jury ■ The Sixth Amendment guarantees defendants the right to trial by an impartial jury, which can sometimes conflict with publicity surrounding trials.

Publicity's role in the outcome of trials is uncertain. As might be imagined, it's impossible to know for certain the effect since we cannot conduct an experiment with real trial litigants where we compare the results in the same case conducted with and without publicity. In the most comprehensive collection of research to date, Jon Bruschke and William Loges concluded, "there is not a pretrial publicity effect that is powerful and able to survive all remedies. There is even some evidence that pretrial publicity might help defendants. There may yet exist a pretrial publicity effect that can be detected with strict control in laboratory conditions, and we

Bedrock Law: Judges are responsible for maintaining decorum in their courtrooms and safeguarding the jury in order to protect the defendant's right to a fair trial.

---

[2]*Sheppard v. Maxwell,* 384 U.S. 333, 339 (1966).
[3]*U.S. v. Burr,* 25 F. Cas. 49, 51 (C.C.D. Va. 1807).

interpret this to mean that there may be a pretrial publicity effect that emerges in some very specific conditions in actual courtrooms."[4]

Legal scholars generally conclude that some sorts of pre-trial information are more prejudicial[5] to a trial than other publicity. It is generally accepted that publishing nothing more than a suspect's name and address is not prejudicial, which begs the question: what sorts of pre-trial publicity are thought to be prejudicial? On various occasions, the Supreme Court has answered that the pre-trial publication of these categories are "presumed" prejudicial:

- Confessions or admissions of guilt[6] or other sorts of "evidence" that would be considered inadmissible at trial;
- Prior criminal record, although the Court softened this stance by saying that reporting criminal record *alone* was not enough to be prejudicial;[7]
- Attribution of serious character flaws or epithets such as "Mad Dog."[8]

News media are not prevented from releasing any of this information, but it could conceivably result in claims by defendants that the impartiality of the jurors has been compromised and that a fair trial is difficult, if not impossible.

PROTECTING FAIR TRIAL RIGHTS

Prior to the *Sheppard* case, some may have thought that the only option when faced with the possibility of prejudicial pre-trial publicity was to restrict the rights of a free press, or risk the possibility of harming the accused's right to a fair trial. The Supreme Court decision offered American courts a variety of ways to protect the fair trial rights of the accused without treading on the free press rights of the media.

Change of venue ■
Moving a trial to a different geographical location.

Change of venire ■
Importing jurors from a different geographical location.

Change of Venue

If a judge is concerned that a jury could be swayed by too much pre-trial publicity, the judge can move the trial to another location. **Change of venue** operates under the assumption that the most publicity about a crime is likely to occur in the locale where it was committed, and that by moving the trial, jurors can be impaneled who are less familiar with the case.[9]

Change of venue raises other difficult questions, though, including a constitutional one. The Sixth Amendment to the Constitution states that the accused shall

---

[4]J. Bruschke & W. Loges, *Free Press vs. Fair Trials* 136 (2004).

[5]The term *prejudicial* itself implies the problem. It is publicity that occurs before the judicial process, and causes judgment to occur before the trial. It is not only pre-trial publicity that can be prejudicial, but that will be discussed later.

[6]*Rideau v. Louisiana,* 373 U.S. 723 (1963).

[7]*Murphy v. Florida,* 421 U.S. 794 (1975).

[8]*Irwin v. Dowd,* 366 U.S. 717 (1961).

[9]Similar to a change of venue is the **change of venire**, wherein jurors from another locale are selected and transported into the court. Both accomplish the same goal of obtaining a jury pool of citizens less familiar with the crime.

enjoy the right to a trial in "the state and district wherein the crime shall have been committed." The Amendment further states that "district" shall be defined, so conceivably it could be as large as a state's boundaries but even so that may not be enough to provide impartial jurors. Imagine a trial for a heinous crime in the state of Rhode Island. It's hard to imagine that anywhere in the state would be outside the coverage of Providence news media, yet the Constitution requires that the trial be conducted in the state and district of the crime. In this modern age, is changing venue of any use at all, or will news coverage simply follow the trial to the new locale?

Another cause for concern with change of venue is the cost involved. It is not cheap. Of course legal scholars are quick to point out that fair trials are costly but that should not be a basis for opposing them.

Continuance

Trials can be delayed. Even trials that are not delayed occur months after the crime was committed. In Sam Sheppard's case, more than three months had passed. If pre-trial publicity is a concern, perhaps a delay would help those prospective jurors who heard prejudicial information to forget it. But there is a Constitutional concern here as well. That same Sixth Amendment mentioned earlier requires a *speedy* trial, and while that term may be vague it clearly argues against any intentional delays.

If **continuance** dulls the memory of potential jurors, it must also dull the memories of witnesses. Courts try to prevent problems in this regard by having witnesses provide depositions. These statements can then be given back to the witnesses so they can read what they said earlier, as a means of refreshing their memories. There is always the possibility that a question can arise at trial that was not covered during the deposition and a witness may not recall that detail.

Continuance ■
Postpones legal proceedings until a later date.

Sequestration

Sequestering a jury is the process of keeping the jurors secluded so that no one talks with them about the trial outside of court. Typically jurors are housed at a local hotel where they can be supervised by the court. Officers can see to it that they do not read newspaper accounts of the trial or watch television newscasts. The jury in the *Sheppard* trial was sequestered only for deliberation. During the course of testimony, jurors were able to talk with anyone about the trial, read newspapers, and otherwise receive prejudicial information.

In addition to the tremendous expense of **sequestration**, it may cause jurors undue stress to be away from their loved ones. With each passing day there is increased pressure to end the trial, prompting some jurors to rush the deliberation process or, worse yet, give in to the majority opinion during deliberations just to get the trial over with. In the long term, the more often juries are sequestered, the more difficult it becomes to impanel a jury as fear of possible sequestration would cause even more people to seek to be dismissed from jury pools.

Sequestration ■
The process of keeping the jurors secluded so that no one talks with them about the trial outside of court.

Voir Dire

While sequestration is an effective tool for keeping jurors who have been selected from hearing prejudicial information, prior to a juror's selection, however, any media coverage of the crime or upcoming trial would be seen and heard, and so the question becomes how much has news coverage of the case formed an impression about the guilt or innocence in a prospective juror's mind.[10] This is a question best answered during the **voir dire**, a legal term that refers to the jury selection process. From the literal French translation, it is "to see to speak." The lawyers in a case have a chance to *see* jurors before *saying* if they are acceptable. Attorneys on both sides in a civil or criminal trial have a chance to interview prospective jurors in order to determine their truthful knowledge and biases regarding the case. They can reject jurors for cause and explain why the juror is not suited to render a fair verdict, or simply issue a peremptory challenge, which requires no explanation. Attorneys have a limited number of peremptory challenges, meaning that they generally try to explain the reason for challenging a juror (for cause) to preserve their peremptory challenges for those challenges the judge might not accept. Jury selection is a controversial process due to the research that informs trial lawyers about the tendencies of prospective jurors to vote a particular way based on their age, ethnicity, gender, education, income, religion, etc.[11]

Voire dire ■ The pre-trial process of jury selection.

Judicial Admonition

The Supreme Court also pointed out that the trial judge in the *Sheppard* case did not do all that he could in **admonishing the jury**: that is, giving them strict rules about what they could and could not do. Instead, the judge's instructions were more in the form of "suggestions" or "requests" that they avoid media coverage, rather than ordering them not to read newspapers, watch television news, or listen to radio newscasts. Judge Blythin asked jurors during the trial if they had seen or heard a newscast stating that Dr. Sam's purported mistress was pregnant with his child. Two of the jurors stated they had. Obviously his order to avoid news reports went unheeded.

Judicial admonition ■ Judges' statements, direction, or advice to jurors, or anyone, at trial.

Control of Courtroom

Unrelated to pre-trial publicity but highly relevant to Sheppard's due process rights, the Court pointed to the importance of the judge's exercise of authority in the courtroom to maintain decorum. The location of reporters, their ability to overhear confidential discussions, their access to evidence and jurors, all played a role in corrupting the judicial process. Reporters might have behaved badly, but only because Judge Blythin allowed them to. We'll never know if his pending election caused him to cater to the news media but many have speculated that it did.

Bedrock Law: Judges can be forceful in asserting that a fair trial *requires* the jury's full cooperation, not just in their attentiveness to the testimony but also in their avoidance of external influences.

---

[10]Two First Amendment scholars have suggested that the issue is not whether prospective jurors have opinions because they likely will have. What is most important is selecting jurors who are capable of setting aside their opinions in deciding the case. N. Minow & F. Cate, *Who Is an Impartial Juror in an Age of Mass Media?* 40 Am. U. L. Rev. 631 (Winter 1991).

[11]Some legal scholars assert that trials are won or lost based on voir dire. Attorneys who are most successful at empanelling jurors sympathetic to their side will win. For a collection of critiques, *see* R. Jonakait, *The American Jury System* (Yale University Press 2003).

Judges have a tremendous amount of authority in maintaining the decorum of the courtroom. Much of this comes from the British legal tradition. Hundreds of years ago, judges were the crown's representatives. They settled disputes in spite of the fact that they may not have even been schooled in law. The judge's robe is a vestige of the king's royal robe. The fact that all rise when the judge enters the court is a sign of the respect paid to the king. As representatives of the king, judges were also given wide latitude in coercing those in the courtroom to behave themselves. **Contempt of court** empowers the judge with the authority to deal with disruptive people by removing them from the court, fining them, or even temporarily imprisoning them. Contempt of court can be a major concern for free press advocates, as judges have also used the power to control the behaviors of people *outside* the courtroom.

CONTEMPT OF COURT

Black's Law Dictionary defines contempt of court as follows:

> Any act which is calculated to embarrass, hinder or obstruct court in administration of justice, or which is calculated to lessen its authority or its dignity. Committed by a person who does any act in willful contravention of its authority or dignity, or tending to impede or frustrate the administration of justice, or by one who, being under the court's authority as a party to a proceeding therein, willfully disobeys its lawful orders or fails to comply with an undertaking which he has given.[12]

The easiest example to understand of a contempt citation is when a person in court is repeatedly disruptive. Even people who have never been inside a courtroom have seen plenty of movies and TV shows where a judge bangs the gavel and calls for order in the court, threatening or actually finding someone in contempt. This type of contempt is known as **direct contempt** because it takes place in court or close enough to be disruptive (such as being noisy outside the courtroom door).

There is also **indirect contempt,** which involves activity away from the courtroom but also results in a disruption of the legal process. When a court issues a **subpoena** (an order for someone to appear in court to testify) and the person does not appear at the appointed date and time, the judge may find the person in indirect contempt. If a judge instructs trial participants not to speak to anyone about the case outside the courtroom and one of the attorneys appears on the evening news discussing the trial, the judge may find the attorney in contempt.

Judges are given tremendous latitude in doling out punishments for contempt but they don't quite have absolute power. A judge might fine someone a million dollars for being disruptive in court or order a reporter to stop writing notes because it's distracting. If a judge's punishment is excessive or a demand is inappropriate, the contempt citation can be appealed. Like any appeal, an appellate judge will review the facts to make a determination. In the case of contempt citations the review is often expedited because of the First Amendment implications.

Contempt of court ■ Any act which is calculated to embarrass, hinder, or obstruct court in administration of justice, or which is calculated to lessen its authority or its dignity. Committed by a person who does any act in willful contravention of its authority or dignity, or tending to impede or frustrate the administration of justice, or by one who, being under the court's authority as a party to a proceeding therein, willfully disobeys its lawful orders or fails to comply with an undertaking which he has given. *See* Black's *Law Dictionary.*

Direct contempt ■ Contempt of court that occurs inside the courtroom, like being disruptive during court proceedings.

Indirect contempt ■ Contempt of court that occurs outside the courtroom, like failure to appear in court when subpoenaed.

Subpoena ■ An order by a court that compels the production of evidence or the testimony of a witness.

---

[12]*Black's Law Dictionary* 319 (6th ed. 1983).

It's important to understand, however, that a judicial order must be carried out until it's appealed. Officers of the court fear that if everyone who disagrees with a judicial order simply ignores it, chaos could result. In 1972, a Baton Rouge, La., judge prohibited reporters in his court from publishing reports based on public testimony given in court. Two reporters violated the rule and the judge held them in contempt and issued a fine. On appeal, the Fifth Circuit Court of Appeals said that the judge's order was a violation of the First Amendment rights of the reporters but in spite of that still upheld the contempt citation. The court opinion stressed that the reporters could have appealed the order rather than simply violating it, leaving it for the court to decide whether the order was justified, not the reporters.[13] There is a little wiggle room, however, if reporters make a good faith effort to appeal what appears to be an unconstitutional order and the appeal is not decided quickly. In such cases, *some* courts in *some* jurisdictions have been willing to invalidate the contempt citation, but this has not been settled by the U.S. Supreme Court and remains shaky ground for journalists.

> **Bedrock Law:** News reporters covering trials should follow the judge's orders, even if those orders appear to be unconstitutional, until they can be appealed.

One settled area of law is that maintaining order in the court does not require people to silence their criticism of judges *outside* the courtroom. In two separate decisions from the 1940s, the U.S. Supreme Court ruled that calling a judge's decision "outrageous"[14] or stating that judges protect criminals more than the public[15] is unlikely to cause judges or courts to lose all respect or damage the process of justice. Saying such things to a judge inside the courtroom might result in contempt, but outside of court such statements are protected.

Civil contempt ■ Civil contempt citations are issued for the purpose of eliciting a particular response, like compelling reporters to testify by citing them for contempt.

Criminal contempt ■ Criminal contempt citations are issued for punitive reasons, like punishing an outburst during court.

In addition to distinguishing between direct and indirect contempt, contempt is divided into categories of **civil contempt** and **criminal contempt**. Civil contempt is used by the court when it tries to coerce cooperation by a party violating a court order. It attempts to get the uncooperative party to have a change of heart. Civil contempt may be invoked when a reporter refuses to testify in a legal proceeding or a television station refuses to provide videotape that has been subpoenaed. On the other hand criminal contempt is punitive. There's no attempt to get a particular response from the person; it is just invoking a penalty for misbehavior. Some actions can actually produce both civil and criminal citations for contempt.

For example, in 2004, two *San Francisco Chronicle* reporters published a book dealing with the use of steroids in sports. The book contained facts about the BALCO investigation (the company purported to supply the steroids to athletes) that were alleged to have been leaked from grand jury testimony. In 2006 the reporters were called to testify before a grand jury to explain how they obtained this information, which should have been kept confidential. The reporters refused to testify. The court was prepared to fine the newspaper $1,000 *per day* that the reporters refused to testify, as if each day they refuse is a new act of contempt. The reporters also faced the possibility of spending up to eighteen months in prison. While the orders were being appealed and before the reporters

---

[13] *United States v. Dickinson*, 465 F.2d 496 (5th Cir. 1972).
[14] *Bridges v. California*, 314 U.S. 252 (1941).
[15] *Pennekamp v. Florida*, 328 U.S. 331 (1946).

were imprisoned, a source voluntarily came forward revealing his identity and ending the grand jury's need to pressure the journalists.

In some cases judges can coerce trial participants to cooperate with requests for information without the threat of contempt of court. In 1979 the Supreme Court ruled that CBS's refusal to provide information during the pre-trial discovery process would allow the judge to presume the claims made by the plaintiff about the journalist's state of mind were correct.[16] Since public figure plaintiffs must prove that the defendant had a knowledge of falsity or reckless disregard for truth, one way to make the argument is by asking the reporter what he or she knew and when. If reporters opt not to answer the question, courts may be forced to accept the plaintiff's assertions. When *60 Minutes* producers would not provide hours of videotape that were requested by the plaintiff in discovery, the Supreme Court said it was reasonable for the judge to assume that the plaintiff's claims about what the tape contained were accurate. The defense had the ability to refute the claims by providing the evidence.

> **Bedrock Law:** Contempt of court citations are used by judges as punishment when trial participants ignore a judge's gag order and in order to ensure compliance with their orders.

GAG ORDERS

One of the many things that Judge Blythin did not do to protect Sam Sheppard's right to a fair trial was to constrain the behavior of the trial participants: the attorneys, jurors, and witnesses. They were free to talk with anyone (including reporters) outside the courtroom. Of course doing so would result in immediate news coverage, which could be read or heard by other trial participants. **Gag orders** are edicts issued by judges for people to keep their mouths shut. It really does evolve from the centuries-old practice that unruly people in the courtroom could be literally bound and gagged to keep them quiet. Today those people would more likely be removed from court, but in the famous 1968 trial of the "Chicago Seven" (radical protestors during the Democratic National Convention in Chicago), Black Panthers leader Bobby Seale was bound and gagged to try to prevent his outbursts (it didn't work and he was later removed). Physical binding and gagging may be outmoded, but insisting that people not speak about a trial even outside the courtroom is still a modern concept that is imposed by judges.

> **Gag order** ■ An order by a judge restricting participants in a trial from making public comment.

Gag orders—also known as suppression or restraining orders—may be challenged, and in some cases the gags have been upheld while in others they have been overturned. Gag orders involve the balancing of two constitutional rights: the First Amendment right of the trial participants to freedom of speech and the Sixth Amendment right of a fair trial.

Among other guarantees of the Sixth Amendment is the right to a trial "by an impartial jury." In determining whether a gag order may be imposed, judges must balance the First and Sixth Amendment rights involved. There is not a magic formula for deciding which one wins. The decision must be made ad hoc each time by weighing the likelihood that a jury will be impartial and comparing that to the extent to which trial participants lose their free speech rights.

---

[16]*Herbert v. Lando,* 441 U.S. 153 (1979).

The fact that the same court has both upheld and overturned gag orders demonstrates the ad hoc nature of the decision. In 1988, the U.S. Second Circuit Court of Appeals found a gag order for trial participants to be constitutional.[17] The federal district court in southern New York had imposed a gag order in a bribery and racketeering trial, and the appellate court upheld the order believing there was a "reasonable likelihood" that a fair trial would be prejudiced by pre-trial publicity.

In a case the very next year, the same southern district court of New York issued another gag order, and the challenge again went to the Second Circuit Court of Appeals. This time, however, the gag order was vacated, and one of the reasons given was that there was no evidence that there was information that would have threatened the defendant's fair trial rights.[18]

So exactly what standard will be applied? Unfortunately, the answer varies by jurisdiction. Research by the Reporters Committee for Freedom of the Press states that the Second, Fourth, Fifth, and Tenth Circuits are more likely to allow gag orders, requiring only a "reasonable likelihood" or "substantial likelihood" that speech outside the courtroom could prejudice a trial. On the other hand, the Third, Sixth, Seventh, and Ninth Circuits are less likely to allow gag orders because they require a "clear and present danger" or a "serious and imminent threat" to the fair trial rights of the accused.[19]

A recent phenomenon has been the request by trial participants that the judge impose a gag order. While attorneys making the request can claim the request is to protect the accused's right to a fair trial, often the true reason is an attempt to avoid potentially embarrassing publicity. In 2002, Kathie Lee Gifford filed a defamation suit in Florida against supermarket tabloid *National Examiner* when the paper claimed Gifford's coddling of her son turned him into a brat. Gifford requested a gag order claiming the trial would lead to "frenzied media interest." The judge denied the request and the case was later settled out of court. Similarly in 2005, Arizona State University requested a gag order when it was being sued by the family of an epileptic student who suffocated when he was handcuffed and strapped face down onto a stretcher. The case had gotten a lot of media coverage and the university requested the judge impose a gag order, which he refused to do.[20]

One settled area of the law regarding gag orders is the Supreme Court's distaste for imposing gag orders on individuals who are *not* trial participants, including the media. The seminal case in this area comes from Sutherland, a small town in Nebraska. In 1975, six family members were murdered and the following day their neighbor confessed to the police. Pre-trial publicity was rampant and the judge was asked by the county attorney to impose a gag order on the media to assure a fair trial. The judge issued the order and the Nebraska Press Association appealed. The Nebraska Supreme Court modified the gag order slightly but otherwise

---

[17]*In re Dow Jones & Co.,* 842 F.2d 603 (2d Cir. 1988).

[18]*In re New York Times Co.,* 878 F.2d 67 (2d Cir. 1989).

[19]A. Gauthier, *Secret Justice: Gag Orders,* Reporters Committee for Freedom of the Press, http://www .rcfp.org/secretjustice/gagorders/effect.html.

[20]*See id.*

left it in place, so the press association appealed to the U.S. Supreme Court. The highest court was unanimous in finding that the gag order was an unconstitutional limitation on free expression.[21] A majority of the Court held there might be instances when gag orders on the media are warranted and provided three issues that a court must examine before gagging the media:

- The nature and extent of the pre-trial news coverage;
- The alternatives to a gag order that would provide for a fair trial; and
- The likelihood that a gag order would actually ensure a fair trial.

The judge in the murder case, like the judge in Dr. Sam Sheppard's trial, never considered the litany of available alternatives. What's more, in a town of just 850 people rumors spread about the biggest crime of the century posed a greater threat to a fair trial than responsible media reporting would.

The 1976 ruling would make it seem that the door was left open for gag orders on news media but that is definitely not the situation. Appellate courts have repeatedly struck down gag orders on nontrial participants that have been imposed by trial courts. As a result of the *Nebraska Press Ass'n* ruling (which was reinforced in another unanimous ruling the following year[22]) there is a nearly insurmountable hurdle when trying to gag anyone other than participants in a trial. One notable exception occurred in 2004, when reporters were gagged while covering basketball star Kobe Bryant's rape case. Some media were mistakenly e-mailed transcripts from closed hearings and the judge ordered the media to destroy them and not to report on any of the information. The appeal was modified by the Colorado Supreme Court but for the most part was upheld.[23] The gag order can be understood as an attempt to correct an error made by the court's own clerks in making public information that should never have been disseminated. Viewed this way, it can be understood as an exception to an otherwise firm prohibition of gag orders on nonparticipants in trials.

When it comes to gag orders on trial participants, the hurdle is a much lower one and there are countless examples of gag orders that either have not been appealed or have been upheld on appeal. Trial participants include everyone *formally* connected to the trial, including the attorneys for either side, the defendant, witnesses, and even the jurors. Obviously judges do not have to gag the trial participants to insure a fair trial, and judges may elect to gag some of the participants and not others (attorneys are more often gagged than jurors) but once the order is issued, those affected must abide by the gag order until the trial is over. It should be noted that the Supreme Court has ruled that in cases *where the media serve as trial participants*, they can be subjected to gag orders just like any other trial participant.[24]

While gagging trial participants usually does not directly affect journalists, such orders always indirectly affect the ability to gather news. Reporters trying to cover noteworthy trials can be frustrated by gag orders that prevent potential sources for a story from speaking to them. There have been instances where trial

---

[21]*Nebraska Press Ass'n v. Stuart,* 427 U.S. 539 (1976).

[22]*Oklahoma Publishing Co. v. District Court,* 430 U.S. 308 (1977).

[23]*People v. Bryant,* 94 P.3d 624 (Colo. 2004).

[24]*Seattle Times v. Rhinehart,* 467 U.S. 20 (1984).

participants have violated gag orders and spoke confidentially to the news media, but those who publish such information face another risk.

Imagine this hypothetical example: Judge Pompous issues a gag order in a murder trial. Sharon Seekrits is a witness who is sure that defendant Freddie Badguy committed the crime. She confidentially speaks to WINO-TV reporter Hugh Bagawind. The next day, Bagawind reports that an "unnamed source" told him about some evidence. Judge Pompous sees the newscast and immediately realizes the only way that Bagawind could have gotten that information was from one of the trial participants, which means whoever spoke to the reporter violated the gag order. The only way Judge Pompous can find out who violated the gag order is to question the reporter. But, can reporters be made to disclose their confidential sources? The next section examines this perplexing question.

COMPELLING REPORTERS TO TESTIFY

One of the most frequent conflicts between the rights of a free press and the right to a fair trial is the court's need to gather evidence. Without evidence, a trial obviously lacks the most basic elements for arriving at the correct outcome. We provide courts with extensive tools to gather evidence. As mentioned previously, courts may subpoena people to require them to appear in court to testify in a trial. A subpoena in no way implies that a person has done anything wrong. A person who receives a subpoena supposedly has information that the court would like to investigate. For that reason, when an attorney requests a subpoena a court is likely to grant it. A judge is not going to expect an attorney to prove beyond a reasonable doubt that the witness has important evidence. Unless a witness has to travel a great distance, the subpoena is a relatively minor burden in most cases.

When a reporter is called to testify, however, the situation is considerably different. The media have claimed that confidential sources need to be protected in order to keep a free flow of information to the public. If confidential sources are divulged by reporters, then those sources may stop providing information. The reasons that sources give for providing information to news media vary greatly. In some cases a disgruntled employee may want to blow the whistle on an employer; in other situations it could be an adversary in a political battle who provides some dirt about an opponent; still other sources could be government employees who disagree with policy decisions and want to see a change in direction. In many cases, confidential sources speak on the condition of anonymity because they face personal or professional retaliation if their identity is revealed. Perhaps the most famous anonymous source in recent history was "Deep Throat," a crucial source of information to *Washington Post* reporter Bob Woodward, who along with Carl Bernstein wrote the series of articles credited with breaking the Watergate scandal that toppled the Nixon presidency in 1974.[25]

---

[25]Deep Throat's identity was protected by Woodward, Bernstein, and the *Washington Post* for more than thirty years until Deep Throat's family revealed his identity in 2005. W. Mark Felt was serving as assistant director of the FBI when he had the late-night meetings to provide Woodward with information. D. Von Drehle, *FBI's Number 2 Was Deep Throat*, Washington Post, June 1, 2005, p. A6.

Despite the value of anonymous sources, media critics charge that news media are too quick to grant anonymity and may be hiding a litany of sins behind the veil of anonymous sources. In 1981 the *Washington Post* won a Pulitzer Prize for "Jimmy's World," a story about an eight-year-old heroin addict. *Post* reporter Janet Cooke later revealed that there was no Jimmy, but that she concocted him as a composite of many people. Cooke had kept the sources for the story anonymous, even from her editors, because she said she had vowed to protect their identities.[26] When her reporting on "Jimmy" was revealed to be a fictional portrayal, Cooke resigned her position at the *Washington Post* and the newspaper returned the Pulitzer Prize.

Apart from the journalistic debate about how and when anonymous sources ought to be used in reporting, the legal question exists as to whether journalists can be compelled to reveal their sources' names by testifying. For the seminal case in this area, we go back in time to the turbulent era of the late 1960s to early 1970s, when illegal drug use and civil disorder were hot topics.

The *Branzburg* Test

What is referred to in legal circles as "the *Branzburg* case" was actually three cases that were heard together by the Supreme Court. The cases involved three different journalists working for three different news media in three different cases. The common thread in all of them was their refusal to disclose the identities of their sources. Paul Branzburg was a reporter for the Louisville, Kentucky, *Courier-Journal*. In 1969 and 1971 he wrote two articles about drug use for his paper that caused law enforcement officials to take notice. In one he explained how marijuana was refined to make the much stronger drug hashish. In order to do the research, he observed people who made hashish. For another story about drug use, Branzburg interviewed a number of drug users and actually observed several of them smoking pot. Law enforcement officials subpoenaed Branzburg as a result of both stories because in each situation he was a witness to the commission of a crime. Branzburg refused to identify his anonymous sources (the alleged criminals) to a grand jury.

In 1970, Paul Pappas was working out of the Providence, R.I., office of a Massachusetts television station when he was sent to cover some civil disorder activities involving "fires and other turmoil." He met with leaders of the local Black Panthers and was allowed inside their headquarters for about three hours on the condition that he not disclose anything he saw or heard except an expected police raid, which never occurred. Pappas was later called before a county grand jury that wanted to know what he learned during his time at the Black Panthers headquarters, but Pappas refused to answer.

A third journalist asked to testify was Earl Caldwell, who was working for the *New York Times*. Caldwell had also been covering the Black Panthers and was subpoenaed to appear before a grand jury to testify about the operations of the militant group. Caldwell complained that the subpoena was so broad and he was

Branzburg **test** ■ To compel a reporter to testify, the government must show 1) probable cause to believe that the newsman has information that is clearly relevant to a specific probable violation of law; 2) the information sought cannot be obtained by alternative means less destructive of First Amendment rights; 3) a compelling and overriding interest in the information.

---

[26]Although dated, a wonderful article outlining the virtues and problems with anonymous sources (available online) is A. Shepard, *Anonymous Sources,* Am. Journalism Rev. (July 1994), http://www.ajr.org/Article.asp?id=1596.

UP CLOSE

The Grand Jury Process

A grand jury is not like the jury in a trial court. It is a group of citizens brought together to hear evidence and decide whether the government ought to go forward in the prosecution of a crime.[a] Grand juries are not usually called just for one individual case but rather are impaneled for a period of time anywhere from one month to three years. While trial juries are drawn from random pools, members of grand juries come from the same potential pool (registered voters or drivers), but are often not random selections at all, with some grand jurors serving multiple terms. In some states grand jurors volunteer for the role. Grand juries investigate; they do not conduct trials of guilt or innocence. Rather than the standard of "beyond a reasonable doubt"

that must be shown in a criminal trial, grand juries are only looking for "probable cause," which is a significantly lower standard. If the grand jury determines that there is probably cause, it will order an **indictment,** a formal written accusation of a crime. Only after there is an indictment does a suspect become a defendant. The grand jury investigation is not conducted by a judge but rather by a law enforcement official, such as a sheriff or county prosecutor. There are both federal and state grand juries (but not all states use grand juries), and both consist of 12–23 members (the term *grand* jury comes from the fact that it is larger than a common jury, known in legal circles as a *petit* jury).

It surprises many Americans who are unfamiliar with the legal system that grand juries are conducted in complete secrecy. No one else is allowed into the proceedings. Witnesses can't even bring attorneys with them when they provide testimony. This is one reason why journalists don't even want to appear before a grand jury. A journalist who enters a grand jury chamber might refuse to answer any questions about a confidential source, but no one can know whether the journalist told everything because the proceedings are secret, and simply appearing before the grand jury for any reason might be seen by news sources as threatening to their anonymity.

The prosecutors have a great deal of control over the whole process: They decide who will be the witnesses, they ask the questions, and they draft the charges. Critics have called modern grand juries little more than a "rubber stamp" for the prosecutor.[b]

---

[a]While there are some "civil grand juries" (in California, for instance) that serve as government oversight bodies, the term *grand jury* is usually used in connection with criminal charges.

[b]American Bar Association, Frequently Asked Questions about the Grand Jury System, http://www.abanet.org/media/faqjury.html.

---

reluctant to appear because of the damage it would do to his relationship with his sources. The grand jury responded that it was investigating a number of serious crimes including conspiracy to assassinate the president and an appeals court ordered Caldwell to testify. He refused and was found in contempt.

It might be useful to remember how volatile the late 1960s and early 1970s were in the United States. In addition to American involvement in Vietnam, drug use and race relations were subjects that often stirred public controversy and protests, sometimes ending in violence. There was a lot of fear at the time: the drug stories by Branzburg and stories about a militant racial organization by Pappas and Caldwell helped to fuel that fear.

In 1972 the U.S. Supreme Court heard the appeals of Branzburg, Pappas, and the government in the Caldwell case (Caldwell's contempt was overturned by the Ninth Circuit). The ruling in the *Branzburg-Pappas-Caldwell* trilogy would provide the test applied by courts when determining whether to require a journalist to testify. One might think that such a solid basis for law might come from a unanimous Court, but in fact the decision was 5–4. It might also be natural to assume the basis would be derived from the majority opinion, but in fact that is not the situation. The majority held that Branzburg, Pappas, and Caldwell did not have the right to refuse to testify before the grand jury.

Yet it is the concurring opinion of Justice Lewis Powell, combined with the dissent written by Justice Potter Stewart that provides the criteria for the test. While the other members of the majority were prepared to turn away any protection for journalists called to testify, Powell was prepared to allow such protection provided conditions that were not present in the *Branzburg* trilogy were met. Combined with the dissent's belief that the reporters should not have been made to testify, Powell's swing vote set the stage for the test, provided in Stewart's dissent. Powell said the freedom of the press and the citizen's obligation to provide testimony must be "balance[d] . . . on a case-by-case basis."[27] The precise criteria for the balancing were then provided in Stewart's dissent. Despite his claim that "all of the balancing was done by those who wrote the Bill of Rights"[28] and that "any test which provides less than blanket protection to beliefs and associations will be twisted and relaxed so as to provide virtually no protection at all,"[29] Stewart provided the three-part test. In order to compel a reporter's testimony, the government must

- Show that there is probable cause to believe that the newsman has information that is clearly relevant to a specific probable violation of law;
- Demonstrate that the information sought cannot be obtained by alternative means less destructive of First Amendment rights; and
- Demonstrate a compelling and overriding interest in the information.[30]

In plain language, the first point prevents law enforcement from going "fishing" for any possible information a journalist might have. To subpoena the reporter, law enforcement ought to know exactly what information the reporter has that is needed.

The second part of the test requires that the journalist be the *only* person who has the information. If other nonmedia sources have the information then the journalist

Indictment ■ A formal accusation that a person has committed a felony or serious crime. After a grand Jury hearing, the grand jury issues either a true bill, in which case the person is charged, or a no bill, in which case the person is not.

---

[27]*Branzburg v. Hayes,* 408 U.S. 665, 710 (Powell, J., concurring).

[28]*Id.* at 713 (Stewart, J., dissenting).

[29]*Id.* at 720 (Stewart, J., dissenting).

[30]*Id.* at 743 (Stewart, J., dissenting).

need not testify. It also implies that coercing reporters' testimony cannot be a substitute for the law enforcement investigation. If a journalist has information that police could discover through their own resources, the reporter should not be made to testify, even if it costs time and money for law enforcement. The expense of an investigation is not as important as protecting First Amendment rights.

The last prong of the test requires that the information being sought is crucial for the investigation. Plenty of testimony is gathered during a grand jury proceeding and the subsequent trial but much of it is not of "compelling and overriding interest." Of course critics assert that sometimes it is impossible to know whether testimony is critical until it is heard.

The importance of the *Branzburg* decision should not be underestimated. Since 1972 more than 1,500 cases have cited *Branzburg* and the case has been mentioned in more than 1,100 law journal articles. In spite of this (or possibly *because* of this) there is a great deal of variation in the "rigor" with which the *Branzburg* test is used in various jurisdictions. Regardless of the degree of support, no jurisdiction grants journalists an absolute right to refuse to testify.

Shield Laws

Shield laws ■ State laws in 39 states which afford *privilege* to journalists to not disclose information (i.e., notes and other materials) obtained during course of their newsgathering.

One attempt to try to afford journalists a greater degree of protection has been the enactment of **shield laws** in a number of states. Shield laws are "state statutes which afford *privilege* to journalists to not disclose information (i.e., notes and other materials) obtained during course of their newsgathering."[31] In 2010 Wisconsin became the thirty-ninth state to have enacted a shield law, with varying degrees of protection.[32]

There are many differences among state shield statutes. For example, exactly who is protected by a state statute? There is no "license" for a journalist, so who qualifies for the privilege?[33] It might be easy to say that a full-time reporter for a newspaper or television station qualifies, but what about a freelancer who is not employed by news media and hopes to sell an article to a magazine? How about bloggers? To use Indiana as an example, the state statute would protect freelancers who have already sold articles to news media but not someone working on a first-time submission.[34] There are no Indiana cases involving bloggers but the language

---

[31]*Black's Law Dictionary* 716 (5th ed. 1983).

[32]The Reporters Committee for Freedom of the Press maintains an online database of reporter's privilege at its website, http://www.rcfp.org/. Check it for the specifics of your state.

[33]At least one scholar suggests that anyone can qualify as a journalist, since we are all able to publish our observations online to a worldwide audience. Such a position would render a definition of journalists obsolete. *See* S. Gant, *We're All Journalists Now: The Transformation of the Press and Reshaping of the Law in the Internet Age* (Free Press 2007).

[34]The relevant portion of the statute reads as follows: (1) any person connected with, or any person who has been connected with or employed by: (A) a newspaper or other periodical issued at regular intervals and having a general circulation; or (B) a recognized press association or wire service; as a bona fide owner, editorial or reportorial employee, who receives or has received income from legitimate gathering, writing, editing and interpretation of news; and (2) any person connected with a licensed radio or television station as owner, official, or as an editorial or reportorial employee who receives or has received income from legitimate gathering, writing, editing, interpreting, announcing or broadcasting of news. Ind. Code § 34-46-4-1 (1998).

▶ UP CLOSE

Privilege

The word **privilege** has many meanings, but when used in the law it refers to a specific power or exemption that someone has which others do not. Diplomatic immunity is a form of privilege we afford foreign officials in order to exempt them from prosecution. In defamation law we speak about the privilege legislators have to be immune from defamation suits while conducting the business of the legislature. Other classes of people use privileged communication, and in such cases, the protected person does not have to divulge the content of that communication. "Executive privilege" exempts the president and the White House staff from having to provide information to other branches of government (Congress or the courts) that could jeopardize the executive's ability to do its job. It also applies to both foreign and domestic communication, but it is not without its limits, as President Richard Nixon discovered when trying to claim the privilege to protect tape recordings made in the Oval Office.[a]

Most people are aware of the privilege that exists in attorney/client communications. Any conversation between a lawyer and his client can be kept confidential; otherwise clients might not be forthright with their own lawyers. Doctors also have the same sort of privilege in communicating with their patients.[b] Most states provide married couples with a privilege that protects them from having to testify against their spouses. Priests have a privilege in communications with penitents who confess to their sins. Opinion is mixed on whether the penitent must be involved in a formal process of confession (such as practiced by the Catholic Church) in order for the privilege to apply.

The claim of a journalist's privilege not to disclose confidential information has been raised by virtually every journalist subpoenaed to testify who has promised his sources secrecy. It is based primarily on a First Amendment argument that the freedom of the press *must* include the right to gather news without government interference; otherwise the right to publish news is eviscerated. With the exception of the spousal privilege, all the others are based on the premise that the professional given the privilege needs to be protected in order to successfully do the job. Just like journalists, they learn the important confidential information in the course of their professional activity. As Branzburg, Pappas, and Caldwell learned, the Supreme Court has not recognized such a constitutional privilege for journalists, thus the proliferation of shield laws.

---

[a] *United States v. Nixon,* 418 U.S. 683 (1974).

[b] Even doctor/patient privilege is not absolute. In many jurisdictions doctors are required to disclose instances of child abuse, sexually transmitted diseases, gunshot wounds, or other conditions considered to be risks to the public at large.

---

of the Indiana statute would appear to exclude them from protection unless they are connected with a blog "issued at regular intervals and having a general circulation." In contrast, a California court extended the state's shield law to include bloggers when it "decline[d] to embroil [itself] in questions of what constitutes 'legitimate journalism.'"[35]

Shield laws also differ in exactly what they cover. Some are specific to the protection of the names of sources of information while others also include any notes

Privilege ■ A benefit, immunity, or exemption extended only to a specific group of people. In journalism, usually immunity from being forced to reveal sources.

---

[35]*O'Grady v. Superior Court,* 139 Cal. App. 4th 1423, 1457 (2006).

or other work product that the reporters have produced. Some states require that sources specifically request anonymity for the journalist to be protected while others do not. Others are clear that the shield law does not apply if the journalist is a witness to the commission of a crime.

Many states distinguish between requests made by grand juries, civil trial courts, and criminal trial courts. For example, Hawaii law protects journalists rather thoroughly when it comes to grand jury requests but affords less protection in felony prosecutions, or even in a civil defamation case.

Ironically, reporter Paul Branzburg was subpoenaed in Kentucky, which had (and still has) a shield law. The Supreme Court was not persuaded that the First Amendment provided him a privilege to refuse to testify, and the Court similarly did not accept the argument that a state law protected him. New Jersey is thought by many to have one of the most protective shield laws in the nation. One of the early adopters, it has had a statute on the books since 1933. And yet, when Myron Farber invoked the shield law in 1978, the Supreme Court of New Jersey did not accept the argument. Farber was a *New York Times* investigative reporter whose crime reporting was a primary reason New Jersey indicted Mario E. Jascalevich for murder. Farber refused to testify or to provide material for *in camera* inspection by the judge and was held in contempt of court. Farber's attempt to defend himself on the basis of the state's shield law was rejected by the court on the premise that the right of the accused to a fair trial, a constitutional right, outweighed the shield law, a state statute.[36]

This is, in fact, one reason why even some journalists oppose state shield laws. As they see it, any attempt to rely on a statute is bound to fail on any occasion where it conflicts with the Sixth Amendment rights of the accused in a criminal trial. A shield law may offer protection in civil cases, perhaps even grand jury hearings, but is less helpful in criminal trials. Further, a journalist of no less renown than Ben Bradlee (who as *Washington Post* editor oversaw the Watergate reporting and its use of anonymous sources) opposes shield laws on the premise that if legislatures have the power to give something, they also have the power to take it away.[37] This position advocates that the First Amendment must be the source of a reporter's privilege, putting it on the same level in the legal hierarchy as the Sixth Amendment right to a fair trial.

Given the fact that a majority of the U.S. Supreme Court has not accepted a reporter's privilege as inherent in the First Amendment, others assert that the best possible protection would come from a *federal* shield law. One such proponent is U.S. Congressman Mike Pence, who also happens to be a former broadcaster.

Given the uncertainty of the situation, practical advice for any journalist is to be reluctant to accept confidential information. Before accepting the offer to protect the identity of a source in exchange for information, the journalist needs to decide if the information is worth the possibility of going to jail. If a journalist believes that the information is that important then a promise of confidentiality seems in order. Even in states with shield laws it could be decided by a court that

---

[36]*In re Myron Farber,* 78 N.J. 259 (1978).

[37]*The First Rough Draft of History,* 33 Am. Heritage Mag. 6 (Oct./Nov. 1982).

the shield law as applied violates an accused person's right to a fair trial and as such cannot be constitutional. *New York Times* reporter Judy Miller spent 85 days in jail in 2005 for refusing to provide the name of her source in the investigation of leaks that led to the disclosure that Valerie Plame was a covert CIA agent.

NEWSROOM SEARCHES

In addition to protecting sources of confidential information, journalists want very much to protect the materials they gather. As in the argument for protecting sources, journalists need to protect their notes, tapes, photographs, digital files, and computers from intrusive eyes so as to be able to continue gathering news without jeopardizing sources. Imagine how frightening it would be to a newsroom to have law enforcement officers storm into the office and begin rummaging through the files. That is precisely what happened to one university student newspaper in 1971.

The *Stanford Daily* had covered some Vietnam War protests involving student demonstrators. Unfortunately, some of the student demonstrators attacked police officers, who had been sent to evict them from the Stanford University Hospital's administrative offices, which demonstrators had taken over and occupied for a day. Two days later a special edition of the paper included an account of the fracas, including photos. Believing the paper might have other photographs that would reveal the identities of the students who struck the officers, the Santa Clara County District Attorney's Office sought and received a warrant to search the paper's offices for evidence.

A search warrant differs significantly from a subpoena. As stated earlier, a subpoena is the traditional manner by which evidence is requested. Had the Santa Clara County authorities followed the normal procedures, they would have appeared at the *Stanford Daily* offices with a subpoena ordering the paper to bring all the relevant material to court by a certain date to be examined. The paper would then have time to gather the material or, if it chose to do so, file a legal request to quash the subpoena (the legal term for voiding it). Up until this time, the legal community considered a subpoena appropriate in those cases where the party being served was not suspected of any wrongdoing, whereas a warrant was preferred when the party involved was suspected of a crime. Certainly if suspected drug dealers receive a subpoena inviting them to come to court and bring the illegal drugs with them it would have little effect, so a search warrant is appropriate. The Fourth Amendment to the Constitution requires that "no warrants shall issue, but upon probable cause, supported by oath or affirmation, and particularly describing the place to be searched, and the persons or things to be seized." Probable cause is not required for the issuance of a subpoena.

Despite the fact that the *Daily* was not accused of any wrongdoing, Santa Clara County asserted that it needed a warrant to negate the possibility that the student publication would destroy evidence that it might have. The *Daily* filed suit claiming that both its First Amendment rights of free press and its Fourth Amendment right to be protected from unreasonable searches had been violated. Although the federal trial court and appellate court both found in favor of the student publication, in *Zurcher v. Stanford Daily*[38] the U.S. Supreme Court over-turned the lower courts and found that the police had not violated the paper's constitutional rights. As might be expected, law enforcement officials praised the decision while media advocates condemned it. Less than two years later, police searched the offices of a Flint, Mich., printer where a muckraking paper was printed and the KBCI-TV newsroom in Boise searching for videotapes that would provide information about a prison riot in Idaho. They, too, were issued a warrant rather than a subpoena, knowing that the Supreme Court authorized such action.

The criticism of the use of warrants was loud and strong. In 1980 Congress passed the Privacy Protection Act, which called on the Attorney General to create guidelines restricting the issue of search warrants to a "disinterested third party." The result was a set of rules that still make it *possible* for law enforcement officials to obtain a warrant in order to search a newsroom but makes it considerably more difficult. Law enforcement agencies are not to search and seize "work product" or "documentary materials" that are believed to have been gathered or produced for "public communication." Work product includes notes, tapes, or other material used in gathering information. Documentary materials are things that would typi-cally be considered finished work, such as a tape for air. But, materials may be seized by use of a warrant if

- The subject of the warrant is suspected of a crime and is not just an "inno-cent bystander." For example, if the reporter is suspected of selling drugs, a warrant may be used.
- There may be injury or loss of life if the material is not immediately seized. For example, if the reporter's notes contain the location of a time bomb.
- There is a belief that documentary materials would be destroyed if subpoe-naed. It's unclear exactly how much proof there would need to be to demon-strate that the journalist would destroy the material rather than turn it over to authorities.
- Earlier subpoenas for the material have been ignored. Journalists can appeal subpoenas but they cannot ignore them.

Journalists in California, Connecticut, Illinois, Nebraska, New Jersey, Oregon, Texas, Washington, and Wisconsin have their own state statutes that afford even more protection than the Privacy Protection Act of 1980.[39]

CAMERAS IN THE COURTROOM

We live in a video world. Surveillance cameras are almost everywhere. YouTube has all sorts of videos, including moments that the participants never knew would be made available worldwide. Official Iraqi video of Saddam Hussein's execution in 2006 ended before showing the actual moment of execution, but someone with a cell phone camera uploaded a complete version of the hanging online where it

---

[38]436 U.S. 547 (1978). James Zurcher was the Palo Alto, Cal., police chief.

[39]Electronic Privacy Information Center, The Privacy Protection Act of 1980, http://epic.org/privacy/ppa/.

could be seen by millions (albeit poor quality). One part of our world where cameras have been tightly controlled has been in the American courtroom. Some states allow no cameras whatsoever, while those that do impose a variety of rules limiting their use. The impact of photographic coverage on a trial's outcome has been the subject of debate for years.

Long before the Dr. Sam Sheppard case, judicial decorum was lacking in another high-profile trial. The controversy actually began in New Jersey in 1935. Bruno Hauptmann was charged with kidnapping the baby of American icon Charles Lindbergh. Photographers were even permitted to take flash pictures in the courtroom. The fallout from this case produced an addition to the Canons of Professional and Judicial Ethics of the **American Bar Association**. The new recommendation was that cameras should be banned from all courtrooms. In 1952 the ABA amended the recommendation to include television cameras in the ban. When the Bar Association makes a recommendation, it does not have the force of law but it certainly has more weight than just an ordinary suggestion. For nearly thirty years, the ABA recommendation was followed with nearly no public comment or criticism. It was accepted as a given for courtroom decorum.

> **American Bar Association (ABA)**
> ■ The United States national bar organization. The bar is a professional organization for lawyers.

That situation changed with a U.S. Supreme Court decision in 1965.[40] Billie Sol Estes was indicted by a Texas grand jury for swindling (cheating people) through a fraudulent fertilizer and cotton business. Due to his association with politically well-connected Texans, including then–Vice President Lyndon Johnson, the *Estes* trial gained a lot of press attention and the court decided to change the venue of the trial (as suggested in the *Sheppard* case). Despite the ABA Canon and a similar one from the State Bar of Texas, and over objections from the defense, the judge agreed to allow television cameras in the trial court. During the pre-trial hearings there were as many as 12 cameras in the courtroom, with cables running everywhere. It was extremely disruptive. By the time the trial began, a booth had been constructed in the back of the courtroom and all cameras were moved inside it. Only certain portions of the trial could be televised live and most of the rest could be only silent video, which was used in portions during regularly scheduled newscasts. Estes asserted that his right to due process was violated by the presence of the cameras. The Supreme Court agreed, stating that the cameras were distracting to the jury, the witnesses, and the judge. In fact the Court used the construction of the camera booth, the restriction on what portions could be televised live, the requirement that video from much of the trial be silent, and the prohibition on shooting the defense's closing testimony as evidence that the cameras caused a distraction. The majority opinion concluded with this prophetic statement: "It is said that the ever-advancing techniques of public communication and the adjustment of the public to its presence may bring about a change in the effect of telecasting upon the fairness of criminal trials"[41] but that was not the present situation. Thus in 1965, the Supreme Court's position was the mere presence of cameras in a court could, and in this case did, result in a violation of the defendant's constitutional right to a fair trial.

---

[40]*Estes v. Texas*, 381 U.S. 532 (1965).
[41]*Id.* at 551–52.

In 1972, the American Bar Association replaced its Code of Judicial Ethics with a new Code of Judicial Conduct, but it still included a recommendation that all cameras be banned from the courtroom.[42] Television technology was rapidly improving with cameras getting smaller, quieter, and capable of shooting in low-light conditions. The prevalence of cameras in society was increasing concurrently, making it less extraordinary to see someone videotaping an event. In 1978 the ABA's Committee on Fair Trial-Free Press proposed experimenting with cameras in local courtrooms provided that the cameras were unobtrusive and the judge maintained strict control. There was mixed reaction to the proposal among ABA committees and governing bodies, but the Conference of State Chief Justices overwhelmingly approved a resolution allowing each state's supreme court to establish its own rules for cameras in their respective states.

Florida established a one-year experiment with cameras in the courtroom beginning in July of 1977. At the end of the 12 months, the Florida Supreme Court extensively studied reports and comments, surveyed trial participants of every kind, and examined the record from six states that already had adopted new cameras in court rules and from ten other states that were considering adopting rules. Florida was satisfied that cameras and a fair trial could peacefully coexist provided certain rules were in place assuring decorum. Florida permitted no more than one camera and one camera operator. The camera had to remain stationary for the entire trial. No extra microphones other than those that might already exist in the court were allowed. The actual videotape equipment itself had to be outside the courtroom. The jury could never be photographed, and the judge had the authority to exempt any individual witness from television coverage.

The very same month that the state of Florida began its experiment, two Miami Beach police officers were charged with grand larceny, allegedly breaking into a well-known Miami Beach restaurant. Officers Noel Chandler and Robert Granger tried to prevent cameras at their trial asserting that the experiment violated their fair trial rights. Their motions were denied and cameras were present. Notably, Florida was one of the few states that permitted camera coverage over the objection of the defendant. In total, less than three minutes of the actual trial were broadcast, but the material used was all from the prosecution's side of the case. Chandler and Granger were found guilty and they appealed their conviction claiming they had been denied a fair trial but presented no evidence as to how the trial was unfair. The Florida appellate and supreme courts rejected their appeal.

In *Chandler v Florida*,[43] the U.S. Supreme Court unanimously ruled that Chandler and Granger's right to a fair trial had not been violated. Chandler attempted to argue that the *Estes* case provided all the proof necessary that cameras were a violation of fair trial rights, but the Court asserted that a close reading of the decision could not conclude that the intent in *Estes* was to ban all cameras from all courts indefinitely. Estes's rights had been denied, but it was not the same as saying all

---

[42]In the Code of Judicial Ethics the admonition had been Canon 35, but in the new Code of Judicial Conduct, the same rule was Canon 3A (7).

[43]449 U.S. 560 (1981).

▶ FROM THE TRENCHES

Cameras as Seen from the Judge's Bench

Judge Louis H. Schiff

For most of the last century, courts were concerned that bringing in cameras and electronic media would be the kryptonite of the judicial system.

The Florida Supreme Court in 1975 boldly began a pilot program whereby cameras and electronic media were allowed in state courtrooms under the condition that journalists follow a strict set of rules designed to open the courts to the public, while protecting the rights of the litigants. The Florida Supreme Court said *In re Petition of Post-Newsweek Stations Fla., Inc.,* 370 So. 2d 764 (Fla. 1979) cameras in the courtroom did not inherently violate the constitutional rights of a defendant. These standards remain in effect today.

The Supreme Court of the United States held the Constitution did not prohibit states from permitting cameras in the courtroom and upheld the Florida Supreme Court in *Chandler v. Florida,* 449 U.S. 560 (1981).

Florida courts at every level have cameras in the courtroom, with the Supreme Court of Florida broadcasting their sessions live on television and over the Internet.

Critics have argued that cameras in the courtroom tend to pose some sort of irreparable harm upon an individual's right to a fair and impartial trial; or they create a "spectacle" like the Hauptmann or the O.J. Simpson trials.

However, under strict rules and guidelines cameras and electronic media serve to inform a citizenship and pull away the curtain of secrecy in the courtroom. As a trial court judge, I have always welcomed journalists using electronic media and cameras into the courtroom. Our system of democracy demands our citizens not only be informed of the goings on in court, but they should see and hear them as well.

Today, judges and media in Florida participate together in forums which educate the third branch of government and the fourth estate on the rules regarding media in the courtroom.

While I am not so naive to believe judges, lawyers, and litigants have not "showboated" while cameras have been in the courtroom, I can say the overwhelming majority of judges, lawyers, and litigants are not affected by electronic media in the courtroom and their behavior is not altered or affected by it. As a judge I am always aware of the presence of the cameras. I realize, whether a camera is there or not, the courts are a very public place with a very solemn purpose, and that purpose is to ensure that justice is carried out. Electronic media can assist the courts in carrying out its duty.

Florida Supreme Court Justice Alan Sundberg said in *Post-Newsweek,* "We have no need to hide our bench and bar under a bushel. Ventilating the judicial process, we submit, will enhance the image of the Florida bench and bar and thereby elevate public confidence in the system. . . ." Electronic media and cameras can bring responsible change to courts and the justice system, and they can add an air of confidence to the public at large that the third branch of government is competently operating in the open.

The Honorable Louis H. Schiff has served as a Broward County (FL) judge since 1997. In addition to his law degree he also has an undergraduate degree in journalism.

cameras in all courts were unconstitutional. "An absolute constitutional ban on all broadcast coverage of trials cannot be justified simply because there is a danger that, in some cases, prejudicial broadcast accounts of pretrial and trial events may impair the ability of jurors to decide the issue of guilt or innocence uninfluenced by extraneous matter."[44] The Court took the firm position that the presence of a camera alone, without any other evidence, will not result in a violation of due process.

Following the *Chandler* decision, more states allowed cameras in their courts, but each established its own set of rules. As with shield laws, each state's rules vary dramatically and professionals in the media need to be familiar with their own state's rules. Some states allow cameras in appeals courts and not trial courts, while it's vice versa in other states, and still others allow both. Only the District of Columbia prohibits cameras in both trial and appeals court hearings. The **Radio Television Digital News Association** maintains an up-to-date database online.[45] RTDNA classifies states according to three tiers of openness: nineteen states (including Florida) afford the most coverage, sixteen states (including Texas) impose restrictions covering important cases or witnesses, and fifteen states (including New York) limit cameras to the appellate courts or impose strict trial court rules that essentially eliminate coverage there.

Radio Television Digital News Association (RTDNA)
■ The largest professional organization for electronic journalists in radio, television, and all digital media, as well as journalism educators and students.

Unlike state courts, federal courts are loath to allow cameras. While the American Bar Association's Canons have *suggested* limiting cameras, the U.S. Judicial Conference has explicitly prohibited them in federal trial courts. In 1946 Federal Rule of Criminal Procedure 53 prohibited any cameras or recording in federal criminal trials, and the rule was expanded in 1972 to include all federal civil cases as well.

In 1988 the Conference recommended a federal experiment with cameras, and a three-year pilot was conducted in six district and two appellate courts. When they studied the results the Conference decided to ban cameras in trial courts but allow the appeals courts to decide for themselves. Cameras are banned in all but two federal appellate courts, the Second and Ninth Circuits.

Chief Justice John Roberts has stated that he has no interest in allowing cameras in the U.S. Supreme Court.[46] Bills have been introduced in Congress as recently as 2007 to require the Supreme Court to permit cameras, but so far none has passed. When the subject came up in 1996, Justice David Souter told the House Appropriations Committee that there would be cameras in the Supreme Court "over my dead body."[47] Souter may be gone from the Court but that attitude is not. In spite of the repeated efforts of newsgathering trade associations and public interest groups, federal trial courts, the overwhelming majority of the appellate courts, and the highest court in the nation are closed to cameras. In 2010, a federal trial judge in northern California was going to allow audio and video to be streamed from his court to other federal courtrooms across the country. The trial court was going to hear a legal

---

[44]*Id.* at 574–75.

[45]*See* http://www.rtdna.org/pages/media_items/cameras-in-the-court-a-state-by-state-guide55.php. Up until 2009, the Radio Television Digital News Association (RTDNA) was the Radio Television News Directors Association (RTNDA).

[46]The Court does release audio from its hearings, available at http://www.oyez.org/.

[47]*On Cameras in Supreme Court, Souter Says "Over My Dead Body,"* New York Times, March 30, 1996, p. 24.

challenge to Proposition 8, an amendment to the state's constitution that would recognize only marriages between a man and a woman as valid. Chief Judge Vaughn Walker was prepared to allow the broadcast of the trial to other federal courtrooms but was blocked by appeals, ultimately to the Supreme Court, which ruled 5–4 that proper procedures had not been followed to allow for the broadcast.[48]

Bedrock Law: Most states allow some camera coverage at either the trial or appellate court level, but it is rare for federal jurisdictions to do so.

MUST COURTROOMS BE OPEN?

If state and federal courts have the authority to determine rules to govern the use of cameras in court (or ban them altogether), do they likewise have the authority to close courtrooms to any and all observers? While the general rule is that trials are presumptively open to the public, not all trials are public, and even for trials that are public, a portion of the trial may be closed.

The presumption that criminal trials are open was made clear by the Supreme Court in 1980. The Sixth Amendment to the Constitution states that "*the accused shall enjoy* the right to a speedy and public trial." If it's the right of the accused to a public trial, might the accused waive that right and ask that a trial be closed? If the Sixth Amendment were the only word on the matter that just might be the case, but history and the First Amendment also come into play. In *Richmond Newspapers v. Virginia*[49] a murder suspect wanted the trial closed and the judge consented. Richmond Newspapers appealed and the Supreme Court agreed that the closure was unconstitutional.

Implicit in the First Amendment is the right to attend criminal trials and the history of the United States bears this out. Allowing defendants to close trials could result in deal making between the participants or the *perception* that something inappropriate was happening behind closed doors, resulting in a loss of public trust in the legal system. The Supreme Court did not assert that *all* criminal trials must *always* be open, but it left for another day the question of precisely what criteria need to be met to close a courtroom.

It used to be that juvenile trials were always closed to the public, and most still are. The rationale has always been that juveniles deserve a higher level of protection than adult suspects. This concern also drives similar laws about nondisclosure of juvenile records (discussed in chapter 9) and media's voluntary nondisclosure of the names of juvenile suspects or victims. In recent years, however, the presumption that juvenile trials must be closed has been revisited. The National Council of Juvenile and Family Court Judges stated, "Traditional notions of secrecy and confidentiality should be re-examined and relaxed to promote public confidence in the court's work."[50] Almost half of the states open a juvenile trial if the charges would be felonies if they were tried in "regular" court. Illinois and California open the trial if the charge is related to "street gang" activity. Some states such as Pennsylvania

---

[48]*Hollingsworth v. Perry,* 130 S. Ct. 705 (2010).

[49]448 U.S. 555 (1980).

[50]D. Oddo, *Removing Confidentiality Protections and the "Get Tough" Rhetoric,* 18 B.C. Third World L. J. 105 (1998).

distinguish between younger and older juveniles, opening the trials of the older ones but not the younger.

Minors might also be protected when they testify in criminal or civil courts by closing the court, but in those situations there must be a compelling reason for closing the courtroom, and only the portion of the trial that deserves the compelling interest is closed. Courts have become less inclined to automatically accept such requests for closure. In 2007 the D.C. Court of Appeals ruled that the closure of a courtroom for the testimony of a twelve-year-old victim of sexual assault was a violation of the defendant's Sixth Amendment right to a public trial. The defendant objected to closure and the appeals court ruled that the judge in the case did not consider alternatives to closure nor demand enough of a showing that closure was necessary. At the time of the request, the only nonparticipants in the courtroom were supporters of the defendant.[51]

While closing courts when minors testify may be allowed, it is *not* constitutional to *require* that the courtroom be closed for minors who testify. The Supreme Court ruled in 1982 that a Massachusetts statute requiring that judges close trials during the testimony of minors who were victims of sex crimes was unconstitutional.[52] The Supreme Court did not say the testimony had to be public: in fact, closure might be warranted. Likewise, though, it might be appropriate for the testimony to take place in an open court and the *requirement* that the trial be closed was an unconstitutional infringement.

The Supreme Court interpreted the Sixth Amendment right of the accused to a public trial in *Waller v. Georgia* in 1984.[53] The defendants were changed with gambling, and they attempted to suppress evidence the prosecution had that was obtained by wiretapping. The court conducted a closed suppression hearing, which the defendants wanted open to the public. The Supreme Court ruled the defendant's Sixth Amendment right to a public trial included pre-trial hearings and could only be closed with a clearly demonstrated "overriding interest." The Court rejected an unsupported claim of a privacy violation to nontrial participants as rising to the level required to close the hearing.

> **Bedrock Law:** With the exception of some juvenile hearings, trial judges can only close the courtroom to the public under extraordinary circumstances when an overriding interest is apparent.

Earlier in the same term, the Supreme Court ruled that the voir dire jury selection process is also part of the trial and subject to the same openness as trials. A California judge closed the courtroom for the entire six weeks of jury selection in a trial for the rape and murder of a teenage girl. The trial court was acting in response to claims that the questioning of prospective jurors in an open court in such a sensitive case would violate the privacy of the jurors and risk the fair trial rights of the accused. In an 8–0 decision, the Supreme Court held that voir dire is part of the trial process and as such should be presumptively open under the First Amendment. As in other cases dealing with closure, the Court pointed out that a narrowly tailored closure in rare instances where there are specific findings that fair trial or privacy rights will be compromised might be permissible, but that

---

[51]C. Zarek, *Appeals Court Reverses Sex Abuse Case for Court Closure,* News Media Update, Oct. 9, 2007, http://www.rcfp.org/news/2007/1009-sct-appeal.html.

[52]*Globe Newspaper Co. v. Superior Court,* 457 U.S. 596 (1982).

[53]467 U.S. 39 (1984).

even in those instances alternative actions that do not infringe on First Amendment rights first must be explored.[54] In those instances, closure could be no longer than absolutely necessary to protect the jeopardized rights.

There may be national standards established by the Supreme Court for the openness of criminal courts, but there is no such definitive answer for civil trials. As with many of the other fair trial issues discussed in this chapter, the answer differs according to the jurisdiction. Most recognize that there is a **presumptive right of access** even to civil trials but the conditions under which they allow closure vary. Some are quite clear while others are less so. California, for example, clearly provides a right of access to civil trials. The issue was decided by the California Supreme Court in 1999 in a case involving actor/director (and mayor) Clint Eastwood and Sandra Locke, a former lover who claimed Eastwood was attempting to destroy her career. California's highest court ruled that closing the trial violated the First Amendment, and that it also violated a century-old California statute that stated "the sittings of every court shall be public."[55] California's standards for civil trials follow exactly the rules for criminal trials: closure only under extraordinary circumstances and only if all the requisite criteria are met.

The Third Circuit Court of Appeals (with jurisdiction over Delaware, New Jersey, Pennsylvania, and the Virgin Islands) has established that there is both a First Amendment right and a common-law right of access to civil proceedings. The case in point stems from a proxy battle between stockholders for control of a publicly traded company. The parties involved asked the judge to close the proceedings which he did, asserting that the hearing was whether or not to make certain information public which would be decided by the press, not the court, if they were in attendance. The Third Circuit ruled that the trial court had not conducted an adequate review, i.e., the request for closure was based on speculation rather than evidence.[56]

North Carolina's Supreme Court also recognized a presumptive right of access to court proceedings, but it did so in a case where it upheld the complete closure of a civil court.[57] In the case, a doctor took legal action against a hospital that had revoked his medical staff privileges as a result of his peer review. North Carolina has a statute that keeps peer reviews confidential. In light of this, the North Carolina high court found in favor of closing the trial.

A federal court in Texas allowed for the partial closure of a civil trial to protect the identities of minor plaintiffs. Three adults and three minors filed suit against the Santa Fe, Tex., school district for policies they believed created an unconstitutional endorsement of religion. To protect them from public retribution, the plaintiffs' identities were kept secret. At an open trial, however, it would be easy for anyone attending to identify the plaintiffs so they requested closure. The federal district court ruled that it would uphold closure for the testimony of the minor plaintiffs but would not uphold it for the adult plaintiffs.[58]

Presumptive right of access ■ The rule in criminal trials (including the pre-trial hearings) is that they are presumptively open to the public and press.

---

[54]*Press-Enterprise Co. v. Superior Court of Cal.*, 464 U.S. 501 (1984).

[55]*NBC Subsidiary v. Superior Court*, 86 Cal. Rptr. 2d 778, 788 (Cal. 1999).

[56]*Publicker Indus. v. Cohen*, 733 F.2d 1059 (3d Cir. 1984).

[57]*Virmani v. Presbyterian Health Servs.*, 350 N.C. 449 (1999).

[58]*Doe v. Santa Fe Indep. Sch. Dist.*, 933 F. Supp. 647 (S.D. Tex. 1996).

Closing Criminal Court

The rule in criminal trials (including the pre-trial hearings) is that they are presumptively open. In order for a judge to close any portion of the trial to the public (and therefore the media):

- There must be a fundamental right (such as privacy or fair trial) at risk if the proceeding is held in public;
- There must be convincing evidence (not mere speculation) that the right at risk will be compromised if the proceeding is not closed;

- There must be no alternative available that will protect the fundamental right which is less damaging to the accused's Sixth Amendment right to a public trial nor the public's First Amendment right to an open courtroom, and;
- The closure must be limited to the specific content that causes problems for the fundamental right being protected.

The State of Florida has declared that all hearings to terminate parental rights are closed. Florida has a statute that declares it so and the constitutionality of that statute was upheld by the Florida Supreme Court, asserting that juvenile proceedings are not presumptively open and that the state had the right to close the proceedings.[59]

While there are some exceptions such as those mentioned in this chapter, under strictly delineated criteria, courts are open. As one nationally renowned legal scholar wrote in 1991:

> By longstanding tradition, the American public is free to view the daily activities of the courts through an expansive window that reveals both our criminal and civil justice systems. Through this window, people can watch an endless panoply of lawsuits, litigants, judges, juries, sometimes garishly illuminated by television lights and dramatized by graphic, occasionally lurid, press reports.[60]

---

[59]*Natural Parents of J.B. v. Florida Dept. of Children & Family Servs.*, 780 So. 2d 6 (Fla. 2001).

[60]A. Miller, *Confidentiality, Protective Orders, and Public Access to the Courts*, 105 Harv. L. R. 428 (1991).

SUMMARY

- The Constitution guarantees a criminal defendant the right to an impartial jury. Juries may be aware of *some* facts of a case and still be impartial, but some sorts of information may have a prejudicial effect on jurors or potential jurors.

- Courts are inclined to do whatever is in their power to protect the rights of the accused in a criminal trial. The *Sheppard* case in the 1950s outlined the Supreme Court's response. When necessary, courts should protect defendants using the tools of change of venue, continuance, sequestration, rigorous voir dire process, stern admonitions to the jury, and maintaining courtroom decorum: all tools that can help to assure a fair trial without impinging on the First Amendment rights of the public.

- Judges have the power to find people in contempt of court to punish them for their misbehavior in court. The threat of contempt can be used to coerce someone to do what the court wants, such as reveal the name of a source. Though not a daily occurrence, there are many instances of journalists having been jailed for their refusal to name a source.

- Another tool judges sometimes use to try to protect the rights of the accused in a criminal trial is to order that no one discuss a trial, otherwise known as a gag order. While these orders limit the information communications professionals can acquire about a case, they are usually constitutional. On the other hand, attempts by judges to gag nontrial participants, especially journalists, have not been upheld.

- A balance of sorts has been struck between the court's desire for testimony and the journalist's desire not to testify. The Supreme Court's *Branzburg* case provides the three-part test to determine whether reporters can be compelled to testify.

- Partly in response to the threat of compelled testimony, a majority of states have created shield laws that attempt to protect journalists from having to reveal information, most notably the names of anonymous sources. Shield laws are far from guarantees for communicators—even in states where they exist, reporters have been ordered to testify or face contempt charges, and some have been jailed. In spite of repeated efforts, there is no federal shield law.

- News media are sometimes subpoenaed when law enforcement believe they have evidence (often pictures or video) that is necessary for an investigation. Media can move to quash the subpoena and a judge will have to decide whether to require the media to produce the evidence. A federal statute prohibits law enforcement from using warrants rather than subpoenas to obtain from news media evidence except in rare instances.

- States decide for themselves whether to allow cameras in courts, and a different set of rules has been adopted by each state to maintain order in the court, which courts can have cameras and what may be televised. A few federal courts have experimented with cameras but the Supreme Court, which sets rules for the federal courts, has not allowed regular camera coverage.

- Criminal trials are presumptively open, and so are the pre-trial activities that are considered part of the process (such as voir dire). Court closure is rare and when it does occur is restricted to the least possible amount of time necessary. More states appear to be moving toward openness for civil trials, but there is no constitutional requirement that these courts be open and the situation varies by state.

Texting in the Court

As technology advances, electronic devices become smaller and less obtrusive. There are some uses of technology in the court that appear to impact a fair trial more than others. A Florida circuit court judge declared a mistrial in a fraud case when it was found that a development official was texting his colleague—who was *on the witness stand* at the time.

We have established that judges have the authority to maintain order in their courtrooms to assure a fair trial is conducted. We have also established that the mere presence of a camera does not result in a disorderly court, and that different jurisdictions have determined different rules for cameras and recording devices. What about newer technologies: laptops, cell phones, PDAs, etc.?

In 2009 U.S. District Court Judge Clay D. Land ruled that sending streaming text messages from the courtroom in the form of the popular Twitter updates constituted broadcasting and therefore could be prohibited from his court (Georgia). That same year in a *different* federal district court (Kansas), Judge J. Thomas Marten ruled that it was acceptable for a reporter to provide tweets (the term for Twitter messages) from his courtroom during a trial.

Is it distracting for a reporter to sit in a courtroom and take notes? One could say that generally it would not be disruptive unless the reporter were making an excessive amount of noise or flailing about with the notepad. What if the same reporter were to take notes using a laptop: would that change the degree of disruption? What if the same reporter's laptop were accessing the Internet via a wireless connection? Would the note taking then be more disruptive?

What limits should be established for the use of electronic devices in a courtroom? Some texters are accustomed to texting in class, in meetings, while at social functions, and even while driving (despite the risks) and might be surprised to find that a judge could hold them in contempt of court for texting from the courtroom. What limits would you establish? Would the criteria be based on maintaining court decorum, preventing the "broadcast" of court proceedings, or some other principle? ■

Freedom of Access

LEARNING OBJECTIVES

After reading this chapter you should know:

- The arguments of public officials for shielding documents from inspection against the news media's arguments for openness

- How to determine whether a record is in fact public

- Where and when public documents may be accessed

- Which U.S. agencies are subject to the Freedom of Information Act and which areas are exempted

- The series of actions a federal agency will take once it receives a FOIA request

- The circumstances in which government agencies do not have to turn over documents

- How to calculate the factors that determine whether an exception applies

- The law's provisions regarding open meetings of the federal government, including circumstances in which elected officials may block access to their gatherings

- State laws concerning open meetings and public records, and be able to demonstrate the differences between state laws and federal provisions

ACCESS IN PRACTICE

Just one day after Barack H. Obama took office as the forty-fourth president of the United States of America, he proposed a new policy for his administration in a memo calling for transparency in the nation's executive branch of government. That memo succinctly stated the principles of freedom of access to government materials, the first one being that "democracy requires accountability, and accountability requires transparency."[1] The president's directive ordered a presumption of openness for fifteen executive departments under his watch and seventy-seven federal agencies. He drew upon the metaphor of Associate Justice Louis Brandeis, who advised in an early twentieth-century *Harper's Weekly* essay, "sunlight is said to be the best of disinfectants."[2]

The Obama administration thus would be less prone to secrecy and far friendlier to openness, or so it seemed. Then came a request for White House visitors' records, and the president began parsing legal terms about media access and FOIA (Freedom of Information Act) requirements. After all, the law specified the "Executive Office of the President," and not the White House office, so it could be inferred the requested access should not be allowed to the news media. After weeks of wrangling with the FOIA request, the White House released almost 500 visitor records and promised to publish visitor logs online each month.[3]

Other run-ins shrouded the White House sunshine statement.[4] When the administration was asked to release new photos of detainee abuse in Iraq and Afghanistan, President Obama realized the images of rape and sexual abuse went beyond anything shown during the Abu Ghraib scandal. He felt the photos would stoke resentment abroad and place American lives in jeopardy and thus reversed his position.

For those who feel the First Amendment protects free expression by granting news media the right to gain access to information whether by public records or covering actual events, the Supreme Court's rulings are instructive. "The Constitution itself is neither a Freedom of Information Act nor an Officials Secrets Act," wrote Chief Justice Warren Burger in 1978.[5] The U.S. guarantee of a free press and its implied access to information is indirect, and demands of citizens or the press to be informed are weighed against other interests, especially national security and local law enforcement.

In the 1960s, the Cold War between the Soviet Union and the United States made the Communist nation of Cuba an especially sensitive island among its Western

---

[1] *See* Memorandum for the Heads of Executive Departments and Agencies: Freedom of Information Act, Office of the Press Secretary (Jan. 21, 2009).

[2] Louis D. Brandeis, *Other People's Money and How the Bankers Use It, compiled from a series in Harper's Weekly* (Frederick A. Stokes Co. 1914).

[3] The decision could be viewed as a victory for Citizens for Responsibility and Ethics in Washington (CREW), a group dedicated to informing the public about government business.

[4] *ACLU v. Department of Defense*, 543 F.3d 59 (2d Cir. 2008).

[5] *Houchins v. KQED, Inc.* 438 U.S. 1 (1978).

Hemisphere neighbors. An American citizen by the name of Zemel wanted to travel there in order to "to satisfy my curiosity about the state of affairs in Cuba and to make me a better informed citizen."[6] Permission was denied. Zemel challenged U.S. Secretary of State Dean Rusk's refusal to allow his passport, and the Supreme Court's ruling in 1965 made clear the distinction between freedom of expression and access: "the right to speak and publish does not carry with it the unrestrained right to gather information."[7]

THE ORIGINS OF ACCESS

The chief framer of the Constitution, James Madison, wrote that popular government without access to information would be "the prologue to a farce or tragedy." American policy with respect to public records and access underscores this quote, but citizens still must convince public officials of their right to view the machinations of government.[8] Some prefer the term *transparency*, and still others name it *public access*, but the conflict over access usually centers on the procedures and penalties that either favor governmental openness or support official secrecy. Advocates of "sunshine in government" represent the right to know, and seek timely procedures that afford a practical means of appealing an adverse decision with penalties exacted against those who create unlawful obstructions to access.

Regardless of the procedures and penalties that vary according to state and jurisdiction, a single underlying principle guides the debate: that decision-making and the governing process should be clear to those affected by the decisions made, which often is not even in the eyes of the U.S. Supreme Court. The thoughts expressed by two associate justices illustrate this point in a celebrated case about investigative reporters and confidential sources. Associate Justice Lewis Powell concluded that the "right to gather news, of some dimensions, must exist" because without the freedom to acquire information, the right to publish would be impermissibly compromised.[9] Justice Potter Stewart argued conversely, "The press is free to do battle against secrecy and deception in government. But the press cannot expect from the Constitution any guarantee that it will succeed." In other words, "the public's interest in knowing about its government is protected by the guarantee of a Free Press, but the protection is indirect. The Constitution itself is neither a Freedom of Information Act nor an Official Secrets Act."[10]

---

[6]*Zemel v. Rusk,* 381 U.S. 1, 4 (1965).

[7]*Id.* at 17.

[8]Ironically, Madison himself was an advocate for utmost secrecy during the constitutional convention, fearing leaks threatened passage of the new constitution.

[9]*Branzburg v. Hayes,* 408 U.S. 665, 728 (1972).

[10]Potter Stewart, *Or of the Press*, 26 Hastings L.J. 631, 636 (1975).

THE CONSTITUTION AND THE COMMON LAW

Historically speaking, laws governing the openness of information only promised access to pertinent records dealing with one's own affairs, but not necessarily to information going beyond that narrow scope. Thus, interpreters of the Constitution and scholars of the common law found a stronger case for confidentiality than for openness. Because the courts traditionally protected only the right to uncover information of personal relevance, facts about the government could remain hidden, potentially leading to abuses of power. One theory, however, suggests both journalists and citizens should have access to official knowledge beyond materials meant only for people with a personal stake at hand. This theory explains one of the first laws intended to open the drawer of federal records for citizens to view, and forms an important, although limited, first step in regulating access to public information.

The Administrative Procedure Act (APA) of 1946[11] arrived at the dawn of the Cold War when secrecy and security needs empowered government gatekeepers from the lower bureaucratic offices up to the White House. The APA gave the right to inspect federal agency paperwork only to those who had "good cause," and who were "properly and directly concerned" with information held by the U.S. government. It lacked a time limit for responding to citizen requests for public records, and it allowed agencies to establish whatever fee they deemed necessary for retrieving documents. Some felt this law did more to prevent disclosure than it did to grant greater access to government-held information.

THE FREEDOM OF INFORMATION ACT (1966)

Freedom of Information Act (FOIA) ■ The Freedom of Information Act (FOIA) is a federal law requiring federal agencies, on request, to disclose agency records unless the information can be kept secret under one of nine FOIA exemptions.

The mood of the nation shifted during the 1960s when civil rights advocates made compelling arguments for more openness in government. President Lyndon B. Johnson signed the first federal **Freedom of Information Act (FOIA)** on Independence Day, 1966. The bill addressed the APA's most awkward language, especially a rather timid public disclosure section that often resulted in curtailment of press access to documents by requiring the requesting party to justify his or her need to know beforehand. This language gave extraordinary custodial power to employees of the government. President Johnson was not necessarily opposed to such potential abuses of power possibly because he feared the law could be used against his own administration.

The FOIA—sometimes pronounced "FOYA"—was meant to expedite the access process. Government agencies in general, and federal bureaus in particular, were tediously slow in responding to citizen requests for records. The length of time it took for handling requests and making documents ready for access discouraged some but not all petitioners. Requests for information in fact grew as more individuals—and businesses in particular—sought all kinds of information, particularly items helping them to best their competition.

Bedrock Law: The FOIA opens access to government records without making citizens prove beforehand that they have a right to know based on their personal interest.

---

[11]Pub. L. No. 79-404.

FOIA Policies and Amendments

In 1976, Congress amended the FOIA with an eye toward speeding up response time, giving government custodians between ten and thirty days to respond to requests. However, these user-friendly provisions met with objections from ranking members of the White House, but the U.S. Congress prevailed and adopted the FOIA deadline anyway, over President Ford's veto. The law has since been amended twice, in 1986 and again in 1996.

Most notably, Congress ordered in 1996 that executive government agencies should post on their websites instructions on how to use the Electronic Freedom of Information Act (E-FOIA). This Clinton-era shift clearly established a more user-friendly approach toward openness in government. E-FOIA asked federal agencies to use digital indexing, electronic searches of data banks, "electronic reading rooms," and the computerization of the FOIA compliance process— even allowing citizens to specify the format of the information desired. It also gave journalists opportunities to have their requests expedited, but it should be noted the law does not give journalists special privileges of access not afforded to the general public.

Policy Shifts

President Clinton's Attorney General Janet Reno embraced this direction in policy and upended the one established earlier, during President Reagan's administration. General Reno's order urged that a **presumption of disclosure,** not confidentiality, should be made when government agencies respond to FOIA requests. She specifically encouraged Department of Justice employees to lean toward transparency rather than conceal-ment. Unless an executive agency "reasonably foresees that disclosure would be harmful," the requested documents should be released, she argued.[12]

That policy of openness, however, would shift again after the terrorist attacks of September 11, 2001. One White House policy instructed federal agencies to maintain closed records whenever there was a "sound legal basis" for doing so. Critics charged this clearly gave preference to privacy over openness; under the new policies, "leaks" could result in the firing of federal employees.

FOIA EXEMPTIONS

According to FOIA policy, a federal agency has to fulfill the requirements of the document seeker, but at the same time protect sensitive government information. There are nine exemptions, all are found in Title 5 of the U.S. Code, § 552.[13]

Bedrock Law: The identity of the person requesting a public record, or the reason for needing it, should not determine whether it is released, but it could impact whether there is a charge involved.

Presumption of disclosure ■ Under FOIA, requests are presumptively granted unless the government can show that the information falls under one of the FOIA exemptions.

Bedrock Law: The press is entitled to no more access to information from the U.S. government than the general public under the Freedom of Information Act.

FOIA exemptions ■ There are nine exemptions to FOIA specified in the statute. The government can deny a FOIA request, and keep information secret, if the requested material falls within one of the nine exemptions.

Government Accountability Office (GAO) ■ The Government Accountability Office is a congressional federal agency that assists Congress in oversight of budget expenditures.

[12]Memorandum from Janet Reno, Attorney General, to Heads of All Federal Departments and Agencies re: The Freedom of Information Act (Oct. 4, 1993).

[13]*See* 5 U.S.C. § 552(b) (FOI Advocates 2008).

Secrets of Energy Policy

President George W. Bush early in his administration encountered an access issue after he appointed an advisory committee, the National Energy Policy Development Group (NEPDG), which began constructing policy under Vice President Cheney's supervision. Public interest advocates wanted to know who was sitting on that White House committee since they were informing the president's energy policy. The advocates were denied access, a fact they found troubling since oil industry lobbyists had contributed mightily to the Bush/Cheney campaign. Some felt those corporate agendas might trump issues advanced by consumer groups and environmentalists. The former Texas energy giant Enron, for example, appeared to influence the president's advisory group when seven recommendations proposed by the Houston-based firm appeared in its final report. Enron later imploded as a result of its discredited business practices, but just how large a role it played in the formulation of the national energy policy became a subject of speculation.

Citizen groups wanted to know more about the committee's deliberations and its membership, but the White House resisted demands for a full disclosure. Advocates for openness in government seized upon the **Federal Advisory Committee Act (FACA)** in their efforts to illuminate the group's activities. This 1972 law was designed to stop lobbyists from shaping policy behind closed doors. Once business employees or private citizens gain membership to an executive advisory committee, FACA theoretically made their

meetings open to the public. There was a problem: no one could say for certain who exactly served on the energy task force. If only government employees were included, then the task force was entitled to meet in secret.

The **Government Accountability Office (GAO)** asked for access to the energy group's records as part of its congressional oversight. If any oil industry representative acted as a member of the task force, the group would be in violation of FACA because the Act was designed to open advisory committee meetings and records to the public. The White House claimed separation of powers, contending that it was not for Congress to inspect the executive branch in this regard. A suit was filed to gain access to the committee's membership, but no access was ever granted.[a]

After the energy task force released its initial policy report, Judicial Watch and other public interest groups entered the debate and insisted the advisory meetings and records be made open to the public. Still the plaintiffs could not access any "official" information regarding the committee's full membership because nothing in the law required it to render a verifiable list apart from its final report.[b]

An even earlier presidential administration fought the advocates of open government and kept the special interest groups at bay. The Association of American Physicians and Surgeons sought Hillary Clinton's health care reform records, but as a government employee, the court ruled she was entitled to meet with her group in secret.[c]

[a] *Cheney v. U.S. Dist Court for the Dist. of Columbia*, 542 U.S. 367 (2004).
[b] *Judicial Watch v. National Energy Policy Dev. Group*, 219 F. Supp. 2d. 20 (D. D.C. 2002).
[c] *See Association of Am. Physicians and Surgeons v. Hillary Rodham Clinton*, 997 F.2d 898 (D.C. Cir. 1993).

The government's interest in protecting records pertaining to national defense and foreign policy is the number one priority for keeping documents confidential. A similar exemption is made for personnel practices and for routine housekeeping rules, such as parking lot spaces or sick leave policies. If executive agencies could be forced to create and dispense such records for public inspection, it might distract the civil servants from more important items of federal business. The legal exemptions to the Freedom of Information Act include the following areas:

1. **National defense**—*National defense or foreign policy information properly classified pursuant an Executive Order. 5 U.S.C. § 552(b)(1).*

   According to this exemption the agency has the right to decline the request for a record that pertains to national defense or foreign policy, if that record is classified by an executive order of the president. This first exemption classifies particular types of sensitive data that are necessary for the welfare of the republic, which are established and updated by the White House. An agency will still review the requested documents to make sure that it legitimately requires some protection from public viewing.[14]

2. **Personnel rules**—*Documents "related solely to the internal personnel rules and practices of an agency." 5 U.S.C. § 552(b)(2).*

   There are two safeguards that fall under this exemption. The first one serves to relieve agencies from assembling and creating access to trivial internal documents and activities, which are generally of no legitimate interest to the public. In *Department of the Air Force v. Rose* (1976)[15], the Supreme Court defined this exemption as, "any matter in which the public could not reasonably be expected to have an interest" (425 U.S. at 369–70). This exemption also serves to safeguard internal agency documents such as internal administrative manuals, disclosure of which "would risk circumvention of law or agency regulations" (FOI Advocates 2008, ¶8).

3. **Statutory exemptions**—*Documents "specifically exempted from disclosure by statute" other than FOIA, but only if the other statute's disclosure prohibition is absolute. 5 U.S.C. § 552(b)(3).*

   This exemption allows the agency to withhold information if it is prohibited from being disclosed by a statute, but only after two criteria are met: "(A) requires that the matters be withheld from the public in such a manner as to leave no discretion on the issue, or (B) establishes particular criteria for withholding or refers to particular types of matters to be withheld." Generally, the courts make three determinations about whether the disclosure can be reasonably denied. If replies to the three questions are yes, then disclosure can be legally denied. The first criterion is the correct application of a specific statute that authorizes or requires the withholding of information. The court also must determine what specific kinds of information the law in question actually forbids from release. Finally, the agency must ask if the record or information that is sought correctly fits the definition of prohibitive information under this exemption.

4. **Trade secrets**—*Documents which would reveal "[t]rade secrets and commercial or financial information obtained from a person and privileged or confidential." 5 U.S.C. § 552(b)(4).*

---

[14]The current executive order on security classification is listed as Exec. Order No. 12958, signed by President Clinton in 1995.

[15]425 U.S. 352 (1976). In this case, the U.S. Supreme Court ordered the release of records of Air Force Academy ethics hearings and held that exemptions 2 and 6 did not apply.

National defense ■ A FOIA exemption for national defense or foreign policy information properly classified pursuant to an Executive Order. 5 U.S.C. § 552(b)(1).

Personnel rules ■ A FOIA exemption for documents "related solely to the internal personnel rules and practices of an agency." 5 U.S.C. § 552(b)(2).

Statutory exemptions ■ A FOIA exemption for documents "specifically exempted from disclosure by statute" other than FOIA, but only if the other statute's disclosure prohibition is absolute. 5 U.S.C. § 552(b)(3).

Federal Advisory Committee Act (FACA) ■ The Federal Advisory Committee Act of 1972 is law which mandates transparency, reporting, and viewpoint diversity when private citizens give advice as part of a commission, committees, or advisory body established or utilized by the president or federal agencies in making policy.

Pictures of Shame

The name Abu Ghraib brings to mind graphic images of prisoner abuse in Iraq and tales of humiliation behind bars under the watch of U.S. soldiers. Americans recoiled in April 2004 when CBS's *60 Minutes II* first showed the images of naked Iraqi prisoners subject to abusive positions and barking dogs in the prison's concrete corridors. Afterward, news spread there were even more photos that had not been released or distributed, and soon citizen groups asked for access to them under the Freedom of Information Act.

In 2005, the American Civil Liberties Union (ACLU) won the release of most of the photos in a U.S. District Court in New York. The government took up the case on appeal, and the U.S. Court of Appeals (2d Cir.) in Manhattan upheld the lower court's ruling for the photos' release and dismissed the Department of Defense's argument that it would endanger "life or physical safety" as too speculative.[a]

In support of the ACLU's position, it was argued that the government would do more good than harm by releasing such photos because it would bring to light all abuses and help expunge the nation of this horrible travesty. The Pentagon felt quite a bit differently, however, and argued that the privacy rights of both U.S. soldiers and prisoner detainees would be violated by the release of any more images of prisoner abuse. Even if their identities could be shielded, making privacy no longer an issue, would not such photographs inflame al Qaeda's followers along with law-abiding Arabs, thus jeopardizing the mission and lives of U.S. soldiers seeking to win citizen support in Iraq and Afghanistan?

President Obama took office in 2009 with a promise of transparency and openness in government; he at first supported releasing the extra photos. But then Congress weighed in with a bill co-authored by U.S. Senators Lindsey Graham (R-S.C.) and Joseph Lieberman (I-Conn). The president apparently was persuaded to rethink his position. He signed the Detainee Photographic Records Protection Act in October 2009, classifying as confidential those photos taken between September 11, 2001, and June 22, 2009, relating to the treatment of individuals engaged, captured, or detained by Armed Forces in operations outside of the United States.

At that point, the ACLU's court case destined for the U.S. Supreme Court became moot. Advocates of access, looking for a silver lining, concluded it was probably better for Congress to ban the photos' release than to have the U.S. Supreme Court issue a more sweeping opinion about how the FOIA should be applied in such circumstances.

[a] See *ACLU v. Department of Defense* (2008), and 5 U.S.C. § 552(b)(7)(F) (2000).

Trade secrets ■
A FOIA exemption for documents which would reveal "[t]rade secrets and commercial or financial information obtained from a person [that is] privileged or confidential." 5 U.S.C. § 552(b)(4).

[This exemption helps to safeguard the competitive practices of businesses that willingly provide reliable commercial and/or financial information to the government.] The U.S. government will decline any requests under the FOIA for data if it finds that the request would hurt the competitive position of the submitting trade organization or business enterprise in the future. "Trade Secrets," according to the case of *Public Citizen Health Research Group v. FDA* (1983) are defined as "a secret, commercially valuable plan, formula, process, or device that is used for the making, preparing, compounding, or processing of trade commodities and that can be said to be the end product of either innovation or substantial effort."[16]

[16]704 F.2d 1280, 1288 (D.C. Cir. 1983).

5. **Agency memoranda**—*Documents that are "inter-agency or intra-agency memorandum or letters" which would be privileged in civil litigation. 5 U.S.C. § 552(b)(5).*

Documents that fall under this exemption are working papers and records that would be shielded from the discovery process in a court-of-law proceeding. Examples include certain studies, reports, or memoranda that are used to reach a decision or are deliberative in making certain recommendations for policy. These records naturally include confidential information between a client and attorney, as well as other types of privileged information.

Exemption 5 includes an executive privilege relating to the president, and protects from disclosure inter-agency or intra-agency memorandum or letters that are part of the decision-making process, which would also prevent the premature disclosure of policies under review (FOI Advocates 2008, ¶24). There is a special priority granted to the president's office requirement for privacy and frank advice from his government agencies.

6. **Privacy**—*Documents which are "personnel and medical and similar files the disclosure of which would constitute a clearly unwarranted invasion of personal privacy." 5 U.S.C. § 552(b)(6).*

This exemption protects the privacy of patients and government employees where the data in their personnel and medical files are involved. Only the private files of individuals qualify for exemption 6, but not the files of corporations or organizations. This exemption protects the individual federal employee from a clearly unwarranted invasion of personal privacy.

7. **Law enforcement**—*Documents which are "records or information compiled for law enforcement purposes," but only if one or more of six specified types of harm would result. 5 U.S.C. § 552(b)(7).*

In order to qualify under this seventh exemption, federal agencies first must make sure the records sought through the FOIA include information useful for law enforcement purposes. Requests for criminal records are exempted only to the extent that the distribution of such records would be reasonably expected to interfere with the prosecution of justice, would deprive an individual of the right to a fair and impartial trial, or would constitute an unwarranted invasion of privacy. Two more elements are involved with this seventh exemption. If the requested record reasonably could be expected to disclose the identity of a confidential source, including a state, local, or foreign agency, or any private institution that has furnished law enforcement information on a confidential basis, then it would be exempt. Finally, this item protects from disclosure the crime-solving techniques and procedures used in law enforcement investigations, especially if their disclosure could be used to circumvent the law, or endanger the life and/or physical safety of any individual.

8. **Financial records**—*Documents related to specified reports prepared by, on behalf of, or for the use of agencies which regulate financial institutions. 5 U.S.C. § 552(b)(8).*

This exemption prevents the disclosure of sensitive financial information to the public, including records that would affect the business of banks, the Federal Reserve, trust companies, insurance agencies, and the like.

Agency memoranda ■ A FOIA exemption for documents that are "inter-agency or intra-agency memorandum or letters" which would be privileged in civil litigation. 5 U.S.C. § 552(b)(5).

Privacy ■ A FOIA exemption for documents which are "personnel and medical and similar files the disclosure of which would constitute a clearly unwarranted invasion of personal privacy." 5 U.S.C. § 552(b)(6).

Law enforcement ■ A FOIA exemption for documents which are "records or information compiled for law enforcement purposes," but only if one or more of six specified types of harm would result. 5 U.S.C. § 552(b)(7).

Financial records ■ A FOIA exemption for documents related to specified reports prepared by, on behalf of, or for the use of agencies which regulate financial institutions. 5 U.S.C. § 552(b)(8).

9. **Oil field data**—*Documents revealing oil well data. 5 U.S.C. § 552(b)(9).*

This exemption prevents the disclosure of geological, geophysical, and topographical information, including maps and locations of oil wells that would be of interest to other drillers. It is analogous in some ways to the protection of trade secrets.

FOIA STEPS TO ACCESS

When government officials refuse to provide requested records, courts are left to decide resulting legal challenges. In such disputes, the first challenge is to agree on legal terms. The law defines *public records* as those materials used, prepared, or kept by government agencies that represent some transaction with the public. Examples include photographs, transcriptions, bills, or electronic records. A **record** is simply "any information that would be an agency record . . . maintained by an agency in any format, including an electronic format." Naturally, this definition cannot apply to public documents that the government has yet to produce, although requests are still sometimes denied for that very reason.

Access to national records is usually at the behest of a federal agency, which is defined as "any executive department, military department, government corporation, government controlled corporation or other establishment in the executive branch of government." Thus, the terms **record** and **agency** are central to the interpretation of access, but these apply to any materials the government office has created, has control over, and holds in its possession. In other words, a "record" can be a letter, map, photograph, or audio or video recording; it can be figures, tables, or data used by an agency to keep track of its activities. But it cannot be something that the agency would have to create just in order to fulfill the FOIA request. It is useful to know that Congress and judicial branches are *not* subject to FOIA access; only executive branch agencies and bureaus fall under its purview.

When citizens seek to gain access under Title 5 of the U.S. Code, § 552, several steps are taken before federal agency records are called up for review. First, the individual government employee charged with fielding FOI requests is contacted, who actually must be maintaining the materials under his or her jurisdiction. The requested material further must be deemed nonthreatening to anyone, and the government employee must determine if any FOIA exemptions apply. After those steps are accomplished, the release of the requested documents might be granted. Even if confidentiality appears warranted, some response is recommended within twenty days. Anyone denied access might receive what is known as the "Vaughn Index," an official list of withheld records accompanied by the reasons for their secrecy.[17]

FOI law obviously demands some judgment on the part of the record holders, who look first to see whether the information has been classified in order to determine what is confidential and what is not. The government custodian cannot decline to release an entire record just because a single sentence, a single page, or even an image is exempted. If a request is denied in whole or in part, and the reasons

---

[17]*See Vaughn v. Rosen*, 484 F.2d 820 (D.C. Cir. 1973).

Freedom of Information Law's Brave New Frontier Is Data

Charles N. Davis, Executive Director, National Freedom of Information Center

The information we once sought hid in manila folders and giant filing cabinets, guarded by earnest clerks bent on secrecy. Today's FOI victories more often than not are stored on thumb drives and can be e-mailed to requesters in seconds, or simply shared online for all to enjoy.

Much has been made of the Obama administration's praiseworthy efforts to open more information in the federal government through what the government has taken to calling "preemptive disclosure." In 2009, the Obama administration began asking for federal agencies to cull through their data sets and post the most frequently requested information. That's a great first step toward making more government information available to more people.

Cities and states are getting in the act, too. San Francisco, Portland, and Washington, D.C., are among the leaders in what could safely be described as a data revolution, in which governments take an active role in pushing data to citizens. Want to know where the snowplows are in your city on a snowy morning, and when you can expect one to rumble down your street? There's an app for that, as they say, in Washington. The state of Illinois will soon deploy technology that allows citizens to report a pothole on their road by submitting a GPS-enabled photograph from their smartphone.

All of this is to say that data, and digital technology, shrink the distance between the governed and the governor, allowing citizen watchdogs to take a more active role in governmental accountability. From state spending ledgers to conflict of interest disclosure forms to auditor's reports, freedom of information law these days often means simply finding data that already exist on government websites.

In fact, the sheer volume of data available freely on government websites could keep an enterprising media mogul busy for years. At least one promising media enterprise, Everyblock.com, has been built on the data kept by municipal governments. Everyblock aggregates data and then makes it searchable at the block level—a news feed for your block, right down to restaurant inspection reports for that little Italian place on the corner you love so much. It's a business model built on the proposition that data can inform us, but only if we can manage the inflow.

Proactive disclosure will never replace good, old-fashioned FOI requests, though, for one simple reason: governments will never proactively disclose that which they know makes them look stupid or corrupt. For the really good stuff, FOI is still the only way.

The ACLU's fine FOI work on Abu Ghraib is a fine example: think the federal government was going to post its records and photos on the notorious Iraqi prison on a website? I think not. It took requests, and appeals, and finally litigation, to wrest that information from the government.

Data-driven FOI represents the future of digital journalism. It engages citizens in their democracy, and does so in ways that empower a much wider range of people than traditional FOI. As we get better at presenting and tell stories from the data produced by FOI, look for even more disclosure. It's a virtuous cycle.

for the denial are not quite clear, then the requestor's next step is to seek the agency's head for an opinion. If that fails, the last resort would be going to court.

Once a lawsuit challenges the validity of government claims for secrecy, federal judges may inspect the classified documents and rule on the correctness of any protected status under the FOIA. Obviously, it would take a powerful argument for any federal judge to rule against a particular agency's authority and question the government official's discernment in keeping safe potentially damaging information that has the potential to harm American citizens, property, and other public interests.

FOIA Initiatives

There is no government form required for making a FOIA request. A letter, with the envelope clearly marked as "Freedom of Information Act Request," should be sent to the agency whose records are sought (see Figure 9.1). It is also a good idea to include a daytime phone number.

Perhaps the most important item in the request is a clear and specific statement identifying the desired record. Vague or generalized requests take up more time and generally meet with inefficient responses. Once the request has been submitted to the government, the agency will send an acknowledgement stating the date of the request's receipt, the case number assigned to it, and whether the records desired are available or not. Obviously, the time taken for each search or review bears on the success of the retrieval, and that too depends on a variety of factors, including the complexity of the search and sensitivity of the materials requested.

FOIA Responses

If an unreasonable number of records are requested, the agency may advise limiting the materials and call for a resubmission of the request. The agency reviews FOIA requests on a first-come, first-served basis and often chooses one of three responses: (1) fulfilling the request, (2) denying the request in part, or (3) denying the request in full. Interestingly, the two federal agencies most besieged by FOI requests are the Federal Bureau of Investigation (FBI) and the Central Intelligence Agency (CIA), both of which have had to hire employees and spend large sums in order to lawfully comply with FOIA requests.

If the executive branch official responds favorably to the FOIA request, it means the agency has jurisdiction over the information, and it has the practical means for recovering it. There are times, however, when the agency deletes information from its records. Once that happens, the government's responsibility is to indicate just exactly why it did so. Either the request is simply denied, or the department fails to find the right information to satisfy the request. If the government does not respond satisfactorily, the sender can appeal to a review panel depending on how the request was handled. Requesters have sixty days after receiving this refusal from the agency to submit an appeal.

Expeditious handling ■
Freedom of Information Act (FOIA) requests are given expedited treatment if the requester is able to demonstrate a compelling need for the requested information.

Accelerating the FOIA Response

There are times when the government can move swiftly to fulfill requests, particularly for journalists. The term used to describe this special efficiency, **expeditious handling,** indicates a compelling need exists for quickly getting the data to the sender, such as "an imminent threat to someone's life or physical safety," to maintain

Agency Head [or Freedom of Information Act Officer]

Name of Agency
Address of Agency
City, State, Zip Code

Re: Freedom of Information Act Request

Dear _____:

This is a request under the Freedom of Information Act.

I request that a copy of the following documents [or documents containing the following information] be provided to me: [**identify the documents or information as specifically as possible.**]

In order to help to determine my status to assess fees, you should know that I am [**insert a suitable description of the requester and the purpose of the request.**]

   [**Sample requester descriptions:**

a representative of the news media affiliated with the _____ newspaper (magazine, television station, etc.), and this request is made as part of a news gathering and not for commercial use.

affiliated with an educational or noncommercial scientific institution, and this request is made for a scholarly or scientific purpose and not for commercial use.

an individual seeking information for personal use and not for commercial use.

affiliated with a private corporation and am seeking information for use in the company's business.]

[**Optional**] I am willing to pay fees for this request up to a maximum of $_____. If you estimate that the fees will exceed this limit, please inform me first.

[**Optional**] I request a waiver of all fees for this request. Disclosure of the requested information to me is in the public interest because it is likely to contribute significantly to public understanding of the operations or activities of the government and is not primarily in my commercial interest. [**Include a specific explanation.**]

Thank you for your consideration of my request.

▌ Sample FOIA Letter

due process, or because the information can prevent substantial harm to some humanitarian interest. There are times when urgent information about actual or suspected federal activities must be rapidly dispensed to the public. The expedited request must be accompanied with the reasons stating the urgent need for such handling, then the government decides whether it is truly warranted or not.

Assessment of Fees

The question of fees involved for access to public information has also been addressed in the law. Federal officials handling a FOIA request will not act upon it unless requestors are willing to pay the fees exacted or can offer some suitable reason as to why the fee waiver is warranted. There are **fee categories** assigned to each request—which vary according to the information desired, the reason for requesting it, and the number of requests submitted—allowing requestors to estimate how much they think the retrieval will cost. If the public interest is involved, which may include reports by the news media or academic institutions, the fee could be zero.

The categories in which the requests are organized include commercial trade, educational and scientific institutions, news media, and others:[18]

<table>
<tr><td>**Fee category** ■
Every FOIA request is placed in a fee category which determines if there is a cost to the requester.</td></tr>
</table>

- *Commercial Use Requests:* Ones that serve to advance the commercial, trade, or profit interest of the person on whose behalf the request is made (22 CFR § 171.11(l)).
- *Educational Institution Requests:* An educational institution means "a preschool, a public or private elementary or secondary school, an institution of undergraduate or graduate higher education, an institution of professional education, or an institution of vocational education that operates a program or programs of scholarly research" (22 CFR § 171.11(m)).
- *Noncommercial Scientific Institution Requests:* Noncommercial scientific institutions are ones whose sole purpose is to advance scholarly research, not just to achieve commercial gain (22 CFR § 171.11(n)).
- *Representatives of the News Media Requests:* Those are made by journalists who collect news for a news organization, whose mission it is to distribute the information to the public. Information, here, refers to news that is of public interest. News media can mean television stations, radio stations, or publishers of periodicals (22 CFR § 171.11(o)).
- *Freelance Journalist Requests:* Freelance journalists have to show proof of publication or likelihood of publication through a representative of the news media, even though they are not actually employed by one (22 CFR § 171.11(o)).
- *All Other Requests:* These are requests that do not fall under the previous categories (22 CFR § 171.11(p)). Fees will not be charged for the first 100 pages and the first two hours spent on the searching process for all except the requests pertaining to commercial use.

Removing FOIA Barriers

Compounding the frustration for the advocates of openness in government is the relatively recent phenomenon of outsourcing federal tasks to private businesses. It took a court fight in Georgia before a private school bus contractor would let the public know of details about the school district's selection of drivers and their

---

[18]*See* Department of State, *Information Access Manual* (2008).

▶ UP CLOSE

The Price of Sunshine

A popular aphorism since 9/11 has been that "freedom is never free," which also applies to certain materials under the Freedom of Information Act. The price paid for government records comes in terms of both the time and money required for researching, reviewing, and responding to requests submitted from the public. Fees vary according to the requester's identity and purpose for searching and reviewing the government records, and the charges for photocopying or duplicating materials electronically.

Congress decided the news media would *not* be charged for researching and reviewing records, but nonjournalistic groups felt their work in the public's interest was also worthy of such favorable terms. In 1989, the National Security Archives expanded the FOIA terms. Custodians of federal records were advised to decide if the request was coming from someone who publishes or broadcast news about current events of interest to the public, but in *Department of Defense v. National Security Archives*, a federal appeals court held the professional description should encompass anyone who "gathers information of potential interest to a segment of the public, uses its editorial skills to turn the raw materials into a distinct work, and distributes that work to an audience."[a]

In 2007, Congress stepped in to codify those terms in the Openness Promotes Effectiveness in our National Government Act, which also included the online world of bloggers, freelance journalists, and columnists. The problem is, not all custodians of those federal records have read the terms, or are willing to enforce favorable rates for FOIA users, and for those who lack the funds to mount a legal appeal, this fact is more than troubling—it is illegal.

---

[a] *Department of Defense v. National Security Archive*, 880 F.2d 1381 (D.C. Cir. 1989).

---

records.[19] The National Freedom of Information Coalition argued that as more government bodies delegate to private contractors, citizens and the media need to be persistent in asking for a freedom of information clause in the local contract to avoid delegating away this information.

Other stifling inhibitions to the quest for public information are the privacy statutes that discourage disclosure of public information because they are either confusing to users or to administrators, or both.

Even though frustration reigns over denials and procrastinations that follow FOIA requests, there are citizen groups dedicated to gaining more efficient access to the mechanisms of government. The National Freedom of Information Coalition proposed that Washington, D.C., adopt an approach similar to what some state governments have done, which is to approve a FOI Commission or Government Records Council that could help petitioners by saving them the trouble of having to go to court to resolve their differences. Informal resolutions either authorized by a committee or a public official obviously would be preferable to tying up judicial bodies with access litigation.

---

[19]*Hackworth v. Board of Educ. for City of Atlanta*, 214 Ga. App. 17, 447 S.E.2d 78 (1994).

Legislation creating an ombudsman-like office within the federal government has been proposed but has not yet won the day. Key to sunshine in government is the creation of a climate of openness that can be either established or thwarted by the political powers overseeing the agency involved. If agency administrators hold in contempt the public's right of access, the policy of disclosure written into the law can be undermined or ignored.

Sunshine in Government Meetings

A 1907 Alabama law prevented closed-door meetings for commissions and boards unless someone's reputation was at stake, and today all states have some laws that govern access to public meetings but they vary widely in terms of their procedures and penalties. Good state open-meetings laws have strong legislative declarations in support of public sessions, specifically defining each one by listing the number of members who must gather to constitute a meeting and declaring void actions taken during a meeting that was improperly closed to the public. Most statutes provide for exceptions to open sessions in order to discuss such matters as personnel actions, real estate transactions, and pending litigation. Florida adopted its open meeting law in 1967, which became a model for many others in requiring advance notice of meetings and published minutes and affirming only public decisions held in open meeting to be official.

UP CLOSE

Presidential Records

Forty years after FOIA was adopted, a question arose about access to presidential records: how long after the death of a president should historians have to wait before they can pore over the records of his administration? In 2007, President George W. Bush issued an order holding up the release of 68,000 pages from Ronald Reagan's library, just as the waiting period was about to expire. It was that order, drafted by then–White House Counsel Alberto Gonzales, that the president used to refuse requests for those public records. As a result, the American Historical Association sought a federal judge's ruling on whether such unlimited veto power was constitutional.

The Presidential Records Act of 1978 expanded protection of executive branch records by placing authority over them in the hands of the National Archives rather than the president.[a] President Gerald R. Ford once remarked, "I firmly believe that after a period of time, presidential papers, except for the most highly sensitive documents involving our national security, should be made available to the public." Calling it an "impermissible exercise of executive power," U.S. District Judge Colleen Kollar Kotelly invalidated that part of the president's discretion and returned the presidential records to the National Archives, where she said they rightfully belonged, thus ending the White House's "expanded protection" of secrecy, and affording greater access to the presidential records in the archives.

[a]*See* The Presidential Records Act (PRA), 44 U.S.C. §§ 2201–2207.

The U.S. Government in Sunshine Act amounts to what might be considered a federal open-meetings law. This law covers about 50 agencies in the executive branch, including regulatory commissions. Members of such government organizations are not permitted to hold secret meetings unless they intend to discuss material that falls into one of ten categories. These categories mirror the FOIA exemptions and also include provisions that permit closed-door meetings to discuss attempts to arbitrate or adjudicate a specific set of legal issues. The law requires the agencies to provide advance notice of meetings and publish an agenda.

STATE GOVERNMENT ACCESS

The first open records law is attributed to the state of Wisconsin in 1848, but in the wake of the Watergate scandal of the 1970s, all states approved some form of law assuring access to their government records. The provisions of state laws vary in which particular offices are required to comply with requests for documents, and how long they may take to respond. States also have different standards for assessing fees and for determining how each request is to be categorized. Statutes around the country have been generous in defining the types of documents that can be dispensed to the public, but enforcement is often weak, especially if the penalties carry no civil or criminal punishment and the prosecuting attorney sees no reason to pursue actions under the law.

Nonetheless, all 50 states have some version of a **FOI statute** and five states have written it into their constitutions. Florida adopted a constitutional amendment that governs access throughout its state government offices. Throughout the nation openness is often based on the interpretation of exemptions regularly used to close open meetings and prohibit access to public records. Exemptions include material specifically excluded by other statutes, law enforcement investigatory information, working papers, and highly personal documents.

Even though all states have laws governing access to documents and meetings, each state varies in the statutory requirements of its access to boards, commissions, and public records. Thus, what individual governments require in their criteria for access and the costs involved delineate the procedures for each jurisdiction. Most states provide for redress in the judicial system if an open records request is refused, however. New York and Connecticut have established commissions that act as arbiters in such matters.

State laws govern all records kept by their agencies, but few apply only to records that are required by law. Some states have a policy that allows exemptions on broad categories of documents, while others finely parse the limits on records or meetings. Some states include e-mail records within the definition of accessible documents. In states where no such access is granted, it is hard to predict where a particular agency will draw the line. The guiding principle is that government carries the burden of proof for denying disclosure, but in actual fact it is usually the *custodian* of records who arbitrarily restricts access. Where the rule of law is silent on such matters, agencies may speak loudly and forcefully—although usually not affirmatively—in favor of citizen access to their records and meetings.

FOI statute ■ All 50 states have some type of access law for records and meetings, but they vary widely in terms of their practical use and enforcement.

Bedrock Law: All states have some type of access law for records and meetings, but these laws vary widely in terms of their procedures, penalties, and enforcement.

E-mails and Text Messages

The mayor of Detroit, Kwame Kilpatrick, learned to his dismay how the Michigan FOI law would be applied to review in public his explicit text messages to his chief of staff, Christine Beatty. The Detroit *Free Press* asked for the records under the state law after the mayor was alleged to be having an affair with his assistant and using a government-issued cellular phone to arrange for their encounters. Eventually, the newspaper did collect the e-mails and publish them, but the *Free Press* battle for release of those romantic text messages raised citizen awareness about freedom of information, and how state laws apply (or not) to messages transmitted by cellular phone or via the Internet.

In New Jersey, for example, a state judge ordered Gov. Jon S. Corzine to publicly release e-mail messages he exchanged with a former companion, Carla Katz, who also happened to be involved in labor contract negotiations with the state. The governor maintained he had an executive privilege and the right to keep those e-mails private, but the court disagreed. Judge Paul Innes ruled the e-mails constituted a public record and should be released under the state FOI act to give the public a chance to evaluate the activities of his administration.

Meanwhile in Missouri, lawyers charged that government employees were asked to destroy e-mail messages in order to prevent their release to the public. A lawsuit was filed encouraging the state's custodian of e-mail messages to release those backlogged e-mail messages. The suit charged Gov. Matt Blunt's staff with intentionally trying to prevent the disclosure of public records. E-mails, text messages, video conferences, and the like are rarely mentioned in state FOI laws, but obviously governments are using these channels of communication more often to conduct the public's business, and so citizens naturally want to read those exchanges in order to gain a better understanding of what their elected officials are doing. It is likely voters will continue to seek e-mail access under the freedom of information statutes in their states.[a]

[a]Freedom of Information Act news items are collected from multiple sources by Charles N. Davis, associate professor and executive director of the Freedom of Information Center at the University of Missouri in Columbia.

LAWS THAT RESTRICT ACCESS

All states and the federal government have laws that specifically exclude certain types of information from the public scrutiny. Today, the right to privacy has expanded as a substantial barrier to access to information held by government agencies.

The federal government has adopted a law protecting the privacy of student records, for example. Congress passed a federal privacy law, which may conflict with the provisions of the Freedom of Information Act. The federal government also has insisted that states pass statutes that control access to criminal history records. The result is that the right to privacy is used frequently to block access to public records at the state and federal level.

Privacy Act of 1974

This law was designed to protect individuals from the willful disclosure of personal information found in government records to third parties. The 1974 law actually calls for the consent of the citizen before such records can be made public or even transferred to another agency. It further allows people to review agency records and correct any mistakes they may find. The Privacy Act of 1974 does provide for legal recourse in terms of damages available to Americans who discover their records were mishandled by the government, but it also allows for certain exemptions in order to permit law enforcement officers to prosecute crimes, census takers to gather data, or Congress to conduct investigations. The move to privacy means that public access is faced with threatened lawsuits or litigation over actions that involve intrusion or misrepresentation, through laws such as the Family Educational Rights and Privacy Act, the Health Insurance Portability and Accountability Act, and the Drivers Privacy Protection Act.

State Driver's License Records

There are times when state and federal bodies come into conflict regarding the types and kinds of confidentiality granted to the public. The U.S. Congress, for example, moved to protect innocent victims of stalkers when it passed the **Drivers Privacy Protection Act (DPPA)** in 1994. That law was the direct result of the stalker murder in 1989 of a Hollywood actress, Rebecca Schaffer, who was gunned down at the front door of her California home. The murderer was able to discover where Schaffer lived after gaining access to her personal records from driver's license data held by the California Department of Motor Vehicles.

The federal law was designed to protect innocent victims from such violent intrusion, but it was less well received by many states that collected revenue from the sale or release of driver's license data. South Carolina considered the DPPA an affront to the Tenth Amendment, which it held was the "legal and spiritual guardian" of states' rights.[20] The U.S. Justice Dept., however, argued DPPA was valid under the **commerce clause** and the U.S. Supreme Court unanimously agreed, thus affirming the act.[21] Chief Justice William Rehnquist held states should not be compelled to disclose certain records, if the federal government determines a legitimate reason for keeping them private.

Drivers Privacy Protection Act (DPPA) ■ A federal law protecting the privacy of state drivers license information.

Commerce clause ■ Article 1, Section 8, Clause 3 of the U.S. Constitution gives Congress power to regulate trade between the states, with foreign countries, and with Indian tribes. Used to justify the government's constitutional right to control broadcast radio by licensing.

Family Educational Rights and Privacy Act (FERPA)

The **Family Educational Rights and Privacy** Act (1974) was intended to prevent schools from releasing academic information about children without consent. Sen. James L. Buckley of New York sponsored it so that schools could keep confidential academic records once they receive federal funding from the Department of Education. Before a student becomes an adult, the law protects parental discretion over academic records, but that right shifts to the students at the age of eighteen.

FERPA also gives students and parents the rights to inspect personal school records and recommend corrections in them if they find information that is inaccurate

Family Educational Rights and Privacy Act (1974) ■ A federal law designed to protect the privacy of children's school information.

---

[20]Carrying its principle over from the articles of confederation, federal constitutional framers felt it prudent to prevent the government from encroaching upon state rights: "The powers not delegated to the United States by the Constitution, nor prohibited by it to the States, are reserved for the States respectively, or to the people."

[21]*Reno v. Condon*, 528 U.S. 141 (2000).

or misleading. The law also requires their signature before any academic authority can release their records to third parties. Posting grades by any easily identifying means (names, initials, or social security numbers) is a violation of the Act. FERPA has provisions guiding state agencies on the transmission of testing data, but it is not airtight. For example, the law does not prevent law enforcement officers on school grounds from obtaining information regarding criminal activities in student files. Whether an honest mistake is made or there is a malicious attempt to obfuscate, universities have sometimes mistakenly believed that FERPA prevents them from releasing information about criminal activity.[22] It also gives accrediting agencies and other academic authorities the right to inspect data in student files. Other reasons for disclosing student records include health concerns, financial aid, and compliance with judicial orders.

Privacy of Health Records

Health Insurance Portability and Accountability Act (HIPAA) ■ A federal law which protects the privacy of individual's health information.

A federal law protecting personal medical information seemed like a good idea at first—it would keep medical records private and require patients to decide whether such information should be made public. This was the intent of language in the **Health Insurance Portability and Accountability Act (HIPAA),** first enacted by Congress in 1996. Title 1 served to protect health care coverage for employees after leaving or changing jobs. Seven years later, Congress added a provision requiring health care providers to ensure confidentiality of medical care records and communications unless they are released from doing so by the patient's signature. Title 2 is known as "AS" for "administrative simplification," where new rules regarding access to patient records have created difficulty for those hoping to gather information.

Unfortunately many hospitals have broadly interpreted the privacy act and have not allowed patient information or condition reports to be released to the families of the hospitalized over the telephone, even if the patient is critically ill and the family member lives out of state. Additional penalties have been implemented for those (mostly nurses) who unknowingly violate HIPAA; some even

---

▶ **UP CLOSE**

FERPA—A Cloak for Athletic Violations?

An Ohio newspaper used the Freedom of Information Act to discover how colleges were treating their star football athletes and to obtain records about possible violations of rules. The paper simply asked the nation's top football programs for public records including travel reports, flight manifests, and reports of NCAA violations. A majority of the schools provided some records, but many moved to censor part or most of the records. The *Columbus Dispatch*

reported three schools refused to release any records of NCAA violations and that others heavily censored student violation reports. U.S. Sen. James L. Buckley (N.Y.) was one of the architects of the FERPA legislation, who saw that its intent was to maintain students' privacy in grading and not to cloak infractions. Schools that were less than compliant with the newspaper's request had added their own interpretation to the law, the senator said.

---

[22]*See Same Game, Different Rules, in Student Press Law Center Report* (Spring 2004).

have been terminated from their positions for accidental blunders that violated their employers' interpretation of the law.

The stringent rules of disclosure apply to materials classified as **protected health information (PHI)** and are an effective ban on the release of details about a patient's health status, financial arrangements, or other provisions of health care. Problematically, liberal interpretations of HIPAA rules easily can conceal any part of a patient's files or medical history.

Journalism and academic organizations have fought for changes in the law in order to more effectively inform the public on major health issues. The University of Michigan demonstrated how HIPAA's enforcement drastically reduced their survey results (96 percent to 34 percent) in terms of heart disease research. Another study detailing the effects of HIPAA enforcement on cancer research showed an even greater decrease in data collection. The informed consent forms required under HIPAA are rife with legal jargon that tends to discourage researchers and patients alike. The end result is a poorer data pool that produces less well-informed decisions about health care management and public health policy.

> **Protected health information (PHI)**
> ■ The class of individual health-care information protected by the Health Insurance Portability and Accountability Act (HIPAA).

PRESS FREEDOMS TO GATHER INFORMATION

The name *Fourth Estate*, as given to the news media, implies a responsibility to gather information and report truthfully on the workings of the branches of government, but the legal distinctions between the right to publish information and the right to access are as divergent as offense and defense.[23] That is to say there is a greater right of the press to defend itself against government encroachment than there is a guaranteed right to claim access. One area where government is less friendly to the public and journalists' inspection are prisons in general, and in particular their access to prison inmates.

Estimates vary, but states generally spend more money on housing criminals than any other single budget item, and with a million people incarcerated in state penitentiaries each day, the workings of the prison are significant to a large number of Americans. Nonetheless, prisons grant only limited access to the public, and this restriction on public property has been upheld by three rulings in the U.S. Supreme Court.

The decisions came at a period when the news media grew concerned with the living conditions faced by inmates; lawyers brought suits to improve their jail quarters. The aim of litigants was to compel states to end inhumane and often violent conditions; and to help improve sanitation, fire safety, health care, and exercise facilities for prisoners. In some cases public action groups actually succeeded, but access was curbed in the 1970s due to three decisions handed down by the U.S. Supreme Court.

The rulings—known as *Pell, Saxbe,* and *Houchins*—ultimately denied any implied right of access to prisons and held that none could be found under First Amendment guarantees.[24] In the California case of *Pell v. Procunier,* the Court

---

[23]C. Edwin Baker, *Press Rights and Government Power to Structure the Press*, 34 U. Miami L.R. 819 (1980).

[24]*Pell v. Procunier*, 417 U.S. 817 (1974); *Saxbe v. Washington Post Co.*, 417 U.S. 843 (1974); *Houchins v. KQED, Inc., supra* note 5.

upheld a penal code rule that refused to grant "press and other media interviews with specific individual inmates." In the second case, *Saxbe v. Washington Post Co.,* Justice Stewart delivered a majority opinion that concluded even though government cannot interfere with a free press it also cannot necessarily "accord the press special access to information not shared by members of the public generally."[25]

Finally, in another public access landmark, *Houchins v. KQED,* the Court bolstered Sheriff Houchins's decision when he stopped a TV news crew from visiting a part of the Santa Rita jail where an inmate was reported to have committed suicide.[26] In this instance, the Court appeared even more determined to ignore any interpretation of the First Amendment that held greater access was owed to the news media than the public at large. These cases have left it up to each state's regulatory and penal code to say just how far they should go in terms of granting access, but it would be a mistake to suppose that prison authorities have grown more liberal toward the news media as a result of *Pell, Saxbe,* and *Houchins.*

Some scholars report that face-to-face interviews create the greatest potential for conflicts, and yet there is no outright ban on media–prisoner interactions. The best way to interpret those three precedents would be to say that prison administrators are expected to grant individual permission for inmate communication if no loss of security or the orderly administration of justice is threatened. Unfortunately, the rise of so-called celebrity inmates has somewhat discouraged granting greater access to the public or news media. The highly publicized incarceration of TV celebrity Paris Hilton underscores the paparazzi phenomenon and the impact it can have on a more liberal policy of inmate access.

In a related matter, attempts to claim a right of access to executions have failed. Despite the fact that prisons invite witnesses to be present, and even in spite of the fact that the prisons have provided closed-circuit television images,[27] there is no access right to executions at the state or federal level.

---

[25]417 U.S. 843, 848.

[26]*Houchins, supra* note 5.

[27]Infamous Oklahoma City bomber Timothy McVeigh was executed at a federal penitentiary in Terre Haute, Indiana. Rather than travel from Oklahoma to witness the execution, family members were allowed to view a closed-circuit transmission in Oklahoma City but its use for any other purpose was prohibited.

SUMMARY

- There will always be a conflict between the government's desire to keep more secrets than it needs to and the media's desire to uncover as much as it possibly can about the government. This natural antipathy usually results in a healthy adversarial relationship that benefits the public. Tensions arise when the need for government secrecy appears to conflict with the rights of citizen to access records and meetings especially at the federal level where the agencies of the executive branch exercise greater powers over the federal bureaucracy.

- Under the Freedom of Information Act, public records are those items necessary for a federal agency to deal with the public and records are those dealings in addition to all documents prepared, used, or kept by the agency pertaining to the public's business.

- Individuals (not just media professionals) may request information from federal agencies under the FOIA. The Act does not apply to Congress or the judiciary, but only the executive branch.

- Once a formal request is received, a federal agency must respond to the request in a timely fashion. If a request is denied, the reason for the denial must be explicit, referring to the specific exemption in the Act. Denials may be appealed. If the denial is determined inappropriate, the bureaucrat who denied access is subject to disciplinary action.

- Analogous to freedom of information, government in the sunshine laws require the same administrative agencies to hold their meetings in public and to provide advance notice of upcoming meetings, including agenda items to be discussed. As with FOIA, parallel exemptions exist to allow some discussions to occur behind closed doors.

- Every U.S. state has some level of freedom of information and government in the sunshine provisions similar to those found at the federal level. Differences exist, but the underlying premise—that openness is the goal—is at the core of the laws.

- Specific areas have been delineated as areas where the public interest in access is outweighed by the privacy interests of individuals. Driver's license data, educational records, and personal health data and medical records are all protected under federal statute and may not be released, even in instances where the states have preferred a more open disclosure.

When the federal government moved at unprecedented speed to shore up the member banks of the Federal Reserve late in 2008, there was an element of secrecy concerning the actual details of the bailout. Journalists became concerned about the size and scope of the $2 trillion effort. Three news organizations asked for details under FOIA, including Fox News and Bloomberg, seeking information including details about the benefiting companies, terms, and rates of the so-called discount window, an emergency lending program for those fed banks.

The Federal Reserve did not favor this effort and so both Bloomberg and Fox News sued in federal court for the release of those financial documents. A district judge in New York City agreed with the Federal Reserve's position that it is not an executive branch agency and held that emergency loans should be kept secret since it would be comparable to revealing trade secrets and other confidential information. Fox News also sought bailout information from the U.S. Treasury Dept. while other news media outlets wanted the records that would inform the American public regarding tax disbursements. The *New York Times* also filed FOIA requests for those financial records from the federal government.

The entire Federal Reserve banking system is a bit of mishmash with a federal agency overseeing it in Washington, D.C., and 12 regional banks that essentially function as private rather than public corporations. Exemption 4 under FOIA protects trade secrets and commercial or financial information from disclosure if the material is privileged or confidential.

In certain states, the definition of a government record is fairly expansive and includes records of both the judiciary and legislative branches of government. The federal government has been less liberal in granting access to these branches of government, and while honoring the nine exemptions for select agencies such as the Federal Communications Commission and the Federal Trade Commission, it has shielded the Federal Reserve Board from all such requests for its records. As the federal government becomes more involved in health care, automotive industries, and other business concerns, should the U.S. Congress grant greater access to documents that will reveal to taxpayers just how their money is spent, and for whose benefit? ∎

Broadcast Regulation

LEARNING OBJECTIVES

After reading this chapter you should know:

- What areas of content and technology the government regulates in broadcast terms
- The constitutional justification for treating broadcasters differently from other media
- Criteria established by the government for licensing radio and television stations
- Offices and powers of the Federal Communications Commission (FCC)

- Steps taken toward the creation of an FCC rule
- Examples of how the FCC seeks to preserve competition, localism, and diversity
- Political rules that influence candidates and campaigns
- Commercial and programming restrictions on television for children

In the 1990s, Americans bought their first high-definition television sets and then eagerly anticipated digital broadcasting to begin. The government put in motion a program of digital migration applying a so-called soft deadline in 2006 to allow analog channels to continue broadcasting until then if 85 percent of the nation's TV households had met the DTV conversion. The soft deadline passed without enough Americans owning digital receivers.[1]

President Bush signed into law a "Digital Television Transition and Public Safety Act," which moved the DTV transition date to February 17, 2009. Washington had a financial stake in the transition because local TV stations were to return frequency bandwidth to be auctioned to other media, including public safety communications and advanced wireless services for broadband networks. The Federal Communications Commission (FCC) and **National Telecommunications and Information Administration (NTIA)** created a coupon program with the backing of Congress in order to subsidize the purchase of DTV set-top boxes and make digital signals visible on analog TV sets. A consumer awareness program featuring public service announcements and a national DTV call center with in-home assistance was implemented. But a snag in the coupon program occurred when a rush of American viewers realized late in 2008 that they needed to make their sets DTV capable by February 2009 or it would cost them a loss of television reception. A third deadline was set after the traditional ratings month of May on June 12, 2009.

Congress called for more public service announcements to urge viewers to purchase a converter box or some other means of watching DTV. This deadline finally arrived and the American switch from analog to digital television broadcasting began in earnest, all in order to free up 108 MHz in bandwidth for fixed, mobile, wireless, and public safety communications. A core area of the TV spectrum was packed with broadcasters from channels 2 to 51, and the newcomers were assigned to frequencies between channels 52 to 69. The FCC netted nearly $19 billion dollars in an auction sale for spectrum rededicated to commercial users.

Broadcasters were not required to provide high-definition programming, only DTV broadcasting, which gives them room to use spectrum space for services such as music channels for audio, Internet data, or even pay-per-view video, but the government requires a fee on their revenues of 5 percent for subscription services. The regulation of broadcasting is dynamic, and the transition from analog to digital television illustrates its state of perpetual flux.

National Telecommunications and Information Administration (NTIA) ■ An agency in the U.S. Department of Commerce that serves as the executive branch agency principally responsible for advising the president on telecommunications and information policies. In this role, NTIA frequently works with other executive branch agencies to develop and present the administration's positions on these issues.

Bedrock Law: Federal regulations place limited control over the fees, technology, and programming content of radio and television stations.

RADIO'S REGULATORY ROOTS

At the crossroads of technology, innovation, programming, and ownership comes broadcast regulation with a history spanning from the century of ship-to-shore communications to the digital era. Along the way, the Federal Communications Commission was formed to oversee "communication by wire and radio so as to

[1] *In re Advanced Television Systems and Their Impact upon the Existing Television Broadcast Service* (MM Docket No. 87–286, FCC 97–115 (Sixth Report and Order, Apr. 21, 1997).

make available, so far as possible, to all the people of the United States a rapid, efficient, nation-wide, and world-wide wire and radio communication service with adequate facilities at reasonable charges."[2] At first, a temporary agency for radio control was formed but the government never did—nor could it relinquish—control over the broadcast airwaves.

Wireless Ship Act of 1910

Before radio broadcasting as we know it today was born, Guglielmo Marconi invented a wireless telegraph transmitter designed to tap out the steady pulse of Morse code. Ocean storms and other perils at sea inspired Marconi's invention to protect human lives and valuable cargo. In 1909, the U.S. Congress noticed how many lives were saved by wireless telegraphy and took action. A steamship collided with a luxury ocean liner near Long Island, N.Y., and passengers of the *Florida* and the luxury liner, *Republic*, were rescued thanks to wireless distress signals.

Following that shipwreck, the U.S. Navy urged Congress to pass a law requiring the "apparatus and operators for radio communications on certain ocean steamers" carrying "50 or more persons."[3] The **Wireless Ship Act of 1910** placed a radio transmitter and wireless operator aboard large oceangoing vessels traveling more than 200 miles from port, and contrary to Marconi's company policy, it became illegal for a wireless operator to refuse to acknowledge or relay a message from a ship using another company's equipment. The 1910 act did not demand twenty-four-hour radio maintenance, which added to the tragedy of the nation's worst ocean liner disaster.

An iceberg floating near Nova Scotia fatally gashed the R.M.S. *Titanic*, the White Star Line's luxury liner, at around midnight on April 14, 1912. The ship's wireless signals of distress went unheeded. A radio operator on a nearby ship had retired for the evening, and the noise from amateur operators interfered with the *Titanic*'s messages, which kept them from reaching radio operators ashore. News of the drowning of 1,500 lives in the icy north Atlantic prompted Congress to rewrite the law.

> The Wireless Ship Act of 1910 ■ A U.S. federal law that required all U.S. ships at sea to carry long range radio equipment. The law was passed in response to a shipping accident where a radio distress call saved over 1,200 lives.

Radio Act of 1912

The Radio Act of 1912 required oceangoing vessels to keep wireless radio operators on duty around the clock. It also authorized the U.S. Department of Commerce and Labor to grant licenses so that it could assign each station its wavelength "for the prevention of interference."[4] When World War I erupted, the issuance of radio licenses was called to a halt in the United States. The U.S. Signal Corps trained soldiers in the use of wireless radio, who returned after the war and began building radio transmitters and receivers. The noisy business of interference plagued radio reception as wireless hobbyists experimented with their transmitters at home.

> The Radio Act of 1912 ■ A U.S. federal law requiring ships to maintain round-the-clock radio watch, and required amateur radio operators be licensed. The sinking of the *Titanic* led to the passage of this law.

---

[2]Communications Act of 1934, 47 U.S.C. § 151 (1976).

[3]*Regulation, in American Broadcasting—A Source Book on the History of Radio and Television* 527 (Lawrence Lichty and Malachi Topping eds., 2nd ed. Hastings House 1976).

[4]Radio channels were measured in meters rather than the frequency of cycles in this early era.

Washington Radio Conferences

U.S. Secretary of Commerce and Labor Herbert Hoover handed out licenses in 1920 with only two frequencies allocated for U.S. broadcasting, which was clearly not enough. Two additional channels were dedicated to broadcasting in 1923, while renegade broadcasters wreaked havoc over the airwaves with static interference. Secretary Hoover felt compelled to take action to prevent a government takeover. He summoned to Washington, D.C., industry leaders to attend four national conferences in the early 1920s to find a way to organize the nation's radio traffic. "The use of a radio channel is justified only if there is public benefit," said Hoover, who saw no conflict between broadcasters and radio listeners. "Their interests are mutual, for without the one the other could not exist."[5] Some stations were forced to share their airtime with others, while the frequency problems persisted and greater government oversight became unavoidable.[6] The lack of effective law enforcement to police the nation's airwaves proved to be a recipe for disaster.

Trial Balloons

Radio was everywhere by 1926; there were 536 American stations broadcasting. Nearly all the three-letter combinations for call signs—WJZ, WOR, WLS, and the like—were exhausted. Frequencies were overcrowded. Adding more broadcast channels from 550 to 1500 kHz helped somewhat, but controlling radio's airwaves without refusing some applicants a license seemed unavoidable. But Intercity Radio Company took Secretary Hoover to court for refusing its application since he "had been unable to ascertain a wave length for use," because of signal interference. In *Hoover v. Intercity Radio Co.* (1923), a federal appellate court found no legal grounds for Hoover's refusal and ordered him to find a channel frequency for Intercity to use with the "least possible interference."[7]

A different radio challenge faced Hoover in Chicago, where the United States had assured Canadian authorities that American radio stations would curtail interfering with their radio stations. WJAZ, owned by the Zenith Corporation, broadcast on a disputed frequency of 910 kHz and challenged the U.S. government orders in court. Zenith won its case when a district judge held that the government had no "express grant of power in the [Radio Act of 1912]" to prevent the broadcasts.[8] *Hoover v. Intercity Radio* and *Zenith-WJAZ*, reached essentially the same conclusion: Secretary Hoover lacked the power to control the nation's airwaves.

---

[5]Erwin G. Krasnow, The Public Interest Standard: The Elusive Search for the Holy Grail—Briefing Paper Prepared for the Advisory Committee on Public Interest Obligations of Digital Television Broadcasters (Oct. 22, 1997).

[6]Andrew F. Inglis, *Behind the Tube—A History of Broadcasting Technology and Business* 84 (Butterworth 1990).

[7]*Hoover v. Intercity Radio Co.*, 286 F. 1003 (D.C. Cir. 1923).

[8]*United States v. Zenith Radio Corp.*, 12 F. 2d 614 (N.D. Ill. 1926).

The Federal Radio Commission (1927)

Congress proposed a new administrative agency to remedy Hoover's legal challenges. Rep. Wallace H. White (R-Me.) and Sen. Clarence C. Dill (D-Mont.) co-sponsored a bill creating the **Federal Radio Commission** (FRC) that would "consistent with the public interest, convenience and necessity, make reasonable regulations governing the interference potential of devices . . . emitting radio frequency energy."[9] White told radio station owners "the broadcasting privilege will *not* be a right of selfishness. It will rest upon an assurance of public interest to be served."[10] In 1927, the FRC began granting licenses to radio stations for three-year terms with the power to refuse a license renewal if the operator was not serving the public interest, convenience, or necessity.

> **Bedrock Law:** Broadcast licensing gives the government legal mechanism to assign frequencies and punish licensees for violating laws or regulations.

The Federal Radio Commission ■ The Federal Radio Commission was created by the Radio Act of 1927. It created a five-member commission with each member representing a geographical area of the country.

Commerce clause ■ Article 1, Section 8, Clause 3 of the US Constitution gives Congress power to regulate trade between the states, with foreign countries, and Indian tribes.

FEDERAL JURISDICTION

What exactly gave the government the constitutional right to control broadcast radio by licensing? The **commerce clause** (U.S. Const. art. 1, § 8) provides for oversight of interstate commerce.[11] In *United States v. Gregg,* the Supreme Court addressed the question of federal authority when a Texas radio station owner operating "The Voice of Labor," chose to ignore the U.S. government's requirement of a license. Paul Gregg felt that his Houston station's signal was too weak to interfere with anyone outside Texas, and so federal oversight would be unnecessary and perhaps unconstitutional. What Gregg failed to realize was that his station's channel was also assigned to radio stations in Louisiana and Florida, which could not reach Texas listeners when his station was broadcasting.[12] That case and another precedent from Indiana established federal authority over broadcast licensing.[13]

Rationale for Regulation

The rationale supporting the necessity of broadcast regulation was based on two principles—the scarcity doctrine and the public ownership of the airwaves. The invisible electromagnetic energy used to transmit broadcast airwaves does not belong to a private entity, but to the American people. Radio and television licensing functions like a "lease" to broadcasters for a temporary period of time that can be withdrawn if necessary. Second, the spectrum of electromagnetic energy is a scarce resource with a limited supply unable to meet all the demand for those who

---

[9]*The Radio Act of 1927, in American Broadcasting—A Source Book on the History of Radio and Television 556 Supra* note 3 (Lawrence Lichty and Malachi Topping eds., 2nd ed. Hastings House 1976).

[10]*See* 67 Cong. Rec. 5479 as cited in *Red Lion Broadcasting Co. v. FCC,* 395 U.S. 367, 381 (1969).

[11]Congress drew upon the commerce clause (U.S. Const. art. 1, §8) which gives it the power "to regulate Commerce with foreign nations, and among the several States" for its rationale to regulate broadcasting, Even if a signal does not migrate across a state's boundary, that station still falls under federal supervision.

[12]*United States v. Gregg,* 5 F.Supp. 848 (1934).

[13]*FRC v. Nelson Bros. Bond & Mortgage Co.,* 289 U.S. 266 (1933).

want to use it. The underlying rationale of the scarcity doctrine is that once citizens are entrusted with a license, they must serve as public trustees.

The U.S. Supreme Court held that "broadcast frequencies constituted a scarce resource whose use could be regulated and rationalized only by the government . . . where there are substantially more individuals who want to broadcast than there are frequencies to allocate. . . ."[14] In 1984, the U.S. Supreme Court ruled in *FCC v. League of Women Voters of California* that the scarcity doctrine could be revised if technological developments warranted it.[15] Similarly, the U.S. Court of Appeals for the D.C. Circuit found there existed an implicit obligation to review the spectrum scarcity rationale.[16]

Broadcasters pay little for the privilege of using a scarce, public resource and, in return, are expected to serve the public's interest. This rationale for government oversight applies even to low-wattage radio transmitters[17] since "unified public control is essential to secure the owners of broadcasting stations an assured channel, which they may use without interference."[18] The FCC does not license broadcast networks, such as ABC, NBC, CBS, or Fox, or regulate organizations such as PBS and NPR that provide programs to public stations. The license is for individual station operators, but because the FCC imposes a greater burden on broadcasting, the legal rationale has been challenged.

Competing Theories

Both the FRC and its lasting successor, the Federal Communications Commission (FCC), license stations to serve the local public's interest. Part of the problem in defining this public interest standard is due to the contradictory theories that guide members of the FCC. Some commissioners believe the public needs to be protected from market-based broadcasting, while others find excessive regulation to be the problem. Communications lawyer Erwin Krasnow summed up the competing legal theories in two terms: "delivering the mail" and seeking the "Holy Grail." Just as the U.S. Post Office is responsible for the mail delivery to Americans, the FCC ensures the delivery of radio and television programming to American households. Krasnow's reference to the "Holy Grail" implies loftier goals for the federal government to fulfill, such as providing services for vision- and hearing-impaired people, providing equal employment opportunities, and meeting children's educational and information needs.

Precedents of Punishment

The First Amendment rights of broadcasters prohibit government censorship, which simply means that the station licensee—not the government—is responsible for selecting the material to be aired. Congress prohibited the FRC from censoring the nation's radio stations in § 29 of its original 1927 act and then proscribed

---

[14]*Red Lion Broadcasting Co. v. Federal Communications Comm'n*, 395 U.S. 367 (1969).

[15]468 U.S. 364 (1984).

[16]*Tribune Co. v. FCC*, 133 F.3d 61, 66 & n.4 (D.C. Cir. 1998).

[17]*See White v. Federal Radio Comm'n*, 29 F. 2d 113 (N.D. Ill. 1929).

[18]A federal judge in Illinois held in *United States v. American Bond & Mortgage* Co. 31 F.2d 448, 453 (N.D. Ill. 1929).

infractions worthy of penalty such as "obscene, indecent, or profane language" that are discussed thoroughly in another chapter.[19] Section 326 of the current act forbids censorship and protects material that may be objectionable because "the public interest is best served by permitting free expression of views," but there are limits.

The FCC does punish broadcasters after the fact and early in its history proved willing to revoke broadcast licenses for outrageous programming. Radio hucksters performing "medical miracles" on the air and outrageous political demagogues tested the FRC's legal authority. "Doctor" John R. Brinkley's KFKB (Kansas First Kansas Best) radio station guaranteed his fabulous "goat gland" surgery would rejuvenate the libido of men by implanting goat testes in them. In 1930, the FRC refused to renew his station license but Brinkley appealed the decision based on his claim of broadcast censorship. "Doc Brinkley" had not suffered any prior restraint but instead was punished by the fact that his license was removed.[20]

Other radio renegades were brought to justice. Rev. Robert P. Shuler of the Trinity Methodist Church South in Los Angeles used his station, KGEF (Keep God Ever First), to rant against politicians, Jews, and Roman Catholics. "Fighting Bob" would announce on the air at times that he had damaging information on a certain listener, whose name would be kept secret so long as that person sent in a donation to the station. This form of broadcast extortion was worthy of punishment, and so the FRC refused to renew his license.[21] The Commission also checked on early broadcast programming for elements of indecency.

One cussing broadcaster in Louisiana chose to sell his station before the government took his license away from him. Radio announcer William K. Henderson frequently swore as he attacked the U.S. government, criticized the spread of "chain stores," and became famous for his on-air tirades. His KWKH radio station in Shreveport tested the FRC's willingness to allow profanity on the public airwaves. The FRC initiated an investigation aimed at his license, but before any action was taken against him, Henderson sold his radio station to another broadcaster.

THE FEDERAL COMMUNICATIONS COMMISSION

Congress felt that once everything was ironed out with new radio station licenses, the FRC would be no longer necessary and it could be closed down as a federal agency. The Secretary of Commerce then would be called upon to issue an "occasional" new license. This expectation proved unrealistic in the view of radio's rising popularity, which became clear six years after the FRC was formed and scheduled for sunset. The **Federal Communications Commission (FCC)** was formed to take its place under the Communications Act of 1934 and was given the responsibility of overseeing both wired and wireless communications, including the technical standards

Federal Communications Commission (FCC) ■ A United States government agency, established by the Communications Act of 1934, that regulates interstate and international communications by radio, television, wire, satellite, and cable.

---

[19]Section 29 reads as follows: "Nothing in this Act shall be understood or construed to give the licensing authority the power of censorship over the radio communications or signals transmitted by any radio station, and no regulation or condition shall be promulgated or fixed by the licensing authority which shall interfere with the right of free speech by means of radio communications."

[20]*KFKB Broadcasting Ass'n, Inc., v. FRC*, 60 App. D.C. 79, 47 F.2d 670 (1931).

[21]*Trinity Methodist Church, South v. FRC*, 62 F.2d 850, 851 (D.C. Cir. 1932).

of broadcasting, telephones, and eventually TV channel assignments. This 1934 act consolidated electronic media under the supervision of one agency.

The Commissioners

Congress delegated the powers of the FCC to ensure the technical quality of broadcast signals while at the same time supervising elements of programming content. The agency is responsible for administering and enforcing laws passed by Congress, which it does by delegating powers to specialized bureaus and offices within the FCC. When it was created, many of the same rules were carried over from the 1927 law and recodified in the 1934 act.

Five men and women are appointed by the U.S. president as **FCC Commissioners** and confirmed by the Senate to serve for five-year terms, although few actually serve that long. The president nominates three commissioners from his own party, and then designates one commissioner to preside as chair. They adopt and modify rules, and establish broadcast policy through their decisions on license renewals or infractions.[22] The FCC's administrative duties are carried on through the offices of seven operating bureaus responsible for homeland security, wireless and wireline media, consumer issues, international affairs, media, and law enforcement. Each bureau is subdivided into divisions, units, and offices, and so far as broadcasters are concerned, the Media Bureau is the most important one as it oversees radio and TV regulation.

FCC Commissioners ■ Five individuals appointed by the president and confirmed by congress that serve five-year terms. The commissioners adopt rules and set policy based on decisions about licensing renewals or infractions.

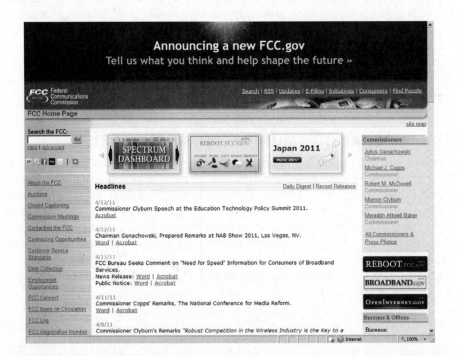

---

[22]The FCC's broadcast rules are contained in Title 476 of the Code of Federal Regulations (CFR), Parts 73 (broadcast) and 74 (auxiliary broadcast), including low-power TV and translator stations.

Rulemaking Process

Federal agencies generally cannot impose new rules or revise old ones without first publicly announcing proposed regulations and inviting public comment. The FCC is no exception; it begins by calling attention to a legal problem by issuing a Notice of Inquiry (NOI). The NOI alerts broadcasters and other interested parties to a specific issue and invites their comments regarding possible solutions. The NOI process is open to all, and comments are made public so that all interested parties can offer replies in support or in disagreement with earlier comments. The Commission's *Daily Digest* publishes the feedback, which is also posted on the FCC's website http://www.fcc.gov/Daily_Releases/Daily_Digest/.

The FCC then sends a message to the broadcast industry indicating a change in the government's rules is imminent. This announcement is called a Notice of Proposed Rulemaking (NPRM), which gives broadcasters a chance to hold forth on the problem and the proposed solutions. After the FCC considers all comments, it generally exercises one of four options: (a) to enact the proposed rule(s) in whole or in part; (b) to revise the rule(s) to be adopted; (c) to reopen public comment to resolve other issues; (d) to maintain the status quo without issuing any rules.

When the agency finally arrives at a decision after the NPRM, it publishes its final Report and Order (R&O). The R&O details what rule will be enforced and the rationale behind it. The R&O indicates whether any amendments are attached and explains why they are preferred. R&Os are accessible in the *Federal Register* published by the U.S. Government Printing Office.[23]

> **Bedrock Law:** The FCC is authorized to draft and enforce rules for electronic media after it invites and receives public comment on the regulatory issue.

Licensing Stations

The FCC administers its functions under the agency's procedures for rulemaking and policy enforcement but licensing is central to its mission, which is to maintain control "over all the channels of radio transmission; and to provide for the use of such channels, but not the ownership thereof, by persons for limited periods of time under licenses granted by federal authority."[24] Simply put, the FCC approves or denies license applications and maintains a record of the broadcasting station's public service.

Licensing Process

The most basic power delegated to the FCC is that of licensing electronic media. For broadcast stations, this poses an initial challenge of finding an available channel for a radio or television station applicant. Some groups rely on technical consultants or a communications lawyer to aid them in this process; they search for public notices to discover where the next station and frequency are available. Once a channel is located, the Media Bureau will show applicants how to fill out the necessary forms in order to submit their request for a license.

The broadcast license is free, but the government assesses an annual fee that varies by market size and medium. That fee could be thousands of dollars a year for a major market station, but quite a bit less—perhaps only a few hundred dollars a

---

[23]*The Federal Register* is also found online at http://www.gpoaccess.gov/fr/.
[24]47 U.S.C. §301.

year—for a small-market radio station. The application process for a new TV or radio station begins with a construction permit, if the license applicant has located a frequency that would not cause any objectionable interference to another signal. The FCC gives new broadcast licensees a specific time period to have the station up and running—usually three years. And if the license is granted, it can be renewed eight years later if the broadcaster has served the public interest without violating the FCC's rules or the Communications Act and has shown no discernible "pattern of abuse."

Licensing Requirements

Washington, D.C., receives far more applications for radio and television station licenses than there are available channel frequencies, which explains why when a channel becomes available, the FCC inspects the application to be sure certain requirements are met:

- The controlling interest of the broadcast organization submitting the license application must hold American citizenship (47 U.S.C. § 310).
- Good financial standing is required, which means the license applicant has sufficient capital to program a station for 90 days without commercial sponsorship. This initial period of time allows the licensee to determine how to best serve the community's public interest rather than simply building up its advertising portfolio. It also discourages the practice of "flipping stations," where one party acquires a station license with the intention of selling it for a fast profit.
- Ownership concentrations limit the number of license applicants per medium (radio, television, cable, newspaper) as well as by market location.
- A good character criterion requires that the applicant have no felony convictions under the U.S. Criminal Code and make no misrepresentations during the licensing process.
- Technical criteria cover audio and video standards must be maintained according to the licensee's coverage maps following the broadcast contours of the transmission tower's signal. The map is drawn to prevent interference with other electronic media.

Public Inspection File

Once a license has been obtained from the government, broadcasters are legally bound to maintain public records for the government and the audience to inspect at the station's office. The public inspection file is available for all to see and includes the license application, station reports to the FCC, contour maps of the coverage area, and letters and e-mails from the audience in addition to similar documents.

The inspection file also includes a listing of problems in the service area and programs designed to address them. The quarterly reports show that the broadcaster has given significant treatment to the issues facing the community of license. Television stations with websites are encouraged to make certain documents available online for easy access, but failure to make the public inspection file available during business hours is forbidden by the FCC. What is not required in the public inspection file are the station's financial records, including profit and earnings statements, payroll accounts, tax forms, or other business records that would put the broadcaster at a competitive disadvantage if publicly disclosed.

Infractions

Theoretically, the government can fine a station for a number of reasons, including the broadcast of obscene or indecent material, soliciting money under false pretenses, advertising or promoting illegal lotteries, or perpetrating a hoax on the public. The FCC moves against violators with fines, or "forfeitures," that are levied after a Notice of Apparent Liability (NAL) has been sent to the station. The agency rarely exacts forfeitures on a station's first offense and even more rarely exacts stiffer penalties. The government routinely renews broadcast licenses about 98 percent of the time. License revocations do occur in cases where false reports are submitted (lack of candor), which are usually compounded by a poor record of public service by the station. Beyond forfeitures or license revocations, the agency can impose lesser penalties on the station that include short-term license renewal, letters of reprimand for the public file, and cease and desist orders given to halt any undesirable practices by the station.

> **Bedrock Law:** The FCC does not censor broadcast stations, but does issue Notices of Apparent Liability, letters of reprimand, forfeitures, and license revocations in rare instances.

Licensing Renewal

Licenses are held for eight-year terms before they are subject to renewal. The station license renewal at one time was considered a "dicey process" subject to challenge, but the **Telecommunications Act of 1996** gave broadcasters some assurance of renewal. Broadcast licenses are secure unless and until they are challenged by advocates armed with substantive reports of violations indicating the public interest has not been well served.[25] The FCC's renewal application indicates whether the broadcaster has submitted to the FCC all required reports; no character issues are left unresolved, including felony convictions, violations of antitrust or unfair competition laws, drug law violations, or fraudulent statements made to the Commission. The agency also checks the Broadcast Equal Employment Opportunity Program Report, and the Children's Television Programming Reports for evidence of public service.

> **The Telecommunications Act of 1996**
> ■ U.S. Federal legislation which updated the 62-year-old regulatory framework of the Communications Act of 1934.

DEREGULATION

In an earlier era, competing stations seeking to broadcast on the same channel frequency would challenge each other in their bid to win an FCC license with high-minded promises and service goals. The National Association of Broadcasters (NAB) lobbied the government to have this competitive process curtailed and lift the license challenges. By the time Ronald Reagan was elected president in 1980, deregulation had taken hold in Congress and the FCC's policies fell under its influence.

---

[25]Until the Federal Radio Commission was formed in 1927, the Commerce Department issued radio licenses for two-year terms, then extended it to three-year terms with the creation of the FRC. The extension to eight-year terms came with the 1996 Telecommunications Act. *See* W. Jefferson Davis, The Radio Act of 1927, *in American Broadcasting—A Source Book on the History of Radio and Television* 556 *Supra* note 3 (Lawrence Lichty and Malachi Topping eds., 2nd ed. Hastings House 1976).

The length of a TV license term was expanded from three years to five, then to seven, and eventually to eight years. The station ownership rules were relaxed in 1985 to allow a twelve-station television chain (up from seven), while the guidelines for advertising along with public affairs and news were abolished. In 1987, the FCC took a bold step by doing away with the fairness doctrine that mandated balanced coverage of public controversies. In 1996 the most dramatic action came in the form of a new law that rewrote the 1934 congressional act.

THE TELECOMMUNICATIONS ACT

It was an auspicious occasion in 1996 when the rules governing electronic media were overhauled by President Bill Clinton's simple stroke of a pen in the Library of Congress. He signed into law the 1996 Telecommunications Act that reestablished the foundation for electronic media during a dynamic era of digital convergence in the United States. It was billed as a competition-friendly law that would speed up the deployment of new consumer services for broadcasting, Internet, and telephone communications. Some rules from the 1934 act stayed on the books, but others were revised or streamlined in five areas. The law's provisions were placed under (1) radio and television broadcasting, (2) cable television, (3) telephone services, (4) Internet/online services, and (5) telecommunications manufacturing.

The nation's broadcast ownership policy was grounded in the **principle of diversity** that the U.S. Supreme Court interpreted to mean "the widest possible dissemination of information from diverse and antagonistic sources is essential to the welfare of the public."[26] That was one of the goals, but two others—**localism** and **competition**—were also a matter of FCC policy. The government is careful to be sure that the playing field is level for communities and broadcasters competing for the public's attention. This calls into question how many stations a single owner can control since multiple-station ownership tends to limit the pluralistic goals of the FCC. The agency must provide a reasoned basis and sound analysis if it chooses to modify or repeal any of its rules.

FCC Analysis of Competition

In order to make its ownership standards clear and maintain a competitive environment, the FCC begins with the premise that larger media markets must be distinguished from smaller ones. In the top twenty U.S. markets, defined by A.C. Nielsen as Designated Market Areas (DMAs), the law allows ownership patterns that include newspaper, radio stations, and TV stations together in different combinations than are allowed in smaller markets. One way of defining the ownership policy is to look at the eight and four test—eight independent voices and only one a top four station—that is to say that at least eight independent outlets (major newspapers or full-power TV stations) must remain as competitors following a merger, and no more than one station among the top four under a single owner's control.

Principle of diversity ■ The widest possible dissemination of information from diverse and antagonistic sources is essential to the welfare of the public; generally focuses on objectives such as maximizing the sources of information, as well as the range of viewpoints and content options to which citizens and/or consumers have access. The FCC and Congress have shown interest in protecting content diversity, ownership diversity, and viewpoint diversity.

Localism ■ Broadcast ownership and program decision-making at the local community level; policy designed to ensure that the programming offered by each radio and television station addresses the significant needs and issues of the community it serves.

---

[26]*Associated Press v. United States,* 326 U.S. 1, 20 (1945), *cited in* Philip M. Napoli, *Deconstructing the Diversity Principle,* 49 J. Comm. 7 (1999).

Television Ownership Limits

The new playing field for TV station ownership fueled the momentum toward mergers and acquisitions. At first, the maximum national limit was based on audience reach and increased the limit from 35 percent to 45 percent of American TV households that any one owner could serve. A federal appeals court stepped in to issue an emergency order blocking the government from enforcing this ceiling because it "employed several irrational assumptions and inconsistencies."[27] Rather than the 45 percent cap, a compromise figure of 39 percent was reached in order to achieve the three principal goals of localism, diversity, and competition.[28] At the local market level, the FCC allows one owner to operate two local TV stations so long as eight independent television stations remain in the market and only one of those two TV stations are ranked among the top four as calculated by Nielsen audience ratings in terms of share points.

Radio Ownership Limits

The Commission says that in small markets with fourteen or fewer radio stations, one ownership group can control up to five commercial radio stations, but no more than three AM or three FM stations. In a market of fifteen to twenty-nine radio stations, one group can control up to six commercial radio stations, but no more than four AM or four FM stations. In a radio market of thirty to forty-four radio stations one group can control up to seven commercial radio stations, but no more than four AM or four FM stations; and in a radio market with forty-five or more radio stations, the limits are eight and no more than five AM and five FM stations.

Duopoly Rule

The term *duopoly* indicates that one owner has taken control of two television stations in a single market. The government originally prohibited any single owner from operating two TV stations per market, but this **duopoly rule** was revised in 1999 to allow two TV stations to be joined together under certain circumstances. Media lawyers filed petitions to have the duopoly rule overturned completely to bring more stations under a corporate umbrella, but they failed.

The duopoly rule allows two TV stations under one owner in the same market if one of the stations is not ranked among the top four stations based on market share. At least eight TV stations must remain to compete before the duopoly merger can be approved. The rule also allows common ownership of up to two TV stations and several radio stations in a market, so long as the whole family of stations does not exceed the local radio and TV ownership limits.[29] There is even the

Competition ■
Competing broadcasters have fair and equitable opportunities to influence the broadcast market; policy designed to ensure that public guidelines and regulations promote rather than limit competition and efficient markets based upon the belief that doing so will create a higher level of supply-and-demand.

Duopoly rule ■
Allows two TV stations to be owned by one owner in the same market if one of the stations is not ranked among the top four stations based on market share. At least eight TV stations must remain to compete before the duopoly merger can be approved.

---

[27] *Prometheus Project v. Federal Communications Comm'n*, 373 F.3d 372, 402 (3d Cir. 2004). The stay was lifted by the Third Circuit in 2010. *Prometheus Project v. FCC*, 2010 U.S. App. LEXIS 20436 (3d. Cir. 2010).

[28] *Fox Television Stations, Inc. v. FCC*, 280 F.3d 1027 (D.C. Cir. 2002).

[29] In the largest markets, an owner may control up to two television and six radio stations—or one TV station and seven radio stations.

Bedrock Law: The 1996 Telecommunications Act revised ownership formulas for radio and television stations based on market size.

possibility of a triopoly with three TV stations allowed per group if the market has more than 18 stations, and if only one of the three is among the top four stations.

The FCC also prohibits any merger among two or more of the four major television networks, but evaluates cross-ownership mergers on a case-by-case basis in order to determine if it would be in the public interest—that is, in furtherance of competition, localism, and diversity.

Cross-Ownership

There are other concerns with the cross-ownership of media, including newspapers and television stations. In 2007, the FCC completed a review of the rules and voted to relax its ban on newspaper/broadcast cross-ownership. The FCC also loosened its restrictions on cross-ownership of TV and radio stations in the top 20 markets under certain conditions. In the case of newspaper/broadcast cross-ownership, the Commission applies four factors before approving a station's sale consolidating media voices in a single market. First, the FCC examines the extent to which the merger increases the amount of local news; second, it determines how each media outlet will exercise independent news judgment; third, it reviews the level of media concentration in the market; and fourth, it calculates the financial status of the newspaper or TV station in order to see if a hardship exists that would be relieved by the merger.

In smaller markets ranked twenty-one or lower, the FCC holds that newspaper/broadcast combinations are *not* in the public interest because such a merger would diminish the diversity of voices in the local community. Some exceptions are made if the newspaper or broadcast station is failing financially, or if the new combination would increase local news coverage.[30] Broadcasters who join together under this "news programming" exception must report to the FCC on a regular basis how much more local news is broadcast.

Rethinking Cross-Ownership

The original cross-ownership rule forbidding partnerships between newspapers and broadcasters was written in 1975, but over the years cable and satellite television channels and Internet sites were added, making the necessity of protecting diversity and competition between electronic media an entirely different matter. Even though more channels are available for consumers, the owners tend to be a few large corporations that have the financial stability necessary to compete in small, medium, and large markets. Newspaper firms such as Tribune, Belo, and Post-Newsweek also control broadcast stations in cities where they own the only daily newspaper in town. The same media groups also seek to buy additional TV stations in markets where they may own cable systems, radio stations, or other outlets.

The 1996 law gave the FCC authority to preempt any local or state ordinance that would obstruct the entry by telecommunications firms that sought to supply

---

[30]Substantial increase in news coverage means an increase of at least seven hours of local news programming per week.

local customers with services for television, telephone, or the Internet. Incumbent services also must allow media competition to interconnect with wired networks in order to reach American households. New modes of technology place telephone and television services in competition supplying the same service through different channels. Americans access long-distance service on the Internet, for example, by using Skype or Voice over Internet Protocol (VoIP), which competes with wired telephone networks. This so-called intermodal competition amounts to selling the same services of television, telephone, and audio by delivering them through different modes of technology.

Spectrum Auctions

Applicants for broadcast stations bid in auctions to win the right to a new local channel by pledging the most money to the government for the station frequency. In order to raise money for the federal government, frequency auctions were established in Washington, D.C., after two previous methods for granting licenses were tried—comparative hearings and lotteries—and abandoned.[31] The shift away from lotteries and the public interest comparison of license applicants to a financial competition was one of several steps the FCC took to further its deregulatory policy. A federal court ruled in 1993 against comparative hearings and Congress did an about-face by giving the green light to competitive bidding. Spectrum auctions threw open the door to virtually any participant who would submit an advance payment for a broadcast station license. In 1997, the government's auction program was expanded and the lottery program was scratched as an alternative means for granting licenses.

After the U.S. Congress decided to shore up its revenue stream for the U.S. Treasury by granting an auction system for radio and television licenses, it devised an online system of bidding. Applicants for a broadcast frequency are invited to participate via their computer in a series of rounds in which eventually one bidder is granted the station's license. The FCC first certifies that the bidders are qualified license holders (U.S. citizens, etc.) and then makes a decision based primarily on the financial worth of the applicant's bid.

LOCALISM AND DIVERSITY

The theory behind station ownership control is the necessity of diversity in the variety of broadcast voices in the local marketplace of ideas, which affords a check on distant corporate powers controlling radio and TV stations. The emphasis is on community because "promoting localism is a key goal of the Commission's media ownership rules."[32] When the FCC came up with new policies regarding the amount and type of local content to be aired and reported, it created a conflict between broadcasters and special interest groups. The FCC's regulatory proposals

---

[31]*See Bechtel v. FCC,* 10 F.3d 875 (1993).

[32]*See FCC Localism Hearing to be Held in Washington, DC, on October 31st, available at* http://fjallfoss.fcc.gov/edocs_public/attachmatch/DOC-277560A1.pdf.

in 2008 established new initiatives designed at increasing localism, including one that broadcasters should establish community advisory boards to discern their public service needs. The FCC proposed rules regarding the staffing and location of stations, and finally more rigorous reporting requirements were made.

Minority Ownership

Before 1978, the FCC granted less than 1 percent of all broadcast licenses to women and minority owners—only 40 stations out of more than 8,500. The agency adopted a tax certificate program under President Carter designed to encourage the sale of cable systems and radio and television stations to women and minorities. This plan created a tax benefit by relieving the stations of having to pay on profits from the sale—a capital gains tax—to the U.S. government. How many broadcast stations and cable system owners were willing to sell their property under this program to a female or minority group? Over about 17 years, more than 350 broadcast and cable deals were signed under this tax certificate program.

► UP CLOSE

Enhanced Disclosure Forms

Localism was driving the government to ask broadcast stations to reveal more about their programming and consult with local advisory boards on the types of programs needed to solve community problems. The FCC wanted broadcasters to boost their local program activities, staff stations with live personnel rather than automation, and locate their studios in the community of their license. Broadcasters objected to the additional burdens imposed under Enhanced Disclosure Order (FCC Form 355). The Commission essentially wanted broadcasters to report their programming in detail on a quarterly basis by listing categories of news, local civic affairs, political campaigns, religious programming, independently produced programming, local programming, and programming for underserved communities.

Each station had to describe how it ascertained the programming needs of its community, whether it met the FCC's closed-captioning requirements, or provided a video description. The enhanced disclosure form also required broadcasters to identify any local marketing agreements with other stations.[a] The National Association of Broadcasters (NAB) filed suit against the FCC to halt these reporting requirements on the grounds that it would require too much money to implement and further shrink broadcasters' revenues.

Some members of Congress joined broadcasters and objected to the enhanced disclosure forms. Sen. John Ensign (R-Nev.) doubted that the FCC rules would actually achieve the goal of increasing local programming or make broadcasters more responsive to local communities. Twenty-three Republican senators joined him in opposition to the proposed localism rules and took exception to the FCC's recommendation for local advisory boards, new license-renewal requirements, and closely regulated content. They argued the FCC localism rules were inherently unfair since they tilted the playing field toward nonbroadcast media by imposing an impractical burden on broadcasters.

---

[a] A Local Marketing Agreement or LMA refers to a pact between two broadcasters where a radio or TV station takes over the programming and commercial sales for most or all of another station's broadcast schedule without actually becoming the licensee or owner of the dependent station.

There was another move toward the diversity in ownership established during President Carter's administration. The FCC encouraged distress sales of broadcast and cable properties to minority and women licensees by allowing the seller to recover some of the market value of their so-called intangible assets. In 1995, however, a major case spelled the end of these programs. In *Adarand Constructors, Inc. v. Peña*, the U.S. Supreme Court ruled against federal programs applying racial criteria unless they were targeted in order to remedy a specific case of discrimination, but not in order to devise general solution for the social ills of prejudice.[33] Congress took action that same year to repeal the tax certificate program by attaching it as a rider on to a health care bill. The result was a slip in TV stations owned by minorities and females. At last report, among more than 12,844 radio and TV stations filing reports, only 460 stations reported minority groups holding a majority voting interest in the company, and even fewer stations (438) reported females holding a majority interest.[34]

In order to improve the situation in 2007, the FCC adopted a Diversity Order that featured reform measures in broadcast transactions, including a ban on discrimination in all such station sales, adoption of a zero tolerance standard for ownership fraud, and nondiscrimination clauses in advertising sales contracts designed to avoid "no urban/no Spanish" requirements. The order also banned the practice of advertisers urging their agencies to avoid Hispanic or African-American media because of supposedly undesirable demographics. The FCC further sought to make capital more accessible to minority groups by creating new distress sale rules for eligible broadcast stations.

Minority Employment

Over the years that the FCC's equal employment opportunities (EEO) rules were on the books, the minority media work force increased from 9.1 percent to 20.2 percent. Women fared better among the employee ranks, gaining more than 40 percent of the available jobs, but only 15 percent were counted among station general managers. The EEO rules required broadcasters to consider minorities and women for job vacancies. No quotas or any particular type of new hires were specified, but the FCC rules did allow the government to pass judgment on hiring decisions after the fact.

The agency, for example, fined two Georgia radio stations in 1991, and granted only a short-term renewal of their licenses for inadequate minority recruitment, but a blow was dealt to the FCC's guidelines when it lost a key case in court. In *Lutheran Church-Missouri Synod v. Federal Communications Comm'n*, the FCC advised two radio stations at Concordia Seminary in Clayton, Mo., that their hiring of minorities failed to comply with EEO guidelines.[35] The agency lost that decision,

---

[33] *Adarand Constructors, Inc. v. Peña*, 515 U.S. 200 (1995).

[34] Female/Minority Broadcast Ownership Data 2004–2005, http://www.fcc.gov/ownership/data.html (last visited Apr. 4, 2011).

[35] *Lutheran Church-Missouri Synod v. Federal Communications Comm'n*, 141 F.3d 344 (D.C. Cir. 1998).

which turned on whether an outreach program for hiring minorities crossed the line from expanding opportunities to disadvantaging nonminorities. In December 2001, the FCC decided the best solution would be to require broadcasters and cable systems to send job-vacancy notices to professional groups representing minorities and women. The agency also called for reporting statistics on the race and gender of job applicants, but there are no sanctions for poor performance, and whatever data are gathered on the increase or decrease of women and minorities hired in electronic media is only to be reported to the government. Basically, all broadcast stations with five or more full-time employees (30-hour work week) must widely distribute information for each full-time vacancy, including to organizations in the community involved in employment activities, and engage in outreach activities, such as job fairs and internships.

PROGRAMMING ISSUES

Structural regulation ■
Many broadcast regulations have more to do with the structure of the media rather than with its content. An example of structural regulation is the rules regarding diversity of media ownership.

As practiced in the United States, media law can be divided into two categories: **structural** and **content** regulation. Any discussion of duopolies, cross-ownership, and the like is based on the industry's structure in terms of legal administration and ownership. There are also important rules regarding programming content. The FCC requires that broadcasters pay close attention to their political programming as it pertains to campaign advertising. Even though the government forbids censorship in § 326 of the Communications Act, it also prohibits suspect information, including hoaxes and distorted news reporting. The agency is especially concerned with programs aired when children are in the broadcast audience.

Content regulation ■ The FCC has many rules regarding programming content, although the FCC is forbidden from censorship by §326 of the Communications act.

Children's Content

Rules for children's television have long been of concern to parents and politicians. Action for Children's Television (ACT) was formed in 1968 in response to cartoons with host characters praising brand cereals and action heroes teaching youngsters their aggressive and sometimes violent solutions to social conflicts. In 1974, ACT urged broadcasters to devote educational time to young people and to be wary of how advertisers approached young viewers. ACT began its battle in 1983 to regulate children's television programs, and seven years later Congress drew up the Children's Television Act, which took effect in 1990. TV stations had to locate three hours in their weekly lineup for educational and informational content. Licensees failing to comply were invited to explain why or risk forfeitures.

Core Programming

Research conducted by the FCC has shown that children between the ages of two and seventeen years old spent an average of three hours watching television a day. After the enactment of the Children's Educational Act of 1990, the FCC began seriously promoting the broadcast of educational and informational programs for children. This type of programming is called "core programming," and is defined as "programming that furthers the positive development of children 16 years of age and under in any respect, including the child's intellectual/cognitive or social/emotional needs." It must meet three criteria:

- Be at least thirty minutes in length.
- Air between the hours of 7:00 a.m. and 10:00 p.m.
- Be at least a regularly scheduled weekly program.

Defining Children's Programs

This rule applies now to television broadcasters, cable operators, and even satellite channels. The FCC was criticized for its refusal to publish a list of acceptable educational programs or to certify whether a program was indeed instructional. As a result some absurd claims were made by stations, such as WFLI in Cleveland, Tennessee, claiming that *The Jetsons* should be considered educational because it shows children what future life might be like.[36] Not wanting to evaluate every program, the Commission's compromise was to require that stations identify their core programs by putting an E/I logo on the screen. At first it was only for the first minute of the program but the rule was amended in 2004 to require the "bug" throughout core children's programs. What's more, parents can access the full list of core children's programs for every U.S. TV station at the FCC website.[37]

During educational and informational shows for children, the number of commercials is restricted. The advertising time is limited to twelve minutes per hour during the week, and ten and one-half minutes per hour on weekends. The FCC is serious about its enforcement of children's programming with regard to commercial advertisers' attempts to skirt the law. A TV show character called Pokemon appeared in a commercial in the same show about Pokemon, and it was all deemed a commercial. The TV station showed limited edition Pokemon Eggo waffles and General Mills "Fruit by the Foot" products during this Pokemon program. Even though the Pokemon characters were fleeting images, the FCC defined it as a program-length commercial out of compliance with the advertising time limits for children's programming (core programming may not contain advertisements using characters that appear within the same core program). Four stations in Texas, Tennessee, and North Carolina were fined by the FCC for violating the limit on commercial time for kids' TV shows, and for not updating their public records.[38] A Chicago TV station also was fined when the FCC identified the entire children's program it aired as an infomercial.

Embedded Advertising

Due to the clutter of advertising messages on television it has become difficult for advertisers to attract the consumer's attention. The advent of digital video technology enables consumers to skip and fast-forward through commercials by using

---

[36] *George Jetson, Teacher,* U.S. News & World Report, Oct. 12, 1992, p. 17.

[37] *See* http://fjallfoss.fcc.gov/KidVid/public/report/12/query.faces.

[38] These decisions are not final and can be appealed. *See* J. Eggerton, *FCC Fined Four Stations, Broadcasting & Cable,* http://www.broadcastingcable.com/article/CA6563094.html (last visited June 28, 2008).

remote controls such as the one devised by TiVo. Commercial sponsors have started to rely on "embedded advertising" to gain the consumer's attention by blending brand names and products into television shows.

The Commission began looking into the matter of product placement in programming with an eye toward possible regulation. The Campaign for a Commercial-Free Childhood (CCFC) protested the lack of protection for children from harmful marketing and implored the FCC to address product placement concerns and brand integration in children's programs. Consumer groups warned the FCC of "Trojan Horse Ads," which sell a product in a program but conceal from the viewer's recognition of the use of that tactic. The CCFC petitioned the FCC for rules that would prevent children's TV programs from invasion by Trojan horses through secret messages that might otherwise be countered by parental safeguards. Consumer groups recognize that the marketers of tobacco and alcoholic beverages conceivably could exploit the lack of regulation for product integration aimed at an audience of children.

Product Placement

The strategy of product placement also involves programming where goods for sale are seamlessly threaded into scripts for such shows as *7th Heaven, The Office, Smallville,* and *CSI,* all of which have hosted brand names such as Oreo Cookies, Staples, Acuvue, and General Motors. Due to pressure from the advertising industry, the FCC was forced to remove the issue from the agenda, but its sponsorship-identification policy requires minimal attention to the practice—larger fonts for the advertiser-identification notices at the end of the show's credits. The FCC reviewed the disclosure credit and found that it appeared so small that it seemed hardly legible to the human eye.

TV Violence and Children

The United States leads the world in violent television programming, and a wealth of data has measured the impact of televised violence on the impressionable child's psyche. A National Television Violence Study found three primary effects that programming violence has on children: (1) aggressive attitudes and behaviors; (2) desensitization to real-world violence; and (3) a fear of being victimized by violence. Children younger than the age of seven generally cannot distinguish between fact and fiction and therefore choose to mimic TV heroes and cartoon violence. In 2003, the government offered a technological solution.

Congress mandated the "v-chip" installation in TV sets with picture screens 13 inches or larger. This hardware solution allows parents to block television programs based on computer ratings encoded for the electronic wiring of the set to read. The v-chip can be programmed to block shows rated TV-PG (Parental Guidance Required), TV-14 (Parents Strongly Cautioned), and TV-MA (For Mature Audiences Only). The Telecommunications Act of 1996 also requires cable systems and multichannel video program distributors (MVPDs) to scramble adult programs that can reach children. By 1999 all of the major broadcast networks and most of the top forty basic cable networks were transmitting ratings through v-chip-equipped TV sets. Certain channels programming news and sports (including CNN, ESPN, and Fox) were exempt.

POLITICAL CONTENT

The government pendulum on political controls for broadcasting content tends to swing between extremes in the United States from regulation to deregulation. For example, the now-defunct fairness doctrine requiring balance in news coverage evolved from a rule against broadcast editorials in 1949, but it challenged both the government and broadcasters in terms of its enforcement for nearly four decades before it was abandoned.

Fairness Doctrine

In an earlier era, the concept of broadcast editorials implied reasoned positions on controversial issues of public importance. The government's goal was to encourage broadcast news coverage in an evenhanded manner in order to resolve such issues. The net effect was that the **fairness doctrine** tended to discourage broadcast journalists, who became sensitive to charges of unfairness especially if they invoked government oversight and second-guessing of the station's news judgment. This so-called chilling effect was blamed for the fairness doctrine's undoing.

> **Fairness doctrine**
> ■ A defunct Federal Communications Commission policy that required broadcast licensees to present controversial issues of public importance and to do so in an honest, equitable and balanced fashion.

According to the doctrine, broadcasters must present an honest and balanced perspective of controversial issues which are of importance to the audience. The FCC rescinded it in 1987, and the periodic moves for reinstatement of the doctrine have been met with fierce resistance.[39] President Bush joined in one campaign against the fairness doctrine's reinstatement, known as the "Broadcaster Freedom Act." He attributed its resurgence to those people who were aligned against conservative radio talk show hosts like Rush Limbaugh. The president stated the fairness doctrine would prevent such talkers from broadcasting their views and vowed to veto any legislation to resurrect it.[40]

Fairness Origins

The fairness doctrine grew out of the FCC's commitment to "the free and fair competition of opposing views," which first appeared in the *Great Lakes* case of 1929, where the FRC emphasized the fairness principle for political candidates and issues of public importance. The *Mayflower Decision* of 1941 prohibited editorializing on the air.[41] In this pre–World War II era, it was felt that broadcasters had an unfair advantage to have their voices heard over those who had no license. *In re Editorializing by Broadcast Licensees* (1949)[42], the FCC's ban on editorials was

---

[39]K. Marre, *Pence Pushes Vote against Fairness Doctrine*, The Hill, Oct. 17, 2007.

[40]John Eggerton, *President Says He Would Veto Fairness-Doctrine Imposition, Broadcasting & Cable*, http://www.broadcastingcable.com/article/CA6540224.html (last visited Mar. 11, 2008).

[41]*In the Matter of the Mayflower Broadcasting Corp. and the Yankee Network Inc.* 8 F.C.C. 323 (1941).

[42]13 F.C.C. 1246 (1949).

replaced with an affirmative obligation to cover public issues in the community, but broadcasters galvanized against it after decades of controversy over its uneven enforcement.

The FCC's Fairness Report in 1985 deemed it a constitutional failure, and the agency took it off the books two years later. A federal panel in 2000 ordered the FCC to also rescind the personal attack and editorializing rules because they "entangle the government in day-to-day operations of the media."[43] The personal attack rule would give private citizens a chance to air a rebuttal against anyone who impugned their personal integrity, but it did not apply to candidates. Another rule was established for the purpose of assessing equal opportunities for politicians.

EQUAL OPPORTUNITIES

Contrary to popular belief, there is no legal obligation that anyone be provided with "equal time" on radio or television. When the fairness doctrine existed, the requirement was "fair" but not necessarily "equal" time. There is, however, a legal obligation that broadcasters provide equal opportunities to candidates for public office, but this is not the same as equal time. If a candidate buys time on a station and an opponent cannot afford to buy as much, the station is under no obligation whatsoever to provide free time. Both candidates are only entitled to the same opportunity to buy time.

American broadcasters are not forced by law to provide equipment or facilities to political candidates, but the law holds that "willful or repeated failure to allow reasonable access to or to permit purchase of reasonable amounts of time for the use of a broadcasting station . . . by a legally qualified candidate for Federal elective office" can lead to revocation of that station's license.[44] The equal opportunities rule holds if a station permits any person "who is a legally qualified candidate for any public office to use a broadcasting station, (the licensee) shall afford equal opportunities to all other such candidates."[45]

Who Is a Legally Qualified Candidate?

The reasonable access requirement applies only to federal candidates, but the equal opportunities rule applies to all elected offices. A candidate is legally qualified if he or she

- Publicly announces his/her candidacy,
- Meets qualifications for office,
- Qualifies for a place on the ballot or is eligible for write-in methods, and
- Is duly nominated by a political party that is commonly known or makes a substantial election showing.

---

[43]*Radio Television News Directors Assn. v. FCC,* 229 F.3d 269 (D.C. Cir. 2000).

[44]47 U.S.C. §312(a)(7).

[45]*See* 47 U.S.C. §315(a), Candidates for Public Office.

Reasonable Access

At the dawn of radio regulation, the bill that created the Federal Radio Commission advised broadcasters they must afford equal opportunities for candidates to air their campaign spots. The law added a stipulation that stations "shall have no power of censorship over the material broadcast."[46] The FCC has a set of rules for political programming and provides advice on issues related to (a) whether equal opportunities for political opponents are warranted, (b) candidate access issues, (c) charging candidates for political advertising, (d) specifics of sponsorship identification, and (e) the FCC's role in enforcing portions of a relatively new law, the Bipartisan Campaign Reform Act.[47] Under § 312 (a) of the Federal Communications Act of 1971, the Candidate Access Rule held that no broadcaster should be allowed to sell airtime in order to support one particular candidate to federal office, and at the same time block the other candidates running for the federal office from gaining access to the airwaves. In theory there is no rule requiring that broadcasters provide access to candidates for local or state office, but they still must act in the public interest, convenience, or necessity, which is why most of them provide access to candidates anyway. If a station were to reject all advertising for local or state office, it might have trouble convincing the FCC that it was acting in the public interest.

Broadcasters can provide political candidates with free airtime or charge them with a fee for that time slot, but the opportunities must be equal for all candidates. These fees are provided under § 312, which states the broadcaster must make available the pricing and discount offers to the political candidates at the lowest unit charge. This bargain occurs forty-five days prior to the date of a runoff or primary election, and sixty days prior to the date of a general or special election, which means basically the amount the station charges its favored commercial advertisers. If a candidate wants a particular time slot when voters are around—say next to the local newscast—the station could increase advertising rates for all to guarantee his or her spot will not be preempted.

Exemptions

There is the question of an inadvertent appearance on television in entertainment programs or films. When candidates log an appearance in a situation comedy or a televised motion picture, does it trigger equal opportunities for their political opponents? In 1980 and 1984, Ronald Reagan's movies were removed from TV program schedules while he campaigned for the White House. So, must broadcasters provide equal opportunity for each appearance by a candidate? The answer is "not always." The law requires equal opportunities for each "use" by a candidate, and then it goes on to exclude certain appearances. It is not considered a "use" (and thus does not trigger a § 315 obligation) if the candidate appears in a

1. Bona fide newscast,
2. Bona fide news interview,

---

[46]47 U.S.C. §315(b)(1)(A).

[47]*McConnell v. Federal Election Comm'n,* 540 U.S. 93 (2003) [ruling on challenges to Pub. L. No. 107–155, 116 Stat. 81 (2002)].

The FCC and Political Advertising

The tone of political advertising can be quite spirited in contests for U.S. public office, and that occasionally puts broadcasters in a precarious position when attack ads are aired. In a U.S. senate race in Louisiana, an incumbent threatened to sue local radio stations if they aired commercial messages that charged him with illicit conduct with women. U.S. Sen. David Vitter (R-La.) claimed the one-minute spots that made these and other allegations were "false, misleading and defamatory" and threatened to sue radio stations that chose to air them. So what should radio stations do?

Attorney Charles Spencer, who serves as general counsel to the Louisiana Association of Broadcasters and was previously on the staff of the FCC, says that radio and TV stations cannot legally censor or select what campaign ads to run and which ones to avoid once

they sell airtime to political candidates in the race for public office. Even when threatened with a libel suit, the station must run the spot and clearly identify the sponsor under the principle of candidate's "use" of airtime.

The term *use* refers to the candidate's voice or image, and the FCC rule forbids any type of broadcast censorship or editorial control over the use of this advertisement. In other words, the broadcaster has immunity from liability for any false or defamatory content, and the FCC has held that the no-censorship provision holds regardless of threats from the candidate's opponent. In fact, broadcast stations are even forbidden from requiring a recording or script of the political advertisement in advance to edit the copy. The only thing a station can do is add a disclaimer but one that cannot be construed as an editorial comment.

3. Bona fide news documentary (if the appearance of the candidate is incidental to the presentation of the subject covered by the news documentary), or
4. On-the-spot coverage of bona fide news events (including but not limited to political conventions and other campaign activities, such as debates).

Newscasts   "Bona fide" newscasts are usually easy to identify; they are those regularly scheduled programs that cover current events. A candidate or station cannot create a pseudo-newscast to avoid equal opportunities obligations. It's easy to understand the need for such an exemption. An incumbent candidate is far more likely to get news coverage while doing the job for which he or she was elected. Stations can't be expected to provide for equal opportunity. Newscasts that are not strictly "hard news" even qualify for this exemption. Entertainment news programs such as *Entertainment Tonight* and *TMZ* also are exempt from § 315.

News Interviews   Similarly, a "bona fide" news interview is a regular scheduled program that routinely deals with news issues. It's easy to understand that Sunday morning talk shows such as *Meet the Press* and *This Week* qualify, but the FCC also has included talk shows such as Jay Leno's and Oprah Winfrey's programs in the exemption.

News Documentaries   The exemption for bona fide news documentaries recognizes that a candidate's appearance in a documentary might have nothing to do with the election. The exemption is conditioned on the candidate's appearance as relevant to the subject of the documentary. For example, if a documentary on the Iraq War included an interview with a U.S. Senator running for reelection, it would be probably ruled as germane to the documentary by the FCC, and as such not deemed a "use" by the candidate. In 2000, A&E Networks asked for and received a declaratory ruling by the Commission that its *Biography* series constituted a bona fide documentary.

Spot News Coverage   The on-the-spot news event exemption was first created to allow full coverage of the Republican and Democratic national conventions. Live coverage of the party conventions isn't a newscast, news interview, or documentary— so another exemption was needed to allow for the coverage. So many candidates for public office attend the conventions that telecasting them without an exemption would trigger literally hundreds of uses if the exemption did not exist.

Debates   The spot news coverage exemption has been expanded to include candidate debates. Usually there are other candidates besides just a Democrat and Republican on a ballot and any one might be able to claim equal opportunity. Since the major party candidates paid nothing to be in the debates, it would require free airtime for the others. In 1960 Congress actually voted to suspend the rule for the famous Kennedy and Nixon debates. For the 1976 Carter-Ford debates, the exemption was broadened to define debates as bona fide news events provided they were conducted by independent third parties (not the candidates or broadcasters) such as the League of Women Voters. Now the rule even allows for broadcasters to conduct the debates themselves. This has allowed debates where only the major party candidates are included. Complaints to the FCC by presidential candidates Ross Perot in 1996[48] and Dennis Kucinich in 2008[49] about their exclusion from televised debates were both denied.

Fine Points of Equal Opportunities

When a use (as defined by § 315) occurs, stations are under no affirmative obligation to inform other candidates. If Sue Doku is running for mayor and buys time on WINO radio, her challengers (or their campaign workers) must go to the station themselves and look through the political file (one of the elements of the public file mentioned earlier) to know how much time they are entitled to purchase at the same price. Sue's challengers have seven days from the date of the broadcast to request the equal opportunity. As stated earlier, if they cannot afford to buy the time the station is under no obligation to give them free airtime.

If, however, WINO were to give Sue free time that constitutes a use (i.e., not one of the exemptions) Sue's challengers could demand equal free time. In 1981, a

---

[48]*In re Complaint of Ross Perot v. ABC*, 11 F.C.C.R. 13109 (1996).

[49]I. Teinowitz, *FCC Rejects Kucinich Complaint about CNN Debate*, TV Week, Jan. 22, 2008. http://www.tvweek.com/news/2008/01/fcc_rejects_kucinich_complaint.php (last visited Apr. 4, 2011).

disc jockey for WSBH radio in Southampton, N.Y., was a Republican candidate for the local town board. The Riverhead Democratic Committee asserted that its candidate was entitled to equal opportunity. The station could not require that the Democratic candidate work as a disk jockey with the time. On the other hand, the radio DJ/candidate's entire three-hour shift was not technically a political use— only the portion of time that the DJ actually was announcing: whether it was news, weather, or introducing songs.

One final technicality about the statute: equal opportunities are afforded candidates for the same office. A candidate for mayor is not entitled to an opportunity equal to the use by a congressional candidate. It isn't that one office is entitled to more or less access than any other, just that any use triggers an equal opportunity only for candidates running for the exact same office. In fact, during the primaries, Republican and Democratic candidates aren't really running against each other— they are running for their respective party's nomination. This means that during a primary, a use by a Democratic candidate only triggers a § 315 requirement for other Democrats for the same office.

In order to ensure that broadcast stations follow the dictates of § 315, the FCC requires records of all campaign commercials and all requests to buy broadcast time from national candidates be inserted in the political file. This file also shows how the station responded to those requests, how many schedules of political commercials were sold for how much, and when the spots actually aired. If a station gives free airtime to a candidate, then that too is kept in records for the FCC to inspect.

PUBLIC BROADCASTING

U.S. law divides radio and television stations into two categories: commercial broadcasters and noncommercial educational broadcasters. The FCC licenses commercial stations to rely on advertising revenue, while noncommercial educational (NCE) broadcasters must meet operating expenses through the support of listeners and viewers, in addition to government funding. The law allows noncommercial broadcasters to acknowledge personal and corporate contributions in terms of underwriting donations through on-air announcements, but NCE stations are prohibited from broadcasting commercial or other promotional announcements on behalf of for-profit supporters. The FCC now accepts what are described as "enhanced underwriting" acknowledgements on PBS stations where for-profit underwriters can broadcast slogans or logos that identify the corporate donor but do not promote any products. The rules allow for value-neutral descriptions of their products or services on the air of an NCE, but prohibit commercial calls to action, or any interruptions in the station's regular programming.

President Lyndon B. Johnson authorized the Public Broadcasting Act of 1967,[50] which established the Corporation for Public Broadcasting and gave the necessary support to form two networks: the Public Broadcasting Service (PBS) and National Public Radio (NPR). President Johnson explained it would show to

---

[50]47 U.S.C. §396.

Public Television's Heroine

When the FCC issued its *Sixth Report and Order* in 1952, the allocation plan included 242 channel assignments for noncommercial educational (NCE) stations. This was due in large part to the work of the first woman commissioner on the FCC, Freida C. Hennock, who encouraged universities and communities to apply for noncommercial educational licenses and advised NCEs on the best ways to gain the support of community leaders and organizations. She enlisted the cooperation of businesses and corporations in affording grants and helped early NCE stations find needed equipment.

The historic battle to set aside spectrum was not easily won because commercial broadcasters fought to prevent federal support of broadcast licensees through tax-based revenues. Hennock, President Harry S Truman's appointment to the Federal Communications Commission, felt differently. Hennock was a Polish immigrant not easily intimidated by commercial broadcasters and recognized the problem was one of stability. When the FCC began reorganizing TV channels in 1951, the agency included dial positions for educational broadcasting, but there was no assurance they would be permanent. Commercial broadcasters were set to win that "television real estate" (VHF channels 2 and 13) but Hennock felt the public needed first to be notified. Her message began to filter down to the American people, who responded in support of noncommercial educational broadcasting.

In June 1953, the first educational TV station took to the air, and Hennock was invited to Houston to speak at KUHT-TV's inaugural program. By mid-1955, twelve educational stations were broadcasting and more than fifty applications for noncommercial licenses had been filed with the FCC. This woman's belief in educational broadcasting was realized thanks largely to her strong will and tenacity; she recognized what was at stake in 1952 when it came time to allocate television channels and to afford commercial-based broadcasting all the VHF bandwidth. More than any other individual, Hennock was responsible for securing the assignment of noncommercial TV channels and eventual creation of the public broadcasting.

the world that the United States offered its people more than just an opportunity to acquire "material wealth . . . we want most of all to enrich man's spirit. That is the purpose of this act."[51]

The 1967 law gave support to educational radio and television stations by providing funds for their facilities and declaring that when noncommercial broadcasters produce programs they should be encouraged to take "creative risks," as they meet the needs of underserved audiences, including children and minorities, all of which serve the public interest. Public television and radio stations, like commercial broadcasters, are required to address local problems through their outreach programs. From time to time, commercial broadcasters have sought legislation to curtail any government funding for noncommercial educational broadcasting, but this is a long-standing fight that has been resolved before in favor of public broadcasting.

---

[51]Remarks of President Lyndon B. Johnson Upon Signing the Public Broadcasting Act of 1967, Nov. 7, 1967, *available at* http://www.cpb.org/aboutpb/act/remarks.html.

BROADCASTING'S OTHER OBLIGATIONS

There are other rules the FCC is asked to enforce from time to time, which do not figure prominently in the legal record and which include broadcasts that might tend to deceive the public or create a dangerous situation. One rule stands against the broadcasting of hoaxes, which is defined as false reports involving a crime or catastrophe that the radio or television station knew were untrue. This rule followed the infamous *War of the Worlds* radio drama that convinced some listeners in 1938 that Martians actually had invaded the state of New Jersey. The other rule involves broadcast journalism and would penalize a station for purposely distorting the news.

Hoaxes and Distortions

In the case of a broadcast that concerned a crime or catastrophe, the FCC requires a showing that the station knew the information to be false and that by airing this false report it caused substantial public harm. The licensee is forgiven such a mistake on the air if it was not foreseeable that broadcasting the false report would have caused this harm. There is a similar rule against announcements that might pose imminent danger and lawlessness to the public.

There is another prohibition against distorting the news by "rigging or slanting the news" which has been called "a most heinous act against the public interest." Again, the government requires a showing that the station knew what it was doing when it falsified or distorted the news before levying penalties against the licensee. The FCC is reluctant to invoke this rule because it places the agency in the position of

---

UP CLOSE

The Holy Grail

One of the so-called holy grail missions of the FCC was initiated in 1996 when the U.S. Congress required broadcasters and multichannel video program distributors (cable, satellite) to **close caption** their programs in order to forge a "critical link to news, entertainment, and information." This rule fulfilled a law adopted in 1990, the Television Decoder Circuitry Act, that required TV set manufacturers to have the electronic circuitry installed for closed captioning. Hard of hearing and deaf viewers found this technology to be useful. In addition, closed captioning opened the door of language learning for non-English-speaking immigrants. Closed-captioning requirements were extended to DTV in 2002. There are exemptions to closed captioning including public service announcements, commercial advertising, and shows aired between 2:00 a.m. and 6:00 a.m.

For visually impaired Americans, the Telecommunications Act of 1996 initiated the broadcasting of Descriptive Video Services (DVS), which can be transmitted on part of the television channel reserved for Secondary Audio Program (SAP) frequencies. PBS became the first network to experiment with its DVS service for the blind in 1990, adding audio narration that was placed between moments of dialogue and sound effects in order for the visually impaired to know what action was taking place on the screen. DVS can also be heard on such popular programs as *The Simpsons* and *CSI: Crime Scene Investigation*; however, the FCC has yet to legally require the DVS technology for all broadcasters, as it has done with closed captioning.

second-guessing the journalistic judgment of the broadcaster. The rule has been used to challenge network programs about hunger and the Vietnam War. The FCC is prohibited from censoring the broadcaster, and thus is not enthusiastic about questioning errors in news judgment unless it recognizes a pattern of abuse.

Station and Sponsor Identification

There are affirmative obligation rules for broadcast stations to identify themselves on the air. The government requires an hourly broadcast of the radio or television station's call letters, and the community of its license. Some stations seize this legal ID opportunity and promote the channel or station frequency in addition to a promotional slogan. Some stations are licensed in one community but actually broadcast from another; in the interest of localism, the FCC requires that radio stations maintain a main studio within twenty-five miles of the community's geographic center in most cases. The law also requires the station maintain a certain level of power over the "principal community contour" for its licensed community and have a telephone number within the city of limit.

When a broadcast program airs for which the station reaps a monetary benefit, the law also requires that the sponsor be identified when the show is aired. Keeping payments secret became a subject of controversy for radio stations during the early rock 'n' roll era when disc jockeys played records for payments and other inducements under the table. Under federal law, a radio station now can only accept money for playing a record if it discloses the advertiser at airtime. In the case of television audiences, local news viewers were left unaware of who was hoping to persuade them with a television story paid for and distributed for local TV newscasts. These video news releases (VNRs) were subject of an FCC investigation that asked local television stations to reveal if they had received any payment ("consideration") for airing VNRs.

SUMMARY

- The FCC was created to oversee both structural and programming issues. Its regulations cover both the structural technology and programming content of radio and television stations. In terms of structure, rules oversee frequency allocation, channel assignments, tower lighting, and the technology of broadcasting. In terms of content, the rules serve the public's interest, convenience, and necessity in areas of political broadcasting, children's television, public broadcasting, journalism, advertising, and other areas.
- The FCC derives its authority from the interstate commerce clause of the U.S.

Constitution, and based on the rationale that American citizens actually own the airwaves, the FCC exercises its legal authority by licensing stations and assigning particular channels. Further, the resource of broadcasting, the spectrum, is limited and lacks the bandwidth to grant licenses to all applicants so broadcasters are given only a temporary license to use them. The FCC is forbidden from any censoring role, but because of broadcasting's pervasiveness and accessibility, the law recognizes the necessity for regulating it.
- Licenses are assigned to applicants with at least 80 percent U.S. ownership, which have enough financial backing to build and operate

a broadcast transmitter for 90 days without commercial support. The FCC can revoke licenses or invoke fines for failing to heed government regulations that are created to protect the public's interest. The FCC reviews its rules regularly and decides whether or not to revise or delete any regulations that are no longer useful or practical.

- Five commissioners fulfill a regulatory role through the administration of the FCC's bureaus and offices where broadcasting policy is crafted. The commissioners are appointed by the president to serve for five-year terms and represent both political parties. They not only oversee broadcasting, but also regulate other electronic media, including cable and satellite channels, telephone, and Internet networks. In terms of infractions and penalties broadcasters might receive from the U.S. government, the FCC enforces its rules by first issuing notices of apparent liability. It can also take action against violators of FCC rules with fines, or "forfeitures," that are levied in addition to letters of reprimand, and if there is a pattern of abuse that violates the public interest, convenience, and necessity, the government can revoke a license. The FCC does enforce political rules designed to afford federal candidates an equal opportunity to reach local voters through the use of broadcast (and cable channels). There are exceptions that cover various kinds of news programming and debates, and the equal opportunity only applies for forty-five days before a primary election and sixty days before a general election. What it does afford candidates for political office is the lowest unit charge for commercial advertisements. A rule regarding the fairness of broadcast coverage for public controversies was repealed in 1987 but has been reintroduced in Congress several times to the loud condemnation of political talk show hosts.

- In order to establish a rule, the FCC first issues a Notice of Inquiry (NOI) that invites broadcasters and other members of the public to consider a problem that the agency feels needs attention. If the FCC decides that some regulatory solution is practical, it will issue a Notice of Proposed Rulemaking (NPRM), which gives broadcasters a chance to respond to the proposed regulation. The final step in the process is the Report & Order that indicates the Commission either will enforce a new rule, revise an existing rule, or maintain the present circumstance.

- Promoting localism, competition, and diversity are central to the FCC's mission, and one way it accomplishes that is through the ownership rules. A sliding scale of media ownership is based on the size of market, and the government upholds a four-and-eight rule meaning that one ownership group should not control more than one of the four most popular television stations in a market and there should be a minimum of eight independent voices of media if one group owns multiple broadcast stations.

- Equal opportunities means that broadcast stations must not favor one candidate over another in terms of selling or offering commercial time on the air during the weeks before an election. The FCC also requires that political candidates be given the best rates for their campaign spots on air during this period.

- Congress has also acted on behalf of children's educational and informational needs by requiring television stations to air at least three hours per week of programs that improve adolescent cognitive skills and meet their emotional needs. The "core programming" must reach children 16 years and younger, be at least a half hour in length and air at least weekly between 7:00 a.m. and 10:00 p.m.

Performance Tax

Like dueling musicians, two opposing groups of lawmakers have been jousting in Congress over the right to impose a performance tax on local radio stations for the music they air. Leading the lawmakers in favor of the performance royalty is Sen. Patrick Leahy (Vt.), who co-sponsored the Performance Rights Act with the support of President Obama's administration. A leader of the opposing group of lawmakers is Sen. Blanche Lincoln (Ark.), who responded to this issue with the "Local Radio Freedom Act," an anti-fee resolution that received bipartisan support in Congress against attempts to impose a performance fee on radio stations.

Under existing law, broadcast radio stations pay royalties to record labels, which means publishers and writers are compensated for their work, but not the owners of sound recordings. This process is contrary to other parts of the world, and the U.S. Department of Commerce supports the performance rights bill for that reason—it would protect performances and producers of sound recordings and revise the law to conform with global standards for the creators of other works. American recording artists lose "substantial royalties for the public performance of U.S. sound recordings abroad (because they) are either not collected at all or not distributed to American performers and record companies," states the U.S. Commerce Dept.

Since 1978 Congress has considered but has refused to impose a performance tax on radio stations due to what broadcasters consider to be a mutually successful relationship between both industries—music recording and broadcasting. The anti-tax group is supported by radio stations led by the National Association of Broadcasters (NAB), which argues that a federal performance fee would be devastating for local radio stations, who give musicians free promotion for the sale of their CDs and concert ticket sales.

In 2011, prominent broadcasters (most notably Jeff Smulyan of Emmis Communications) implied a willingness to support performance fees if Congress would attach an unrelated requirement that cellular phones be built with radio receivers. This helps demonstrate two truisms: laws are often passed by compromise, and trade associations are powerful influences in the process of legislation. ■

Telecommunications

LEARNING OBJECTIVES

After reading this chapter you should know:

- How cable television was "invented"
- The origins of a common carrier
- That cable television evolved from a natural monopoly to a competitive environment of multichannel video program distributors (MVPDs)
- Content regulations and their impact on MVPDs

- Cable regulation has swung from almost no regulation to heavy regulation and back to a middle ground
- The impact that the breakup of AT&T had on telecommunications
- How the debate over network neutrality impacts the future of video services online and the Internet in general

A LEVEL PLAYING FIELD

Seven billion dollars may seem like a lot of money, but the U.S. government often speaks in terms of trillions for economic recovery, so it was only a drop in the bucket—though a rather large drop. The U.S. Congress, in its efforts to stimulate the economy, set aside billions of dollars to establish the Broadband Technology Opportunities Program (BTOP). The idea was to reach underserved or even unserved areas with broadband channels as part of the American Recovery and Reinvestment Act of 2009 (ARRA). The BTOP made infrastructure grants available to give Americans faster access to the Internet. The grants would be important to the future of both old and new media, including the most popular medium of all, television. The question raised by policy makers was by what rules the money would be allocated to upgrade public computing centers, community colleges, and public libraries. "Nondiscrimination" became the key word for industry and political leaders who sought to level the playing field for new competition with so many federal dollars at stake.

Television, whether transmitted by cable, satellite, or the Internet, has never been more plentiful in the United States, and the competition to sell it never greater. Digital video services offer subscriptions to reach viewers in their homes, offices, via mobile phones—virtually everywhere. Congressional concern often looks toward keeping the competition between all media fair, or maintaining a level playing field as it's often described, especially since older media outlets are losing momentum. Less than 10 percent of American households view free TV channels by home antennas, while basic cable viewers in the United States are now less than 60 percent of the market. Can free broadcast television compete when more and more Americans subscribe to a bundle of video, mobile, and Internet services? That is the question regulators and policy makers now face.

The battle to satisfy the consumer's communication appetite has produced rules that affect not only competition, but also ownership issues, access obligations, franchising requirements, taxable revenues, and technical standards. Regulation of broadcasting and cable systems is a given, but the telecommunications revolution has added new media to the equation and that means regulatory bodies must keep up with the innovations in telecommunications.

> **Bedrock Law:** The government regulates telecommunications carriers and their companies in a dynamic field that requires constant revision of regulations.

In the Beginning . . .

At first, Americans tuned in to see black-and-white TV screens by tilting rabbit-ear antennas atop the wood and glass boxes in their living rooms. If they were lucky enough to live within the range of the about one hundred original TV stations located in large cities they could see "radio with pictures," but most Americans in 1948 lived beyond the signal of a local TV station. In fact, the Federal Communications Commission (FCC) stopped licensing new TV stations for four years in order to redraw its channel allocation map and divvy up new licenses for the nation. In addition, the government had to choose between competing systems of color television technology to replace black-and-white pictures, and that took time.

This hiatus for broadcast licensing inspired appliance shopkeepers and amateur electricians to find ways to bring big city TV stations to rural homes by erecting community antenna television (CATV) towers and capturing distant signals. They placed the poles in good spots of reception and crossed the terrain with coaxial cables that brought early TV pictures to American homes. By 1950, an estimated 14,000 Americans were watching 70 CATV systems in communities like Astoria, Oregon, and Mahoney City, Penn., where community antenna television began its remarkable journey.

The first CATV systems carried channels to service "white areas," where no broadcast channels could be received at all. In those communities where one or two TV channels were viewed, CATV provided the necessary fill-in service, importing the missing network stations. They leased towers from microwave firms to import distant signals from TV stations, which eventually created legal disputes that began defining the new medium in legal terms.

Defining the Messenger

The government appeared at first to be uncertain of its role in cable television's regulation. The FCC's position for most of the 1950s was that CATV fell beyond its jurisdiction, but that stance did not set well with American broadcasters who saw federal oversight as an imperative. An early case in point involved the use of microwave towers for CATV. The Carter Mountain Transmission Company wanted to relay broadcast signals along microwave towers in Wyoming and import TV programs from Denver, Colorado. A broadcaster in Riverton, Wyoming, KWRB-TV, did not appreciate the new competition and challenged the microwave relays. An FCC hearing examiner first decided that CATV relays were acceptable, but the full Commission reversed his decision and sided with the broadcaster.[1]

Common carrier ■
In transportation, moving people or goods for a fee. In communications, transporting the communications of others via wire or airwaves. In either case, non-discrimination of passengers or messages is required.

CATV clearly posed a problem in terms of regulatory definition. Sure, it was retransmitting broadcast programming but without any editorial control—so how should it be defined? Was it a broadcast medium or a **common carrier**?[2] The term *common carrier* evolved from a transportation term for services that were available to all. Freight traveled via common carriers like trains, and busses accepted all passengers willing to pay the fare. In media terms, a common carrier defined a communication system that offers its information transmission services to the general public without manipulating the content. Common carriers include the telephone and telegraph, which have been under the watchful eye of federal regulators for years, and yet cable television seemed more like a small network of TV channels for sale than something akin to the phone company or telegraph office. Rather than confuse the issue, the FCC simply avoided defining this new medium in legal terms, but it did eventually recognize its jurisdiction.

FCC JURISDICTION

The arrival of high-powered TV channels via cable from Los Angeles threatened local TV stations to the south in San Diego, and that case forced the government's hand. In 1968, the Supreme Court ruled in *U.S. v. Southwestern Cable* that the

[1]*Carter Mountain Transmission Co. v. Federal Communications Comm'n*, 321 F.2d 359 (D.C. Cir. 1963).
[2]*Frontier Broadcasting Co. v. Collier*, 24 F.C.C. 251 (1958).

FCC should exercise its authority over cable and enforce regulations based on its congressionally mandated oversight of radio and wired communications. The FCC's "regulatory authority over CATV is imperative" in order to assure local broadcast television is preserved and equitably distributed around the country, according to the high court's reading of the Communications Act of 1934.[3]

The province of jurisdiction was placed in the commission's hands so long as its CATV rules were "reasonably ancillary" to broadcast services. The federal authority over cable was needed to protect broadcasters, but soon the agency adopted even more expansive rules. The FCC asked that cable companies register for a certificate of compliance and set the franchise agreement terms, cable's technical standards, signal carriage standards, and standards for syndication programs.[4] Some of these policies were later revised or deleted altogether, but not before several legal decisions were made that directly impacted cable's regulatory landscape.

Early Competitors

In Los Angeles, Preferred Communications operated a cable company that made a bid to compete in the market by establishing its right to overbuild the local cable system already in place.[5] The Los Angeles Department of Water and Power had refused to grant access to the poles needed for hanging additional cable lines, claiming they would interfere with the municipal aesthetics, and cause a "permanent visual blight" for the city. The appeals court in this case held that the city of Los Angeles needed to do more than just argue that ugliness was the reason to stop competition, and a more developed record of evidence was needed. The U.S. Supreme Court ultimately held that cable television systems were entitled to compete unless a city could conclusively show that its utility system could not support two cable systems at the same time.

When cable television systems encounter competition, the operative term is *overbuild*, as in a telecommunications firm is *building over* a system in a market already served by one **MVPD**. EchoStar's DISH and DirecTV are considered cable television's chief **overbuilders**, but broadband and telephone services also have taken to the playing field. RCN, for example, is a Virginia-based corporation that became popular in the northeast and Chicago for its marketing of the triple-play option. This merchandising tool of bundling telephone, cable television, and Internet services into one package for the subscribing customer has attracted new business to firms like RCN. By 2006, RCN claimed 424,000 domestic customers and 130 cable franchises.

Natural Monopoly

At the economic level, cable television systems were first viewed as a **natural monopoly**. By looking at their public utility features the term seemed to fit. Cable systems used an electronic wired infrastructure requiring right-of-way easements,

MVPD ■
Multichannel Video Program Distributor. The term for services providing bundles of video channels, such as cable systems, home satellite dish providers, video over internet protocol, etc.

Overbuilders ■
New entrants into an existing telecommunications market are referred to as overbuilders, as in building over the existing system.

Natural monopoly ■ A natural monopoly occurs when the cost of producing something outweighs the benefit to the producer. If the goods are public goods that are still needed, the government may become involved since ordinarily, free markets will not produce goods at a loss. Traditional examples are public goods like sewerage or lighthouses.

---

[3]392 U.S. 157 (1968).
[4]*See* 1972 *Cable Television Report & Order*, 36 F.C.C. 2d 143 (1972).
[5]*Los Angeles v. Preferred Communications, Inc.* 476 U.S. 488 (1986).

and their customers were served a monthly bill. Natural monopoly also seemed practical in terms of cable competition at the local level because there was only so much room available on poles or underground casements for extra wires. Cities found that accommodating just one cable system posed challenges, technically and economically. The so-called natural monopoly characteristics also were associated with economies of scale, which meant cable's Multiple System Operators (MSOs) could concentrate on acquiring more cable systems and providing more services.[6]

Competition eventually shattered the natural monopoly perspective, but not before mergers and acquisitions catapulted MSOs into huge media conglomerates and put out of business the original "mom & pop" systems selling cable television to neighbors, families, and friends. Congress finally disposed of the natural monopoly view through its passage of the Telecommunications Act in 1996. By then, the MVPD competition had evolved into what some would consider an *oligopoly* with a few major players dominating the phone, television, and Internet markets. Professor Noam observed, "we may have to get used to the idea of living with oligopoly in telecom rather than the hoped-for competition."[7] The natural monopoly days are gone, and yet some local communities appear reluctant to welcome new competitors despite the fact that federal law requires it. No town or city can unreasonably refuse to allow competition and prevent an additional telecom franchise from doing business alongside the cable company. If a city refuses to grant a rival MVPD a franchise, then it must demonstrate its just cause, and note that the aspiring competitor to the incumbent system has a right to appeal the decision.[8]

> **Bedrock Law:** Cable television has evolved from a natural monopoly to many competitors in the marketplace of multiple channel video program distributors (MVPDs).

PENDULUM OF CABLE REGULATION

For years, regulators engaged in a tug of war with cable systems over a variety of issues, but it was not just between the FCC and telecommunications carriers. The Internal Revenue Service (IRS) decided to levy an excise tax of 8 percent on CATV systems in 1951. The nascent industry responded by gathering at a hotel in Pottsville, Penn., and forming the National Community Television Council. A district court of appeals subsequently threw out that excise tax, but that legal battle did serve to create a voice for the industry. The National Cable & Telecommunications Association (NCTA) is a direct descendant of the Pottsville delegates and represents cable system operators and their program networks on a host of public issues.

In 1991, the question of taxing cable companies was raised again in the case of *Leathers v. Medlock*.[9] The ruling held that cable television was a medium deserving of First Amendment protection, but the U.S. Supreme Court allowed for the state to tax its cable system revenues—that is so long as that tax was unrelated to its freedom of expression and was nondiscriminatory in terms of any particular viewpoints.

---

[6]Eli M. Noam, *Is Cable Television a Natural Monopoly?* 9 Comm.Int'l J. Comm. Res. 241 (1983–84).

[7]Eli M. Noam, *The Emerging Cyclicality of the Telecom Industry,* in *Global Economy and Digital Society* (E. Bohl, S. Levi, N. Sung, and C.H. Yoon eds., Elsevier Science 2004).

[8]47 U.S.C. § 555.

[9]499 U.S. 439 (1991).

Copyright Issues

An early issue raised was over the question of cable's use of broadcast television property. The distinct possibility that CATV was infringing on copyright ownership came before the U.S. Supreme Court in *Fortnightly Corp. v. United Artists* (1968). Fortnightly operated two CATV systems in the rolling hills of West Virginia where a broadcast signal faced the natural obstacles of hill and dale.[10] United Artists argued Fortnightly's retransmission of its motion pictures on television was a copyright issue. This reasoning came from a 1909 law that considered it to be copyright infringement when a performance was restaged without permission from the original owners for the privilege. The Court did not feel that viewing distant TV channels in West Virginia amounted to a "performance" since "CATV systems basically did no more than enhance the viewers' capacity to receive the signal."[11]

Broadcast television stations were under the impression that their licensing agreements with networks, syndicators, and show producers would entitle them to receive copyright payments from cable systems. That was not the case. In 1976, the Copyright Act gave cable operators the freedom to retransmit TV shows so long as their systems bought the compulsory licenses. A copyright royalty panel was established to collect money based on a share of each cable system's receipts. Those cable revenues were deposited with the Copyright Royalty Tribunal (CRT), which converted it into royalty payments for the TV program owners.

In 1993, Congress replaced the CRT with federal arbitration panels appointed by the Librarian of Congress to address copyright issues for program owners. Twice a year, cable systems file a statement of account regarding their revenues with the licensing division of the copyright office in the Library of Congress. The cable firms are then assessed a fee based on gross receipts of local and distant TV channels. TV copyright holders receive royalties for the cable programs based on these fees.

Syndicated Exclusivity

The conflict over syndicated programming between broadcast and cable television has produced additional twists and turns in the legal road map. Syndicated programs such as *Seinfeld* and *Oprah* are offered to local TV stations and aired as either second-run network productions or original syndication often licensed for exclusive showing to a local broadcaster. Once a TV station buys a license to air a syndicated program, it might lose both ratings and advertising revenue if the same show is on a competing channel. The FCC's rule of **syndicated exclusivity** or "syndex" calls for the deletion of competing cable programs to protect local TV broadcasters from viewer migration to cable channels.

This syndex rule was abolished in 1980 in order to encourage cable's development, but that policy was reversed once it became clear that local broadcasters were harmed by its absence. Nielsen confirmed that audience ratings suffered for local TV channels when superstations like WGN-TV in Chicago and WTBS-TV in

Syndicated exclusivity (syndex) ■ An FCC regulation which allows local television stations to enter into exclusive contracts for syndicated content, and requires MVPDs to honor those contracts.

---

[10]*Fortnightly Corp. v. United Artists*, 392 U.S. 390 (1968).
[11]392 U.S. 157 (1968).

Ratings dilution ■
Refers to the effect
on local stations
when cable channels
air programs previ-
ously purchased by
the local station.
This is one of the
effects syndicated
exclusivity was
intended to prevent.

Atlanta duplicated syndicated fare. This negative impact became known as **ratings dilution**, which translated into depressed rates for local commercials on syndicated programs.

In 1988, the FCC reinstated its syndex rule, an action that was upheld by a federal appeals court one year later.[12] This rule is actually an assurance that broadcasters who pay a premium for the exclusive contract to televise a syndicated program will have the force of law supporting that contract. Not all syndicated shows have exclusive contracts though; it's cheaper for a local TV station to obtain a nonexclusive program. A lot of older shows are sold nonexclusively so that the syndicators can sell to both local stations and cable networks, but many first-run shows (like *Jeopardy*) are only available by exclusive agreement. The rule allows for cable systems to choose *not* to delete syndicated programs in some cases, including programs on a "significantly viewed" channel in that market. Given the business model of broadcasting, most TV stations want to reach as many households for their advertisers as possible, and that means a guaranteed spot in the cable dial.

Must-Carry Regulation

Must-carry rule ■
The FCC mandates
that cable compa-
nies carry various
local and public
television stations
within a cable
provider's service
area. *See Turner
Broadcasting Sys. v.
Federal Communications
Commission,* 512 U.S.
622 (1994).

The original **must-carry rule** was adopted in 1965, and it required that a cable system retransmit all local TV stations within a certain radius of its service area. Generally, a cable system with twelve or more channels has to carry local TV stations on up to a third of its programming tiers, but then cable channels became popular and systems began to sell local advertising time to interested businesses. Cable was competing with broadcasters for commercial advertising, which created a problem when cable operators were forced to carry local TV stations. Cable operators also felt that the must-carry rule had robbed them of valuable channels that were assigned to broadcasters, thus preventing more lucrative opportunities for cable programming. Cable operators also were able to persuade the courts in the 1980s that their position had legal merit.

In the *Quincy* and *Century Communications* cases, must-carry rules were twice rejected because they were an encroachment on the First Amendment freedom of cable systems as a form of forced speech. These lower court rulings declared must-carry obligations to be in violation of the cable operator's constitutional rights.[13] Congress settled the question in a 1992 act by giving broadcasters the choice of either seeking compensation from the cable company or demanding must-carry rights. Early retransmission deals were usually for carriage of a second channel rather than in exchange of money from cable systems to retransmit their primary channel.[14] It was inevitable that cable systems would wage a legal fight against this measure, and Ted Turner, acting on behalf of his cable empire, chose to fight the new must-carry rule by taking the FCC to court—twice.

[12]*United Video v. Federal Communications Comm'n,* 890 F.2d 1173 (D.C. Cir. 1989).

[13]*Quincy Cable TV, Inc. v. Federal Communications Comm'n,* 768 F. 2d 1434 (D.C. Cir. 1985); *Century Communications Corp. v. Federal Communications Comm'n,* 835 F.2d 292 (D.C. Cir. 1987).

[14]Cable Television Consumer Protection and Competition Act of 1992, Pub. L. No. 102-385.

Turner I & II

The cable industry had hoped to set a standard similar to newspapers, and the lawyers for Turner Broadcasting argued that it would be no more reasonable for the government to require cable systems to carry local TV stations than it would be to legally demand a newspaper to publish a particular columnist. This analogy of newspapers to cable access was persuasive to four of the Supreme Court justices who thought the must-carry rule was not content-neutral and ran afoul of the First Amendment, particularly since broadcast channels were gaining access and others were not. Yet, the majority of the Court came to believe that must-carry was content-neutral and therefore deserved only a test of intermediate scrutiny, which meant the public interest—in this case the cable industry's interest—was important, although not compelling. This means of achieving it—must-carry—was reasonable though not the least restrictive means. In other words, it was treated as a structural rule rather than content mandate removing it from concerns with free expression.

The *Turner* case was remanded for another trial in federal district court in Washington, D.C., which found the must-carry rule carried no threat to free expression nor encroached upon the editorial discretion of the cable system. The U.S. Supreme Court took the case once again on appeal, and in 1997 ruled that it was the best way to deal with cable's competitive advantage over broadcast television stations. In *Turner* I, the Court barely upheld the new must-carry rule by a 5–4 vote that gave broadcast stations the right to ask for a guaranteed spot on the local cable system dial.[15] The majority recognized the national interest in keeping weaker television stations on the air in light of competition from cable. In *Turner* II, the government "has an independent interest in preserving a multiplicity of broadcasters," said the Court, which is what the law was designed to do.[16]

Dissenting voices in the *Turner* decision felt the wrong test had been applied. Associate Justice Sandra Day O'Connor held that must-carry rules were content-based and promoted the speech of broadcasters over cable operators. She and other dissenting justices would have applied strict scrutiny to the must-carry regulation and struck it down for favoring local broadcasting over national cable television. The majority, however, saw no constitutional violation in that the must-carry obligation gave no unfair advantage to any particular viewpoint.

Bedrock Law: The must-carry rule was judged to be content-neutral and therefore remains on the books because it did not interfere with the First Amendment rights of cable systems.

Retransmission Consent Agreement

The flipside of the must-carry obligation was the retransmission consent obligation, which meant that broadcasters have the right to enter negotiations every three years with the local cable system. Early on, broadcasters were wary of demanding cash for fear that cable systems would refuse their demands and sought retransmission agreements in exchange for carrying a second channel. Local TV stations had the option to start a local weather channel, or twenty-four-hour news

---

[15]*Turner Broadcasting Sys. v. Federal Communications Comm'n*, 512 U.S. 622 (1994).
[16]*Turner Broadcasting Sys., Inc. v. Federal Communications Comm'n*, 520 U.S. 180 (1997).

Dallas and Its Cable Dilemma

It was the sort of made-for-television drama that viewers might see promoted as a reality show: "What happens when broadcasters and cable firms tangle over a local TV channel?" The Dallas–Fort Worth market is headquarters for Belo Broadcasting and its flagship Channel 8, WFAA-TV, but customers of Charter Communications were surprised to learn they might be losing their hometown station late in 2008. Negotiations had reached an impasse between Charter and Belo, which was hoping to get retransmission fees from the cable firm. Instead it appeared as if the ABC affiliate would lose its place on the local cable system menu of channels.

Broadcasting and newspaper groups like Belo face increasing competition from the Internet, which shrink their advertising revenues. Cable systems say their resources are stretched as well, and they cannot afford to pay broadcasters extra for their channels. In Dallas, the Belo group demanded a penny per day for each one of the cable subscribers, and it became a contest of who would blink first during the

negotiations. Neither the cable company nor the broadcaster wants the agreement made public for fear of giving a negotiating advantage to a competitor. Eventually, the cable company and Belo came to terms and concluded their retransmission negotiations successfully.

This Texas conflict illustrates the contentious nature of retransmission consent agreements, in which some fights become so hardnosed that local cable customers might find their favorite TV station has disappeared from sight. The two rules involved are related but separate—must carry and retransmission consent. Every three years, commercial broadcasters choose whether to pursue retransmission consent fees from the cable company or demand must-carry rights—they cannot do both. Consequently, cable and satellite firms obtain permission from the broadcaster for televising its signal by paying a fee, or if the local TV station cannot bargain for lack of audience, it can demand its must-carry rights in order to avoid deletion from the cable system.

Cable Act of 1984
■ Congressional amendments to the Communications Act of 1934 that deregulated cable pricing and established a national policy for the regulation of cable systems.

channel, or shopping channel. Nationally owned stations often sought carriage of a new national cable channel owned by the parent company (Fox's fX and NBC's CNBC forged carriage agreements this way). In the twenty-first century, retransmission agreements have been all about the money.

Cable Act of 1984

When it came time for Congress to measure the extent to which the FCC could apply its jurisdiction over cable, it did so by substantially amending the Communications Act of 1934. The **1984 Cable Franchise Policy and Communications Act** was drafted by Sen. Barry Goldwater (R-Ariz.), and it freed cable systems from some of the more extraordinary demands imposed by local franchising authorities through their legally binding agreements.[17] Its economic protections, for example, relieved escalating franchise fees that were capped at 5 percent of gross revenues.

---

[17]Pub. L. No. 98-549, 47 U.S.C. § 521.

In general, the 1984 cable law delineated how much authority the federal agency could exercise over cable system operators. Cable franchising had to be handled by either state or local governments, so that cable systems would serve communities on the basis of the franchise agreement. The new law protected cable systems from overly ambitious contracts that might impose stricter standards than the ones specified by the FCC. It also prevented franchise authorities from terminating a contract without just cause by establishing a rationale for the local franchise authority to renegotiate in cases where the cable operator failed to fulfill its promises necessary for a successful operation.[18]

This congressional intervention in 1984 came as a breath of fresh air to the cable industry, which seized the opportunity to expand its systems' channel capacity, increase the number of households served, and raise the charges billed to local subscribers. Seven years later, it appeared that cable system operators had exploited their newfound freedom at the expense of customers who complained loudly about their cable bills that were rising three times faster than the inflation rate. It was not long before Congress was back at the reregulation table drawing up a new measure of legislation for cable television, not nearly as magnanimous as the 1984 law.

Cable Consumer Act of 1992

The **Cable Television Consumer Protection and Competition Act of 1992** established a variety of subscriber-friendly measures. Its provisions kept cable rates in check and upheld new standards of competition. Under this 1992 act, the FCC adopted a plan giving local franchising authorities the responsibility for regulating basic cable rates and equipment. This law stipulated that no cable operator should establish an exclusive franchise without a signed agreement.

Before a cable system can begin operation under the 1992 law, it must send the name and contact information of its system operator to the FCC along with the date it plans to provide cable services to at least 50 subscribers. The cable company also must identify all broadcast television channels it plans to carry, and if six or more full-time employees are involved in the system's operation, it must submit an equal employment opportunity form to Washington, D.C. In addition, the system operator signs a registration statement that indicates its compliance with all federal standards.

The government specifies both technical and service obligations for cable systems. There are, for example, measures to protect subscribers from disruptions in cable service, guidelines regarding billing, and even installation practices for cable systems to follow. Cable bills must be readable and comprehensible with clear, concise language including an understandable itemization of all costs. The cable system also must meet a particular time period for customer notification of a change in its rates, thirty days, which coincidentally is the same time frame given to resolve billing disagreements. The law requires an advisory note if a change in the cable channel's position or dial location takes place. The FCC even requires cable companies to answer service calls within a certain number of phone rings. Most importantly, this

Cable Consumer Act of 1992 ■ A U.S. federal law designed to ensure diversity of local programming on cable. It required cable systems to carry local broadcast channels and forbade them from charging to carry the signal for local channels. The law was superseded by the 1996 Telecommunications Act.

---

[18] *See* Cable Communications Policy Act of 1984, 47 U.S.C. § 546.

1992 law secured cable access for local TV stations, rekindling a debate that has characterized the relationship between broadcasting and cable systems for years.

The Telecommunications Act of 1996

Telecommunications Act of 1996 ■
This act rewrote the provisions of the Communications Act of 1934 and changed federal communication policymaking, increased competition in the broadcasting industry, promoted the industry of cross-market communications, prohibited the transmission of indecent and obscene material to minors, and increased Congress' role in policy making.

The **Telecommunications Act of 1996** was the first major overhaul of American media law in more than six decades and its objective was to allow any media company to compete in terms of offering customers subscription-based telephone, television, and Internet services. It was passed in an era when policy makers envisioned an "information superhighway" and spoke of the need to provide public access via all of its thoroughfares. This law divided electronic media into radio and TV broadcasting, cable television, telephone services, Internet, and online media.

The advantage to consumers would be greater choice in subscription media services. The telephone companies had a special advantage by owning the well-established infrastructure of wires and pole attachments to offer delivery of television and broadband services to the home. Traditionally, telephone companies are subject to common carrier regulation and the "telcos" have resisted attempts to reregulate their services. Some state governments became involved and joined in the franchising process as telephone companies expressed their preference for a regional rather than a local agreement for their media services. However, state lawmakers found this embrace a difficult one to manage, since municipalities relied on existing revenues from local franchise agreements (LFAs). Incumbent cable operators argued that it would be unfair competition for them to face new rivals who obeyed a different set of rules set at the state level rather than by municipal government.

Effective Competition

The FCC tried to ensure more competition in the MVPD market after discovering in 2007 that some cities were dragging their heels in affording cable competitors the chance to forge a franchise agreement at the municipal level. The Commission noted "buddy clauses" in some LFAs, and began to suspect noncompetitive practices at the local franchise level. The barriers to entry included negotiations that would last for months with new telecom carriers and contracts that forced cable rivals to construct facilities beyond their service area, including new public access studios. Some cities even required franchise fees above the 5 percent legal limit and levied additional charges for noncable services including the Internet. The government had permitted local franchise authorities to more closely regulate their systems if fewer than three broadcast channels were in competition.

The government lifts federal regulations when effective competition exists between the cable system and other MVPDs, based on its formula of effective competition. Generally, small cable operators are exempt from rate regulation if they represent less than 1 percent of all cable viewers and have fewer than 50,000 subscribers. If there is no effective competition, it is possible that cable systems could be subject to individualized rate regulation. The FCC uses several tests to determine if the cable company has effective competition before it undertakes special oversight. These include calculating the share of household subscribers the cable company serves in comparison with other MVPDs doing business in the franchise area. With the proliferation of MVPDs (notably satellite) each year fewer carriers are subject to rate regulation.

Vertical and Horizontal Integration

The video marketplace is increasingly competitive with more choices for television viewing than ever before. Nonetheless, government's involvement in ensuring effective competition prevents exclusive contracts between cable operators and satellite-delivered networks. In this way and others, the government seeks to eliminate the dangers of vertical and horizontal integration. **Vertical integration** describes the powerful position a media conglomerate can have in owning shares of everything from the creation of the content down to the delivery of the content to the consumers' homes. **Horizontal integration** occurs when two or more companies in the same line of business join forces, which can limit the viewpoints that citizens to have access to. The concern with such practices by large vertically integrated cable operators is intended to protect the public and the content producers and to uphold competition.

The 1992 Cable Act required companies that supply affiliated cable systems with programming via satellite to offer that same programming to cable competitors, such as the satellite systems DirecTV and DISH. This law also prevents cable systems and programmers from entering into exclusive contracts or conspiring to limit access to choice programming in order to compete unfairly. The ban on exclusive agreements between cable programmers and operators was set to expire in 2002, but it was extended until 2012. Some MSOs own part of regional sports or news channels that are distributed by microwave or fiber-optic lines, and so they do not have to share these networks with their competitors.

In 1992, Congress authorized the FCC through § 613 of the 1992 act to "prescribe rules and regulations establishing reasonable limits on the number of cable subscribers a person is authorized to reach," and the Commission's response was a 30 percent limit on audience reach. The FCC took additional action to discourage vertical integration by limiting the number of cable networks owned by large system operators, especially the ones carried on its systems. No more than 40 percent of the first seventy-five channels could be used for programming affiliated with the cable system's owner, and the remaining 60 percent had to be made available to broadcast or other channels in which the system's owner owned no more than a 5 percent share. The two largest cable MSOs at the time, Time Warner and AT&T, challenged the rules and the D.C. Circuit Court of Appeals found the limit reasonable at first, but in 2001, it overturned the rules because the Commission had failed to adequately justify either the horizontal or vertical limits.[19] In 2007, the FCC issued another order using new calculations to justify maintaining the 30 percent horizontal limit, but it has yet to identify a new calculation for the vertical limits.

Vertical integration ■ When a media company owns businesses or operations all along the production and distribution chain that increase market power.

Horizontal integration ■ When a media company expands its ownership through acquisitions and mergers of businesses or operations that are at the same level producing similar products.

---

[19]*Time Warner Entm't Co. v. FCC*, 240 F.3d 1126 (2001).

The 70/70 Rule

In 1984, Congress felt that there could be a day when federal regulation would be necessary in the form of price controls for cable. A trigger was added to the law declaring that federal intervention would only come after cable corporations passed 70 percent of the nation's households and sold cable subscriptions to 70 percent of those potential customers. This so-called 70/70 threshold was a feature of the Cable Act of 1984, and it gave the FCC authority to make changes in the leased access channel rules for cable services with at least 36 channels.

In 2008, the FCC took the position that it was time under this policy to move toward reregulation. Cable's rates were rising, and its services were eroding. Consequently, FCC officials argued the 70/70 threshold had been met and it was time for Washington to establish new rate controls on cable systems. The problem was that the percentages providing the trigger for tighter federal controls were actually quite equivocal.

The cable industry conceded more than 70 percent of the American TV households had access to basic cable, but nowhere near 70 percent of those potential subscribers actually subscribed to cable television. Cable operators further challenged the underlying rationale as flawed since multichannel video services from satellite and telephone companies were available in most markets throughout the country, affording more effective competition than envisioned in 1984.

70/70 Rule ■ If the Federal Communications Commission finds a cable service is accessible to 70% of households and 70% of those homes subscribe, the FCC can implement any additional rules to make certain there is a diversity of information sources.

Tiered Model of Regulation

Each cable tier follows a different set of rules. The FCC used a benchmark rate that is based on the number of channels, cable subscribers, and pay services. The tiers of service are divided into three types: pay-per-view, cable program channels, and basic. Basic is the lowest tier of service, which includes all over-the-air TV channels as well as any public access channels built by the system. The basic tier of channels is actually rather small and not a popular choice for subscribers (mainly because it has none of the popular cable channels).

The second tier of cable program channels (sometimes called "expanded basic") includes those beyond the basic service package such as superstations and advertising-supported networks like ESPN and CNN. These cable channels are not subject to rate regulation, and they can be grouped and sold in different tiers. Pay-per-view channels are classified as premium tiers, which are also free of any rate regulation.

A La Carte Channels

A la carte cable would allow customers to tailor their program selection to a personally selected menu of channels and thereby eliminate offensive program channels. Rather than subscribe to one hundred or so cable channels, viewers simply would choose only the ten to twelve channels they usually enjoy watching—even if that meant fewer choices than the tiers to skim through to reach their usual favorites. Consumer advocates argue it would save customers up to 13 percent on their bills if they could start buying cable channels a la carte.

Proponents claim that a majority of Americans would prefer to have this type of personalized menu of cable channels to the current cable system. Nonetheless, a coalition of network executives representing the largest television enterprises warned the FCC chair in 2008 that any attempt to force a la carte pricing of cable would meet with devastating consequences. Cable rates continue to spiral past the rate of inflation at about 2 percent to 6 percent per year and the industry's refusal to consider a la carte pricing has provoked some to call for a tightening of cable rules in Washington. A la carte opponents argue that individual channel pricing would result in *fewer* channel choices because dozens of channels would not get adequate support—many of those channels being the ones that provide the sort of diversity MVPD systems provide.

PUBLIC ACCESS OBLIGATIONS

The FCC asked cable television systems to serve communities with local programming by building studios for public access television that would feature **public, educational, and government** (PEG) programs. Public access channels were envisioned as an ideal forum for democracy that would give viewers an opportunity to produce their own shows on a first-come, first-served basis. In reality, they became amateur hours periodically threatened by radicals of various stripes eager to test the bounds of the First Amendment through their unconventional behavior and rhetoric. Cable system operators understandably sought to reduce both the expense and the controversy that arose with PEG channels by eliminating them. The courts, however, have stood by public access television, declaring it to be an important medium of community self-expression and an effective way to respond to growing concentrations of media ownership.

Public, educational, and government (PEG) ■ Public access channels that are mandated by a local franchising authority—not the federal government—to provide increased channel diversity.

Midwest Video Cases

In one U.S. Supreme Court case, public access television was found to be within the federal authority to impose legal demands on cable system operators. The Court affirmed the FCC's oversight role regarding cable television's obligations in terms of local TV origination.[20] The 1972 ruling in *United States v. Midwest Video Corp.* upheld FCC rules requiring that cable systems create their own programming and build production studios for public access shows. In 1976, these channels were legally required if more than 3,500 subscribers were served by a twenty-channel system. They were intended to give third-party access to the cable system and increase citizen involvement in local public affairs.

The FCC required **leased-access channels** depending on how many channels the cable company sold to its subscribers. Leased-access channels are outside the editorial control of the cable system operator but are offered to the public to use

Leased-access channels ■ Channels that provide reduced rate airtime on a cable system to independent cable programmers and producers.

---

[20]*See United States v. Midwest Video Corp.*, 406 U.S. 649 (1972). In addition, this decision also preserved syndication agreements that prevented cable systems from airing a syndicated program from a distant channel if the local TV station had already secured the rights to it.

on a commercial basis. In this regard, they function somewhat like a common carrier such as the telephone. Cable systems were asked to dedicate at least 10 percent of their channels for leased access if they had thirty-five or more channels on their systems.[21]

In the second *Midwest Video* case, the U.S. Supreme Court decided the FCC had overplayed its hand with this rule requiring cable systems with twenty or more channels to allocate four access channels to inexpensive use by the community, including public, educational, and governmental (PEG) studios. The 1979 ruling in *FCC v. Midwest Video* prevented the government from regarding cable systems as common carriers like the telephone company. Congress stepped in five years later, however, and passed the 1984 Cable Franchise Policy and Communications Act that gave local governments the right to require PEG channels and prevented system operators from exercising any editorial control over the content while absolving them of liability for whatever content the access channels televised over their systems. As the law stands today, franchise authorities (whether statewide or local) *may* require cable companies to provide one or more access channels but do not have to.

SATELLITE TELEVISION REGULATION

Cable's power to retransmit television channels and offer new programming options, such as premium channels and pay-per-view, has meant serious competition to local TV stations. The FCC encountered political pressure during the 1970s to stop cable systems from competing against broadcasters especially through their purchase of movies for cable distribution. That was when Home Box Office (HBO) came along, and began by offering movies without commercial interruption, which seemed to be just what television viewers wanted. However, HBO was stymied by FCC rules that would control the quality and age of motion pictures available for cable viewing.

In 1977, the U.S. Supreme Court sided with cable and against regulation in *HBO v. FCC* (1977).[22] The Court found the FCC had gone too far in its efforts to protect broadcasters with rules that would prevent the showing of movies on cable for at least three years after their release to theaters. Consequently, the ruling gave HBO and other cable channels the freedom to televise satellite-transmitted movies. So-called **anti-siphoning rules** also prevented cable channels from purchasing sports programming that had been "traditionally" provided by free over-the-air broadcasters. If such rules were still in place, ESPN would be prohibited from carrying college football bowls or NFL games.

Anti-siphoning rules ■ Defunct rules introduced by the Federal Communications Commission in 1975 that were designed to prevent subscription-based cablecasters from purchasing rights to televise important and culturally significant events that had been traditionally aired on free-to-air television.

Open Sky Policy

In the 1970s, communication satellites were launched into space and began bouncing broadcast signals back down across the global terrain, where earth relay stations became a key feature in telecommunications development. The FCC encouraged

---

[21]*Federal Communications Comm'n v. Midwest Video Corp.*, 440 U.S. 689 (1979).
[22]567 F.2d (D.C. Cir. 1977), *cert. denied*, 434 U.S. 829 (1977).

cable networks to draw upon satellite signals by adopting an **Open Sky policy** in 1972. This action gave the green light for cable companies to enter the domestic satellite business so long as they had the essential technical know-how and financial backing. In 1975, satellites began feeding HBO shows to cable viewers, which created a new system of television networking. Competitors were watching, however, and soon satellite firms were auctioning off transponders—satellite circuits—leasing them to carry programming from earth to space and back again for all sorts of programming channels. Cable channels multiplied quickly as subscribing viewers eagerly signed up for premium tiers of service.

The Showtime network challenged HBO for cable viewers in 1978 with its lineup of new motion pictures and original programming. Pay cable enabled subscribers to buy programs by charging them more than the basic monthly fee. Cable's business model evolved to a system based on tiers, which afforded a menu of programming options to customers according to various channel subscription plans. Cable television systems principally rely on two sources of revenue—subscriptions and advertising. Some channels like VH1 and CNN carry commercials, while others, like American Movie Classics and HBO, rely solely on subscriber fees. Some cable channels barter commercial time slots to the local cable system for their sale to advertisers.

Direct to Home Satellites

The FCC has authority to regulate Direct Broadcast Satellite television services such as DirecTV and Echostar's DISH network due to their use of the electromagnetic spectrum. Satellite television does not transmit over the airwaves directly to the general public, and so the law treats it as a subscription service rather than as a broadcaster. In its adoption of the 1992 Cable Act, Congress gave the FCC authority to regulate satellite television by drafting must-carry provisions and dealing with other content issues.[23] In 1999, the FCC adopted an access rule requiring satellite television services to set aside 4 percent of their channel capacity for noncommercial education and information programming.

In the same year, Congress passed the Satellite Home Viewer Improvement Act (SHVIA) that permitted satellite television systems to provide local broadcast TV channels to all subscribers in a designated market area (DMA). SHVIA 1999 revised the 1988 law and allowed satellite television to offer local broadcast channels to all subscribers within the local market area. It also permitted satellite companies to provide distant network broadcast stations to its subscribers. There were about ten million households in the United States taking satellite television, but that number would double in ten years' time. SHVIA had the effect of placing satellite television on a level playing field with cable in terms of broadcast channel selection. By 2002, the FCC required satellite television companies like DirecTV to carry all local TV channels in markets where they carried any at all, which became known as the "carry one, carry all" rule. That same year, the government dealt with the picture quality standard, which it called its "good quality signal" rule and

[23]Cable Television Consumer Protection and Competition Act of 1992, *supra* note 14.

Open Sky policy ■
A 1972 Federal Communications Commission policy that permitted private industries to use private communication satellites for broadcasting television programs.

essentially held that satellite carriers were entitled to the same quality signal from local broadcasters that competing cable systems had sold to their customers.

Alternative Subscription Services

Satellite master antenna television systems (SMATV) are small self-contained networks providing television to motels and apartment complexes. The U.S. government classifies them as nonregulated private cable systems beyond the reach of state or local regulations. The FCC has authorized SMATV systems were to be free of the impositions of franchise fees or other service obligations at the community level familiar to public cable systems. If a SMATV system crosses a public right of way, however—a street or alley—it could be reclassified and regulated as a public rather than a private cable system.

Wireless Cable (MMDS)

Wireless cable ■
Also called multi-channel multipoint distribution service (MMDS). An MMDS system transmits television via microwave signal, and the FCC regulates its services.

Another subscription TV service to customers in smaller sub-communities is known as **wireless cable** or multichannel multipoint distribution service (MMDS). An MMDS system transmits television via microwave signal, and the FCC regulates its services due to the use of the spectrum that could cause interference with other forms of wireless communication. In the interest of competition, these wireless cable systems are guaranteed access to cable programming channels under the 1992 Cable Act. Wireless cable services also must comply with a retransmission consent rule if they seek to carry local broadcast TV stations. MMDS systems can offer Internet access in competition with cable modems or the phone company's DSL lines, but this subscription TV service is free of state or local regulations.

DIGITAL DELIVERY OPTIONS

A different rulebook applies to different telecommunication carriers based on the media channels involved. Whether the television supplier is a cable company located in smaller communities of residences, linked to growing networks through the Internet, or part of the expansion of telephone services, the regulatory features vary somewhat according to technology and jurisdiction. When electronic media began converging in digital technology on the Internet, the U.S. Congress acted in 1996 to pass the most substantial rewrite of its original law governing broadcasting, cable, and other telecommunication carriers.

Telephone Competition

As a result of the 1996 Telecommunications Act, Congress gave telephone companies the right to compete with traditional video services by means of wired or wireless delivery systems. Different portions of the law govern telephone companies, broadcast stations, and cable systems but the law changed the basic understanding of telephone services as only a common carrier. Under the 1934 Communications Act, Congress defined telephone companies as common carriers that were to provide nondiscriminatory services at similar rates to anyone wishing to send and receive messages by voice. During the early years of the cable industry, telephone companies became involved in cable system ownership, and cable systems reported difficulty gaining access to telephone poles needed for their wires to home subscribers. Cable operators complained that the phone companies were refusing to rent them space at a reasonable rate on their poles.

Breakup of the Bell System

The FCC recognized the potential for anticompetitive behavior in terms of the poles and lines to prospective customers' homes, and established a cross-ownership ban on cable and telephone system ownership. Congress codified that rule in the 1984 Cable Act that prevented all phone companies in the United States from owning or operating a cable television system.[24] That state of affairs would change twelve years later after a monumental shakeup in the telephone industry.

The court-ordered settlement requiring that American Telephone & Telegraph divest itself of regional properties (Regional Bell Operating Companies or RBOCs) created the so-called seven baby bells, and added new competition to the marketplace.[25] The companies of Ameritech, Bell Atlantic, BellSouth, NYNEX, Pacific Telesis, Southwestern Bell, and U.S. West eventually placed their stake in telecommunications. The 1984 ban on telephone–cable cross-ownership was challenged and found to be unconstitutional in 1993, after a federal district court ruled the phone company should be entitled to enter the video services business following which several other baby bells sued and won settlements along the same lines.[26]

The passage of the Telecommunications Act of 1996 simply codified what the courts had already seen fit to do and set the stage for competition in new media services. It eliminated the telephone–cable cross-ownership ban, and it allowed local phone companies to provide video programming as a common carrier or as a wireless cable provider with its own programming channels. The legal term defining this hybrid enterprise was open video system, or OVS. If a telephone company chose to enter the television subscription business and compete against cable or satellite television, it still faced the prospect of franchising. Typically, state governments entered the picture in order to retain the right to franchise telecommunication systems or delegate it to local jurisdictions.

New Wireline Competition

The new corporate giants that have emerged in the telephone business, Verizon, Qwest, and the new AT&T, were interested in having the same access to content, technology, and customers that had been granted to satellite and cable systems. In *Verizon Communications v. Federal Communications Comm'n*, the U.S. Supreme Court held that smaller competitors should have reasonable access to cable

---

[24]*See* 47 U.S.C. § 613(b) (1984).

[25]*United States v. American Telephone & Telegraph* Co., 552 F. Supp. 131 (D. D.C. 1982).

[26]*Chesapeake & Potomac Tel. Co. of Va. v. United States*, 830 F. Supp. 909 (1993).

programming channels at reasonable rates.[27] The emphasis moved toward a national information infrastructure that would give broadband access to as many Americans as possible.

Common carriers that offered video services were regulated as cable systems were unless they fell under the open video systems provision of the Telecommunications Act. Local exchange carriers (LECs) could provide video services under the open video provisions and would not be required to grant access to all. In an attempt to spur competition between cable operators and LECs, Congress provided that cable systems operators were not required to obtain additional franchise approval for offering telecommunications services.

Telecommunication companies rivaled cable for subscribers through direct broadcast satellite (DBS), the telephone company, and the Internet. The telephone company's accelerated marketing of video products indicated the fierce competition for subscription television marketed by Verizon's FiOS—fiber optic service—and AT&T's U-Verse. Qwest also sold television channels to its customers through a co-marketing agreement with satellite television suppliers EchoStar and DirecTV. The future prospects of Internet television gave rise to broadband service providers (BSP) such as Hulu, Joost, and TiVo. In 2005, the FCC adopted a policy encompassing Internet broadband principles designed to encourage such new media ventures. The principles emphasized how Americans should be able to access Internet content of their choice and run legal applications and services, while also connecting to legal devices on the Internet that were not harmful.

Most significantly, American consumers were entitled to benefit from the Internet competition among network, application, and service providers. Some say there should be a fifth policy for nondiscriminatory practices on the Internet, which was prompted after Comcast was found in violation of FCC policy because it blocked some peer-to-peer file transfer, and earlier a North Carolina communications company was cited for blocking Voice over Internet Protocol (VoIP) services.

Triple or Quadruple Play?

The majority of Americans rely on a bundle of digital services—television, telephone, and Internet—usually marketed as a "triple play" with the government doing its best to keep up with regulations that ensure fair competition. If a fourth option, mobile, is involved, it becomes a quadruple play. Within three years after the startup of digital cable, the number of digital cable customers in the United States surpassed 22 million, and it continues to grow daily through an array of services offered by cable, including Internet telephone. By mid-2004, there were 16-million cable modem users in the United States, and Internet telephony or Voice over Internet Protocol (VoIP) reached 2.5 million cable subscribers.

Voice over Internet Protocol

VoIP is more than just telephone over the Internet. It must be defined as either a telecommunications or information service, but which one? The local exchange

---

[27]535 U.S. 467 (2002).

carrier (LEC) wireline service traditionally is identified as a common carrier, which in the eyes of the law is an *information* service. If a LEC is classified as a *telecommunications* service, it can deliver video programming and a different set of rules will apply. If VoIP is an information service, it is adaptable to analog telephones and should offer emergency 911 access. It also is legally subject to providing services for people with disabilities. If VoIP is a long distance carrier similar to Skype (computer-to-computer technology), then a different set of rules come into play.

The legal definitions tend to blur under such distinctions. When the federal government first sought to define Voice over Internet Protocol or VoIP, it found a business that provides customers with local, long distance, and international calling services by means of the Internet. As a result, the FCC has yet to achieve the distinction for VoIP as either information or telecommunications service.[28]

IPTV and Regulation

Rather than flipping through conventional broadcast and cable channels over a TV set, IPTV (Internet Protocol Television) basically means watching television programs over a computer, although the definitions vary according to what type of video is seen over the computer and how it might be delivered. Telecommunications giant AT&T began offering IPTV services in 2006 for local residents in eleven cities, and within three years was advertising high definition channels in those markets. The principal limitation is the rollout of broadband networks, but that impediment is temporary as telecommunication firms envision the IPTV future in terms of subscriber competition. Thus far, IPTV has been defined as a multiple program transport streams (MPTS), but that term does not resolve all regulatory issues. The FCC must decide exactly how it will apply regulations such as closed captioning and emergency notification to IPTV. Fairness is involved since telecommunication services with heavier legal burdens will suffer in the media marketplace.

For example, the cost of adding closed captioning to broadcast and cable channels was substantial, but for IPTV carriers it would be less cumbersome. On the other hand, if emergency alert messages are required of IPTV—as they are of broadcasting and cable systems—how will the viewers be located for the emergency alert messages and how will the IPTV get the urgent words to the right computer?

Network Neutrality

Who owns or directly controls the wire that provides the information and entertainment channels is also part of the legal equation. There are challenges of **network neutrality** and access. IPTV allows TV and video on demand (VOD), so the question of whether broadband networks bringing online services to homes and offices should be regulated and fairly grant access to all to protect the degrading of content by

Network neutrality
■ Refers to the general principle of equal access to internet resources and content, as opposed to a tiered structure, which preferences certain users, technology, and content over others.

[28]*See Implementation of the Telecommunications Act of 1996: Telecommunications Carriers' Use of Customer Proprietary Network Information and Other Customer Information*, CC Docket No. 96–114, Report and Order and Further Notice of Proposed Rulemaking, 22 F.C.C.R. 6927 § 54 (2007).

download speeds or bandwidth limitations is important. The engineering involved for the so-called last mile of cable where broadband providers enter the home or business can be controlled or even blocked unless a law prevents such interference.

In December 2010, the FCC voted 3-2 (along party lines) to mandate network neutrality for wired Internet Service Providers (wireless services were exempted). Reaction was immediate—in fact, too immediate. The D.C. Circuit Court of Appeals threw out a challenge to the rules from Verizon and MetroPCS because the suit was filed even before the FCC rule had been written into the Federal Register. In Congress, the Republican-dominated House of Representatives voted to preempt FCC authority over net neutrality, but as of this writing the Democratic-dominated Senate was unlikely to pass the bill and even if it did, President Obama vowed a veto. The issue is likely to be debated long after this book goes to press.

Models of Regulation

It is a natural tendency for a government to regulate new technology based on old models. The common carrier concept was superimposed on telephone regulation based on a previously existing transportation scheme. When trying to decide how (or whether) to regulate cable television, the FCC and courts actually debated whether cable was more like broadcast or newspaper, because regulatory schemes existed for those. The World Wide Web has created similar issues for Congress and the FCC. Attempts to regulate the Internet as it would newspapers or broadcast have been repeatedly challenged. Courts struck down laws based on a broadcast model for regulating Internet indecency (discussed in chapter 7). The Digital Millennium Copyright Act protects web "publishers" from liability in libel suits where a third party publishes the defamation in an unmoderated space, yet a newspaper that publishes a defamatory letter to the editor can be held liable.

The problems are only exacerbated in a worldwide context because of the inability to regulate beyond a country's borders. The United States has regulations that prohibit certain forms of activity online. The United States as a whole and many individual states strictly regulate gambling within their borders, including Internet gambling, yet a multitude of Americans gamble online, mostly through websites that are operated outside of the United States, beyond the reach of U.S. regulators.

Despite the need for new regulatory schemes, government regulators tend to fall back on what they know. To be fair, Congress and the FCC make concerted efforts to create appropriate regulatory schemes for different media. The electromagnetic spectrum is divided into dozens of categories of service, only one of which is broadcasting. The rules for broadcast spectrum do not apply to aeronautical or radio astronomy users. Even within categories of service the laws vary. Broadcast television has children's programming requirements but broadcast radio does not. In spite of these differences, different media have overarching regulatory frameworks that help Congress and the FCC in making determinations about the need for (or the need to avoid) certain regulations.

In decades past, wires that carried telephone calls did only that and the telephone service was simply regulated as a common carrier. In the 1970s such a classification was overly simplistic, so a two-tiered system of regulation was created. Title I is the category for "information services" rather than "communication services." When an ATM communicates with a bank's computer it is merely data that is being transferred. That is a Title I service. Traditional telephone, which is traditionally seen as a means of communicating between people, is a Title II service. Title II services are much more heavily regulated than Title I services are. The "basic" telephone of old has always been treated as a common carrier. Just as today the same wireless smartphone handles data and voice, wired phone services carried both voice and data, as many homes and businesses connected to the Internet via a modem. If communication over a telephone line was completely "transparent," with no undue processing by the phone company, it was subject to common carrier laws. If, as with the enhanced services, there was some degree of coding or processing, such as would be the case with storage and retrieval (voicemail) systems, these services were not subjected to common carrier regulation.

Even proponents of network neutrality may not be advocating for the regulation of broadband equivalent to the Title II regulation of basic phone services. In 2010 FCC Chairman Julius Genachowski called for a "third way" of regulating broadband: a sort of hybrid of Title I and Title II regulation.

SUMMARY

- Cable television in American began as Community Antenna Television (CATV): a means by which people could get clearer reception of over-the-air broadcast signals. As the decades passed cable became both more prevalent and increased its content offerings, both of which impacted the perception of whether cable needed to be regulated.

- Derived from transportation law, the concept of a common carrier has been applied to telecommunications and refers to services that must be open to all willing to pay for them. Much as public transit, common carriers may have different fees based on different classes of users but their services must be open. Traditional, basic telephone service is a common carrier. The Supreme Court has ruled that cable television is not.

- When coaxial cable was the only way to deliver cable television, most communities in the United States that had multichannel video program distributors had only one. The capital outlay was far too great to try to overbuild in most places, creating natural monopolies in most communities. With the advent of other MVPD services (such as satellite and video over telephone lines), few MVPDs have a complete monopoly in any community and regulation has reflected this change.

- Cable television regulation includes various content restrictions. Cable companies must honor existing exclusivity contracts between stations and content providers, even if it means blacking out a program. Local television stations may require a cable company to include their channels in a cable company's offerings. Franchising authorities (local or state) may impose public access channel requirements, a power which has been upheld by the courts.

- Originally broadcasters were happy to have cable television as a means of increasing the reach of their signals (thereby increasing the amount they could charge for advertising), but that climate changed as cable began importing distant signals to compete with local stations, began creating content of its own to compete with broadcasters, and began competing with broadcasters

for advertisers and becoming profitable.
As a result, an industry that had little regulation in the 1950s became rather heavily regulated in the 1970s. As technology provided alternatives, some of that regulation was loosened in the 1990s.

- For much of the twentieth century, national telephone service was dominated by AT&T. In the early 1980s the Justice Department worked to break up the monopoly and subsequently more companies were created. Government and industry compromised to develop rules that would allow new companies to develop while allowing existing companies to enter businesses they had previously been prohibited from entering (most notably,

cable television). Today the same companies offer telephone services and cable television.

- Internet Service Providers (ISPs) have traditionally charged a flat fee to subscribers for "all you can eat" Internet access. The fee may be higher for higher-speed service, but systems have not discriminated against which websites will load faster or slower. As video, with its vast bandwidth demands (especially when uploading), has become more prevalent online, some ISPs have asserted a need to manage their networks and their capacity. Network neutrality is a push for regulations that would prohibit ISPs from favoring or disfavoring the load speeds of any source or type of download, treating all bits equally.

Universal Service

One of the basic tenets of basic telephone service in the twentieth century was the concept of universal service. The idea promoted by AT&T in the 1920s was that telephone service increased in value as more people had telephones, so it ought to be a matter of policy to try to increase the number of households with phones. Under a monopoly system, it was relatively simple for AT&T to redistribute its income in order to cross-subsidize higher-cost services. For most of the twentieth century, local telephone service costs were kept lower by inflating long distance costs, and the cost of providing rural phone service (higher because of the lower density of homes) was cross-subsidized by more profitable homes that were easier to serve. With the deregulation of phone service in the 1980s, and the new technologies that made distances less relevant to phone charges in the 1990s, this model of cross-subsidy has disappeared. But the discussion has returned, in a new form.

It can be more costly to provide broadband services to rural areas than to other locales primarily because of the density of homes. Extending a fiber optic line one mile is relatively the same whether there are two homes (i.e., potential subscribers) along that mile or fifty. Pricing for rural broadband would be prohibitive in many locations were it not for some means to support it financially. One possible solution is to allow some sort of government support for rural broadband in the same way that rural telephones received funding for universal service. Instead of asserting that the network is more valuable as justification for subsidy, rural broadband proponents make the argument that health care, education, and commerce all rely on broadband connections. Increasingly, Americans must even go online to contact federal agencies such as Social Security. If broadband connection is essential in the modern world, the assertion is that there must be support for broadband to areas where it would not be profitable for a private provider to offer service, and that is primarily rural areas.

An interesting twist has been the provision of broadband by local government in some communities. Municipal broadband has been seen as one means of building out a network that would provide services more equally regardless of profitability. Ironically, though, a number of municipal broadband projects have been built or proposed not in rural areas but in communities with more density. Critics argue that governments ought not be in the business of providing services that are available commercially. Even in places where commercial service is not *yet* available, government involvement precludes future entry by commercial providers if and when private companies would see fit to invest.

In the meantime, though, must rural communities miss out on educational, medical, and entertainment opportunities? One compromise has been for local governments to build broadband networks that serve only noncommercial entities such as schools, libraries, and law enforcement, leaving the commercial sector to private providers who may come along later. That may seem like a reasonable compromise, but these noncommercial services are the high-volume users that just might drive interest by a broadband provider. If these institutions are already being served (and not needing to subscribe to a commercial service), there is less potential revenue for a commercial provider.

It is without question that broadband has become a major component, if not essential, to the vitality of twenty-first-century communities. Businesses are less likely to locate in a community without broadband, making it an essential part of economic development. Broadband deployment is not just about the ability to download movies at high speeds. It can mean the

(*continued*)

difference between growth or loss of residents and jobs, which results in less revenue to the community, which results in reduction in services, fewer schools, and so on.

What should be done? Should national policies create a modern universal service scheme to extend broadband? Is the solution to require a cross-subsidy to fund broadband deployment? Is it a problem that does not need to be addressed because the marketplace will eventually correct whatever discrepancies exist? At the risk of sounding overly dramatic, for some rural communities this is a matter of life or death. ■

Advertising Law

LEARNING OBJECTIVES

After reading this chapter you should know:

- How advertising has evolved from no First Amendment protection to its current status
- The Supreme Court decisions that have established the basis for advertising laws
- What the *Central Hudson* four-part test is and how to apply it
- How the role of the Federal Trade Commission evolved in the regulation of advertising
- The three elements of a deceptive advertisement
- The difference between factual claims about a product and statements of opinion

- The special rules that apply to testimonials, especially celebrity endorsement of products
- The actions that may be taken by government agencies when an advertisement is ruled deceptive
- Advertising regulation is not the sole purview of the Federal Trade Commission
- Advertisers engage in self-regulation as a means of pre-empting government regulation

PATERNALISTIC APPROACHES TO REGULATING ADVERTISING

Medical information is certainly confusing. With all the variables involved in personal health care, it's hard to keep up with all the possible treatments. Doctors and pharmacists are required to take years of specialized training in order to understand, and still they cannot possibly know everything there is to know. Two cases from Virginia decided in the 1970s set the stage for First Amendment protection for advertising.

Prior to the 1973 landmark *Roe v. Wade*[1] decision guaranteeing women a right to an abortion, each state established its own rules for abortions; while some states had no rules, others made the procedure illegal. In the state of Virginia, not only was abortion itself illegal but publishing information "encouraging" an abortion was as well. On February 8, 1971, the *Virginia Weekly* (published in Charlottesville, Va.) published an advertisement for a New York company that would assist women in obtaining an abortion in the state of New York, where abortion services were legal. The managing editor, Jeffrey Bigelow, was charged with violating the Virginia statute, found guilty, and fined $500, only part of which he would have to pay if there were no repeated violations. Bigelow's conviction was upheld by the Virginia Supreme Court, finding it an acceptable use of the state's police power, "to ensure that pregnant women in Virginia who decided to have abortions come to their decisions without the commercial advertising pressure usually incidental to the sale of a box of soap powder."[2]

The U.S. Supreme Court overturned the Virginia court's decision, finding that the state's **paternalistic** interests in protecting pregnant women were outweighed by the First Amendment.[3] To begin with, the Court refuted the belief that expression loses its protection simply because it is commercial speech. For quite some time courts had made it clear that advertising was not entitled to *the same* protection as other types of expression (most notable political speech, which is at the core of the First Amendment), but the Supreme Court made it clear that *less* protection was not the same as *no* protection. In declaring that advertising was worthy of protection, the Court asserted that even though the ad's purpose may have been commercial it still "conveyed information of potential interest and value to a diverse audience."[4] It was a recognition that advertising is rarely if ever exclusively about a commercial transaction—that valuable marketplace of ideas implications might be involved. "The relationship of speech to the marketplace of products or of services does not make it valueless in the marketplace of ideas."[5]

In 1968, Virginia passed a law that prohibited advertising the price of prescription medications. The Virginia Board of Pharmacy considered it unprofessional conduct if a pharmacist "publishes, advertises or promotes, directly or indirectly, in

Paternalistic ■ The theory that it is beneficial to control, usually by government regulation, what consumers see and hear in order to protect them better than they can protect themselves

---

[1]410 U.S. 113 (1973).

[2]*Bigelow v. Commonwealth*, 213 Va. 191, 196 (1972).

[3]*Bigelow v. Virginia*, 421 U.S. 809 (1975).

[4]*Id.* at 822.

[5]*Id.* at 826.

any manner whatsoever, any amount, price, fee, premium, discount, rebate or credit terms . . . for any drugs which may be dispensed only by prescription."[6] Florida, Pennsylvania, and Maryland had had similar laws, but those states' laws were removed after legal challenges.[7] In 1974 Virginia's law was ripe for challenge, and the Virginia Citizens Consumer Council, the Virginia AFL-CIO, and an individual who took daily prescription medication took the case to federal district court.

In spite of repealed laws in other states, Virginia believed it could regulate the advertising. After all, the Supreme Court had been quite clear that purely commercial speech did not deserve as much protection as other forms of expression. As a licensed profession, pharmacists' behavior is controlled by a state board with duties that include "maintaining the integrity" of pharmaceutical services. The law had been challenged by a drug company in 1969 and was upheld.[8]

What was different from the earlier case was the interest of the plaintiff. When a drug company challenged the constitutionality of the Virginia regulation, the court abided by earlier rulings that gave limited protection to commercial speech when balanced against the state's interests. Drug companies wanting to advertise their prices were merely engaging in commercial speech. But when the assertion was the rights of the *consumer* to learn of the prices of prescription medication, the whole equation changed. It was the First Amendment rights of the consumers to *hear* the price information that was being asserted rather than the right of the pharmacists or drug companies asserting a commercial interest. The federal district court ruled in favor of the consumers, and the decision was upheld by the U.S. Supreme Court.

The Supreme Court pointed out that there were discrepancies in the prices of prescription medication from one pharmacy to another. As such, consumers had a vested interest in obtaining price information in order to make informed decisions about where to purchase prescription medications. The Court also made it clear that speech was *not unprotected* simply because it was determined to be commercial speech, even if the speaker's interest is "purely economic," with no intention to contribute to a marketplace of ideas. The Court recognized that oftentimes it is just this sort of information that is of the most interest to citizens:

> Moreover, there is another consideration that suggests that no line between publicly "interesting" or "important" commercial advertising and the opposite kind could ever be drawn. Advertising, however tasteless and excessive it sometimes may seem, is nonetheless dissemination of information as to who is producing and selling what product, for what purpose, and at what price. So long as we preserve a predominantly free enterprise economy, the allocation of our resources in large measure will be made through numerous private economic decisions. It is a matter of public interest that those decisions, in the aggregate, be intelligent and well informed. To this end, the free flow of commercial information is indispensable.[9]

---

[6]*Virginia State Bd. of Pharmacy v. Virginia Citizens Consumer Council*, 425 U.S. 748, 750 (1976).

[7]In 1969, 1971, and 1973 respectively.

[8]*Patterson Drug Co. v. Kingery*, 305 F. Supp. 821 (W.D. Va. 1969).

[9]425 U.S. at 765.

The Supreme Court rejected the paternalist argument that price advertising might drive consumers to purchase from cost-cutting pharmacists, which might not be in their own best interests.

The *Bigelow* and *Virginia Board of Pharmacy* cases provide a framework for understanding that advertising is a protected form of expression because it provides information that citizens want, even if that information is little more than just prices. Governments (city, state, or federal) cannot restrict advertising with a vague assertion that doing so will be in the public's best interest. Paternalistically claiming that it is best for citizens to have *less* information will not pass constitutional muster.

There are many times, however, when government regulation of advertising is acceptable. Our focus for the remainder of this chapter will be to understand when and where those restrictions will be permitted.

ROOTS OF ADVERTISING REGULATION

Although never explicitly overruled, most constitutional scholars consider the Supreme Court's ruling in *Valentine v. Christensen*[10] to have little relevance today. *Valentine* was the first case in which the Court explicitly addressed commercial speech. In that case, the Supreme Court upheld a New York City ordinance that prohibited distribution of advertising materials in the city's port. F. J. Christensen wanted to promote the fact that he had a submarine in the port available for tours (for 25 cents per person). In order to evade the rule, Christensen printed his handbills with his advertisement on one side and a protest of the city regulation on the reverse. Christensen tried to assert that his advertisement was not purely commercial speech, and because it contained political expression it ought to be entitled to First Amendment protection from the New York ordinance. The U.S. Supreme Court ruled against Christensen, arguing that his "political speech" was merely subterfuge for purely commercial speech, which was not entitled to protection.

In subsequent decisions, the Supreme Court has repeatedly limited the scope of the *Valentine* decision. In 1964 the Supreme Court made a major step in limiting the precedent in *Valentine*. In *New York Times v. Sullivan* (covered extensively in chapter 5), a police commissioner filed suit against the *Times* for an advertisement that he considered libelous. The commissioner tried to claim that an advertisement has no First Amendment protection and cited *Valentine* as precedent, but the unanimous Supreme Court disagreed. "That the *Times* was paid for publishing the advertisement is as immaterial in this connection as is the fact that newspapers and books are sold."[11] Thus, the Supreme Court began its long history of distancing itself from *Valentine*.

In 1969, the National Organization for Women filed a suit against the Pittsburgh Commission on Human Relations. Pittsburgh had an ordinance that prohibited

---

[10]316 U.S. 52 (1942).
[11]376 U.S. at 266.

discrimination in hiring by gender, yet the *Pittsburgh Press* continued to segregate classified ads under "Help Wanted Male" and "Help Wanted Female" categories. NOW forced the Commission to examine the *Press*'s advertising practices, and the Commission ruled they violated the city's ordinance. The *Pittsburgh Press* then filed suit challenging the constitutionality of the ordinance.

In 1973, the U.S. Supreme Court ruled 5–4 that the ordinance was constitutional and that the newspaper could be prevented from using the discriminatory designations.[12] The majority asserted that the illegal behavior of discrimination is not protected by the First Amendment, just as libel would not be protected. In balancing the paper's First Amendment rights with the protections afforded against discrimination, the Court narrowly sided with the latter. What may be most informative, however, are the dissenting opinions, which point to *Valentine* and express concern that the Court was trying to return to that line of thinking. Justice William Douglas, who had been part of the *Valentine* Court, explicitly stated, "My views on that issue have changed since 1942."[13]

The decisions in the *Bigelow* and *Virginia Board of Pharmacy* cases mentioned earlier further limited the *Valentine* ruling. The Court recognized that advertising had value both to the speaker *and* to the consumers, and that commercial speech had value, just not as much value as other forms of expression (most notably political speech). The "thermometers" provided in chapter 2 explain that not all expression is equally protected. The Supreme Court has asserted that commercial speech does not need the same protection as political speech:

> Two features of commercial speech permit regulation of its content. First, commercial speakers have extensive knowledge of both the market and their products. Thus, they are well situated to evaluate the accuracy of their messages and the lawfulness of the underlying activity. In addition, commercial speech, the offspring of economic self-interest, is a hardy breed of expression that is not particularly susceptible to being crushed by overbroad regulation.[14]

Commercial speech is more easily verified than political speech. Imagine the difficulty of trying to verify the "truth" of political statements compared to whether a toothpaste actually whitens your teeth. Commercial speech is hardier than political speech because advertisers with a commercial interest are more likely to persevere where lone political activists fighting for a belief may not have the resources.

All this begs the question. We get the idea that commercial speech is less protected than political speech, but that still doesn't answer when a government regulation that restricts advertising is constitutional (like the one in Pittsburgh) or when it isn't (like the two in Virginia). If only there were a test that could be applied to determine when the government has created a restriction on commercial speech that will pass constitutional muster. There is.

---

[12]*Pittsburgh Press Co. v. Pittsburgh Comm'n on Human Relations*, 413 U.S. 376 (1973).

[13]*Id.* at 398 (Douglas, J., dissenting).

[14]*Central Hudson Gas & Electric Corp. v Public Service Comm'n*, 447 U.S. 557, 564, n. 6 (1980) (citations omitted).

THE *CENTRAL HUDSON* TEST

In 1973 the United States was facing an energy crisis, and many communities even faced fuel shortages. In December, the New York State Public Service Commission ordered all its state's electric utility companies to stop any advertising promoting the use of electricity. Three years later fuel shortages were no longer a problem, but the Commission decided to continue the ban in the interests of energy conservation. Central Hudson Gas & Electric Corp. opposed the ban on First Amendment grounds. New York courts upheld the ban but the U.S. Supreme Court reversed.[15] In doing so, the Court provided the seminal four-part test.

It's extremely important at the outset to understand *what* it is that the **Central Hudson** test actually tests. The test sets up a formula for understanding whether any governmental entity (city, state, or federal, legislature, university, or commission) is allowed to restrict advertising in a specific way. It is *not* a test of whether an advertisement is legal: it is the *regulation* that is being tested, not the communication. We will now move through each of the four parts of the test.

> *Central Hudson* test ■ A four-part test used to determine the constitutionality of any law that limits commercial speech. (1) The speech must not be misleading and concern lawful activity, (2) the asserted state interest promoted by the restriction must be substantial, (3) the restriction must directly advance the asserted state interest, and (4) that the regulation does not restrict speech any more than necessary.

1. *Is the commercial speech entitled to protection?*
   Very simply, there are two forms of commercial speech that are not protected.

   ■ Advertisements for illegal products or services;
   ■ False or misleading advertising.

   Regulations that restrict either of these types of advertisements do not create constitutional issues. For example, the government is within its rights to regulate advertising for illegal drugs. In fact, one Supreme Court decision even allowed a community to regulate advertising that was "marketed for use *with*" illegal drugs. Hoffman Estates, Ill., required such shops to obtain a license, which was challenged by the Flipside, a Hoffman Estates store that sold novelty devices, including a variety of drug-related items. The Supreme Court ruled that the Village of Hoffman Estates was within its right to require the licensing, despite the fact that the products themselves were legal. The Court noted that the drug paraphernalia was sold alongside publications that advocated illegal use of drugs and commercial speech for illegal products could be regulated.[16]

   The examples of government regulation of false and misleading advertising are extensive, and we will discuss several in a later section. An entire division of the Federal Trade Commission devotes its time to determining whether advertisements are misleading. The FTC and its activity are constitutional, despite the fact that they affect expression. If the commercial speech is not false or misleading or for an illegal product or service, we must address the second part of the test.[17]

---

[15]*Id.*

[16]*Village of Hoffman Estates v. Flipside*, 455 U.S. 489 (1982).

[17]Some law texts consider *Central Hudson* a three-part test, removing this part and focusing on the other three. There is some logic to this, since this prong of the test doesn't really test the government's behavior but rather the nature of the communication. We use four because the Supreme Court referred to it as a four step analysis in *Central Hudson*. Whether the test is seen as three or four parts, the result is the same: governments are permitted to regulate false or misleading advertising as well as advertising for illegal products and services.

2. *Does the government have a* substantial *interest in regulating?*
Government regulations are subject to different levels of scrutiny by the courts. When discussing regulations of political speech we usually talk about the strict scrutiny that the court applies to government regulation. Courts expect regulators to be able to show an overriding, significant, or compelling interest in regulating political speech. As has already been discussed, commercial speech is not entitled to the same level of protection, so the level of scrutiny is somewhat less. The government can show that it has a substantial or legitimate interest with very little trouble. Usually governments have a substantial interest anytime they are trying to protect the public. Protecting the morals of the public is legitimate, as is protecting public health and safety.

In a narrow 5–4 decision, the Supreme Court ruled that Puerto Rico could prevent casino gambling advertisements directed to the citizens of the Commonwealth of Puerto Rico. The Court held that "the Puerto Rico Legislature's interest in the health, safety, and welfare of its citizens constitutes a 'substantial' governmental interest."[18] The regulation allowed casino advertisements targeting tourists and non-casino ads targeting local residents for hotels that contained casinos, but not casino advertisements targeting local residents.

So if it is so easy for governments to satisfy the second prong of the *Central Hudson* test, then why is it even necessary? Some might contend that it really isn't: that the threshold for the government is so low that it will always be able to claim a substantial government interest. The third prong of the test is tied to the second, though, and that is not so easily met.

3. *Does the regulation actually* advance *the government interest asserted in Part 2 of the test?*
It is one thing to claim that the government has an interest in protecting health and safety, morality, or even the aesthetic beauty of a community. It is another thing entirely to be able to make a case that a regulation *directly* advances the government's stated interest. If the government has an interest in the health and safety of its citizens, it might want to discourage excessive drinking of alcoholic beverages by banning advertising the prices of alcoholic beverages. Rhode Island attempted to do just that with a law it passed in 1956. The law was challenged in 1985 on two fronts: a Rhode Island liquor store wanted to advertise in a Massachusetts newspaper (the store was in a border town), and a Rhode Island newspaper wanted to accept Massachusetts liquor store advertisements. When the case reached the U.S. Supreme Court the law was struck down in part because it could not satisfy the third prong of the *Central Hudson* test. The Court's opinion noted the fact that there was a "lack of unanimity among researchers" as to whether liquor advertising impacts the amount of consumption.[19] It further stated that the government had the burden of proving the regulation advances the state's interest "to a material degree."[20]

---

[18]*Posadas de Puerto Rico Associates v. Tourism Co.*, 478 U.S. 328 (1986), at 341.
[19]*44 Liquormart, Inc. v. Rhode Island*, 517 U.S. 484 (1996), at 493.
[20]*Id.* at 505.

This is where the Court departed from the earlier thinking in the *Posadas* decision. When Puerto Rico asserted that advertising targeting local residents would result in an increase in their gambling and harm poor residents, the Supreme Court accepted the assertion with little or no evidence. In the intervening decade, the Court "tweaked" the *Central Hudson* test, no longer accepting claims that the regulation advanced the government interest without the presentation of concrete evidence.

4. *Is the restriction on expression narrowly drawn?*
This part of the test requires that a regulation of advertising does not go far beyond what is necessary by restricting speech more than necessary to achieve the desired end. In the *Central Hudson* case itself, it is this fourth prong where the Court determined that the ban on advertising that encouraged energy consumption was unconstitutional. New York had a substantial government interest in energy conservation (Part 2 of the test) and under less stringent evidence requirements was able to assert that there was an "immediate connection between advertising and demand for electricity"[21] (Part 3). The reason the Court found the New York regulation unconstitutional was because the rule went too far. The power company was able to demonstrate that the law prevented it from advertising about efficient uses of energy, such as purchasing a heat pump to improve energy efficiency. This would mean the regulation prohibited *too much* expression. What's more, the Court stated that an alternative law might permit the ads but require that they contain certain energy efficiency information, much as tobacco advertisements require statements about smoking's impact on health.[22]

More recent Court decisions have made it clear that a regulation does not have to be a "perfect fit" with the substantial interest but rather "narrowly drawn" to achieve the goal. It would impose quite a burden on the state to prove that every regulation of advertising was the least restrictive means possible. If any petitioner could claim a scheme that would be less restrictive, the regulation would have to be ruled unconstitutional. The Court did not accept such a position.

American Future Systems sold housewares to college students by gathering ten or more students together for a demonstration. Hosts for the demonstration were enlisted by providing gifts to the host based on the amount purchased by those attending. The State University of New York had a rule restricting commercial enterprises on campus. In 1982 an AFS representative who had been invited by a resident to conduct a demonstration in a dormitory on the Cortland campus was asked to leave by campus police. When she refused she was arrested and charged with trespass. Her challenge went all the way to the U.S. Supreme Court, where the Court applied the

---

[21]447 U.S. at 569. About the only "evidence" provided was the assertion, "Central Hudson would not contest the advertising ban unless it believed that promotion would increase its sales. Thus, we find a direct link between the state interest in conservation and the Commission's order." *Id.*
[22]*Id.* at 571.

Central Hudson test. The Supreme Court refuted a claim by the district court that the New York rule had to be the "least restrictive" measure possible to pass the fourth prong of the *Central Hudson* test. Instead, the Court stated that there must be a "fit" between the "legislature's ends and the means chosen to accomplish those ends . . . not necessarily perfect, but reasonable."[23] In other words, the Court was prepared to show some degree of deference in deciding the fourth part of the test.

Summary

Commercial speech doctrine has evolved in the twentieth and twenty-first centuries, and it is not too daring to speculate that it will continue to be defined as more cases are tried. We have moved far from the 1940s thinking of *Valentine* that commercial speech is not protected at all to the position that even commercial speech that does no more than advertise prices should be entitled to some degree of protection. The *Central Hudson* test is an attempt to strike the balance between no protection and full protection, and it continues to be refined with each subsequent commercial speech decision.

THE FEDERAL TRADE COMMISSION

Government attitude toward advertising regulation a century ago can be best summed up in a familiar two-word Latin expression: *caveat emptor* (let the buyer beware). There was no government agency charged with protecting consumers. In 1914 Congress passed the Federal Trade Commission Act, which created the five-member Commission. Although today the agency enforces all sorts of regulations on advertising to protect consumers, that wasn't the reason Congress created the FTC. The major thrust for the Commission's creation was to prevent anti-competitive business practices. Monopolies and monopolistic business practices were a major concern for President Woodrow Wilson early in the twentieth century. At the outset, the FTC regulated deceptive advertising on the premise that it was a form of unfair competition. In 1922, the FTC was challenged when it ordered an underwear manufacturer to stop labeling underwear as natural wool when it contained only 10 percent wool. Winstead Hosiery contended that the FTC lacked any authority to regulate advertising: that the Commission was limited to policing unfair competition. The U.S. Supreme Court ruled that any advertising that attempted to deceive consumers was a form of unfair competition.[24]

---

[23]*Board of Trustees of the State Univ. of N.Y. v. Fox*, 492 U.S. 469, 480 (1989) (quoting *Posadas*).
[24]*Federal Trade Comm'n v. Winstead Hosiery*, 258 U.S. 483 (1922).

But the FTC still lacked Congressional authority to protect consumers. In 1931 the Raladam Company challenged the Commission's authority to regulate an "obesity cure" being marketed by the company. The FTC made the claim that the cure did not work but the U.S. Supreme Court sided with Raladam because the FTC's authority was protecting businesses from unfair competition, and there was no showing that any competitor had been harmed.[25]

It was years later under President Franklin Roosevelt's administration that the Federal Trade Act was amended to authorize the FTC to protect consumers. The Wheeler-Lea Act passed Congress in 1938 and decreed "unfair or deceptive acts or practices in commerce are hereby declared unlawful."[26]

**Federal Trade
Commission (FTC)**
■ Created in 1914 to prevent monopolies and unfair methods of competition in commerce, the FTC also regulates advertisements. The FTC requires that all advertisements be truthful, non-deceptive, and fair, and also states that advertisers must have evidence to back up their claims.

The Federal Trade Commission has five members who are appointed by the president and confirmed by the Senate. Members serve rotating seven-year terms[27] (so no more than one Commissioner's term expires in any given year) although many leave office before completing their terms. No more than three members can come from any one political party. Generally, three commissioners come from the President's party. The President appoints the Commission Chair. While the commissioners are the most visible part of the agency, a good deal of the day-to-day work is performed by the staff members who populate the various divisions and bureaus. Generally commissioners are not involved in enforcing deceptive advertising rules but leave those tasks to the Bureau of Consumer Protection.

In spite of a staff of about 900 employees, it would be impossible for the FTC to monitor the millions of advertisements in print, on the air, or online. The FTC relies on complaints from consumers and businesses (about competitors) to inform it of possible legal infractions.[28] Like other administrative agencies, it must also be responsive to the wishes of Congress, both explicit and implicit. Congress can pass legislation that requires action by the FTC or modifies the Act, which the FTC is bound to enforce. Sometimes Congress may simply conduct an investigation without passing any legislation, but the signal is heard loud and clear at the FTC. Remember that Congress controls the agency's appropriations and can vote to increase or decrease funding as it finds appropriate.

The Commission sometimes provides guidance to industries through industry guides outlining what is and is not acceptable for advertising within a certain industry. The guides serve as advice to industries and, although not the same as law, are referred to if complaints are registered against an advertiser. Some of the industry guides include *Rebuilt, Reconditioned and Other Used Automobile Parts Industry; Fuel Economy Advertising for New Automobiles*; and *Dietary Supplements*.

---

[25]*Federal Trade Comm'n v. Raladam*, 283 U.S. 643 (1931).

[26]15 U.S.C. § 45(a)(1).

[27]The anomaly of five members appointed to seven-year terms is a result of the reduction in the Commission's size from seven to five members as part of the government reduction of the Regan administration. Agencies vary: the Federal Communications Commission has five members who serve for five years; the Federal Election Commission has six members who each serve a six-year term, and; the International Trade Commission has six members who each serve for nine years. Some say commission size and terms of office are rather arbitrary.

[28]Complaint forms are available online at https://www.ftccomplaintassistant.gov/.

Occasionally the FTC will rescind industry guides when they outlive their usefulness, as the FTC did in 2002 with the *Guides for the Household Furniture Industry*. The guides were adopted in 1973 and the Commission had not received a single complaint under the guides.

The Commission goes beyond guides when it enacts administrative law in the form of FTC Rules. Unlike guides the rules *are* law and advertisers who are not in compliance can be fined. A well-known FTC rule is the 1964 decision to require cigarette companies to include health warnings in advertisements and on the packages. A 2003 FTC rule created the National Do Not Call Registry, limiting the ability of telemarketers to contact those wanting to avoid such calls.

The FTC is a quasi-judicial agency in that it not only enforces law but also has a branch responsible for hearing legal challenges to its decisions. If a company wants to contest an allegation by the Commission, that company's case would first be heard by an administrative law judge. ALJ decisions can be reheard (or appealed) to the full five-member Commission for a ruling. The case before the FTC actually substitutes for a federal district court decision. If an FTC decision is then appealed, the appeal is heard by the U.S. Court of Appeals.[29]

DECEPTIVE ADVERTISING

One of the major tasks faced by the FTC is to take action against unfair and **deceptive advertising**. Liability for deceptive advertising can be placed with the product or service, the advertising agency that creates the ad, the medium that carries the ad, or all of them. Later in this chapter we will discuss specifically what action the FTC can take. For now we must define deceptive advertising. Fortunately there is an explicit definition (although there is still a degree of subjectivity). A deceptive advertisement is

> A representation, omission, or practice that is likely to mislead a reasonable consumer and is material to a decision to purchase a product or service.

Be careful to notice that *nowhere* in the definition of deceptive advertising is there any mention of the truth or falsity of a claim. A statement that is 100 percent true may be considered to be deceptive while one that is completely false may be not deceptive. For example, in 1972 the FTC found that Ocean Spray Cranberry Juice was being deceptive when it claimed that cranberry juice contains more "food energy" than orange juice.[30] Ocean Spray never mentioned in the ad that it was defining food energy as calories, which, after all, is the source of a body's energy. As defined, the advertisement was absolutely true, but the FTC found it to be deceptive because information was omitted that was likely to mislead a reasonable consumer, who might then make a purchase based on that information.

Conversely, an advertiser may be able to make a completely false statement that would not be considered to be deceptive. For years, Red Bull Energy Drink

Deceptive advertising ■ According to the FTC's Deception Policy Statement, an ad is deceptive if it contains a statement—or omits information—that is: (1) likely to mislead consumers acting reasonably under the circumstances, and (2) is "material"—that is, important to a consumer's decision to buy or use the product.

---

[29]Challengers also have the option of filing suit against the FTC in a local federal district court.

[30]*Ocean Spray Cranberries et al.*, 80 F.T.C. 975 (1972).

has used the slogan "Red Bull gives you wings." Their television commercials even contain animated characters that sprout wings after drinking the product. This claim is completely false: no one grows wings after consuming Red Bull. And yet the ad is not considered deceptive because no reasonable consumer believes the outlandish claim. It is an example of **puffery**, an over-inflated claim about a product or service that is not intended to be taken seriously.

Puffery ■ An over-exaggerated claim about a product that is too out-landish to be believed by a reasonable person, and as such is legal.

In *Pizza Hut v. Papa John's*,[31] Pizza Hut filed suit against Papa John's advertisements claiming that the Papa John's slogan, "Better ingredients. Better pizza." was deceptive.[32] Pizza Hut claimed that the ads were deceptive in that they showed Pizza Hut workers using canned sauce but did not show Papa John's using canned sauce, which they do. Pizza Hut asserted that the claim "better" in this context was deceptive, and the trial court agreed. In appeal, however, the appellate court ruled that the slogan was an example of puffery. Without a showing by Pizza Hut that the ads were likely to deceive, the court decided in favor of Papa John's.

Note also that nowhere in the definition of deceptive advertising is there any mention of the *intent* of the advertiser. It really doesn't matter whether an advertiser purposely or accidentally deceives consumers. The FTC has gone so far as to state that advertisers must correct misleading advertising, whether intended or not.

We now turn to each of the three criteria for defining deceptive advertising, with examples of ads that have been adjudicated as deceptive or not.

1. Likely to Mislead

How is it possible to know whether an advertisement is "likely to mislead"? Certainly false advertising that would be believed by consumers (unlike puffery) is likely to mislead. Truthful advertising might also mislead, however, as evidenced by the Ocean Spray example mentioned earlier. Advertising can be likely to mislead because of information that is included *or* excluded. The fact that the cranberry juice ad omitted important information made it deceptive. Information might be included but in such a way as to be incomprehensible, which is also likely to mislead. The use of technical language that might not be understood by consumers may be likely to mislead, as would be disclaimers in advertisements that would be too small to read. Ads that have dual meanings will be considered misleading if *either* of the meanings is likely to mislead. Examples of practices that the FTC has ruled likely to mislead include misleading price claims, inadequate disclosure of dangers associated with hazardous products, the use of "bait and switch" techniques,[33] and failure to meet the express obligations in a warranty.

---

[31]227 F.3d 489 (5th Cir. 2000), *cert. denied*, 532 U.S. 920 (2001).

[32]In addition to action by the FTC, a company can file a suit against a competitor for deceptive advertising by claiming that the deceptive advertising damages their business. Remember that the FTC not only protects consumers but prevents unfair business practices.

[33]*Bait and switch* is the term for illegally advertising a low-priced product to entice a customer into a store only to be out of the advertised item, at which time the staff tries to pressure the customer to buy a more expensive version. To avoid such accusations most stores advertise "quantities limited" or offer rain checks.

A representation can mislead even when an advertisement's words do not. In 1982 Tropicana Orange Juice advertised that it was "pure pasteurized juice as it comes from the orange." Tropicana was in fact pure and it was pasteurized. The problem was that the television commercial showed an Olympic champion squeezing an orange and pouring the juice into a Tropicana container. The deception was the misleading visual. The juice was pasteurized, which meant that after it was extracted from the orange it was heated, but the visual showed the juice going straight from the orange to the carton. The FTC considered it a misleading representation.[34]

The FTC can "presume" that a practice is likely to deceive but in some cases it requires evidence that an advertisement or practice is likely to mislead, not just a claim that it might. The Commission dismissed a claim that selling unmarked products in Alaska misled consumers into believing that the products were handmade by natives. The FTC said elaborate proof was not necessary but that at least "some extrinsic testimony evidence" needed to be provided by the complainants.[35] In determining whether an advertisement is likely to mislead, the FTC often relies on expert testimony or consumer surveys.

2. Reasonable Consumer

While evidence of someone actually deceived by an advertisement helps make the case that an ad is deceptive, it might not be conclusive. If a million people see an advertisement and one person is misled, that will not be considered deceptive. If a consumer is not "reasonable" the FTC will not hold the advertiser liable for any misunderstanding. More than 40 years ago the FTC stated:

> An advertiser cannot be charged with liability with respect to every conceivable misconception, however outlandish, to which his representations might be subject among the foolish or feeble-minded. Some people, because of ignorance or incomprehension, may be misled by even a scrupulously honest claim. Perhaps a few misguided souls believe, for example, that all "Danish pastry" is made in Denmark. Is it therefore an actionable deception to advertise "Danish pastry" when it is made in this country? Of course not. A representation does not become "false and deceptive" merely because it will be unreasonably misunderstood by an insignificant and unrepresentative segment of the class of persons to whom the representation is addressed.[36]

It is possible, however, that adverting which targets a specific population might be considered deceptive *to that population*, in which case the Commission will find it deceptive. Obviously children's discernment skills are not as well developed as those of adults, so ads targeting children might be ruled deceptive when the same advertisement would not be deceptive if seen by adults. The U.S. Supreme

---

[34]*Coca-Cola v. Tropicana*, 690 F.2d 312 (2d Cir. 1982).

[35]*Leonard Porter*, 88 F.T.C. 546, 626 n.5 (1976).

[36]*Heinz W. Kirchner*, 63 F.T.C. 1282, 1290 (1963).

Court has endorsed this doctrine, stating "The determination whether an advertisement is misleading requires consideration of the legal sophistication of its audience."[37] A toy company agreed to stop showing commercials where a ballerina doll pirouetted on one toe unassisted when in fact the doll could not do so.[38]

Children are not the only unique audience. The FTC has pointed out that terminally ill patients "might be particularly susceptible to exaggerated cure claims."[39] Even weight loss claims might be judged based on the target audience, which might be considered more susceptible to exaggerated claims: the Commission stated, "To these corpulent consumers the promises of weight loss without dieting are the Siren's call, and advertising that heralds unrestrained consumption while muting the inevitable need for temperance, if not abstinence, simply does not pass muster."[40]

It matters how a reasonable consumer interprets the *entire* message, not just selected words or images. Disclaimers can be effective means for fending off a claim of deception if those disclaimers can be clearly understood. This is an extremely difficult and subjective judgment. In the same case, the FTC found one instance where fine print in an advertisement was an adequate disclosure and another where it was inadequate. Litton Industries advertised its microwave ovens in newspapers and magazines with a headline stating "76 percent of the independent microwave oven service technicians surveyed preferred Litton." Readers had to look to the fine print to realize that only Litton authorized service technicians were surveyed, and the FTC considered the disclosure insufficient. On the other hand, a fine print disclosure that "independent" meant the technicians worked on Litton and one other brand was sufficient.[41] The FTC has been attentive to the behavior of reasonable consumers: whether they are likely to be attentive to a particular disclaimer because of its relative size or technical nature, or the likelihood that a consumer would read it.

3. *Material* to Purchasing Decision

Deception is material if it is about product characteristics that sway consumers to buy or not buy a product. An individual who makes a purchase based on deceptive advertising has been injured, so a material deception is one that causes an injury. It's easy to understand examples at the extremes. Obviously the cost of a product or service is material to a purchasing decision. In 1980 the FTC ruled that a New York City publishing company and its Chicago subsidiary were deceptive in their advertising of correspondence courses.[42] The violations included not only

---

[37]*Bates v. Arizona*, 433 U.S. 350, 383 n.37 (1977).

[38]*Lewis Galoob Toys, Inc.*, 114 F.T.C. 187 (1991) (Consent Order).

[39]FTC Policy Statement on Deception; *appended to Cliffdale Associates, Inc.*, 103 F.T.C. 110, 174 (1984). Though more than twenty years old, this document provides an excellent review of what constitutes deceptive practices.

[40]*Porter & Dietsch*, 90 F.T.C. 770, 864–865 (1977), *aff'd*, 605 F.2d 294 (7th Cir. 1979), *cert. denied*, 445 U.S. 950 (1980).

[41]*Litton Indus.*, 97 F.T.C. 1 (1981), *aff'd as modified*, 676 F.2d 364 (9th Cir. 1982).

[42]*MacMillan, Inc.*, 96 F.T.C. 208 (1980).

omissions of information about admissions and misrepresenting the job market for graduates, but also inadequate information about the costs that a student would incur.

On the other hand, deception is not material if it's the sort of misinformation that has no impact on purchasing decisions. If a magazine advertisement happened to make a printing mistake and show a perfume bottle as a different color, the ad might mislead a reasonable consumer to believe the bottle was blue when in fact it was green. It's not the sort of deception that will affect purchasing decisions, which means it is not material, which means it is not deceptive.

Most advertising claims will be considered material. After all, if advertisers are by definition trying to persuade people to purchase products, most of what they include in their ads will be material. To date, however, no successful claims have been made against advertisers for the sort of implied messages that advertising relies on to sell products. Sex appeal has been used to sell everything from automobiles to toothpaste, yet no ad has been found deceptive for suggesting that drinking a particular brand of beer will make a man more popular with the ladies.[43] An unsuccessful suit was filed in California claiming that minors were being deceived by tobacco ads that glamorized smoking, but the California Supreme Court rejected the claim.[44]

But there are some implied messages that will be considered deceptive. The FTC ruled it was deceptive for a mattress manufacturer to use a picture of a man in a white jacket next to the word *orthopedic*, implying the mattress had somehow been endorsed by medical professionals or had in some other way been designed for medical use.[45]

Ads can have material deception even in cases where the deception *shouldn't* matter because the average consumer doesn't know any better. The FTC ruled that Carnation was deceptive when it claimed that its instant breakfast product contained as much "mineral nourishment as two strips of bacon."[46] The ad was deceptive because bacon may provide lots of protein, but not much in the way of minerals. A Baggies commercial was ruled deceptive because it showed that a sandwich dunked underwater and swirled in a Baggie stayed dry while a competitor's bag allowed water in. The FTC stated that the demonstration would deceive viewers into believing that the demonstration showed superiority at keeping food fresh when temperature, moisture, air, and a "myriad" of other factors are what affect food freshness.[47]

[43]In 1997 the National Council on Drug Dependence and Mothers Against Drunk Driving filed an unsuccessful petition with the FCC requesting that counter-advertisements be required for alcohol advertising on television in part because of the deceptiveness toward minors of the sex appeal of the advertising.

[44]*In re Tobacco Cases II*, 41 Cal. 4th 1257 (2007). *cert. denied sub nom. Daniels v. Philip Morris*, 2008 U.S. Lexis 2467 (2008).

[45]*In re 2361 State Corp.*, 65 F.T.C. 310 (1964).

[46]*In re Carnation Co.*, 77 F.T.C. 1547 (1970).

[47]*In re Colgate-Palmolive*, 77 F.T.C. 150 (1970).

Sometimes the demands of creating an advertisement require that simulations or mock-ups are used in advertisements. For example, if an amusement park wants to produce a television commercial, it might want to include a scene with a family eating an ice cream cone as they walk through the park. If the commercial has to be shot on a hot day, it might be difficult to get a shot without having ice cream running everywhere. The production company might elect to substitute something that looks like ice cream but would not melt as fast, such as mashed potatoes. Clearly the mock-up of an ice cream cone in an ad for the amusement park would not be material or deceptive. On the other hand, if a mock-up is material and deceptive, the FTC will act.

The historic example of a deceptive mock-up is from 1965. In a television commercial, Rapid Shave shaving cream "demonstrated" how it softened so well it could soften a piece of sandpaper so that it could be shaved clean. One deception in the ad was ruled to be the fact that Rapid Shave did not disclose that the sandpaper had to soak in shaving cream for over an hour to be shaved. In addition, Rapid Shave used a mock-up in the ad: what it showed shaved clean was not a piece of sandpaper but rather a piece of plexiglass, which would be rather easy to "shave" clean. Rapid Shave attempted to assert that it was simply using production techniques necessary to show a TV audience how the product worked. The FTC disagreed and ruled the advertising deceptive, a decision upheld by the U.S. Supreme Court.[48] The FTC made it clear that mock-ups and simulated demonstrations would be permitted as long as they were not material, or if they do not misrepresent a material characteristic of the product.

FACTUAL CLAIMS

It is reasonable to expect that if an advertisement claims a product can do something, then the product must in fact be able to do what is claimed. Relatively speaking, this is easy to discern. If an advertiser claims that a product "kills germs" it is simple to test whether or not this is a **factual advertising claim** by applying the product to a surface and measuring whether the germs have been killed. If it is claimed that "9 out of 10 dentists surveyed say . . ." there had better be a survey, conducted legitimately, where 90 percent of the dentists surveyed respond as alleged.

The requirement that there be valid evidence for factual claims does not require an advertiser to include negative representations. For years Pepsi conducted "The Pepsi Challenge" in which people coming out of grocery stores were asked to blind taste Pepsi and Coke and select their favorite. It is not deceptive to show *only* people who selected Pepsi so long as the advertisement does not imply that *everyone* chose Pepsi.[49]

The use of certain terms in advertising can constitute a factual claim. Calling a piece of furniture "antique" is a factual claim, as is calling an automobile tire "safe." The Federal Trade Commission ruled that Firestone misled customers

Factual advertising claims ■ FTC guidelines state that any claims stated as facts by the advertiser must have a reasonable basis for making such a statement.

---

[48]*Federal Trade Comm'n v. Colgate-Palmolive*, 380 U.S. 374 (1965).

[49]No deceptive advertising claim has been lodged against "the Pepsi Challenge," and Pepsi was always clear that Pepsi was chosen by *more* people, not *all* people.

Legitimate Evidence

An advertiser cannot ask ten of his best friends if they like his product and then claim that "9 out of 10 people surveyed prefer our product." It would not be considered a valid survey. Making a claim that people prefer a product in a "blind taste test" requires that the test be conducted fairly: no serving the preferred soft drink in a crystal glass while serving the competitor in a paper cup. Conscientious advertisers usually hire research firms to conduct the independent testing of their claims.

There are legal ways, however, that allow advertisers to get the results they want. A lot can be done with the phrasing of questions, order of questions, or approach to solicit the "right" answers.

Consider the phrase "Nine out of ten dentists surveyed recommend sugarless gum for their patients who chew gum." The phrase may seem to imply that dentists recommend sugarless gum, but that's not quite right. The clause "for their patients who chew gum" qualifies it. Ninety percent of the dentists are actually agreeing with the statement "If your patient is going to chew gum no matter what, would you prefer that patient chewed sugared gum or sugarless gum?" That's quite different from asking whether dentists *want* their patients to chew *any* gum.

If an advertiser uses the plural "surveys show" or "tests prove" then legitimate evidence would require results from at least *two* surveys or tests.

when it claimed to be "The Safe Tire." When the FTC asked Firestone to prove its claim, the company simply asserted that since the tires passed all the company's inspections they were safe. The Commission ruled the ad deceptive.[50]

WHAT ABOUT STATEMENTS OF OPINION?

Is it deceptive to claim that your product "tastes great"? What evidence can an advertiser provide for individual taste, which is such a subjective judgment? If a statement is *purely* an **opinion advertising claim** (e.g. a statement of opinion), no evidence or substantiation is required. To claim that something tastes great or smells fantastic is a pure statement of opinion and therefore not deceptive. If an advertiser claims that "most people say it tastes great," a consumer could easily infer that a survey or test has been conducted to determine what most people believe. Also the FTC has advised that presenting the opinion of an expert will be generally considered as a statement of fact rather than opinion. A commercial that shows a physician saying it is her "opinion" that a medication is safe is likely to be heard by consumers as a scientific statement of fact.

It's not always easy to tell whether a statement is purely opinion. The FTC ruled that an advertiser claiming its television antenna to be an "electronic miracle" was making a claim that the product was superior to others.[51] The advertiser tried to claim that the term *miracle* was simply a form of puffery and should not be actionable but the Commission disagreed, asserting that "in the context of . . . grossly exaggerated claims" consumers might be deceived.

> **Opinion advertising claims** ■ Cases based on subjective opinion claims (taste, appearance, smell) are generally not actionable. Claims based on opinions are actionable, however, if they are not honestly held, if they misrepresent the qualifications of the holder or the basis of his opinion, or if the recipient reasonably interprets them as implied statements of fact.

[50]*Firestone*, 81 F.T.C 398 (1972), *aff'd*, 481 F.2d 246 (6th Circ.), *cert. denied*, 414 U.S. 1112 (1973).
[51]*Jay Norris*, 91 F.T.C. 751, *aff'd*, 598 F.2d 1244 (2d. Circ.), *cert. denied*, 444 U.S. 980 (1979).

UP CLOSE

The Special Case of Testimonials

Testimonials and endorsements are special sorts of statements with a formal set of FTC guidelines.[a] "Endorsements must always reflect the honest opinions, findings, beliefs, or experience of the endorser."[b] If someone claims that a pain reliever worked, the FTC expects it to be true. This is quite different from a commercial where someone acting in the role of a person with a headache "pretends" to get relief from a pain reliever, or a voice-over announcer who provides the "voice of the company." In advertisements that appear to use "actual consumers," the people in the advertisement must in fact *be* actual consumers.

If a consumer claims in a testimonial ad that he got excellent results from using a product, the testimonial might be deceptive even with substantiation, if the average consumer could not expect similar results. This is why often testimonial advertisements include the phrase "Results not typical. Actual results may vary."

The rules also require that anyone claiming to use a product actually use it. This is especially relevant with celebrity endorsements where fans of a celebrity can be influenced to use a product based solely on the celebrity's popularity. If people believe that Tiger Woods uses a specific brand of golf ball they may purchase it assuming that someone as good a golfer as Tiger Woods must certainly know which golf ball

is best. Pop singer Pat Boone endorsed an acne medication in the 1970s claiming that all of his daughters used it. The FTC asserted that the Boone children did not use the product and initiated action against the medication company and the singer.

Astronaut Gordon Cooper attracted the FTC's attention when he endorsed G.R. Valve, a gadget that claimed to increase the fuel efficiency of automobiles. The fact that Cooper had an engineering degree might cause the misimpression that he understood fuel efficiency (his degree was in aerospace engineering). The FTC contended that Cooper implied expertise in fuel efficiency when he had none.

Consumers will naturally assume that people in advertisements are compensated for their appearance. An advertisement where a celebrity endorses a product does not require a disclaimer stating that the celebrity was paid for the appearance. The same is true of actors appearing in commercials. The situation is different, however, if it appears that the person in a blind taste test has selected one soft drink over another, or that the people in the restaurant being observed by hidden camera have shown amazement that they were served instant coffee. Audiences will naturally assume that those individuals were *not* compensated for their endorsements and if they are advertisers have an obligation to provide that information in the ad.

[a]*FTC Guides Concerning Use of Endorsements and Testimonials in Advertisements,* 45 F.R. 3873 (1980). Public comment was sought in review of the rules in 2009. *Notice of Proposed Changes to Guides,* 73 F.R. 72374 (2008).
[b]*FTC Guides* at §255.1.

If an advertiser makes any kind of factual claim that the FTC questions, the FTC may simply say "prove it." Consumers *should* base purchasing decisions on facts about a product or service, and it is realistic to expect that the advertiser has "reasonable basis" for any claims being made.[52] If the advertiser lacks substantiation, the ad is considered deceptive.

[52]*FTC Policy Statement Regarding Advertising Substantiation, appended to Thompson Med. Co.,* 104 F.T.C. 648, 839 (1984), *aff'd,* 791 F.2d 189 (D.C. Cir. 1986), *cert. denied,* 479 U.S. 1086 (1987).

The Case of Paid Endorsers

Michael C. Lasky

The current relationship between the Federal Trade Commission (FTC) and the public relations (PR) industry is one characterized by greater scrutiny and quite possibly, on the side of the FTC, mistrust. The tension between FTC and the PR industry reached a fever pitch in 2005 when it was revealed that conservative pundit Armstrong Williams was paid to promote the Bush administration's "No Child Left Behind" law, a fact that Williams did not disclose when promoting the law on talk shows.

Since the Armstrong Williams scandal, the FTC has been paying closer scrutiny to disclosures of material connections in nontraditional media, such a talk shows and social media. In 2009, the FTC issued its revised *Guides on the Use of Endorsements and Testimonials* (*Guides*) to make clear that material connections that consumers would not normally expect between an endorser and a marketer must be disclosed in new media forms, such as in blogs, social media posts, and on talk shows.

After enacting the revised *Guides*, in 2010, the FTC resolved its first action for unfair and deceptive practices arising from noncompliance with the *Guides*. The action was against Reverb Communications, Inc., a PR agency in the video game industry, and its sole owner, Tracie Snitker. The settlement resolves claims that Reverb and Snitker engaged in deceptive marketing by having employees pose as ordinary consumers and post reviews on iTunes of a game application they were hired to promote. According to the FTC, Reverb and Snitker's postings did not disclose that employees posting were hired to promote the products or that Reverb's fee often included a percentage of its client's sales of the game applications. This action has shown that the FTC is intent on enforcing the revised *Guides'* disclosure requirements, not only with respect to the companies whose products are marketed, but also with respect to the public relations agencies who market those products.

The FTC's settlement with Reverb Communications should be viewed as a warning message to the PR industry that it is now more important than ever to adopt the ethical disclosure practices set forth in the revised *Guides* and to err on the side of more disclosure to consumers regarding the relationships between public relations agencies, their hired spokespeople, and the marketers they represent.

Michael C. Lasky is a senior partner and co-chair at Davis & Gilbert LLP Attorneys at Law.

ACTIONS

The FTC has a number of tools in its arsenal when dealing with deceptive advertising. As with any enforcement agency, whether to politely ask a company to stop doing something or take harsh legal action, with penalties attached, is completely up to the Commission. Here are the various enforcement mechanisms.

Staff Advisory Letter

The FTC staff can inform an advertiser of their opinion as to whether a particular ad or practice is deceptive. Such an advisory letter does *not* have the force of law.

It is not considered to be the Commission's official position but rather is intended to prevent possible (expensive) legal proceedings. For example, in 1997 Network Solutions, Inc. requested a staff opinion about the practices of Internic Software. Network Solutions had the contract from the National Science Foundation to register Internet domain names, and did so through "InterNIC," an acronym for Internet Network Information Center. Internic Software, a company located in Sunbury, Australia, was getting a lot of hits at its website by people who *believed* they were contracting with Network Solutions. While www.internic.*net* would land someone at the official Network Solutions site, www.internic.*com* would direct the search to Internic Software. Staff opinion was that a reasonable consumer would be misled and the URL for Internic was a deceptive practice.[53]

Consent Agreement

Consent decree ◼
The FTC may agree not to prosecute the advertiser if the advertiser agrees not to repeat the offense. A consent decree cannot be appealed unless it can be proven that it was based on fraud by one of the parties or a mutual mistake.

When the FTC believes than an advertiser has engaged in unfair or deceptive advertising, the advertiser might actually accept the claim by the Commission and willingly enter into a settlement. A **consent decree** is a judgment agreed to by both the FTC and the advertiser that the matter is settled. The agreement may be a simple wrist slap or may involve a much harsher penalty. The advertiser, however, does not have to admit to any wrongdoing. In 2000, the FTC and Bayer Aspirin entered into an agreement that Bayer would spend $1 million in an educational campaign to inform the public that not everyone ought to take aspirin to reduce the risk of heart attack or stroke, and that a physician ought to be consulted before anyone begins taking aspirin regularly. Bayer also consented to refrain from making claims about the benefits of a daily aspirin regimen without mentioning potential risks (simply saying "Just ask your doctor" was not considered good enough).[54]

Cease and Desist Order

It has been the FTC's tradition to try to come to agreements with advertisers, so often cease and desist is actually part of a consent agreement that an advertiser willingly accepts. In 2003 the FTC filed actions against the makers of weight loss supplements containing ephedra. The Commission asserted that the advertisements made claims that the product was safe and would result in rapid, substantial and permanent weight loss without diet or exercise. Health Laboratories of North America signed off on a consent agreement to cease and desist in addition to paying a $370,000 settlement.

On the other hand, cease and desist orders can be unilateral: they do not have to be agreed to by the advertiser but can be an order to immediately stop doing what the FTC considers to be deceptive. In 1996 the FTC issued a cease and desist order to the Home Shopping Network for making unsubstantiated claims about a number of vitamin sprays. HSN did not willingly enter into any agreement: in fact the FTC had to file legal action to enforce the ruling.

---

[53]FTC Staff Advisory Letter, Aug. 21, 1997, *available at* http://www.ftc.gov/os/1997/08/internic.let.htm.
[54]Consent decree, *available at* http://www.ftc.gov/os/2000/01/sterlingdecree.htm.

Corrective Advertising

One of the more creative ways the FTC tries to correct the false impression made by deceptive advertising is to require the advertiser to correct the misimpression. This remedy is not used too frequently but when it is imposed, it often attracts a fair amount of media attention. The FTC says **corrective advertising** is appropriate when challenged ads substantially create or reinforce a misbelief that is likely to continue if not corrected.

The FTC first ordered corrective advertising in 1971. Profile Bread had been advertising that it contained fewer calories than other bread. When compared slice to slice, the claim was true, but this was because Profile was sliced thinner than its competitors. Ounce per ounce, there was no significant difference in calories. The FTC ordered that the company devote 25 percent of one year's advertising budget to correcting the misimpression they had made.[55]

In 1999 the FTC ordered Doan's Pills to correct the unsubstantiated claim that the product was more effective at treating back pain than other over-the-counter medications. The Commission said the product was an effective pain reliever but the implication that it was superior to others was considered to be deceptive.[56] The Commission required the parent company to spend $8 million on advertising to correct the unsubstantiated claims. It based the amount on what was spent annually to advertise Doan's Pills over the eight years of the campaign.

The FTC can order corrective advertising but it cannot order language that is punitive of an advertiser. For years Listerine mouthwash had claimed that it helped prevent colds. The FTC took Listerine to task because it could not substantiate its claim and ordered parent company Warner-Lambert to spend $10 million in advertising that included the message that "contrary to prior advertising" there was no evidence that Listerine prevented colds. Warner-Lambert appealed the FTC decision and the D.C. Circuit Court of Appeals upheld the $10 million corrective advertising order, but it struck the requirement that the ads contain the phrase "contrary to prior advertising."[57]

The FTC can also order an advertiser to disclose certain facts to prevent from being deceptive. Aspercreme is a topical medicine for arthritis pain. The name itself almost implies the product contains aspirin, but the company went further in a commercial asserting "When you suffer from arthritis, imagine putting the strong relief of aspirin right where you hurt. Aspercreme is an odorless rub which concentrates the relief of aspirin." The D.C. Circuit Court of Appeals upheld an FTC ruling that the company must disclose that the product contains no aspirin.[58]

A Final Note about FTC Action

Cynics complain that most of what the FTC does with regard to deceptive advertising is too little, too late. An advertiser can create a false impression with

Corrective advertisement ■ The FTC may order an advertiser do more than cease and desist its deceptive advertising, and also refrain from future advertising for a specified period of time, unless it corrects the misleading impression that its prior false advertising may have created.

---

[55]*ITT Continental Baking Co.*, 79 F.T.C. 248 (1971).

[56]*Novartis*, 1999 F.T.C. Lexis 90 (1999), *aff'd*, 223 F.3d 783 (2000).

[57]*Warner-Lambert v. FTC*, 562 F.2d 749 (D.C. Cir. 1977).

[58]*Thompson Med. Co. v. FTC*, 253 U.S. App. D.C. 18 (1986), *cert. denied*, 479 U.S. 1086 (1987).

impunity for weeks or even months before the Commission is notified, goes through a lengthy investigation process, and then takes action, which of course can be appealed. Most often, when the Commission does take action it is via consent decree (in more than 90 percent of cases), requiring no more than an agreement to stop the deceptive practice. The preponderance of advertising campaigns do not extend beyond a few months, so advertisers usually don't suffer very much by an order to stop a particular ad. In those few instances where a deceptive advertisement results in a fine from the FTC, even that is often seen as just the cost of doing business. In 1962, the Commission began its investigation and action against the makers of Geritol, a vitamin supplement marketed primarily to older Americans. Geritol was advertised as a way of dealing with tiredness. The FTC believed the ads were deceptive because tiredness is only occasionally the result of vitamin or mineral deficiencies, which the advertiser did not make clear. In 1964, the Commission issued a cease and desist order but Geritol continued to advertise in the challenged way.

In 1966 the FTC called on the Justice Department to intervene, and in 1973 Geritol's parent company was fined $800,000, but in 1974 the U.S. Second Circuit Court of Appeals ordered a new trial. Finally in 1976 Geritol was ordered to pay a $280,000 judgment. For fourteen years Geritol was able to engage in what the FTC considered a deceptive practice, and it did so at a cost of $20,000 per year. Given advertising budgets, that amount seems insignificant and allowed the company to continue making the claim.

OTHER AGENCIES AND ADVERTISING

In addition to the FTC, several other agencies can become involved in advertising regulation and enforcement. The Food and Drug Administration can become involved when advertisements relate to food, drug, or cosmetic products. The FDA is especially active in the area of labeling these products.

Advertisements for stocks and bonds come under the purview of the Securities and Exchange Commission. Companies that advertise stock for sale are strictly regulated by the SEC and a deceptive advertisement in this arena can be judged to be securities fraud, which can result in both civil and criminal penalties. Not only are the advertisements subject to regulation but so might any other material that a publicly traded company provides that might encourage investment based on false information. If a corporation's annual report purposely ignores a liability or is unduly optimistic about revenues, that can be seen by the SEC as a fraudulent attempt to manipulate the market.

While the Federal Election Commission does not directly monitor advertising, it does regulate campaign financing for elected federal offices. Not only the candidates themselves are regulated, but so are those groups active in the election or defeat of federal candidates. Political action committees are groups formed, as the name implies, to engage in political action including supporting or opposing candidates for office. The FEC monitors this activity and limits each PAC to a $5,000 contribution per candidate per election. PACs may spend as much as they like *independent of the candidate* to support or oppose federal candidates. In other words, a PAC may contribute $5,000 directly to Polly Tician's campaign for U.S. Senate but it may also spend a million dollars (or more) airing commercials supporting Polly for Senate as long as there is no coordination between the PAC and Polly's campaign (thus the required disclosures during the PAC's commercials). PACs must register with the FEC and provide a public accounting of all expenditures on behalf of candidates. Disclosure of who paid for an ad is required for any candidate ads, whether directly by a candidate, by a political party, or by a PAC.

Of course the Federal Communications Commission gets involved in the regulation of radio and television advertising. The best-known regulation of radio and television advertising, the ban on cigarette advertising, is not imposed by the FCC, though; it is by federal statute passed by Congress. In 1967 the FCC responded to public criticism of cigarette advertising by instituting a rule requiring radio and television stations to carry free antismoking public service announcements if they accepted paid advertising that promoted smoking. In the 1960s the Fairness Doctrine was still enforced (discussed in the broadcast chapter), and cigarette smoking was deemed to be a controversial issue that required fair treatment by broadcasters, hence the edict that PSAs "balance" the cigarette commercials. The FCC conceded that it need not be an equal, one-to-one balance of cigarette commercials to PSAs but would be satisfied with one PSA to every two paid commercials. After a couple of years of wrangling between the FCC, tobacco industry, and public interest groups, the Commission was considering a total ban on cigarette advertising when Congress acted, passing the Public Health Cigarette Smoking Act, which banned cigarette advertising from radio and television as of January 1, 1971. In 1986 the law was expanded to prohibit smokeless (i.e., "chewing") tobacco ads as well.

SELF-REGULATION

One of the best ways for industries to fend off the threat of regulation from the government is to regulate themselves. Self-regulation exists in most industries in the form of codes, guidelines, and standards.

Several organizations self-regulate advertising but the most active is probably the National Advertising Division, an extension of the Council of Better Business Bureaus. The NAD investigates deceptive advertising claims much the same way the FTC would, but it lacks any enforcement authority to impose sanctions. The NAD may rule than an advertiser should "cease and desist" but it has no power to enforce such a ruling. It relies in large part on the publicity that its decisions attract to influence advertisers in the court of public opinion.

In 2009 the NAD responded to a complaint from Stanislaus Food Products about advertisements and labeling for Hunt's Tomato Sauce. The NAD agreed with some of Stanislaus's complaint but disagreed with part. The NAD sided with Hunt's claim that the sauce is made from "all-natural vine-ripened tomatoes" but found the product label deceptive because it said "packed full of Hunt's 100% natural vine-ripened tomatoes." The NAD had no problem with a claim that the sauce was "made from" or "prepared from" vine-ripened tomatoes, but because the sauce came from a puree (concentrate) and water, the 100 percent claim was deceptive. Parent company ConAgra issued a statement that it respectfully disagreed with the finding but would still follow the NAD's decision and cease making the claim.[59]

Self-regulation is often more attractive than government intervention not only because self-regulation is less likely to be as harsh, but also because the costs associated are significantly less. NAD judgments are often favorable to legal action because they do not have to adhere to the disclosure rules that the courts or the FTC must follow. NAD keeps all data confidential, releasing only the decision and the participants' positions. Finally, NAD decisions occur more quickly than government action could ever occur since NAD's policy is to offer a written decision within sixty business days (about four months).

Dispelling Some Myths about Advertising Regulation

There is a lot of misinformation about advertising regulation. What has been industry self-regulation has been believed by many people to be a legal requirement. Here are four of the most often stated myths.

1. Television commercials are not allowed to show anyone drinking beer, wine, or hard liquor. There has never been such a prohibition. The National Association of Broadcasters *used to* have a recommendation in its Television Code that advertisements not show the consumption of alcoholic beverages. The TV Code was dropped by the NAB in 1982 after the Justice Department won an antitrust suit, because the code also suggested the maximum number of commercial minutes per hour that stations could air. Rather than just "fix" the portions that violated antitrust, the Association decided to discontinue the Code. Despite the fact that the Code was eliminated more than 25 years ago, advertisers and TV stations still self-regulate and choose not to show alcohol consumption in commercials.

2. "Hard liquor" ads are prohibited on over-the-air broadcasting. Another example of self-regulation from the National Association of Broadcasters. In this instance, both the Radio *and* Television Codes prohibited the ads. Though never a law, the first advertisement on a licensed station for hard liquor did not occur until 1996 (for Seagram's Crown Royal). Despite some public criticism and requests from President Bill Clinton and FCC Chairman Reed Hundt that broadcasters voluntarily refrain from airing liquor ads, no legal prohibition was enacted. Though still not pervasive, more radio and television stations have accepted hard liquor ads.

3. There is a legal limit to the number of commercial minutes in an hour of radio or TV programming. Once again, this myth is a vestige of the National Association of Broadcasters' codes. Both the Radio and Television Codes prescribed maximum numbers of commercial limits and the rules were purely

---

[59]National Advertising Division Press Release, *NAD Examines Advertising for Conagra's Hunt's Tomato Sauce*, Jan. 15, 2009, *available at* http://www.nadreview.org/DocView.aspx?DocumentID=7153.

self-regulation, not law. In fact an entire hour of content can be commercials (precisely what an infomercial is).

There is one area in which the law *does* restrict the number of commercial minutes: children's television. Within the three hours of children's core programming required of every television station (including over-the-air, cable, and satellite providers), stations may not exceed ten and a half minutes of advertising per hour on weekends or twelve minutes per hour on weekdays (children's television rules are discussed in chapter 10).

4. Advertisers must use "Brand X" or some other alias in ads comparing their product to a competitor rather than using the actual name of the competitor. Quite the opposite is the case. In its policy statement on comparative advertising, the FTC states that it "encourages the naming of, or reference to competitors" in comparative advertising, but cautions that such ads must be clear and not deceptive.[60] The Commission's policy statement on comparative advertising points out that it has been industry self-regulation that has often discouraged comparative ads because of their tendency to "disparage" a competitor's product, but that the FTC does not prohibit disparagement as long as it is truthful and not deceptive.

SUMMARY

- No more than 50 years ago, the Latin phrase *caveat emptor* (let the buyer beware) was the operative term. The U.S. government did not, for the most part, engage in the regulation of advertising. Consumers were expected to be skeptical of any and all advertising.

- In 1942 the U.S. Supreme Court ruled that "purely commercial speech" was not entitled to First Amendment protection. Since then, the Court has acknowledged that a great deal of information is conveyed through advertising and that while it may not be on the same plane as political speech, it still deserves some degree of protection.

- In order to establish a line between permissible government regulation and rules that would be unconstitutional, the Court created the *Central Hudson* test. The four-part test first asks whether the advertising in question is protected (i.e., a nondeceptive ad for a legal product), and then examines whether the government regulation advances a substantial government interest in a narrowly defined way.

- Originally created to protect businesses from one another, the Federal Trade Commission's role of prohibiting anticompetitive behavior has been expanded to include consumer protection. In effect, deceptive advertising is a form of unfair competition.

- The three criteria for defining deceptive advertising are (1) is the advertisment likely to mislead; (2) does the advertisement deceive a reasonable consumer; (3) could the advertisement be material to a purchasing decision?

- Advertisers who make factual claims about products can be made to substantiate those claims. Opinion enjoys more protection, but sometimes lines between factual statement and opinion can be blurred.

- The FTC assumes that the public is particularly susceptible to testimonial claims,

[60] 16 C.F.R. § 14.15.

especially those made by celebrities. Testimonial claims must be backed by evidence, and celebrities claiming to use a product must actually use it or the ad will be seen as deceptive.

- The FTC has various enforcement tools in its arsenal, ranging from simple warnings in a Staff Advisory Letter up to fines and the requirement that the advertiser run corrective advertising to fix any public misperceptions.

- Advertising can also fall under the jurisdiction of other agencies, including but not limited to the Food and Drug Administration, the Securities and Exchange Commission, and the Federal Communications Commission.

- Advertisers have created a number of self-regulatory schemes to preempt government regulation. The National Advertising Division of the Better Business Bureau investigates misleading advertising claims without involving government action. A number of advertising restrictions that the public believes to be laws are instead self-regulated restrictions.

Is It Advertising or Isn't It?

In the modern age, more and more people turn to the Internet to investigate anyone and everything. Blind dates are no longer "blind" because people going out on them enter their dates' names in a search engine to check their backgrounds (and see pictures). Students turn to websites to check the evaluation of professors before enrolling for their classes. In a legendary story of the power of blogs and social networking, Dell Computers was almost put out of business by bad reviews and revived by the online reaction to the company's renewed responsiveness.

Travel service websites that allow customers to book hotel rooms often provide an opportunity for customers to provide reviews of their experiences. This service can be extremely useful but can be subject to abuse by individuals with an ax to grind. One customer who received poor service might go online and write 10 different reviews under different aliases. Instead of appearing to be one complainer, the critic can look like a whole group of people who have gotten poor service.

Travel service websites might actually be able to limit such problems *if* they limit reviews to only those people who have actually paid for reservations through the service. This would prevent the hypothetical problem stated above, and a few websites do restrict comments in a similar way. But what about websites that have restaurant reviews? Must a restaurant reservation be made through a site in order to post a comment? Most diners don't reserve online and it would drastically reduce the number of reviews if such a system were implemented. The reverse is also possible. What about the likelihood of a restaurant going online and posting false positive reviews about itself?

In 2009, Yelp, a website that provides reviews and recommendations for restaurants, shopping, and entertainment for major cities in North America and Europe, was accused of allowing businesses to "bury" bad reviews by purchasing advertising. Whether the company actually did so is not resolved, but the question remains whether such activity ought to be legal. Can a business diminish the accessibility of criticism by purchasing advertising?

Corporations have learned the power of online reviews and have begun to take advantage of them in new and strategic ways. Popular bloggers have been provided with free products and/or payment to provide reviews of products, often without disclosing that they have received any compensation whatsoever. In broadcast law, this is called payola or plugola and is expressly illegal, but on the web? While most ethicists consider it a clear breach, the law has not caught up. Do we need laws that prohibit "advertising" that is not clearly labeled as advertising? If so, what about product placement in television programs and motion pictures? The credits for those programs usually contain a line for "promotional consideration," but it is usually so small or on the screen for such a short time that audiences have no way of seeing it. ■

Media Business Law

LEARNING OBJECTIVES

After reading this chapter you should know:

- What a contract is, and the elements that make up a legally binding contract

- How release forms act as a sort of contract

- That media professionals often sign labor contracts containing no compete and/or morals clauses and how each clause is exercised

- That media companies are subject to the same antitrust laws as other corporations; the First Amendment is not a shield against the regulation of commerce

- The obligations of media organizations in dealing with labor laws

- Whether corporations have rights of free expression

- Restrictions that exist on the speech of people with "insider information" about publicly traded corporations

Despite the fact that high-profile legal cases dealing with topics such as libel and obscenity get more attention, it is the more routine business affairs of the media that are the subject of day-in, day-out consideration for the companies that own and operate newspapers, television and radio stations, and other American media. Media outlets are businesses and, just like other businesses, are subject to laws regulating commerce. While many of the individual soapbox speakers and pamphleteers may be promoting their ideas, most American media exist to make a profit for the shareholders, and that enterprise involves contracts, government regulations, and labor relations.

In the 1930s the Supreme Court made clear that the laws regulating commerce are applicable to media businesses as well. The National Labor Relations Act (1935) prohibits businesses from firing or otherwise punishing employees who engage in union activity. Morris Watson was an Associated Press (AP) employee who was fired in 1935 for his union involvement. The National Labor Relations Board (NLRB) began an investigation on behalf of Watson, but the AP refused to cooperate, claiming the First Amendment protected it from labor laws. The news wire service argued that subjecting itself to such government scrutiny was a violation of the free press guarantee of the First Amendment. The NLRB even issued a ruling requiring the AP to reinstate Watson but the news organization ignored it, claiming constitutional protection. The U.S. Supreme Court did not accept the AP's argument. It was adamant that media are not above laws regulating businesses. The Supreme Court agreed with the assertion that "[n]ews and intelligence are, in disregard of the First Amendment, treated as ordinary articles of commerce, subject to federal supervision and control." The decision further held:

> The business of the Associated Press is not immune from regulation because it is an agency of the press. The publisher of a newspaper has no special immunity from the application of general laws. He has no special privilege to invade the rights and liberties of others. He must answer for libel. He may be punished for contempt of court. He is subject to the anti-trust laws. Like others he must pay equitable and nondiscriminatory taxes on his business.[1]

As a result, the AP joined the nation in recognizing the right of labor to organize in order to enter into collective bargaining negotiations for its employees.

Entire books are dedicated to the subject of business law, and it is well beyond the scope of this text to try to cover all of business law. Instead we will focus on those business regulations that are specifically relevant to media businesses enterprise and begin with a brief explanation of contract law in America.

> **Bedrock Law:** Laws regulating commerce are applicable to media business as well.

CONTRACTS

A basic understanding of contracts is essential to communication law. Employees often sign contracts when they start work with a media company. Sometimes those contracts contain clauses that impact the employee's personal life, or even that

[1]*Associated Press v. National Labor Relations Bd.*, 301 U.S. 103, 132–33 (1937).

employee's behavior *after* leaving the company. Motion picture studios sign contracts of all sorts: with actors and other "contractors" for their skills, with distribution companies for carriage of their products, and with investors who contribute sizable amounts for the completion of major films. Radio and television stations sign contracts with syndication companies and networks that contain all sorts of stipulations about what will happen if a station does not air a program at the regularly scheduled time, or if the program provider does not deliver the program as promised. What's more, there are occasions when contractual obligations may exist even if there is no contract.

In 1982 Minnesota reporters promised a source, a campaign associate, that they would not reveal the source's identity in a story about a rival candidate for

> **Bedrock Law:** Oral agreements can be as binding as a written contract.

lieutenant governor that featured material about minor offenses. The two newspaper reporters decided that the minor offenses, which resulted in no criminal prosecution, were not much of a news story, but the juicy item was the "smear" campaign being conducted against the candidate by his opposition, who had been given assurance of confidentiality.

Promissory estoppel ■ A statement may be treated as a promise by a court when the listener relied on the statement to her detriment. See § 90 The Restatement (Second) of Contracts.

Both the *Minneapolis Star* and the *St. Paul Pioneer Press* used the source's name, Dan Cohen, in the story. Cohen was subsequently fired from his job. Incensed, he filed a lawsuit, which was decided by the U.S. Supreme Court in 1991.[2] In the 5–4 ruling, the Court did not find the journalists in breach of contract but instead found they had violated state rules of **promissory estoppel**, a doctrine that in essence requires individuals to honor promises they have made if breaking the promise would somehow harm the individual. Although not technically a contractual issue, the Supreme Court did endorse the notion that oral agreements do have the force of law. Media professionals also must honor more formal agreements, which means understanding the basic elements of a contract.

Elements of a Contract

Three conditions must exist in order to have a valid, enforceable contract.[3] They are:

■ Offer, ————————> MENTALLY CAPABLE
■ Consideration, and
■ Acceptance.

Offer ■ A specific promise, conditional on acceptance, that is communicated with the intent of forming the terms of a contract.

An **offer** is very simply one individual or corporation of sound mind voluntarily agreeing to provide goods or services to a second party. Note that there are a couple of qualifications. A person must be mentally capable of entering into a contract in order for it to be binding. Suppose a friend offers to sell you his car for a certain amount of money. As long as he is mentally capable (not drunk or a child) and has not been forced to make the offer, the first condition of the contract has been met. Now you may not like his offer, in which case you'd simply ignore it or explicitly reject it. Perhaps you think the price is too high, and instead offer a lower

---

[2]*Cowles v. Cohen*, 501 U.S. 663 (1991).

[3]It can be argued that there are more than three, and in fact some legal texts list more. The Texas Building and Procurement Commission, for example, lists six on its website.

amount. You have made a **counter-offer**, which in effect is a new offer. Now it is up to your friend to decide whether to accept or refuse your offer. Either of you might choose to **revoke** the offer before the contract is completed. For example, if someone came along and offered him more money for the car before you had accepted the offer, he would be able to retract it. Now if someone offered him more money *after* you both had a contract, it would be too late to retract the offer. Once all three elements are met, both of you would have to agree on the retraction or the terms of your contract could be enforced.

Consideration involves some sort of compensation for the goods or services provided. If the offer is to buy his car with cash, money is the consideration. Money is the most common form of consideration in contracts but there are other exchanges that can take place. He might offer to give you his car in exchange for mowing his lawn for one year. Regardless, there must be some kind of consideration exchanged. Otherwise, if he simply promises to give you his car and then changes his mind, there has been no **breach of contract** because there was never a valid contract to begin with. The worst you would be able to say is that he broke his word to you, but *not* that he violated a contract.

Acceptance is your agreement to accept his offer. Acceptance can be **express** (signing the written contract, shaking hands, or saying "It's a deal"), **implied** (as would be the case if you said something like "I'll bring the money tomorrow"), or **conditional**. Conditional acceptance means you accept the offer if certain other conditions are met. This happens in real estate contracts where people agree to buy a home provided they are able to sell their current home, or provided that certain repairs are made to the property.

Once a contract is accepted it may be tough to get out of it, even if conditions change. The well-known actress Brooke Shields found that a contract her mother signed when she was a minor was still enforceable, even though Brooke had become an adult and wanted to rescind the contract.[4] Brooke's mother had signed a contract with a photographer that granted him the use of photos taken of Brooke as a child. When she became a young woman she attempted to stop use of the photos through repeated legal action and, though successful in preventing their use in pornographic publications, she was unable to completely invalidate the existing agreement.

Offer, consideration, and acceptance constitute a legally enforceable contract. The contract need not be written, although it is in both parties' interests for the terms of the agreement to be in writing. If it's not written, how does anyone prove exactly what the terms of the contract were? A court battle is likely to involve a lot of allegations about what each person thought with little evidence to prove either argument. A vivid example of this occurred with the children's video series *VeggieTales*. Lyrick Studios was licensed by Big Idea to distribute the cartoon. A series of telephone conversations and faxes went back and forth but no formal signed contract existed. When Lyrick tried to sue Big Idea for issues including rights to DVD distribution (Lyrick had been distributing VHS tapes) and stuffed animals, a federal appeals court ruled that no contract existed.[5] There's a joke among lawyers that an oral contract is not worth the paper it's written on.

Counter-offer ■ A conditional promise in response to an offer that changes the terms of the original offer, and thus requires acceptance.

Revoke ■ Revocation of the offer by the offeree before acceptance.

Consideration ■ Each party must receive something of value for the mutual promises to be enforceable as a contract. Money, goods, and services are the most common form of consideration, but it can take many forms and need not have any monetary value.

Breach of contract ■ A legal cause of action based on damages resulting from the failure of a party to a contract to perform according to its terms.

Acceptance ■ An offeree's assent to the terms of an offer by the means specified or expected by the offeror.

Express acceptance ■ Acceptance that is evident based on the explicit statements of the offeree.

---

[4]*Shields v. Gross*, 58 N.Y.2d 338 (1983).

[5]Brooks Boliek, *"VeggieTales" Off Justices' Menu*, Hollywood Reporter, Apr. 4, 2006, at 4.

Bedrock Law: Three elements define a contract—an offer that is based on some form of compensation that is accepted by at least two parties.

Implied acceptance
■ Acceptance that is only evident due to context, rather than explicitly stated by the offeree.

Conditional acceptance ■ A conditional acceptance, where the offeree's acceptance is conditioned upon a change in the terms, is not acceptance. It is a counter-offer.

Bedrock Law: If one of the participants does not fulfill the obligations of a contract, then a breach has occurred that can result in a court order.

A breach of contract occurs if one of the parties does not fulfill the agreed-to terms. A breach doesn't always result in legal action, though. Sometimes a breach of contract might be considered so trivial as to be immaterial. If the contract for selling your friend's car stated his mileage was 100,000 miles and he delivered the car to you with 100,001 miles on the odometer, then that would be considered an immaterial breach. Strictly interpreted he would be violating the agreed-to conditions of the contract but the breach would be so inconsequential that it would not invalidate the deal.

A material breach of contract might result in a legal order. If he refused to sell the car to you because he got a better offer, a court might require him to sell the car to you at the agreed-to price. If he breached the contract by selling you the car with 200,000 miles on it rather than the stipulated 100,000 miles, the court might require him to give you your money back or adjust the price appropriately. Rather than spend all the money on taking a breach of contract to court, many times the dispute will be resolved by a mediator or through arbitration. Essentially these routes require an independent third party to negotiate with the people involved and find the necessary resolution. Arbitrators can be found in the yellow pages of the phone book in most major cities.

Releases as a Contract

Most people are familiar with a simple release form. As a child you probably had to bring one home for your parents to sign so that you could participate in a class field trip. It was intended to release from liability the school, teacher, and bus driver should anything happen to you on the class trip. The release served two different functions: It assured the school that your parents knew and approved of you going with the class, and it also prevented any lawsuits should anything unexpected occur on the trip.[6]

Release forms are used by motion picture studios, advertisers, and video producers to obtain permission for the use of people's images in their work. Someone shooting a television commercial at a grocery store must be certain to have a release form signed by everyone who appears in that commercial, otherwise people later may be able to claim that they were used without their consent and as such have a right to compensation, or even the right to have the commercial removed from the air. In order to prevent this, producers have everyone sign a release form that specifically states their willingness to appear in the commercial.

In the typical release form, offer, consideration, and acceptance are easy to see. The producer invites the participation of those who appear in the commercial, their acceptance is in writing on the release form, and consideration is offered in the form of a payment. But what about those occasions when individuals agree to appear in an advertisement or some other commercial use of their image without

---

[6] These releases are actually quite limited in protecting the school from liability. If the bus driver had an accident in which you were injured and it was determined that the driver had been drinking, the release would not likely protect the school from a lawsuit given the extenuating circumstance of his actions.

getting any compensation? Does this mean the signed release form is not a contract? Not necessarily. Frequently student filmmakers will involve friends, family, and other volunteers as actors in their films without any payment. While some universities pay students for the use of their image in brochures, on websites, and in other promotional material, others do not. A properly worded release form will state that consideration is being received in some other way. For example, the University of Texas's Talent Release Form begins, "For valuable consideration."[7] The University of Nevada, Las Vegas, Photo Release Form states "I hereby grant permission . . . without further consideration."[8] In these and many other instances, the wording is such as to imply some form of existing consideration. It can be legitimately argued that there is a value in having one's image used in an advertisement. A student with no modeling experience can gain portfolio examples by being included in advertisements. Aspiring actors can add lines to their résumés.

There are actually times when a signed release form may not exist but a producer or photographer can show that an individual had **implied consent**. In other words, the person whose image is being used obviously knew the image was going to be used and voiced no objections. For example, if you were making a video about your university and interviewed fellow students about the reasons they chose to attend your school, you might assert that by voluntarily sitting down in a video studio with you and answering your questions, they were implying their consent to appear in the video. Obviously they knew they were being taped. It might be arguable whether they knew how the video would be used, and that's why a signed release form outlining the use of the video (or providing blanket permission to use the video in any way) is always better than trying to assert implied consent. If you had told students that you were making a video for classroom use and then the video ended up in a national TV commercial, your claim of implied consent would not work because what they had consented to and what you used it for were two different things. It's a lot easier to assert implied consent in a situation such as the taping of a television talk show, where the actual use of the video is well known. Members of the studio audience for *Oprah*, for example, know before going in that they may appear on television. They could not later claim that the producers did not have their permission to use their picture.

Implied consent ■ A sometimes controversial form of consent that is not evident from a person's express statements, but from circumstances. For example, all licensed drivers in the United States have implied their consent to a field sobriety test.

Bedrock Law: The use of a person's image or persona for commercial purposes requires either implied or stated consent, as in a written release.

Labor Contracts

It can be very intimidating to be given a multipage contract when being hired for your first job after college, but this is the situation many graduates find themselves in when joining media corporations. This is especially true for those people who will have on-air positions in large markets, but it is becoming more the norm in smaller markets, as well as for news producers and people in sales and advertising. There are a couple of clauses in particular that are of special interest in media labor contracts.

---

[7]University of Texas System Office of General Counsel, http://www.utsystem.edu/ogc/intellectualProperty/contract/release.htm.

[8]University of Nevada, Las Vegas, http://web.unlv.edu/pdf/photo-release.pdf.

No compete clauses ■ A clause in a contract which prevents a person, often an employee, who has learned trade secrets or skills, or company from competing after employment terminates.

No compete clauses are rooted in the principle of protecting businesses from unfair competition.[9] They have traditionally been used when individuals have sold their businesses. The buyer wants to be sure that the seller won't simply turn around immediately after selling the business and begin a new company doing the very same thing and probably "stealing" all the clients from his former company. The buyer agrees not to compete in that business for a specified length of time.

In labor contracts, no compete clauses are conditions added to a contract by an employer to prevent employees from taking jobs with a competitor. The most common example of this is where scientists have been working on a formula for a particular company, or computer programmers have worked on some cutting-edge software. The no compete clauses in their contracts keep them from taking to a competitor the fruits of what they have been working on (and getting paid for) for months or perhaps years. In media, a no compete clause for labor is common for local on-air talent contracts. For example, imagine the news anchor at the ABC-affiliated television station in your city getting an offer for more money from the CBS-affiliated television station. In other professions it might not matter, but in TV news, that station has invested significant resources in promoting that anchor's image. The ABC station probably has billboards all around town advertising the news team. The station may have run ads in the local newspaper or *TV Guide*. A major reason the CBS station now wants to hire this anchor is because of the recognition the person has in the community: recognition created by the ABC station. A no compete clause in the contract would prohibit the anchor from appearing on the air on a competitor's station. There are two important stipulations. No compete agreements must be for a limited duration and scope. Most no compete clauses in labor contracts extend six to twelve months.[10] In our hypothetical example, the ABC station could prohibit the anchor from appearing on the air of one of the competing stations for up to a year *after* ending his/her employment with the station. A Massachusetts case invalidated a no compete clause for a television station employee because the three-year covenant was considered by the court to be too long.[11]

Employees are often shocked to find that no compete clauses can be enforced even beyond their employment. It seems extremely unfair to them that an employer can control their fate even after they no longer work for the company, but that may be the case. What's worse, imagine a scenario where an individual has been fired by a station. The station has essentially said it believes the employee is no longer of use to the company. Is the no compete clause still enforceable? Much to the chagrin of the employees, the no compete is still enforceable. Imagine from a management perspective a situation where this is not the case. An employee gets a better offer from a competitor, but there is a no compete clause in the contract. If the employee can get out of a no compete clause by getting fired, the employee might purposefully do a poor job, be lazy, or even stop coming to work just to get fired, at which

---

[9]A good survey article is Note: *Switching Stations: The Battle over Non-Compete Agreements in the Broadcasting Industry*, 27 Okla. City U. L. Rev. 693 (2002).

[10]There is at least one instance of a court upholding a two-year no compete agreement in broadcasting, but this is rare. *Murray v. Lowndes County Broadcasting*, 284 S.E.2d 10 (Ga. 1981). Generally media contracts contain no competes of 12 months or less.

[11]*Richmond Bros. v. Westinghouse Broadcasting*, 256 N.E. 2d 304 (Mass. 1970).

point the employee would be free to accept a higher salary from the competitor. For whatever reason, no competes are enforceable even beyond the term of employment (for a limited time).

A no compete clause also must be limited in scope. An anchor can't be prevented from taking *all* jobs with competing TV stations, just those on-air.[12] If an anchor were to take a job with a competitor as a station manager the no compete clause would not likely apply. There are many instances where on-air talent from a newscast (news, weather, or sports) has been hired by a competitor and been allowed to work in that department but has been unable to appear on-camera until the expiration of the no compete period. A TV meteorologist hired by a competitor might work on the forecasts, build the weather graphics seen on the air, update the station website, etc., until the time restriction has passed, and then join the newscast. It also would be difficult for a station to enforce a no compete clause for a local anchor moving to another market. A New York television station would not be able to use a no compete clause to stop an anchor from taking a job in Los Angeles. An Atlanta radio station tried to enforce a no compete clause to prevent an employee from working on a competitor's air not only locally, but in any other market where the owner had stations. A court invalidated the no compete clause as unreasonable since the geographical restriction went beyond what was necessary to protect the station's interests.[13]

With media personalities recognized nationally, no compete clauses are not usually an issue. Perhaps because trying to enforce a no compete clause nationwide is too grand in scope, or perhaps because the celebrity status of national media personalities allows them the negotiating power to refuse to sign a contract with a no compete clause, national media outlets generally do not have no compete clauses in contracts with national celebrities.[14] It is true that they sometimes have exclusivity clauses (prohibiting personalities from appearing on competing airwaves) but those only exist while the celebrity is employed with them.

In contracts with salespeople, the scope of the no compete clause might actually cross different media. The reason for no compete clauses for salespeople is that people in sales have clients they have developed, so moving to a new job would allow them to take the client list they have developed with them, and that too would mean effectively "stealing" business from their former employer. The logic is similar to that where those selling their businesses agree not to compete for a certain amount of time. Someone selling advertising for a television station could actually cultivate those same clients to buy advertising on radio stations, or in newspapers, or even billboards and telephone books. A no compete clause could

---

[12] It may even be more narrow than that. A Pittsburgh newscaster left her job for a public relations job with an in-home walking company. She claims her no compete prevents her from doing news, not a "healthy lifestyle" program. *See* Rob Owen, *KDKA's Antkowiak Prepares to Walk Away from News Desk*, Pittsburgh Post-Gazette, Apr. 21, 2006, at C-5.

[13] *Wake v. Crawford*, 114 S.E. 2d 26 (Ga. 1960).

[14] Exceptions exist. Financial reporter and analyst Lou Dobbs said he had a no compete clause in his contract with CNN. Andrea Thompson left *NYPD Blue* to work in news for a New Mexico television station, then on to CNN. After leaving CNN she said she was under no compete restrictions. *TV Notes*, Pittsburgh Post-Gazette, Jan. 21, 2003, at B-4.

be written to prevent employees from taking sales jobs with any of these potential competitors.

One of the newer labor groups to find no compete clauses in their contracts has been television news producers. They are not seen like anchors, nor do they have client lists that they have cultivated, but they do have sources and skills that were acquired at the station. The media companies claim the need for no compete clauses for news producers is due to the wealth of contacts and resources the producers develop. It would be a disadvantage to stations if those sources could be taken from them to a competitor. A cynic might assert that the real reason producers are now seeing no compete clauses in contracts is because there is a shortage of news producers, and stations do not want to have to get into a bidding war to attract or keep competent ones. Regardless of the reason, no competes are increasing in the media professions.

As might be expected, no compete clauses are seen as unfair by most labor groups, and they have been effective at getting some states to pass legislation to prohibit them, or restrict them to only encompassing trade secrets.[15] Massachusetts, Arizona, and Maine have labor laws to prohibit no compete clauses in the broadcast profession.[16] Illinois has passed a statute that specifically prohibits no compete clauses in broadcast contracts, although the restriction does not include sales or management staff.[17] California prohibits any contract "by which anyone is restrained from engaging in a lawful profession, trade or business of any kind."[18] Such a rule would prohibit stations from enforcing a no compete clause against a news anchor, who could continue to draw a living from their recognized persona, or celebrity status at another station in the market.

Bedrock Law: No compete clauses in media contracts must be for a limited time period and within a reasonable geographic area to be enforceable.

We are a celebrity-conscious culture, and celebrity status is worth a great deal of money in our society. There are some athletes who earn more money from endorsements and personal appearances than they actually do from the sport itself. In 1999, Tiger Woods signed a five-year deal with Nike for $100 million. That was only *one* of his endorsement deals. Whenever a new motion picture is released, the stars will appear on television talk shows to promote the film (it's the *only* time some stars will agree to do talk shows). The studios know that the promotional value of those personal appearances will affect the box office. Radio and television personalities attract audiences to parades and local charity events. Because the image of these individuals is so important to the media companies they represent, most of them have a **morals clause** in their contract.

Morals clause ■ A provision in a contract that prohibits specific behavior in a party's private life.

Morals clauses in contracts hold individuals responsible for any behavior that may damage their reputation, and thus effect the reputation of the media company or product with which they are associated. In 2003, when basketball star Kobe Bryant was accused of sexually assaulting a hotel worker, he lost $11.5 million in

---

[15] An excellent reference for checking the specific laws for any state is Brian Malsberger, *Covenant Not to Compete: A State-By-State Survey* (BNA Books 2005).

[16] Mass. Gen. Laws ch. 149, § 186 (West 1998); Ariz. Rev. Stat. § 23-494 tit. 23 (Lexis 2005); Me. Rev. Stat. Ann. tit. 26, § 599(2) (West 1999).

[17] Broadcast Industry Free Market Act, 820 Ill. Comp. Stat. 17/10 (2002).

[18] Cal. Bus. & Prof. Code § 16600 (West 2001).

endorsement deals, including $5 million from Coca-Cola. Note that the contracts only require a reputation to be damaged, so even before a trial occurs or even if someone is found innocent of wrongdoing, a company can claim that allegations are enough to result in a canceled contract. Celebrities accused of wrongdoing are "damaged goods" and less likely to attract consumers to the products they endorse.

Broadcast companies are especially concerned about the image of their high-profile employees. NBC fired famed sports announcer Marv Albert in 1997 after he pleaded guilty to sexual assault charges. Michael Nader was an actor on the soap opera *All My Children*. In 2001 he was arrested for selling cocaine and ABC terminated his contract. Nader attempted to have his contract reinstated by claiming he was being discriminated against, but the courts upheld the morals clause of his contract.

On a local level, many broadcast stations have morals clauses in the contracts with their on-air staff. If a newsperson gets drunk at a bar and causes a disturbance, stations argue that the audience will lose respect both for the person involved and the station for which he or she works. Celebrities (and local broadcast talent) must

The clause in Michael Nader's contract that resulted in his termination from *All My Children* is fairly typical. It read:

If, in the opinion of ABC, Artist shall commit any act or do anything which might tend to bring Artist into public disrepute, contempt, scandal, or ridicule, or which might tend to reflect unfavorably on ABC, any sponsor of a program, any such sponsor's advertising agency, any stations broadcasting or scheduled to broadcast a program, or any licensee of ABC, or to injure the success of any use of the Series or any program, ABC may, upon written notice to Artist, immediately terminate the Term and Artist's employment hereunder. In the event ABC terminates Artist's services pursuant to the provisions of this Paragraph, ABC shall be discharged from all obligations hereunder by making any and all payments earned and payable on account of services performed by Artist prior to such date of termination. The guarantee, if any, applicable to the cycle in which such termination is effective shall be automatically reduced to the number of programs produced in such cycle and on which Artist rendered services prior to the effective date of such termination. In addition to whatever other right ABC may have, ABC may also remove Artist's credit, if any, from all such programs on which such credit may have appeared.*

* *Nader v. ABC Television*, Inc., 330 F.Supp. 2d 345, 346 (S.D. N.Y. 2004), *aff'd* 150 Fed. Appx. 54 (2d Cir. 2005).

▎ Sample Morals Clause

recognize that their actions are subject to scrutiny, even while not at work, and even if miles away from home. In 2003 a Youngstown, Ohio, newscaster was vacationing in the Florida Keys after recovering from a serious illness. In her celebration she participated in a wet T-shirt contest and eventually was photographed completely naked. She resigned when pictures of her started showing up on the Internet. Local radio and television celebrities commonly have morals clauses in their contracts and may have their contracts terminated—not just for illegal activities but for embarrassing behavior as well.

Hold-Harmless Clauses

Hold-harmless clause ■ A provision in a contract where one party agrees not to hold the other party responsible for any damages. This is a unilateral indemnification of one party by another, but it can be reciprocal among multiple parties.

In certain outlets of the media—advertising and public relations, for example—an employment contract can make a discernible difference in terms of how vulnerable the employee is to a corporate lawsuit. In the realm of public relations, there are safeguards—indemnification, or **hold-harmless** clauses—that essentially free the professional from personal responsibility should a harmful company release be approved by higher executives. Such fine print in an employee's contract relies on mutual and informed assent by both the boss and the practitioner. It also will not be worth the paper it is printed on if the terms shift the burden of responsibility to the weaker party in the deal.

MEDIA AND ANTITRUST

Nothing in the U.S. Constitution says anything about the ownership of media, but there are a number of federal regulations that control media ownership. The issues only became contentious in the twentieth century as media conglomerates grew and some people feared undue control of the marketplace of ideas by only a few voices. As noted at the beginning of this chapter, media are subject to the laws of commerce, which include prohibitions against antitrust violations.

Sherman Act ■ United States federal law passed in 1890 that prohibits monopolistic behavior by businesses and has been used to break up a number of powerful monopolies or near-monopolies, such as Standard Oil.

In 1890 Congress passed the **Sherman Act** in an attempt to prohibit the growing concentration of economic power. The Act prohibits monopolistic behavior by businesses and has been used to break up a number of powerful monopolies or near-monopolies, such as Standard Oil in the early twentieth century. The Sherman Act and its progeny (the Clayton Anti-trust Act of 1914) prohibit behavior that encourages the monopolization of a market, but not all behavior. For example, if there are three newspapers in a community, one of them may be able to drive out the other two newspapers by doing a better job of covering the news, or by lowering the price of the newspaper, or by providing superior customer service. All of these might drive out competition but none would be illegal.[19] On the other hand, if two of the newspapers colluded to lower their price that would be illegal. It might appear at first that the consumer would benefit—after all, two of the three newspapers would decrease in price. Competitors are prohibited from colluding with one another because the result is likely to be less competition. By lowering their prices, the two newspapers

---

[19]In fact, lowering the price of the newspaper *could* be a violation of antitrust regulations if the price drop were determined to be predatory pricing. But that discussion is beyond the scope of this text.

could successfully drive out the third competitor, at which time the two papers might actually raise their prices with no existing competition.

Throughout much of the 1930s and 1940s, the Lorain *Journal* was the only daily newspaper in Lorain, Ohio. The mere fact that it operated a monopoly was not illegal. The paper had done nothing to cause the single-newspaper market in which it found itself. In 1948, a new radio station entered the market, and WEOL threatened to be a true competitor for the *Journal*. The newspaper decided to take drastic action. It instituted a policy of refusing to accept advertising from anyone who also purchased advertising from WEOL. The *Journal* hoped to force advertisers to choose between the two competitors and as the dominant medium in the market, the newspaper expected to be the overwhelming choice. Recognize that generally there is no law against refusing to accept advertising. In most cases the result is a loss of revenue for the medium and there may be more harm to the medium than the advertiser. The newspaper attempted to defend itself in court with that very argument: that it had the right to decide whether or not to sell advertising to anyone. In this situation, however, the purpose of refusing to sell the advertising was to encourage the monopolization of the market. In court several Lorain County businesses testified that they stopped advertising on WEOL or never started due to the policy. When the case was appealed to the highest court, the unanimous decision held that the actions of the newspaper were a violation of antitrust law because it was a blatant effort to monopolize the market.[20]

In 1940, the only two Tucson, Ariz., daily newspapers decided to enter into an agreement that would allow them to compete in some ways and cooperate in others. The *Star* and the *Citizen* each maintained autonomy in the news and editorial departments but agreed to pool their resources on the business side, combining the papers' production, distribution, and advertising departments. In doing so they were able to reduce their expenses while still maintaining two different voices in the marketplace of ideas. The plan was successful, as combined profits for the newspapers grew from $27,000 in 1940 to nearly $2 million by 1964. After the government claimed the agreement violated antitrust laws, the Supreme Court ruled in 1969 that some forms of joint operations might be permissible but that provisions for price fixing, market control, and profit pooling were monopolistic and illegal.[21]

In part as a reaction to the Supreme Court decision, Congress passed the Newspaper Preservation Act in 1970. At the time of the *Citizen Publishing* decision, there were 22 joint newspaper operating agreements in various cities across the country. The fear was that if all of these agreements were found to be antitrust violations and dissolved, some newspapers might go out of business. Congress tried to protect these failing newspapers through the Newspaper Preservation Act. The rationale behind it was that if a community could not fully support two competing newspapers, the marketplace of ideas would be better off if they were allowed to cooperate in some ways rather than having one of them cease to exist. As long as both publications maintained independent voices it might be worth relaxing antitrust rules to allow for this exception. Since Congress created the

---

[20]*Lorain Journal v. United States*, 342 U.S. 143 (1951).

[21]*Citizen Publishing v. United States*, 394 U.S. 131 (1969).

antitrust rules they certainly had the authority to fashion an exception. The law has many critics. They assert that if newspapers are entitled to their very own Act of Congress to create an exception to antitrust rules others should be able to receive similar exemptions. Some feel that the Act actually achieves the opposite of its intended purpose by keeping a "marginal" newspaper afloat and by blocking other potential market entrants that might be able to survive on their own. In 2011 there were six remaining Joint Operating Agreements: the one involving the two Tucson papers ended in 2009 when the *Tucson Citizen* folded.

There are actually other instances where Congress has exempted businesses from antitrust rules. While the Newspaper Preservation Act helps media companies, the exemption provided for professional sports does not. National television broadcasts of sports were still in the early stages in 1961 when Congress passed the antitrust exemption that allows professional sports leagues to enforce blackouts on telecasts.[22] Without this exemption, the NFL would not be able to dictate that neither television stations nor cable operators may provide a live telecast of a game within that market unless that game was sold out by seventy-two hours before game time.

LABOR LAWS

Newspaper Carriers

If one of the lessons from this chapter is that the First Amendment is not a shield to protect media from the same laws for operating businesses that other companies must follow, then how do we reconcile the law concerning newspaper carriers? Most states have laws that

- Establish a minimum age for workers,
- Establish a minimum wage for workers,
- Require employers to provide workers' compensation in case employees are injured on the job, and
- Prevent employers from making employees work seven days a week.

And yet, when it comes to the person who delivers the daily newspaper, none of these rules seem to be enforced. The person who delivers the morning paper might be only thirteen years old (below the minimum age), earn less than the standard hourly wage, have no insurance, and be expected to deliver the newspaper each and every day, Sundays and holidays included (with no extra holiday pay). So, how could this happen?

The answer is that the newspapers do not actually *employ* the person who delivers the newspaper. That individual is actually seen as an independent contractor who has entered into a contractual arrangement to provide a service to the newspaper. In at least one instance a state has found that newspaper carriers had to be treated like employees regardless of the fact that the contract they signed stated they were independent contractors.[23] Yet in many other states newspaper carriers

---

[22]15 U.S.C. § 1291.

[23]*News Carriers Are Employees for Unemployment Purposes, Kentucky High Court Says*, 13 Ky. Emp. L. Letter, March 2003. http://sandulligraceonline.com/?p=118

are still treated as independent contractors, and courts in Minnesota,[24] Kansas,[25] Illinois,[26] and Florida[27] have endorsed the arrangement.

Child Actors

What about using underage children in movies and television shows? Why doesn't that violate child labor laws? The simple answer is that states create special rules just for child actors.

A lot of labor law is created at the state level, so you might expect that states where movies are most frequently produced would be the ones that have labor laws specific to the video industry. California undoubtedly has the most extensive guidelines regarding the use of children in movies and TV. The laws specify the working hours and conditions that are permissible. In most cases, special permission must be granted from the state to employ especially young children: those too young to obtain work permits. The hours a child may work are usually set on a sliding scale: older children are permitted to work longer hours. In California, for example, infants (six months of age or less) may only be allowed to be present at the work site for two hours, but may actually *work* no more than 20 minutes per day. Older children may work as long as eight hours per day. This is the reason why identical twins are so often hired for film and television production. When production began on the TV series *Full House* in 1987, Mary-Kate and Ashley Olsen shared the acting duties for their character, Michelle Tanner. This enabled the producers to use each girl the allotted amount of time, yet double the amount of time they were able to shoot with "Michelle." In addition, school-aged children must be provided with a teacher at the work site.

One other labor law specific to children in this industry was enacted in California in the late 1930s. Jackie Coogan was a famous child actor who appeared in a number of short films and features with major stars, such as Charlie Chaplin. By the time he was an adult he had appeared in more than 20 films and would have had a handsome bankroll as a result except that his parents would not give him the money. A court decision upheld the right of the parents to keep his earnings. An outraged California legislature passed a law requiring any producer using child actors to pay at least 15 percent of the child's fee to a trust account, which only can be accessed by the child himself once he becomes of legal age. The law is referred to by the Hollywood community as "Coogan's Law."

[24]Barbara Jones, *Accidents Involving Newspaper Carriers Present Thorny Issues*, The Minn. Lawyer, April 10, 2006. http://www.accessmylibrary.com/coms2/summary_0286-14878393_ITM.

[25]*Contractual Exclusion from Benefits Plan Upheld*, 4 N.M. Emp. L. Letter, Aug. 1998.

[26]*Circuit Court Held That Newspaper Carrier Was Independent Contractor*, 5 Ill. Workers Compensation L. Bull., May 19, 1997. http://www.pa-newspaper.org/web/2005/10/independent_contractors_newspaper_handbook.aspx.

[27]*First DCA Held That Newspaper Carrier Was Independent Contractor*, 1 Fla. Workers Compensation L. Bull., June 26, 1995. http://www.poynerspruill.com/publications/Pages/IndependentContractororEmployeeRecentCourtOpinionsProvideGuidance.aspx.

Equal Employment Opportunities

Congress has created federal legislation requiring employers to provide equal employment opportunities (EEO). As a practical matter this prohibits businesses from making hiring or firing decisions based on race, gender, color, creed, or national origin. In addition to such general laws applying to all businesses, specific regulations exist governing electronic media.[28]

EEO laws are *not* quota requirements. No court would allow a law requiring a percentage of employees to be of a certain gender or race to stand. EEO requires *opportunities*, and what is critical in cases involving broadcasters is whether there have been opportunities available to learn about job openings and apply for them. Broadcasters and multichannel video providers (like cable and satellite TV systems) are required to take affirmative action to be certain that information about vacancies in their business is widely disseminated. It is not enough to simply post a job in the local newspaper, but the law requires becoming more proactive by reaching out to underrepresented persons through minority channels. For example, Hispanics might be more likely to read a Spanish-language publication than a general circulation daily newspaper. The FCC advises electronic media to provide notice of all full-time job openings to recruiting organizations and *widely* distribute the information, which would include multiple publications, local educational institutions, and on-air announcements. What's more, employers are expected to conduct "recruitment initiatives," including job fairs, internship programs, and other community events. Beyond ethnic concerns, media enterprises must be aware of other legal issues regarding employee discrimination.

There have been a few high-profile cases where on-air talent at television stations claimed they were discriminated against because of their age. The case that received the most attention was that of Christine Craft, a TV news anchor at KMBC in Kansas City. The station removed her from the anchor chair, allegedly because she was "too old, too unattractive and not deferential to men." Craft filed a discrimination suit against the station and was originally awarded $500,000 by a federal district court jury.[29] A federal district court judge set aside that award, and a second jury reduced the figure to $325,000.[30] However, the Eighth Circuit Court of Appeals overturned the verdict and Craft received nothing.[31] The Supreme Court refused to hear the case.[32]

Craft's suit may have been the most publicized but it is certainly not the only example. Deserved or not, television news has a reputation for being more accepting of "mature" looking men than it is of older-appearing women. In most cases, as Metromedia argued with Craft, stations provide research data to show that the women being removed or demoted have lost some of their appeal to audiences. Is it discrimination for a station to remove an anchor who has lost the ability to

---

[28]See, for example, 47 C.F.R. § 22.321.

[29]William MacDougall, *Ahead: Rising Role for Women in TV News*, U.S. News & World Report, Aug. 22, 1983, at 56.

[30]*In the News*, 5 Entertainment Law Reporter, Dec. 1983.

[31]*Craft v. Metromedia*, 766 F.2d 1205 (8th Cir. 1985).

[32]*Craft v. Metromedia*, 475 U.S. 1058 (1986), *cert. denied*.

attract an audience? There have been instances where women have won discrimination suits against stations. Sara Lee Kessler won a $7 million judgment against WWOR-TV in New York in 1999.[33] In many instances stations and anchorwomen have reached settlements without having to go to court, reducing the embarrassment and legal costs for both sides.

LABOR UNIONS

The misery of the Great Depression led to the organization of labor unions to protect members from abuses at the hands of their employers. These groups represent media professionals in contract disputes and other negotiations. The National Labor Relations Act (§ 7) gave American employees "the right to form, join or assist labor organizations, to bargain collectively through representatives of their own choosing, and to engage in other concerted activities for the purpose of collective bargaining or other mutual aid or protection."[34]

Four labor unions organize employees in the media, the National Association of Broadcast Employees and Technicians (NABET), which joined with the Communications Workers of America (CWA) in 1994; the American Federation of Television Radio Artists (AFTRA); the Screen Actors Guild (SAG); and the International Alliance of Theatrical Stage Employees (IATSE). They tend to be more active in states where right-to-work legislation has not been adopted. These include twenty-two states located predominantly in the South and Midwest—so-called red states based on their conservative voting patterns. Typical of the right-to-work statutes common to these states is the one adopted in Louisiana: "No personal shall be required as a condition of employment to become or remain a member of any labor organization, or to pay any dues, fees, assessments, or other charges of any kind to a labor organization."[35]

Pro-labor states, such as Illinois, take a different tack. When the owners of a Chicago Spanish-language station, WSNS, resisted organizing efforts among station employees, the state senate intervened. The Illinois lawmakers authorized a resolution that essentially told the Chicago broadcaster to "negotiate in good faith" with its employees, but AFTRA's local executive was more blunt. "It's time for NBC and Telemundo to recognize the fact that Spanish-language employees have earned the right to the same quality of benefits and working conditions as English-language employees."[36]

This is not the only example of labor negotiations that encountered friction. Spanish-language media workers began planning for collective bargaining rights at a Miami television station, when one of the leading union advocates was dismissed from his job. AFTRA's Executive Director in Miami, Herta Suarez, said that others had been threatened with dismissal, and that employees had been forced to work

---

[33]Kessler's suit includes charges of discrimination based on age, gender, religion, and disability. Ann Beck, *An Age-Old Problem*, Broadcasting & Cable, Oct. 31, 2005, at 12.

[34]National Labor Relations Act, 29 U.S.C. at § 157

[35]La. Rev. Stat. Ann. § 22:983 (1976).

[36]Roger Feder, *Tracking: Senate Takes Sides*, Chicago Sun Times, June 8, 2005, *available at* http://www.findarticles.com.

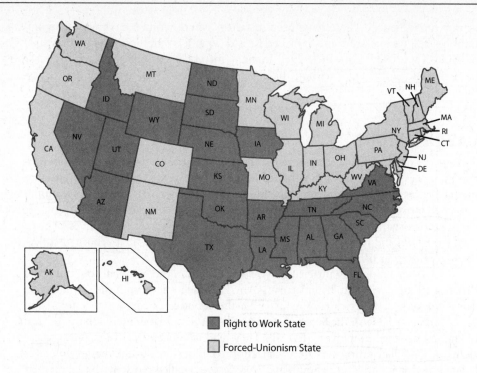

■ Right to Work State

□ Forced-Unionism State

without breaks for meals. The union also observed that there were no basic benefits written into employee contracts.[37]

Union groups have been struggling at some major media outlets. In January 2006, NBC News anchors and correspondents voted to sever ties with AFTRA and decertify their representation. It did not take long for the network management to praise the outcome of the vote. "We are grateful for the trust our employees have placed in the company," said the NBC News release. Conceding defeat, the union simply said, "we wish all NBC News broadcasters the best of luck and look forward to the day when they will again be part of the community of AFTRA's broadcast journalists."[38] At PBS, a majority of the members of the National Association of Broadcast Employees and Technicians-Communications Workers of America (NABET-CWA) approved a separate contract with the network after negotiations reached an impasse. Meanwhile, National Public Radio's largest union, AFTRA, claimed NPR violated its contract by assigning new technical duties to its members without union approval. Some of the changes were due to the transition to digital editing, which eliminated exclusive union responsibility over audio technician work. Basically it boiled down to whether union engineers would be the only ones who were allowed to mix the sounds heard on *All Things Considered* and programs like it. AFTRA leaders argued that NPR producers would have to spend

---

[37]*Spanish-language Media Workers Seek Union Representation at Miami's America TeVe Channel 41,* Shoptalk, newsletter@TVspy.com, Aug. 12, 2005.

[38]Jesse Hiestand and Paul J. Gough *NBC News Parts Ways with Union,* Hollywood Reporter, *republished in* Shoptalk, newsletter@TVspy.com, 1 Aug. 16, 2006.

more of their time technically mixing and recording the sounds of stories at the expense of writing and reporting them.

Unions also have been diligent in their fight against no compete clauses. AFTRA's leaders were given credit for outlawing such contractual obligations in the states of

---

▶ UP CLOSE

1893 IATSE)

Media Labor Organizations

Of the four national unions representing broadcasters and media workers, the oldest one is the International Alliance of Theatrical Stage Employees (IATSE), which was founded in 1893 and chartered by the American Federation of Labor. Originally, IATSE joined stagehands of the theater with cinema projectionists to bargain collectively with their managers over job contracts. In the years since, IATSE has opened local shops for film and television technicians and producers of audio/visuals and computer graphics at casinos, conventions, and industrial shows. It claims to have achieved some of the highest wages and best working conditions for its employees by keeping up with technical innovations and by "vigorously pursuing a policy of organizing non-union workers."

The National Association of Broadcast Employees and Technicians (NABET) began in 1934 as the Association of Technical Employees (ATE) in order to represent radio and film personnel. The union changed its name to NABET in 1940 and merged with the Communications Workers of American in 1994. When ATE was formed, it was basically serving the employees of NBC radio's Red and Blue networks, but by the time it became affiliated with the Congress of Industrial Organizations (CIO), it had grown to arbitrate 23 independent contracts. Since 1997, it has represented the Newspaper Guild and around 10,000 broadcast workers in the field. By virtue of its ties to CWA, which serves telephone workers, there are 60,000 other employees enrolled in this union. NABET now represents about 10,000 broadcast workers in 35 local unions.

The Screen Actors Guild (SAG) has perhaps the most colorful history of America's labor unions as the original Hollywood bargaining collective that fought to keep the studios from taking advantage of actors and actresses during the golden age of motion

pictures and to protect them during the anti-Communist era of the 1950s. One famous leader was actor, Ronald Reagan, who became the SAG union president in 1947. When the union became involved in the McCarthy era in the House Un-American Activities Committee (HUAC) hearings, it tried to save the careers of the famous "Hollywood Ten," who were blacklisted for alleged ties to socialist organizations. With 20 branches nationwide today, SAG represents nearly 120,000 actors in motion pictures, television, commercials, and music videos.

In much the same way that the Screen Actors Guild has represented movie actors, the American Federation of Television and Radio Artists (AFTRA) was founded and governed by its members to represent performers in radio and television in contract negotiations. AFTRA claims 80,000 members including radio and television announcers, anchors and reporters, and singers and recording artists. Its two largest local unions are Los Angeles, California, and New York City, New York. The media contracts AFTRA negotiates guarantee minimum salaries, but never maximum figures. AFTRA not only represents its members in contract negotiations, but also seeks residual payments for secondary uses of their performances, and arbitrates health and pension benefits. AFTRA claims to be the first union of its kind to have established employer-paid health retirement plans; a separate foundation provides scholarships and other charitable benefits for its members and their dependants.

Labor unions, such as IATSE, SAG, NABET-CWA, and AFTRA are principally dedicated to increasing members' compensations and work benefits while ensuring that their working conditions are maintained with some measure of health and safety protections in mind.

Arizona, Illinois, Maine, and Massachusetts, while pressuring other state legislatures such as the ones in New York to follow suit and end the contract practice.

CORPORATE SPEECH

The First Amendment was drafted well before the marketplace of ideas became the province of large media corporations, and an obvious question became how much free expression was owed to businesses hoping to get their viewpoint across to reach voters. Later in this chapter, we will discuss the doctrine of commercial speech and campaign controls, but the question of corporate speech beyond product promotion has a direct bearing on the role that public relations practitioners play in our society. The key question in the 1978 case was whether a state law that would ban banks and business from influencing voter approval of referendum issues might be considered unconstitutional. The decision in *First Nat'l Bank of Boston v. Bellotti* affirmed First Amendment rights for corporate entities based on the belief not in the seller's interests but in the free exchange of ideas.[39] It was a close vote of 5–4, which held the Massachusetts criminal statute prohibiting such funding of messages designed to influence the political process at the ballot box was unconstitutional. Those opposed to the ruling criticized its rationale based on the listeners' rights as opposed to an analysis of speaker's rights in light of corporate power.

The doctrine of corporate personhood was adopted early in the nineteenth century. The case involved Dartmouth College, and an attempt to convert the private school into a state university. The ruling held that even though the word *corporation* is nowhere to be found in the Constitution, a corporate charter is a contract that cannot be reshaped by government.[40] The ruling limited the government's power to control corporations, so states began to write controls into the charters they granted.

In the case of *Kasky v. Nike, Inc.*, a California activist, Marc Kasky, sued Nike for publicity issued about its use of overseas manufacturers.[41] Nike appealed the case to the Supreme Court but the justices decided to dismiss the appeal. The limited rules influencing corporate political speech had a wider berth than consumer groups may feel is warranted. Those who feel otherwise point to constituents and investors, which corporations must answer to, and how the Securities and Exchange Commission (SEC) plays a role in the process.

INVESTING IN MEDIA

It's easy to understand why large media conglomerates depend on the capital generated by stock investments. Securities brokers dealing in publicly traded securities not only have a sharp impact on who owns the media, but ultimately on what we see, hear, and read over television, radio, and Internet channels. If you were to take

---

[39]*First Nat'l Bank of Boston v. Bellotti*, 435 U.S. 765 (1978).
[40]*Dartmouth College v. Woodward*, 17 U.S. 518 (1819).
[41]*Kasky v. Nike, Inc.*, 27 Cal. 4th 939, 969 (2002).

over the media conglomerates of Disney, Time Warner, Viacom, Bertelsmann, News Corp., and General Electric, you would own close to 90 percent of the nation's news and entertainment outlets. That reality places the packages of stocks sold into these companies squarely on the radar screen of federal regulators. It also means Congress minds how the game of securities is played on the frontier of American investment. Capitol Hill gave its sternest look at stock sales more than seventy years ago.

During the depths of the Great Depression, the Securities Act of 1933 changed the way Americans invest in their businesses. First and foremost, that law defined what facts should be disclosed and which ones are to be kept quiet until securities are ready for sale. Even before media stocks are sold, the corporation must file a registration statement with the SEC, and wait before they start promoting their stock sale. If word leaks out during the twenty-day waiting period, *gun-jumping* is the term used by SEC agents who cite § 5 of the 1933 Act that prohibits this sort of priming the pump for stock sales before the government has approved them.

The strict law on promoting stock sales before their time is not quite so cut and dry. Some believe loopholes exist or as the government likes to call them, "safe harbors." Media corporations seek shelter under Rule 134, for example, which is called the "tombstone advertising" safe harbor—an indication allowing the simple facts involved in the potential sale. While this rule forbids providing a full prospectus or supplement to potential stock buyers, sellers can offer information on how investors can sign up to participate in the offering once it begins. Another safe harbor falls under Rule 168, where forward-looking information in press releases is allowed due to its factual business nature.

A good example would be the report on the business wires by Raycom, Inc., which sold twelve of its television stations to Barrington Broadcasting. Since the transaction had yet to be blessed by the government, press releases carefully referred to the Private Securities Litigation Reform Act of 1995, where the safe harbor of Rule 168 is found. Normally, lawyer language accompanies advance press releases warning investors of "risks and uncertainties" involved, including changes in interest rates, advertising sales, taxing authorities, and other financial conditions might have an impact.

What remains are restrictions against announcing the initial public offerings (IPOs) before the media firm files its prospectus. Most of these offerings are managed by investment banks, which act as underwriters. Not all media companies are publicly traded firms, but those that are fall under the registration requirements to be filed with the SEC, and the annual forms and quarterly reports that keep the company's business fully disclosed to its investors. Publicly traded media impart loads of data to their investors, a lot of statistics to be sure, but also corporate reports to indicate just how healthy their businesses are each year.

Media corporations are legally bound to be vigilant in rooting out "misrepresentation, deceit, and other fraudulent acts and practices" that might influence the sale of securities.[42] It also is a matter of case law that media corporations guard

---

[42]The Securities and Exchange Commission, *The Work of the Securities and Exchange Commission* (1974).

their investors from fraud, while promoting honesty and fairness. Yet the focus remains on certain types of fraud and deception. Rule 10b-5 under the Securities Exchange Act of 1934 says if a stock seller makes an untrue or a misleading statement of a material fact, she or he will be subject to liabilities resulting from anyone acting on that misinformation.[43]

Insider Trading

Perhaps the most famous example of stock trading gone wrong is the case of Martha Stewart, the homemaking maven who spent five months in prison for lying to federal investigators about why she sold her stock in Imclone System Inc. in December 2001. Stewart first had been convicted of a criminal charge in 2004, but she also suffered liabilities in civil court for **insider trading** and ended up paying the government $137,019, which was three times the amount of losses she avoided in her sale of stock.

Insider trading ■
An illegal business practice where market participants base decisions on information that is known to be confidential and not generally available in the market. For example, officers of a company buying stock in the company at a current market price below what they know will be announced in the future as a buyout price.

Reporters can also run afoul of SEC rules when they become involved in the reporting of publicly traded companies. When reporting on business matters, a reporter who makes a negative comment about a publicly traded company can actually cause the stock to drop. The announcement of a major discovery or development can cause a company's value to rise. An unscrupulous reporter who knows this information could have a tremendous financial advantage by buying or selling stock in the hours between learning of a development and reporting on it. The *Wall Street Journal* is well known and well respected for its business reporting. In 1987 R. Foster Winans was found guilty of securities fraud. He was not a stockbroker, but as one of the journalists contributing to the *Journal*'s "Heard on the Street" column, he had the ability to influence a number of investors. He took advantage of this position by buying and selling stock before the stories that affected their price appeared in the paper. Winans was found guilty of securities fraud by the Second Circuit Court of Appeals.[44]

Merger Mania

The urge to merge media enterprises has prompted the government to ask for reports from the company who seeks to take control of one of its competitors. If the takeover is a tender offer, then the buyer must disclose who the target company is, how many shareholders are involved, the reason for the bid, and where the buyer wants to take the newly acquired company. SEC rules on what constitutes the beginning of the tender offer. The tender offeror must submit financial statements to the government or face sanctions from the government. SEC Rule 14(d)

---

[43]See Rule 10b-5—Employment of Manipulative and Deceptive Devices under General Rules and Regulations promulgated under the Securities Exchange Act of 1934: "It shall be unlawful for any person . . . a. To employ any device, scheme, or artifice to defraud; b. To make any untrue statement of a material fact or to omit to state a material fact necessary in order to make the statements made, in the light of the circumstances under which they were made, not misleading, or c. To engage in any act, practice, or course of business which operates or would operate as a fraud or deceit. . . ."

[44]*Carpenter v. United States*, 484 U.S. 19 (1987).

states that publicity about the purchasing of the company must include the identity of the bidder, and information about how stock holders can find more about the pursuing form. If anything is found false or deceptive, it is not out of the question that the SEC could sue the lawyers and the company. There are both civil and criminal penalties for violating the security laws.

SUMMARY

- A contract is an agreement between two parties that must contain three elements to be legally binding: an offer, consideration, and acceptance. Oral contracts are legally enforceable but most contracts are written because it reduces the disputes about what was promised and by whom.
- A release form is a variant of a contract often used by media companies. Production companies often require people appearing in their videos to sign talent releases stating that the producers can use the video in a variety of ways. Sometimes consideration is in the form of money but not always.
- Not everyone who has a job signs a lengthy legal contract, but in media industries many people do have contracts and those contracts contain a lot more than just salaries and job descriptions. Some media contracts include morals clauses that prohibit employees from engaging in any activity *off the job* that might reflect badly on the employer. Media employees' contracts sometimes contain no compete clauses that prevent them from taking jobs with a competitor for six to twelve months.
- Antitrust laws prevent businesses from engaging in anticompetitive practices, and those laws apply to media companies just like any other businesses. There are a couple of notable examples of legislation that has exempted certain activities that would otherwise run afoul of antitrust law, such as competing newspapers sharing facilities or sports blackouts rules.
- Labor laws are also applicable to media companies, but like antitrust exemptions, special niches have been carved out that have allowed media to employ children, and television stations have been able to remove anchors because of their ages without losing age discrimination suits.
- Corporations have *some* rights of free expression but not to the same extent as individuals.
- Corporations that sell stocks have a special obligation to protect their stockholders (i.e., "owners") by treating them fairly. People within corporations who have access to insider information could take advantage of their positions by buying company stock just before announcing a great discovery, or selling the stock just before terrible news about losses is announced. The laws prohibit insiders from trading on such knowledge, and journalists who have access to such information before the public in some instances can be held similarly responsible.

Limiting Celebrity Behavior

Tiger Woods has attracted a lot of attention as a professional golfer, but never as much as he attracted in 2009 when allegations of marital trouble and multiple claims of infidelity came to the public's attention. In the weeks following, media stories speculated on his future with his wife, but many also speculated on his future as a multimillion dollar pitchman. Some companies canceled sponsorship contracts while others did not. Coca-Cola canceled its endorsement deal with Woods, but Nike never dropped the golfer and continued to pay his $30 million endorsement fee.

Some legal scholars have suggested that celebrity endorsers ought to be held to an even higher standard and that there ought to be a "reverse morals clause." Under such a scheme, celebrities who tarnish their images (and consequently those of the products they endorse) would have to *pay* compensation for the damage they've done. To date this is just talk: no one has yet come forward to say s/he has such an endorsement contract, but in the future, who knows?

If someone breaks the law it is easy to understand how the enforcement of a morals clause is both ethical and legal, but what about instances where there are no allegations of illegal activity? Tiger Woods faced no criminal charges. Neither did the Ohio newscaster mentioned earlier in this chapter who lost her job.

In addition to morals clauses, other celebrities are having their communications "curbed" in the interest of protecting the employer. Professional athletes are being restricted in their external communications with the public. Some players are well known for tweeting to large followings. The NFL restricts players from using their Twitter accounts immediately prior to or during a game. Players can also be fined for criticism of the league or officials, speech that would otherwise be protected.

Should corporations be able to terminate a contract with a celebrity or fine that person for behavior that is outrageous but legal? ■

Intellectual Property

LEARNING OBJECTIVES

After reading this chapter you should know:

- The legal basis for copyright protection and the "bundle of rights" that make up copyrights
- The way music authors license their music to collect royalty payments
- The tremendous value of derivative works
- What can and cannot be copyrighted
- The advantages of registering a copyright

- How long a copyright lasts
- The four elements of fair use and how it is applied
- Whether devices that facilitate copyright infringement can be prohibited
- What a trademark is
- How intellectual property rights are enforced—or not

Joel Tenenbaum was a typical 16-year-old growing up in Rhode Island when he found himself caught up in larger-than-life situation. Like many other teens he enjoyed music and liked sharing songs with others. Thanks to the development of peer-to-peer (P2P) file-sharing software, Joel was able to share music via the Internet using Kazaa, a service that allowed users to download MP3 files from others' computers. In 2003 Joel was contacted by the Recording Industry Association of America (RIAA) and told that he was liable for violating the copyrights on seven songs he downloaded. RIAA requested a payment of $5,250 ($750 per song). Joel never tried to deny downloading the songs but instead sent a check for $500 claiming that as a high school student, it was all he could afford. The check was returned and nothing more happened for four years.

RIAA had engaged in actively pursuing claims against individuals for allegedly illegally downloading music. Joel was just one of thousands who received notice from the RIAA, offering the chance to "settle" out of court so both parties could avoid expensive legal battles. RIAA even set up a website to facilitate credit card payments from those it alleged had violated copyrights. According to the Electronic Frontier Foundation, more than 28,000 people were threatened with legal action.[1]

In 2007 Joel was sued by major recording labels Sony BMG, Warner Brothers, and three others for allegedly downloading 30 songs belonging to the plaintiffs. He responded after a year-and-a-half, admitting to having copied the songs but claiming that the downloading was a "fair use," a copyright doctrine that allows limited copying under specific qualifications. Fair use will be discussed in detail later in the chapter but for now it is enough to explain that Tenenbaum tried to argue that because his use was noncommercial (no money changed hands: he made no profit from file sharing), a jury ought to be allowed to decide whether his file sharing was a copyright infringement or not. His strategy was really rather radical. His defense was dependant on a jury of his peers whom Tenenbaum hoped might see his violation as "no big deal." The federal district court called Joel's defense strategy "so broad that it would swallow the copyright protections that Congress created."[2] The court never allowed the case to reach a jury, issuing a summary ruling that his copying was not a fair use. Tenenbaum's argument was that file sharing did not harm the record industry's revenues (he provided no evidence for this argument), but the court rejected this assertion, stating that copyright enforcement does not require looking at overall sales but rather whether sales of each individual work is affected. The court stated it is obvious that "continuous, high volume file sharing" would impact the sales for copyrighted works (although the court provided no evidence for the argument).

The court noted that both the plaintiff and the defendant were in agreement that:

- The main purpose of the file sharing was personal enjoyment;
- Entire songs, but not entire albums, were downloaded;
- The works were not "transformed" in any way (Tenenbaum did not try to remix songs or turn them into new creative works);

---

[1]*RIAA v. The People*, http://www.eff.org/riaa-v-people (last visited June1, 2010).
[2]*Sony v. Tenenbaum*, 672 F. Supp. 2d 217. 221 (D. Mass. 2009).

- The file sharing spanned more than four years and involved different software, and;
- The file-sharing software made more than 800 songs available for download by others from Joel's computer.[3]

Tenenbaum's fair use argument was rejected by the court, as was his attempted appeal. While not a Supreme Court decision, the case provides strong evidence that the centuries-old concept of copyright still exists. Even in a digital age, copyright holders have enforceable rights.[4]

A CONSTITUTIONAL RIGHT? REALLY?

Some legal scholars trace the evolution of U.S. copyright law back to seventeenth-century Britain with the creation of the Licensing Act of 1662, but the first law granting a fixed term of ownership to authors came in 1710 with the Statute of Anne. The British law granted rights to authors but also limited their ability to control a work once it had been purchased by others. It was clearly the precursor to U.S. copyright law, as the arbitrary fourteen-year limit on copyright was precisely the length selected by the U.S. Congress when it passed the first Copyright Act.

Article I, Section 8 of the U.S. Constitution is that very important (and often litigated) portion that outlines the powers of Congress. Among the list of powers, Congress is given the authority:

> [T]o promote the progress of science and useful arts, by securing for limited times to authors and inventors the exclusive right to their respective writings and discoveries.

Authors are granted the exclusive right to their work via copyrights, and inventors are given exclusivity by patents. As this text deals with communication law we will not examine patent law, which varies from copyright law but comes from the same constitutional root.

To understand the philosophical underpinning of copyright, it is important to pay attention to the clause "to promote the progress." The reason for protecting copyright is to encourage people to produce more. Everyone has to provide for basic needs and most of us do that by doing work that results in earning money, which we then use to buy the things we need and want. A few authors may be motivated to write by a burning desire from within, but a lot more will write if they believe they can make a living doing it. Could any of our best-selling authors

---

[3]*Id.* at 222.

[4]Tenenbaum was originally ordered by the court to pay $675,000 (about $22,000 each for the 30 tracks he pirated), but in July 2010 a federal judge reduced the amount of the award to $67,500. Federal District Court Judge Nancy Gertner said the reduction was appropriate given that the awards in cases involving commercial entities that violate copyright (such as unlicensed bars and restaurants) are often far smaller. *See Judge Reduces Fine in File-Sharer Case,* MediaPost, July 9, 2010, http://www.mediapost.com/publications/?fa=Articles.showArticle&art_aid=131728 (last visited July 12, 2010).

afford to stay home all day and write if everything they wrote could be freely copied without any payment to them?

But another part of the constitutional admonition is that the copyright is granted for a limited time. The logic here is that authors have the right to control their works only for a certain length of time. After that, others ought to be able to use those works. There is a great history of people taking the works of others and building upon them. In 1676 the famous scientist Isaac Newton remarked that he was able to advance science because of those whose work had come before. "If I have seen a little further it is by standing on the shoulders of giants."

Thus we have the classic copyright debate summed up in just a few words. Authors must have their copyrights protected in order to promote creativity, but authors can't have unlimited copyright protection so as not to stifle the creativity of others.

Of course constitutions are just frameworks, so there must be statutes to "flesh out" the meaning of copyright protection. The first U.S. copyright statute came in 1790, just three years after the Constitution. As mentioned previously, the U.S. government adopted the fourteen-year limit on copyright first created by Britain in 1710. Unlike current copyright law, there was a provision allowing for a copyright renewal. The 1790 act allowed authors to renew the copyright for an additional fourteen years. Why not simply copyright the work for twenty-eight years to begin with and be done with it? Once again, the law attempted to strike a balance between the rights of the authors and the public's interest in making works available for others to use. If an author died or no longer had an interest in the copyrighted work, it would pass into the **public domain** at the end of the fourteen years. If the author renewed the copyright, it would then extend the author's exclusive right to the work for another fourteen years.

Public domain ■
Works are in the public domain if they are not currently subject to any private intellectual property right: either because they never were, like published court cases, or because the copyright has expired.

What Is Copyright?

An overly simplistic way to think of copyright is to dissect the word: the right of copy. Controlling who may copy a work (such as in cases involving illegally downloading music) is *part* of copyright law but only a portion of the law. Most legal treatises refer to copyright as a *bundle* of rights. The creator of a book, play, poem, film, song, or any other copyrightable work actually has the exclusive right to control:

- *Reproduction*—Reproduction rights allow the author to decide who may copy a work or what fee must be paid for copying (such as with music downloads).
- *Performance*—Copyright holders also have a right to be compensated when someone performs their works. A songwriter is paid a royalty when a piece of sheet music is sold, but that songwriter also receives a royalty when someone performs that song. Buying a piece of sheet music does *not* come with the right to publicly perform the song. A radio station that plays copyrighted music needs to pay performance rights (more on this later).
- *Derivative works*—A derivative work is a work based on a copyrighted work. Someone who makes a movie based on a book needs the permission

of the book's author, and someone who makes a new arrangement of a copyrighted piece of music needs the author's permission.

- *Distribution and public display*—Taking a picture of a copyrighted work of art may or may not be a reproduction but publicly displaying that photo is clearly a public display, which the owner of the copyrighted work has a right to control. Control of the rental or lease of copyrighted works is the right to control distribution.

In each case, the copyright holder can keep all of these rights or may contract to give a portion of the rights to some other entity while retaining other rights. The best example of this has happened in the music industry.

> **Bedrock Law:** The legal protection of copyright gives the owner exclusive rights to copy the material, derive other works from it, perform it, display it, and distribute it.

Licensing Performance Rights

An author who writes a piece of music owns the entire bundle of rights listed above. That author might find it rather tedious to try to keep track of every performance of any of his or her songs, then to try to collect money from restaurants, music halls, or radio stations that used the music. For that reason, a group of music rights holders created the American Society of Composers, Authors and Publishers (ASCAP) in 1914. It did not take long for a case to find its way to the Supreme Court. By 1917 in fact, *two* cases were heard together by the Court. The Vanderbilt Hotel was playing "From Maine to Oregon" in its dining room each night. Shanley's Restaurant was performing "Sweethearts" for the enjoyment of its patrons. Because no one was paying to hear the performances (it was part of the dining rooms' ambiance) the owners tried to assert it was not performed "for profit" (a stipulation of the 1909 Copyright Act). The Court reversed the appellate court's decision and found that such a performance did, in fact, infringe on the songs' copyrights.

> If the rights under the copyright are infringed only by a performance where money is taken at the door they are very imperfectly protected. Performances not different in kind from those of the defendants could be given that might compete with and even destroy the success of the monopoly that the law intends the plaintiffs to have. . . . The defendants' performances . . . are part of a total for which the public pays. . . . It is true that the music is not the sole object, but neither is the food, which probably could be got cheaper elsewhere.[5]

Licensing the use of music in restaurants continues today, as well as malls, grocery stores, and even universities. But it was the addition of radio station performance rights beginning in 1923 that really increased music revenues for ASCAP. Radio executives became frustrated with ASCAP's ability to demand just about whatever it wanted from stations, since they had no alternative if they wanted to perform copyrighted music. In 1939 they founded Broadcast Music Incorporated (BMI) as a way to try to break the monopoly and provide stations with more negotiating power. A third licensor, SESAC, started in 1930 to license European authors

---

[5]*Herbert v. Shanley*, 242 U.S. 591, 594–95 (1917).

but has made a concerted effort to increase its library of U.S. composers. Today almost all U.S. songwriters license their music performance rights through ASCAP, BMI, or SESAC.

When a songwriter signs with a licensor, that agency takes responsibility for collecting fees and distributing them to its members based on some established formula. The vast majority of licenses are for *blanket* usage of music. A blanket license allows users to pay a flat fee for an entire year's worth of music regardless of how much they use. Users pay based on their revenues and what portion of their business depends on the use of licensed music. Radio stations in larger cities typically pay more than those in smaller towns, and a restaurant will pay less than a radio station in the same town. Typically licensors ask the establishments they license (radio and TV stations, bars, restaurants, etc.) to keep track of all the music they use during a sample week. That helps them fairly distribute royalty payments to their authors.

The licensing agencies collect the fees, but they also work to expand the list of establishments paying fees. They travel the country in search of bars, restaurants, stores—even local YMCAs—looking for places that are "profiting" from copyrighted music without paying for it, just like the restaurant cases a century ago. In some instances venues that should be paying copyright fees are unaware, so licensing agencies "educate" them by offering to sign them up for blanket licenses rather than taking them to court for copyright infringement.

In 1998 Congress passed the Fairness in Music Licensing Act as a way of trying to balance between the rights of music authors and the needs of small businesses. The law sets an arbitrary size limit on restaurants, bars, and grills. Any establishment smaller than 3,750 square feet (all spaces included—even rest rooms and broom closets) does not need a license to play radio or TV music. Retail establishments smaller than 2,000 square feet also qualify for exemption, but again the exemption is only for broadcast music: recorded music or live performance would still need to be licensed. Larger establishments might also be exempt if they "use six or fewer speakers with no more than four speakers in any one room or use audiovisual equipment consisting of no more than four TVs, with no more than one TV in each room, and no TV having a diagonal screen size greater than 55 inches, together with the same speaker restrictions."[6]

One other category of user that is exempted from paying copyright is retailers who sell the music. Normally, if a store plays a CD from beginning to end, it is considered a "use" for copyright purposes and the owner of the store is then required to pay a performance fee. Obviously if a store is selling the CD, it wants to play it to entice shoppers to purchase it. This "record store" exemption has existed for decades but has been expanded to allow the use of copyrighted work not only to sell just *that* work, but also as a means of demonstrating the *devices* that play the work. A store that sells TVs and stereos needs to be able to demonstrate how well the equipment works. Use of copyrighted works to sell playback equipment, just like selling the music, does not require copyright payment.

---

[6]17 U.S.C. Chapter § 110 (2010).

UP CLOSE

The Unusual Case of "Happy Birthday"

What could be more natural than celebrating a birthday by going out to dinner? Families and friends gather and someone tells the restaurant (either publicly or secretly) that someone at the table is celebrating a birthday. At the end of the meal the restaurant staff may bring over cake, ice cream, or some other treat with some degree of fanfare. The whole wait staff may deliver the dessert to the table, and they will probably draw the attention of everyone in the restaurant. The one thing they likely *won't* be doing is singing "Happy Birthday." Why not? Because they don't want to have to pay the sizeable

fee for a public performance. It is for this reason that most restaurants celebrating birthdays usually do so with a song of their own invention or some other substitute.

"Happy Birthday" was registered for a copyright in 1935, although the tune is attributed to sisters Patty and Mildred Hill, who wrote it for their kindergarten classes in Louisville, Ky., in 1893. The copyright has changed hands a couple of times and as of this writing is owned by Summy-Birchard Music, a division of media giant Time Warner. "Happy Birthday" brings in an estimated $2 million per year in royalties.

For many larger establishments, the solution is to pay a music service to deliver music with the licensing already paid. Perhaps one of the best known of these services is Muzak, which has been providing background music (despairingly referred to as "elevator music"[7]) since 1934. Some large chains find it more efficient to just create their own audio service for use in their stores. These in-store "networks," like Muzak, pay licensing fees on the music they use so that the individual stores, hospitals, restaurants, etc. don't have to.

It is extremely important to note what licensing agencies do *not* do: they do not handle rights other than performance rights. There is a huge misunderstanding among many in media industries about this. A radio station that pays a blanket license to ASCAP, BMI, and SESAC has permission to perform (play) all the music in their libraries, but it would be a violation for that station to burn CDs of the music to give away to listeners (reproduction) or to use a portion of a song as the music bed for a commercial (derivative work).

It's important to see this from the point of view of the songwriter. Imagine having written a song about a topic that you feel strongly about. You want the song to get as much airplay as possible, not only because your licensing agency will pay you more but because you want the world to hear your thoughts on the topic. You see this song as more than just a nice tune but a political statement: you're exercising your First Amendment rights to their fullest. Now imagine that someone else takes your song and uses it for something completely unrelated, like a dog food commercial on TV. Imagine the most inane setting possible, including animated dogs singing and dancing to what you considered a ballad of epic proportions.

---

[7]Muzak actually started by providing music for use in elevators, to calm the fears of people afraid of riding in elevators. The company has grown and evolved to offer dozens of different music channels for dentist offices, zoos, hotel lobbies—and even the White House.

Production Music

Like any other productions, low-budget video productions need music. The vast majority of corporate and industrial videos don't have adequate budgets to pay rights fees for popular music like feature films would. Low-budget videos usually turn to production music libraries that provide everything from a few seconds of music to dozens of CDs filled with hours of music. As with performance rights, synchronization rights can be purchased on a per use basis or by paying a blanket-licensing fee covering unlimited use of any music in the production library. Some libraries provide **buy-out licenses**. Unlike blanket licenses that require the payment of annual fees, buy-out libraries own production music that is purchased in perpetuity. Obviously this is cheaper in the long run but the music quickly sounds dated. A quick Internet search for "production music" will yield dozens of companies that provide stock music.

Buy-out license ■
Unlike blanket licenses that require the payment of annual fees, buy-out libraries own production music that is purchased in perpetuity.

Synchronization ■
A form of derivative work, a synchronization license allows a copyrighted work, such as a song, to be integrated with other media, like a video.

As the songwriter, shouldn't you have the *right* to say "no way"? You do. Putting music to video is known as **synchronization,** which is a derivative work—part of the author's bundle of rights. Authors have the right to allow their music to be performed while at the same time preventing other uses. There are legends of artists who refuse to allow their works to be used in commercials at any price, and other stories of authors who "sold out" for huge payments. Whether the stories are true or just hype to increase the value of their work doesn't really matter.

Unfortunately for people wanting to do the right thing and seek permission from authors for synchronization rights, it's not an easy thing to do. Years ago the Harry Fox Agency used to license synchronization rights. They even had a low cost license that low-budget video producers could obtain for $75 with just a simple form, but HFA stopped that service in 2002. Now it can sometimes take days or weeks to locate a copyright owner, request permission, and wait for a response. If you've ever wondered why there are so many lawyers listed in the credits at the end of a movie, getting licensing for copyrighted material used in the film is one of the reasons.

Derivative Works

Derivative works can often result in more money for an author than any royalties resulting from reproduction or performance rights. A movie based on a book can bring in bigger revenues, especially in a worldwide market. Not only are movies defined as derivative works if based on books, but the characters in those books and movies can spawn other creative works that are then obligated to pay the original author for the use of the intellectual property. It is well known among television writers that it can be profitable to introduce a character. If that character recurs in future episodes, the writer responsible for the character's creation continues to collect royalties whenever the character appears, even if the writer who created the character no longer writes for the show.

The *Star Trek* franchise can demonstrate the value of derivative works. Gene Roddenberry created the original series in the 1960s, and the show ran for only three years on the NBC television network. After it was canceled in 1969, it aired in syndication and continues its television run to this day. Gene Roddenberry died in 1991, but because copyright continues beyond the death of the author, his estate continues to receive royalty payments from his creation. But the story does not end there. Movies based on the TV show were produced beginning in 1979. Other TV series based on the Star Trek concept, but without the original characters, were created, starting with *Star Trek: The Next Generation* in 1987. After Rodden-berry's death, additional movies and TV shows were produced that obviously he had no involvement with, yet because they involve intellectual property based on the original, his estate still receives remuneration. Klingons, Vulcans, and Star Fleet, as well as their specific attributes, are protected intellectual property and their use requires a contract usually involving some form of compensation.

It's not just the TV shows or movies that were spawned from the original, but all the derivative works *based* on the derivative works that also require licensing. If a new *Star Trek* movie is released, the licensing of toys, Halloween costumes, or even McDonald's drink cups based on characters from the film also can produce royalty payments for the original copyright holder.

As the *Star Trek* example shows rather clearly, income from derivative works can easily exceed the royalties paid for the initial performance or reproduction right.

An Exception to Distribution Rights

Just like reproduction and derivative works, copyright owners are empowered to exercise control over the distribution of their copyrighted works. If a book author wanted to, the author could give exclusive distribution rights to one bookstore over others. Authors usually don't do this because there is no financial incentive for them to do so, but occasionally there may be an exclusive release to one distrib-utor a day or two before it is available to others.

Congress did create one exception to distribution rights, which is known as the **doctrine of first sale**. Once a copy of a work is sold, the author no longer con-trols the copy: the author still owns the copyright on the intellectual property but has no right to determine what is done with the individual copy of the work.

Have you ever thought about how unfair a library is to a book author? A library pays for a single copy of a book, yet dozens of people then get to read it for free. That means dozens of book sales that may be lost for the author. Multiply that times the thousands of libraries in the United States[8] (even more worldwide) and the author of a popular book could potentially lose the royalties on the sale of thousands of books.

Even an individual who purchases a book and lends it to a friend or sells it in a garage sale potentially reduces the author's royalties. Should someone need an author's permission to lend a book to a friend or pay a royalty if a book is resold? The doctrine of first sale strikes a balance between the copyright holder's rights and the purchaser's rights. The basic premise is that the author was compensated in the original sale and that any subsequent redistribution does not entitle the

Doctrine of first sale ■ After a particular copy of a work is sold, the author no longer controls that particular copy: the author still owns the intellectual property, but that individual copy belongs to the purchaser.

---

[8]The American Library Association estimates there are more than 122,000 libraries in the United States.

Bedrock Law: The doctrine of first sale simply means a copyright holder's right to control the change of ownership ends with the first sale of a copy of the work.

author to a payment. It is important to note that this does *not* apply to making copies but only to the original work, on which a copyright was paid. Purchasing a CD of music and making a copy for a friend is *not* protected under the doctrine of first sale. Neither is purchasing sheet music of a song and then performing it in concert.

Contrary to popular belief, copyright holders do not receive royalties when people rent DVDs. The doctrine of first sale stipulates that the author was compensated by the sale of the DVD to the rental store and the author need not be further compensated. Obviously a DVD rental store wants more than one copy of popular titles so it will have to purchase multiple copies, the sale of each one resulting in a royalty to the author. The store cannot copy any of the works to rent but must purchase as many as it needs. Once it does, though, it owes the copyright owner nothing whether the video is rented once or 1,000 times.

There are a couple of exceptions to this exception. In 1984 Congress passed a statute that prohibited redistribution of records (the old vinyl sort), and a 1990 amendment restricted the redistribution of computer software. In both cases, the essence of the rules was a recognition that borrowers or renters of this sort of content were more likely to violate copyright by making illegal copies rather than just using the content and returning it to the owner. Non-profit schools and libraries are exempt from the statutes, which is why people can still check out copies of music CDs and computer software from the local library but the local video store isn't able to offer them for rental. In recent years there has been a good deal of disagreement over computer software. With the ability to easily duplicate the digital files, software creators fear the potential loss of millions of dollars in sales. In order to try to bolster their claims for protection, software companies generally use **shrink-wrap licenses,** claiming that as soon as customers remove the wrapping from a piece of software, they have consented to the terms and conditions of the license stated on the box. Shrinkwrap licenses place all sorts of stipulations on the use of the software, often limiting the purchaser to installing the software on only one device. Opinions vary as to the enforceability of these "contracts."

Shrink-wrap licenses ■ Software companies generally claim the consumer removing the wrapping from a piece of software constitutes acceptance of the offered terms and conditions of the license stated on the box.

Copyrightable Works

In order for a work to be copyrighted, it must be an original work, contain an element of creativity, and be in a fixed medium. According to the U.S. Copyright Office, copyrightable works include:

- Literary works;
- Musical works, including any accompanying words;
- Dramatic works, including any accompanying music;
- Pantomimes and choreographic works;
- Pictorial, graphic, and sculptural works;
- Motion pictures and other audiovisual works;
- Sound recordings; and
- Architectural works.[9]

---

[9]U.S. Copyright Office, *Copyright Basics, available at* http://www.copyright.gov/circs/circ1.pdf.

While pantomimes and choreographic works are listed above, note that in order to be copyrighted, works must be fixed in a tangible medium. A live dance performance is not copyrighted, but if recorded or written out the choreography is copyrighted.

A creative work must be more than just an idea to be copyrighted. Ideas, if fleshed out as film treatments or book outlines, become more than just ideas and can be copyrighted, but an idea alone is not copyrightable. "Someone coming from another planet with powers that humans don't have" is an idea that has been manifested dozens (maybe hundreds) of ways: as the comic book hero turned movie hero, Superman; as the TV series and movie *My Favorite Martian;* as the TV series *Mork and Mindy;* as the plot of the Jerry Lewis movie *Visit to a Small Planet;* and many more. Can one claim that another violated copyright by copying the idea? Not a chance. Ideas, procedures, and methods are not copyrightable, but their descriptions or illustrations may be.

There are certain sorts of works that are not copyrightable. One narrow class of works not subject to copyright claims are those produced by the U.S. government. Since 1895, federal law has stated that the U.S. government does not hold any copyrights to its works. This means the many offices and agencies of the federal government produce materials that can be reproduced, performed, or adapted without payment or permission. Members of the President's Commission on Obscenity and Pornography may not have liked it in 1970 when Earl Kemp decided to take their report and illustrate it, but there was no "bundle of rights" that they could control, since federal government agencies cannot copyright their works.[10] This lack of copyright applies only to the federal government, not the states, and only applies to work produced *by* the government and not to works that may be *purchased* by the government. For example the Federal Communications Commission might produce a research paper on cell phone use by Americans. That report would not be copyrighted. But if the FCC paid an independent researcher (such as a university professor or research institute) to produce the report, the work would be subject to copyright.

> **Bedrock Law:** Documents and other works created by the U.S. government are placed in the public domain unless produced by a third party working for the government.

Facts are not copyrightable, although the way in which they are presented might be. It is a fact that Hawaii is the fiftieth state to join the United States. No one can claim copyright on that fact but a history book can state that fact and be copyrighted. This is a concern for media every day. A radio station could not do its newscast by simply reading the news stories straight from the local newspaper. That would be a copyright infringement. Every fact in that newspaper though—even those contained in "exclusive" stories—could be reported by the radio station without violating the newspaper's copyright.

Titles, names, short phrases, and slogans cannot be copyrighted, although they may be trademarked. Trademarks will be discussed later. For now it is enough to say that "Coca Cola" is a registered trademark but it is not copyrighted.

---

[10]Kemp was indicted for sending pornography through the mail but not for any copyright infringement. *See* John Semonche, *Censoring Sex: A Historical Journey through American Media* (Rowman & Littlefield 2007).

Finally, works that lack originality, regardless of how much work they took to create, are not copyrightable. Copyright is not a reward for sweat of the brow. Rural Telephone Service, a telephone company in Kansas, tried to claim that Feist Publications infringed their copyright when Feist "copied" white pages listings (the part of the phone book containing the alphabetical listing of names, addresses, and phone numbers except for those who have paid to be unlisted) from Rural's telephone books. Feist tried to get Rural to license use of their white pages but Rural refused to sell to a competitor. Feist then decided to copy the listings for inclusion in their own phone book. Rural sued for copyright infringement and in 1991 the case made its way to the U.S. Supreme Court, which unanimously ruled that Feist did *not* violate copyright, despite the fact that it was an undeniable copying of Rural's work. "[O]riginality, not 'sweat of the brow,' is the touchstone of copyright protection in directories and other fact-based works."[11] The Court pointed out that the yellow pages with their enhancements such as display advertising and categorization of businesses would be quite different from simply the nonoriginal alphabetical order of phone customers.

> **Bedrock Law:** Some works cannot be copyrighted due to their historical or factual nature, including lists of names or certain facts available to all. It is the creativity found in original tangible fixed expressions that afford copyright protection.

Copyright Registration

Among the many revisions that have occurred in U.S. copyright law is the change in the registration requirement. Copyright exists from the moment a creative work is fixed in a tangible medium, such as a poem written on a piece of paper, or a song recorded in a magnetic medium. Do not be fooled by the word *tangible:* computer files that can be easily erased are still tangible. Under older laws, prominently displayed **copyright notices** were required that included the word "copyright" or the copyright symbol ©, the copyright owner, and the year of copyright. While these notations are still a good idea (how can anyone find out whom to contact when trying to license a copyrighted work if there is no notice?), notification rules are no longer in effect.

Copyright notice
■ Under older laws, prominently displayed notices were required that included the copyright symbol ©, owner, and the year. While these notations are still a good idea, notification rules are no longer in effect.

Even though copyright exists from the moment an original work is fixed in a tangible medium, people who want to protect their copyrights from infringement are wise to take the time and expense involved in registering their copyrights. In order to file a lawsuit for copyright infringement, the author must have a work registered. If an author proves a copyright infringement and the work was registered within three months of the publication or prior to the infringement, the author might be able to recover court costs and collect punitive damages. This would be a significantly larger award than just actual damages, which is what an author receives when the infringed work is not registered or was registered *after* the infringement occurred.

Even registering a copyright doesn't necessarily mean that a person is guaranteed the exclusive right to a work. When the U.S. Copyright Office registers a work, it does not go back searching through the hundreds of millions of copyrighted works to find if there is one of substantial similarity. Each year the Copyright Office

---

[11]*Feist Publications v. Rural Tel. Serv.*, 449 U.S. 340, 359–60 (1991).

receives more than a half-million copyright registrations. It is conceivable that a work registered this year may later be discovered to have infringed upon a work published a decade earlier. Registration is evidence of possession on the date of registration.

Under old copyright law, authors who wanted to avoid paying a copyright registration fee would engage in a practice known as the "poor man's copyright." This involved sealing a copy of the work in an envelope and mailing the copy to oneself, making certain that the postmark covered the seal. This served not as a copyright but as evidence that the author had the work on the date it was postmarked. If someone came along later with a copy of the work, the author could prove that he or she had it first. Since copyright registration is not much more than the date of possession evidence, many saw this alternative as a suitable, low-cost means of doing the same. Because of the 1978 copyright law revisions that limit the award of damages if a work is not registered, saving the copyright registration expense by using the poor man's copyright does not appear to be a good investment under the current system.

The Copyright Office has made the process fairly simple. Most copyrights can be registered electronically online by uploading the work and paying a $35 fee. The "old fashioned" forms and registration are priced higher ($65 at this writing) because the paper processing requires more time and expense. Those filing electronically also receive certification sooner than those filing paper forms although the copyright date in either instance is the date the Copyright Office receives the registration request, not the date the author receives certification.

> **Bedrock Law:** An original fixed expression has copyright protection from the moment of its creation, but in order to recover legal damages for infringement it is necessary to have the work registered with the federal government.

Copyright Duration

Congress has periodically extended the length of time for copyright. In 1831 Congress extended copyright to twenty-eight years, with the opportunity for authors to renew copyright for another fourteen years (for a total of forty-two years). In 1909 the Copyright Act was again revised, this time providing authors with exclusive rights to their works for twenty-eight years and a possible renewal of twenty-eight years (fifty-six years total). In 1976 Congress made U.S. copyright protection conform to international standards by making the length of a copyright equal to the life of the author plus fifty years. Of course there are lots of creative works that are not authored by a person at all, but rather by a corporation. An owner's manual for a car, appliance, or electronic device isn't the creative work of an individual but rather a company. Individuals write the manuals but the intellectual property belongs to the company that paid for them to be created. These types of intellectual property are known as **works for hire**, and the 1976 act set their copyright duration as seventy-five years. Employees of media companies usually produce works for hire. A newspaper or television reporter's work belongs to the paper or station, not to the individual reporter, so it is a work for hire.

The 1976 changes made it more difficult for anyone who wanted to use a work to know exactly when the copyright expired. Previously all one had to do was check the date of the copyright and add 28 or 56 years in order to figure when the copyright expired. With the 1976 Act you had to know when the

[handwritten margin note: 28 yrs 1831 & 42 yr 1909]

Works for hire ■. Copyrightable material that is made as a condition of employment. For example, the author of a work may have been a salaried employee who produced the work while on company time using company resources, so the company would own the copyright.

Works for Hire

According to the Copyright Act of 1976:

A "work made for hire" is—

1. a work prepared by an employee within the scope of his or her employment; or
2. a work specially ordered or commissioned for use as a contribution to a collective work, as a part of a motion picture or other audiovisual work, as a translation, as a supplementary work, as a compilation, as an instructional text, as a test, as answer material for a test, or as an atlas, if the parties expressly agree in a written instrument signed by them that the work shall be considered a work made for hire.[a]

Works for hire are generally those copyrightable works that are made as a condition of employment. This means that the author of the work was a salaried employee who produced the work while on company time using company resources. There is some ambiguity, however, about works that are created by nonemployees who are paid for their work, such as freelance writers and photographers. In 1989 the Supreme Court had to decide whether a sculptor who was commissioned to create a Nativity scene depicting the Holy Family as modern-day homeless people was entitled to the copyright of his work. The not-for-profit group that commissioned the work claimed it was a work for hire and therefore the group owned the copyright. The Court unanimously decided the case by examining the Copyright Act and finding that Congress had enumerated nine types of works for hire (listed in (2) above), none of which could be interpreted to include this particular sculpture.[b]

Magazines often purchase articles and photos from freelancers. Who holds the copyright on these works? Unless there is a contract that states it differently, the author of a freelance work owns the copyright and merely sells the one-time publication rights to the periodical. Increasingly though, publications are writing contracts that require the authors provide more than just a one-time publication before they will consent to publish their works. The issue became acute in the digital age, when a photograph or article published in a magazine could be accessed later in an electronic database.

In the early 1990s, six freelance writers sold articles to the *New York Times, Newsday,* and *Time.* The publications unquestionably had the right to publish their articles in the print publication, but the authors took issue with the fact that the publications then made their work available through the electronic database Lexis/Nexis and on CDs, both of which the publishers were paid for. The authors did not receive additional compensation. The freelancers were frustrated that the publications were continuing to profit from the databases that contained their works, but they received no additional compensation. A federal district court ruled in favor of the publications but that was reversed by the Second Circuit Court of Appeals, and the U.S. Supreme Court agreed that the freelancers' copyrights were being violated by the publishers.[c] Publishers paying freelance writers were only entitled to the original use unless a contract stipulated otherwise.

The result of the *Tasini* case has been an increase in the freelance writer contracts that contain clauses granting publishers the right to include freelancers' work in databases without additional compensation. Of course freelancers have the right to decline but they risk losing the sale of their articles to other freelancers willing to agree to those terms.

---

[a]17 U.S.C. § 101.
[b]*Community for Creative Non-Violence v. Reid,* 490 U.S. 730 (1989).
[c]*New York Times v. Tasini,* 533 U.S. 483 (2001).

author expired and add 50 years in order to determine when the copyright expired.

The most recent change in the length of copyright came in 1998 when Congress passed the Sonny Bono Copyright Term Extension Act, which added twenty years to the copyright's duration, making it the life of the author plus seventy years or ninety-five years for works for hire. The Act was named for the deceased Congressman and former singer-songwriter (half of the Sonny and Cher team) who had argued for extending copyright protection.

> **Bedrock Law:** Works for hire become the intellectual property of the employer so long as the work's creator has forged that agreement in writing.

The 1998 extension was quite controversial. Proponents of the extension argued that the government needed to extend copyright protection to be more in line with other countries, most notably the European Union, which had already extended copyright protection to life of the author plus seventy years. The argument was primarily an economic one: American authors who had twenty years less protection than their European counterparts were economically disadvantaged in world markets. An increasingly significant portion of the sales of creative works, not just books but movies and music, are marketed for sale to large international audiences.

Opponents of the extension argued that Congress was protecting a few large corporate interests, most notably Disney, which had valuable film assets that would soon pass into the public domain if the copyright period was not extended. In 2001 a group filed suit against the U.S. Attorney General's office claiming that this extension of the life of a copyrighted work violated the "limited time" prescription of the Constitution. The case made its way to the Supreme Court, which ruled 7–2 that this extension was constitutional, and that Congress was within its authority to extend it to the life of the author plus 70 years.[12]

[Handwritten margin note: 1998 life of author (+) 20yrs or 95yr for works for hire]

THE DOCTRINE OF FAIR USE

Copyright holders have a bundle of rights, but they are not able to absolutely control the use of their copyrighted works. The rights of the copyright holder must be balanced with the free expression rights of others who would like to use copyrighted works, regardless of the author's wishes. The copyright holders of this book ought to be able to prevent readers from photocopying the entire book. Should they be able to prevent readers from photocopying a *single page* of the text? Doesn't that seem a bit extreme? Filmmakers probably like to get good reviews of their movies and probably like it a lot less when a review is harsh. Should filmmakers be able to allow only those who like their films to use brief clips of it in their movie review? That seems wrong, doesn't it?

The balance that has been struck between the rights of authors and those of consumers is to provide for the **fair use** of a copyrighted work. If use of a copyrighted work is considered a fair use, copyright holders have no right to prevent its use nor are they entitled to any compensation for its use. Section 107 of the Copyright Act clearly spells out the factors to be considered in determining whether a specific use is fair.

Fair use ■
Section 104 of the copyright act allows copyrighted material to be used for fair use, which is determined by considering 1) the purpose of the use, 2) the nature of the work, 3) the amount of the work used, and 4) the effect on the market for the work.

---

[12]*Eldred v. Ashcroft*, 537 U.S. 186 (2003).

FAIR USE !

> **Bedrock Law:** The fair use test requires the application of all four standards, including purpose and character of the use, nature of the work, substantiality and amount of the use, and the impact on potential markets.

1. The purpose and character of the use, including whether such use is of commercial nature or is for nonprofit educational purposes.
2. The nature of the copyrighted work.
3. The amount and substantiality of the portion used in relation to the copyrighted work as a whole.
4. The effect of the use upon the potential market for, or value of, the copyrighted work.

ALL four factors must be considered in determining whether a use is fair. It is not enough, for example, to state that a work is for educational nonprofit purposes and is therefore a fair use. If that were the case, school districts across the nation would only need to purchase one copy of any textbook and make all the copies needed for their students. The use would be educational and not-for-profit but it would definitely be a copyright infringement. We will examine each of the four factors in turn.

Purpose and Character of the Use

The first consideration in determining whether use of copyright material will be considered fair use is to consider the purpose and character of the use. Nonprofit educational uses have an almost mystical appeal. Educators everywhere often justify any copying they may do as fair use because it is for educational purposes and certainly educational use is the sort of purpose Congress was trying to protect in the statute. Congress specifically mentioned nonprofit educational purposes in its description of an appropriate fair use, but it is not the only acceptable purpose. Review and criticism is also an acceptable purpose. Certainly a critic commenting on a book, play, or movie ought to be able to include excerpts of the copyrighted work to provide examples to the audience. Research, scholarship, and news reporting are also acceptable fair use purposes.

In 1994 the Supreme Court made it clear that parody was also an acceptable purpose for the fair use of copyright material. In 1989 the rap group 2 Live Crew wrote and recorded "Pretty Woman," a song that by the group's own admission was a parody of the 1964 Roy Orbison hit "Oh, Pretty Woman." The rights to the Orbison song were controlled by Acuff-Rose Music, and the publishing company did not want 2 Live Crew to produce the parody. Contrary to Acuff-Rose's wishes, 2 Live Crew released the song and shortly after found itself the defendant in a copyright suit. A federal district court dismissed the suit but the Sixth Circuit reversed. When the case made its way to the U.S. Supreme Court it attracted a good deal of attention. *Amicus* briefs are often filed by third parties interested in the outcome and this case was no exception. As might be expected, the National Music Publishers' Association, Nashville Songwriters' Association International, and National Academy of Songwriters along with well-known songwriters Michael Jackson, Dolly Parton, and the estate of George Gershwin all lined up to support the right of authors to control their works from parody use. Conversely, parodists including the Harvard Lampoon, *MAD Magazine,* and the Capitol Steps (a well-known Washington, D.C., comedy troupe specializing in musical parody of politics) supported 2 Live Crew. In a unanimous decision, the Court ruled that

2 Live Crew's use was not a copyright infringement but a legitimate fair use. The Court removed any doubt as to whether parody was an acceptable purpose when it held that "parody, like other comment or criticism, may claim fair use under §107."[13]

> **Bedrock Law:** The transformative value of parody affords greater freedom to use the copyrighted material for humorous purpose without being subject to infringement claims.

Nature of the Copyrighted Work

This second criterion is the least debated of the four. At issue is whether the author of the copyrighted work created something that should be open to fair use. Generally speaking, most work is suited to news reporting or criticism or educational use, but there are exceptions. The most notable one would be an unpublished work. Someone might produce poetry with no intention to ever publish it. The poems would be copyrighted as soon as they were fixed in a tangible medium, but the author might keep them forever in a desk drawer, or only share them with the lover who is the subject of the poems. Publishing excerpts of those poems for the purpose of comment or criticism might constitute an acceptable purpose for a fair use, but the nature of the copyrighted work would be such that the use would not be fair. Commentary and criticism are appropriate for work that the author has made public, especially work that the author has attempted to commercialize, but that is a difficult argument to make when the author has chosen not to make the work public.

Fair use generally is easier to claim with nonfiction works than with works of fiction. Facts cannot be copyrighted and the public benefits from the dissemination of information so it is easier to claim that the nature of a nonfiction copyrighted work is suited to news reporting, research, and scholarly activity, although it is still possible to make that claim for fiction works, too. Most law texts assert that scientific articles are more suited to fair use than "creative" content but there is no case law to substantiate this.

Finally, "consumable" works are considered less suited to fair use than other sorts of intellectual property. Workbooks are created with the intent to be used one time. Unlike books that can be read and passed along to another reader, a workbook depends on each use to "consume" the content. Photocopying a portion of a book is much more likely to be seen as an acceptable fair use than photocopying a similar portion of a workbook.

The Amount and Substantiality of the Use

Most people can easily understand that a fair use of a copyrighted work requires using only a limited amount. In the example above, it's easy to see that photocopying an entire textbook and making enough copies for an entire school district is not a fair use. What's not so easy to suppose is just how much of a work can be used while still qualifying as a fair use, and Congress provides no formula to help with the guesswork.

---

[13]*Campbell v. Acuff-Rose Music,* 510 U.S. 569, 579 (1994).

One factor that is known is that the phrase "amount and substantiality" refers to both a qualitative and quantitative measurement. To know whether a use is fair requires knowing whether too much has been used, but it also requires knowing whether the amount copied was so significant as to constitute the heart of the copyrighted work. Television shows or websites that provide reviews of movies often use brief clips—sometimes only a few seconds but never more than a couple of minutes of a movie. As a percentage of the content, this constitutes only 1 or 2 percent of the film. Under normal circumstances this would not be too much quantitatively. But what if the two minutes were to reveal the "whodunit" in a murder mystery, or the surprise ending of a movie? It could be that the heart of the movie would be taken, and that qualitatively the amount copied would be significant.

This is precisely what happened in 1979 when *The Nation* magazine rushed to press with a 2,250-word article containing excerpts from the soon-to-be-released memoir of former President Gerald Ford. *Time* magazine had an exclusive contract with publisher Harper & Row for prepublication excerpts from the book. Once *The Nation*'s article appeared in print, *Time* canceled its contract and refused to pay $12,500: the second half of the agreed-upon amount for the rights. The article contained fewer than 400 words that were direct quotes from the unpublished manuscript. Quantitatively the quoted material was a small portion of *The Nation* article, an even smaller portion of the planned *Time* magazine 7,500-word excerpt and an even smaller portion of Ford's book on which both were based. But qualitatively the quotes were substantial. With all due respect to President Ford, as a half-term president who was never elected to either the presidency or vice presidency, the greatest interest in his memoir was the portion dealing with his succession to the presidency and speculation as to whether he had a deal with former President Nixon to provide Nixon with a pardon in exchange for the presidency. The other chapters about his youth or as a member of Congress had significantly less market value outside his native Michigan. Inquiring minds wanted to know about the pardon.

In 1985 the Supreme Court ruled 6–3 that *The Nation* infringed on Harper & Row's copyright, and the article was not an acceptable fair use. In addition to the fact that the substantiality of the work was significant, the Court also noted that the copied material was used before it had been published (emphasizing the nature of the copyrighted work as one of the criteria) and that the market value was affected.[14]

Effect on the Market

Copyright infringers who do not profit from their infringements often wrongly assume that their use of copyrighted material falls under fair use. They incorrectly believe that because they do not profit from the infringing use they are innocent of wrongdoing. It is important to note that copyright infringement is not about others illegally profiting from a copyrighted work but instead about denying copyright holders the fruits of their intellectual property. Infringement is not about putting money in the infringer's pocket but about taking money *out* of the pocket of the

---

[14]*Harper & Row Publishers v. Nation Enters.*, 471 U.S. 539 (1985).

copyright holder. As with the example of a school district copying a textbook, the district would not profit by providing free photocopies to students, but it would definitely subtract profits from the copyright holder. This chapter opened with the story of Joel Tenenbaum's illegal downloading of music and his attempt to assert that his downloads were a fair use—an argument the court rejected. The court operated under the assumption that downloading the songs without paying for them had an effect on the market. The authors missed out on receiving royalties that they would have received had the songs been legally purchased.

In the earlier case involving 2 Live Crew, the Supreme Court explained that parody is transformative, that is, it actually is quite different from the original work. Unlike a new arrangement of an old song or a group doing a "cover" of an older song, a parody would not be the sort of thing to replace the earlier version. A cover song is a derivative work, not a fair use, and the author would receive a royalty on the sale of the original song or the cover. On the other hand a parody is not a substitute for the original work. The Court had a hard time imagining someone in a music store wanting to purchase a version of "Pretty Woman" but not certain whether to buy the Roy Orbison or 2 Live Crew version. The sale of a 2 Live Crew parody would not be likely to result in one less sale of the original. In the case of President Gerald Ford's memoirs, however, the Supreme Court believed that the unauthorized use of copyrighted material by *The Nation* would reduce the number of people willing to pay to read the excerpts in *Time* magazine or the entire memoir by Harper & Row publishers.

It is understood that all four factors must be considered in determining whether or not a particular use of copyrighted material is a fair use, but if one factor has a little more weight than others it is probably the determination of the effect on the market.

Trying to Do the Right Thing

Neither Congress nor the courts have provided any precise measuring stick to indicate exactly what constitutes a protected fair use. It's easy to imagine teachers, researchers, authors, filmmakers, and others who want to operate within the law but just don't know what they can and cannot do.

The Center for Social Media at American University has provided some help through its guidebooks of "best practices" for media literacy education, online video, and documentary filmmaking. CSM provides those trying to do the right thing with a consensus of opinion on the use of copyrighted materials and fair use. The best practices are not a formula, and certainly lack the force of law, but those who adhere to them stand a better chance of claiming that their use falls within the purview of acceptability than by just argument.[15]

In 2001, Creative Commons was founded as a not-for-profit organization hoping to change the culture and dynamics around copyright. It encourages copyright holders to share more of their creative works. Under traditional copyright,

---

[15]The guides can be accessed through the Center for Social Media's website, http://www
.centerforsocialmedia.org/.

there are two extremes and nothing in between. At one end, the copyright holder controls the entire bundle of rights discussed earlier. This position is expressed by copyright holders by the phrase "all rights reserved." At the other extreme are works in the public domain for which there is no copyright holder, or the copyright holder has forfeited all rights. Creative Commons has created a middle ground, where copyright holders can make it clear that they will accept certain uses of their copyrighted works. A Creative Commons licensee can authorize sharing according to six different levels. At every level, the copyright holder must receive attribution (see Creative Commons Licenses figure).

The Creative Commons website lists a number of participants. The popular photo-sharing website Flickr is the world's largest source of Creative Commons licenses. Those who post pictures to the site are given the option of making their photos more or less free for use by others. The rock group Nine Inch Nails was able to share its music through Creative Commons while still bringing in substantial amounts of money and selling out a concert tour. All content taken from the collaborative encyclopedia Wikipedia is available through a Creative Commons "Share Alike" license.

Of course there are commercial services that will help those wanting to pay for uses that do not qualify as fair use. The Copyright Clearance Center is a commercial service that allows businesses and schools to purchase duplication rights for books and articles either through a blanket license or per use. The Harry Fox Agency no longer licenses synchronization rights but will still provide licenses for mechanical rights (such as those including a previously recorded song in a compilation CD) or ring tones.

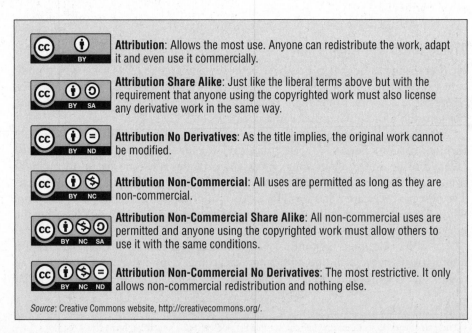

Attribution: Allows the most use. Anyone can redistribute the work, adapt it and even use it commercially.

Attribution Share Alike: Just like the liberal terms above but with the requirement that anyone using the copyrighted work must also license any derivative work in the same way.

Attribution No Derivatives: As the title implies, the original work cannot be modified.

Attribution Non-Commercial: All uses are permitted as long as they are non-commercial.

Attribution Non-Commercial Share Alike: All non-commercial uses are permitted and anyone using the copyrighted work must allow others to use it with the same conditions.

Attribution Non-Commercial No Derivatives: The most restrictive. It only allows non-commercial redistribution and nothing else.

Source: Creative Commons website, http://creativecommons.org/.

Creative Commons Licenses

DEVICES THAT FACILITATE INFRINGEMENT

Copyright violators are responsible for their own actions, but should anyone *else* assume a degree of culpability for copyright violations? Since photocopiers are so often used as instruments for violating copyright, should their manufacturers also have to accept some share of the responsibility?

Analog Tape Recording

The seminal case in this area was decided by the U.S. Supreme Court in 1984. In *Sony v. Universal*,[16] Universal Studios wanted the Court to hold Sony responsible for copyright infringements based on the fact that the Sony Betamax video recorder was being used to violate copyright. Universal and other studios tried to assert that Sony was marketing the recorders as a way for people to record copyrighted movies and television programs and that Sony and the retailers that sold the equipment ought to be responsible. In a 5–4 decision, the Court ruled that the simple process of "time shifting" (recording a program for later viewing) was a fair use that did not harm the market for the copyright holder. Fred Rogers of public television's *Mr. Rogers' Neighborhood* testified that he endorsed noncommercial home taping of his program to allow families to watch it at a convenient time. Even if the recording of the programs had been a copyright violation by the video recorders' owners, Sony was not somehow "vicariously liable" for the actions of those who purchased the recorders. The legal doctrine of "contributory infringement" had been previously used to show a relationship between an infringer and someone who had provided the means for infringement. In those cases, however, there was a continuous relationship between the infringer and the "contributor."[17] Sony's relationship ended as soon as the recorder was purchased and as such it did not "contribute" to any possible copyright infringement. Certainly there was a potentially illegal use of Sony's video recorder, just as there were many legal uses for the machine, and Sony could not be held liable for the illegal uses.

Digital MP3 Recording

The *Sony* case was a concern for manufacturers of audio cassette recorders as well as video recorders, some of which were manufactured with two tape slots: one for a "play" tape and one for a "record" tape to allow copying of tapes. Photocopier manufacturers also had a vested interest in not being held responsible for the copyright infringements committed by the users of their machines. When the Supreme Court found that Sony was not liable, it was a great relief to a wide assortment of recording equipment manufacturers.

---

[16]464 U.S. 417 (1984).

[17]In the Sony case, the Court cited the "dance hall cases" as examples of an ongoing relationship between a business and a copyright violator. Violations were facilitated by a racetrack, a cocktail lounge, and dance hall. In those cases there was a continuous relationship between the copyright infringer and the "facilitator." *Id.* at 437–38.

It was nearly fifteen years later when Shawn Fanning started college at Northeastern University in Boston and almost immediately developed Napster, a peer-to-peer (P2P) file-sharing service. Napster was not the first P2P service but it became quickly popular because it focused on MP3 music files and had an easy-to-navigate interface. The combination made it simple for anyone with an Internet connection to share music with other music lovers around the globe. The service became enormously popular especially with college students who had access to fast Internet connections through their campuses and who were the sort of early adopters easily engaged by digital technology. When the service became available in 1999, 15,000 users downloaded the software in just the first week with no promotion or publicity. The number of users and files grew rapidly. In less than two years, more than two billion files (mostly songs) were being traded each month.

Had Napster remained just a small group of Fanning and his friends sharing music it's unlikely the service would have garnered much attention, but that was not to be the case. Napster became the lightning rod for the music industry's concern over file sharing. The Recording Industry Association of America (RIAA) filed the first of several lawsuits against Napster in 1999. Heavy metal band Metallica was outraged when one of its songs was shared on Napster before the band had even publicly released the music. In 2000 the band filed suit against the P2P service, which was followed by one filed by rapper Dr. Dre, then a third suit filed by a collection of recording companies. A federal district court presided over the case and essentially put Napster out of business[18] by ruling that even though Napster itself was not violating copyrights, it was liable for "contributory" and "vicarious" copyright infringement: a ruling upheld by the Ninth Circuit.[19] Although the defendants attempted to argue that Napster was just like Sony and that the service should not be penalized for the illegal uses that some people might engage in, the Ninth Circuit did not accept that premise. The court noted that Napster still had control over the use people made of the service, unlike those who purchase a video deck and then never interact again with the manufacturer. Napster's involvement with copyright infringers was continuous. The court also noted that Napster's index system, which was used by file traders to search for the songs they wanted, could also allow Napster to search the files for copyrighted material and remove it from the system—a capability that Sony never had. While Sony never had the ability to police the behavior of its equipment users for infringements, Napster had that ability and opted not to use it.

The story doesn't end there though. File-sharing network Gnutella was created in 2000, and Kazaa, Morpheus, BitTorrent, and Grokster rolled out in 2001. Each service, like Napster and Sony's Betamax video recorder, was capable of legal uses as well as copyright infringements. The *Napster* case never made its way to the Supreme Court, but in 2005 the Court decided a case involving Grokster and Morpheus, a service of StreamCast. The P2P services were sued by a group of movie studios, songwriters, music recording companies, and publishers. A California

---

[18]The Napster name still exists as a legal paid music service of Best Buy but bears no resemblance to the P2P service it was founded as.

[19]*A&M Records v. Napster*, 239 F.3d 1004 (9th Cir. 2001).

federal district court and the Circuit Court of Appeals for the Ninth Circuit had found in Grokster's favor, largely by an analysis that followed the *Sony* rationale. The P2P services had legitimate uses, and the "manufacturer" should not be held liable for the illegal uses made by some of the customers. On appeal, the Supreme Court issued a strongly worded reversal of the lower courts' decisions. The second sentence of the Court's opinion read "one who distributes a device with the object of promoting its use to infringe copyright, as shown by clear expression or other affirmative steps taken to foster infringement, is liable for the resulting acts of infringement by third parties."[20] Writing for a unanimous Court, Justice David Souter noted that "from the moment Grokster and StreamCast began" they promoted themselves as free services that would allow users to download copyrighted works.[21] He noted that both services made concerted efforts to attract Napster users looking for an alternative service after the injunctions that stopped Napster's file sharing. The companies made no effort to prevent copyright infringement and appeared to thwart efforts by anyone to monitor whether or how much infringement was occurring. The Supreme Court stated that the lower courts had misapplied the *Sony* decision because *Sony* should not be interpreted as protecting any product simply because it is *capable* of substantial lawful use. The Supreme Court declined to provide some formula to the *Sony* decision and rather to "leave further consideration of the *Sony* rule for a day when that may be required."[22]

The Supreme Court may someday provide more direction on devices that have legal uses and are used for illegal copying, but we can already see lower courts interpreting the importance of a company's attitude and involvement in policing its users. YouTube is an amazing story. Founded in 2005, it had 8 million videos viewed per day by the end of the year. By 2010, YouTube had exceeded 2 *billion* views per day. Google purchased YouTube in 2006 for $1.65 billion. In March of 2007, media giant Viacom filed suit against YouTube and its parent company for $1 billion, claiming that YouTube encouraged copyright infringement similar to what had been done by Grokster and others.

YouTube acknowledged that it may have had some copyrighted material on its site but defended itself by asserting that it was not encouraging copyright infringement. Quite the contrary, YouTube asserted that it responded immediately to any request it received to take down copyrighted content. The Digital Millennium Copyright Act (DMCA), which criminalized any equipment or actions that attempt to defeat digital rights management software (the software that prevents unauthorized copying of digital work) also provided protection for online services that might be used for copyright violation, provided those services quickly complied with any takedown requests. The so-called safe harbor in the DMCA protects good faith efforts by those who don't violate the copyrights but whose websites provide opportunity for others to infringe copyright. Website operators such as YouTube won't be responsible for infringements if they quickly respond. YouTube has been so quick to respond that others have accused YouTube of

---

[20]*MGM v. Grokster,* 545 U.S. 913, 919 (2005).

[21]*Id,* at 923–24.

[22]*Id,* at 934.

removing material that should be protected, such as parodies that would be considered fair use. YouTube's policy has been to remove material when requested to do so and then later reinstate it if it is determined that the copyrighted material may still be used. This decision, though likely to be appealed, has come as a great source of relief to the multitude of websites that allow the sharing of videos, pictures, text, and so forth.

From the *Sony* case to the present, the message appears to be that creating a means for violating copyright is not a problem if there are also noninfringing uses. Promoting something as a means of violating copyright, or creators who fail to take action within their ability, may be culpable.

TRADEMARKS   10yr validation + Renewal

Another form of intellectual property is a trademark. The simplest way to think of a trademark is as a means for customers to identify a product. Some people might not taste a difference between Coke and Pepsi, but others would be very upset if they were sold one soft drink when they thought they were getting the other. Trademarks are a way of distinguishing one product from another. Well-known trademarks (like Coke and Pepsi) are recognizable worldwide, and the companies that own the marks spend millions of dollars protecting them from infringement.

In the United States, companies register their trademarks through the U.S. Patent and Trademark Office. As with copyright, registration can be done online and requires the payment of a fee. The duration of a trademark is quite different from copyrights, though. A trademark registration is valid for only ten years, but it can be renewed an indefinite number of times. Coca-Cola was first registered as a trademark in 1893 and has been continually renewed.

On the other hand, trademarks may be sold or transferred. A company may go out of business and no longer need the name, so it can be sold just like any other assets. Brands USA Holdings is a company that acquires trademarks and then resells them. In 2010 they held an auction where they sold brand names like Handi-Wrap for $30,000, Meister Brau (a former beer) for $32,500, and Shearson (former financial company) for $45,000.

Company names can be trademarked but so can other distinctive attributes, such as nicknames, slogans, or logos. Coke is a trademark of the Coca-Cola Company, and the name Coca-Cola is also trademarked. For years Coke had trademarked the slogan "Coke is it," but that particular trademark was canceled in 2004. Coca-Cola still maintains the trademark on the phrases "This calls for a Coke" and "Coke add life." A variety of Coke logos are trademarked, most notably the name "Coca-Cola" in distinctive red script.

What may be surprising to some is that the contoured bottle unique to Coke not only was patented[23] in 1917, but it was granted a trademark as a distinctive symbol of the product in 1977.

---

[23]Patents are exclusive rights to inventions. Like copyrights, they are constitutionally protected and are registered with the federal government. A thorough discussion of patents is beyond the scope of this book.

Companies invest in protecting their trademarks for several reasons, primary among them is the fear that failure to aggressively protect a trademark may result in a company losing its exclusivity to the name. There is an extensive history of trademarks that have been lost over time because companies did not do enough to protect their trademarks. Aspirin was developed in the 1890s and was once the exclusive trademark of the international drug company Bayer, but the term became so commonly associated with any company's version of acetylsalicylic acid (the scientific name of the chemical compound) that Bayer could no longer claim the exclusive right to use the name.[24] The same fate has happened to trademarks for escalator, kerosene, and trampoline. All were once exclusive trademarks that have since become generic terms. Companies like Kimberly-Clark and Johnson & Johnson collectively cringe when consumers use the terms *Kleenex* and *Band-Aid* as generic names for tissues and adhesive bandages respectively. Each year Xerox places advertisements that tout its trademark and discourage its use as a verb (you can copy a document; you cannot "Xerox" it). This is why companies notify media whenever they see their trademarks have been misused. If a reporter happens to mention needing a "Kleenex," a Kimberly-Clark attorney may contact the television station advising them not to use their trademark as a generic term. It provides evidence that the companies have aggressively protected their trademarks: a consideration used in determining whether the trademark deserves renewal.

One of the Coca-Cola Company's registered trademarks

A second reason for protecting a trademark is to prevent it from losing its commercial value. In 1972, Coca-Cola filed legal action again a company that was making posters that said "Enjoy Cocaine" in the same script that "Enjoy Coca-Cola" was using. Gemini Rising attempted to defend its poster by asserting that Coca-Cola had not shown any loss of income as a result of the posters, and that no consumers were shown to have been misled into thinking the posters were a product of the Coca-Cola Company. A federal district court in New York found in favor of Coca-Cola and ordered a halt to the posters for three reasons: (1) associating cocaine with Coca-Cola disparages the product; (2) consumers might be confused into believing Coca-Cola was somehow involved in the poster (the trademark claim), and; (3) the poster is likely to damage Coca-Cola's business reputation.[25] In the years since this case, Congress has added legislation that makes it easier for companies to protect their trademarks from dilution: the legal term for use of a trademark by others that diminishes the uniqueness of the mark, regardless of whether the use is competing or results in lost revenue.

---

[24]While "aspirin" is considered a generic term in the United States, it is still a registered trademark in dozens of countries, including Bayer's international headquarters of Germany.

[25]*Coca-Cola v. Gemini Rising*, 346 F. Supp. 1183 (E.D. N.Y. 1972).

On the other hand, another federal court found the near-replication of a trademark as entitled to some protection. One of the best-known logos around the world is the Nike swoosh. From 1977 to 1991, Nike spent more than $300 million advertising its trademarks. Along came commercial artist Michael Standard who decided to parody the famous symbol by producing t-shirts and sweatshirts with a swoosh and the name "Mike," just one letter off from the athletic company's name. Standard then marketed the clothes to people named Mike, admitting that the whole intent was for people to see the similarity to the famous Nike logo. A federal district court issued a summary judgment and enjoined Standard from marketing his parody logo, but on appeal the Seventh Circuit found that the evidence was not as clear as the district court implied. Standard had provided a list of customers who knew they were not purchasing Nike clothing while Nike provided no evidence of any consumer confusion.[26] Unlike the Coca-Cola poster, there was no claim that the product had been somehow disparaged or the brand damaged by the parody and the appellate court was unwilling to enjoin the use of the logo without evidence of consumer confusion. Whether Michael Standard would win today given the new federal statutes is open to speculation, but certainly is not a sure bet.

Trademark dilution can be used by companies to prevent their trademarks from being devalued, but not in every instance. The federal Dilution Act protects trademarks, but not from the sort of uses that would be similar to fair use exemptions on copyright. Use of a trademark in a comparison ad, for example, is not considered trademark dilution. When Pepsi runs commercials that show someone preferring the taste of Pepsi over that of Coke with a trademark bottle or logo clearly visible, there is no trademark dilution.[27] News media use of trademarks is not a dilution of a trademark either, nor is the inclusion of a Coca-Cola logo in this text.

Unlike copyrights, trademarks are registered *after* they have been in use. The claim for a trademark by a company is that a word, phrase, or logo has come to be associated with a product and that takes some time to establish. Certain words or phrases have more or less protection based on their distinctiveness. Names of companies that exist nowhere else have a strong claim as *distinctive* trademarks and are able to enforce their trademark across all industries. Company names like Kodak, Verizon, and Exxon are unlike other company names or English-language words.[28] As such, these company names are distinctive trademarks that can be enforced in other industries. Even though Kodak is not involved in oil exploration and refining, it could prevent another company from coming along and starting the Kodak Oil Company. Similarly Exxon could prevent any other company from making an Exxon digital camera.

---

[26]*Nike v. "Just Did It" Enters.*, 6 F. 3d 1225 (7th Cir. 1993).

[27]Of course the advertisement must be accurate otherwise it could be misleading—a topic covered in chapter 12.

[28]The creation of the Exxon name has become a legend in trademark circles. In 1911 the Supreme Court broke Standard Oil into 34 companies, one of which was Standard Oil of New Jersey, which used the name "Esso" (a vocalization of the abbreviation S.O.). Because of the other Standard Oils that existed, Standard Oil of New Jersey could only use Esso in parts of the United States. In the early 1970s the company changed its name to Exxon. The name was an attempt to resemble Esso while creating a name distinctive enough to withstand trademark challenges worldwide. The double-X does not naturally occur in any major language.

Comparing Apples to Apples

Apple Computer provides an example of how seemingly different businesses might become interrelated and thus create trademark confusion. In 1978 Apple Corps, the company that owned the Beatles' record label, was concerned that Apple Computer would infringe the record label's copyright. The situation was further complicated by the fact that both international companies were based in different nations (the record label in the UK, the computer company in the United States) with different trademark laws. For nearly thirty years the two Apples negotiated, with Apple Computer paying Apple Corps and both companies agreeing to stay out of each other's core business. In 1978 the similarity in brands was not much of an issue but in the twenty-first century, Apple Computer became a major player in the music industry with its iTunes service. Apple Computer successfully defended itself against a trademark infringement claim in a British court in 2006 and a new agreement was signed between the two companies in 2007, with rumors that the computer company had paid the record label half a billion dollars for trademark rights. The two companies "settled" for the first time in 1981 but the ensuing decades proved the issue was anything but settled.

In contrast, other perfectly valid trademarks can be created that are *fanciful* rather than distinctive. Fanciful marks combine words in an odd combination that makes them unique for that industry. What does an apple have to do with a computer? Absolutely nothing. Combining the words makes Apple Computer an enforceable trademark, but not beyond the confines of that specific industry. Apple Computer would not win a claim of copyright infringement against Big Apple Grocery in San Francisco, Apple Tree Daycare in Connecticut, or Apple Bail Bonds in New Jersey. Consumers are not likely to be confused into believing that the same company that makes the computers operates the grocery store, daycare, or bail bonds service.

Unlike distinctive or fanciful trademarks, a descriptive trademark is one that describes the product through the name. It's more difficult to obtain a trademark if the name is simply descriptive because of the possible confusion to the consumer. Raisins and oat bran flakes form a cereal that is familiar to Americans and multiple cereal companies provide their own versions, but none of those companies can trademark "raisin bran." Kellogg's Raisin Bran, on the other hand, is a registered trademark because of the inclusion of the distinctive name "Kellogg."

A company can get a trademark for a descriptive trademark if the mark takes on a secondary meaning. "Coppertone" certainly sounds descriptive: in fact it is used to describe the color that the product intends to produce. Since 1950, the Schering-Plough Company has held the trademark registration first for hair coloring and later for suntan products and then expanded it to include moisturizers, sunglasses, insect repellants, clothing, and other products generally associated with the beach. Trademark questions always revolve around consumers and whether they are likely to recognize a trademark as an indication of a specific company's product. Coppertone has successfully asserted its mark as recognizable by consumers and not merely some generic descriptor of the product. The recommendation from most trademark attorneys is that companies should avoid descriptive trademarks as much as possible but rather try to create marks that are distinctive (fanciful), if possible.

Celebrity names create unique issues in trademark law. Julia Roberts is a well-known movie actress who has performed in dozens of motion pictures, appeared on television, and is regularly the subject of tabloids. Certainly her name is associated with her, and when most people hear "Julia Roberts" they tend to think of the actress. Should Julia Roberts be able to trademark her name? If so, does that mean other people who happen to be named Julia Roberts are not entitled to use the name?

Famous people do have the right to trademark their names, if (as with any other "product") consumers are likely to associate the specific name with that product. Even though there may be dozens of Jennifer Lopezes in the United States, the singer/actor/entrepreneur claims the right to use the name and to prevent others from using the name *even if it happens to be their name*. Trademark laws attempt to protect the consumer, so if it is believed that consumers may be confused into believing that a song or piece of clothing with the name "Jennifer Lopez" on it came from *the* Jennifer Lopez then trademark law requires that the use be denied.

Celebrities want to protect the exclusive use of their names on all sorts of products and on the Internet as well. Julia Roberts had to fight a legal battle to prevent someone else from using the URL "juliaroberts.com." In 2000 she was successfully able to assert that the URL had been acquired by a "cybersquatter": a person who stakes a claim on domain names for the purpose of exploiting their fame. In some cases, people used to cybersquat intending to "ransom" valuable URLs for large sums of money. In 1999 Congress passed the Anticybersquatting Consumer Protection Act (ACPA), specifically in response to a number of complaints about entrepreneurs who tried to extract large payments from individuals and companies that wanted to acquire the URL resembling their names. Despite the fact that Roberts's name was not trademarked at the time, she was able to demonstrate that her name had acquired a "secondary meaning" and as such she had common-law trademark rights. One of the major considerations in deciding that she was entitled to the URL was the bad faith actions of the cybersquatter who tried to make money by selling the rights for much more than he paid, and the fact that he had acquired a number of URLs for just such a purpose. Had the same URL been acquired by a Julia Roberts fan club with the intention of posting news about the star and not attempting to profit from her, or by a *different* Julia Roberts who happened to use it as her own personal page, Roberts may have had a much more difficult time.

Just as trademark law does not prevent others from naming a product when criticizing it, neither does the ACPA prevent others from using a name in a URL when criticizing that person or company. While there is no Supreme Court case on the issue, in 2003 the Court of Appeals for the Sixth Circuit ruled that a web designer in Texas who used the name of a mall in six different URLs did not infringe the mall's trademarks.[29] One of the websites had mall information but provided a prominent disclaimer that it was not the mall's official website and a

---

[29]*Taubman v. Webfeats*, 319 F.3d 770 (6th Cir. 2003).

link to the official site. The other five websites were "complaint" sites, all containing "sucks" as part of the URL. The mall may not have liked the websites, but there was no doubt that any visitor to the sites would recognize them as *not* being operated by the mall. "Sucks" sites have become rather common on the web and most major corporations have some complainant who has started a website to complain about them. Some companies have attempted to buy up URLs that might be used against them, but there are just too many possible combinations. Even if walmartsucks.com is not currently a gripe site, Wal-Mart has to contend with gripe sites at walmartsucks.org and walmart-blows.com. It's not just major corporations that have gripe sites. Every pop culture icon from the *Twilight* books and movies (twilightsucks.com) to the TV show *Survivor* (survivorsucks.yuku.com) have gripe sites. People for the Ethical Treatment of Animals has even created milksucks.com to discourage human consumption of animal milk.

THE RED LIGHT AT 3:00 A.M.

Intellectual property law is tremendously detailed and sometimes tedious. There are many times that people wonder whether their copyright infringement will ever be noticed, and even if it is, whether a copyright holder would ever bother filing suit. After all, they assume, in most cases the infractions are small and the likelihood of being caught is small as well.

An ideal metaphor for thinking of this is a traffic light. Red means stop whether the light is at a busy intersection or on a country road. It's the same whether it's the height of rush hour or the dead of night. The law doesn't change, although the possibility of being caught is radically different in different situations.

Many copyright infractions can be thought of as running a red light at 3:00 a.m. They are still violations but they are less likely to be discovered. There are probably hundreds of high schools in the United States that have put together some sort of slide show for seniors using the Green Day song "Good Riddance" (also known as "Time of Your Life"). That's a synchronization that should be licensed. When a person buys a CD and makes an *illegal* copy of that disk for a friend, that's a violation of copyright law just as certain as if someone pirated the CD and made it available on a file-sharing service, but it's a whole lot harder to detect the former than the latter.

Police *do* sometimes catch people running red lights at 3:00 a.m. though, and sometimes what might have been thought to be a minor copyright infraction is litigated. A fraternity at the University of Central Florida probably never expected legal trouble from *Playboy* when it put the bunny logo on party tickets without *Playboy*'s permission. Nonetheless Kappa

Alpha Psi was notified by *Playboy* in 2004 that it was going to find itself the defendant in a lawsuit.[30]

It's also safe to assume that the Girl Scouts never thought about the copyright problems they might face by having campers sing copyrighted songs around the camp fire, yet in 1996 ASCAP started pursuing licensing fees from the Girl Scouts. Just like the ambiance of a restaurant is enhanced by the music in the dining room, the camp experience is enhanced by the copyrighted songs sung at camp. ASCAP had the right to demand compensation, and several camps started to pay fees, but the licensing agency did not foresee the public relations nightmare that would result. When news media across the country started reporting that Girl Scouts would have to stop singing camp songs or face possible litigation, ASCAP was characterized as a bully picking on little kids, and quickly recanted. ASCAP is still adamant that it has the right to collect fees, but licenses the Girl Scouts for $1 per year.

There are countless stories, some apocryphal, of someone who had committed what appeared to be a minor copyright or trademark infringement and was persecuted (or prosecuted) for having done so. ASCAP and BMI have employees who visit restaurants and other establishments that they know have not paid licensing fees to determine whether licensed music is being played without authorization. Professional and collegiate sports teams are constantly looking for unauthorized use of their trademarks and logos on clothing. YouTube receives take-down notices daily from authors claiming copyright infringement. For centuries there have been more violations of intellectual property rights than can ever be discovered, regardless of the technology.

The traffic light metaphor helps to understand this situation. There are a lot more people who run red lights than are ever caught. Law enforcement could never possibly have enough staff to catch all the people who break the law. But laws, whether they are traffic laws or intellectual property laws, rely on enough violators being caught to discourage illegal behavior by others. It's not necessary to catch all lawbreakers to maintain an orderly system. What matters is that people know that the possibility exists that they will be caught if they break the law, which discourages many (perhaps most) from engaging in illegal behavior. Publicity about enforcement actually helps. Drivers who know that the police occasionally stake out a particular intersection are less likely to run that particular red light. When news media report on a Joel Tenenbaum being fined for copyright infringement, it frightens some people just enough to prevent them from illegally downloading content. This sort of cat-and-mouse game has always existed. Technological advances have exacerbated the problem but it's still about having enough enforcement to keep violations to a tolerable amount.

College campuses have been seen as breeding grounds for digital piracy. Campuses usually have lots of bandwidth that facilitates high-speed downloads. The distributed nature of campus computing makes it ideal for sharing files in multiple locations. Students are bright and are generally among the early adopters of new

---

[30]*Playboy Suing UCF Fraternity over Use of Logo for Party*, WFTV-TV, *available at* http://www.wftv.com/news/3588705/detail.html.

technologies. The RIAA has decided that there might be more benefit by putting some pressure on universities to prevent widescale copyright infringement on their campuses than from pursuing individual pirates. In 2008 Congress passed the Higher Education Opportunity Act, part of which contained requirements that universities implement guidelines on illegal file sharing. Universities vary in the steps they have taken: everything from informational brochures on copyright laws to loss of Internet use and even expulsion for repeat offenses.[31]

> **Bedrock Law:** There is a big difference between whether something is a copyright infringement and whether it is likely to result in legal action.

SUMMARY

- Copyright is constitutionally protected and is actually a bundle of different rights that include copying (reproduction) but also rights to control performance of the work, derivative works, distribution, and public display of the work.

- Music authors usually collect royalties for the performance of their works via one of three major licensing agencies: ASCAP, BMI, or SESAC, all of which will act as licensing agents for the authors and collect fees from those using their music (broadcasters, restaurants, etc.).

- Derivative works may have even greater value to an author than the original work itself. A book author's royalties on a few thousand copies of a book could be tiny compared to the movie rights if the book is turned into a major motion picture.

- Original creative work in a fixed medium can be copyrighted but ideas and facts cannot.

- One owns copyright whether or not the work is registered. Without registering, though, the remuneration a copyright holder can receive for an infringement is significantly less.

- For single-authored works in the United States today, copyright lasts for the life of the author plus seventy years. The length of copyright has been changed repeatedly by Congress, most recently in 1998.

- Even a copyright holder cannot prevent fair use of a copyrighted work. This can be complicated. There is no concrete list of acceptable and unacceptable fair uses—only a list of four criteria to be considered: the purpose and character of the use; the nature of the copyrighted work; the amount and substantiality used; and the impact on the market.

- Creating hardware and software that *could possibly* be used for copyright infringement (like a video recorder) is not legally actionable, but creating or promoting devices as ways to violate copyright will surely run afoul of the law.

- Trademarks are words, short phrases (like slogans), logos, or physical attributes that help consumers identify a product as belonging to a particular vendor. Trademark law is based on the premise of consumer protection.

- Copyrights *could* be enforced a lot more often that they are. Some infringements are unlikely to be discovered by the copyright holder. In other cases the copyright holder simply decides it's not worth the effort to pursue legal action. Just because someone gets away with a copyright infringement once, twice, or one hundred times doesn't mean an infringement is legal and copyright might be asserted the one-hundred-and-first time.

---

[31]*See* Greg Sandoval, *Federal Rules on Campus File Sharing Kick in Today,* Cnet News, July 1, 2010, http://news.cnet.com/8301-31001_3-20009386-261.html?tag=mncol.

Harmless Hobby or Copyright Infringement?

Fan fiction is writing that is done by fans using characters and premises from TV shows, movies, or books.[a] The works are generally not approved by the original owners of the intellectual property from which the fan fiction is derived. Some copyright holders are quite comfortable with fan fiction, believing that it keeps fans engaged with characters and may even attract new fans to the original work. Other copyright holders are vehemently opposed to fan fiction, fearing that fans may denigrate characters or story lines. J.K. Rowling does not categorically oppose fan fiction of her Harry Potter character, but her lawyers sent a cease and desist letter to the operator of a particular fan fiction website in 2002 that involved the characters in sexually explicit activity. There is the additional concern that a fan who publishes a derivative piece of fan fiction might in the future attempt to claim that the original copyright holder "stole" work to incorporate in a later book or film.

Authors of fan fiction attempt to assert that their work is fair use. Examining the four requirements of a fair use defense, it appears at least arguable that the derivative work does not impact the market for the original, and in most cases the amount and substantiality of the original used would not be excessive. It could be asserted, though, that those websites are "profiting" from the intellectual property of the original copyright holders without just compensation. The websites that carry fan fiction do not pay for submissions, although even fanfiction.net carries a minimal amount of advertising.

In spite of the many fan fiction postings that exist (there are tens of thousands based on the *Star Trek* franchise alone), there has been surprisingly little legal action. There have been authors who have been vocal about their opposition to fan fiction, and reputable sites such as fanfiction.net will not allow postings of derivative works by those authors. Of course the Internet makes it easy for those denied access at one site to post their work elsewhere, but if it can be found by readers it can be found by the authors. At present there seems to be a sort of standoff between most authors and fan fiction writers.

There is no question in copyright law that derivative works are included in the bundle of rights held by copyright owners. Is it worth it to copyright owners to seek out others creating derivative works based on their originals? Do fiction authors need a licensing agency like music authors have ASCAP, BMI, and SESAC to enforce their copyrights? Licensing agencies survive by extracting a portion of the licensing fees. Would fan fiction authors who write for no money pay licensing fees? Assuming that there is no profit to be made from licensing fan fiction, should authors be allowed to control the uses of their intellectual property? Should fan fiction be allowed to do anything with characters taken from others' work, including involving them in content offensive to the original author? ■

---

[a]Fan fiction can also be based on comic books, plays, video games, or any other narrative form. For a comprehensive list, visit http://www.fanfiction.net.

GLOSSARY

70/70 Rule   If the Federal Communications Commission finds a cable service is accessible to 70% of households and 70% of those homes subscribe, the FCC can implement any additional rules to make certain there is a diversity of information sources.

Absolute privilege   In libel law, absolute privilege means a privileged statement can never be the basis for a libel cause of action. An example is the absolute privilege given to legislators in their formal deliberations.

Acceptance   An offeree's assent to the terms of an offer by the means specified or expected by the offeror.

Actual damages   Also called compensatory damages, this is the monetary compensation designed to remedy the losses suffered by the plaintiff.

Actual malice   The requirement in cases of libel against public officials that the publisher acted with knowledge of falsity or a reckless disregard for the truth.

Administrative law   Law that derives authority from being part of the regulations set out by executive agencies.

Agency memoranda   A FOIA exemption for documents that are "inter-agency or intra-agency memorandum or letters" which would be privileged in civil litigation. 5 U.S.C. § 552(b)(5).

Agency   Under FOIA, a federal agency is "any executive department, military department, government corporation, government controlled corporation or other establishment in the executive branch of government."

American Bar Association (ABA)   The United States national bar organization. The bar is a professional organization for lawyers.

Anti-siphoning rules   Defunct rules introduced by the Federal Communications Commission in 1975 that were designed to prevent subscription-based cablecasters from purchasing rights to televise important and culturally significant events that had been traditionally aired on free-to-air television.

Appropriation   This privacy tort protects people from having their likenesses used for commercial gain without their consent. *See* right to publicity.

Arraignment   A hearing where formal charges are read against a criminal defendant and the defendant is expected to enter a plea.

Bad tendency test   A standard which allows government to criminalize speech if it has a bad tendency to contribute to collapse of the government. *See Patterson v. Colorado; Gitlow v. New York.* Contrast with Clear and present danger test, which allows less restriction of speech.

Beyond a reasonable doubt   The burden of proof in criminal cases.

Bill ignoramus   When a grand jury does not find enough evidence to charge a crime, it returns a no bill, or bill ignoramus, instead of a true bill. *See also* grand jury, true bill.

Bill of Rights   The first ten amendments to the U.S. Constitution.

Branzburg test   To compel a reporter to testify, the government must show 1) probable cause to believe that the newsman has information that is clearly relevant to a specific probable violation of law; 2) the information sought cannot be obtained by alternative means less destructive of First Amendment rights; 3) a compelling and overriding interest in the information.

Breach of contract   A legal cause of action based on damages resulting from the failure of a party to a contract to perform according to its terms.

Burden of proof   Refers to the threshold of certainty a party in court must meet to prove a matter in dispute.

Buy-out license   Unlike blanket licenses for music that require the payment of annual fees, buy-out libraries own production music that is purchased in perpetuity.

Cable Act of 1984   Congressional amendments to the Communications Act of 1934 that deregulated cable pricing and established a national policy for the regulation of cable systems.

Cable Consumer Act of 1992   A U.S. federal law designed to ensure diversity of local programming on cable. It required cable systems to carry local broadcast channels and forbade them from charging to carry the signal for local channels. The law was superseded by the 1996 Telecommunications Act.

Censorship   An act of government to prevent expressions of speech or publications.

***Central Hudson* test**   A four-part test used to determine the constitutionality of any law that limits commercial speech. (1) The speech must not be misleading and concern lawful activity, (2) the asserted state interest promoted by the restriction must be substantial, (3) the restriction must directly advance the asserted state interest; and (4) that the regulation does not restrict speech any more than necessary.

Change of venire   Importing jurors from a different geographical location.

Change of venue   Moving a trial to a different geographical location.

Child pornography   Material depicting sexually explicit acts involving a minor. On its face, this class of material has no constitutional protection.

Chilling effect   A criticism of vague restrictions on speech which may cause speakers to restrict themselves from saying certain things for fear that they might subsequently be punished, when in fact the speech in which they would engage would be constitutional.

Civil contempt   Civil contempt citations are issued for the purpose of eliciting a particular response, such as compelling reporters to testify by citing them for contempt.

Civil law   The body of law that regulates disputes between private parties.

Clear and present danger test   Speech that presents a clear and present danger is outside the protection of the First Amendment. This test was first articulated by Justice Oliver Wendell Holmes in *Schenck v. United States,* with the example of a man shouting "fire" in a crowded theatre.

Commerce clause   Article 1, Section 8, Clause 3 of the U.S. Constitution gives Congress power to regulate trade between the states, with foreign countries, and with Indian tribes. Used to justify the government's constitutional right to control broadcast radio by licensing.

Commercial speech   Commercial speech is speech with a profit motive. The classic example of commercial speech is advertising. This type of speech is much more subject to regulation and restriction than other forms.

Common carrier   In transportation, moving people or goods for a fee. In communications, transporting the communications of others via wire or airwaves. In either case, non-discrimination of passengers or messages is required.

Common law   Law that represents the precedent set by courts in past decisions.

Compatible use doctrine   Allows restriction of speech when "the manner of expression is basically incompatible with the normal activity of a particular place at a particular time." *See Grayned v. City of Rockford,* 408 U.S. 104 (1972).

Competition   Competing broadcasters have fair and equitable opportunities to influence the broadcast market; policy designed to ensure that public guidelines and regulations promote rather than limit competition and efficient markets based upon the belief that doing so will create a higher level of supply-and-demand.

Comstockery   Named after zealous advocate of Victorian morality Anthony Comstock, Comstockery is advocacy of censorship on the basis of perceived immorality.

Concurring opinion   When justices agree with the result reached by the majority, but they think the majority's rationale is wrong, the justice may author a concurrence which agrees with the result but offers a different rationale.

Conditional acceptance   A conditional acceptance, where the offeree's acceptance is conditioned upon a change in the terms, is not acceptance. It is a counter-offer.

Consent decree   The FTC may agree not to prosecute the advertiser if the advertiser agrees not to repeat the offense. A consent decree cannot be appealed unless it can be proven that it was based on fraud by one of the parties or a mutual mistake.

Consideration   Each party must receive something of value for mutual promises to be enforceable as a contract. Money, goods, and services are the most common form of consideration, but it can take many forms and need not have any monetary value.

Contemporary community standards Jurors apply contemporary community standards to determine what is obscene. This rule localizes the definition of obscenity, and was first adopted by the United States Supreme Court in 1957 in *Roth v. United States*, 354 U.S. 476 (1957).

Contempt of court Any act which is calculated to embarrass, hinder, or obstruct court in administration of justice, or which is calculated to lessen its authority or its dignity. Committed by a person who does any act in willful contravention of its authority or dignity, or tending to impede or frustrate the administration of justice, or by one who, being under the court's authority as a party to a proceeding therein, willfully disobeys its lawful orders or fails to comply with an undertaking which it has given. *See* Black's *Law Dictionary.*

Content-based restrictions Content-based restrictions do not apply equally to all speech, but only restrict certain speech content. Content-based restrictions are subject to strict scrutiny.

Content-neutral restrictions Content-neutral restrictions do not single out certain viewpoints; they apply equally to all speech. Content-neutral restrictions are subject to lower scrutiny than content-based restrictions.

Content regulation The FCC has many rules regarding programming content, although the FCC is forbidden from censorship by § 326 of the Communications Act.

Continuance Postpones proceedings until a later date.

Copyright notice Under older laws, prominently displayed notices were required that included the copyright symbol ©, owner, and the year. While these notations are still a good idea, notification rules are no longer in effect.

Corrective advertisement The FTC may order an advertiser do more than cease and desist its deceptive advertising, and also refrain from future advertising for a specified period of time, unless it corrects the misleading impression that its prior false advertising may have created.

Counter-offer A conditional promise in response to an offer that changes the terms of the original offer, and thus requires acceptance.

Criminal contempt Criminal contempt citations are issued for punitive reasons, like punishing an outburst during court.

Criminal law The body of law that defines conduct prohibited and punished by the state.

Criminal libel An antiquated crime in which a publisher could be charged with defamation by the government. In modern United States jurisprudence, the crime of criminal libel does not exist.

Criminal syndicalism Violent insurrection and anti-government protests.

Damages Money awarded to the plaintiff in a civil suit, to be paid by a defendant.

De novo From the Latin "from the beginning," when an appellate court reviews a non-jury trial record, it may conduct the review de novo, meaning to look for error in the judge's findings of fact, as well as matters of law.

Deceptive advertising According to the FTC's Deception Policy Statement, an ad is deceptive if it contains a statement—or omits information—that is: (1) likely to mislead consumers acting reasonably under the circumstances, and (2) is "material"—that is, important to a consumer's decision to buy or use the product.

Defamation Holding up of a person to ridicule, scorn, or contempt to a respectable and considerable part of the community.

Defamatory language In libel law, the plaintiff must show that the libelous material was defamatory, meaning it asserts an untrue fact that would cause harm to the plaintiff's reputation in the mind of "right thinking persons."

Defendant The accused in a criminal legal proceeding, or responding party in a civil proceeding initiated by complaint.

Demurrer A motion that challenges the legal sufficiency of a claim set forth in a filing by an opposing party.

Depositions Out of court sworn oral testimony that is transcribed for use at trial.

Direct contempt Contempt of court that occurs inside the courtroom, like being disruptive during court proceedings.

Discovery Pre-trial phase in which each party is entitled to request and gain access to evidence possessed by the other side.

Doctrine of first sale After a particular copy of a work is sold, the author no longer controls that particular copy: the author still owns the intellectual property, but that individual copy belongs to the purchaser.

Dominant theme According to the first prong of the *Miller* test, a work is only obscene if its dominant theme taken as a whole appeals to the prurient interest. For example, a specific sexual scene in a movie can't be taken alone without considering the rest of the film. *See Miller v. California,* 413 U.S. 15 (1973).

Drivers Privacy Protection Act (DPPA) A federal law protecting the privacy of state driver's license information.

Duopoly rule Allows two TV stations to be owned by one owner in the same market if one of the stations is not ranked among the top four stations based on market share. At least eight TV stations must remain to compete before the duopoly merger can be approved.

Equity law Historically, courts of equity were able to grant equitable remedies, which require the parties to perform, or refrain from, certain actions rather than simply requiring a defendant to pay monetary damages. Modern U.S. courts are a unified system, with access to both equitable and legal remedies.

Executive branch The executive branch of government has authority for execution of the laws. In the federal government, executive authority derives from the president.

Executive orders Issued by the president to direct the executive branch as to how it should execute the law. Many executive orders carry the force of statutory law by congressional consent.

Expeditious handling Freedom of Information Act (FOIA) requests are given expedited treatment if the requester is able to demonstrate a compelling need for the requested information.

Express acceptance Acceptance that is evident based on the explicit statements of the offeree.

Factual advertising claims FTC guidelines state that any claims stated as facts by the advertiser must have a reasonable basis for making such a statement.

Fair use Section 104 of the copyright act allows copyrighted material to be used under the doctrine of fair use, which is determined by considering 1) the purpose of the use, 2) the nature of the work, 3) the amount of the work used, and 4) the effect on the market for the work.

Fairness doctrine A defunct Federal Communications Commission policy that required broadcast licensees to present controversial issues of public importance and to do so in an honest, equitable and balanced fashion.

False light An invasion of privacy claim where the plaintiff must show that the defendant's publication, with actual malice, placed him or her in a false light that would be highly offensive to a reasonable person. A false light cause of action is not recognized in all jurisdictions. Often the same set of facts that give rise to defamation claims can provide the basis for a false light claim.

Falsity In libel law, a defendant cannot be found liable for defamation unless his/her statement was false.

Family Educational Rights and Privacy Act (1974) A federal law designed to protect the privacy of children's school information.

FCC Commissioners Five individuals, appointed by the president and confirmed by congress, who serve five-year terms. The commissioners adopt rules and set policy based on decisions about licensing renewals or infractions.

Federal Advisory Committee Act (FACA) The Federal Advisory Committee Act of 1972 is a law which mandates transparency, reporting, and viewpoint diversity when private citizens give advice as part of a commission, committee, or advisory body established or utilized by the president or federal agencies in making policy.

Federal Communications Commission (FCC) A United States government agency, established by the Communications Act of 1934, that regulates interstate and international communications by radio, television, wire, satellite, and cable.

The Federal Radio Commission The Federal Radio Commission was created by the Radio Act of 1927. It created a five-member commission with each member representing a geographical area of the country.

Federal Trade Commission (FTC) Created in 1914 to prevent monopolies and unfair methods of competition in commerce, the FTC also regulates advertisements. The FTC requires that all advertisements be truthful, nondeceptive, and fair, and also states that advertisers must have evidence to back up their claims.

Fee category Every FOIA request is placed in a fee category which determines if there is a cost to the requester.

Fighting words Speech which by its very utterance inflicts injury or tends to incite an immediate breach of the peace.

Financial records A FOIA exemption for documents related to specified reports prepared by, on behalf of, or for the use of agencies which regulate financial institutions. 5 U.S.C. § 552(b)(8).

FOI statute All 50 states have some type of access law for records and meetings, but they vary widely in terms of their practical use and enforcement.

FOIA exemptions There are nine exemptions to FOIA specified in the statute. The government can deny a FOIA request, and keep information secret, if the requested material falls within one of the nine exemptions.

Fraud An intentional material misrepresentation of fact by the defendant that the plaintiff relies on to his or her detriment.

Freedom of Information Act (FOIA) The Freedom of Information Act is a federal law requiring federal agencies, on request, to disclose agency records unless the information can be kept secret under one of nine FOIA exemptions.

Gag order An order by a judge restricting participants in a trial from making public comment.

Government Accountability Office (GAO) The Government Accountability Office is a congressional federal agency that assists Congress in oversight of budget expenditures.

Harmless error Error found by an appellate court to have occurred at trial that did not sufficiently prejudice the outcome to warrant reversal.

Health Insurance Portability and Accountability Act (HIPAA) A federal law which protects the privacy of an individual's health information.

Hicklin rule This early standard finds obscenity if any part of an explicit work influences the most susceptible mind. _See Regina v. Hicklin_ (1868), LR 3 QB 360.

Hold-harmless clause A provision in a contract where one party agrees not to hold the other party responsible for any damages. This is a unilateral indemnification of one party by another, but it can be reciprocal among multiple parties.

Horizontal integration When a media company expands its ownership through acquisitions and mergers of businesses or operations that are at the same level producing similar products.

Identification In libel law, plaintiffs must show that they were identifiable from the libelous material.

Implied acceptance Acceptance that is only evident due to context, rather than explicitly stated by the offeree.

Implied consent A sometimes controversial form of consent that is not evident from a person's express statements, but from circumstances. For example, all licensed drivers in the United States have implied their consent to a field sobriety test.

Incorporation doctrine Neither the U.S. Constitution nor its amendments apply to the states as a whole. However, once specific parts of the Constitution are individually incorporated into the 14th Amendment by the Court, they become applicable to states through the 14th Amendment's limitation on state action.

Indictment A formal accusation that a person has committed a felony or serious crime. After a grand jury hearing, the grand jury issues either a true bill, in which case the person is charged, or a no bill, in which case the person is not charged.

Indirect contempt Contempt of court that occurs outside the courtroom, like failure to appear in court when subpoenaed.

Injunction A form of equitable remedy which requires a party to refrain from doing things specified in the injunction.

Injunctive relief A form of equitable remedy; but rather than commanding action, injunctive relief commands inaction, prohibiting the respondent from acting.

Innocent construction rule A rule some courts use to interpret allegedly libelous statements that might have multiple interpretations according to the most innocent interpretation, or the one that most favors the defendant.

Insider trading An illegal business practice where market participants base decisions on information that is known to be confidential and not generally available in the market. For example, officers of a company buying stock in the company at a current market price below what they know will be announced in the future as a buyout price.

Intermediate scrutiny The middle level of scrutiny courts apply when reviewing laws. Intermediate scrutiny requires the law serve an important state interest in a way that is substantially related to the public interest.

Interrogatories Written questions pertinent to the case posed by attorneys for both sides in the discovery phase of a trial.

Intrusion This privacy tort protects people from intrusion into their private space and their private data. Since the right protects against intrusion, publication is not required.

Judicial admonition Judges' statements, direction, or advice to jurors, or anyone, at trial.

Judicial branch The judicial branch of government, established in Article III of the U.S. Constitution, is the court system. In the federal government, judicial authority rests in the Supreme Court, and whatever lower federal courts congress may establish.

Judicial review The doctrine under which the judiciary is the final interpreter of the constitutionality of executive and legislative actions. First established in *Marbury v. Madison* (1803).

Landmark rulings Cases that establish new legal principles.

Law enforcement A FOIA exemption for documents which are "records or information compiled for law enforcement purposes," but only if one or more of six specified types of harm would result. 5 U.S.C. § 552(b)(7).

Leased-access channels Channels that provide reduced rate airtime on a cable system to independent cable programmers and producers.

Legislative branch The legislative branch of government, established in Article 1 of the U.S. Constitution, has the authority to pass laws. In the federal government the legislative authority rests in congress.

Libel Traditionally, libel was thought of as printed defamation, as opposed to spoken, which is slander. Libelous statements are untrue and cause harm.

Libel per quod Consists of words or phrases that require contextualization in order to identify the harm.

Libel per se Consists of those words which in and of themselves are so damaging as to be considered defamatory, meaning use of the words is prima fascia evidence of defamatory language.

Limited public forum A forum that has traditionally only been open to public expression and assembly for specific limited purposes.

Limited purpose public figure In libel law, plaintiffs who are not otherwise public figures might be considered to be if they have gained notoriety by voluntarily injecting themselves into a matter of public controversy in an attempt to influence the outcome.

Localism Broadcast ownership and program decision-making at the local community level; policy designed to ensure that the programming offered by each radio and television station addresses the significant needs and issues of the community it serves.

Marketplace of ideas The justification for freedom of expression that holds that the best way to find truth is to allow conflicting ideas to compete. Typically associated with philosophers John Stuart Mill or John Milton.

Memorandum order Indicates the winning party but does not explain why. In such cases, the Supreme Court may be suggesting that precedent should stand and there is no special significance to that case.

Miller Test A three-prong test under which material is obscene if the average person applying contemporary community standards would find the dominant theme of the work taken as a whole 1) appeals to the prurient interest, 2) depicts patently offensive sexual content, and 3) if a reasonable person would find the work lacks serious literary, artistic, political, or scientific value. *See Miller v. California*, 413 U.S. 15 (1973).

Miranda Warning Requirement to apprise suspects of their rights that arose out of the 1966 case *Miranda v. Arizona*.

Morals clause A provision in a contract that prohibits specific behavior in a party's private life.

Multichannel Video Program Distributor (MVPD) The term for services providing bundles of video channels, such as cable systems, home satellite dish providers, video over internet protocol, etc.

Municipal broadband The provision of broadband by local government in some communities.

Must-carry rule The FCC mandates that cable companies carry various local and public television stations within a cable provider's service area. *See Turner Broadcasting Sys. v. Federal Communications Commission*, 512 U.S. 622 (1994).

National defense A FOIA exemption for national defense or foreign policy information properly classified pursuant to an Executive Order. 5 U.S.C. § 552(b)(1).

National Telecommunications and Information Administration (NTIA) An agency in the U.S. Department of Commerce that serves as the executive branch agency principally responsible for advising the president on telecommunications and information policies. In this role, NTIA frequently works with other executive branch agencies to develop and present the administration's position on these issues.

Natural monopoly A natural monopoly occurs when the cost of producing something outweighs the benefit to the producer. If the goods are public goods that are still needed, the government may become involved since ordinarily, free markets will not produce goods at a loss. Traditional examples are public goods like sewerage or lighthouses.

Negligence Breach of a duty that results in reasonably foreseeable harm.

Network neutrality Refers to the general principle of equal access to Internet resources and content, as opposed to a tiered structure, which gives preference to certain users, technology, and content over others.

Neutral reportage In some jurisdictions, this is recognized as a defense to libel which asserts that, so long as a medium accurately recounts all sides of an argument, it acts as a neutral conveyor of information and should not be responsible.

Nolo contendere A plea entered by the defendant in a criminal proceeding, which admits neither guilt nor innocence, but does not contest the charge.

No compete clauses A clause in a contract which prevents a person, often an employee, who has learned trade secrets or skills, or company from competing after employment terminates.

Non-public forum A forum that has traditionally not been open for public expression and assembly.

Offer A specific promise, conditional on acceptance, that is communicated with the intent of forming the terms of a contract.

Oil field data A FOIA exemption for documents revealing oil well data. 5 U.S.C. § 552(b)(9).

Open Sky policy A 1972 Federal Communications Commission policy that permitted private industries to use private communication satellites for broadcasting television programs.

Opinion advertising claims Cases based on subjective opinion claims (taste, appearance, smell) are generally not actionable. Claims based on opinions are actionable, however, if they are not honestly held, if they misrepresent the qualifications of the holder or the basis of his or her opinion, or if the recipient reasonably interprets them as implied statements of fact.

Overbuilders New entrants into an existing telecommunications market are referred to as overbuilders, as in building over the existing system.

Patently offensive According to the second prong of the *Miller* test, obscene material must be patently offensive base on contemporary community standards. *See Miller v. California*, 413 U.S. 15 (1973).

Paternalism The theory that it is beneficial to control, usually by government regulation, what consumers see and hear in order to protect them better than they can protect themselves.

PATRIOT Act (USA PATRIOT Act) Uniting and Strengthening America by Providing Appropriate Tools Required to Intercept and Obstruct Terrorism Act of 2001.

Penumbra (right of privacy) A penumbra is an aura of light shining through a filter like a glistening sunset, as if through a partial shadow above the horizon. Although the Constitution does not explicitly contain a right to privacy, courts have recognized a penumbra of the right emanating from the 1st, 3rd, 4th, 5th, 9th, and 10th Amendments.

Per curiam order A decision rendered with an opinion, but not signed. This type of ruling is "by the Court" as a whole.

Peremptory challenge A challenge to a juror in voir dire that is not for cause. Most jurisdictions afford attorneys one or more "strikes" without giving a reason for striking the names.

Personnel rules A FOIA exemption for documents "related solely to the internal personnel rules and practices of an agency." 5 U.S.C. § 552(b)(2).

Plaintiff In a civil trial, the party bringing the action.

Political speech Political speech is the most protected form of speech due to its key role in support of representative government.

Preponderance of evidence The burden of proof in criminal cases.

Presumption of disclosure Under FOIA, requests are presumptively granted unless the government can show that the information falls under one of the FOIA exemptions.

Presumptive right of access The rule in criminal trials (including the pre-trial hearings) is that they are presumptively open to the public and press.

Principle of diversity The widest possible dissemination of information from diverse and antagonistic sources is essential to the welfare of the public; generally focuses on objectives such as maximizing the sources of information, as well as the range of viewpoints and content options to which citizens and/or consumers have access. The FCC and Congress have shown interest in protecting content diversity, ownership diversity, and viewpoint diversity.

Prior restraint   A form of censorship in which the government, in advance of publication, orders a publisher not to publish certain material.

Privacy   A FOIA exemption for documents which are "personnel and medical and similar files the disclosure of which would constitute a clearly unwarranted invasion of personal privacy." 5 U.S.C. § 552(b)(6).

Privilege   In libel law, privilege is an affirmative defense in which the defendant asserts a justification for having defamed the plaintiff.

Promissory estoppel   A statement may be treated as a promise by a court when the listener relied on the statement to his or her detriment. See § 90 RESTATEMENT (SECOND) OF CONTRACTS.

Protected health information (PHI)   The class of individual healthcare information protected by the Health Insurance Portability and Accountability Act (HIPAA).

Prurient interest   Shameful or morbid interest in nudity, sex, or excretion. *See Roth v. United States*, 354 U.S. 476 (1957).

Publication   For the purpose of a libel claim, the term *publication* refers to any dissemination of a defamatory statement, not strictly in print. In order to damage someone's reputation, a defamatory remark must be made public.

Public disclosure of embarrassing private facts   Protects people against publication of private facts about them that are not newsworthy and are so intimate as to outrage the public's sense of decency.

Public domain   Works are in the public domain if they are not currently subject to any private intellectual property right: either because they never were, like published court cases, or because the copyright has expired.

Public, educational, and government (PEG)   Public access channels that are mandated by a local franchising authority—not the federal government—to provide increased channel diversity.

Puffery   An over-exaggerated claim about a product that is too outlandish to be believed by a reasonable person, and as such is legal.

Punitive damages   This type of damage award is not intended to make the plaintiff whole, but to act as an additional deterrent to the type of conduct the defendant engaged in.

Qualified privilege   In libel law, qualified privilege means a privileged statement may or may not be the basis for a libel cause of action, based on the specific facts. An example is the qualified privilege given to journalists to fairly and accurately report the contents of a police report, even if it contains harmful untruths.

The Radio Act of 1912   A U.S. federal law requiring ships to maintain round-the-clock radio watch, and required amateur radio operators be licensed. The sinking of the *Titanic* led to the passage of this law.

Radio Television Digital News Association (RTDNA)   The largest professional organization for electronic journalists in radio, television, and all digital media, as well as journalism educators and students.

Ratings dilution   Refers to the effect on local stations when cable channels air programs previously purchased by the local station. This is one of the effects syndicated exclusivity was intended to prevent.

Record   For the purposes of the FOIA, a letter, map, photograph, audio/video recording or figures, tables, or data used by an agency to keep track of its activities.

Remanded   A higher appellate court may send back, or remand, a case to a lower court for some subsequent action.

Respondent   The responding party in a legal proceeding, particularly in appellate proceedings or proceedings initiated by petition.

Revoke   Revocation of the offer by the offeree before acceptance.

Reversible error   Error found by an appellate court to have occurred at trial that sufficiently prejudiced the outcome to warrant reversal.

Right of privacy   Privacy rights include the broad categories of rights that flow from the right to be personally autonomous and the right to be left alone. Although the U.S. Constitution does not explicitly contain a right to privacy, courts have recognized a penumbra of the right emanating from the 1st, 3rd, 4th, 5th, 9th, and 10th Amendments.

Right of publicity   Protects famous people who wish to protect their likeness, voice, or image from others exploiting it for commercial gain. *See* appropriation.

Right to impartial jury   The Sixth Amendment guarantees defendants the right to trial by an impartial jury, which can sometimes conflict with publicity surrounding trials.

Sedition   The common law crime of advocating and intending to bring about harm to the government.

Seditious libel   The common law crime of punishing speech harmful to the government.

Sequestration   The process of keeping the jurors secluded so that no one talks with them about the trial outside of court.

Sherman Act   United States federal law passed in 1890 that prohibits monopolistic behavior by businesses and has been used to break up a number of powerful monopolies or near-monopolies, such as Standard Oil.

Shield laws   State laws in 39 states which afford *privilege* to journalists to not disclose information (i.e., notes and other materials) obtained during course of their newsgathering.

Shrink-wrap licenses   Software companies generally claim the consumer removing the wrapping from a piece of software constitutes acceptance of the offered terms and conditions of the license stated on the box.

Slander   Traditionally, slander was thought of as spoken defamation, as opposed to libel, which was written defamation.

Social contract   A concept in political philosophy first proposed by Jean-Jacques Rousseau, which justifies the power of the sovereign ruler by the existence of a social contract between free subjects, who voluntarily and mutually submit to the sovereign authority for the good of all.

Stare decisis   The legal doctrine that judges are bound to follow the decisions of past courts, or precedent, in deciding similar cases.

Statutory exemptions   A FOIA exemption for documents "specifically exempted from disclosure by statute" other than FOIA, but only if the other statute's disclosure prohibition is absolute. 5 U.S.C. § 552(b)(3).

Statutory law   Law that is enacted into statute by a legislative body.

Strict scrutiny   The highest standard of scrutiny courts apply when reviewing laws. Strict scrutiny requires the law 1) serve a compelling government interest, 2) be narrowly tailored to achieving the goal, and 3) use the least restrictive means to do so.

Structural regulation   Many broadcast regulations have more to do with the structure of the media than with its content. An example of structural regulation is the rules regarding diversity of media ownership.

Subpoena   An order by a court that compels the production of evidence or the testimony of a witness.

Summary judgment   A final judgment for one party without trial when a court finds either no material fact is in dispute, or when the law alone clearly establishes one party's claim.

Supremacy clause   Article VI, paragraph 2, of the U.S. Constitution mandates that federal law is supreme whenever a conflict arises between federal and state law.

Symbolic speech   Speech is more than just words. Actions or symbols can also be considered speech protected by the First Amendment.

Synchronization   A form of derivative work, a synchronization license allows a copyrighted work, such as a song, to be integrated with other media, like a video.

Syndicated exclusivity (Syndex)   An FCC regulation which allows local television stations to enter into exclusive contracts for syndicated content, and requires MVPDs to honor those contracts.

Tariff Act of 1842   Banned the importation of all indecent and obscene prints, paintings, lithographs, engravings, and transparencies, and gave government the authority to dispose of pornographic cargo from France or other foreign ports.

The Telecommunications Act of 1996   U.S. Federal legislation which updated the 62-year-old regulatory framework of the Communications Act of 1934.

The First Amendment   "Congress shall make no law respecting an establishment of religion, or prohibiting the free exercise thereof; or abridging the freedom of speech, or of the press; or the right of the people peaceably to assemble, and to petition the Government for a redress of grievances."

The *Tinker* test   Schools cannot restrict symbolic speech unless it causes a substantial material disruption. School officials' desire to avoid a substantial, material disruption. The desire of school officials to avoid the unpleasantness of an unpopular or controversial view is not enough, without substantial disruption.

Tort   From the Latin "break," a tort is a civil wrong that involves the breach of a duty to someone else, resulting in foreseeable harm.

Trade secrets   A FOIA exemption for documents which would reveal "[t]rade secrets and commercial or financial information obtained from a person [that is] privileged or confidential." 5 U.S.C. § 552(b)(4).

Traditional public forum   Refers to public property that is open for expression and assembly, such as streets, sidewalks, and parks. Public forums have strong First Amendment protection.

Treason   Generally, the crime of betraying your sovereign nation. In United States law, treason is levying war against the Unites States or giving aid and comfort to its enemies.

Trespass   A common law tort that protects people against interference with their person, land, and possessions. Often the same set of facts that is the basis for an intrusion claim is also the basis for a trespass claim.

Universal service   An idea promoted in the 1920s, particularly by AT&T, that the value of the telephone increased with the number of households that had telephones.

Vacated   A vacated judgment voids a previous judgment.

Variable obscenity   According to the doctrine of variable obscenity, the harm of the explicit material varies according to the consumer's level of maturity. Under this principle, the sale of erotic though not necessarily obscene materials to minors can be prohibited.

Vertical integration   When a media company owns businesses or operations all along the production and distribution chain that increase market power.

Voire dire   The pre-trial process of jury selection.

Voluntary self-regulation   Industry forming sets of rules and regulations for itself without government oversight or enforcement.

Wireless cable   Also called multichannel multipoint distribution service (MMDS). An MMDS system transmits television via microwave signal, and the FCC regulates its services.

The Wireless Ship Act of 1910   A U.S. federal law that required all U.S. ships at sea to carry long range radio equipment. The law was passed in response to a shipping accident where a radio distress call saved over 1,200 lives.

Works for hire   Copyrightable material that is made as a condition of employment. For example, the author of a work may have been a salaried employee who produced the work while on company time using company resources, so the company would own the copyright.

Writ of certiorari   A writ the U.S. Supreme Court issued to review a lower court's decision.

Writ of mandamus   Issued by courts to command lower courts or government officials to perform specific actions.

CREDITS

Text Credits

Definition of "contempt of court" from *Black's Law Dictionary,* 6/e, 1983, 1990, p. 319. Reprinted with permission from *Black's Law Dictionary,* 6th, © 1983 Thomson Reuters.

Figure, "Measuring the Climate for Free Expression."

Figure, "Sample FOIA Letter" from Freedom of Information Center at the University of Missouri School of Journalism, http://www.nfoic.org/sample-foia-letters. From the National Freedom of Information Coalition and the Freedom of Information Center at the University of Missouri School of Journalism. Reprinted by permission.

From the Trenches: Cameras as Seen from the Judge's Bench by Judge Louis H. Schiff. Reprinted by permission of the Honorable Louis H. Schiff.

From the Trenches: The Case of Paid Endorsers by Michael C. Lasky. Reprinted by permission of the author.

From the Trenches: The FCC and Political Advertising by Charles Spencer. Source: Background information from Charles Spencer.

From the Trenches: Using the Freedom of Information Act by Charles N. Davis, National Freedom of Information Center, University of Missouri, Columbia. Reprinted by permission of Charles N. Davis, Director, Freedom of Information Center.

"Geographic Boundaries of United States Court of Appeals and United States District Courts" from http://www.uscourts.gov/images/Circuitmap.pdf.

Screen captures of fcc.gov and gpo.gov. From fcc.gov and gpo.gov.

Photo Credits

Page 1, Jonathan Larsen/Shutterstock.com.

Page 3, Kumar Sriskandan/Alamy.

Pages 4, 31, 35, 50, 62, 98, 104, 110, 123, 132, 143, 145, 170, 171, 179, 195, 204, 221, 236, 279, 282, 301, 317, 352, 357, & 363, Icon rendered based on clip art found at http://www.bbc.co.uk/scotland/learning/bitesize/standard/physics/transport/forces_at_work_rev1.shtml.

Page 18, Chuck Kennedy/Newscom.

Page 20, Courtesy of FindLaw, a Thomson Reuters business.

Page 26, Charlie Newham/Alamy.

Page 26, OtnaYdur/Shutterstock.com.

Page 29, Photos.com/Thinkstock.com.

Page 43, Ryan Rodrick Beiler/Shutterstock.com.

Page 47, Asterixvs/Dreamstime.com.

Page 66, PDImages/Shutterstock.com.

Page 78, Christi Tolbert/Shutterstock.

Page 86, Library of Congress.

Page 103, National Archives.

CASE INDEX

INDEX